THE FIRST WORLD WAR

The First World War

Personal Experiences

Volume I.

Charles à Court Repington

Simon Publications

2001

Library of Congress Card Number: 20022246

ISBN: 1-931313-71-7

Distributed by Ingram Book Company

Printed by Lightning Source Inc. La Vergne, TN

Published by Simon Publications, P.O.Box 321,
Safety Harbor, FL 34695

PREFACE

THESE records of my personal experiences during the war
are a contribution towards the elucidation of the truth so
far as I was able to ascertain it at the time, and will, I
hope, enable many to understand better the events of these
memorable years. A certain amount has been omitted on
the recommendation of eminent counsel, and some names
have also been left out, but for the rest the entries in my
diary have been left substantially as they were written, and
are a faithful record of my impressions during this extraordinary and eventful epoch.

My grateful thanks are due to some most kind friends
for reading the proofs and giving me much valuable
advice; to Lady Maude for allowing me to use her late
husband's letters to me; and to the writers of other
letters for giving me permission to publish them.

CONTENTS OF VOL. I

CHAPTER I

OUR MILITARY UNDERSTANDING WITH FRANCE, 1906-14

CHAPTER II

THE FIRST YEAR, AUGUST 1914–SEPTEMBER 1915

CHAPTER III

THE OUTLOOK, AUTUMN 1915

CHAPTER IV

SALONIKA AND THE DARDANELLES

CONTENTS

ix

CHAPTER V

THE OUTLOOK FOR 1916

CHAPTER VI

EQUALITY OF ALLIED AND GERMAN STRENGTHS

CHAPTER VII

A VISIT TO THE FRENCH FRONT, MARCH AND APRIL 1916

CHAPTER VIII

RECRUITING AND SUBMARINE TROUBLES

CHAPTER IX

A TOUR IN ITALY, JUNE 1916

CONTENTS

CHAPTER X

THE SOMME BATTLE, JULY 1916

CHAPTER XI

MR. LLOYD GEORGE AS WAR SECRETARY

CHAPTER XIV

MR. LLOYD GEORGE AND THE MILITARY MOLOCH

CHAPTER XV

MR. LLOYD GEORGE PRIME MINISTER, DECEMBER 1916

CHAPTER XVI

THE QUESTION OF JAPANESE CO-OPERATION
JANUARY 1917

CHAPTER XVII

MR. LLOYD GEORGE AND MAN-POWER, 1917

CHAPTER XVIII

MR. LLOYD GEORGE REVIEWS THE SITUATION
MARCH 1917

PAGES

CHAPTER XIX

OPENING OF THE 1917 CAMPAIGN IN FRANCE

CHAPTER XX

ARRAS AND CHAMPAGNE, APRIL 1917

CHAPTER XXI

THE AMERICAN PROGRAMME

CHAPTER XXII

MESOPOTAMIA AND EGYPT, 1917

CHAPTER I

OUR MILITARY UNDERSTANDING WITH FRANCE
1906–1914

Russia's defeat in 1904-5—Danger of a German attack on France—
Discussions with the French Military Attaché—Sir Edward Grey's
view—Opinions of Admiral Sir John Fisher, Lord Esher, Sir George
Clarke, and General Grierson—Unofficial submission of questions to
the French Government and their replies—The French plan of concentration—Differences of opinion on strategical questions—Meeting
of Sir Edward Grey and Mr. Haldane—Sir Henry Campbell-Bannerman's attitude—Official relations opened between the French and
British General Staffs—The French Press divulges the truth—Co-
operation of the two Staffs, 1906-14.

THE origin of our military understanding with France
is a page of history which has not yet been written. I
happened to be concerned with it, and as it explains much
that followed I cannot better preface this account of my
personal experiences in the First World War than by
describing how our most fruitful military co-operation with
France was first brought about.

The story dates back to the end of 1905 when Germany
showed an evident disposition to pick a quarrel with France
over the Morocco question, and to profit by the temporary
eclipse of Russian power which had been caused by Russia's
defeats by Japan in the Far East in 1904-5, and by the
internal troubles within Russia which followed. This
menace to France drew to a head in December 1905 at the
moment when Mr. Balfour's Government had fallen, and the
General Election which placed the Liberal Party in power
had just opened.

Russia was *hors de combat* for the time, and of little service to France as an Ally. She was France's only Ally, and though our *entente* with France had happily been effected by Lord Lansdowne in 1904, we had done nothing whatsoever to prepare joint military action and to gain close touch with French military circles. It was Germany's chance. I had been watching her closely ever since she had begun to display hostility towards us, and I knew enough of her doctrines and preparations to realise how serious the danger for France was. Germany at that time had permeated England with her influence in social, political, financial, and commercial circles. Her tentacles reached everywhere, and not the least symptom of her intentions was the endeavour which she made at this time to attract us to her side by every kind of insidious propaganda. I have described in a little volume of pre-war memories [1] how on Dec. 27, 1905, I wrote in the *Times* an article dealing with the growing hostility of Germany towards France, and how I ended it with a warning to Germany that she would endanger her vital interest if she staked upon a doubtful hazard the results achieved by the great founders of German unity. I warned her that a war might unchain animosities in unexpected quarters, and I did not pretend a friendliness which I did not feel.

This article had considerable effect and was widely quoted, but on the following day, Dec. 28, Major Huguet, afterwards General, the French Military Attaché in London, a close friend of mine for many years, dined with me, and I found that we were both exceedingly anxious about the situation. He told me that his Embassy people were worried because Sir Edward Grey, who had just taken over the Foreign Office, had not renewed the assurances given by Lord Lansdowne. Major Huguet regretted Lord Lansdowne's departure because M. Cambon, the French Ambassador, could not speak English well, and the Embassy believed that Sir E. Grey could not speak French. M. Cambon was very reserved, and feared that he might not

[1] *Vestigia.* Constable, 1919.

catch the exact meaning of a conversation on such a delicate subject in another language. Moreover, M. Cambon was now on leave till Jan. 12, and the Algeciras Conference was due to meet on the 16th. I asked why the Councillor of the Embassy did not go to the Foreign Office at once to clear the air. Major Huguet replied that he could not, in the absence of the Ambassador, open such a grave conversation without precise instructions, but that if Sir E. Grey would broach the subject at the next diplomatic reception, the French Embassy would be much relieved. They knew that our sympathies were with them, but they wanted to know what we should do in case Germany suddenly confronted them with a crisis.

Major Huguet thought that the situation was delicate, and that no one knew what the Kaiser really wanted. He told me that the French Navy had already taken certain precautions and was prepared. He knew that our Navy was ready, and trusted it, but did not know what it would do to co-operate in case of trouble. The French Army, he said, was ready, and reservists were already coming to barracks to ask for orders. Major Huguet thought that the Germans might attack suddenly, and probably through Belgium. I urged him strongly to advise his people at once not to dream of violating Belgium, since the violator would stand fatally condemned in the eyes of our public. He wanted us to stiffen the Belgians if war came, and believed that the Germans could not break through on the French frontier. We walked back together to his rooms and talked till 12.30 A.M.

I communicated the purport of the conversation on the morning of the 29th by express letter to Sir Edward Grey. The General Election, which eventually replaced the Balfour by the Campbell-Bannerman Administration, was in full swing, and Sir Edward Grey was away, but the letter was sent after him to Northumberland. On Saturday, Dec. 30, Lord Esher and I lunched together and discussed the whole situation. In the afternoon I saw the First Naval Lord, Admiral Sir John Fisher, at the Admiralty. We talked of many things, but in relation to the Franco-German crisis he told me that he was forming a new Western Fleet with Headquarters at Berehaven. He was taking two battleships each from the Atlantic, Mediterranean, and Channel Fleets, and was adding six armoured cruisers, and destroyers recalled from China and the Mediterranean, in order to create the new fleet, and the destroyers were, at that moment, on their way home, touching at French ports in North Africa *en route*. As I knew that this would soon become known to the Germans and would alarm them, I thought it good news. The Admiral thought that the Germans would beat the French. The latter had discussed co-operation with him, but all that he wanted from them was submarines at Dunkirk. He assured me that Admiral Wilson's Channel Fleet was alone strong enough to smash the whole German Fleet, and said that he, Fisher, was prepared, on his own responsibility, to order our fleets to go wherever they might be required. He told me that he had seen on paper Lord Lansdowne's assurances to M. Cambon, and that they were quite distinct in their tenor. He had shown them to Sir Edward Grey, and declared that they were part of the engagements taken over from the last Government, and would hold good until denounced.

On Monday, Jan. 1, 1906, came Sir Edward Grey's reply from Fallodon, dated Dec. 30. He said, ' I am interested to hear of your conversation with the French Military Attaché. I can only say that I have not receded from anything which Lord Lansdowne said to the French, and have no hesitation in affirming it.' I had asked Lord Esher to communicate with Sir George Clarke, Secretary of the Defence Committee, and this Monday morning there came a letter from the latter from Bournemouth suggesting that I should take certain steps at the French Embassy. Sir George disapproved of the idea of our joining the French Army in case of war, and also of our supporting the Belgian Army unless Germany violated Belgium. Clarke and Fisher were for a certain course of action, Admiral Wilson for another, and the soldiers, I expected, would be for a third. General Grierson, then head of the Operations Branch, Major Gorton, head of my old section of the Intelligence Branch, and I dined together at ' The Rag ' on Wednesday, Jan. 3, when Grierson opposed all the Fisher-Clarke ideas of a serious military attack on the German coasts in case of war, and I quite agreed with him. He said that, on the assumption that Germany violated Belgium, we could put two divisions into Namur by the thirteenth day of mobilisation, and all our field army of that period into Antwerp by the thirty-second day.

Major Huguet came to my house on Friday, Jan. 5, and stayed to lunch. I walked back to the Embassy with him, and we discussed Sir G. Clarke's letter and alternative operations. He assured me definitely, as his personal opinion, that France would not violate Belgian neutrality, but he said that the French did not realise, and had nothing to go on to make them realise, that a German violation of Belgium would automatically bring us into the field, as I believed it would. Huguet was as much opposed as I was to the Fisher-Clarke plan of attack on the German coast in case of war. He preferred that our help, in case of need, should come either in Belgium if Germany violated her neutrality, or on the left of the French line of deployment between Verdun and Mezières if she did not.

That same evening I saw Lord Esher and Sir G. Clarke at Whitehall Gardens, when we fully discussed the situation together. It was becoming uncommonly serious. The Morocco crisis was coming to a head, and there might have been an explosion at any hour. All our new Ministers were away electioneering, and as at that time a General Election lasted many weeks, there was almost a complete separation between responsibility and the executive. We were well aware that the Germans knew how to profit from such a situation. We thought it indispensable that something should be done, and as both Lord Esher and Sir G. Clarke were serving in an official capacity and I was a free lance, it was eventually agreed between us that I should sound the French Government through Major Huguet, and that when the French views were thus privately and unofficially ascertained we should pass the matter on to our Government, which would be completely uncommitted and able to continue the conversations or to drop them as they pleased. Huguet then arranged to leave for Paris on the 7th, and to see General Brugère the Generalissimo, and General Brun, Chief of Staff, on Monday, Jan. 8.   Before he left I gave him a short list of questions upon which I desired a good French opinion.

Huguet returned from Paris on the evening of Jan. 11, and came to my house at 11 A.M. on Jan. 12, remaining till 1 P.M. He had submitted my questions, dated Jan. 5, to M. Rouvier, Prime Minister, and to M. Etienne, Minister of War, on Saturday evening, Jan. 7. They were then placed before M. Thomson, Minister of Marine, and his naval staff, and before Generals Brun and Brugère. My questions and the French replies to them were as follows :

My Questions.

1. Have the Conseil Supérieur de la Guerre considered British co-operation in case of war with Germany ? In what manner do they consider this co-operation can best be carried out : (*a*) by sea, (*b*) by land ?

The French Replies.

1. La question de la coopération de l'armée britannique sur terre a été étudiée— on estime que, pour être le plus efficace, son action devra :— (*a*) être liée à celle de l'armée française, c'est-à-dire, être placée sous la même direction, soit que les deux armées agissent sur le même théâtre d'opérations, ou sur des théâtres différents. (*b*) se faire sentir dès le début des hostilités, en raison de l'effet moral considérable qui en résultera. Il serait à désirer qu'un certain nombre de corps anglais, quels que soient leur nombre et leur effectif (1 ou 2

My Questions (continued)

The French Replies (continued)

divisions si possible), puissent être débarqués vers le 5me ou 6me jour, de manière à être transportés sur le lieu de leurs opérations, en même temps que le seront les corps français. Ils pourraient partir à leur effectif de paix en doublant les unités ; les réservistes rejoindraient ensuite pour porter les unités à leur effectif normal de guerre. Le reste de l'armée exécuterait sa mobilisation régulièrement, et partirait quand il serait achevée.

Sur mer, la situation particulière de l'Angleterre, la grande supériorité de sa flotte, la possibilité qu'elle a de prendre à l'avance toutes les mesures préparatoires qu'elle juge utiles, la mettent à même d'établir un plan mieux que la France, qui ne jouit pas de la même liberté d'action parce que :—

(1) Elle ignore quelle serait l'attitude de l'Italie.

(2) Elle ne peut, pour cette raison et aussi pour éviter des récriminations, prendre à l'avance les mêmes mesures que l'Angleterre.

2. May we take it as a principle that France will not violate Belgian territory unless compelled to do so by previous violation of Belgian territory by Germany ?

2. Oui, d'une manière absolue.

My Questions (*continued*)

The French Replies (*continued*)

3. Do the French realise that any violation of Belgian neutrality brings us into the field automatically in defence of our Treaty obligations ?

3. La France l'a toujours supposé, mais n'en a jamais eu l'assurance officielle.

4. Assuming that Germany violates Belgian territory, what plan of operations do the French propose for co-operation between the French, English, and Belgian forces ?

4. On compte peu sur une action de l'armée Belge qui, croit-on, se contenterait de se retirer à Anvers en protestant contre la violation de son territoire. Dans le cas où elle serait décidée à défendre son sol, on proposerait une action commune immédiate, sous une diréction unique, action qui ne peut être définie à l'avance, parce qu'elle dépendra des circonstances.

5. What is the French opinion concerning landings on the German coasts ? If we could send 100,000 men for such operation and assisted France with transports, could she supply another 100,000 men, and in what time and from what ports ?

5. Vu la supériorité numérique probable des Allemands, une opération de ce genre au début de la campagne paraît très délicate, et ne semble pouvoir être tentée que dans des circonstances exceptionnelles.

6. Do the French look to us to propose a plan of joint action by sea ?　Have they any plan ready to suggest to us ?

6. Voir réponse à la première question.

7. Would it be possible for France to capture Togoland and the Cameroons, if we captured German E. and S.W. Africa and German possessions in the Pacific ?

7. Au point de vue militaire, l'opération sera facile à exécuter et notre intention est de l'exécuter.

My Questions (continued)

8. Would it be agreeable to France that all captures of German ships and colonial possessions by France and England during the war should be pooled and held as a set-off against any possible German successes in Europe ?

9. Should we establish it as a principle, except for the operations described under 7, that the English shall command at sea and the French on land ?

10. What share should the Netherlands be asked and expected to take in the war, or what precautionary measures should she be asked to take ?

11. In general terms, what line of action do the French expect the Germans will adopt in case of war ? How soon will they be concentrated, and upon what lines are they ex-

The French Replies (continued)

8. Cette question est surtout d'ordre diplomatique et devra être traitée diplomatiquement au moment voulu.

Toutefois, à priori, il semble probable que — l'Angleterre devant avoir à ce point de vue le role le plus brillant — la France s'en remettra entièrement à ce que décidera l'Angleterre.

9. Oui ; l'unité de direction étant absolument indispensable, soit sur terre, soit sur mer.

10. On n'est pas fixé à cet égard. Si les Pays-Bas veuillent résister on leur conseillera de s'opposer par tous les moyens possibles à la violation de leur territoire ; de résister pied-à-pied, et de se retirer sur le gros des forces françaises, en détruisant les voies ferrées et tous les ouvrages d'art. Défense passive, s'ils n'osent, comme il est probable, opposer une défense active.

11. D'une manière générale, on estime que l'effectif probable de l'armée allemande sera de 1,300,000 à 1,400,000 hommes. Le gros des combattants aura achevé la con-

My Questions (continued)	*The French Replies (continued)*
pected to advance, in what numbers and in what time ?	centration vers le 11me ou 12mo jour, les convois vers le 15me, ou le 16me.
	Le réseau ferré allemand semble indiquer que la concentration se fera entre Metz et Thionville. Une offensive immédiate très énergique dans la direction de Paris est ensuite à prévoir.

Jan 5, 1906.

Major Huguet's account of the profound astonishment of the 2me Bureau of the French General Staff, when he announced to them the mission on which he had come, was most amusing. He found them deeply engaged upon the elaboration of an academic plan for the invasion of England, and when he told them of the friendly British invasion which some of us contemplated, their jaws dropped, their pens fell from their hands, and they were positively transfixed with surprise. All went well. The French Ministers, soldiers, and sailors did everything possible to facilitate his mission. He was sure that everything possible would be done officially to prolong the conversations and make the necessary arrangements for co-operation the instant that we, on our side, gave our consent.

Meanwhile Major Huguet told me that M. Cambon, who had returned earlier than he had intended, had seen Sir E. Grey on Jan. 10, when the latter had said that he could not speak for the Government who were all scattered on electioneering work, but that his private opinion was that we should not be able to keep out of a war if Germany attacked France. M. Cambon had then suggested official intercommunications by the respective Staffs, but Sir E. Grey had said that they were impracticable at present, and that we must wait until the elections were over and the Government installed. M. Cambon had judged that Grey was privy to the private and unofficial conversations in progress.

Major Huguet next explained to me, to my amazement, that the French plan of concentration was an adaptation of the Napoleonic lozenge ; an *armée d'avant-garde* of the 6th, 7th, and 20th Army Corps, and the rest of the armies on a front of only forty kilometres, echeloned in depth with reserve divisions in third line. I could not stand this at all, protested vehemently, and pointed out that the German tactics of envelopment would destroy the lozenge speedily ; that the French would be unable to use their arms, and that I saw no more certain means of ruining their army. Subsequently I elaborated my objections in detail[1] at Major Huguet's request, and fortunately this terribly dangerous plan was given up, to my great relief. It alarmed me more than anything else at this time, and made me suspicious of the French strategists and tacticians.

I took my questions, the French replies, and some explanatory notes to the Defence Committee the same day, and discussed them at length with Lord Esher and Sir G. Clarke, who shared my views of the lozenge concentration. Clarke agreed to see Sir John Fisher on the subject of naval plans, and on the following day, Jan. 13, telephoned to me that his talk had been very unsatisfactory, and that Fisher was not prepared to meet the French half-way.

I wrote my opinion of Sir John Fisher's attitude to Lord Esher, and saw Clarke at his house on the 14th. Admiral Fisher, said Sir G. Clarke, would not let the French into any plans of ours ; he was not prepared to guarantee the passage of our Army across the Channel, and he was opposed to the employment of our troops on the continent of Europe. He wanted to fight his own war his own way. It would not have mattered to me had he confined himself to naval operations. But he wished to impound our Army and to use it for naval ends. He was all for scratching in the

---

[1] My criticism of the French tactics appeared in the *Times* of January and February 1911. It was reprinted in *Essays and Criticisms* (Constable and Co.), chapter xvi.

Baltic, and wished the Army to help him and not the French. *Pour comble de malheur* I learnt that Sir John French was for the Fisher plan, and at this time opposed union with the French on French soil. This was very exasperating, and I objected that nothing counted in comparison with weight at the decisive point, and that fooling in the Baltic was the sort of stuff amateurs were teaching the Navy, whose leaders seemed to be completely ignorant of strategy and of the necessity of making as sure as our means allowed the victory of France in the first great shock of battle.

Things were not looking so well, and I could not give Major Huguet the answer which he desired about the shifting of the conversations to an official basis. But meanwhile Sir E. Grey and Mr. Haldane had news of what was going on, and determined to meet in spite of their electioneering. They did so, at the greatest personal inconvenience, and to their everlasting credit agreed to take upon themselves the responsibility for continuing the conversations in a semi-official manner. They met at Berwick. Sir E. Grey's concurrence was largely due to the fact that, owing to the growth of foreign Navies, we were no longer able to remain isolated and aloof. Mr. Haldane then came on to London to see Sir Henry Campbell-Bannerman during the week-end of Sunday, Jan. 14. He obtained the new Prime Minister's approval, and then gave Sir Neville Lyttelton and General Grierson permission to carry on.

On Jan. 17 Major Huguet informed me that Grierson had opened relations with him that morning, and that he felt himself entitled to consider that Grierson would not have done so without authority from the Minister for War and the Government. I thought that he was perfectly justified in arriving at this conclusion, and informed Huguet that my share in the conversations was now at an end, and that it remained for the French Staff and ours to get to work and go ahead. The matter was not fully *en train*, of course, until the approval of the new Prime Minister, Sir Henry Campbell-Bannerman, had been secured. I had some doubt about the manner in which he would view it, but in his talk with Mr.

Haldane he was very firm and clear on the point that we should be prepared for all emergencies, and that conversations between the two Staffs, without any binding agreement between the Governments, were permissible measures of prudence. It was arranged that a paper should be signed by Grierson and Huguet stipulating that the conversations should not commit either Government, and this was done. C.-B. was a fine old Tory in Army matters. He was also a warm friend of the French, and quickly realised the whole position. How he explained matters to certain members of the new Cabinet I did not ask, and it did not matter. I believe that he considered it a departmental affair, and did not bring it before the Cabinet at all at the time.

I was quite well aware that the secrecy of conversations of this character could not be long preserved, and I was therefore not astonished when a French paper—the *Figaro*, I think it was—revealed the truth one fine day in a veiled but perfectly patent manner. I saw no harm in the indiscretion for which the French were solely responsible. Except in keeping my editor, Mr. Buckle, informed of the trend of affairs, I never mentioned the matter to a soul. Perhaps the Germans scented danger even before the *Figaro* article. They were very well informed, and Paris was always very leaky. But, obviously, the greatest good for peace could only be derived by German knowledge of the fact that the Anglo-French Entente, which Lord Lansdowne had effected in 1904, had been supplemented by a plan of naval and military co-operation in the event of German aggression. It was bound to give the Germans pause, and to make them dread the consequences of finding England across their path if they ventured on a war of aggression against France. I have no doubt that it did so, and that a revision of the war plans of the German Admiralty and Great General Staff necessarily followed. In any case, the menace to peace was removed, and gradually the storm-cloud passed away for the time. That we did not profit fully from the respite of seven years which preceded the break with Germany was a cardinal error for which the whole responsibility must be assigned to the statesmanship of the time.

The Anglo-French military conversations, officially begun in January 1906, continued uninterruptedly till the outbreak of war in 1914. They led to close co-operation of the British and French Staffs, and to the gradual working out of all the naval, military, and railway projects for the delivery of our Expeditionary Force in France. I believe that I suggested the name of the Expeditionary Force. It was first called the Striking Force, and I thought that this would alarm the Radicals unduly. As the improvements in our military affairs at home went on, the plans were constantly changed to take account of them, and this entailed much hard work in the days of General Grierson and of General Ewart who succeeded him. I was kept informed of the general plan of the arrangements, and was mainly concerned to watch that the principle of our military co-operation at the decisive point should be maintained intact. Our General Staff never deviated from this principle, which ultimately led us to make our main effort in the right quarter when war came. Why the principle of unity of command by sea and land dropped out [1] I have never heard. We fortunately found in Prince Louis of Battenberg a sailor to guarantee the safe passage of the Channel by our Army, and the Fisher Baltic plan was ultimately ruled out. Colonel Huguet's co-operation was perfect. He remained with us till the outbreak of war, and then accompanied our G.H.Q. in the field.

With the Staff reconnaissance-rides and other arrangements between the French and English Staffs, which followed after the definite settlement of the character of our military intervention, I had nothing to do. My impression is that in the years immediately preceding the war some of our soldiers and the French came to false conclusions

---

[1] 'I wish you distinctly to understand that your command is an entirely independent one, and that you will in no case come in any sense under the orders of any Allied general.'—Instruction of the Government to Sir John French : see *1914*, 1st edition, p. 15.

on the subject of a German attack, gravely underestimated the enemy's strength, misunderstood his strategy, and never took sufficiently into account the danger that the Germans would make their main effort through Belgium, often though I alluded to it in the *Times*.[1] We were within an ace of being ruined by the poverty of our strategic intelligence.

In the year 1895, when in charge of the French Section of the Intelligence Division, I had estimated that Germany could at that time place over 3,000,000 men in the field, and that the blow against France would be delivered by 1,250,000 to 1,500,000 Germans. Eleven years later no higher estimate was placed by the French upon the German figures, despite the continuous growth of the German Army in the interval. There followed a series of German military laws up to the outbreak of war, all of which increased the German power and were fully recorded by me year by year in the *Times*. The reasons why the German effort was underestimated have to be explained by those responsible for the miscalculations.

To the best of my present knowledge, Germany placed in the field, on both fronts, 61 Army Corps, besides Line of Communication troops and Landsturm formations. In October there appeared 6½ new Army Corps and a division of Marines, to be shortly followed by a second. By January 1915 the number of fighting formations placed in line was 69½ Army Corps, composed as follows:

	Army Corps.
Active Army Corps . . .	25½
Reserve Corps	21½
Ersatz Brigades . . .	6½
Reserve Corps of new formation .	7½
Landwehr Corps . . .	8½
Total .	69½

It was supposed by the French G.Q.G. at this time, January 1915, that about half, or 4,000,000 men, of the

---

[1] These allusions can be found in *Essays and Criticisms*, chapter xvi., and in *Vestigia*, chapter xxii. (Constable and Co.).

German still-existing recruiting resources were in the field, and that 3,500,000 men were still available, excluding 500,000 exempted as indispensable, and allowing 1,000,000 for the German casualties up to date. These resources were increased, year by year, by the annual contingents, and by anticipating coming contingents, each contingent being 550,000 gross, and giving an average net figure of under 400,000.

The weight of the initial effort made by Germany should increase our respect for the valour of those, mainly Frenchmen, but also British and Belgians, who checked the first onsets and won the victory of the Marne. Not until the whole of the available manhood of Germany had been thrown into the field, and had been well beaten, did Germany give up. The character of this war of attrition must always remain in our minds when we read the story of the First World War.

CHAPTER II

THE FIRST YEAR

AUGUST 1914—SEPTEMBER 1915

The outbreak of war—Divisions within the Cabinet—Mobilisation delayed—The violation of Belgium unites the whole country—Lord Kitchener's appointment as Secretary of State for War—His plans of organisation and view of the general situation, August 15—My views of the military situation on the eve of war—The Expeditionary Force leaves for France—Disclosure of the German concentration, August 12—Early defeats of the Allies and the retreat from Mons— The Marne victory—F.M. Lord Roberts's last offer of his services— My first visit to the Army in France—Life at Sir John French's G.H.Q.—Visits to the French and Belgian fronts—General Foch at Cassel—He asks me an interesting question—French and English languages—The King and Queen of the Belgians—The question of the shells—Reiterated demands for shells—War Office promises not kept—The situation on May 9, 1915—Heavy casualties in British attacks—The 2nd Battalion Rifle Brigade at Fromelles—My telegram of May 12—The Dardanelles drain on the munitions in France—Sir John French informed that he can expect no more reinforcements for a considerable time—A disquieting situation—Captain Stanley Wilson, M.P., and Mr. Bonar Law—Proposed action by the Unionist Leader—Mr. Lloyd George's action—Censoring of my telegram in France—My paper exposing the facts—Reconstruction of the Government—The Coalition Ministry—Creation of the Ministry of Munitions —Lord Kitchener stops my visits to Sir John French—Injudicious article in the *Daily Mail*—The Russian campaign—The Dardanelles— Recruiting difficulties—Suppression of my articles—Public service of Lord Derby at this time.

THE ostensible cause of the outbreak of the war was the murder of the Austrian Archduke Franz Ferdinand at Serajevo on June 28, 1914. This murder was followed by an Austrian ultimatum to Serbia of the most rigorous and exacting character, and though Serbia humbled herself, and agreed to almost all the terms, Austria pretended to regard the reply as unsatisfactory, and at once declared war.

This ultimatum was, I believe, drafted by Count Forgach, my old friend of the Hague days, in collaboration with

Count Berchtold and the German Ambassador at Vienna. Sir Edward Grey told me soon afterwards that the annotated text of it had been seen, before it was sent off, on the table of one of the chiefs of the Foreign Office in Berlin. The German military party, determined to wage war at the first favourable opportunity in order to forestall the impending expansion of the Russian Army, reckoned the moment propitious and the pretext adequate for war, and from the first Germany blocked all the openings to peace.

How much the Kaiser had to do with the decision, history will tell us later. My own feeling is that he did not wish for war, but was carried along by the tumult of events. In any case, his old friends Colonel von Leipzig and his wife suddenly appeared in London during the last days of July, as they had done at other times of crisis, and came straight to me. Von Leipzig was utterly opposed to war, and tried to concert means for stopping it even at this late hour. He proposed that we should admit the occupation of Belgrade by Austria as a satisfaction to her, and that operations should then cease pending an arrangement. I passed this on to the Cabinet, and some attempt was made to act in this sense, but it was much too late, for measure was followed by counter-measure, the German military party were in control, and all the efforts of Sir Edward Grey and the Tsar to avert the greatest catastrophe of history were rendered fruitless.

During the first ten days of Aug. 1914 it positively rained ultimatums and declarations of war, and very soon all the great Powers of Europe, except Italy, were at war. Though war had often been expected, it had been expected for so long, and so many crises had been successfully overcome by diplomacy, that it came in the end like a thief in the night, quite unexpectedly. We were far from being united in our determination to stand by our friends, for the whole spirit of Gladstonian Liberalism hated war like the plague, and most of all continental war, which was positively anathema to the party in office. These divisions were marked within the Cabinet, but when Germany sent an ultimatum to Belgium, demanded a right-of-way on the plea of military necessity, and thereby broke the faith of treaties to which she had set her hand, all doubts and differences vanished, and we went into the war wholly united and in a good cause.[1]

All my anxieties during the days immediately preceding the war, which began between us and Germany at 11 P.M. on Aug. 4, were centred upon the timely mobilisation and concentration of our land and sea forces. From July 27 onwards I urged in the *Times* and privately that our fleets should be sent to their war stations, and that the order for mobilisation should be issued to the Army.

Thanks to Mr. Churchill and Prince Louis of Battenberg, the order went to the fleets on the night of Wednesday, July 29, and it was a great relief when this was known, for it was not realised by us that Germany was unready for war at sea, and had not anticipated that we should take part in the war so soon, if at all. The German ultimatum to Belgium reached Brussels at 7 P.M. on Aug. 2. It was not known in London until after the Cabinet meeting on that day. The mobilisation of the Army was delayed until 11 A.M. on Monday, Aug. 3, when Lord Haldane, instructed

---

[1] The dates of the various declarations of war were as follows :—

	War declared by Central Powers.	War declared against Central Powers.
Serbia	July 28, 1914	August 9, 1914.
Russia	August 1, 1914	November 3, 1914.
France	August 3, 1914	August 3, 1914.
Belgium	August 4, 1914	April 7, 1917.
Japan	August 27, 1914	August 28, 1914.
England	November 23, 1914	August 4, 1914.
Portugal	March 9, 1916	November 23, 1914.
Rumania	August 29, 1916	August 27, 1916.
Greece		November 23, 1916.
United States		April 6, 1917.
Italy		May 23, 1915.
Italy (with Germany officially)		August 28, 1916.
China		August 14, 1917.
Brazil		October 26, 1917.

There also declared war, Montenegro, San Marino, Panama, Cuba, Siam Liberia, Guatemala, Nicaragua, Haiti, and Honduras.

by part of the Cabinet overnight, gave the order for it to the Army Council. The first day of mobilisation was Aug. 4, leaving us two days behind the French. All our military plans had been laid for a simultaneous mobilisation, and the delay of the Cabinet was partly responsible for the defeat at Mons, since we arrived there late, and with the Expeditionary Force not at full strength. I attacked the Government about this delay in the *Times*, and saw Sir Charles Douglas, then Chief of the General Staff, to urge action upon him. I found that he had warned the Cabinet explicitly of the dangers which they were running, but that they had not listened to him, and the only excuse was that the Cabinet were not united on the question of war until the violation of Belgian neutrality was an accomplished fact. The Germans invaded Belgium on Aug. 4.

After Colonel Seely had left the War Office as a consequence of the troubles in Ireland, Mr. Asquith, the Prime Minister, had taken charge of it. It was impossible for him to hold such an office in a great war with all his other responsibilities, and on Aug. 3, with the approval of the editor of the *Times*, Mr. Geoffrey Robinson, I made the first proposal in the Press that Lord Kitchener, who was at home on leave from Egypt, should be appointed War Minister. This proposal was warmly taken up all over the country and soon bore fruit. Lord K. sent Sir Henry Rawlinson to see me and find out what political game was behind my suggestion. I told him that I knew of none, and that I had made the suggestion in the public interest without any prompting from anybody.

It needed Lord K.'s immense military prestige to carry the public forward in the great work that lay in front of us. From no one else would the people accept the great military schemes needed for the expansion of the Army, while it seemed certain that Lord K. would keep the Cabinet up to their work, and would never allow them to make a disastrous peace. No one else could have asked the country for millions of volunteers, and no one else had the foresight to say that the war would last for three years. Even if Lord K. had done nothing more than this, his taking office would have been an inestimable service to the country, while although he had scarcely a friend left in the Cabinet at the end, the public retained their faith in him to the last in the most touching way. The tall, grim, silent figure—silent at least in the public estimation—whose impressive portrait appeared on every wall and on the recruiting posters, was the central feature of the war ; and if at any time the country had been asked to choose between him and the Cabinet, the latter would have come off second-best. This is not a soldier's appreciation only, it is a fact. Lloyd George admitted and deplored it to me more than once.

I was on the best of terms with Lord K. at the opening of the war and told him that I would do my best to support him if he would trust me. We had several talks, and a few days after he had taken office he sent for me to meet him at Lady Wantage's house in Carlton Gardens, when we had a long talk for a couple of hours about his plans. The purport of this conversation I published in the *Times* of Aug. 15, and as he revised my proof of the article, and approved of it, it stands as an authoritative account of his views at the time. Lord K. saw clearly that we were in for the greatest war of our history, and were bound to rise to the level of our responsibilities. He said that we had to create the armies of our needs, and that our enemy was a nation in arms of 70 million people who meant to crush us if they could. He allowed that we had stout Allies, but said that France was throwing the whole of her manhood into the field, leaving little behind except the successive annual contingents of recruits, while Russia, with all her immense capacity for defence, had untried and unproved offensive powers.

He thought, in these circumstances, that the war would last very long, and that it was his duty so to prepare our land forces that by their steadily expanding numbers and constantly increasing efficiency they should enable us to play a part worthy of England, and at the peace to impose terms in consonance with our interests. We must, he said, neglect for a time the works of peace and apply ourselves sternly to the business of war in defence of a righteous and impregnable cause. He allowed me to hint at the need for 500,000 additional men as a beginning, and thought that at the moment when other Powers were exhausted, we should prove to be most capable of continuing the war. There must, he declared, be no question of peace except on our own terms, and he proceeded to outline and discuss with me his plans for the Regulars, the Territorials, and the New Armies, all of which plans were subsequently carried out.

The publication of this article aroused the greatest public interest, but, by a perverse stroke of fate, it became the determining cause of our estrangement. He sent for me one day and told me that the Radical editors had made the devil of a fuss about his having given me the exclusive knowledge of his plans, and that he had been bitterly attacked in the Cabinet on this subject. He was, with all his power at this time, terrified of the politicians. He said that it was as much as his life was worth to see me again, but told me that I could always see one of his Staff, and that they would tell me anything I wanted to know. But it was not the same thing, and though I occasionally called to see FitzGerald, most capable and loyal of Lord K.'s men, great questions arose on which I could usefully speak to my old Chief alone, and in the natural course of things, when I could not get things done which I knew ought to be done, I drifted away from him. His method of doing everything himself made it useless to talk to any one else, as I knew full well from having served on his Staff. Poor Sir Charles Douglas, a slave to duty, and the most honest and trustworthy of men, died very soon, and was succeeded as Chief of the General Staff in London by Sir James Wolfe Murray, who was a good man in his day, but was too gentle to stand up to Lord K. As a result, the General Staff lost its rightful position, and Lord K. usurped most of its duties without knowing how to perform them. Lord K. was pre-eminently an administrator. He knew little about our political system and Army organisation at home. He had not seen nor studied European Armies and countries, and was not versed in all the great military problems which had been exercising European General Staffs in our time. Sir Henry Sclater, the Adjutant-General, was a hard worker, but was as wax in Lord K.'s hands, while Sir John Cowans restricted himself to the Q.M.G. work, which he did splendidly, but he knew little of other things going on.

My view of the general military situation at the opening of the war was given in the *Times* of Aug. 3 on the eve of the declaration of war. I showed in that article that though Russia had 4,000,000 trained men, it would take her a month to place from twelve to sixteen Army Corps on the Austro-German frontiers; that the 2,000,000 French of the Active and Reserve Armies expected to meet the German masses between the fourteenth and twenty-first days of mobilisation; that by the fourteenth day Russia could give but little help; that Germany would leave from three to five Army Corps of the First Line to face Russia, and would mass her main forces against France, which would find against her a superior Army; and that if we failed at the rendezvous,—which seemed possible at that moment, for France had mobilised on Aug. 2 and we had not—history would assign our cowardice as the cause.

Things fell out precisely in this manner, with the exception that Sir John French arrived with four divisions and the cavalry in time for the first encounters, or nearly so. All the work of mobilising and moving this force to France was admirably, secretly, and expeditiously accomplished, and I am not sure that the Germans knew that we were in front of them till Aug. 22. The passage of the steamers was covered by the Navy. All the previous work of the French and British Staffs from 1906 onward bore fruit, and it may almost be said that the army took wing without the public at home being aware of what had happened. The Territorials dropped into their places for home defence, and some went abroad even at this time, while scores of thousands of recruits trooped in voluntarily to join, though there were neither quarters, clothing, equipment, nor arms for them. There had joined, by the third week in May 1915, no less than 1,239,312 Regular recruits and 469,611 Territorials, the largest intake in any one week being in the week ending Sept. 5, 1914, when 174,901 Regulars enlisted. The work thrown on home staffs, and especially on the Q.M.G.'s department, by this avalanche was simply overwhelming.

The best journalistic *coup* that I brought off at this time was the publication on Aug. 12 of a map showing the concentration of the German Armies on the French frontier, giving the position of every Army Corps. The concentration was not quite complete since the 2nd, 5th, and 6th Army Corps were not yet up and were not shown, but all the rest were given, and I think with fair exactitude. Such a *coup* had never been brought off before contact of the armies by any newspaper in any war. This map completely exposed the German aim of enveloping the French left by a march through Belgium, and had the proper conclusions been drawn by the French Staff from the indications on which the map was based, the great misfortunes of the opening of the war would have been avoided. Directly I had made and studied the map I began to preach a defensive until the advancing hosts had broken their heads against our prepared positions, and I am persuaded that if the French had held their left defensively from Namur through Brussels to Antwerp, as they might have done in co-operation with the Belgian and British Armies, they would never have lost Western Belgium, nine departments of France, and the great harbour on the Scheldt. The information on which my map was based was known to the French on Aug. 10. The first encounter between us and the Germans did not take place until Aug. 22, and there was ample time to have acted as the information really dictated.

But things happened that I feared would happen. The French had their own plans which had been long prepared for certain eventualities which did not happen, and when the conditions changed the French plans did not sufficiently change with them. The three French attacks in Alsace, Lorraine, and the Belgian Ardennes were launched regardless of the menace in the North, and our unfortunate Army was left to be positively overwhelmed by a flood of enemies. It fought superbly and saved the French left from being enveloped and destroyed, but the real trouble was that no French general at this time had the prestige and the power to order a defensive attitude to be temporarily observed when the contrary tactics had been preached for so many years.

After a long retreat, great losses, and much suffering, the Allied Armies turned on the Marne, and from Sept. 6 onward there began that wonderful series of battles in which the French re-established the campaign and drove the enemy back in rout to the Aisne. The action of General Joffre and of his Army Commanders and their valiant troops during this period filled me with admiration, and, except in July 1918, there was perhaps never such an abrupt reversal of the rôles between two contending armies as there was at this famous time. I also thought that Sir John French's decision to cross the Aisne in pursuit was one of the boldest ever taken by a commander, and the behaviour of our troops in that fight seemed to me most glorious. Our Army then moved to the left and began that series of wonderful actions which culminated in the defeat of the second great German effort to overwhelm us in the West, and eventually ended in the establishment of rival lines of defence, and in the crystallisation of the fighting into the trench warfare which endured throughout the years 1915, 1916, and 1917.

One episode during this early period remains firmly in my mind. Only a few weeks before his death in France, Field-Marshal Lord Roberts drove up to my house at Hampstead one morning, and his alert and active figure suddenly appeared at my library door. 'I have come to talk strategy with you : get out the maps,' he said. He then proceeded to unfold to me a plan which he thought should be carried out, namely, a landing on the Belgian coast, the outflanking of the German line of battle, and the ruin of its communications. He thought that the stroke

should be delivered by 150,000 men, and asked what I had
to say about it. We discussed it up and down ; the troops,
ships, escort, landing, organisation, forward march, and so
on, and we finally decided that though it was an operation
of great risk and difficulty, it was the right stroke to deliver.
The Field-Marshal then rose and walked sharply up and
down the room, deep in thought. 'Yes,' he said at last,
'yes, it must be done . . . and I must go in command of
it.' The old Field-Marshal, at the age of eighty-two, was
prepared to risk his great fame, his reputation, and his life
in command of an expedition attended with infinite risks,
and more suited to a man of half his age. I said nothing,
but as I accompanied him to his motor car I pressed his hand
and could only say, 'Field-Marshal, you are splendid!' He
went off to suggest the stroke and to offer his services in
the command to Lord K. first, and to the Prime Minister
afterwards. His offer was not accepted, but his grand
soldier's spirit shone out in this last and supreme offer of
his services to his country.

I had plenty to do in writing constantly to the *Times*
upon the campaigns in East and West, in seeing important
people, in looking over many hospitals due to private
initiative, such as the Duchess of Bedford's hospital at
Woburn, which was a model undertaking, and in visiting
our camps at home to watch the progress of the new
troops. But when the campaign in France settled down
I thought that the time had come when I should not be
too much in the way if I went out, so I accepted an invitation from the Field-Marshal to visit the Army in France,
and reached St. Omer, then Sir John French's Headquarters, on Nov. 23, 1914.

It was the first of many visits which I paid to the Army
in France, thanks to the friendship and hospitality of
the Field-Marshal. During these visits I went round the
British lines several times, saw and talked with most of the
chief Army and Corps Commanders, discussed matters with
the heads of services, had many conversations with officers
and men of all arms and all ranks, and, last but not least,

enjoyed many a long talk with the Field-Marshal alone, and with his two successive Chiefs of Staff, Sir Archibald Murray and Sir William Robertson, who were two of my oldest and most valued soldier friends.

I will first describe the G.H.Q. itself. An ignominious peer on one occasion got up in the House of Lords and made himself the echo of malicious rumour which had spread the report that cards were played and ladies entertained at G.H.Q. The Field-Marshal was not a card player, but if a rubber of Bridge had been played I should certainly have taken a hand at it. I never saw a pack of cards during my many visits, and am convinced that the life was much too strenuous for any amusement of this kind. I saw no ladies at G.H.Q. except a nurse who accompanied Lady Horner when her boy was badly wounded, and I am sure that this peer's charges were as silly as they were mendacious.

Sir John lived very simply. He occupied an ordinary house in an ordinary street, and except the two sentries at the gate there was no display of any kind. Sir John and a few of his Staff occupied the building in which were usually lodged the young Prince of Wales and his com-panion, Lord Claud Hamilton, while in a house opposite the few guests were lodged, and here there lived Billy Lambton, his military secretary, Brinsley FitzGerald, his private secretary, Major Watt and Freddy Guest, his A.D.C.s, and Colonel Barry, who was looking after the Prince. Vesey, the assistant military secretary, Lord Percy and Major Swinton, who at first acted as 'Eye-Witnesses' and wrote accounts for the Press, were also installed here, but were not in the G.O.C.'s mess. Murray had been in it at one time, but the constant flow of messages from the front so interrupted meals and disturbed the Field-Marshal's calm that Murray at last wisely withdrew, while all the other Chiefs of Services had messes of their own in various parts of the town. The living was plain and good. Sir John sat at the end of the table facing the windows. There were generally six or eight persons at meals, but now and then some of his particular cronies, such as Philip Chetwode and

Cis Bingham, turned up and had a seat. There were just the dining-room, Sir John's sitting-room, and the A.D.C.s' room, besides the kitchen on the ground floor. Meals were short. The others thought it best to give the Field-Marshal's mind a rest by talking of things not connected with the war, telling good stories, and indulging in friendly unconventional talk. There was no display, and no formality. We all dropped in when we liked.

The Prince of Wales was under twenty-one in the late autumn of 1914. He looked much younger, and his fair hair and pink and white complexion added to his youthful appearance. He was full of energy and go, and his idea of perfect happiness was to join his Grenadiers in the trenches. He was a tremendous walker, making light of a toe and heel of ten miles before breakfast, and he drove his own car at a fast pace. He made capital maps of his various trips, some of which he showed me, and wrote in his room till all hours in the morning. He was most punctual in all his duties and saluted every officer senior to him with the greatest precision in true Guards fashion. He was very much liked, but was treated like any other subaltern, and no one made any fuss about him. A rare education for a Prince of Wales !

If fighting was going on, Sir John was either at or went off early to his *poste de commandement*, which was nearer the front than St. Omer, and from this point he controlled affairs. Most days at St. Omer he had breakfast at 8 A.M., and at 9 A.M. the various heads of departments reported to him; namely, the Chief of Staff, Q.M.G., A.G., P.M.O., Director of Intelligence, and so forth. The Field-Marshal issued orders, if any were necessary, and then went off and spent the day visiting his Army Commanders, any point of the line of special interest, the hospitals, or some particular service or department. Often he visited the French generals in his neighbourhood, and was visited by them, while occasionally he travelled by car to Chantilly to see General Joffre. The liaison officers also reported to him regularly. They were good men like Lord Loch, Sidney Clive, Hugh Dawnay, etc., and they kept

him *au courant* with all that was going on.   In the evening
the heads of services came again with the reports of the day,
and by all these means Sir John was kept well posted in the
whole situation of his own troops and that of his enemy.
One day crossing the Channel I had a talk with the F.M.
about the strategy of the campaign, and suggested that an
offensive down both banks of the Meuse seemed to me the
proper direction for our efforts.   The F.M. surprised me by
saying that he had never discussed these things with Joffre.

Most days when I was at G.H.Q. I had at least two long
talks with the Field-Marshal alone, usually early and late,
and I was impressed by his complete grasp of the whole
military situation, and by his intimate knowledge of all the
details of his troops and their services.   He possessed the
sacred fire of leadership in a rare degree.   I never knew him
to be depressed.   He was the incarnation of confidence, and
he inspired confidence in all.   Though he had been through
such terrible experiences during the retreat, he was remarkably well, alert, and in all his mental and physical vigour.
Nothing escaped him, and the rapidity of his decisions was
most remarkable.   But he was greatly enraged at the con-
tinual interference of Lord K. with the operations, and at
the constant worrying about small subjects on the part
of the War Office at home.   He did not at all approve of
Lord K.'s visits to France, considering him a Civil Minister
who had no right to pose as the leading soldier in Sir John's
domain, and even at this early date of Nov. 1914, Sir John
was much hampered by, and exercised about, the supply of
guns and shells.   I did my very best to try and make him
keep on good terms with Lord K. for the sake of the cause,
but each time that I went out to France I found that there
had been more friction, and that the relations between the
two men had become more strained.   I could do nothing at
home on account of the attitude which Lord K. had been
compelled by the politicians to adopt towards me, and there
seemed to be no one else sufficiently intimate with the two
Field-Marshals to smooth things over.   Each had true
friends, but each had different friends.

During my visits to France I had a car placed at my disposal, started early and came in late, spending as much time as I could with the commanders and troops. Frequently I was accompanied on these tours by one or other of the King's Messengers, who arrived every morning and was at a loose end during the day preceding his return. The K.M.s were hard-worked men. The idea that their job was a soft one was only entertained by people who did not know what was implied in almost continuous travel to all parts of Europe in war time. I thought it a good thing to help these men to hear and see all that they could, so that the truth of the situation might be known at home. There was nothing to conceal. The Germans had all the best of the ground at the end of the operations in November, and had a great superiority of guns, but their two great attacks had been shattered, and I found all our officers and men in the best of health and spirits, and imbued with that invincible belief in their superiority which Sir John's boldness did so much to inspire. He was confidence itself. Every day the Armies under him were growing, and the troops waited with impatience for the moment when their time would come to attack.

I went to France as often as I could, because in view of the attitude which Lord K. had adopted I scarcely ever went near the War Office at this time. In France I was told everything, and was especially able to keep touch with the German dispositions, thanks first to General Macdonogh, the extremely competent head of our Intelligence Service, and subsequently thanks to the French G.Q.G. and their excellent officers. Macdonogh was a first-class man at this work, very hard-working, methodical, sure, unenthusiastic, and perfectly indefatigable in his pursuit of the truth. Colonel Dupont of General Joffre's Staff, and subsequently Colonel de Cointet, were worthy colleagues of his, and I can only say that the information concerning the enemy was so good that we knew the positions of almost all the regiments of the enemy. The air service, which began with small things—forty-five planes, if I remember right—and gradually worked up so wonderfully, was most valuable, and from the photographs taken by them there were compiled plans showing all the German trenches in detail.

I also visited the French and Belgian fronts. Foch was then commanding on our left, with his Headquarters at Cassel, a town on a hill with many windmills and a fine view over the surrounding country. General, afterwards Marshal, Foch was certainly, even in 1914, one of the most distinguished of the French generals in the war. His services at the Marne, during the great battle of Ypres, in Artois, then on the Somme, and finally in the Supreme Command, were of incalculable value to the cause, and he had a special gift for the offensive, which suited his fiery temperament. He was a good comrade, and understood us better than most of his colleagues. All my recollections of him are of the most pleasant character, and as he spoke his mind to me on matters small and great I never failed to look him up when I found myself within reach of him, and I learnt much from him whenever I paid him a visit, as this diary will show. He was dead against the Salonika expedition, which was my pet aversion amongst all the follies that we committed during the campaign, and he was a man who was always learning from events and endeavouring to improve the handling of his troops.

I recall one curious episode which showed that even the most illustrious and enlightened of French g nerals never quite understood in those early days our British policy. At the close of one day which I spent with him in 1914 he took me into his sanctum, and having shut the door, said, in a most impressive way, that there was one subject upon which he seriously desired my opinion, for he said that he could not ask any one else, and he knew that I would not misinform him. I wondered what it could be. He took up a map of northern Europe, spread it out, and asked me solemnly how much European territory we should expect for ourselves at the end of the war. I could not help laughing, and said, ' But, my dear General, not an inch of continental territory at a gift ! ' He seemed surprised and incredulous, whereupon I asked him if he knew who founded the British Empire. He mentioned various names, and I said 'No' to them all. Well then, he said at last, who founded it ? I replied, 'Joan of Arc,' and went on to point out that from the moment when we were driven out of France our visions of continental domination ended, and that we had turned to the sea and gradually created our Oceanic Empire. I told him that I confidently expected to see a statue to Joan in Palace Yard one day, and on it the inscription, ' Founder of the British Empire ! '

One of the difficulties which beset us in the war was the inability of almost every French general to speak a word of English, and the almost equal ignorance of most of our senior officers at first of French. This was a real hindrance to relations, and I think it was particularly harmful to us in political and military affairs, for we made an effort to converse in French, and here our good Allies had all the best of us, and regularly talked us down. There was practically no leading statesman or soldier on our side who could speak French fluently and hold his own in a conference in French. I never met a French general or statesman during the war, Clemenceau excepted, who even attempted to speak English, and though the younger liaison officers on both sides were in most cases good linguists, it was throughout a serious defect that the leaders could not converse rapidly and with ease in each other's tongue. The extraordinary thing was that the rank and file of the Army, though not knowing a word of French at the start, and uncommonly little at the finish, seemed to get on very well with the French people, and especially with the girls. I saw soldiers sitting talking with girls times out of mind, and they got on famously though mutually ignorant of each other's tongue. It was a very extraordinary position. Here was the pick of our youth in a foreign land, quartered in the houses of the people, and with all the able-bodied Frenchmen gone away to fight. What the results of this extraordinary state of affairs may be the future historian will have to tell us, but Frenchmen openly spoke of the building up of a new race and regarded the inevitable consequences of the position with apparent satisfaction. I must say that I never heard of any serious charges brought against our men, and I think that their conduct was quite exemplary on the whole, and that we had every reason to be very proud of them.

When at La Panne I visited the King and Queen of the Belgians and had lunch with them. They were very civil to me, and I had long political and military talks with them. They were living in the most bourgeois style in quite a small seaside villa right upon the shore with the dunes at the back. Countess Ghislaine de Caraman Chimay, my old friend of Brussels days, was in attendance. The Queen one day made me go and see a long, low cottage hard by as she thought that it would interest me. It certainly did. It was full of books, every room, and evidently the home of a literary man. On inquiry I found that it had been taken before the war by a German, Dr. Reich, who had selected La Panne because it was such an unsophisticated spot and had no soldiers near. Here the good man established himself to write a book on Universal Peace, and the war surprised him in the midst of it. He had selected by inadvertence the Headquarters of an Army in the greatest of wars. Reich was interned, and his cottage became a barrack for gendarmes, whose swords and pistols were seen hanging in front of his precious but neglected books. Truly an example of the vanity of human wishes !

The King of the Belgians had shown himself to be one of the great figures of the war. The Queen was a very brave woman. She had been in the front trenches and occupied herself in hospital work. The royal villa was very exposed to attack, both from sea and air. While I was there one afternoon the German aeroplanes were over it and under fire from Belgian guns, but the Queen went on with her tea with perfect calmness and unconcern.

General Tom Bridges, the head of our mission, was away at this time, but Prince Alexander of Teck was there, also Major Tyrrell, who ought to have been at the Dardanelles as he had been Military Attaché at Constantinople, and some others,—a very cheery party.　Lady Dorothie Feilding, who was doing fine work with the sick and wounded, came in one day,—a remarkable character—and she was afterwards decorated for her gallant conduct in attending to the wounded under fire.　Thousands of our women of all classes were already distinguishing themselves by rare devotion to duty at home and abroad.

The episode which aroused the greatest public interest, so far as I was concerned, during the first months of the war, was the share which I took in the revelation of the want of shells in the British Army.　I had been able, during my frequent visits to France, to ascertain how lamentably short we were of high explosive shells for our field artillery in particular, and it was with this gun and this projectile, at this period of the war, that we prepared the way for the infantry assault.　We were also short of heavy guns of all calibres, in which the enemy enormously outnumbered us, and of shells for those which we possessed ; we were short of trench mortars, of maxims, of rifle and hand grenades, and, in fact, of almost all the necessary instruments and materials for trench warfare ; and the trouble was that Lord K. did not comprehend the importance of artillery in the war, took no effective measures to increase our supplies of it, and concealed the truth of the situation from his colleagues in the Cabinet.　There were no regular Press correspondents with our Army at this time.

I shall never forget the look on our soldiers' faces when they came out of the trenches after a long hammering by the German artillery to which ours, at this time, could make little reply.　It was a look of utter and complete weariness and it haunted me.　They seemed almost dead to the world.　Our G.H.Q. in France had quickly realised their deficiencies.　They had started with scarcely any H.E. shells for field guns, but, from their experiences on the Aisne, they raised their demand to 15 per cent. of H.E. in September.　On Oct. 10, 1914, they raised the proportion to 25 per cent., and on Dec. 31, as the result of further experience, to 50 per cent.　Sir Archibald Murray was haled over to London to see Lord K. at the end of December about this demand for 50 per cent. of H.E. for field artillery guns, and was roundly abused about it. Murray told me at the time that Lord K. had informed him that he was not fit to be a General Staff Officer, and that the British Army ought to be able to take positions without artillery. He even instanced the Atbara as a precedent, proving himself to be totally unacquainted with the lessons of the campaign. The request for 50 per cent. of H.E. was refused.

I suppose that General von Donop, the M.G.O., did his best, but all that I can say is that all deliveries promised in France were late, and that our Army, on every occasion during the earlier battles of the war, was completely out-matched by the guns, shells, and maxims of the enemy. I believe that the War Office had given our contracts to men of straw who were unable to produce the goods, but I do not think that this absolved the M.G.O. I had watched the state of our ammunition in France with great anxiety and growing anger. Every time that I went over I heard of promises from the War Office, and found on my next visit that the promises had not been kept. Representation after representation had had no effect. I found our trenches being plastered with shells, and our guns restricted to a few rounds per day. Three times I endeavoured to see Lord K. on this subject, and three times I failed. It was useless to see any one else, and I found that my allusions to the subject in the *Times*, censored as everything inconvenient to the Government was censored during the war, were not enough to rouse the country to the facts. The Army in France knew the situation. Lord K. and the M.G.O.'s branch knew it. The public knew nothing, and it was not certain that the Cabinet was any wiser.

I knew that the great Anglo-French offensive in the spring of 1915 was due to begin on May 9, and I went over some time before it, hoping to find that after the lapse of so many months we might have approached to the 50 per cent. standard. I found, on the contrary, that we had only 7 per cent. Our 700 field guns represented at that time tho bulk of our armament, and we had only 71 guns of larger calibre than 5 in., so that we were obviously not in a position to prepare an infantry attack as experience had shown it should be prepared. I went up to the Ypres front to see the end of the heavy fighting which followed the first German gas attack. I was incensed by the little return which we could make to the German guns. We had 51,000 casualties between April 22 and May 9, mainly from this cause. Whereas, again, the French on our right in Artois, on May 9, used 240 rounds of H.E. shell per field gun per day, and prepared their attack by a violent and continuous bombardment lasting for four hours, we could only afford forty minutes' similar bombardment; and while the German trenches in front of the French were knocked to bits, those in front of us were not similarly treated. Much barbed wire remained uncut, the German defences remained but little injured, and the very numerous machine guns of the enemy were not placed out of action. I witnessed the attack. We obtained insignificant results at the cost of heavy loss. I visited the 2nd Battalion of my old regiment, the Rifle Brigade, and saw its commanding officer, Colonel R. B. Stephens, immediately after the action at Fromelles. He gave me a paper showing that the battalion had gone into action with 29 officers and 1090 other ranks, and had come out, 24 hours later, with only one young company officer, who had been in the Cambridge Eleven the previous year, and 245 other ranks unwounded. I was enraged by this loss which was attributed by the troops solely to the failure of the guns, due in its turn to want of shells.

I therefore determined to expose the truth to the public, no matter at what cost. I sent off to the *Times*, on May 12, without consulting any one, a telegram which became famous, and stated, amongst other things, ' that the want of an unlimited supply of high explosive shells was a fatal bar to our success.'[1] These words were my own,

---

[1] ' Never before perhaps in the history of the world, certainly of war, have sixteen words in a newspaper produced such epoch-making results.' —*Adventures in Interviewing*, p. 124, by Isaac F. Marcosson (U.S.A.).

and were not suggested by Sir John French. The original of my telegram contained much more than saw the light when it was published on May 14. General Macdonogh censored it, and cut out all allusion to the Rifle Brigade casualties, as well as all my remarks about the want of heavy guns, howitzers, trench mortars, maxims, and rifle grenades. I believe that Sir John French never saw the telegram, though he told me afterwards that he approved of it. Macdonogh consulted Brinsley FitzGerald, who told him that he felt sure that Sir John would approve, and away the fateful telegram went, dreadfully bowdlerised, it is true, but still containing, in the one little phrase, enough high explosive to blow the strongest Government of modern times into the air.

On Friday, May 14, I picked up at St. Omer Captain Stanley Wilson, M.P., a King's Messenger, motored with him to Hazebrouck, where Sir John's Headquarters were temporarily located, and took stock of the situation. On Saturday, May 15, I went, again with Captain Wilson, to Le Couteau, where we climbed the church tower and witnessed from the top of it a bombardment preparatory to a night attack. We returned to Hazebrouck at 5 P.M., where I saw the Field-Marshal and heard some exceedingly disagreeable news. He had been ordered to send a large proportion of our precious and exceedingly small reserve of shells to the Dardanelles, with one or two of the largest of our heavy guns, and had received another communication which I can only describe as heartbreaking.

This was a letter from the War Office signed by Mr. Cubitt, but emanating, I was afterwards told, from Lord K. himself. I think that the date of the letter was May 14, but am not sure. It began by saying that the Admiralty, in consequence of the new dispositions of the Fleet, were no longer able to safeguard the shores of England from invasion by the enemy on a large scale, and that, in view of this statement, the War Office were no longer able to fulfil their promises with regard to reinforcements for the Army in France. It said that the Territorial regiments at home were not up to full strength, and that consequently the War

Office would be unable to promise drafts for the Territorials in the fighting line in France. This was most grave, as the strengths of these regiments were very low. The letter went on to say that, with regard to the New Armies, Sir John had already received the 9th Division and was expecting the 14th, but that it was now uncertain whether the latter could be sent at present, and that, if it were sent, no further reinforcement of any kind whatsoever could be expected for a considerable period of time.

Such was the general purport of the communication, and the exact wording I do not pretend to reproduce. It was most disheartening, and though no one questioned the Admiralty opinion, or the deductions drawn from it, it was certainly extraordinary that our Commander in France should be placed in such an unenviable position a week after opening his operations agreed on with the French. It seemed impracticable for Sir John to fulfil his promises to our Allies were his few shells to be taken away, and the flow of his reinforcements to be suspended at such a critical moment. I believe that on May 16 we had only four rounds per gun in reserve on our Line of Communication instead of 150.

I told Captain Wilson the facts and asked him to see what he could do in London. He crossed the following day, Sunday, May 16, saw Mr. Bonar Law at 5 P.M. at the Carlton Club the same day in the presence of Mr. J. A. Grant, M.P., and informed him how matters stood. In view of Captain Wilson's communication, and my telegram which had already appeared, Mr. Bonar Law informed him that he would see Mr. Asquith at once and would tell him that he intended to move in the House of Commons for the appointment of a Committee to inquire into the exact position with regard to munitions and reinforcements for our Army in the field. But first he desired to be placed in communication with me, and as I was due to arrive that evening in London at 9 P.M., Captain Wilson promised to meet me at Victoria, and he there informed me of Mr. Bonar Law's wish.

I had been furious about the censoring of the telegram, and had hastened to London to expose the facts. Mr. Asquith, immediately before, doubtless on the faith of false information supplied to him, had declared in a speech at Newcastle that we had no lack of shells; and while I was in France he had refused to consider even the idea of a Coalition Ministry. He was obliged, and very hurriedly, to alter his note. It was Mr. Lloyd George who, as he frequently told me afterwards, applied the match to my train of gunpowder. I saw him on my return, and he told me that immediately he had read my telegram in the *Times* of May 14, he had gone to the Prime Minister and had informed him that he would be unable to go on. I was astonished at his ignorance of the facts. He had been on the Cabinet Munitions Committee appointed in Oct. 1914, and was on another Special Committee assembled in April 1915 to deal with war material. Yet he seemed to know nothing of what was happening. I gave to Lloyd George a hastily-drafted paper exposing all our deficiencies in munitions and guns of all types, and giving the history of the shortage. I had no need to make a further disclosure to the public, for I found a first-class political crisis in full blast. Having posted up Lloyd George with the facts, and having his promise that he would go straight to the Prime Minister, I saw Lord Curzon, Mr. Bonar Law, Sir Edward Carson, Sir F. E. Smith, and other Unionist leaders; and at dinner at Bonar Law's house, when Carson was present and F. E. came in later, I told them all I knew, and neither minced my words nor concealed my feelings. My exposure was fully sustained by the report which Sir John sent over. The Unionist Party informed the Prime Minister that there would have to be a debate, and the Prime Minister, realising that he had been inaccurately informed, that he would be beaten, and that he had no defence, ran for shelter under the Opposition umbrella and decided to accept the Coalition Ministry which a week before he had rejected with contumely.

Thus fell from office the old Gladstonian Liberal Party which had never understood foreign politics, and had neither foreseen the war nor prepared for it. Questions were asked in the House of Commons about my telegram, and Mr. Tennant had the imprudence to declare that it was not censored in England, thereby inferentially throwing the blame upon Sir John French and his staff for exposing the Government, though God knows it was time they did. But Freddy Guest was at home and flew down to the *Times* when I gave him the original of my telegram as it reached the *Times* office with the London Censor's stamp upon it, and I begged him to throw it down on the table of the House of Commons, and to inform Tennant, with my compliments, that he was mistaken. But whether Guest saved his own Liberal people, or whether Tennant learnt his mistake by some other means, he withdrew his statement and saved his skin. I learnt long afterwards that my telegram had been taken by Colonel Cockerill to Major-General Charles Callwell, then D.M.O., and that Cockerill had asked that it should be passed. Both knew the real situation, and Callwell replied, ' All right, carry on.' The telegram never went before the Press Bureau, and how the Censor's stamp came to be on the telegram I do not know. On such slight accidents do great events turn !

This explosion was followed by the reconstruction of the Government and the establishment of a Ministry of Munitions under Lloyd George, who handed over the Chancellorship to McKenna. The general provision of an adequate supply of munitions of all descriptions dates from this convulsion, but Lord K. was so furious with me about it that he ordered Sir John, in a private letter which the F.M. showed to me, not to allow me to visit his Headquarters any more, and it was not until the battle of the Somme that I was able to see with my own eyes the complete transformation in the relative strength of the two artilleries, effected by a year of Lloyd George's administration of his new office. This was a grief to me, but the only thing that really mattered was the safety of the Army and the success of the cause.

The reconstruction of the Government, and the disappearance of many Radical politicians to make room for the Unionists in the new administration, made me shoals of enemies. Every endeavour was made to show that I had been engaged in an intrigue against the Government or was acting under the orders of Northcliffe, and various reptiles bit me whenever they could. It is not an intrigue to endeavour to save an Army from defeat by a necessary public exposure when all official representations have hopelessly failed. Northcliffe, whom I had neither seen nor consulted on this matter from first to last, made things much worse by coming in late upon the scene, five days after the publication of my telegram, and publishing in the *Daily Mail* a most ill-judged personal attack on Lord K. This article had precisely the contrary effect of what was intended. The *Mail* was burnt on the Stock Exchange on May 22, and for some time its circulation fell. The best of the joke was that the *Daily Mail* subsequently proclaimed itself to have been the organ that exposed the shell shortage. It had nothing to do with it, nor had Northcliffe, though the latter did the Army some good turns later, as my diary will show. All that Northcliffe did by this particular attack was to get Lord K. the Garter, and, by causing a revulsion of feeling in Lord K.'s favour, to confirm him in his office.

I thought it best in Sir John's interest not to deal much with affairs in France after this episode, and occupied myself mainly with following the terrible Russian campaign, and in endeavouring to arouse people to the need for men and for compulsory service. The German attack upon Russia, which had begun on May 1, 1915, continued all this year well into September, by which date the Russians had been driven out of Poland, Courland, and the best part of Galicia, mainly, though not entirely, owing to their lack of rifles, guns, and shells. The Russians fought gloriously, often almost without arms, but were overwhelmed by the superior leading, organisation, and armament of the enemy. The campaign was well conducted by the Germans, who made an immense number of prisoners and captured a vast quantity of rifles and guns, leaving the Russian Army in the end almost at the point of extenuation, but never out of heart. Many of us feared that the Germans would follow up their victories when the frost came, and march on Petrograd, but they made the supreme blunder of leaving their work half finished at this time, and of returning in the winter of 1915–16 to the West, leaving a thin veil of troops on a huge front of 700 miles in the East, and allowing the Russians time for recovery.

This campaign, which filled me with profound interest, I regarded as the turning point of the war at the time, and from June to September I was mainly occupied in following and commenting upon it. The Dardanelles expedition was not a subject that I was able to write about freely, for although I admired greatly the bold landing of Ian Hamilton and the superb gallantry of his men, I recognised that we could not, for a long time, have sufficient military resources to win in France and at Constantinople at the same time; and for this reason,—though I thought Constantinople a right objective, and had so informed Hankey, the Secretary of the Defence Committee, at the opening of the war with Turkey—I disapproved of the Dardanelles adventure. I believed that there were three times as many Turks at the Dardanelles, or within short call of it, as there were British in Sir Ian's little force, and I never perceived any sound basis or plan for the glorious but hopeless proceedings which followed. Sooner or later, I thought, we should have to meet army by army, and our strength was never sufficient to offer Sir Ian a fair chance of winning. By dividing our armies between France and the Dardanelles it seemed probable that we should be too weak for victory in either theatre, as indeed we proved to be, and as I could say nothing good for the expedition to the Dardanelles, and the Censor mangled the few articles which I drafted on this operation, I relapsed into silence. The first Report of the Dardanelles Commission has revealed most of the facts, and I need say no more about it here.

Of even greater interest was the question of recruiting at home. The preliminary enthusiasm of our people gave us in the first months a huge number of men, and as we were unable to arm these men, or even to equip and clothe them, for many long months, the question of recruiting was not at first of great moment. But it became evident during the second quarter of the year 1915 that we were not obtaining by voluntary recruiting the regular flow necessary for maintaining our strength in the field, and the creation of new divisions had to cease. Lord K. had made the mistake of ignoring the County Associations and the organisation which Lord Haldane had left behind him as the foundation of a future National Army, and the New Armies had no real territorial connection and no depots or reserves. Lord K. knew nothing of modern military organisation, and he had not a strong Adjutant-General in Henry Sclater. Lord K., when numbers began to fail, concealed the fact from the Government and the public, as he had done in the case of the shells. Whole articles which I wrote on this subject were suppressed by the Censorship, and matters steadily went from bad to worse. Had Asquith or Lord K. come forward at any time to announce the need for Compulsion, the country would joyfully have accepted it, but both hung back, and it was not until Lord Derby and his assistants invented the Group System that things began to mend. Derby, in my view, performed a great public service at this time, and deserved the gratitude of the country. His system merged easily into full-blown Compulsion when the situation of the Army had become wellnigh desperate, and the Asquith Government were obliged to move.

Posterity will probably wonder how this generation regarded the casualties, which were severe from the first and ran into 6000 and 7000 a day during the stiffest fighting later in the war. What happened at first was what M. Thiers long ago predicted would happen, namely, that after the first great battles all our best families were in mourning, and many humble homes besides. The heroines who suffered in the glorious deaths of those whom they loved set a noble example of fortitude, and it was thanks to their early example that public opinion subsequently remained so steady. There was considerable doubt among leading people in London how the country would stand the inevitable losses of a war like this, but no unworthy plaints ever soiled the roll of honour, whether at first, or later when the losses became distributed over all classes of the people. The people of the home country and the Empire displayed un-exampled courage in hundreds of thousands of stricken homes, and in this and every other sacrifice demanded by the war, were perfectly splendid. Nothing could exceed the steadiness with which they took good and evil news alike, or the tenacity with which they set themselves to suffer anything rather than to lose the war. There was nothing, at any time, that the people would not have done in response to a call from their leaders.

Less valiant, we must admit, were certain members of the Government. The effect of the heavy losses upon some of these, from Sept. 1915 onwards, was to cause them to question the correctness of our strategy in France. They did not all firmly bear in mind that the overthrow of the main German Armies in France was the only road to victory, and that this road was a hard and stony track which had to be followed with implacable resolution amidst blood and tears till the end. They sought ways for evading these losses, and looked round for theatres of war where they might, as they vainly thought, win victory at little cost. The thing was never practicable, but the tale was passed round that there was a stalemate in the West and that we could never win the war there. We consequently never, till after our defeats in the spring of 1918, made the effort necessary for victory in France, and we sent Armies to many theatres where success, no matter how brilliant, could not have brought Germany to her knees. From this weakness, the war was prolonged and our casualties enormously increased. We were indeed brought to the very brink of ruin, but the people had no responsibility for these errors, which were due to the Government alone.

But I am not now writing the history of the war, and will proceed to trace the succeeding phases of this mighty con-flict by the entries in my diary.

CHAPTER III

THE OUTLOOK, AUTUMN 1915

Mr. Lloyd George's views of the situation, Sept. 29, 1915—Mr. Churchill on the Dardanelles and naval matters—Sir William Robertson on the situation in France and the attack at Loos—The Salonika Expedition—Opposition of French and British Staffs—The first Zeppelin raid on London—Mr. Lloyd George's views, Oct. 18—Criticisms of the Battle of Loos—Dissatisfaction with the Government—Ignorance of the people concerning events—General Joffre and Lord Bertie in London—The New Armies at Salisbury—Sir Archibald Murray on the conduct of the war—Lord Kitchener goes to the Eastern Mediterranean, Nov. 1915—Sir Arthur Markham's views—Sir Arthur Lee at the Munitions Ministry—Lord Derby and Recruiting—Mr. Churchill joins up—Russia's day, Nov. 18—The Dardanelles and Salonika—General Townshend in trouble after Ctesiphon—Lord Curzon on his colleagues.

Wednesday, Sept. 29. Lunched with Lloyd George at 11 Downing Street. Met Mr. and Mrs. Edwin Montagu. The host in good form ; he monopolised the conversation. After lunch the others went away, and L. G. and I sat by the fire, while he smoked a big cigar for an hour. He wants me not to hustle about compulsory service just now, as the thing must come, and is more likely to come soon if we do not raise too much Radical opposition. We discussed the campaign up and down. He thinks that the Russians have done wonderfully, though the Germans have a little the best of it. They are like two dogs fighting, neither of which can get on top. He does not think that the Russians have 1,000,000 rifles left, and said that they have been fighting one rifle against three, and one shell against ten. The Russians will not be armed before May next year at the earliest. He thinks that the Germans will try to press on and capture Petrograd and the Russian factories of munitions, when the snow freezes. He does not think that the Germans will give the Russians time to recuperate, if they can possibly prevent it. He is getting on well with his shells and rifles, and declares that there will be a tremendous flow of everything next spring and onwards. Woolwich, he declares, is very badly organised. The filling and issuing departments are most inadequate, the result being that hundreds and thousands of empty shells are waiting to be filled. He has got men down from Vickers to expand these departments, and to get rid of the present narrow neck of the bottle. He was most critical of Lord K., and said some very severe things about him. Evidently something has cropped up, and the story that K. had a very bad week in the Cabinet is confirmed. There must be something more than mere obstinacy or L. G. would not have spoken as he did. He continues to be opposed to the Dardanelles, and is mildly in favour of the Salonika affair; but, on the whole, is most anxious to keep up the strength in France. He asked me what I would do about the Dardanelles, and I said, 'Take away the troops and put some of them in Egypt, and have transports so that 20,000 men can raid the coast of Syria, *à la* Sidney Smith.' He agreed, and asked me to come to his office and ask for Davies whenever I wanted to see him.

Dined with Winston, Lady Randolph, Mr. Lowther, and Lady Gwendeline Churchill, at 72 Brook Street—Lady R.'s house. Everybody talked at once. Soon after dinner, W. and I adjourned to his study upstairs, and went through all his alleged failures at the Admiralty. He showed me that he had been the first to suggest the withdrawal of the patrol, composed of the *Cressy, Aboukir,* and *Hogue,* and this was because he heard a young officer with the Grand Fleet talk about the 'live-bait patrol.' He was so impressed by this description that he determined to warn the First Sea Lord. The date of his note was two days before the ships were torpedoed. The court of inquiry laid the blame for the affair on the Admiralty. It appeared to me that Prince Louis of Battenberg had been playing a very restricted part, and that the Secretary of the

Admiralty had been acting as a kind of Chief of Staff to Winston, with whom a great deal of the initiative originated. I told him that if he had been content to administer his department, and not to dabble in strategy, he would have been still at the Admiralty. He rather agreed, but said that sailors had no initiative and understood very little about war and movements, and were so hopeless in the higher branches of strategy that, unless he moved, nobody did anything. As for Kit Cradock's fight off Chili, he told me of the coveys of ships which were chasing the Germans in various waters, including a Japanese squadron which were following the Germans down from the north. Cradock had distinct orders not to fight without the *Canopus*. But I said that I thought that as this was a slow ship, Cradock knew that his only chance to fight was to do so without the *Canopus*; it had always seemed to me that Cradock had taken the most honourable course. Winston then went into Antwerp, and I saw the telegrams from which it certainly appeared that the French were prepared to help with a couple of territorial divisions, but I did not see it stated that they made any distinct promise to line up at any particular place or date, and the whole thing seems to have been a rare bungle, into which Winston, apparently encouraged by Lord K., had thrown himself out of sheer love of adventure. As regards the Dardanelles, his position is that he cabled to Carden to ask him if he could force the Dardanelles. The latter replied that he could not rush them, but thought that he could take them by deliberate attack. His plans were sent home, and approved by the Admiralty. Two days before the attack Carden went sick; Winston then cabled to De Robeck, who had succeeded Carden, to ask whether he approved of Carden's plans, and was prepared to carry them out. Robeck answered 'Yes,' and the attack went on. After the loss of the three ships, Winston said that the Admiralty declared that they were prepared to lose twelve ships, and wished to go on, though Jack Fisher was already hesitating. Winston cabled privately to De Robeck to urge him to go on, but the latter now said that he preferred that the soldiers should take on the job, and although Winston disliked this course he consented to it. The military plans were approved by Lord K., who practically ran all the military part of the expedition. In short, Winston's position is that he was only directly responsible for the naval attack ; that he only used old ships which were useless for any other purpose ; and that the attack by the ships was not pressed home. He read to me the statement that he was to have read in Parliament but refrained from reading. He admitted that these failures had greatly impaired his usefulness, and he was rather despondent about himself. I stayed until about 2 A.M., and had to telephone to the Turf Club for a taxi, which came with only half a gallon of petrol, not enough to get up to Hampstead—so like the rest of the war arrangements.

Tuesday, Oct. 12. I saw Sir William Robertson, the new Chief of Staff of the Army in France, at Somerset Hotel at noon, and had a long talk with him. The situation of the Army in France appears now on the whole to be good. They have enough though not plenty of men, guns, and ammunition. For the recent attack at Loos—Sept. 25 and the two following days—they had accumulated over 900 guns on the main front of attack south of the La Bassée Canal, and this attack was successful. We still hold the chief points gained in the attack, but the troops in their eagerness pressed on much further than was intended, and got into the third German line, from which they were driven out by the German counter-attacks. We have in front of this main attack, from our left to our right, the 7th German Army Corps, a Guard Brigade, the 117th and 123rd Divisions, and the 4th Army Corps. It is generally agreed that 14 German divisions have left the Russian front, of which about 8 have come to France, including, I think, the Guard and the 10th Corps. All these, with 7 other loose German divisions not actually holding the trenches, have been drawn in for the various German counter-attacks, including that of last Friday, Oct. 8., when 28 battalions attacked our front and lost 8000 men,—so we say—while our losses were only 150. In the three days, Sept. 25-27, our losses were not so high as has been rumoured. They were nearly 47,000, a great deal caused by the inexperience of new troops who had pressed on too far without consolidating their captures. Robertson thinks that the German reserves are now temporarily exhausted on the Western front. The estimate of the German numbers in the West as a whole at the opening of the attack is 1,070,000 rifles, nearly 4000 field guns, and about 2000 heavy guns. The Germans have never scored a point against us for a very long time. Robertson thinks that there is no better policy than to go on hitting them.

The main attack is being conducted by our 1st Army under Haig, because they hold the most important part of the position, and are in touch with the French on the right. The front of the 2nd Army has no clear objective. The Ypres salient is difficult to debouch from, while the fortress of Lille is here on our front with three defensible river lines behind it. Our 3rd Army, under Monro, is holding a front of thirty miles with ten divisions, some of which are quite new troops, and consequently this Army is not in a position to attack.

On the right of our 1st Army is General Foch, but he has only one Army now, which is under D'Urbal, and Robertson evidently thought that two leaders here were inadvisable. We then spoke of affairs in London. Apparently General Sarrail, who was *dégommé* by Joffre, has much influence in Paris, and compelled the French Government to search about for another high command for him. They first thought of large operations south of the Dardanelles. This was negatived; then there came up the Salonika plan. Viviani, the French Prime Minister, as I already knew, came over to the Cabinet last week, and was full of sending 400,000 men to Salonika; but on investigation this plan was ruled out, as nothing could be hoped from it within the time available. I had been told by a friend that our General Staff had sent in a very good memorandum to the Cabinet two days ago—signed by Sir A. Murray and by Jackson the First Sea Lord—which, up to a point, recommended the policy which I have so frequently advocated of concentrating every effort in France and Flanders, and strongly deprecated dispersion in any form, unless it was quite obvious that troops could be spared, and that we could completely satisfy all our wants in the Western sphere. But, in the last paragraph, Murray, unfortunately allowing himself to be influenced by Kitchener, gave some sort of conditional approval to the further prosecution of the Dardanelles expedition, thus vitiating the whole argument. It must here be explained that K. went to see Joffre a few days ago, and, though bringing nothing back in writing, declared to the Cabinet that Joffre had told him that he would be unable to continue his offensive seriously for another three months, and Robertson thinks that it is on account of ammunition, of which the French have been very prodigal, and of which they have less than they say. K. represented all this, and it became a reason for checking our offensive in France, and continuing the Dardanelles adventure. The Cabinet yesterday agreed to despatch from France eight divisions to the Mediterranean. Robertson says that this is the best way to lose the war that he can think of. He doubts that Joffre holds the views that K. attributes to him, and is afraid that there is a Radical-Socialist cabal in France, and that it is making things very difficult. No one knows what the Allied troops which have been sent to Salonika are expected to do. He asked K. what their orders were, and was told that they were to go to Salonika, and that was all.

I hear that Carson, who threatens to resign, wishes to send an ultimatum to the King of Greece, and also to tell the Serbians—who are pressing us to say what we propose to do—what our plans are ; but all the Cabinet appear to have told the Serbians is that we cannot send them any troops this month. Carson thinks that this is dishonest, for it sounds as if we meant to send them next month, whereas, in fact, we do not mean to send any at all. Apart from the folly of detaching troops from France, Robertson points out that the time question is all important.

We are going on with our attack in France to-morrow, and no troops can be taken out of the line for another fortnight at least. It will take the Admiralty six weeks to carry the eight divisions to Egypt, and ships have already been taken up with this object in view. It will take another fortnight before troops can be put ashore from Egypt in the Dardanelles, where apparently they are to be landed at Suvla Bay. This means that the operations in the Dardanelles cannot begin till January and the General Staff calculate that the Germans may have knocked out the Serbians by then, and may be at Constantinople by the end of November. Comment is needless.

There still appear to be two parties in the Cabinet, one for Salonika, and one for the Dardanelles. The chief advantage of the Salonika party is that they wish to take the troops away from Gallipoli. Some say that this cannot be done, but Robertson doubts this, and says that in any case we shall lose fewer men by withdrawing them than by leaving them there for three months. Curzon and one or two others oppose the withdrawal from the Dardanelles on account of the loss of prestige, and the resulting danger in Egypt and India, so that this increases the difficulties of the whole situation.

Asquith, searching for a compromise that would please everybody, suggested that the eight divisions should be taken from France and put on board ship, their destination to remain a subject of subsequent consideration. Thus for months this important body of troops will be inutilisable in all theatres. The worst of it is that owing to the unfortunate paragraph which slipped into the General Staff's memorandum at Lord K.'s instigation, the Government will be able to affirm that this action is initiated on the advice of the General Staff. It would appear that if these calculations of time and distance be correct, the Germans will be in Constantinople before we can get to Salonika.

Wednesday, Oct. 13.   I wrote an article strongly condemning the proposal to withdraw our troops from France. This article was more mangled than usual by the Censor, but the main points of the argument were allowed to remain. Found everybody very excited about the subject of the crisis in the Cabinet, and about the proposed despatch of troops to the Mediterranean.   The King reported to be very angry about the decision of the Cabinet.   In the course of the day things have altered a little, and L. G., who originally proposed the Salonika expedition, knocked out Gallipoli, and substituted Salonika.   The proposal is to take 250,000 men from France.   The question is how to kill this scheme most effectually.   I am told that Joffre last week only consented to the withdrawal of three British divisions and not eight, and this only with reluctance on account of our predominant interests in the East.   It seems therefore most improbable that he should have agreed, as Viviani declared in his speech in the Chambers, to the despatch East of 400,000 Anglo-French troops.

Northcliffe sent a man to-day to Joffre to warn him what was in the wind, and another to Clemenceau, who is of our way of thinking.

Thursday, Oct. 14.   Zepp. raid last night, bombs on the Strand, including three theatres, and on Woolwich, Croydon, and Hertford.   They began at 9.30 P.M.   I was dining with Mrs. McCreery, 1 Grosvenor Crescent ; Lady Colebrooke and Bulkeley-Johnson also there.   Our hostess was rather alarmed, but when the guns stopped we settled down again. No damage was done to any of our friends.   Drove Lady C. home, and went on in her motor until I found a taxi, of which there were very few about.

Tried to find L. G. this morning, but discovered that he was staying down at Walton Heath with a bad headache and neuralgia, and had asked the dentist down to take some teeth out.   Had a talk with his secretary, Davies.   I told him that L. G.'s enemies were using L. G.'s approval of the Salonika adventure in order to prevent him from becoming Prime Minister ; and that Lord K., who had no love lost for L. G., was asking people how they would like a Prime Minister who had such wild-cat schemes. Davies, who is evidently the echo of L. G. and seems a smart fellow, asked whether we had not a million more men in France than the Germans, and whether we could not spare the troops. I said 'No,' we could not spare them; that Salonika was useless, unless Greece and Rumania came in too, and that we ought to send an ultimatum to Athens; that our troops would arrive much too late to save Serbia. I shall try to see L. G. to-morrow when he comes up.

Met several people who approved of my article to-day.

Monday, Oct. 18. L. G., Northcliffe, and Jack Cowans lunched with me. We had a tremendous talk over the war; on the whole most unsatisfactory. L. G. says that he has the most unpleasant reports about Russia from Sir George Buchanan. The political state of Russia is as bad as can be, and German influence predominates everywhere. There are serious riots, and in many cases Russians are selling their rifles to the Germans. He does not anticipate any useful results from Russian fighting this year, or even next spring, and he thinks it quite possible that the Germans will try to get to Petrograd when the snow freezes. It seems to me that the picture is a little overdrawn. He thinks that Germany has plenty more men, and so does Northcliffe. L. G. says that the great difficulty is to find any one to tell the truth, especially about Russia, but also about recruiting and the Balkans. He thinks that a large Cabinet is useless, and wants a small War Cabinet. The conduct of the war is where, in his opinion, we have failed most. He thinks that the offensive in France has definitely failed with enormous loss, but no one will tell this to the country. Cowans and I told him how much opposed he and I were to the Balkan campaign, and how useless it was to send troops into this country without the proper guns and pack transport. Cowans told him that it would take a month to make the pack saddles required for a single division, and we both told him that it would take three months to carry a large and properly organised force from

the West to the Balkans, when it would be too late to help
Serbia. He seemed very much struck by our arguments,
and I expect that the Cabinet will hear about it. He
told us that Carson had definitely resigned, and Northcliffe proposes to get Carson to make a full statement of
his reasons, and to tell the country the whole truth about
the war.

I asked L. G. whether it was true that Joffre had gone
back on his undertaking to allow a large Army to go to the
Balkans, and he said that this was correct, and that Joffre
must be untrustworthy, as he, L. G., could not conceive
that one of his—L. G.'s—own colleagues had deceived him.
Whereat we all laughed, and I think that there is no doubt
that Lord K. brought back from France last week an inaccurate impression of Joffre's opinions, just as Robertson
thought. L. G. still believes that the British public will
insist on helping Serbia if she puts up a good fight, but he
admits that he does not know what our forces at Salonika
can do. He evidently finds Asquith and Balfour in the
Cabinet very trying, but he did not give any hint that he
personally would resign or take any drastic course. We
stayed and talked for a couple of hours over the events of
the war, and L. G., as usual, was very bright and sympathetic,
and ready to listen to us all. He certainly has a great
charm. I told him I wanted him for Prime Minister, and
Carson for Minister of War, and that the Dardanelles force
ought to be withdrawn, and a strong force placed in Egypt
with transports to carry 20,000 men to raid the coast of
Syria. I think that we all regard Serbia as done for, barring
a miracle. We have not enough time to send troops
properly organised.

Thursday, Oct. 21. Dined last night with Lady Colebrooke at Claridge's. Mrs. Astor, who dined with us, was
looking a picture. I was half an hour late for dinner,
being unable to get a taxi. Lady Cunard had a party
at a neighbouring table. She and Lady Randolph,
Wolkoff, young Horner (recovered from his serious wound),
Mrs. Duggan, and a few more. They came up and had a

talk to us after they had finished their dinner. Winston is back in Cromwell Road again. We had a great talk at dinner about politics, love affairs, and all sorts of questions, one fair lady holding that a man was the nicest thing in the world when he did not make love to you, and another objecting that such companionship was quite incomplete and impossible, and that there was nothing in it. We heard a good deal about American opinion, which is said to be deteriorating on account of the Censorship, and all the stupid things we have done over here, and I am not surprised. Heard this morning that Cyprus was going to be given to Greece. Rang up my editor, Geoffrey Robinson, and protested most strongly.

Lunched at Prince's Grill; Lockett, M., and X. home from the 2nd Cavalry Brigade in France. He was very interesting. Admitted that the whole attack had been a failure, and laid the blame on Douglas Haig. The cavalry, he said, had been prepared for several months to break through a gap of ten miles when it was made, and to raid right up to Antwerp. Considering the whole country in front of us is full of hostile troops, can only be traversed by the roads, and is unjumpable, the scheme seems perfectly mad.

X. said that the 21st and 24th Divisions of the New Armies were given orders to penetrate as far forward as they could get. The error of Neuve Chapelle, which seems to have taught our people nothing, was repeated. These troops were badly cut up here. If they had had a limited objective assigned to them, they could probably have attained it. X. thinks that the offensive in France is over for a year, and that D. Haig has become dreadfully aged. He says that cavalry horses are all going to be sent back to the coast, where they will be looked after by 100 men in each regiment, drawn from the reserve regiment ; that the cavalry are being taught bomb-throwing, and will be more or less equipped like infantry ; and that they will take their turn in the trenches like infantry. They loathe the idea of another Flanders winter. He says that our artillery bombardment completely levelled the German trenches and destroyed the barbed wire, but that it killed very few Germans, as they were in dug-outs thirty-five feet deep. He does not think that we killed more than 8000, but in the counter-attacks the Germans lost a lot. He does not think that we hold either the Hohenzollern Redoubt, or the Quarries, or Hill 70, all of which figure in the recent reports, and he is very critical of the Staff, especially of the 1st Army Corps—the usual stories that are circulated in London when anything goes wrong.

Had a letter from Sammy Scott this morning from somewhere in the Mediterranean, probably the Ægean. He says an Austrian submarine, commanded by a German, popped up within 2000 yards of them while they were rescuing the men of a French collier. He thinks that the transport would certainly have been sunk had the submarine been British. As it was, they fired a few small guns, and down she dived. It must have been a narrow squeak. He says that there is a lot he would like to tell me, and suggests that things are bad in the Dardanelles. But this is no news !

Friday, Oct. 22. Went to talk to Lady Ridley about the political situation, and what was to be done. We discussed the whole situation up and down, the incompetence of the Cabinet, the indecision of the Chief Ministers, and the troubles into which we were drifting on all sides. She has a very good head, and always gives good advice. We thought that if the King would take these affairs into his own hands, the country would be sure to be with him. We both wanted the King to send for L. G. We thought that the King might write a letter to Lord Derby or some neutral statesman to explain the reason for his action, but of course we saw the difficulties. Another alternative was for me to write a letter to the *Times*, which I have done to-day, but I do not expect the Censor to pass it.

The ignorance of the people concerning the war, owing to the Censorship, is unbelievable. Lunching at the Hautboy, on my way to my mother's, near Ockham, the other day, the proprietor—a good-class intelligent man—told me that the Serbians were going to beat the Germans ; that there was nothing in front of our Army in France ; and that we were going to be in Constantinople in ten days' time.   These are the kind of beliefs into which the country has been chloroformed by the Censorship.   Incidentally, I met at the Hautboy, which is the quietest of country inns, a certain couple who were much taken aback when I walked in.   I expect I was the last person they wanted to meet.   What a ridiculous little world it is !

Dined last night at Mrs. McCreery's ; Princess Hatzfeldt, Jack Tennant, Lady Colebrooke, Ashmead-Bartlett, Mrs. Bingham, Dunlop Smith, Lady Paget, and one or two more. A pleasant dinner ; Lady P. full of her matinée at the Empire for the Red Cross, which I had shirked.   She made £2000. The Queen and everybody perfectly delighted.   It lasted from 2 till 6.   I had taken Lady Paget to see Doris Keane in *Romance* some time before, and we had chosen a scene out of the first act, which was about the most dainty dish to set before the Queen.   We went round to Doris's dressing-room to arrange about it.   It was a great success this afternoon, and Doris was frightfully pleased, and says that it will do her a lot of good in America.

Monday, Oct. 25.   I spent the week-end at Coombe.   Mrs. Astor drove me down.   We found Sir A. and Lady Paget, and the two boys, the Aga Khan, Lord and Lady Charles Beresford, Lady Drogheda, Mrs. Bingham, Baroness de Forest, Mr. Roberts, Mr. Cora of the Italian Embassy, and an American diplomatist from Bukharest.

A wet day Sunday.   The American from Bukharest told us that the Rumanians would come if we put 300,000 men in the field, and that, short of that, they would not move. He said that our military attaché at Bukharest had declared to him that the Bulgarian mobilisation was a bluff, and that the Bulgarians would never attack Serbia.   He said that the Austrians have about 250,000 men on the Rumanian frontier, and the Rumanians rather more than this ; also that the Rumanian Army is practically mobilised, and ready to come in at a few days' notice.

The Aga Khan was very interesting, and I found him more or less in accord with all my views. He thinks that to capture Bagdad is impossible with our present force, and asked whether we could hold it at such a distance from the sea when the Germans reach Constantinople, and begin to arm the 1,000,000 Turks who are waiting for arms and equipment. He says also that the Germans are training 90,000 Persians, and that the main road to Persia from Turkey passes eighty miles north of Bagdad, so we shall have to occupy a further stretch of country. This is pretty well what I have already said to Archie Murray. Sir Arthur said that he was very short of reserves, and that unless something was done our organisation would collapse. He cannot get battery commanders for his divisions of the 4th Army.

Jack Cowans came down to lunch. He said that the French had crossed the Serbian frontier, and that our 10th Division were south of the frontier waiting instructions what to do. The Cabinet was still in a state of indecision, and had taken the 22nd and 28th Divisions away from Sir John French. They were to begin to embark from Marseilles to-day, but only the infantry, as our horse ships at Marseilles had been lent to the French who had cavalry ready to start. He repeats that it will take a month to equip a single division with pack transport. We both regard the Salonika enterprise as insanity.

Went through events at sea with Charlie Beresford. We compared views on our future strategy on the Eastern Mediterranean. Lady P. still tremendously pleased at the success of her matinée, and is getting up another for the Russians next month, when Lydia Kyasht will appear, and will produce a Russian ballet.

Saw Geoffrey Robinson in the afternoon. I showed him an important letter from France, received Oct. 23, and discussed the situation with him. Our politics, strategy, and diplomacy all seem to be in a rare muddle. Fortunately events are likely to forestall the action of the Allied Army at Salonika before too much harm is done.

Friday, Oct. 29. I dined last night at the Café Royal. Went off after dinner to see Lydia Kyasht, who was leaving for Russia next morning. She had asked me specially to come and advise her about an important matter. I found her alone at her new house, 37 Avenue Road. The house is perfectly charming, very nearly finished, and in excellent taste. Lydia had sent for me to say that her husband had broken down after fifteen months of fighting in Russia with his regiment, the Rifles of the Guard, and wished to be attached to John French's Staff, and could I arrange it ? Lydia is due in Petrograd, Nov. 15. Captain Ragosin, her husband, will be there on leave, Nov. 7, for a fortnight, so that this matter must be fixed up, if at all, before Nov. 21. I promised to do my best for her. She showed me round the house : very delicious, furniture from a Belgian château, and altogether a great improvement on her last house in Knightsbridge, where we had the mad supper party.

Lunched to-day with Lady Herbert, Olive, Mrs. Astor, Mrs. Sneyd, Lord Bertie our Ambassador in France, Mr. O'Beirne our Minister at Sofia (just returned after Bulgaria's outbreak), and the Prince Aga Khan. Learnt that Joffre is here at last. The Government will now know for certain his views, which have been differently expounded by different people. Bertie says that General Gallieni, who is to be the new French Minister of War, is very unfriendly to Joffre, but that possibly his ambitions will be satisfied by being made War Minister. Mrs. Astor gave me a short character sketch of M. Briand, the new French Premier. I fancy that some French politicians will try to get rid of Joffre, in order to appoint a man who is completely in their hands. Bertie does not think that the French Army will stand this, but we shall see. O'Beirne very interesting with his experience of Sofia. He thinks that the Serbians have committed suicide by not agreeing to allow the Bulgarians to occupy the contested territory. He dates the Bulgarian decision to come in against us to the fall of Warsaw, which had a bad influence. He says that the Bulgars hate the idea of fighting against England or France, but are united about Macedonia, and that the war will be fought with a savagery never before surpassed.

Tuesday, Nov. 2. Met some boys from the late battle at luncheon. They all seemed to agree very cordially with some mild criticisms of Sir John French's despatch of Oct. 15. One of them belonging to the 15th Division told me the whole story of the attack of his Division on Loos, on Hill 70, and on the Redoubt behind it. They had penetrated almost to Cité St. Auguste, reaching the latter point about noon. They were then attacked by German reserves, and having lost nearly 75 per cent. of their strength, were driven back. No reserves at all appeared to help them throughout the day. Their artillery, under Alexander, co-operated beautifully. McCracken commanded the Division, and of the Brigadiers, two were from the K.O.S.B.s The boys could not say why no reserves came up, but probably all communications were cut. There are some fairly acrimonious criticisms of this battle in some of the papers to-day, and I think matters ought to be looked into. I have many communications agreeing with my article of this morning. We hear that Kragugevatch, the Serbian arsenal, has fallen, and that the enemy is now close on Nish, the fall of which, I suppose, we cannot prevent. The German spies sit in rows on the quays at Salonika smoking large cigars, and note down every man, horse, gun, and ton of stores landed. This is a nice way to make war ! Up to the last week these spies reported that we had landed 76,000 men. There is going to be a nice mess here soon.

Wednesday, Thursday, Friday, Nov. 3-5. Went down to Salisbury to stay with Sir Arthur Paget. Found Crowe, his chief Staff Officer ; Bethell (Westbury's son), his A.D.C. ; and Charles Bathurst, M.P., acting on the Administrative Staff. Had a great talk about the war. Prevailed upon Paget not to write what he contemplated to K. about the leading and the number of cavalry generals in high command. He decided to see Lord K. and talk the matter over with him, which is much better. Lady Paget and his Staff were much relieved. We went out both mornings and saw the troops. There are seven divisions of the 4th New Army on the Plain, most of them ready, but only three with their full complement of rifles, and all the artillery very backward. The 33rd and 30th are Paget's best divisions. There are also going out the 31st, 32nd, 34th or 35th, and 38th. The first three will leave their artillery behind, and will take over the guns of the Indian divisions in France, and of the two Territorial divisions. As each division is taken away from France, one of the 4th Army divisions will take its place. There is a great absence of reserves. Recruiting appears to be poor, in spite of Lord Derby's boom. We shall sadly need some fresh divisions next year. Saw the attack of two divisions from trenches against other trenches ; one attack was done well, and the other not so well. There are only one or two Regular officers per battalion. The troops lack experience, but they are a very fine lot of men, with some good boys among the officers, and all as keen as mustard. When they are gone there will only be the 5th Army divisions left, and they will not be fit for anything for some months.

We tried to get Lady Pembroke over to dinner, but she was away in Ireland. Paget living at a nice old-fashioned house, owned by one of the Cathedral dignitaries. During the trench operations, Paget, who was born in 1851, bounded like a stag over trenches full of infantry with fixed bayonets. I had to follow, and then remembered that he was our crack hurdle racer in old days.

Saturday, Nov. 6. Had a long talk at the War Office with Archie Murray, the C.I.G.S. ; also with Kiggell, the Director of Home Defence—an old comrade of mine on Buller's Staff. Kiggell all for concentration in the West. He says that he is trying to get the Navy to make a fresh statement of what they can do respecting invasion, and says there is no fresh standard against invasion since Lord Roberts and I got it raised from 10,000 to 70,000 after our fights with the Defence Committee. Found Murray in thorough accord with all my views. He had just come from an afternoon War Council. He says things are tending to the evacuation of Gallipoli.

He was opposed to the Salonika expedition, but Joffre had compelled our people to go in for it. He hinted that Sir John French would not remain much longer in command, and supposed that Haig would replace him. He told me that he and his directors, with Admiral Jackson, meet regularly in the room where we were talking, and sign memoranda in common for the Cabinet. He was not keen on the advance on Bagdad, and thought that the expedition should have halted at Basra or Kurna, as I advised him when he consulted me about the advance; but at that time no General Staff was in existence, or at all events permitted to advise, and so the troops went on. India has been told that we could not support them in Mesopotamia, and possibly not keep up the strength of the white troops, but India had accepted full responsibility and had determined to go on. The result is that all the resources of India will be committed to an operation which, even if successful, can scarcely influence in any degree the main issue of the war. He showed me that there are eighteen Austro-German and nine Bulgarian divisions against the Serbians. I heard in the evening that the War Council to-day were apparently alarmed at the position—as well they may be—and suggested our coming away. But they had been told that they could not go on changing their minds every day, and as they had acted against the advice of the G.S., they must go on with it and make the best of it. I am not sure that this is good advice, for there is no point in persisting in folly.

Sunday, Nov. 7. Went down to Coombe last week-end, in spite of a bad cold. Hoped to find Bertie Paget, but he could not get over from France as the boats were not running. There were Mrs. Leeds, Lady Granard, and some other people. A long talk with Sir Arthur about the question of the command of the Armies in France. He is representing that there are too many cavalry officers in high commands, and that this is the cause of many of our recent disappointments. He has written a letter which he is sending to the Prime Minister and to Balfour. I was asked to try and stop the letter, but Sir Arthur is set on sending it this time, as he is the senior serving officer of the infantry. Returned with him on Monday. Had a long talk with Mrs. Leeds about Greece. She says that all Greece is pro-Ally, but that they are afraid of the Germans, and do not want to fight; consequently they are all with the King.

A great deal of talk about Lady Paget's Russian day, and all the plans of making it a success.

Monday, Nov. 8. Lunched at Prince's with E.; Percy Stout of the Egyptian Service also there. He told me that all the Indian troops in France, except the cavalry, were off to Mesopotamia next week. We discussed Syria, which he knows very well, and the difficulties of landing there. We agreed that Kitchener, who left the War Office last Thursday night on a visit to the Eastern Mediterranean, would probably winter in Cairo, and remain there. Dined with the McLarens, 69 Eaton Place. Met Sir Arthur Markham. We had a very interesting talk on the whole war. He is the most severe critic of the Government, and is evidently a tremendous worker, and very well informed. He is going for the Government to-morrow, Wednesday, and was going to attack Archie Murray, but I think I have headed him off that track. He hates Asquith and Kitchener. We discussed munitions, recruiting, General Staff, diplomacy, operations, and much of the inner history of the last few months. Markham has a pretty good insight into things, and is very anxious to advance national interest, and to eliminate all the duffers who infest politics. He is transparently honest and sincere. I think that he is a man who would attack his best friend without compunction if he thought him wrong. He told me what the Government were saying of me, namely, that I was using my friendship with Sir John French and Murray to find materials for attacking the Government in the interest of Lord Northcliffe. This made me laugh, but people will invent any tale when they are found out. I told him facts about my visit to France, and the shell shortage, and that I took no orders from any one in expressing my opinions on military affairs. I think on the whole that we were completely in agreement.

Tuesday, Nov. 9. Wrote an article on the New Armies telling my experiences at Salisbury, showing the need for fresh troop formations, and demonstrating that unless we set about the creation of thirty new divisions by Aug. 1916, we should not be doing our duty. I showed the differences between the Government's point of view, which would subordinate the Army to the needs of our home trade, and the military view, which places the Army first. I also wrote a letter to the *Times* to show that Curzon was misinformed when he stated in the House of Lords that the articles of military correspondents were not censored, but the letter which I wrote seems to have been censored too ! With a Censorship, it is as easy for Ministers to retain office as it is for them to romance.

An article of mine on the Conduct of the War, published on Monday. Dined in the evening with Mrs. Bingham at 4 Walton Place ; Lady de Trafford, Lady Granard, Lord D'Abernon, Sir Vincent Corbet, and Baron Michiels. Found D'Abernon's views and mine about affairs were much the same. Lady de Trafford very pleasant. Not much news.

Wednesday, Nov. 10.   Went to see Arthur Lee at the Ministry of Munitions (Armament Buildings). Found him very full of his work and the war. He regards a disaster, or disasters, at Salonika and the Dardanelles as probable, and considers that the Prime Minister has been very astute in the manner in which he has unloaded Lord K., who, he thinks, will never come back to the War Office. Lee does not want to replace him, and agrees with me that Derby is the best choice if L. G. is not available. L. G. seems to have a wonderful Staff at his new Ministry, composed of men formerly drawing huge salaries in business life ; for example, Stephenson, the managing director of Walker's Whisky, who gave up £14,000 a year to come and work for nothing. The office is full of this type of man. Woolwich has now been taken over by the North Eastern Railway Staff with wonderfully good results. Lee says that there is only one civil service man in the whole office, and that it is extraordinary how easily the work goes on with all these business men in charge. Heard a good lot about guns, shells, and rifles. The maxims are the greatest difficulty on account of the extreme nicety of the gauges, while big guns are the easiest to get of all, it seems, and there is no difficulty about shells. Lee and Dr. Addison are the two heads under L. G., one military and the other civil. Lee was contemptuous of the strategy of the war and of Lord K.'s administration.

Lunched with Mrs. Astor to-day; Wolkoff, Lady Johnstone, and a party of Americans. Afraid that Mrs. Astor has definitely decided to go to America, Dec. 16, and see her girl. Quite a cheery party. Lady Johnstone very amusing. The ladies wrangled about what nationalities— men, that is to say—are most valiant and enterprising; by common consent they all voted British. One lady had a delightful phrase which I must try and recall about the disappointed vexations of a woman who came home in fear and trembling in the dark expecting to be accosted, and no one took any notice of her. Talked with Lady Johnstone about Kühlmann's iniquities at The Hague. My impression is that he is not doing much to hurt us.

Thursday, Nov. 11. Went off early to see Lord Derby, and had a long talk with him. In the month that has passed he has gathered 160,000 recruits, or about three times as many men as were taken in a similar period before he came in; but he is paying less attention to the number of recruits than to the creation of a system which will enable Compulsion to be applied. He is instituting Local Tribunals, supervised by Parliamentary Committees, with whom are associated in each constituency War Office representatives with their Advisory Committees. The starring of men presents great difficulties. The armlets given to those willing to serve will, he thinks, make all the older men, and married men, his recruiting agents. They will know that their turn will come unless the unmarried men are made to go, and this will make them push the latter out. Derby's greatest difficulty is with the various departments, all of which are trying to keep their own men. The Board of Agriculture and the Home Office have been curiously obstructive, and Derby has had to put his foot down. Derby was asked one day to find 300 bakers for the A.S.C., and at the same time he received a letter from Lord Lansdowne to say that no more bakers were to be enlisted. He does not expect to be able to make a statement on the recruiting situation until the beginning of January, as many of the papers will not so much as go out until Nov. 20. He is less certain than he was that compulsion will come. He has been given a list of 160 trades from which he is not to enlist men, and, of course, at this rate it is hard to get on. I told him that the safety of the country was in his hands, and that we should never get recruiting right until we told the country the truth. He said that he intended to do so, and that I could make quite sure of it. He was much more critical of Lord K. than I expected. He said that he had prevented K., time after time, from making the most horrible mistakes, but at the same time it remained true that Lord K.'s name had more influence and more prestige with the public than anybody else's. He thinks that Lord K. should have been made Commander-in-Chief, and not placed in the Cabinet or at the War Office. The General Staff's views had never been presented to the Cabinet properly, for Lord K. had his own ideas. We fully agreed that neither of us will ever again support the appointment of a soldier to be Secretary for War. I found him very keen to be War Minister, from which I judge that he knows that Lord K. will not come back, at all events in that capacity. Derby thinks that Curzon is his chief rival, and that he, Derby, may not get the post because so many Cabinet Ministers dislike his independence and frankness. He showed me a letter which he had written to the Prime Minister, stating very clearly the need for saying exactly how many men we had, and how many we needed, and declaring that K.'s figures of our requirements per week, namely, 30,000 men, were much below the mark, and should have been 35,000 to 40,000.

Derby is a useful public servant, tall, bluff, hearty, and

always smiling ; not clever, but very shrewd, a man of the world with very good sense, and at this moment is popular with all classes, including labour and the Army. I do not see anybody better than he for the post of War Secretary if L. G. does not want it. But I question whether it is wise for me or the *Times* to advocate Derby's appointment. I am inclined to think we had better wait and let things work out naturally.

Arthur Lee told me that if Lord K. wanted to come back, his colleagues would not have him, and that there were twenty members in the Cabinet against him. The War Office now wears one broad contented smile, and having lost Lord K., there is a deep sigh of relief all round. What Lord K. will do in the Mediterranean no one can tell. He may go to the Dardanelles to endeavour to continue the attack, although Charles Monro has recommended evacuation. There is a pretty kettle of fish in the Middle East, and we shall see how he deals with it. Lee thinks that K. knows that he has failed, and that if he fails in the Mediterranean, or sees failure coming, he will try to get to India. But who knows what the Sphinx really thinks or means ? On the Tuesday before he left he asked a friend of mine to Broome for the week-end, and Lady Salisbury was to drive down with him on the Saturday. But on Thursday night, he went off suddenly without beat of drum. I have asked no one the reason yet, but I imagine that when Monro proposed evacuation L. G. was ready with a suggestion that Lord K. should go out and report on the whole situation ; that all his colleagues supported this view ; and that K. could not refuse. In any case, if the Cabinet can prevent his return they will do so. The difference in the opinion of Lord K. held by those behind the scenes and by the rest of the public is astonishing.

Wednesday, Nov. 17. Went to see Northcliffe at 22 St. James's Place, and found Winston with him. Winston was in great form and tearing spirits. He leaves for France to-morrow to rejoin his regiment, abandoning what he calls his 'well-paid inactivity.' It is rather splendid of him. To give up £4000 a year and go off soldiering is certainly noble, except from the point of view of his family. He had come to ask us to treat him in a gentlemanly way when he is away, which I hope we shall. He talked a great deal about his colleagues. He urged the continuance of the Dardanelles operations once more, but, I thought, with less conviction in his voice than formerly. He thought that Salonika was coming out badly, and that he would have stayed had he been kept on the War Council, but as he was taken off he felt justified in leaving the Government. He spoke of the mess his colleagues would be in when the Salonika adventure came to grief, and he described how every morning fresh chunks of responsibility seemed to fall from him. He was critical of Kitchener, and was evidently disposed to put down most of the misfortunes of the war to him. We had some talk of the war in France, but most of the time it was politics.

Thursday, Nov. 18. Russia's day. Wrote in the morning, lunched with E. and party, and then went to the Alhambra to Lady Paget's matinée. Sat next Mrs. Grahame White, a lady with a very pretty wit. We found to our vexation that the two plays that formed the chief feature of the programme had been banned; *The Theatre of the Soul*, because it was supposed to be too advanced, and Doris Keane's play of *Catherine of Russia*, because Count Benckendorff, the Russian Ambassador, considered that it was impious to suggest that Catherine was warm-hearted. Poor Doris had to do the third act of *Romance* at the last moment, and the scene was lost on the large stage. The performance was not very good, and there was nothing really first class in any of the turns. Queen Alexandra was there. Benckendorff had a box, and various other people. I saw Lady Randolph, Lady Cunard, Lady Diana Manners, and a lot more. Mrs. Bingham and Mrs. Astor selling flowers and flags, looking very pretty. I went off before the end. Dined afterwards at the Carlton with Lady Paget; our party including Mrs. Leeds, Mrs. Astor, Lady Drogheda, the Grand Duke Michael who was in uniform, Bertie Paget, and Wolkoff. We had an excellent dinner, with a Russian menu of course, and afterwards went to a concert in the hotel (also Russian), and finished up about midnight. Mrs. Astor and I counted her gains of the day from her bag into a money box: it came to £42 in coins of sixpence upwards, which was pretty good for one woman selling flags and flowers. Lady Paget and the other ladies nearly dead with fatigue.

Friday, Nov. 19. Dined with Lady Charles Beresford; Lady Johnstone, Lady Kitty Somerset, Miss Bertha Capel, Sir Edward and Lady Carson, Mr. Bonar Law, Arthur Stanley, Colonel Stuart, and a few more. Found Miss Capel amusing and original. Arthur Stanley was opposed to his brother going to the War Office, but I think that I rather brought him round. A great deal of talk about the war with Bonar Law and Carson. The former gave me to understand that the Salonika expedition was a bad egg, and that no further hope of success was entertained. He was evidently in favour of a withdrawal from the Dardanelles, and questioned me closely about it to see what I thought. I told him that I approved, and he said he saw no use in leaving 50,000 men at the tail of the peninsula to be held up by the same number of Turks or less. He asked me my views about the defence of Egypt, and I gave them to him, and afterwards expanded them in the form of a letter to him. He seemed much interested. Both Carson and Bonar Law were very critical of K. When I said I could not understand why the Government sent out Charles Monro to report about the Dardanelles, and then did not take his advice, they both said that they had said the same thing to the Cabinet themselves. We had a discussion about the Aga Khan's influence with the Mohammedan troops, which Stuart declared to be very slight.

Saw Sir A. Murray in the afternoon after the War Council. He told me that the flow of troops to Salonika was going on, but that they were not going beyond the port. He showed me the situation on the map, the Serbians all shepherded in a small corner towards Novi Bazar and Mitrovitza, and a large block of Bulgars between us and them. We have, of course, been too late, as every soldier knew we should be. He was anxious about Sarrail's position, which was in an exposed salient, but expected the main effort of the Bulgars on the flanks. He had written a paper against an advance along the Vardar Valley, and against the coercion of Greece. How on earth they are going either to get these troops away or to get them to do anything useful I cannot imagine, for obviously the whole of the enemy's forces will eventually concentrate upon us, and will take no account of the Greek frontier or of Greek semi-neutrality. He told me that everything was tending towards the evacuation of Gallipoli, and that there was a chance of a great mess before the withdrawal was carried out. Apparently the fate of Sir John French still hangs in the balance. I think that Sir William Robertson has the best chance of succeeding him.

Sunday, Nov. 21. Wrote an article just giving the bare facts and bringing the history of the Salonika expedition up to date. It needs no comment.

Wednesday, Nov. 24. Dined with Olive Guthrie; Mrs. Jack Leslie, Lady Cunard, Lady Belle Herbert, Sir Ernest Cassel, and Pat Guthrie. A report had come of a disagreeable set-back to our operations in Mesopotamia. Cassel knew nothing of it, but I telephoned to the *Times* and found that Townshend's division, after capturing the Turkish position at Ctesiphon, had to retreat four miles for want of water. The affair does not look very well, but if the Cabinet will send a weak division into the heart of a sub-continent, 600 miles from the sea, to fight a warlike people with a million soldiers, they are bound to get us into trouble. It is a pity they did not take my advice, and stop at Kurna. It is also stupid to have fought before the two divisions came from France. Lady Cunard very full of her sale, and of her coming concert.

Thursday, Nov. 25. Wrote an article in the *Times* this

morning on ' The Military Situation,' explaining my reasons for not wishing to fight in the Balkans, giving an outline of my ideas for defending Egypt, and saying that I agreed with Bonar Law that the outlook would be favourable after the liquidation.   Lunched with Mrs. Leeds.   We had a political talk, and then she told me a lot about her boy.   He is at Morton's school, where young Lord Herbert now is.   The Leeds's boy is being brought up as though he were the son of a poor man.   She gave me an amusing example.   He had written to tell her that he was obliged to take half of a half-crown tin of Bovril every day, and he wished to consult her whether he could afford at the same time to buy a ' Charlie Chaplin ' outfit.   She had written to tell him that as health was the first consideration, he could have the Bovril, but the outfit would have to wait until Xmas.   He gets £2 a quarter from the Matron, and is not allowed to have tips.   It is very Spartan, but I expect that this young man will some day want a good many more outfits than that of Charlie Chaplin's.   She explained that nearly all the sons of millionaires in America have become vicious and useless owing to the possession of too much wealth, and she and her husband had determined this boy should only have it if he proved worthy of it.   She told me that she had spent £15,000 this year on British War Hospitals, and she was now practically keeping thirty of them at the rate of £200 a month, which is pretty good for a foreigner.   But the point was that the Government charged her not only tax but super-tax for these gifts, and that as her taxes in May came to £5700, she proposed to transfer her donations to the French who did not charge any tax.   I must write to McKenna and put the case before him, for more hide-bound stupidity I never heard tell.

At 5.30 I had an appointment with Lord Curzon. Found him deep in papers, correcting proofs of memoranda for the Cabinet.   The telephone kept ringing, and he returned rather short answers to his interrupters.   The main point I wanted to know was whether Lord K. was coming back, and if not, whether Curzon wanted to be

Secretary of State for War. Curzon told me that nearly all Lord K.'s colleagues would be very glad if K. remained in the East to control the campaign there, but that K. had taken the seals of office with him and might turn up again at any minute. He said that it was not the practice of Cabinets to review the proceedings of any particular Minister, and that the only person who could review them was the Prime Minister, who probably in this case would not do so. I gathered that Curzon would like the War Office or the Foreign Office, as he considers that his administrative gifts are not being used, but he thought that the Prime Minister would try to give all the best posts to his political friends, and that Lloyd George would probably get the War Office if Lord K.'s rule ended.

Dined with Mrs. McCreery; Princess Hatzfeldt, Lady Colebrooke, Lady Clonmel, Mrs. Portman, Lord Bateman, Lord Athlumney, Almeric Paget, and a few more. Wrote an article on the Serbian campaign, which is going to be infernally unpleasant before long.

CHAPTER IV

SALONIKA AND THE DARDANELLES

A visit to Wilton—General Joffre and Salonika—General Du Cane
at the Ministry of Munitions—A tale from the East—Mr. Washburn
on the Russian Armies—The Dardanelles and Salonika—Divergent
views—Dispute about the Battle of Loos—The evacuation of the
Dardanelles—Sir Ian Hamilton's views—Sir John Simon's attack on
the *Times*—The defence of Egypt—Lord Derby on Recruiting—
Reasons for General Townshend's advance after Kut—F.M. Sir John
French replaced by Sir Douglas Haig—Mr. Asquith's reasons—The
Dutch mails—Transport losses in the Mediterranean—A visit to
Hackwood—Lord Curzon of Kedleston on Salonika decisions—A con-
versation with the Queen of the Belgians—Withdrawal of troops
from France for Salonika—A speech to the Northern Association of
Unionist Agents—Success of the evacuation of Gallipoli and Anzac—
German strength in E. Africa—Lord Kitchener opposes General Staff
plans—Rasputin—Russian munitions—Trade or Victory?—More
reasons for Sir John French's recall—Allied and German Armies in
France—Home Defence Forces—A New Year's party.

Week-end, Nov. 27-29: Saturday, Sunday, Monday. Went
down to Wilton for the week-end as Reggie was back from
the front. Only his fourth visit since the war began.
Reggie and Lady Pembroke, Mrs. Rupert Beckett, Sir Fritz
Ponsonby, Colonel Kincaid Smith, and the Duke of
Sutherland.

A very cheery party; played games after dinner.
Walked in the morning and afternoon of Sunday. Returned by an early train on Monday with Reggie who is
returning to France by the midday boat. It is wonderful how much Bee has done to the house in the last few
months. The north entrance front has been much
changed. There is a large window in the big tower, and

the covered porch has been removed and replaced by pillars. The dining-room has been lowered by 12 feet, and is now a very handsome and well-proportioned room— an immense improvement on the gloomy old panelled room of the past. Aunt Liz's old room has been lengthened, and the fireplace changed. The old smoking-room is now a billiard-room, and a couple of rooms behind it form a much better smoking-room. Electric light has been laid on, but it is not yet in use. Most of the best pictures have been cleaned at last, and the effect is superb. The Vandycks, Holbeins, Titians, and Reynoldses all come out in new glory. It is a revelation now that the centuries of dirt have been removed. The Vandyck of Philip Pembroke is especially astonishing, and is a glorious work of art. The great Vandyck is also seen for the first time, in the memory of this generation at all events, and it will be a great moment when the wonderful Double Cube room is lighted up with electric light for the first time. All these changes and great improvements have been done under the supervision of Lady Pembroke, and I think Reggie is a wonderfully lucky man to have such a charming and accomplished wife.

We had a good deal of talk about the war, and Fritz, who was rather a cripple from lumbago, told us some good stories about Queen Victoria. The one I liked best was her correction of a draft letter written by Fritz, to say that the Duchess of Connaught was to join the Queen's train at some place or other. The Queen wrote in pencil on the draft, ' You should always describe the Duchess as " Her Royal Highness," to show that she is *not a common Duchess.*'

On returning to London we read the German wireless. They claim that the Serbian Army is completely knocked out. I fear that this is true, and that the whole pack will now come down on us.

Nobody seems to know anything about the Russian Army on the borders of Bessarabia.

Dined with Sir Ernest Cassel at Brook House ; Mrs. Bischoffsheim, Countess Hofberg, Mrs. Leslie, Mrs. Cis

Bingham, Olive and Pat, Mrs. Arthur James, Lord Lurgan, Sir Vincent Corbet, and Charles Swaine.

The big house rather cold; the palatial dining-room hung with Vandycks. The huge round table had a depressing effect upon the conversation. A good host and everything done exceedingly well.

Tuesday, Nov. 30. Had an absurd experience to-night. A thick fog. Dined with the Charles Beresfords at 1 Great Cumberland Place. Started at 8 o'clock; fog like pea soup; had to go at a foot's pace all along Regent's Park. Arrived half an hour late for dinner, and found a large party at two tables; majority men, for the first time since the war began. The Italian Ambassador and the Marchesa, Wolkoff of the Russian Embassy, Lady Paget, Belle Herbert, Ashmead-Bartlett, Charles Whibley, Austin Harrison, Ronny McNeill, M.P., and a few others. Kept my taxi; lent it to Bartlett after dinner; it went off into the fog and was never seen again. I went home by tube, crawling along the roads holding on to the railings. Heard afterwards that some of the guests could not get away at all, and had to sleep there. Lady Paget took two hours to reach Belgrave Square.

Rather an amusing evening. Bartlett, not realising that Wolkoff was Russian and a diplomat, held forth on the subject of Russian iniquities, declaring that Russia ought to have taken Constantinople, if she wanted it, and not to have thrown the burden on us. Wolkoff, who held his tongue and smiled benignantly, told me afterwards that Russia would have been very glad, but she could not get there. He told me that all the Embassy telegrams were now about rifles and ammunition, instead of diplomatic questions. The rifles were coming in fast, and they hoped to send a large force to Bulgaria through Rumania. McNeill and I had a long talk about Carson, and the proceedings in the House next Tuesday.

General Joffre arrives on Thursday. He is apparently quite converted to the idea of Salonika. It is a great blow to me. Two divisions have been diverted to Egypt and will

not be available for another fortnight. It will be two months
before the rest arrive, and by that time the situation in
Serbia will be changed so much that I hope we may be able
to keep out of the war in the Balkans.

Wednesday, Dec. 1. Went to the War Office and found
all military opinion among the soldiers, including Archie
Murray, Robertson, and Cowans, utterly opposed to the
Salonika adventure. Drove down to Coombe ; found the
Beresfords, Lord and Lady Lytton, the Aga Khan, Colonel
Stuart from the Dardanelles, Almeric Paget, Mrs. McCreery,
Mrs. Duggan, the twins, and a few more. Talked to Sir
Arthur most of the afternoon about events. Lady Charles
at tea declaimed against Curzon. Mrs. Duggan was sitting
next to her. Drove back with the Aga Khan in his car.
Looked in at Portman Street to apologise for shirking
a promised rubber. Found Olive, Mrs. Astor, Seymour
Fortescue, and Pat playing Bridge. George Street, X., and
Charles North dined at Maryon. X. full of the war and
extremely critical of the Generals and Staffs in France.

Thursday, Dec. 2. Busy reading and commenting on
Sir John French's despatch of Oct. 15.

Friday, Dec. 3. Went to see Johnny Du Cane at
Armament House, Ministry of Munitions. The announcement of his appointment appeared in Monday's paper, and
I wanted to know what it all meant. He told me that he
does not know whether the whole thing was a sort of departmental *coup d'état*—the day before Lord K.'s return
from the Eastern Mediterranean—in order to provoke a row
and a crisis, or whether it was a serious attempt on the part
of the Government to mend matters with regard to munitions, which are nothing like right yet. He was invited by
Lloyd George to take up the work. He replied that he
would rather remain in France, but would come to London
if the opinion was that he could be of more use there. He
had stated to Lloyd George, and to the Prime Minister,
that he had to make two conditions, the first being that he
should be given the officers that he required for carrying
on the office, and the second that the M.G.O.'s branch should

not remain over the road in a dummy state and interfere with, and hamper, the work of the Minister of Munitions.

He was apparently promised that these conditions should be fulfilled. He informed Von Donop what was in the wind, and imagined that the M.G.O. would be left in charge of fortifications. But Cowans then seems to have proposed to hand over the Ordnance Stores, and all that appertained to them, to the M.G.O., but this was finally negatived. Du Cane's idea is practically to become M.G.O. himself, and to leave to the General Staff only the duty of defining the needs, and to the Ordnance Branch of the Q.M.G. Department the work of distribution. This seems a good scheme, if Du Cane's conditions are fulfilled. But the disappearance of Von Donop and the D.F.A. are essential preliminaries, otherwise there would be two branches doing the same work. The Prime Minister apparently fell in with Du Cane's proposals, but the Army Council met and ruled that they viewed the proposal with great alarm. The Prime Minister overrode this opinion, and declared that the decision to act as Du Cane wished had been taken by the Government itself. He further said that Von Donop should be given another appointment. This is how the matter stands at present, and it is that which Lord K. will have to deal with on his unexpected, and, to many, unwelcome return to London to-day. Du Cane at present has a table and a chair and a temporary secretary, but no office proper, no officers, and is merely a skeleton of a branch. I think that the whole should be under the War Office, though a separate branch of it, and that its head should hold the same important but still subordinate position that M. Thomas does in France. The question is what Lord K. will do when he comes back and finds his department has been cut in bits in his absence. There will probably be a great row. I fancy that the Army Council think that the change was made in rather a shabby manner behind Lord K.'s back, as indeed it was. This accounts for their attitude, and for the display of some hostility towards Du Cane, who really had nothing to do with the matter.

Lunched with Mrs. Leeds, Dr. Page, the American Ambassador and his wife, Lady Strafford, Lady Paget, Sir Sidney Greville, and Bogey Harris. An excellent lunch, and an amusing talk. Dr. Page told us some great stories of people who wrote from America to the Embassy, men wishing to find pretty English widows, and women wishing to adopt soldiers' children.

Drove to Totteridge to see Northcliffe, who was in bed with a bad cold. Found an agent back from the Continent. He told me that according to some evidence which he had collected, there were four German Army Corps (160,000 men in all) assembling north of Switzerland for the invasion of Egypt. They were all young men who had not yet served in the war. This Army had a lot of 15 to 21 centimetre guns newly turned out by Krupp. The men were being trained to harness and ride camels ! They were to be sent to Constantinople via Belgrade and Sofia, as soon as the railway was reopened, and they were expected to reach Constantinople in January. They will be joined by 350,000 Turks, and the whole will march upon Egypt ! It is a pretty tall story, but Lord K. and the War Office appear to believe it. The agent is going off again to Belgrade and Constantinople, and it will be interesting to see if his report turns out to have a vestige of truth.

Went to see Stanley Washburn in a private hospital. He is back from Russia, and is going home to America on leave for a few weeks. He told me that he thought that the Russians had $1\frac{1}{2}$ million rifles, and would have $2\frac{1}{2}$ million combatants next spring. He declared that the Tsar was much more intelligent than the Grand Duke Nicholas, but that he had not the decision of the latter. Alexeieff, the Tsar's Chief of Staff, has decision, but appears to be a very modest, retiring sort of man, with no advisers but only assistants. The Germans are now well dug in all along the Russian front. Had the Russians 500,000 more rifles they could drive the enemy away. It is all a question of rifles, but Washburn says that the Armies are not stiff with guns, and have lost a lot. He thinks that

Evert, who commands the Central Armies, is a very steady fellow, who will do what Alexeieff tells him, but that Ruszky in the north and Ivanoff in the south are rather more independent, while Ruszky hates Alexeieff. There is evidently a danger of want of concord along the front, and Washburn quoted a case of a commander of the Guard Corps, Besobrazoff, who refused to support the 3rd Army in a recent fight, was dismissed, and then put back by the Tsar's favour. He does not think that the Germans will be able to do any more this winter. He cannot say what force the Russians have on the borders of Rumania, but fancies that they are the 17th and 15th Armies, of which the latter are probably young troops, as the Germans describe them to be. He is inclined to think that the Russian reinforcements are to be thrown mainly at the centre. Archangel is still open, and may be open all the winter. The railway to the new northern port will not be ready till February at the earliest. He says that there are certainly 2,000,000 men standing in reserve, and awaiting rifles. He sails on Dec. 13.

Saturday, Dec. 4. Lunched at Ciro's; E. and others. One of the ladies apparently wants to bring me to the idea that when all women have a vote there will be no more wars. I told her that there would be twice as many.

Went to the War Office after lunch, and saw some friends. I found out some interesting things. The War Council had decided to evacuate Gallipoli, but the Cabinet rejected their advice. This is a flagrant instance of the futility of the new arrangement, and it has now been shown that the War Council reject the advice of the General Staff and the War Staff, and that the Cabinet in its turn reject the advice of all three, with the result that indecision reigns supreme, that nothing is done, and that the wretched garrison at Gallipoli remain exposed to the gathering cloud of enemies. The Cabinet, after deciding to evacuate Salonika, found that the French refused to agree, saying that if we went they would remain. In consequence, some Ministers and soldiers, including the Prime Minister and

Balfour, with Sir A. Murray and one or two more, go over to France to-day to consult with Briand, Gallieni, Joffre, and others. They were expected back on Monday, but returned this evening after 3½ hours' conference at Calais.

At present we have 140,000 men, including 50,000 French at Salonika, 120,000 at Gallipoli, and 85,000 in Egypt, or about 300,000 men in the Eastern Mediterranean.

We have had a nasty knock near Bagdad. We seem to have advanced very rashly with our single division under Townshend, who met superior forces, and in the end was forced to retire, after suffering heavy loss. Who sent him there with his insignificant little force ?

Sunday, Dec. 5. Went down to Coombe this afternoon, and had a long talk with Sir Arthur. A large party of people trooped in at various odd times. Mrs. Leeds, Mrs. Astor, Lady Ridley, Lady Paget and the twins, Mr. Vansittart of the Foreign Office, the Aga Khan, Bogey Harris, and some others. Had two long walks in the morning, the first with Sir Arthur, and the second with Mrs. Astor. We had a big luncheon party. Walked over with Sir Arthur in the afternoon to call upon the Ripons. Found them at home with Mrs. Sneyd and the Marquis de Soveral. Had an interesting talk about the command in France, when Queen Alexandra was announced, and I was caught and could not get away. She was very charming, but very deaf. I wonder why Royalties will stand up for so long, and make every one else stand. I slipped away as soon as I could against all rules, and found the Warren House ladies rather cross that all the men had gone off by themselves. We had a cheery evening, and I drove back with Sir Arthur on Monday morning.

Monday, Dec. 6. Orders were issued on Sunday for the evacuation of Salonika, but I saw de la Panouse, the French Military Attaché to-day, and he told me, as did others, that the French Government has gone back on the decision of the Calais Conference. We should have to wait for two or three days before learning what was finally decided.

It seems to be the practice of all these various committees and conferences to cancel each other's decisions, with the result that there is a general muddle. Also, as no notes appear to be exchanged in writing,—or at least very seldom —and as few of our people can speak French, and none of the Frenchmen can speak or understand English, all the elements for a misunderstanding are present. L. G. was asked the other day whether he could understand French. He said that he could not understand the Frenchmen when they spoke French, but that he could understand Grey perfectly when he did !

Wednesday, Dec. 8.   Had a talk in the afternoon with a member of our Headquarters Staff in France.   He told me that Sir John and Douglas Haig had both sent in reports about the failure to use reserves at the battle of Loos.   He did not think that any one here was competent to adjudicate between the two.   He doubted whether the question of superseding French had ever come to the point, but that French had many enemies, and that if his health suffered this winter, the opportunity of getting rid of him would be seized upon.   He said that French had ceased to trust Douglas Haig, and that we should not see the next action confided to this general.   He said that we were now all right as regards munitions, but that we were getting short of men, having a deficit of 35,000 in the front line alone. There was no doubt that the Germans had brought up a lot of men and guns in the West, that there was a great chance of a scrimmage, and that many people thought it the best thing that could happen.   We compared notes about Lord K.

Thursday, Dec. 9.   Saw Sir Ian Hamilton in the afternoon.   He was just finishing his Dardanelles despatch. He was not able to do so before, because all the reports from the Suvla Bay troops had been sent home to Sir F. Stopford, who had sent his report direct home to the War Office, and Sir Ian had to send for them all before he could complete his own draft.

He was very interesting on all the story of the Dardanelles.

He was grieved to think that we were coming away. He had been asked about it before leaving the Dardanelles, and reported against it, mentioning large figures as the probable price of evacuation. He had been able to obtain the opinion of Corps and Divisional Commanders, who changed their views after he had come home.

Monro had advocated withdrawal. Generals Davies, Birdwood, and Byng, had now all recommended evacuation. Lord K. had told the Cabinet that they would have to give in. Lord K. thinks evacuation possible, and places the loss at a lower figure than that anticipated by Hamilton. The latter declares that troops sent out to him had always been sent out too late, but he admits that for the Suvla Bay affair he got all he wanted. Lord K. told Sir Ian that there was no fault to be found in his conduct of operations, and that he could always hold his head high. Sir Ian naturally replied that in that case he did not know why he was at home. The men he asked for were Rawlinson and Byng, but K. had said that the man selected must be senior to Mahon. Sir Ian had then asked for Bruce Hamilton, and had received a reply that the Prime Minister thought Bruce too old. Lord K. then offered him Spencer Ewart, but Sir Ian replied that Ewart was not physically up to the work.

There are not enough ships to take away the Dardanelles and Salonika forces at the same time. Monro is at Mudros and is apparently in charge of the two expeditions. Maxwell is in Egypt. Sir Ian thinks that he has been holding up 240,000 Turks at the Dardanelles. He thinks that these troops will now be dribbling down to Syria, and he agrees that an attack will probably be made on Egypt this winter. He thinks that the forces at Salonika should be able to stand up to the enemy for some time, which is lucky if true, as there are no ships to carry them away. I suppose all this will fall in with the French ideas of not wishing to evacuate Salonika, on which point their Press is still very warm, and as I am the chief exponent of the contrary policy I am a good deal attacked.

A military conference has been going on for the last three days in Paris ; French, Robertson, and Murray are our representatives, and all these are strong opponents of the Salonika expedition. Sir Ian looks worn, and tells me that his weight has gone down to nine stone. I expect he has suffered a good bit, and that his cheery smile is just for the sake of appearance. He says that Birdwood is worth a million to the Empire and commanded the Australians magnificently, and that Birdwood would never have recommended evacuation so long as he, Sir Ian, was there. Ian thinks that we may be able to get away half our guns, then the reserves, and then the supports ; but that the firing line, part of which is ten yards from the Turks, together with 100 guns and most of the three weeks' supply stored on the beach, will be sacrificed in the event of retirement, and that such losses will drag down Lord K. and the Government.

He evidently does not think that Lord K. has treated him very well, or shown any skill in the general management of the war. He said it was as hard to get troops out of him as to get butter out of a dog's mouth. He says that our defences at Gallipoli are extremely strong, and he still holds that had he been sent 100,000 men and the 50,000 new rifles which he had asked for, after the Suvla Bay affair, he would have got through.

I cannot help thinking, however, that the unanimity shown by Monro and the other generals, is pretty clear proof that the game is up. It is merely a question now of the price to be paid in cutting the losses.

Dined with the Ancasters, 95 Lancaster Gate,—the Mintos' house. Lord and Lady Wolverton, Lady Edmund Talbot, Fox McDonnell, Lord Falconer, Mrs. Higgins (Lady A.'s mother), and Evan Charteris. An excellent dinner ; hostess very brilliant. Lady Wolverton resplendent. I discussed political affairs at dinner with Lady Edmund. She was very furious with Gulland, the Liberal Whip, for having concealed from Edmund Talbot the fact that Sir John Simon was going to raise a debate against the *Times* on the adjournment. She said that not even the Cabinet knew it, or at all events not the Unionist members of it, and that Simon had arranged it with the Prime Minister behind the back of the Cabinet. This procedure met with a merited failure. I found everybody very rabid with the Ministers, and all heartily approved of the strong article which I had published this morning on Simon and his wiles. Wolverton says that our Japanese rifles are all being sent to Russia. I wonder if our division on the coast have now got any rifles at all.

I found an invitation from Lord Haldane to dine alone with him on Wednesday ; he says that the position is very serious—as if we did not know it !

Friday, Dec. 10. Worked in the morning, and lunched with Mrs. Astor in Grosvenor Square. We discussed her trip to America, and I gave her a letter from Steed, showing what she could do to help the cause over there, and gave her the addresses of our New York and Washington correspondents. We had a great talk over the question of the union of the English-speaking races.

Saw Sir Archibald Murray in the afternoon, and we discussed the defence of Egypt. He does not think that more than seven divisions will be required, plus cavalry, and proposes to go forward to Katia, so as to deny this oasis to the Turks and Germans. He did not seem very keen on my plan of attacking the communications of the Turks in Palestine. He thinks that we must leave one division in reserve to watch the raiders on the Western frontier.

There are about 40,000 Turks in Palestine just now, and we have 85,000 men in Egypt, but scarcely any of the larger units. We have nearly five divisions in Salonika now, with three French. We have to hold this place through the winter, but the enemy may try to take it if it is any use to him. There are gathering in front of us nine Bulgarian divisions and two German. We discussed the evacuation of Gallipoli. The 2nd Mounted Division is already away safely. We also discussed Mesopotamia. Charles Townshend's division was only 11,000 combatants (all ranks) at Kut, and 9000 at Ctesiphon, and yet Crewe said in the Lords that he had more than a division, *i.e.* more than 20,000 men. The Cabinet appear to know less about our affairs than any other body of men.

Dined with the Charles Beresfords, the young Duchess of Sutherland, Lady Ridley, the Ralph Petos, Lord Dunraven, Edmund Gosse, the Aga Khan, Lord and Lady Edmund Talbot, and some others.

Took in Lady Ridley, who was very interesting. The Admiral monopolised the conversation after dinner, and held forth at great length about Labour politics. There was some violent speaking against poor old Haldane, in which neither Gosse nor I joined, and I know we both totally disagreed. One might as well try to dam Niagara with a toothbrush as stop an anti-Haldane talk just now. Talked to Edmund Talbot when we went upstairs. He asked me my views on Commanders and Staff Officers, and I gave them. He confirmed what Lady Edmund had told me that the Cabinet were not informed of Sir John Simon's intention to adjourn the House and attack the *Times* the other day. The Tories very angry at Simon's tactics.

Saturday, Dec. 11. Saw Lord Derby at Derby House. He could not give me the figures as he was reserving them for Asquith to announce, but I gathered that he was fairly satisfied, though the starring had been very badly done. There were a tremendous lot of men of all sorts. He said that owing to the number of reserved trades and occupations, he did not think that even Compulsion would give us enough men to keep going the seventy divisions which we are said to have promised to French. His honour was entirely involved in the married men not going until all single men had gone, according to his promise.

He had not made up his mind what he was going to do in case the Prime Minister did not make a complete statement of the facts, but if the worst came to the worst he would resign, and make a quite clear public statement. He was in a difficult position because he had figures before him which were confidential, but I think he means to see the thing through, and have all the facts brought out. There is little doubt in my mind that he would like to go to the War Office as War Minister. He would like Lord K. to be Commander-in-Chief, and free of the War Office administration. But he suggests that Lord K. should still be head of the General Staff, and this would never do, for he would never allow it to represent its views freely to the Cabinet. If Lord K. were made C.-in-C. he would become opposite number to Joffre, who has just been advanced to the same position in relation to all the French armies, instead of Chief of the Army of the North-East alone. Meantime, Lord K. is comfortably installed and does not look like moving !

Had lunch with Mrs. Astor—a send-off party. Jack Cowans, the Aga Khan, Lady Belle Herbert, Colonel Walker (a Yankee who wanted to meet me), Wolkoff, and one or two Foreign Office people, with Colonel Stuart and Lady Paget. Belle Herbert sat next to me, and we had a very amusing talk. Lady Paget vows that we have lost sixteen ships in the Mediterranean. Jack told me that they had taken 600,000 Derby recruits up to Friday, and expected 100,000 more to-day, but these are gross figures. I told him that we were 300,000 men short of our establishments, and that I should have to make a row about it. Mrs. Astor very charming. We were all sorry to say Good-bye, but she hopes she will not be long away.

Sunday, Dec. 12. Mrs. Townshend and John Walter came to lunch at Maryon ; the latter, who is forty-two, is going to take up soldiering again ; he has been seven years away from the old Volunteers.

Mrs. Townshend interesting about her husband's experiences in Mesopotamia. She brought his despatch of the battle of Kut for me to read. A well-planned and well-executed battle. He had 11,000 men, and did not wish to go on without reinforcements, but apparently India pressed for an advance for the sake of our prestige in Persia, which would have profited by the capture of Bagdad ; so Townshend went on and fought the battle of

Ctesiphon with 9000 men, or less than half the strength of a division, against not 8000 Turks but 30,000. Our intelligence service must have been very bad. His casualties were about half his force. In the India Office, judging by what Austen Chamberlain seems to have said to Mrs. Townshend, they had not expected him to get back without a disaster. Lord Crewe's statement in the House of Lords, that Townshend had more than a division, is evidently completely inaccurate; but this may have been said to deceive the enemy. We must not make a fuss about it at present.

Mrs. Townshend amusing about French politics, the Salonika expedition, and the higher commanders of the French and the English. She vows that the French are rather wild with us, but apparently with no reason. The idea that we did not send men enough, or quickly enough, to the Balkans, is stultified by the fact that we have 100,000 men and the French 60,000 now on the spot, though we lent ships to carry the French. The enemy is attacking our troops in the Balkans and pushing back our 10th Division, which is protecting the French right.

Monday, Dec. 13. Lunch with Ireland and Kitty at the Berkeley. He is expecting to go off to France at any moment. Dined at Ciro's with Lady Colebrooke, Lady Sarah Wilson, and Sir Seymour Fortescue. A pleasant dinner and good cooking; not too many people as there usually are at lunch. We adjourned to the Commodore's delightful rooms at St. James's Palace. All news from the Balkans is bad.

Wednesday, Dec. 15. Lunched with Mrs. Leeds and had a long talk with her. Dined with Lord Haldane. He showed me the diary of his visit to Berlin in 1912, and wishes that it could be published. I did not gather very much that was fresh from it. I told him that the main points which weighed against him were that he had admitted his anxiety about the situation in 1912, but had not warned the public, and, secondly, that he had claimed in an article that the public had to instruct the statesman and not vice versa.

Thursday, Dec. 16.   Announcement made that F.M. Sir John French is to be replaced by Douglas Haig in France.

Saw Sir John at 94 Lancaster Gate in the morning. Brinsley FitzGerald also there. The F.M. looking fit and well. The P.M. had written to him that the F.M.'s age and the great strain made it advisable in the public interest that he should come home, but that the P.M. would not insist or recall him. It was practically a recall, and it is absurd to speak of the action having been taken ' at the instance ' of Sir John French. The F.M. is glad to be out of it, as during the last few months the Government had so pestered him with all kinds of worries, that he had not been able to attend properly to his work. They had also vexed him with a system of espionage in France and round his London house, though I suppose they will say that they were after some one else. Sir William Robertson is to come home too and to take Murray's place, which is a mean trick to play on the latter when he has done so well. French says that Murray is to have a Corps. He says that he and I can meet again now. We spoke of the F.M.'s new work, and I told him that he would find chaos and have a great deal to do, and that a good A.G. would be indispensable. Drove off with Brinsley, and we discussed the Drexel divorce.

Lunched with the Dutch Minister and Madame van Swinderen at 32 Green Street—Ribblesdale's house. Baron Michiels, Count Limburg-Stirum—just appointed Governor of the Dutch East Indies—and his wife, and Sir Eyre Crowe of the F.O. Van Swinderen believes that Grey will not return to the F.O. He was furious with us for abstracting Dutch mails in our territorial waters, and declares that Grey was away fishing and that Nicholson knew nothing about it. He attacked Crowe on the subject. Lord Curzon rang me up at lunch at the Legation, and said that the Queen of the Belgians had arrived in England, and wished me to go down to Hackwood to-morrow to meet her. Walked back with Crowe and had an interesting talk.

Dined with Lady Sarah Wilson, 21 Hertford Street.   Lord

and Lady Alington, Sir Charles Hartopp, Sir C. Metcalfe, Mrs. Leeds, and Mrs. Ley from the U.S. Consulate at Berlin. Lady Sarah very pleasant. Mrs. Ley would not talk much, and I doubt that she knows much of the German situation. She has got into hot water for having talked too freely about the merits and strength of the Germans, and had evidently been warned.

Friday, Dec. 17. Lunched with Mrs. Toby Long, 55 Seymour Street. Vansittart of the F.O., and Trefusis, late of the Scots Guards, on parole from Holland. Went on to the Ritz to meet Lady Paget, Mrs. Leeds, Lady Headfort and Jack Cowans. Jack said that they had lost one transport a day during November in the Mediterranean. But the spirits of people in England are proof against all adverse fortune, and it is a great source of strength. Incidentally, they do not know anything.

Down to Basingstoke by train and thence motored to Hackwood. Found the Queen of the Belgians, Countess Ghislaine de Caraman Chimay, Count de Grünne, Mr. Henry Chaplin, Lady Irene Curzon—grown very handsome—and her two sisters.

An agreeable dinner. Chaplin most amusing, and Curzon full of good stories as usual. During dinner the question came up whether a cow's ears were in front of or behind its horns, and above them or below them. We all had different views except Chaplin, who has been Minister of Agriculture, and said that he had not the faintest idea! Sat between Ghislaine and Lady Irene. The former rather depressed and with less than her usual spirits. She had been six months in Paris, and Paris is depressing in this war. Lady Irene I found quite charming. After dinner talked to the Queen all the evening till she went to bed, and then with Curzon up to 1.30 A.M. Curzon told me that Millerand had come over and had stampeded the War Council. The Cabinet then took it up and negatived the Salonika expedition, of which Curzon entirely disapproved. Then Briand came in and sent Joffre, who practically made the War Council commit themselves, and the Cabinet's hand was forced.

Curzon seems to approve on the whole of French's super-session, because the regimental commanders had lost confidence in him—so he says. Curzon had also disapproved the advance on Bagdad, but declares that any one who knows any particular subject connected with the war is sure to be overruled when the subject is discussed. He says that the question of Sir John's recall was never submitted to the Cabinet, and he knew nothing of the Robertson-Murray change before I told him. He was grieved about Murray and sent to him some flattering messages by me. We discussed recruiting and the Derby boom at great length. I hope, if the P.M. fails in his duty, that Curzon and the conscriptionists will leave the Cabinet in a body. L. G. has told Curzon that he will stand by them.

I heard from Cowans to-day that we had taken over 2,000,000 names by the Derby scheme, and that Derby imagines that only a quarter of them will be utilisable. I passed this on to Curzon and advised him to learn the present deficit in the Army from the A.G.

Saturday, Dec. 18. The Queen came down early and sat at breakfast with me. We then went for a long walk together till my car came. She took several photos of me. She thought, and said the King thought, that the position was very serious. They had now 115,000 Belgian troops at the front, and 30,000 in reserve—a good result in the circumstances. She deplored Salonika, and took me all over the various fronts, I telling her my views and she telling me hers, which were shrewd and much to the point. She knew that our Allies had dragged us to Salonika and desired that we should adopt a firmer attitude. She said that the Belgians in Belgium were found by the Germans to be most intractable, more so than the French in the occupied territory. A Belgian soldier at the Paris Conference had brought back a report that the Russians were short of *men*, not rifles, but this can scarcely be right. She quoted Commandant Gallet as saying that the Anglo-French manner of conducting the offensive was wrong, with which I agreed. She was anxious about Loreburn and Courtney's speeches

about peace, but I reassured her and said that they had no
following, that we were going on no matter what happened,
and that the Russians would do the same, even if the French,
owing to their losses, found some need to spare their men.
We agreed that the Germans could go on for some time,
but I told her that we and the Russians ought to be able
to place more men on the front next year than Germany
could freshly raise, and that our men and munitions combined would give us the pull. We discussed the Yser inundations and how to use them in case of a frost. The
Queen had been in the trenches, and as far forward as a
bridge-head across the Yser within 50 yards of the Germans.
Except Alexander of Teck, there was no one left of the old
English Mission with the Belgians, and the Queen did not
know who was to replace Tom Bridges, who had got a
division. The Queen made me promise that I would visit
her at La Panne when I next went to France.

Returned to town and went to see Sir Archibald Murray at
the W.O. in the afternoon to condole with him. He showed
me the P.M.'s letter, very flattering to him, saying that now
he was to succeed Monro in the Mediterranean. Thus the
change of the higher command in France entails the shifting
of Robertson, Murray, and Monro, three of the best soldiers
we have. What a mess! Lord K. had been very curt with
Murray, and had simply said that he had meant to make a
change.

We have taken eight divisions from France, where our
front, after the arrival of some five New Army divisions, will
be two to three less on balance. The Boches will indeed be
pleased. The Army for the defence of Egypt is to be eight
divisions and eight mounted brigades. We are undertaking
our main work of evacuation at Gallipoli to-morrow night—
a terrible anxiety. We hold the right at Salonika, and the
French the left—an extended line. The G.S. had just drafted
a memo. on the general situation. It dealt in divisions,
not entering into recruiting, and showed first how many
divisions were needed for defensive purposes. Murray
thinks that the Allies on the main front must agree to act

simultaneously, and that on each front there must be a general attack where we stand. In this manner the enemy will not be able strategically or tactically to deplete one front, or one part of the front, for the profit of another.

Robertson is coming in next Friday. Dined with Colonel MacFarlane and a party of men.

Sunday, Dec. 19. Lord Haldane called in the afternoon. We deplored the Staff changes. His idea of the psychology was that the Cabinet were too weak to order Lord K. to Egypt, and therefore put in Robertson to neutralise him and stand up to him. We both thought that Murray was the best man in London, and R. invaluable in France. Discussed recruiting, but I found Lord H. still in the old Radical strain, and I expect no help from him. Lord H. would prefer Haig as C.I.G.S., and Balfour as War Minister. I should not.

Monday, Dec. 20. Went to see Laszlo's portrait of Mrs. Leeds. A great success. A fine piece of work, and a most companionable picture. Lunched with Mrs. Leeds, Lady Sarah, Mrs. George Keppel, and some others.

Dined at the Hotel Cecil with the Northern Association of Unionist agents. Lockett Agnew presided with great verve over a large body of capable men, mostly from Lancashire, Yorkshire, Cheshire, etc. I addressed them on the war, not mincing matters. Made an effective speech. Steel-Maitland also spoke, and was as critical of the Government as I was.

Mrs. Keppel told me to-day that Lord K. had been offered India and refused it. Steel-Maitland, however, says that Austen Chamberlain vows that he will leave the India Office if K. is made Viceroy. All the Ministry are pining to dispose of K., but no one can bell the cat. K. is not on the pinnacle he once was, but the mass of the people hold to him.

Tuesday, Dec. 21. We heard this morning that our troops had evacuated Gallipoli and Anzac successfully ; a great relief to us all, and especially to the Government, which would probably have been turned out had the operation

cost as much as was feared by Ian Hamilton and others.
Spoke to Callwell at the W.O. about the share of the General
Staff in the initial military attack on the peninsula of
Gallipoli.   He assured me that the G.S., as such, were
never consulted, nor had been asked to express an opinion.
Lord K. alone was responsible.   Maurice and Whigham are
coming back with Robertson, and Kiggell goes out as C.G.S.
to Haig.

Saw a friend and discussed the general situation.   The
continuation of the allied pressure on the three main fronts
is in our opinion the best road to victory.

We agreed upon the uselessness of the Balkan theatre
to us, and exchanged views about the danger of an oversea
attack on us at home, especially if we make our main
offensive elsewhere than in France.

I am told that Murray says that the attack on Egypt
may come sooner than expected.   He sails next Tuesday.
He will have exclusive command, but will allot to Maxwell
responsibility for the Sudan and Western fronts.   Several
Ministers, notably Balfour, have deplored his departure.

We discussed East Africa.   The Germans have 2200
whites, perhaps 20,000 blacks, and 63 guns.   The raising
of the S.A. Levies for the war had to await the close of the
late elections in S.A., and they will now not be ready before
the rainy season (April-July) comes on.   So the proceedings
this winter will be preparatory only, and the German posts
inside our frontier will be beaten up.

Lord K. strongly dissents from the G.S. proposal to attack
German East Africa.   He seems to have written like a
cross schoolgirl, and his paper is said to be nearly as feeble
a production as his instructions to Sir Ian when the latter
started for the Dardanelles.

Dined with Lady Sarah Wilson, Lady Colebrooke, and
Sir S. Fortescue at the Commodore's rooms in St. James's
Palace.   A capital dinner and a good talk.

Wednesday, Dec. 22.   Engaged upon a summary of the
year when I want to be at much more important work.
Dillon attacked me in the House of Commons last night.

He says that I ' might be described as the 23rd member of the Cabinet; very much more powerful than the other 22 members ' (official report). I wish he had heard my speech at the Cecil !

Lunched with Mrs. George Keppel, Lady Sarah Wilson, and a few more. Heard some interesting things.

Dined with Lydia Kyasht at her house, 37 Avenue Road, Regent's Park. A very pleasant dinner. Lydia full of her late visit to Russia, describing the state of destitution as awful, and declaring that a revolution is imminent, and that the only question is whether it can be postponed till May. She says that the Army is all right, and they will have 7 million men in the spring, but I fear only 2 million will be armed. The Army want the Grand Duke Nicholas back, but some regiments will stand by the Tsar. Society is now all for revolution, but whether they will profit by it is another matter. Her description of the influence of the favourite so-called monk, Rasputin, who is an illiterate peasant, unable to read or write, is most astonishing. He is said to have the Tsar and the Tsaritsa completely under his influence. Unheard of tales are told of his goings-on. He told the Grand Duke that he was coming to bless the Army, and the Grand Duke replied that he would hang him if he came. The next day the Grand Duke was dismissed and sent to the Caucasus. Many, including Prince Orloff, have tried to open the Tsar's eyes to the rascality of this Russian Piers Gaveston, but all have failed, the Tsar saying that he will allow no one to interfere in his private affairs. Even allowing for exaggerations it is a pretty distressing state of things ; and it seems to be true, as Benckendorff tells his intimates, that no one is governing in Russia, and that things are drifting.

Friday and Saturday, Dec. 24-25. Met Johnny Du Cane and Peter Granet, Xmas Day, on my return from Ockham. Johnny said that they had just succeeded in detonating ammonal, and he was very pleased about it. Our H.E. shells supplied since June had been on the 80 to 20 basis, and 50 per cent. of them had proved ineffective. Partly owing to this, and to the fact that many shells had burst at the muzzle, and to the conservatism of the artillery, which would not easily transform itself from a shrapnel to a H.E. artillery, we had used 500 rounds of shrapnel to 60 of H.E. at the Loos battle. Things were coming on, but we all agreed that the rearmament of Russia was a primary interest of all the Allies. Knox had come back from the British Mission in Russia stating that they had only 800,000 rifles left after the retreat. It is thought that they cannot have more than 1,500,000 by the spring, as U.S.A. supplies will not come in until well on into next summer. Du Cane said that the Russians had first made their own contracts in America. Then it had been decided that all orders should go through England, whereupon the Russian man in America, who thereby lost his commission, refused to pass the rifles in America! How can one win a war when these things happen in such a grave crisis?

Looked in at Olive's Xmas tree. Pretty Bridget kissed me under the mistletoe.

Sunday, Dec. 26. Wrote an article on 'Trade or Victory.' It will make the Radical Press howl. But after all, if you give the Army men you get victory, and if you keep them back for trade you don't get victory, and then eventually get no trade. Victory gives all. Q.E.D.

Monday, Dec. 27. Dined at the Carlton with H.H. the Aga Khan, Lady Paget, and Mrs. Cis Bingham. Lady P. sure that the P.M. and Lord K. would soon be out of office. The A.K. and I doubted about the P.M. We all imagined that the Cabinet to-day at 3 P.M. on the Derby scheme would lead to no decision, and in fact this was so. Mrs. Bingham described Sir John French's departure from the Army. All the cavalry, 35,000 men, lined the two sides of the road and cheered him to the echo. Cis Bingham found the tears rolling down his cheeks, and when the F.M. stopped to shake hands with him he was so overcome that he could not say a word.

We went on to a very silly play called the *Spanish Main,* and saw an act and a half of it, which was more than enough.

Had no chance of a good talk with the Aga Khan about Eastern affairs.

Tuesday, Dec. 28.   The *Daily News* attacks my last article and makes a precious hash of its reply.   The Cabinet meets again to-day at 11.30.   Some think that it will break up on the question of compelling single men to serve.

Went to see F.M. Sir John French at 94 Lancaster Gate and had nearly two hours with him.   Sir John told me more fully the story of his giving up the command.   When the P.M., Balfour, and Lloyd George were in Paris, Sir John heard rumours of a change, and drafted a letter to say that unless he had the entire confidence of the Cabinet he preferred to resign.   But Esher, then at G.H.Q., asked him to hold the letter up, and posted off to Paris, saw each one of the three Ministers separately, and was told that they had not thought of any such thing.   Shortly after, when Lord K. had gone East, Esher came over to France with a verbal message from the P.M., saying that on account of the F.M.'s age, and because the P.M. wanted him at home, it would be better for the F.M. to resign.   Sir John then went to London, and arrived one Saturday night when the P.M. was away.   Sir John consulted Walter Long, who was all for a personal interview, and the F.M. saw the P.M. on the following Monday evening at 5.   The P.M. was very nice to him and told him that he, the P.M., had been Lord K.'s only friend in the Cabinet, but he was now unable to put up with him, and consequently wanted Sir John to Command-in-Chief at home, so that the Cabinet might have his military advice.   He said that there was no hurry, and that if Sir John himself did not decide to return, he, the P.M., would not insist.   Sir John said that he had to consider whether he was justified in leaving the Army which had fought so bravely under him ; secondly, to consider what view history would take of his action ; thirdly, to know who was to succeed him.   The P.M. agreed, and as to the last point, said he would consult the F.M., who eventually nominated Robertson, but without success.   He then returned to France after telling the P.M. that he was in consultation with Walter Long, a course of which the P.M. approved. A few days later Lord K.'s unexpected return was made known to be imminent, and Walter Long wrote to Brinsley FitzGerald saying that the P.M. really wanted French badly at home, and advised resignation. On this advice French acted.

We discussed the whole affair. Sir John thinks that the P.M. really wants him, and had told him that home defence was in a state of chaos, but French also thinks that there was an intrigue against him and in favour of Haig, who proposes to make X. his military secretary, a post for which X., despite his good points, is not very suitable. French thinks that it suited the P.M.'s book to fall in with this arrangement. However, we are agreed that the Cabinet were not consulted on this change, or on any of the others recently announced, and that there is still some mystery about the P.M.'s decision which must be cleared up.

French thinks that we have 35 divisions and the French 96 in the West. We had a combined superiority of 700,000 men in September, but since then the Germans have brought 12 divisions from the East, while we and the French have lost 8 for Salonika, and we could not count the New Army divisions recently sent out to France because they are no good yet. In fact, taking 10,000 men as the average fighting strength of a division in rifles, we have 350,000 only, and the French 960,000, making 1,310,000, and the German 103 divisions equal 1,030,000, so that the balance in our favour is only 280,000 rifles, while we have to remember the German superiority in heavy guns and machine guns. He gives the Germans only 45 divisions, or under 500,000 rifles, on the Russian front. The German units are kept up better in France than in Russia. The German division should have 13,000 rifles, but in the West companies are down to 150–180 men in the place of 250, giving about 10,000 rifles per division, and he doubts whether in Russia the German battalions are so high. He does not believe that the Germans have more than 1,000,000 men left in reserve. He practically rules out the Russians for the rest of the campaign. Note that 350,000 rifles for 80 miles of front held is only $2\frac{1}{2}$ men per yard, even if all were there.

In his new job the F.M. will not get into his office for two days. He is to have training and home defence, and the inspectors will be under him. He had half an hour with Lord K. and Sclater (the A.G.) this morning, and jotted down a few notes about numbers, but is quite ignorant of his command. He imagines that he will have the last five of the New Army divisions, and thirteen 2nd-line Territorial divisions, but the former go abroad in February and March, and the latter will follow, when he will only have 300,000 scratch volunteers, at present unarmed, and about 1,000,000 others, chiefly recruits, depots, special reserves, invalids, and garrisons—a motley crew, but, as ever, Sir John disbelieves in invasion, and would send all his men to France if asked.

His Staff for operations will be at the War Office, but I told him that his head man at least should be with him at his office. He promises to look very carefully into strengths and rifles, and to see all the weak commanders. He gets on perfectly with Robertson. The latter insisted on full powers when appointed. Sir John says that Robertson is not like us ; he takes nothing on trust, and finds out himself. He has already had to be very firm with Lord K.

Friday, Dec. 31. A New Year's party at 35 Belgrave Square. Lady Paget, the Duchess of Westminster, Lord and Lady Ancaster, Lord and Lady Colebrooke, Mrs. Cis Bingham, Belle Herbert, Jack Cowans, Mrs. Duggan, Mr. O'Beirne, Sir Louis Mallet, the Aga Khan, and one or two others whom I forget. A very cheery evening. We dressed up in the hats from the crackers, ragged a good deal, went out into the square at midnight to hear the chimes, and then back to drink an excellent punch and sing 'Auld Lang Syne.'

CHAPTER V

THE OUTLOOK FOR 1916

Lord Kitchener and Sir William Robertson—The deficit in our Army
strengths—General Robertson's plans—Derby recruiting estimates—
The Compulsion Bill introduced—Gallipoli finally evacuated without
loss — Sir Ralph Paget and Mr. O'Beirne on Balkan politics —
Sir Ian Hamilton on the Dardanelles—Visit to Sunninghill Park—
Home Defence chaos—M. Coleyn on German numbers and British
strategy—Lord Derby on recruiting—German losses—Sir W. Robertson's views of events—Sir F. E. Smith's arrest in France—Russia's
rifle strength.

Tuesday, Jan. 4. Saw Sir William Robertson for the first
time since he was installed as C.I.G.S. He told me that
he had had to drop his first plans of being wholly independent of K. because orders had to go out in the name
of some Secretary of State to be valid, so he could not make
the War Council his Kaiser as he had wished. He now
preferred to range up alongside Lord K., and to act with
him. Lord K. had accepted the position that all orders
should go out through R., and an Order in Council would
shortly come out in this sense. K. had at one time practically resigned, and the P.M. had accepted the resignation,
but R. had met K. at Calais, had travelled to Paris with
him, and had induced him to carry on. R. is having much
trouble with a section of the Cabinet. McKenna and
Runciman are urging that finance and trade require that
we should have a small Army. R. advocates the comple-
tion of 70 divisions. We have now actually 67, including
3 in India (Territorial), and 6 Canadian and Australasian.
He says he believes that at one of the Calais meetings it
was agreed that we would supply 70 divisions.

I told him that I knew we were short of establishments,

and to keep up the strengths for three months by 338,000 men. He calculates that the Derby recruiting will give us, if we get Compulsion, these needs, and enough men more to go on for nine months—a total need of about 1,500,000 men for the year. He has advised that all the divisions should be raised to war strength, and he cannot do more at present. He has not put this on paper, but has verbally stated the case to the P.M. McKenna was opposing the 70 divisions, but he did not apparently know that they all existed, or that their staffs, guns, cadres, and transport were already provided. It apparently costs 7½ millions to keep up a division, and all found, for a year. To cut off the thirteen 2nd-line T.F. divisions at home would save McKenna less than 100 millions, which would not go far to pay the 600 millions a year which we lend to our Allies.

R. thinks that there is chaos in our arrangements, but hopes to get it right in a few weeks. All the generals now report to him. He has 200,000 men in Egypt, but can only find two formed divisions out of them, as they are mostly odds and ends. He is working up for 12 divisions in Egypt. The Helles lot will try to come away when the weather serves. He considers troops at Salonika useless, and laughs at Garvin's and Strachey's admonitions, in the *Observer* and the *Spectator* respectively, to make a great campaign in the Balkans. He has not altered the memorandum, the *magnum opus* as he calls it, of Murray and Kiggell, and has given the Cabinet a short summary of it under a few heads, saying that he has nothing better to propose. He hopes to strengthen the force in France with more troops (4 to 6 divisions) and plenty of heavy guns soon. He will take the troops from Salonika when he can. He says, to my surprise, that Joffre is dead against Salonika, and has thanked R. for opposing the expedition ! Why then did he advocate it here on Oct. 29 ? R. thinks from political motives. R. is not at all sure what the Germans will do. We discussed invasion. R. says that there are 1,200,000 men at home here, and Sir John may be able to do a great work in setting them in order. R. disbe-

lieves in invasion. He thinks that Balfour and Austen
Chamberlain advised the advance on Bagdad, which
Nixon had stated he could take but not hold. K. was
against the advance. We discussed the chances of a fresh
attack on us in the West, and I gave my views. Grey,
McMahon, and K. all insist on Maxwell remaining in command in Egypt, though Murray has gone out to command.
An absurd line of demarkation has been drawn along the
canal. R. strongly opposed this and wanted one commander, and the poor P.M. was in a quandary to decide
between R. and K. Finally he supported K., and R. did
not think it worth while to resist any more. But the
P.M. will make Murray full General, and then in case of
need he can order Maxwell about. R. sees little sign of a
Turkish attack on Egypt, but admits that our information from these parts is defective. He has brought Macdonogh home to run his Intelligence Service here, which
pleases me very much.

Dined at Olive's ; Belle Herbert, Lady Colebrooke's
pretty daughter-in-law Mrs. Murray, Colonel Wyndham
Portal, Lady Randolph Churchill, and Pat. Was very late,
but so were some of the others. A very pleasant dinner,
and we had a rare gossip afterwards. Lady Randolph in
great form, and most bitter against Lord K.

The figures of the Derby recruiting scheme came out this
afternoon. We should get, according to these estimates :

Unstarred attested men	343,386
„ married „	487,676
Unattested single „ (651,000), say .	300,000
Direct enlistments taken	275,000
Total .	1,406,062

This is only an estimate, but if it works out all right
Robertson will get the men he needs for 1916 at all events.

Wednesday, Jan. 5. Went down to hear the P.M. bring
in the Compulsion Bill. Had a seat under the clock in the
Sergeant-at-Arms' box. A packed house. The P.M. very
quiet and undemonstrative. He spoke so low that he was

invited to speak up. A great want of magnetism, and judged by this speech his powers are failing, but it may be only a trick. He gave no explanations of the military necessity for the Bill, but restricted himself to the political side, to his pledge, and to the terms of his Bill. Sir John Simon, who has happily left the Government, got up next and made an unhappy speech for a Minister who has had all the facts before him. He was cheered by the riff-raff of the Left, but he made a bad impression.

Thursday, Jan. 6. The Bill passes first reading, majority 298. Bonar Law, Ward, Barnes, Samuel, and Balfour made the most effective speeches. The Labour Conference passes a resolution by a supposed large majority against Compulsion.

Friday, Jan. 7. Dined with Lady Charles Beresford. Congratulated her and the Admiral on the peerage. Lady Norreys, Mrs. Maguire, Lady Kitty Somerset, Lady Paget, Lord and Lady Lytton, etc. A pleasant dinner and a good talk afterwards about politics and strategy. Charlie B. holding forth with shrewd good sense and much to the point.

Saturday, Jan. 8. Went down to Coombe for the week-end. There were either there or came over on Sunday, Sir A. and Lady Paget, Lord and Lady Granard, Lord and Lady Charles Beresford, Sir John Cowans, Sir Charles Hartopp, Mrs. Peto (who was Ruby Lindsay), Mrs. Keppel, Sir Ralph Paget (late Minister to Serbia), Bogey Harris, and Mr. O'Beirne (late Minister at Sofia). A pleasant party, but we sat up too late. Jack Cowans told us on Sunday night that the last part of Gallipoli had been successfully evacuated without loss. This was good news. Official estimates led people to fear the loss of between 30,000 and 50,000 men. He told us that we had now 1000 ships in the Mediterranean, and that the cost was something frightful. He mentioned one that had been at Mudros since the spring, and was costing £90,000 a month, and another that was travelling about with a heavy gun which could not be landed anywhere, and had already cost the country £11,000. He had telegraphed to tell them to throw the gun into the sea and come home.

I had a long talk, first with Sir Arthur Paget, and then with O'Beirne, in the morning of Sunday, and in the afternoon I walked over with Mrs. Keppel to call on Lady Ripon. We found Gladys and Juliet both at home; also that shrewd judge of affairs, Soveral. Topps and O'Beirne came in after us. We had a great political talk. Gladys very amusing about the French Ministry, many of whom seem to be mixed up with different ladies, and their colleagues all make it warm for them in consequence. Mrs. X. tells me that she met a French Army Commander who assured her that France could not go on any more, and that it was necessary to think of terms of peace. Gammon!

There is a great difference of opinion about McKenna and Runciman, who are making themselves rather a nuisance just now.

Had an interesting talk at breakfast with Ralph Paget and O'Beirne about Balkan politics. Each of these ex-Ministers takes the point of view of the country to which he has been accredited, Paget holding that the Bulgars are liars and thieves, and O'Beirne holding that the Serbs committed suicide by not giving up to Bulgaria the contested territory. Paget thinks that the war will be over very soon owing to the exhaustion of the Germans. He says that there are very few Germans left in Serbia, and that they have all gone off again to the Russian front, and to watch Rumania. His account of the Serbian retreat is very interesting. The Ford cars seem to have done best on the rough roads. He thinks that about 120,000 of the Serbians are left one way or another, but that the submarines make a difficulty in getting them away from the Adriatic to Salonika. Lady Charles amused me very much by asking 'what the Baron was saying.' I could not think what she meant, but it was Charlie B. holding forth at the other end of the table. There is some feeling because he took the peerage from Asquith, whom he attacked so severely, but I don't think that this is fair criticism, for in a

Coalition Government Lord Lansdowne has his own list for honours.

Jack produced a lot of stories and verses. The supposed French *communiqué* was rather good.

Tuesday, Jan. 11. Wrote an article on 'Amateur Strategy' in the morning, but it was banned by the Censor. Lunched with Sir Ian and Lady Hamilton at 1 Hyde Park Gardens. He and I at once plunged into the history of the Dardanelles expedition. He told me that the largest number of effectives that he had ever had under him at any time was about 130,000, and that the Turks had available on the peninsula, or within easy reach of it, 240,000 men. I told him my views which I had written down in my article in the morning, namely, that the matter really resolved itself into a fight between two main Armies, in which case his Army was not strong enough to gain victory. I told him that I did not think, if he had captured the heights above the Narrows, that the Navy could have compelled the Turks to make peace, and that therefore the objective assigned to him was not a correct one. He admitted that the whole thing had been planned in a most sketchy manner between him, K., Callwell, and Braithwaite during an hour's vague talk before he went out, when Kitchener scarcely thought that a landing would be necessary, but said that, if it was, Ian was to restrict himself to the peninsula. There was no paper before this meeting for consideration, and the whole thing was left exceedingly nebulous. Sir Ian thought that the Navy would have expected to dominate the Sea of Marmora and to starve the Turks by controlling the railway which fringes the Asiatic shore of the Marmora, but the submarines had exercised this command to a large extent for a long time without starving the Turks, and the latter could still have got supplies over the Bosphorus from Asia Minor or from Thrace, Bulgaria, and Rumania. He showed me the correspondence about his subordinate commanders, from which it appears he had asked for Byng and Rawlinson, as he had told me before, but had been refused because

K. did not wish to supersede his old friend Mahon in the command. Mahon was a senior Lieut.-General, and there was hardly any one senior to him worth taking. We looked at the Army List and I saw no one except Lake and Willcocks worth thinking of. K. had offered him Spencer Ewart, and Ian had replied that he would not do as he could not get about in the trenches. He unfortunately added that Stopford would do better than Ewart, so that in a sense he was responsible for Stopford coming out. Sir Ian also showed me a letter from Birdwood about Lord K.'s visit to Gallipoli, from which it appeared that 'Birdie,' in changing his opinion about the evacuation and in approving it, was influenced by K.'s, Maxwell's, and McMahon's opinions about the imminence of an attack on Egypt, and by the fact that the Army in this case would not pull its weight in the boat by remaining at the Dardanelles.

We are told some amusing stories about the evacuation. Ingenious contrivances were made to fire off guns and rifles mechanically when the troops had left, and then went on firing for half an hour after the troops had embarked. There does not appear to be the slightest truth in the rumour which naturally goes round that the Turks were bribed.

Wednesday, Jan. 12. First meeting of the Hampstead Tribunal. The Mayor, Mr. O'Bryen, the Town Clerk, and four or five others, rather inclined to be Jacks-in-office, and even to dispute the right of Colonel Sheffield and myself to appear, as we had not our credentials with us. I had asked our Advisory Committee to come up and listen to the meeting and see how things were done and worked, but the Mayor put them all out, saying that he did not want their help, which is not the point at all. The harm had been done before Sheffield and I had arrived. They took $2\frac{1}{2}$ hours to do ten cases, and Heaven only knows how long we shall be when the Compulsion Bill comes into force. I have had no dealings with Municipal authorities before, and did not know their idiosyncrasies.

Thursday, Jan. 13. Lunched with Mrs. Keppel; Lady

Paget, Lord Ilchester, Lady Juliet Duff, and Mr. and Mrs. Leishman (who represented the U.S. in Constantinople and Berlin), Violet Keppel, and Bogey. Found Leishman a very intelligent and well-informed old gentleman. His wife has been a great beauty. We had an amusing lunch, and all chaffed a good deal. Juliet in great good looks. I was glad to see Violet again ; she is such a clever girl, and so attractive ; but I told her that she frightened me to death, for she is the best mimic in London, and a noted caricaturist—two most dangerous accomplishments. I heard her taking off some people at Mrs. Rupert Beckett's after dinner one night last year ; she is inimitable and acts each part to the life. Lady Minnie in good form and full of amusing stories.

I am attending a meeting of the Advisory Committee at the recruiting office in Finchley Road, and go there again to-day. The Advisory Committee consists of one barrister, one Labour man, and five local tradesmen of the better class. Mr. David, K.C., is chairman. They are a good lot of fellows to work with, and are very fair in examining claims. Our trade unionist is the hardest man of all on the poorer classes.

Friday, Jan. 14. Things are going badly with Montenegro, which looks like losing her capital and getting quite knocked out. The Italians have been very slack in the Adriatic, where their interests are most involved. I don't wonder that the French Press are sarcastic about them. The *Giornale d'Italia* asked me for another interview to tell them what I think of the Adriatic, but I have not answered the invitation as I should not have anything pleasant to say about them. Last time they interviewed me, their man did not send me the account before it was published, as he promised to do, and apparently he made me say all sorts of awful things, for all kinds of protests came from various countries, and I was shown a long telegram from our Minister at Bukharest, complaining bitterly about it. So it is best to keep these gentlemen at arm's length, even though this paper is the Italian Prime Minister's organ.

Monday, Jan. 17. Went down on Saturday to spend the

week-end at Sunninghill Park, near Ascot, with Mrs. Duggan.
Travelled down to Windsor by train with Lady Sarah
Wilson. Jack Stirling came to say Good-bye at Padding-
ton ; he is off to France to-morrow, and hopes to get command of a battalion. We had some talk before the train
left. Motored through Windsor Great Park, and then to
the house. A large, comfortable, early-Victorian house,
with 1000 acres of park and farms, and a large lake bordered
by woods. Our party consists of Mrs. Duggan and her three
children,—including a perfectly adorable little girl of eight—
Lady Sarah, Lady Paget, Sir George and Lady Arthur, Lord
Curzon of Kedleston, Lord Ribblesdale, and Lord Drogheda.
There also came over on Sunday afternoon Colonel Ames
from Windsor and Lady Downshire and party from East-
hampstead Park. Lady Downshire the second wife of
the 6th Marquess : a beautiful woman with great natural
dignity.

The house has some treasures in it, especially some of
the pictures, but also a good few early-Victorian horrors.
A very comfortable house to stay in, and a very charming hostess. We did a great deal of talking and
walking. I had some good talks with George Arthur
about Kitchener, whose private secretary he is. Lord K.
seems much more free now than he was. Had some
long talks with Curzon about politics and the war. He
thinks that Sir John Simon made a miscalculation, and
fancied that he was going to find himself at the head
of a strong party instead of the riff-raff. I told him
about the money received from Germany at the time of
the last railway strike, and suggested that they should
publish the facts now in order to dish the strike-makers,
who are still opposing Compulsion. He seems still hurt
that he is not on the War Council. I am not surprised.
We had an interesting talk about the manner in which the
history of this time will be written, and he wondered whether
any Cabinet Minister wrote an account to some woman or
another of what was happening. He felt sure that no
Cabinet Minister kept a diary. He did not think that there

was going to be a big affair in France just now as is
rumoured. We had a good deal of chaff with Wolkoff
about the Russian offensive movement in progress now.
Wolkoff could not understand why the Russians were
attacking alone, nor could we.

Tuesday, Jan. 18. Dined with Mr. and Mrs. Edward
Stonor, the Marquis d'Hautpoul, Baron Michiels, and Lady
Colebrooke. Good pleasant conversation, and first-rate
Bridge ; both d'Hautpoul and Michiels play admirably.

Thursday, Jan. 20. Lunched in Belgrave Square. Lady
Paget, Prince and Princess Victor Napoleon, Mrs. Duggan,
Wolkoff, and Max-Muller of the Foreign Office. The Princess
very nicely dressed, and charming as usual. Mrs. Duggan
was in the most attractive widow's weeds imaginable.
Callaud of Paris makes a speciality of mourning for war
widows apparently. These particular weeds included a
very pretty hat in crape, with a veil hanging down behind,
or rather streamers, and a narrow band of white crape round
the hat next her face, and also under her chin. The dress
had a white waistcoat of tulle, and open at the neck ; in fact
she looked like a fascinating nun. Laszlo has painted her
in this dress. The Princess raved about her afterwards.
We had an amusing lunch, and a good talk about
Belgium, France, America, and the blockade. I walked
away with Max-Muller, who has been writing all the confidential reports about German trade, and he told me that
his opinion was that economic pressure would never bring
the war to an end, but would require to be supplemented by
military successes. I had hardly left him before I met
Count Wrangel, the Swedish Minister, who told me that
military successes would never bring the war to an end,
but that economic pressure would. Moral, try both.

The Tribunal met at Hampstead to-night, and did its
work well.

Friday, Jan. 21. Had a lot of letters about my article
on ' The Western Front,' which appeared in yesterday's
Times, all approving except Ian Hamilton, who was critical
but inexplicit, so I wrote to ask him to define an alterna-

tive policy. Had an interesting letter from Northcliffe giving his reason why I should not enter Parliament. I had been approached to learn whether I would stand for an important provincial town where one of the sitting members offered to retire in my favour. Northcliffe says that we can open fire with much better effect from the *Times* platform, and that my position is absolutely unique.

Lunched with Lady Paget and met Doris Keane and Mrs. Duggan again. I bet that she would not come in the same widow's weeds, but she did, to our joy. Doris Keane was perfectly delightful, and told us all sorts of stories about her play, *Romance*, and all the letters she had about it every day. She made a profit of £1000 last week, and she puts all her success down to Lady Paget and me for having got her to act before the Queen. There is no doubt that this play goes deep down into the hearts of all classes, and the wonderful acting of this little lady has conquered London. There were 500 people turned away last night. But it is comical that until Doris acted before the Queen no one went to her play, and she was losing £7000 over it. Now all the so-called literary sets think that they have made a great discovery. They have not. They have simply been snobbish sheep.

Saturday, Jan. 22. Wrote an article on the Committee of the Compulsion Bill. Feel somewhat doubtful whether we will get the figures that Lord Derby anticipates, owing to the many exemptions in the Bill and the long lists of reserved trades that are constantly being added to it. In the afternoon went down to see ' Viscount French of Ypres.' French went at great length again into his reasons for coming away from France, and the attitude of the P.M., etc. His account did not vary materially from that which he gave me before, and I find that he still believes that the P.M. wished him to come home to take command owing to the disorganisation here. He said that I had been quite right in warning him that he would find chaos. He had done so. He had found an immense mass of troops, something like a million and a quarter or a million and a half, but with no organisation worth the name, and most indifferently armed. Out of his Central Forces under Rundle, nominally 170,000 strong, he declares that there are only 30,000 armed. He is to abolish the generals in command of the Training Centres, except Hunter at Aldershot, and to appoint his senior generals, namely Paget, Bruce Hamilton, Lawson, and perhaps Ewart, in charge of a sector each. He proposes to organise each sector on the lines of the defences in France, and to fight on the coastline, and with plenty of guns if he can get them. He is going to take a tour of the commands, and when he has seen into things he will decide what is best to do. He has not at present a complete Staff. He has taken away from the General Staff the Directors of Military Training and Home Defence, namely Lowther and Shaw—both good men; but he has not an Adjutant-General nor a Q.M.G. branch, though there is one member of the A.G.'s department working with him. He is inclined to suggest that the New Army formations should terminate, and that the whole business of maintaining in the field both New Armies and Territorials should be left to County Associations. I begged him to insist upon having a complete Staff, telling him that the chief part of his work at first would be an Adjutant-General's question, and that I thought that he could easily dismiss to civil life 200,000 men now at home, namely convalescent, sick, and immature and useless men. He is inclined to think the same. He is still on very good terms with Robertson and has no difficulties with Lord K. for the moment, but thinks no real good will be done until Lord K. has been got rid off. I recommended that he should have a good look round, and begin by sending in a paper, describing fully and faithfully the existing situation of Home Defence, and giving numbers, armament, fitness for service, and general usefulness or otherwise of the troops for Home Defence. I advised him not to find fault with any one in this paper, or to crusade against anything, but to make it a plain matter-of-fact business statement, so that the Cabinet should know exactly where they stood.

I had a talk to George Moore afterwards and found him as bitter as anything against Lord K., and much amused at the excitement in London about him this year. We had a talk about private affairs. Lord French quoted something which amused me, namely, the remark that Lord Cardigan made to the man who came to apologise for running away with his wife, 'My dear sir, you have done me the greatest service that one man can render to another.' I was very glad to hear that he meant to keep on Sir Arthur Paget as one of his sector commanders.

Sunday, Jan. 23. Worked in the morning, then had a pleasant drive down to Mother's. Called at Olive's on the way back, and found that her father, Sir John Leslie, had died that afternoon at the age of ninety-three. A wonderful figure ; he was a good artist, a great sports man, lived through many reigns, and was probably the last living witness of Tom Sayers's great fight. He told Olive the other day that he had had only one disappoint-ment in his life, and that was when, after winning the Grand Military in England, he had failed to win it in Ireland. He and Lady Constance were both very good-looking and very fascinating. She bears the blow well. The funeral is to be at Glaslough. Olive and Mary Crawshay are going over for it.

Tuesday, Jan. 25. Lunched with Mrs. Townshend at the Ritz. Saw Townshend's last letters. It is still in doubt whether he can be relieved. After lunch M. Coleyn came to see me. He was Minister of War in Holland for three years, and is just back from a trip in Egypt and to the Dutch East Indies. Van Swinderen, the Dutch Minister, arranged for our meeting. Coleyn expressed himself entirely in agreement with my article of last week on 'The Western Front.' He thinks that the Germans had a total available 11,000,000 men to fight, and that they have lost 3,500,000, and have 1,000,000 on work of national interest. This leaves 3,000,000 men over, after deducting the field forces; and he said that he found large garrisons at Carlsruhe, Düsseldorf, Wesel, etc., including young men in training. He gives the Germans 18,000,000 men 18 to 45, and 11,000,000 deducting the physically unfit. Not all the 3,000,000 remaining can be placed at the front, but perhaps 2,500,000, so with wastage at 200,000 a month the effectives may be maintained for another year. He does not think that the Germans can do much more in Russia, and is disposed to think that they will throw for a victory in the West. He scoffs at Salonika, and thinks that our presence there merely keeps the Bulgarians in the field. The folly of our strategy which keeps 1000 ships in the Mediterranean causes freights to rise and is a tax on our people. He does not think that the attack on Egypt will be very serious. He says that the superior internal organisation of Germany has prevented the blockade from being very effective, and agrees that we shall never wear the Germans out with economic pressure. If we tighten up the blockade we shall meet with the same disappointment. It would be better to let in food and compel the Germans to export gold. He believes that the German desert railway is within 25 miles of El Kantara, but that a single narrow gauge railway cannot do much. Coleyn suggests that it was perhaps the loans which France gave to Serbia after the Balkan war that made her drag us off to save that little country, and he considers that this action was penny-wise and pound-foolish, as we have already spent on the expedition more than the whole value of the loans. We do not now know how to get away, and it will take a long time to get away. We are doing no good there. With nearly all these views I entirely agree. Went on to the *Times* office to see some people for Northcliffe, then had a great discussion with Geoffrey Robinson and Mackenzie on the subject of German casualties. We decided to await my dinner with Haldane next Friday, when I shall see his figures and the premises on which they are based.

Wednesday, Jan. 26. Saw Lord Derby at 10.30 A.M. at his house. We had an hour's talk about the Military Service Bill and its prospects. He still thinks, on the whole, that he will get the numbers that he anticipated in his report. He is most alarmed about the lists of reserved trades, several of which have been published since he made his reports, and, secondly, about the clause dealing with conscientious objectors, the effect of which is very hard to define. He is more afraid of the Government departments than he is of the Tribunals, and I agree with him. The Tribunals are all right. I asked him who was responsible for all the linoleum trade being exempted on one of these lists, and was much amused by his answer. Derby thinks that the Ministry of Munitions has been very bad about the exemptions, and declares that they have starred 800,000 men. I went into some of the points of the administration of the Group System, and told him where I wanted some changes made. I am to put them on paper and let him see them. He does not think that there is any chance at present of Lord K. going, and he says he, Lord D., is sometimes very despondent at things that go on at the War Office. He wants to get his 1st-line of Lancashire Territorials filled up abroad, but cannot manage it, although the 3rd-line is 1200 strong. He says that Bethune is a good fellow enough, but is always all things to all men, and being partly under the A.G. and partly under Tennant, is the shuttlecock between the two, and nothing gets done. He says that Lord K. is likely to change his A.G. We discussed means of effecting a change, but he says that the Territorials are under the U.S. of S. and so he, Derby, can't get hold of them. He has managed to raise the T.F. establishments in France from 800 to 1050, but his Lancashire battalions at the front stand on an average only about 700. In England the territorial battalions are only 650 men. He thinks that this is enough, but I don't. He says that K. is frightened to death of the Cabinet, in which he seems to have many enemies. He says that I can take it that no power on earth will make the Cabinet raise the number of divisions in the field above 70, but says that the reason is political and not military. He says that the infantry recruits are now going to pass to the front after three months' training, which is little enough in all conscience.

Thursday, Jan. 27. Dined last night with Mrs. Cis Bingham and a party of ten or twelve : Lord and Lady Wolverton, Mrs. Keppel, Lady de Trafford, Mrs. Hope, Sir Fritz and Lady Ponsonby, Wolkoff, and Tommy Maguire. A very pleasant dinner. I had Lady Wolverton and Lady Ponsonby next to me at dinner, and they both talked well. Lunched to-day with Lord Grimthorpe at the Café Royal : Dr. Dillon, Mr. Gully, and Lord Weardale. A very interesting talk, Weardale quite unregenerate about the Military Service Bill. He still talks great nonsense about Compulsion, and thinks Sir John Simon is the only statesman we've got, and will be the future head of the Liberal Party. He declares that we should only get 100,000 men by the Bill. When we asked him how he would have got the number of men without the Bill, he had not a single argument worth answering. We all agree about abusing the ' Higher Direction of the War ' on the part of the Government, and in criticising all the adventures abroad. Dr. Dillon full of good stories of all his experiences, and gave examples of Russian peculation. Went down to the Foreign Office to see Max-Muller, and told him that Mr. Marshall had a very good character as a journalist in America. We discussed the propaganda question in the Middle West of America, and are quite clear how it is to be done ; but that is altogether a different thing from getting it done. Our Government departments are full of boobies.

Friday, Jan. 28. Dined alone with Lord Haldane, and had a great talk over all points of the war. The special object of our meeting was to find out how many casualties the German Army had suffered, and what effectives they can provide in the future. He gave me a mass of statistics which I took away with me. They date mostly from August last, but as many of them are concerned with establishing the basis on which one should estimate casualties, they are still quite valuable. The Press Bureau appear to trust more or less in the German casualty returns. Macdonogh, however (lately the head of the Intelligence in France, and now at the War Office again), declares that these statistics are inaccurate, and he wants us to add fifty per cent. to the German records of killed, missing, dead, and severely wounded, in order to get at the net wastage of the German Army. He would also add 420,000 per annum for the permanent loss by sickness in 3,500,000 German troops in the field. I don't think that he has quite made out his case, but certainly there are many omissions in the German lists, and one must add something on this account—possibly 10 per cent. Dr. Brownlee's estimates of the total number of men of the military age of Germany and Austria-Hungary, and of the number of these that can be spared for fighting, I found very interesting, but in the papers there is no firm conclusion on the whole subject from any responsible person or body, and there are certainly wide differences of opinion. I should say that the Germans will be able to keep up their strength for the greater part of the year. Lord H. is against Derby going to the War Office in Lord K.'s place.

Sunday, Jan. 30. Northcliffe came up in the morning, and we had a long walk on the heath till lunch time. We flitted from subject to subject about the war, and never got to the bottom of any of them. He says that the Government are going to take all the mass of paper that he has so carefully collected for his various journals, and distribute them among the Radical papers that are short; in fact, wise virgins will be made to give up their oil to the unwise, which is against Biblical teaching. Talked to him of George Moore's coming action against the *World*.

Monday, Jan. 31. Lunched at the N. and M., and had long talks with Sir James Willcocks, late Commander of the Indian Army Corps in France; John Baird, M.P.; Peter Granet, now commanding the 58th Division; Valentine Allison, commanding a division at Chelmsford; Dick, the King's Messenger; Sir George Armstrong, and others. They are very anxious about the Mesopotamian expedition, and about Townshend. It seems impossible to discover who ordered the advance on Bagdad. All that is certain is that Townshend officially protested against it. He wrote the same thing to his wife and to me. Curzon was certainly against it, and Willcocks and I agreed that it was folly when we discussed it months ago. However, there it is. Robertson wrote to me this morning that Monro says that the advance on Egypt is a mare's nest. Probably they know that we have 300,000 men there, and are directing all their attention to Mesopotamia. Willcocks is told that Lake has come back sick, but I am not sure. Met Jaffray, who offered to make 4-inch shells for the Government at 6s., and was told to tender through the Suffolk Munitions Branch, who now charge the Government 7s. As Jaffray makes 1000 a week, this is £50 dead loss a week to the country for no reason. I am afraid that this is the sort of thing that is going on. Jaffray's firm was making glass bottles somewhere down in the S.E. corner of England before the war.

Tuesday, Feb. 1. Had a busy day. Dined with Mrs. Higgins, and was late. Lord and Lady Ancaster, Tommy Maguire and his wife, Lady Essex, and Mr. Benson. Very pleasant dinner. Found the last taxi in London to get home with.

Wednesday, Feb. 2. To *Romance* in the afternoon. Doris acted superbly; Owen Nares rather less well, I thought, than when the play began. Anson as Vantyle was quite excellent. House crammed full. The more I see of this piece the more I think that Doris is one of the finest actresses that we have seen on the stage in our time.

Went on to see Sir William Robertson at Queen Anne's Mansions. He is fairly satisfied about the general position. He hopes that the politicians will let him alone, and not expect him to take any part in political manœuvres against Lord K., with whom he seems to get on very well. Robertson agrees with me that Lord French will require an Adjutant-General's Staff, and that the affairs in England

are in a rare muddle, for we have a million and a half men
and make no adequate use of them.　R. complains specially
that the Territorials of the reserve formations will not
come forward to support their 1st-line units in the field.　It
is the old story of the Militia wanting to go out with their
own men and under their own officers, and not caring for
the Army point of view.　R. is dissatisfied with the Munitions Ministry, against which Lord K. has been stirring
him up.　R. says that it is ridiculous that the munitions
should be separate from the War Office, and that the right
system is that of France, where M. Thomas is Under-Secretary of State for War.　This is not the position here on
account of the rivalry of Lord K. and Lloyd George.　Meanwhile Von Donop stays on as M.G.O. and has a D.F.A.
and the normal Staff, although practically all the duties,
including the control of the Ordnance Committee and the
responsibility of the designs, have passed to the Munitions
Ministry, where the sentiment is hostile to K. and Von
Donop.　The rifles do not seem to be coming in very fast,
and I judge that we are not through our troubles yet.　But
all this comes from the initial failure to understand the
munitions problem, and as L. G. and his men are putting
it right, I consider that it is best to leave them alone.
R. still agrees with me that the Western front is the theatre
of war of chief importance.　We have forty divisions there
now, and more will come for the same theatre, including
perhaps some from Egypt later.　R. has seen Joffre twice
this last week.　Joffre thinks that the Germans are going
to attack him.　This they may do, but R. thinks that they
ought to be well beaten if they try.　He thinks that all
the splash and noise made on the Galician side by the
Germans are to distract attention.　The French have had
heavy losses, and are supposed to be no good for more than
one more serious and costly effort.　They played the main
part last year, and expect us to do so this year.　This we
are prepared to do, but at present the ground in front of
us in Flanders is too sodden for movement.

We discussed aerial warfare, which is now being handed

over from the Admiralty to Lord French. The Admiralty took over all our light little dirigibles, and have none, or nothing to speak of, for North Sea scouting. We discussed the big air raid of the last day or two. R. does not know how they are to be countered except by building similar craft and executing reprisals on German towns. R. was very cross that the Home Office had not published yesterday morning's statement handed to them at the War Office about 10.30 A.M. R. has not heard of any particular movements of concentrations on the German coast. He does not appear in a hurry to call away the troops from Salonika, and thinks that they mystify the Germans. I doubt it. We have no assurance that there are 50,000 Germans south of the Danube. R. has no particular news about the attack on Egypt and does not believe in it. The best season for such an attack is slipping away. Murray has something like twelve divisions in Egypt. There are 50,000 Australian drafts. The whole thing is gradually being put in order. He thinks that there must be 300,000 men there.

We talked a lot about Mesopotamia, and I promised to send him all my papers about Townshend. R. wants to have authority over the C.-in-C. in India for the general control of the operations in Mesopotamia and elsewhere, a point of view with which I thoroughly agree. We discussed the responsibility for the advance on Bagdad. The G.S. here were misled by the bad information from the Mesopotamian front. He is not sure whether Townshend can hold on for more than three weeks. He seems to place a great deal of responsibility for the advance on Austen Chamberlain, and says that K. opposed it. It is one of the most sensible things that he has done since the war began. We have four divisions in Mesopotamia, not counting Townshend's force. Apparently it takes three weeks to get a division from the Persian Gulf to Kut-el-Amara, and six weeks to get a division from Egypt to Kut. R. is against the advance on Bagdad, and proposes to have a defensive campaign, which was my idea from the start. Some wandering officer of ours appears to have seen the Grand Duke Nicholas in the Caucasus and to have concocted a scheme for co-operation. He was told to mind his own business, and the Grand Duke was told what our policy was—without phrases. Meanwhile the Grand Duke is attacking Erzeroum. Thus while we were passive they were active, and now it is *vice versa*. It is hard to win campaigns with this manner of proceeding.

R. thinks that the Russians will have 2,100,000 rifles by April next, and nearly 1,000,000 more behind of the odd-job lots provided by England, France, and Italy. American contracts of rifles for Russia are still many months overdue, and R. thinks that there is German money at work to stop them. I sketched to R. my idea of what he could do with the Press if he took it in hand with the idea of misleading the Germans about our plans, and he promised to consider it. R. has now his own man with Joffre, and Joffre has sent a man to him. This is a good arrangement, except that Lord K. and Gallieni, the French War Minister, also have exchanged Staff Officers, and the two lots may not always see with the same eyes. On the whole R. is fairly satisfied, considering that we began this war without an Army. He says that Haig is not distinctly under Joffre, but is told to conform with the plans of the latter, and is practically in the same position as Lord French was.

Friday, Feb. 4. Finished rather an important article about the German casualties, making out that they have lost 150,000 men a month since the war began; that is the permanent net loss including sickness. I find that my article on ' The Western Front ' is regarded as unanswerable, and is generally agreed with by the most important people. Had various visitors in the afternoon, and was unable to get down to London. Lovat Fraser came up to go into the Mesopotamian affairs with me. He declares that it is Arthur Balfour who persuaded the Cabinet to throw over George Curzon's advice, and to advance on Bagdad. My papers from Townshend are with Robertson, so I could not show them to him. We agreed that Townshend is in a very tight place. We do not feel sure that Aylmer, with two weakened divisions and two more dribbling up to join him, will be able to relieve Kut. It is still very difficult to find out exactly how this foolish movement originated. I told him how much better it would be if Robertson were in general charge of all these operations, and were able to issue directions to the C.-in-C. in India.

The men coming up under the Military Service Act are due to appear on March 2, so I expect that we shall have a very heavy month dealing with claims for exemption. It is very interesting work, for one gets an insight into the home life and the circumstances of numerous people and classes whom one never mixes with. I do not find any signs of shirking, but no doubt there are many cases in which it is a great hardship for a man to go. The work gives one a very clear impression of the social upheaval caused by compulsion in any form.

Saturday, Feb. 5. Wrote an article on 'Plans and Projects '—ours and Germany's. It is very difficult to decide what the Germans are going to do. Is it to be the East or the West ? or is it England ? This time no one can tell ; from all appearances one would judge that they will have a go at us in the West first, and then take on Russia in May, worrying us all the time in Mesopotamia and in Egypt. I don't think we have anything to do but go on steadily killing Germans in the West. We have just heard that one of the Zepps. has been destroyed in the North Sea on its way home. One of our trawlers refused to save the crew of the Zepp.

Sunday, Feb. 6. Jack Cowans sent his car to take me down to Coombe. Our party: Sir Arthur and Lady Paget, Mr. May (a Belgian), Mr. Gunther of the American Embassy (very nice fellow), Mrs. Duggan, Lord Castlerosse, Mrs. Stanley, Sir F. E. Smith, and Jack Cowans.

May was very interesting about the condition of Belgium, declaring that the country would starve but for the American feeding arrangements. He said that there were 175,000 Belgian refugees in England, and 80,000 in Holland, and that the Belgians would not work for the Germans, and if America goes to war with Germany, and Germany feeds the Belgians, she will make them work. Gunther seems to think that America will go to war with Germany sooner or later, but I expect later, black, or rather white, as things look at present. Had a long talk with Sir Arthur about Home Defence, and the state of his troops on Salisbury Plain. Of his two 2nd-line Territorial divisions one has Japanese rifles, with only 200 rounds per rifle, and no reserve; the other has the old Lee-Enfield, and no ammunition. They both have their guns, one the 18-pounders with no horses, and the others some mixed guns, partly converted 15-pounders. Paget is all for fighting the enemy on the coast when he comes. Jack Cowans showed me some figures of what he is spending. It is about a million a day, and he has spent over 400 millions already.

I made F. E. tell me the story of his arrest in France. It was too ludicrous. He went with Bonar Law and Lloyd George. He called on Macready the A.G., and upon Haig. The latter's A.D.C. telephoned to arrange that F. E. should see Winston in the trenches. He then got into uniform, and as his chauffeur had a pass, he thought that he was quite in order, and went off to the Division, whence he was sent on to the trenches, accompanied either by an officer or an orderly. This is exactly what I have always done. He met Winston in his dug-out, where they had a talk. Some time afterwards there arrived the Assistant Provost-Marshal of the Division, and informed F. E. that he had been ordered to place him under arrest, and send him back to Headquarters. There was nothing to be done, so he went off, arriving at St. Omer again early in the morning. He was taken to the Provost-Marshal's office, and after half an hour's delay, the latter's assistant came down, and was severely taken to task by F. E., but still the arrest persisted, and he was sent off to the Hotel du Commerce, where a room had been taken for him for the night. The assistant told him that he had to go before the Adjutant-General in the morning at a very early hour, whereupon F. E. said that he would see the A.G. in hell first. At this time it was about 4 A.M., and a few hours later the A.P.M. turned up again and ordered him to go before the A.G. in half an hour. F. E. refused, and said that he intended to sleep for half an hour more, and then take an hour to dress. Then he went off with his escort and saw Macready. F. E. was still in uniform, and told Macready that he would like to go off and put on civilian clothes unless he would grant him the same liberty as if he were in civilian clothes. M. said he would, whereupon F. E. gave him a good deal of his mind, telling him that he, F. E., had been outrageously treated, and that Macready was an officious blunderer. Macready vowed that he had never issued orders for his arrest, and made the A.P.M. confirm this. Macready said that the mistake had arisen owing to errors in repeating telephone messages, and said that he had only invited F. E. to come and see him. Macready then wrote an apology. F. E. had deposited this apology with Sir R. Brade at the War Office, where I must go and see it. F. E. then went back to bed, saying that he was not to be disturbed by anybody, even by Haig himself. Haig had meanwhile heard of the story, as Macready had reported to him. Haig sent Philip Sassoon to ask F. E. to lunch. F. E. was not approachable, and Sassoon was kept trotting backwards and forwards all the morning. At last he went to lunch and sat, as he said, on Haig's right hand, and all was peace. It is not true, as is currently reported, that F. E. was marched on board ship a prisoner. He went off with Bonar Law and Lloyd George.

We spoke about G. Moore and the libel action.

Monday, Feb. 7. Drove back with Sir Arthur, who dropped me at the house of a certain statesman who gave me some important documents to take away and read, and told me that the number of Russian rifles was now 1,398,000, and will be 2,200,000 at the end of April, at which time they will also be making 200,000 rifles a month themselves.

CHAPTER VI

EQUALITY OF ALLIED AND GERMAN STRENGTHS

Wednesday, Feb. 9. Finished my examination of the papers,
then went down to the Reform Club. Lunched with Colonel
A. M. Murray; his editor, Mr. A. G. Gardner of the *Daily
News*; and our host's brother, Sir George Murray, late of
the Treasury. We had a pleasant lunch. Mr. Gardner is
a self-made man, alert, independent, and sensible. It was
very amusing to be lunching with him, considering how
often the *Daily News* and the *Star* fall foul of me, but
I found all the same that we were in agreement on most
subjects. A. M. Murray preached from his usual texts in
favour of campaigns in the East, while George Murray was
sarcastic about everything Radical. The latter told me
that Vickers had just launched the finest battleship in the
world, but he would not tell me the calibre of the guns.

Dined with the Ancasters. We had Sir F. E. and Lady
Smith, Sir Fritz and Lady Ponsonby, Mr. and Mrs. Henry

Higgins, Sir Lionel Earle, and a few more. Earle tells me
that he has not been able to effect his brother's exchange
yet, but the Germans are ready to exchange him for one
of equivalent rank. He is dreadfully wounded in the
head, arm, and leg, and is almost blind. Such a splendid
specimen of humanity too !

Thursday, *Feb*. 10. Northcliffe came up to see me this
morning, and I showed him the papers, about which he
made some shrewd remarks. Went to 35 Belgrave Square,
where I found Colonel and Mrs. House. He is President
Wilson's confidential emissary, and is just back from
Berlin and Paris. Lady Minto, Soveral, Dr. Dillon,
and Madam Grouitch, the wife of the Serbian Minister.
Found Mrs. House very pleasant. She said that Berlin
was decidedly empty, that no one now had a motor car, not
even Gwinner of the Deutsche Bank. She saw plenty of
troops in the streets coming and going. The tap of the
drum was constantly heard. The Kaiser was not in Berlin
while she was there. She thought that his illness was only
a cold. There were scarcely any wounded to be seen in
the streets. I liked the look of Colonel House. He is short
and reserved looking, a thoughtful, pleasant face, and
has a difficult part to play in pretending to be friendly to
all countries alike. We had a little talk and agreed to
meet again and talk quietly before he goes back to America.
Sir Arthur came in later. He is off to Russia again to take
a Field-Marshal's baton to the Tsar. I am afraid that this
means that he will have to give up the Salisbury centre.

Friday, *Feb*. 11. Northcliffe telephoned that he thought
the statesman had some object in giving us those papers,
and that we ought to be careful about them. I told
him that I did not care who gave me the papers
so long as we had the information. N. asked about
the black troops in Africa, and whether it was true
that we had 38 millions of blacks, and the French 28,
and why we should not do more with them. I said that
the exact figures were not in my mind, but certainly we
could raise great masses of black troops, and that it was

unpardonable of us not to have done so. In the fighting in East Africa the Germans have 30,000 natives in arms.

Lunched with Mrs. Harry Higgins: Mrs. Peto, Mrs. Duggan, Lady Horner, and Wolkoff. Mrs. Duggan told me that George Curzon was back, and that the Belgian part of the mission had been satisfactorily performed, and that the King and Queen of the Belgians were very well satisfied. Curzon appears to have been nearly caught by a shell while visiting Winston, and he also went up in an aero-plane, but was not allowed to cross the German lines. He does not appear to be so well satisfied with the general situation.

Wolkoff and I walked off together, and I told him what I knew about the state of the Russian armament, and the way in which American contracts for rifles in Russia had been delayed by the Russian Inspector in the U.S., who had refused to pass the rifles when the orders were sent through us because this course deprived him of his usual commission. Wolkoff says that there are a great many people in Russia who want hanging. He confesses that he has been frightened to death by the political situation in Russia lately, but that the dismissal of Goremykin had been very satisfactory, that M. Stürmer had been receiving deputations from Zemstvos, and that the Duma was to assemble without any date being fixed for its prorogation. Wolkoff says that we were very near an explosion; and that the whole of Russia, including the Army and even the Guards, were of one mind. This confirms what Lydia Kyasht told me. He was deeply interested, and did not know what would happen when the Duma met. He told me various stories of the famous monk, Rasputin, which again confirmed Lydia's tales. He said that the Tsar remarked to some one who ventured to object to the monk, *mieux vaut un moine que vingt hystéries.* Apparently the monk keeps the Tsaritsa quiet. It is true that he is illiterate, and indulges in the most wild fancies, but he seems to have the most extraordinary fascination for the ladies, and indulges in every kind of folly. Wolkoff said that one woman tried to assassinate him, but did not quite succeed. Wolkoff said how extraordinary it was that at the moment of a tremendous crisis like this, such a lunatic should have such a sway, but he thought that this war made many people mad, and he instanced the power of a clairvoyant with certain ladies of our acquaintance. He had just seen some telegrams from Russia which made him very much happier about everything. He had not seen Yermoloff lately. Evidently there is some jealousy between the Embassy and Yermoloff, with whom the Grand Duke collaborates. He told me that there was a neck of Russian territory running into Norway, and within a short distance of an open fiord southwest of the North Cape, and that the Norwegians were allowing the Russians to use this as a line of communications. I suppose the coast-end has reindeer transport. He was very sick indeed with the way in which Italy had allowed things to slide in the Adriatic, and complained greatly of their want of initiative. He is still anxious about Rumania, and wants us to advance from Salonika to keep the Bulgars in play. They seem to know that Robertson was against this course and is all for the Western front.

Saturday, Feb. 12. Dined with Sir John and Lady Horner ; Lord Haldane and Lady Leslie also there. We had a great talk about German casualties with reference to my article in the *Times* of Feb. 9, and about the war generally. Lord Haldane thought that my figures were conservative, but he did not shake me in any way by such few criticisms as he made. We went over the interminable question of National Service again, and found the ex-Chancellor quite unmoved. He browses about in the pre-war Radical pastures, and assumes that we shall go back to old heresies after the war. He was very interesting, and we were full of reminiscences of his term of office.

Sunday, Feb. 13. I lunched with the other F. E. Smiths in Hampstead, and old Mrs. Earle, author of the book *In my Surrey Garden*, and a very clever old lady. Sir Lionel

Earle also there and talked well, and is very keen about his work, which is in the Board of Works. His idea is to bring all interned prisoners down to the ports to relieve the congestion, and I don't see why this should not be done, if we can get any one in a Government office to stop pampering the Boches.

Drove down in the afternoon to Mother's in a taxi and back again.

Monday, Feb. 14. Wrote a letter to the *Times* on ' German Losses,' in reply to a great number of letters from correspondents, and answering them all. I spent the whole of the afternoon on the Advisory Committee, and we got through a mass of cases. No claim yet before us under the Service Act. Got home very late. Our Advisory Committee: Mr. David, K.C., chairman; Mr. Green, of Green and Edwards; Mr. Briscoe, a barrister; Mr. Fraser, who is a sort of rag merchant; and Mr. Pratt, a labour member; our secretary is Mr. Smith. We now sit at the Town Hall, which is very inconveniently placed in the outskirts of the borough.

Tuesday, Feb. 15. Lunched at the club expecting to meet Sir James Willcocks, but found that I had made a mistake about the date. Had a talk to Jenner, who is running the personnel of the Intelligence; also met Lord Midleton, with whom I am to have another talk. He rather thinks that Lord K. does the least harm where he is. He is intent upon getting Grey out of the Foreign Office.

Went down to the Horse Guards and found Lord French in his office, where everything seemed much the same as when he occupied the same rooms as Inspector-General. Lowther, Watt, Barry, and Dawnay in attendance. We had a little talk in the A.D.C.s' room about George Moore's impending action against the *World*. Watt thinks that the real object of the enemy is to aim at Lord French through his friendship with George Moore.

Had a long talk with the Field-Marshal. He has sent in his views of the situation. He is still without an A.G.

and Q.M.G. branch. He says that Asquith is most kind to him, but that certain other influences are very hostile. Lord K. has been over to France the last four days. French cannot imagine why K. should go over to France. We discussed the air problem. Air Defence has now been handed over to him. It is a *damnosa hereditas*, and I told him that he would get into trouble over it; that in the absence of dirigibles on our side to counter-raid, nothing could prevent night raids by Zepps. and day raids by aeroplanes until we have good anti-craft guns and efficient aeroplanes, and plenty of them, and that the public would become incensed against him for not succeeding. He agreed, but said that Home Defence had been handed over to him, and as Air Defence was part of it, so he could not shirk it. He is reorganising it as well as he can with David Henderson's help. London is divided into eight districts, including Woolwich and Waltham. Machines as well as guns and lights are allotted to each. This machinery of defence is being extended elsewhere, as well as a system of communications and warnings, but he has no dirigibles. He knows of none being made, though the Navy have a few themselves, and as the best thing is to fight dirigibles with dirigibles, they are also the best means for counter-raiding. He can neither guarantee to stop dirigibles when they come nor counteract them by reprisals. He is working with David Henderson, who is a close ally of his, of course, and David advises him not to attempt to order his airmen when and where to fight in the air, but to trust to his air commanders, who alone know what they can do, and what is possible. Lord French looks uncommonly well.

Wednesday, Feb. 16. Worked in the morning. Lunch with Sir James Willcocks, and afterwards sat and talked with him and Sir William Knox, General Kempster, and Smiler Kennedy. We had a great talk over all the fronts of the fighting. Willcocks tells me that his Indian Corps in France was never over 25,000 men, often down to 18,000 and less, had had 25,000 casualties, and went off to Mesopotamia without a Thank-you from anybody except the Prince of Wales. I told him that the last two Indian divisions are being withdrawn from France, perhaps to take the place of the British divisions which went out a month or two ago, and are now on their way back to France from Egypt, including Eddy Wortley's North Midlanders.

We imagine that India will be furious at having the command of Mesopotamia taken out of her hands and confided to Robertson, but we all thought that it would be a very good thing.

We discussed Zeppelin raids, and Kennedy told us that they came only a thousand feet from the top of his house at five o'clock in the afternoon, 16 miles from Cromer, and bombed freely but hurt nobody. The bombs made great craters about 15 feet broad and 6 feet deep, so they must have been pretty heavy ; 49 were dropped in this particular locality. There was some artillery near by, but they could not get sufficient elevation, and the wires from the watch station to the artillery were cut, both at the time of this raid and at the time of the last. The Zepps. returned later on in the night the same way as they had come ; our people tried to get a searchlight on to them, but failed, and the anti-aircraft guns seem to have all been moved to London.

Went round to Bond Street to see the wonderful Rembrandts of Lockett Agnew, and a very beautiful eighteenth-century commode. The Rembrandts were dated 1632 and 1631, the former from the Duc de Broglie's collection, and the latter of a monk reading, and the face hidden by a cowl. Very mystic and wonderful, and the paper from which he is reading has a white light on it, and stands right out from the picture. It is a good piece of work. Sir Claude Phillips was there, and admired these beautiful things very much.

Friday, Feb. 18. Tribunal work most of the day. Dined with Lady Strafford at Chandos House, Cavendish Square. The Italian Ambassador and the Marchesa Imperiali, the Spanish Ambassador and Madame Merry del Val, the Speaker and Mrs. Lowther, and the Councillor of the American

Embassy and his wife. Found Mrs. Lowther full of talk, and
charmingly indiscreet. The Americans quite confirmed the
good news which I had heard of the possibility of American
intervention.

A lovely house in the Adams style, dated about 1760,
with nice old-English furniture, very comfortable and restful.
We played Bridge afterwards ; Madame Merry del Val very
bright and amusing, but not quite so good at the game as
her husband is at diplomacy ; fortunately we were playing
for very low stakes.

Saturday, Feb. 19. Tribunal most of the morning, and
arranged about checking the lists of starred men. Went
off to Oakham in the afternoon to stay with Lord Lonsdale,
and to discuss various German matters. Travelled down with
Foster of the Blues, who manages to get about wonderfully
considering his lost leg. Was met at the station by an
eighteenth-century yellow coach, on ' C ' springs very high in
the air, driven postillion fashion. The postillion and the
tiny tiger who sat upon the box had yellow-faced liveries
and fluffy yellow beaver hats. We seemed to be a century
or two out of date. Foster, in his motor, screamed with
laughter as I drove off. Drove to Barley Thorpe with our
pair of chestnuts. This house was once an inn where a
previous Lord Lonsdale used to keep his horses ; it has been
added to, and the grounds and stabling laid out afresh. A
comfortable house, an excellent cook, early-Victorian furniture, no electric light, and house full of sporting prints,
pictures, caricatures, and curios. Lady Lonsdale ill in
bed, so Lord Lonsdale and I had the house to ourselves, only
young Lady Londonderry coming over on Sunday afternoon.
We had a talk on leading men now in Germany, and
about German affairs. Lord Lonsdale still holds that the
Kaiser is not responsible for the war, which was brought on
by the war party regardless of him or his wishes. He
told me some curious stories about the Kaiser and the
Crown Prince. The former told Lord Lonsdale that the
Prince had never grown up, and that his brain had never
come on since he was sixteen years of age. L. thought

that Falkenhayn was about the best of the Germans. Mackensen was the grandson of a Scotsman called Mackenzie. We had forgathered to talk German politics, but got on to ladies and horses, and soon forgot all about the Boches. We had a great talk about the late King Edward and his associates, about whom we told each other a string of amusing stories. He also told me the tale of his famous match with Lord Shrewsbury. There was a copy of the Tranby Croft gaming-table picture from *Truth*, and this led us to exchange confidences about the chief actor in that drama.

I was much interested in Lonsdale's dogs. There were nine of them in the dining-room, and I never knew it till we got up to sit after dinner before an old mahogany horse-shoe table in front of the fire. Then he called them, and they all came from the corners in which they had been lying; each dog had his corner, and never took the corner of another dog. L. has evidently a marvellous knowledge of, and power over animals, and they seemed very fond of him, and under perfect discipline. They followed him from room to room, and in each room each dog had his corner. When a new dog joined the pack, he was shown his corner, and if he moved from it, he was gently but firmly taken back and reproved; if he moved again, he was again taken back to the same corner without any unkindness or beating. There was a lurcher, a Westmoreland collie dog, two retrievers, a spaniel, two Cottesmore terriers, a big yellow dog, a Labrador, and one other. The most extraordinary collection.

Sunday morning we went round to the horses, of which he had about one hundred and fifty. It is evidently a kind of parade. A pair of yellow gloves are handed to him as he enters the stable yard, and as he enters each fresh stable a basket of sliced carrots is brought to him. The stables are very perfect, and his weight-carrying hunters are quite superb. All the harness horses are chestnuts.

We then went on to see the kennels, where there are a nice lot of terriers and a pack of miniature bloodhounds, which hunt deer and hares. They were brought from

Germany by the Prince Consort, and dispersed at his death. Lonsdale found some in Devonshire and restored the breed. The dog I coveted most was a Cottesmore terrier, a little square-built fellow with short legs and most engaging manners. We ended up by telling each other more stories of the beauties of the late-Victorian and Edwardian period, and never came to L.'s German documents at all! The pretty ladies, the horses, and the dogs had made us forget the war for one brief week-end.

Monday, Feb. 21. Came back by an early train. Lunched with Arthur Balfour at 4 Carlton Gardens. Miss Balfour, Lord and Lady Rayleigh, and Mr. Bonar Law. We discussed the war. There is no doubt that Balfour is largely responsible for the advance on Bagdad, but he declared that they had been misled by bad information, and that the whole of the military authorities in India and at the front had told them that the advance could take place without danger and with the greatest of ease. It was merely a question whether the Turks might bring up reinforcements six months later to turn us out. He had never heard of Townshend's objection to advance, and when I told him the details he was astonished and said that it was necessary to probe the facts. Bonar Law quite confirmed what he said. We had an interesting discussion about the officers of the New Armies, and about the issue of posthumous decorations to those who had fallen. I made them see that the Indian troops had been badly treated. Balfour told me that Jellicoe had just been down from the north and had complained bitterly at the want of small craft and mine-sweepers. The Germans had, he said, undoubtedly been laying mines recently with submarines. He was not at all disposed to underrate the danger of the German threat due for fulfilment on March 1. I said that it was the old cry of want of frigates, and he agreed that it was so. He said that the Battle Fleet was strong enough, barring accidents in a mine field, but he had, of course, to run the risk of having no ships in the south. The Grand Fleet was still based on Scapa Flow, the Moray Firth, and the Forth, and this was a long way from the south of England, but I agreed that it was the best jumping-off place, as I had said many years ago when all our fleet was in the south. But I saw that Balfour was decidedly anxious, and he is not at all a timorous person. He said that the Germans had a lot of bogus battleships, and undoubtedly ample transports to carry large forces. He spoke of a big neutral shipowner who frequently came to us with good information: his latest news on the whole was favourable to us. There is a rumour that Prince Henry had been given a separate command in the Baltic, and A. J. B. was not at all displeased about it, as it will suit our book. He seems to have heard of the American Wollcott's reports. This man was agent for Rockefeller, and for the provisioning of Poland. He has been to Germany, and has been all round. He says that the Germans are making big preparations for a heavy blow in the West[1] and consider the Russians as of no account. I asked Balfour what he thought of the command in France, and gather that his advices about Haig, whom he did not know personally, are all second-hand. He had also no very good reports about generals in Mesopotamia, and when I was asked by Bonar Law whom I would send there, I said Willcocks, who in my opinion had been very badly treated. Bonar Law agreed and said that Chamberlain thought the same. I walked with Balfour to the Admiralty and he took me up to his rooms, but M. Painlevé arrived just then, so we had to break off talk.

Friday, Feb. 25. Saw Sir William Robertson at Queen Anne's Mansions at 6.15 P.M.; had a good talk about the war. He is not so pleased with Lord K. as he was, and begins to think that we shall not get on until K. goes. He has been over twice to see Joffre lately. On two occasions in the last fortnight the French had tried to induce us to send more men to Salonika. They wanted us to send 100,000, and the Italians the same number. Cadorna refused, and so did Robertson with the support

[1] The German attack on Verdun began this day.

of the War Committee which is now solid behind him. He is bringing over to France the 29th Division from Egypt, as well as the North Midland Territorials. As regards the troops in Egypt, he is acting on the principle that it is better to have a small number of troops back in the West now than a larger number later on, and he hopes to be able to get some troops from Salonika. I advised him to make our Cabinet speak stiffly to the French about this folly. It is extraordinary that the French should want to burden us with this expedition when they are being heavily attacked since Feb. 21 at Verdun, and nine French provinces are in German hands. When Joffre told Robertson that he wanted more troops, Robertson told him that the French had better supply them themselves, and he said that he did a little thumping on the table on his own account in the approved French style. Joffre said that they could not spare any, so Robertson said, 'Then why ask us to send them as we are all in the same boat?' Joffre replied, 'Well, there are no more in France.' Robertson came home thinking that he had convinced Joffre, but the next day came a fresh request from the French with the same old story, but our people remained adamant. Robertson used all my old arguments, of the want of an objective in a mountainous country, the absence of roads, little mountain artillery or mule transport which would take months to collect, a single line of rail, partly damaged and destroyed, to serve the needs of French, British, and Greeks, and so on. Why any sane man can continue to advocate this folly, when the Germans are known to have 118 divisions on the West front and maybe more, while we have only 140 and weaker, is one of those mysteries which no one can fathom. He agreed with me that the Navy were anxious, and thought that even if they lost a few ships they ought to come south now and then to initiate offensive operations just to keep their hands in, and to give the Boches fits.

We spoke of the forces in Egypt. Robertson does not think that the Turks in Syria are strong. I told him that a stroke at Adana would upset the whole of the Turkish communications by rail with Mesopotamia, the Caucasus, and Egypt, and I gathered from him that some operation of this kind was in project. He had bad news on the whole from Mesopotamia. He had asked the Indian Government if they could receive and maintain Joe Maude's 13th Division, and India answered ' Yes,' whereupon the 13th was sent to the head of the Persian Gulf ; but on their arrival India cabled that they could not send them up the river and feed them without starving the rest of the Army. This is what they call receiving and maintaining a division ! I recommended him to send Jimmie Willcocks out to take charge of the whole affair, as it seemed to me to be in charge of a pack of imbeciles. Townshend could hold out, he said, until the middle of April. Aylmer will have 30,000 men there in a week's time ; that is three weak divisions ; the fourth apparently is not yet up. He says they are searching everywhere from the Thames to the Irrawaddy for light river-boats. The old Indian Marine seems to have charge of the river transport, and appears to have made a mess of it.

We went into the question of the Derby system, and the supply of men. I explained the machinery of the Tribunals, etc., of which he seemed to know very little. I advised him to do certain things : first, to get the Prime Minister to compel the Board of Trade to revise its lists of reserved occupations, which, in my opinion, were killing recruiting ; second, to make Lloyd George reduce the number of men of military age engaged on munition work ; third, to tell the Advisory Committees to beat up their starred men by using the pink cards of the Registration Act to find the names of employers ; and fourth, to send a confidential letter to the Tribunals that every man was needed. He promised that he would take all these steps at 10 to-morrow morning, and I think he will.

Thursday, March 2. Went to see Derby in the morning. He said that the results of the recruiting under his scheme could only be described as appalling. They were not one half of his estimates, but it was impossible to give figures at present, because if one said that four groups of 86,000 men had only produced 18,000, it might be that the result of postponement might still produce another 18,000. He told me that he was still Director of Recruiting in a civil capacity, and that Mackinnon was merely given the title of Director-General for administrative reasons. He, Derby, only spent 1½ hours at his office every day. He had told the Prime Minister that if he could not get enough work he would go back to Lancashire, so he was made Chairman of the Air Committee, where he had nothing whatever to do with Air Defence, and was mainly there to use tact and judgment in order to prevent the Army and Navy from falling out. He was not Air Minister at all, and thought that he was being attacked by the *Daily Mail* because Northcliffe wanted his own nominee put in. The *Daily Mail* campaign was impairing his usefulness, and was doing a great deal of harm. Could I stop it? There was no chance of his succeeding Lord K. at present. He thought that if he succeeded Lord K., it would be disloyal to the latter, whereupon I said that I only recognised loyalty to the country in a great crisis like this. He was going down to the House of Lords this afternoon, and was going to trounce the Government and Simon, also McKenna, Runciman and Co. I advised him to produce the list of starred occupations, and to fling it at the Government. There ought to be some fun if his speech comes up to his intentions.

Thursday, March 9. Have been meeting lately the American, Mr. Wollcott. At one party we had Donald, editor of the *Chronicle*; Gardner, editor of the *Daily News*; Austin Harrison, and Harry Brittain to bring him out. He came over here to help in the French Loan; when this was put through he was asked to take up the plan of feeding the starving Poles. He got his passports and went off to Germany, and visited some of the chief towns, as well as the Headquarters of the Armies. He saw Von Beseler, Governor-General of Warsaw, visited Hindenburg's Headquarters at Kovno, was in Berlin, then on the Western front, where he saw Von Bissing the German Governor of Belgium, and talked with many German generals and staff officers. He made no secret of the fact that his main object was to feed the Poles. He says that the Germans have not got enough to feed the Poles, that Poland to a large extent has been devastated, and that they want us to allow in 15 million marks' worth of food a month, which the Germans will pay for in gold, and they will find the ships to carry it in. Wollcott supports his plea with the argument that it will stop the Germanisation of Poland ; that it will draw gold out of Germany ; and that it will prevent the despatch to Germany of 1 to $1\frac{1}{2}$ million Poles, who will set free a similar number of Germans for fighting ; and, lastly, that it will prevent a crusade against us for our brutality in starving the Poles.

We were not all convinced by this argument, but he has certainly brought back a very unpleasant picture of Poland, and also a large supply of photographs, showing the devastation wrought among the starving people, of whom there are said to be 15 millions altogether.

He says that the German generals talk quite differently from the way they make their Press talk. They admit that they made the war in order to forestall Russia's great military programme, and they glory in all the frightfulness which they have carried out. They admit that they cannot win the war, or succeed at sea, or win in the economic struggle against England, but they think that their Army cannot be beaten, and that the war will end somewhere in the region where the respective Armies are now situated. They believe that they have got the advance in the air warfare, and they mean to keep it. They laugh very much because they have made fools of the English, and have attracted such large armies to Salonika and Egypt, and they are out for a big throw in the West, for which they are prepared to lose half a million men. He said that all the German Staffs read my articles regularly. Scarcely any other foreign articles are seen. My military articles are read by officers who understand English, and become the subject of general conversation among the Staffs each evening. Practically no English articles are read and discussed except mine.

He says that the figures told him by the Germans as to the number of reserves tally closely with mine given in the *Times*, and he says that people of importance in New York meet together every week and discuss my articles.

He heard nothing said by the German Staffs of any oversea operation by the German Army and Navy combined. He thought that the German Navy was rather foreign to all the German military set, and that the latter did not much bother about it. He thought Falkenhayn and Beseler two of the best German leaders. Hindenburg was old, but a national hero ; Mackensen he had not met.

He wants to do the feeding of Poland through the organisation which is feeding Belgium, but I am doubtful whether any of our people will look at it.

I like Wollcott ; he is acting for Rockefeller, and the Germans are good to him because they want American financial help after the war. In any case I have confidence in the general accuracy of his statements. He told people here of the approaching attack on Verdun a fortnight before it began, and he declared that he had been watching the preparations made for it since January. This is not the information which a pro-German would convey.

Friday, March 10. Yesterday George Moore won his case against the *Chronicle* (Manchester), which had copied the *World's* libel about him and Lord French. The Manchester paper ate humble pie.

I went to see Lord French to-day, walking down to the Horse Guards with Sukky Barry from the club. Saw General Shaw and Colonel James in charge of the Home Defence under French. They complained bitterly that they were not fighting the Germans, but the Home Office, the Treasury, and the Finance branch at the War Office.

French was fairly well, and said he would soon be all right if he were a trifle less hampered. When he took office Lord K. told him that there were 1,600,000 men in England, and 1,000,000 fit to fight, and that 1,300,000 recruits were coming on this year. French made a note of these figures at the time, and showed me the note in his writing. When French got to his own office he told his officers to look up the states, which they did, and he showed them to me. They showed that the total number of men drawing rations in England was 1,019,000; the total number of men fit to fight was 540,000, with about half a million rifles, of which 350,000 were ·303. He said that he supposed that Lord K. would deny having given the figures, although Sir Henry Sclater, A.G., was present. I told French that in his position I would have sent a note to Lord K., putting down the figures that Lord K. had given, and requesting confirmation, and French regretted that he had not done so. He said that chaos was still considerable, but that things would gradually improve. He could not tell me whether the Government knew the facts, but he had told Walter Long, who was with him for an hour just before I came in.

Shaw, by the way, scoffs at the idea of an Air Minister in the shape of a civilian, to direct the movements of a fighting force. But if he were only to administer the new department, that was another matter, and this is a very sound point of view.

French declared that according to Macdonogh there were only 10 German divisions in reserve unexpended on the Western front. There were 115 German divisions in all in the West, 3 unaccounted for, including the 22nd Corps, and I think $50\frac{1}{2}$ in the East, including 3 (101 to 103) in Serbia. Therefore the idea seems to be that Germany cannot do much more, but this depends entirely upon the strength with which Germany chooses to hold the rest of her line in France, and I am not yet convinced, as our people appear to be, that the Germans will not make another push.

Lord French was not hopeful that we would be able to do much, as he did not see whence the force was to come for doing it. He was very severe on our detachments in the

Eastern Mediterranean, and put down our troubles to those who had initiated the military part of the Dardanelles expedition.

Saw General McGrigor to-day just back from Mudros, which is now cleared out. He says that there are over twenty big German submarines in this sea, and that the moving about of troops entails great risks. He was quite near to the *Provence*, which was sunk the other day, and as he was in a 10-knot ship he did not much care about it. He was very sarcastic about the Naval Division.

There were immense trenches now east of the Suez Canal, and many great swinging bridges. One small party of Turks had come across the desert with a mine, which they managed to place in the Canal during the night, and it nearly sunk one of our old battleships. He scoffed at the idea of a Turkish attack. There were said to be 36,000 Turks at Beersheba, but K., Maxwell, and McMahon had been talking about 250,000. Their information was most defective, and had been a very expensive mistake.

Wednesday, March 15. I have been seeing more lately of Wollcott, and also of Mr. Simonds, the editor of the New York *Tribune*, who is here on a visit. I have met them frequently at Lady Sarah's, Olive's, and Mrs. Astor's. The latter is just back from New York, and has brought her girl, who is pretty and charming.

Wollcott says that the Charleville Headquarters are linked by direct telephone and wire to all the Armies, and that they sent a message from there to Hindenburg's Head-quarters at Kovno at 10 A.M., and had a long answer back by 1 P.M.

Wollcott was chiefly interesting to-day at Lady Sarah's about German finance. The Reichsbank, by dint of massing all the gold in circulation, etc., and by drawing 27,000,000 of gold from Austria apparently, had managed to collect 187,000,000 sterling in gold, but, owing to the mass of paper issued, the gold, which at the beginning of the war repre-sented 87 per cent. of the notes issued, now only repre-sented 19 per cent. The result was that the current price of the mark was still inflated, and it was worth only 25 per cent. of its par value. He said that the thing could go on, but directly the veil was lifted after the war there would be a catastrophe. A German, for example, who had £5000 in the bank, would already have had taken away £1000 for contributions, and his £4000 would be worth only £1000, out of which he would have to pay war taxes. It was a perfectly rotten situation, and they could not go on much longer. The chief German bankers whom he had spoken to did not conceal their anxiety from him. I asked him why all the clever financiers of the world allowed the mark to be quoted at an inflated price, and he said that it was because they did not know how bad things were. He was much struck by the claim for an indemnity having disappeared from the latest edition of the German peace terms sent to us from America after the return of Colonel House from his trip to Europe. Wollcott is very sure that the Germans are making a gigantic effort to place themselves in a favourable position to make peace on good terms. He said that they did not talk of Paris, but only of Verdun.

Mr. Simonds was extraordinarily interesting at Mrs. Astor's the other day. He says that the Germans have been far more clever than we have been in America. They were stupid at first, and Dernburg tried to promote his propaganda by making speeches, and so forth, but soon found out that Roosevelt's system was the best. This was to be accessible, and to use the American Press, which acts in America in a more important manner than ours, and has greater influence in politics. So Bernstorff keeps open house in Washington, and will always discuss any question with a pressman over a cigar and a drink. They also feed any papers that they may eventually want with stacks of advertisements. There is little or no direct bribery Simonds thinks.

Our Embassy meanwhile is useless. Sir Cecil Spring-Rice is too much of a diplomatist, and the Embassy is no good as a centre of news to the American Press. Mrs. Astor says that our attachés out there are very nice fellows, but she describes them as ' cavemen,' and she says they go to the club and keep to themselves in the old British manner, instead of circulating and spreading the gospel.

Simonds says that he has been here three weeks, and has practically seen no one but Balfour. His London correspondent, Draper by name, has had even worse luck, and from being very strongly pro-Ally, has become almost pro-German. I think that Simonds is tending that way from sheer neglect on our part. Simonds says that London is almost written off American journalism on account of the inaccessibility of our chief men, and is reckoned as no more important than a suburb of New York, and the best men will not come. He says that people do not realise over here how unpopular England was in America before the war, and how much Germany has been able to trade on this feeling. He thinks that Wilson's Government is purely opportunist, and that it will follow the line of least resistance in order to succeed in the next Presidential Election. We therefore have to be very careful, and should leave no stone unturned.

Thursday, March 16. Lunched with Sir Arthur Herbert and his wife at 1 Hill Street, Knightsbridge. He has been two years in America, and told me pretty much the same story as Marshall, Simonds, and Wollcott. He has been trying to do propaganda, and has come back here hoping for a job in connection with it. He described how the business over here was in water-tight compartments, one run by Gilbert Parker, another—the Pilgrim Section—by Brittain, and the third by Willie Siyerell of the Press Bureau ; no co-ordination.

Sir Arthur is not very keen about the Marshall plan of putting first-class American journalists in charge over here, and another at New York in charge of the distribution service, but he gave me no reasons for thinking that this was not the best plan, as I think it is.

Friday, March 17. Lunched with Colonel Sykes of the Flying Corps at the Ritz. He is just back from the Dardanelles, and has been given the C.M.G. by the Admiralty, having had nothing from the War Office in spite of his good work—so like our people. There were at the lunch, Mrs. Townshend, the Duchess of Marlborough, Lord Percy, Geoffrey Robinson, and Commandant Bertier de Sauvigny, who is the new officer *de liaison* between General Joffre and Sir William Robertson. Had a great talk with Bertier, and arranged to go over and pay a visit to General Joffre and General Castelnau the week after next, if possible.

Prince Victor Napoleon came in after lunch. I introduced Bertier and Sykes to him. Bertier says that the Germans had nothing to do but to attack the French. His argument is much the same as that given in the *Times*. He says that the Germans are nearly ruined, and are short of men. They had to make a great effort and score a striking success in the West, and they chose Verdun because of its importance in the eyes of the mob. He thinks that they have failed, and that there are no more than six to eight fresh German divisions at their disposal for continuing. He declares that as soon as the Germans are exhausted, we must counter-attack and prevent them from having leisure for recovering themselves. Joffre's view, he says, is that every one who is not in France on the Allied side by May 15 had better stay away altogether, for they will be useless. What Joffre evidently implies is that he means to have a good smack at the Germans by that date. When we were deploring the want of action by our troops, Bertier said that that might come too, but he would not say much. He was glad about the divisions coming to France, but he tried to support the policy of Salonika, and when I drove him into a corner about it, and showed the inutility of this operation, and the wastefulness of it all, he could only argue that the shipping did not permit more than the divisions from Egypt coming West at present, which is quite another matter. He did not think that the Serbians at Corfu could be any use for three or four months, for they were practically a mob, without arms, clothing, equipment, or guns. Joffre wanted us to put every division we could into France from England, but, of course, could not dictate to the British Government what they should do. Bertier said that even second-rate troops could hold the trenches and release some good divisions for the offensive. The game was for all the Allies to attack simultaneously in May, a view which I have always held. If the Russians were not quite ready they would have to come on and do their best with what they had. As for Joffre's view about troops arriving after May 15, this is an exaggeration. We must try and keep up a constant stream of fresh troops. Bertier thinks that Germany is like a groggy boxer who is trying for a knock-out in desperation before he is himself finished. The only question is whether the adversary has strength enough to hit him hard enough. He probably won't be owing to the waste of men and munitions at Salonika.

Sykes and I had some talk afterwards about the Flying Corps.

Monday, March 20. Published an article on 'Recruiting' in the *Times*; it was held up two days by the Censor.

Had a long sitting of the Tribunal; cases very interesting. A longer experience has given me a higher opinion of this body. If we can judge by Hampstead, the Advisory Committees and Tribunals perform their work admirably. They are careful, sympathetic, and thorough, and I consider their decisions are very just. Of course, to apply a measure like this is foreign to all our habits, and our people meet with extraordinary difficulties. We have to create our own precedents, and to act by the light of nature, as in some cases our instructions do not help us out. There is very little shirking among the people, but there are so many bolt-holes in the new law, and the lists of certified occupations which Runciman has put out through the Board of Trade are so long, that there are an intolerable number of claimants for exemption.

Tuesday, March 21. Spent the afternoon hearing Lord Northcliffe's account of his visit to France. He is full of praise of the French Army and French generals. He said that all the French people and all the French Staff were reading my articles and discussing them, as they do in Germany, but I was criticised about Salonika, as I can well believe. If they would only give me a military reason for this idiotic adventure, I should be very pleased, but they never will, because there is none. Northcliffe did rather a smart thing journalistically. He motored to Paris from Verdun, and sat up all night to put his story together, so defeated a rival who was with him. Steed is also back, very full of the noise of the cannonade at Verdun and the danger of the trenches in Champagne.

Dined with the Agnews; met Lady Byng, Sir Theodore Brinckman, and Sir Savile Crossley.

Wednesday, March 22. Met Dr. Hughes. We had a great talk about the economic question, he holding that we could do Germany an infinity of harm by the coming economic conference in Paris, and I maintaining the thesis that victory alone counted, and if one had victory everything else came with it.

Dined with Reggie and Bee Pembroke, 10 Belgrave Square. Mrs. Asquith, the young Duchess of Sutherland, Belle Herbert, Admiral Sir Hedworth and Lady Meux, Mr. Bonar Law, Mrs. Sneyd, Lord French, and Lord Derby. Very pleasant dinner. Had a little talk with Bonar Law afterwards, and some talk with Lord French, who told me that he had had to go to the Prime Minister in order to get Sir Arthur Paget and Sir Bruce Hamilton appointed to the commands under him in the United Kingdom, as Lord K. had steadily obstructed their appointment. He also admitted that he had dismounted many of the Yeomanry at home, partly for financial reasons and partly because they were just as good as cyclists.

After dinner Mrs. Asquith and Bonar Law played Bridge against the Admiral and the Duchess. Lady Pembroke, Belle, Derby and I, and Mrs. Sneyd had a great talk afterwards, and a good deal of chaff. Reggie was in great form, and full of good stories as usual. He is just back from Russia, where he went with Arthur Paget to give the Tsar his Field-Marshal's baton, and he is off back to France to-morrow.   Derby told me to-night that they were doing some real good work in cutting up the lists of certified trades.

Thursday, March 23.   Lunched with Lloyd George at 11 Downing Street.   Mrs. Lloyd George and Scott, editor of the *Manchester Guardian*.   L. G. just back from the War Committee looking very fresh, young, and spruce, much better than last time I met him.   We had a fascinating talk about the war.   He said that even now he had not been able to get out of Lord K. the demands of the Army for munitions between the outbreak of the war and the time when I began the row of May 1915.   He turned to Scott and said, ' Is it not extraordinary that the whole Cabinet only knew the truth from Colonel Repington, and could not get it from any one else ? '   I told him that recruiting was as great a scandal as that of munitions, and he agreed. The whole trouble had come from Lord K.'s inability to understand the question and foresee the future.   L. G. was gloomy about numbers, and thought that we would not get them this year.   He thought that the best way to deal with the case of the married men was to extend the Courts Emergency Powers Act, and to see that no process was served against married men who were with the colours.   This seems a good way out of the difficulty.   L. G. thought that it would prevent a family who had means from claiming relief automatically when they could afford to pay, but, of course, it only postpones until after the war the real financial difficulty of the problem.   L. G. is not very sanguine about the future.   He told me that he read my papers on German casualties very carefully, and was amused that the chief criticisms in the Press of them were that they were too pessimistic.   He thought the contrary.   He gave the enemy—Germany and her Allies—13,000,000 men still upstanding, and could not see the way to victory this year.   He asked me if I could, and I admitted that I could not.

He liked Robertson and thought that he had played

the game. L. G. said that he was employing 2,000,000 people, men and women, in Army and Navy munition work. The least he could do with was 1,000,000 men, of whom 300,000 would be of military age. He was working Ireland for all she was worth to create his factories, as Ireland did not come under the Service Law. He confirmed what Du Cane told me about sending 60,000 shells a day to France, and said that by about June we should be ready for practically unlimited expenditure of munitions in every way. He did not think that Russia was anything like ready, and he thought that their supply of munitions was not greater than ours, although we had a 100-mile front, and theirs was 1000 miles. He thought that they were gambling in the present attack, and would have done better to wait and pile up ammunition, but he says the Russians gamble whenever they have any money, and so they gamble with their munitions without any real thought for the future.

We told each other stories about Lord K. L. G. said that when he, L. G., came into office, not only were the heavy guns not ordered, but not even the machinery to make them existed, and it had been a tremendous task to get the whole thing moving. L. G. said that he was in favour of the General Service Act—looking fiercely at Scott as he said so. I asked the latter what he thought, and he said he was prepared to assent to it on terms.

L. G. was inclined to think that the Germans would go at the Russians again in the summer.

Friday, March 24. Lunched with Sir Arthur and Lady Paget, Max-Muller, and some ladies whose names I forget. We had a great talk about Russia. Sir Arthur produced two orders set in brilliants which the Tsar had given him. They were really quite superb, and I think that one was the Alexander Nevsky, and the other the St. Stanislaus, but I am not quite sure. He and Reggie had done a long journey, and had been to the Russian G.H.Q., which were at Minsk, I fancy, or somewhere in that direction. They had a great function. He says that there are nearly

2,000,000 rifles now and 1,000,000 with the reserves. They called up 1,400,000 men a short time ago, and will call up 400,000 more a month! Polivanoff, the new Russian War Minister, told him everything. There are going to be no new formations except some small bodies in the Caucasus. The output of rifles in Russia is only 95,000 a month, and not 200,000 as other reports have suggested. They are short of heavy guns, and do not think they will be able to resist an attack, *à la* Verdun, in the East, but Sir Arthur says that the men are very splendid and physique magnificent. What they lack is young men of the officer type and our N.C.O.s, but the training will be better this year than towards the end of the retreat last year. He expects that the Russians will make their main effort in the South as before, partly in order to bring Rumania in. He says that he disabused the minds of the Russians of the belief that we could do anything from Salonika of a really serious character. The Russians were anxious about the Riga front owing to the manner in which the ice melts in the Baltic, *i.e.* earlier in the south of Riga Bay than in the north, but they all seemed determined to fight things out. Sir A. Paget is rather disposed to think that some of the Russian Army Group Commanders fight on their own initiative, and he says that when the thaw comes all operations will have to stop for a time.

Saturday, March 25. I have had a look into our affairs to-day with the help of much information recently conveyed to me by political people, and I see no reason why we should expect victory yet. All the following statistics are unknown to the public. We have 6,300,000 men of the Allies in the chief theatres of operation, and our enemies have 6,000,000 or about the same. With equal numbers we must expect drawn battles unless our leading and quality are superior, and this we cannot affirm, taking all the Armies together. The German reserves, including the 1917 and 1918 Classes, promise 2,500,000 exclusive of recovered wounded. The French have about 750,000. The Italians have 2,750,000, but have neither the cadres nor the guns to increase their forces much. The Austrians have at least 1,000,000. For the Russians the reserves are still ample, but we have to count rifles rather than men. The Russians say that they have 1,400,000 rifles, and will have 2,200,000 at the end of April.

Robertson has always refused to place a figure on our needs, and has said plainly that no limit can at present be placed upon the numbers which we may have to find to win the war. We have raised 70 divisions in the U.K., of which 50 are now abroad, 3 T.F. divisions in India, 13 2nd-line T.F. divisions at home allotted to Home Defence with only 600 men per battalion, and 4 New Army divisions getting ready to go abroad. We have also 3 British and 2 Indian cavalry divisions in France, and about 1,000,000 miscellaneous troops at home, including 600,000 reserves of all branches of the Regulars and T.F.

Our divisions are below strength and we have immediate need of over 200,000 men to fill up strengths and meet wastage for three months, even after allowing for all our reserves at home. If we can work up to 62 divisions abroad we shall need 123,000 drafts a month to keep them going according to our past experience, at all events during the fighting seasons. There is no doubt that we can spare these men without industrial disaster and therefore ought to get them, but the German reserves are also large, and they can give tit for tat. We have about 2,750,000 men on the W.O. pay list, exclusive of Dominions.

Our debts are already near £2,000,000,000. The Army costs nearly 600 millions a year, grants or loans to Dominions and Allies 600 millions, munitions over 400 millions, Navy over 200 millions, and charges for debt 134 millions. These are the main items per annum, and the hardest drain on us of all, namely, the loans to Allies, is not likely to diminish. L. G. has ordered between 4000 and 5000 heavy guns and howitzers from 4·5-in. to 15-in. and they are coming along finely. We are lending Russia 300 millions a year, Italy 120 millions, Dominions 100 millions, France 48 millions, Belgium 30 millions, and so on, but we have also released France from the obligation which she undertook last year of sharing with us equally the burden of the loans to some of our Allies. This amounts to 150 millions. We also help France in freight and coal below market rates, and pay them for using their railways to defend them. No one of the public is aware of any of these facts. If France did all the things for us that we are doing for her we should be over 400 millions richer a year. It is a hard war for England.[1]

[1] By the end of the war our Allies owed us £1,700,000,000, exclusive of advances for reconstruction purposes. Out of this total, France and Italy each owed us 470 millions.

CHAPTER VII

A VISIT TO THE FRENCH FRONT, MARCH AND APRIL 1916

The struggle over Salonika—Our strength in France—Visit to Chantilly—Views of Generals de Castelnau and Pellé—System of work at the French G.Q.G.—By motor Paris to Souilly—Situation at Verdun —Visit to the battlefield—French confidence that they can hold Verdun —General Pétain's views—His use of artillery—The 2me Bureau, 2me Armée—German divisions used—German prisoners—Visit to General Gouraud—The French trenches described—The French 5me Armée Headquarters—Their views of the situation—Visit to General Joffre—His views on artillery, British strengths, Salonika, black troops, and French losses—Visit to the French War Minister— Conversations with M. Briand and M. Berthelot—A version of the Constantinople affair—A visit to La Panne—Belgian strengths.

March, 1916. Commandant Bertier having arranged with the French G.Q.G. that I should visit the French front, I left London on Monday, March 27, went to Southampton, and embarked on the boat for Havre. It was blowing great guns, and I slept on board. We started at 7 A.M. on the morning of March 28. Fairly quiet until we got into the Channel. We saw a line of nets extending across between the forts, and there were various patrol boats at anchor in the neighbourhood, and some destroyers further out. We passed the line of nets between two old hulks which mark the Channel much too clearly. When we got into the Channel we found a gale blowing. Had a most tempestuous crossing, nearly everything in my cabin was smashed. However, it must have been much too rough for the German submarines to come to the surface, and so we duly arrived at Havre, and, after having a very poor meal, went on to Paris at 5.23, arriving 9 P.M. I found that none of the registered luggage had come with us, and most of us had nothing but

what we stood up in. Went to the Ritz. Telephoned to
Bertier, who was in Paris, and told him that I could not
go to the G.Q.G. (Grand Quartier Général) until Thursday.
He undertook to make arrangements. Wrote to Sir William
Robertson that I was in Paris; he is here for the Conference of the Allies. Took leave of Gerald Campbell, who is
leaving Paris; he is on his way to Switzerland for the *Times*,
and his book on the Vosges fighting is just coming out.

Wednesday, March 29. Robertson came round to see
me at 9.45 A.M. He said that he and Joffre had agreed
not to discuss military matters and strategy before the
sixty to one hundred persons who are taking part in the
Conference. They had decided only to refer to military
affairs in general terms, but they had agreed to an Anglo-
French Conference, which seems to have been rather breezy.
The French had brought Gilinsky, the representative of
the Russian H.Q. Staff, and Robertson said that had he
known that they were going to do this, he would have
brought Cadorna to balance matters. The great struggle
was to try and make the French send the Salonika troops
to France. He did his best, and both Asquith and K.
supported him. They found the French quite immovable.
Joffre got angry, or pretended to be, and stormed and
thumped the table, complaining that Robertson was *un
homme terrible*. R. was not quite sure what this meant,
and asked me whether it was a kind of *enfant terrible* in
a grown-up form. I said that I thought that the French
would bring the troops back too late, and R. agreed. He
complained bitterly that our Ministers did not take the
lead in the debates, and that none of them, except Lord
K., could speak French properly. Asquith and others
spoke in English. There was a very good translator discovered by Lloyd George. He apparently let them speak
for a quarter of an hour, and then spoke the speech in
French for them. R. said that the translator's speech was
much better than the original, but that the whole thing
was babble and did not lead anywhere. R. said that we
should soon have 40 divisions in France, 2100 field guns,

600 howitzers, and 600 heavy guns, also a total of 4,000,000 rounds in reserve for the field guns in France, and 1,000,000 for the heavy guns. He thought that our position as regards ammunition was now good. We went over the points that I meant to make in my conversation with the French over here, concerning which R. and I are in entire agreement.

Lunched with the Le Roy-Lewises. Met Mrs. Leeds, who is staying at the Ritz. Bertier came to lunch and then went off back to England.

My uniform had now come, so Lieut. Pernot of Joffre's Staff and I started off for Chantilly at 2.40 P.M. It is about one hour's run. I saw General Pellé first. I had met him in Mecklenburg at the German manœuvres in 1911, and knew his value. A very pleasant and capable man. He called for Colonel Dupont, who is head of the 2nd Bureau at French G.Q.G. We discussed Verdun and German plans. First of all, it appeared that the French had only 3 reserve divisions —namely, the 61st, 63rd, and another—on the N.E. front where the Germans first attacked. General Herr commanded them. They had a very bad time as the enemy was so superior. Herr had in all 9 divisions in the fortified region of Verdun. Herr had put Joffre wrong by vowing that the Germans would never dare attack. The first four days were very serious—21st to 25th; then, on the 25th, General Pétain, commanding the 2nd Army, was placed in charge of the whole operation, and there were placed under his orders also the 3rd Army (Humbert) and Herr's divisions. The 2nd and 20th French Army Corps attacked on the 26th and checked the German advance. The Germans had used 24 divisions, of which 20 had attacked seriously. We had a long talk on various subjects, and then I saw General Castelnau, Chief of the General Staff, whom I had met before both in Paris and England. He has already lost three sons in the war. He said that the Germans had already lost 137,000 men at Verdun. Others think they have lost more. The French have lost about half this number. There were now, according to Castelnau, only 8 fresh German divisions left over at disposal on the whole Western front, and they were all in front of the British. Robertson had told me that he thought the Germans were off the Russian campaign, and intended to continue the offensive in France. Castelnau was of the same way of thinking. He said that he thought that the Germans expected to take Verdun in a few days by their rush tactics under the fire of their numerous guns ; otherwise they would not have omitted an attack on the left bank of the river. He said they had used woods north of Verdun to conceal their guns, that there were such masses of the latter that the French artillery had been exceedingly effective. He said that in one zone, 1200 metres by 400, the Germans had fired 370,000 shells. During the fight the Germans had withdrawn 10 divisions, and, after completing them with men from the field depots, had sent them back to the fight. The French, on the other hand, drew their divisions out of the fight before they had lost their quality, and sent in new divisions from the reserve. The French had 20 divisions employed in all. The Germans adopted their system from want of divisions in reserve, and the French thought their own system best. The French now think that they have information two days before any fresh German troops come up from the interior of Germany or from other sections behind the line. The French have all their plans ready to replace any one of their divisions at any point in their front line at a moment's notice, so they can always follow any German change by a corresponding movement.

Generals Castelnau and Pellé asked me many questions about our troops in England, and I enlightened them concerning our situation. De Castelnau made rather a good suggestion which I passed on to Sir W. R. the same night, namely, that the Allied diplomacy should call upon Greece and Rumania to take part in the war by June at the latest and aid an offensive of our troops in Salonika. If they come in, well and good ; if not, then we leave at Salonika 50,000 men, French and English, and 120,000 Serbians now reforming at Corfu, and bring back 150,000 men to France.

I told him that I thought this a very sound proposal, but he rather surprised me by saying that he did not know what the Allied diplomacy was doing. From other sources I have heard that there is considerable jealousy in Paris of the powers of the French G.Q.G.

This G.Q.G. at Chantilly is placed in an immense hotel, formerly much crowded in the racing season. It is about one hour from Paris by car. It is not a bad place, and the service of order is quite good. They are away from Paris and from the atmosphere of the capital, which is not always healthy. The system they work on is to have their *rapport* at 8 A.M. and 8 P.M. every day. The information which enables the *rapport* to be drawn up comes by telephone. This means a great saving of time. It requires only two hours for the reports from a Brigade to pass through Divisional, Army Corps, and Army H.Q. to the G.Q.G. The Army Group Commanders do not seem to be involved in this chain, but the Armies duplicate the *rapports* to them, and the Group Commanders appear to be engaged mainly upon special missions such as those given during this war to Foch, Castelnau, and Pétain. But when an order is issued by G.Q.G. it goes out through the Group Commanders when they exist.

I hear that the French are making 175,000 shells a day. We are sending 60,000 a day to France. We had some talk of the Russians on the German front. It is thought that the Russians are taking the offensive just as the thaw sets in, in order to prevent the Germans from using their heavy guns, but as the Germans are already in position I am not sure that this will help them much. The French say that the German line in Russia is not continuous. It is a broken chain of points of support. General de Castelnau gave me to believe that there are eight French lines west of the Meuse. There is no sign of the Prussian Guard yet appearing before Verdun. There is only one Ersatz division of the Guard in this region. Two divisions of the Active Guard are in the line further west, two in reserve behind the line opposite the British, and one division in Russia. One Army Corps, they say, has been recently taken away from the Belgian front.

I saw some of the other heads of departments of the G.Q.G. Janin, who is Major-General of the operations in the North-East, has under him : Bell for personnel ; Dupont, 2nd Bureau, for information ; and Renouard, 3rd Bureau, for operations. General Pellé is Major-General of what they call the T.O.E., namely, the Theatre of Exterior Operations. The heads of his 3rd Bureau are Dessier, Deuvigné, and Billotte. Pellé and Renouard struck me as the best, and Renouard gave me the above information about the manner of working the *rapports*. It is on these *rapports* that the daily *communiqués* are drawn up morning and evening for the Press.

I asked Castelnau about the written promise said to have been given by us to the French to keep seventy divisions in the field. He said that if there were such a paper he had never seen it, so I must ask Joffre about it when I see him.

My talk with Castelnau ended by his saying that ' rather than accept slavery at German hands, the French race will die upon the battlefield.'

Dined with the Lewises at the Ritz. Lewis said that by taking over the front held by the 10th French Army [1] we have set free ten French divisions. We have seven in reserve. Lewis makes a point of the supposed German ignorance of our order of battle. I don't believe a word of it.

Thursday, March 30. Saw Mrs. Leeds in the morning, and had a long talk.

Lieut. Pernot came in from the G.Q.G. and lunched with me. We started at 2.15 in a Belleville-de-Launay landaulette, and went by Vitry le François and Bar-le-Duc. Stopped at Vitry for tea. We have two stout fellows in helmets and goatskins to drive us. We travelled from sixty to eighty kilometres an hour. The roads were in capital order, and not overcrowded. At Sommesous we

---

[1] These were the 9th, 12th, 17th, and 33rd Army Corps and the 130th Division.

found a depot for woodwork for the trenches. After passing Epernay we found all the towns full of troops, who appeared to be very well clothed and equipped, and the furlough parties were going off to the stations as if nothing were happening. We then came into the old Marne battlefield, when signs of war devastation began to multiply. All the farms are capitally kept, and the fields are in excellent condition. It is said that the arrangements for bathing and cooking are very good. Pernot says that after heavy fighting units require rest of from six weeks to two months for restoration of their moral, but physically they are restored much quicker. There is a system of reading all the soldiers' letters sent home or received from home. A summary is made of them, and sent to each Army H.Q. In this way the General keeps his finger on the pulse of the Army and the country. The spirit of the Army is said to be good. I was subsequently shown one of these summaries, and it quite confirmed all the opinions which I had heard. A glorious spring day with no wind. We put up at the Hotel du Commerce. Poor quarters and worse food.

Friday, March 31. Hotel produced only crusts of stale bread and water for breakfast. Started at 6.30 A.M., arrived at General Pétain's 2nd Army H.Q. at Souilly at about nine. Had a talk with Commandant de Cointet, head of the 2nd Bureau, and with Commandant Faucher, Joffre's liaison officer at Pétain's H.Q.—both good men.

I saw General Pétain first in his working room. A fair Pas-de-Calais man of medium height, with a firm and reserved aspect and a masterful regard; a soldier before all, and one with strong will and decided opinions. I was much attracted by him.

Pétain took command at Verdun on the evening of Feb. 25, when affairs were looking rather black. He counter-attacked Douaumont on the 26th, the 20th Army Corps on his right, the 2nd on his left; General Balfourier led this attack, which re-established affairs in this quarter. Pétain has now his own Army (the 2nd) under him, also Humbert's 3rd Army—the right of which rests on the Avocourt Wood

—and Gen. Herr's old garrison of Verdun which withstood the shock of the first five days alone. Faucher, Pernot, and I went on to the Fort de la Chaume, where we had an excellent view of the whole position. It was a fine clear day, and my Zeiss glasses were much in request. There was a general bombardment in progress, not so remarkably heavy as I had expected to find it. On the left bank of the river, the French main positions about the Bois Boissu were in full view, and all the gun positions behind it. We had also a fine view of the right-bank positions. I was impressed by the importance of the artillery positions which the Germans were holding at Beaumont, and the adjacent woods and hills. The situation of Douaumont, which the Germans had captured in the evening of February 25, and were holding strongly, is also very dominating and important. The Poivre Hill is much lower, and is wooded, except near the river facing the Woevre plain. The French position seems to be satisfactory on the Woevre side. The German batteries here are not able to move much off the roads, and are given a bad time by the French guns. They seem ready enough to stop shooting if the French do so. The Germans are bombarding Vaux Fort, Poivre Hill, and Bois Boissu, including the Fort de la Marre, making pretty bad practice at the latter, and seemed unable to find the French batteries in the rear of it. It seems that last night the Germans had captured part of Malancourt, and Pétain was contemplating the abandonment of this bit to-night, as he had made the Germans pay the price. It is a really indefensible salient. He explained to me that they were much exposed to the German fire from the Talou Hill, where the Germans must also be suffering a good deal. I watched the fight of the aviators. The French seem to have the mastery very distinctly. The French anti-aircraft guns are now very good; no German airman seemed to get over our lines, but we were all over theirs. It was about March 8 that the French obtained the mastery of the air. The Germans may have about 2000 guns at Verdun. This artillery is in two main groups, one north of Mort Homme, and one about Beaumont. The direction of this artillery is poor. The French fire is good. Pétain has a genius for heavy guns, which he manages now with great facility, and their *feu d'écrasement* is believed to do much damage. Pétain also uses the *feu de barrage* with great effect. The German fire seems to be more scattered than the French. The hostile guns were better at first in their prepared positions, and then they had not so many French guns against them, but as they advanced they became much less effective. Pétain cannot hold the Malancourt positions, because his guns cannot get forward enough, as they would be raked from the right bank. Pétain suffered at first from lack of communication trenches (*boyaux*), but these seem now to be extending in rear of all positions. No one here seems to believe for a moment that the Germans can take Verdun. They are, however, throwing incendiary shells into the town, and doing what damage they can to the place. I was shown a particularly vile and detestable German trick. The compressed forage sent from America contains a lot of needles and sharp, bent pieces of steel and smaller splinters. These are intended to pierce the intestines of animals eating this forage, and the French lost many horses and mules before finding it out. The Duc d'Auerstadt told me he had lost seven horses from this cause, and I was shown a specimen of this forage with the steel in it, and have no doubt that the outrage is deliberate, and is traceable to the German-Americans in the U.S.A. Moral : Use no American compressed forage or tinned goods.

I saw many French troops. All the villages and towns west of Verdun full of them, and many hundreds going on furlough, which does not look as if they were much alarmed by the German attack. The moral of the Army is really magnificent.

Lunched with Pétain and his Staff, including General Herr, commander of the old Verdun garrison; there was also one of the Army Corps commanders—about ten or a dozen in all. Pétain congratulated me on my writings, and said that he had used the arguments of my article on ' The

Western Front,' of Feb. 20, for some official appreciation, and cordially agreed with it. He said that his reading of the situation was that the French had to thank me and the English people, but not the English Government. He was very critical of Lord K., and cordially disagreed with many things that he had done, especially in Egypt, which could, he thought, be held by a handful of men now. He was strongly in favour of an attack on Alexandretta. He had been against the despatch of troops to Salonika, but was not now for their coming away. He reminded me that he had never seen a shot fired before this campaign. I told him that he was doing fairly well for a beginner ! He told me that he had been at the École de Guerre as professor under Foch ; his arm was the infantry, but he had realised since September 1914—and he appealed to his artillery commander to say if he had not said so— that artillery now conquers a position and the infantry occupies it. So he had gone all out for the guns, and had, above all, tried to make his heavy guns *supple* so that they could quickly concentrate their fire on different objects and destroy them by the *feu d'écrasement*. He owed his successes to following this principle. The French artillery fired all day and night. They denied the roads to the enemy at all hours, and so the Germans took to the woods, but the French airmen reconnoitred the *pistes*, and then these were also shelled by night. If 250,000 German infantry attacked, it was imagined that 120,000 men of other arms and services would also have come under fire. The Germans, like the French, suffer more when in reserve than when in the first line, since the cover is inferior. There are comparatively few losses in front-line trenches on quiet days when there is no infantry attack.

Pétain asked me what I thought the Germans were going to do. I said that he was in a much better position to judge than I was, but that I thought they would continue to peg away in the West, because there was nothing else for them to do. He impressed upon me, as Castelnau had done, that the battle was not yet over. Pétain asked me how many German spies had been shot in England, and I said about a dozen, so far as I knew.

I went after lunch to the 2nd Bureau of the 2nd Army, where de Cointet gave me a useful map and some papers ; he also showed me the *dossier* of all the German regiments. From this one can follow the positions and strengths of all the German regiments, battalions, and companies since the beginning of the war. It is very well done and always kept up to date from the evidence of prisoners. I find that our Intelligence book on *The German Army in the Field* is highly appreciated, and they all ask for more copies to be sent when the next edition is published.

The situation is that the Germans have now brought up thirty divisions in all to Verdun. These are shown in the map given to me, and they include the 1st Division of the 1st Corps, which is reported to have arrived at Étain from Russia. This is not absolutely certain as yet. This number of thirty includes the 3rd and 18th Army Corps, which are now licking their wounds in the second line. The other German divisions held in reserve in the whole of·the Western front number ten in all, of which eight are in reserve behind the German troops facing the British. It would appear from this distribution that the German troops are either preparing an attack against us, or expect us to attack them. Another hypothesis is that they may bring the eight divisions from the reserve on our front up to Verdun.

A company of German prisoners was paraded for my inspection. They were captured in Avocourt Wood a few days ago. They are a villainous-looking lot with bad faces, and many were miserable-looking specimens of humanity. Two aspirant officers reported their platoons, clicking their heels and saluting us in the best Potsdam manner. There were all sorts of men. There were Poles who were delighted to be free ; others were short of fingers or were deaf ; others had joined in February and were captured within two months. From the Bavarian prisoners one learnt that the 11th Bavarian Division had been first in Russia and then in Serbia, afterwards at Antwerp, and then before Verdun. There was scarcely any man who would have been taken by the German Army in peace-time, except half a dozen who had been taken out of munition works to be taught bombing. But it appeared on examination that they had not thrown any live bombs until the day of the fight in which they had been captured. The French interpreter of the 2nd Army was a savage-looking little man, who had been two years a student at Bonn. He made short work of the prisoners, telling them that they must say all they knew, or the consequences would be awful. He told me that out of 12,000 prisoners whom he had examined since the beginning of the Champagne offensive in 1915, not more than five or six had refused to speak in the end, officers included. We asked a lot of questions of the prisoners ; they all said that they were dead sick of the war in Germany, and that everybody wished that it would end. I should say that Bavaria had emptied her gaols to produce the rascals whom I saw.

Motored on to Châlons and arrived at 6 P.M. Dined with General Gouraud and his Staff that night. He commands the 4th Army, and had been badly wounded at the Dardanelles, losing his left arm, and was also very lame. It was a Turkish gun from the Asiatic side that had got him. A very gallant and noble gentleman, perfectly charming. I talked to him most of the evening, largely of extra-European affairs. He is a strong pro-Salonikan. His own front for the moment was quiet, but he said that the Germans were working down the slopes towards him, and that he expected an attack, but that he did not know where they would now find the troops. Commandant Henri was at the head of his 2nd Bureau. He told me that one German division had been taken away from the front of the 4th Army for Verdun, and that he knew of its impending departure a fortnight before it happened. The German strengths in front of the 4th Army are well maintained. The company in the field ran from 160 to

180 in addition to the *abkommandirende*. Note that the German Guard has now its two regular divisions at the angle turn of the German line in the West. Two reserve Guard divisions are behind German troops facing the British; one Guard Ersatz has just come up at Verdun; the 3rd Guard Division is still in Russia.

Saturday, April 1. Rose early, made some chocolate in my Etna, and with it and the biscuits fed Pernot and self. Motored to Donchery; stopped on the way short of Rheims. Davoust Duc d'Auerstadt of Gouraud's Staff and Captain d'Humières of the cavalry joined us on the way.

An exciting fight of aeroplanes over our heads at the village where we got out. The bugle sounded and everybody else took cover, for the French anti-aircraft guns were raining shrapnel upon the German airman whose progress was marked by the little puffs of bursting shrapnel which looked like scraps of cotton wool in the blue sky. Unfortunately the Boche got away, having had his look. I expect he tried the Montagne de Rheims, which is a good place behind which to assemble troops for a surprise.

We visited the trenches of the 4th Army, which are held on their left by the 7th Cavalry Corps. A long walk through woods and *boyaux* to a ruined farm, and on through four or five positions to the first line called the 1re *bis* or line of resistance. In front is the first line of all, which is an outpost line held by a small number of men and a few machine guns just to check the enemy and to split up an attack. All these trenches are protected by wire, mostly barbed, but not altogether so; and as it is the order in the 4th Army to add two yards of depth to one or other of the lines of wire entanglement every week, the result is a perfect sea of wire. In the low ground the defences are almost entirely breastworks, very much like some of ours, but theirs are concealed by the woods, which Gouraud very wisely does not allow to be cut. After leaving the low ground we reach the chalk, where the trenches are extremely good. The chalk, of course, stands up almost perpendicularly when frost and thaw do not crumble it.

In the lower ground the *boyaux* have still much water in them, but there are duck-boards which allow one to get along dry. Further up, the trenches are very dry and clean. Units remain in these trenches for ten days. The cavalry in the trenches are mixed with the Territorials; the latter have an *équipe* to look after the *boyaux* and act as *cantonniers*. They keep the trenches in perfect order, and quickly repair all damage done by the shells. Under a farm was the colonel's quarters with a stag's head to ornament them. This head was blown 1200 feet by a shell, and was brought back by the Territorials. We went down to see the colonel's kitchen, which is sunk very deep in the ground under the road. It seemed like a huge cavern. The colonel has an excellent *batterie de cuisine*. The roadway of the *boyaux* is sunk some eight to ten feet below the ground line. All turnings are marked with notice boards. There are steps here and there for getting out, and there is much barbed wire on all sides. The dug-outs are very deep, with good wooden bunks, one above the other, for the men to sleep in. There are blankets and straw in the bunks. Each dug-out has at least two entrances, in case one is blown in by a shell. The approaches to the advanced lines are zig-zags, but each bit of the *boyaux* is defended by parapets or traverses with loop-holes for rifle fire, so that not much progress can be made by the enemy along the *boyaux*, even if he gets into them. The parapets are arranged for rifle fire, but there seems to be a great absence of head cover. The machine guns and 37-mm. guns are placed in concealed pits flanking the lines and covering all approaches. The tops of them are covered with canvas and pieces of bracken or branches. Along each *boyau* there run a dozen or more telephones which diverge along the branches. There is one line buried under the ground, one metre deep, in case the other lines are destroyed. I was told that a *feu de barrage* takes from 40 seconds to 3 minutes to turn on, and that a field battery covers 400 by 400 yards with one shell every minute every 10 yards. At one point we stood up about 300 yards from the German trenches in order to look round, and no one fired at us. It was very different from Flanders, where we should all have been shot at if we had shown our noses above the parapet. I fancy that the French and Germans are less vicious than we and the Germans. They fight a battle harshly enough, but in the intervals they like to keep quiet. We go on fighting all the time.

The observers in these front trenches are protected by little steel cupolas, and even when there is much bombing they are fairly immune. On the parapets of the front trenches are what look like window flower-boxes. They contain chemical materials for making a smoke screen to *lift* the German gas when it comes. All the rats in the trenches congregate round these smoke boxes when the gas comes, as they realise that they save them from suffocation. This process of lifting the German poison gas was discovered quite by chance. During a gas attack some straw was set on fire by accident and forced the German smoke up. The rats came in swarms to squat round the burning straw and gave the French the hint. There is a special *boyau* for a 60-centimetre light line of rail, which is laid down with the metal sleepers attached to it. It runs under cover within a few yards of the front line, and the trucks are pushed by hand. All the supplies, including the wood for the dug-outs, come this way. Strong and close wire-netting is used to support the earth, where it does not stand by itself. All these trenches are clean, comfortable, and natty. The discipline is excellent. Every man we met in the trenches saluted, and all seemed very cheery. I am told, however, that these Champagne trenches are better than anywhere else. A man was killed close to us. We walked back in the open, and went on by car to the Montagne de Rheims, which is a strong artillery position. It is within range of the German guns, but people are at work on the vines everywhere as if there were no war. I remember my last voyage here with the Vicomte de Polignac and his pleasant party. A fairly large population still remains.

The statue of Joan of Arc still stands untouched in front of the Cathedral, but the latter is a scene of vandalism and desolation.

Drove on to Donchery to lunch with General Franchet d'Esperey, commanding the 5th Army, but he had just gone off to the Vosges to confer with General Dubail, so we lunched with his Staff. All very pleasant and friendly and informal. They were billeted in the house of a Hun who, of course, had disappeared. I went into the 2nd Bureau and had a talk with them all. There was a capable captain there, by name Fagalde, in charge of it, and several other officers, including a Japanese. The captain's view was that the Germans would go on till the last gasp. He admitted 2,000,000 as a possible number of reserves still available, counting at half a million each yearly class, 1916-18. We studied the maps of the German distribution, and found that there were absolutely no German troops in reserve in front of the 5th Army, which has 105 kilometres to look after. In this front there were 10 German divisions all holding the trenches with nothing higher than single battalions for local reserves. The German positions in front of the 4th and 5th Armies have the best of the ground, which is shown by an excellent panorama in General Gouraud's sitting-room. I told Gouraud that if he could place himself on the top of these hills, all the world would be at his feet. Captain Fagalde thought that except for eight divisions in reserve in front of the British, there were no other German troops to spare between Verdun and the sea.

Motored on to Chantilly in the afternoon. Had tea with Henry Yarde-Buller at the British Mission. Henry the same as ever, very cheery, bright, and pleasant. Le Roy-Lewis told me some time ago that Lord Bertie cannot bear him, but I don't know why. Then went on to see General Joffre, who occupies a big house facing the race-course. He is a big man, even vast, especially in breadth. He has a big head, big shoulders, big arms and hands. He greeted me civilly, but at first with some formality.

As we talked all the formality wore off, and he became cordial and eventually almost expansive. He started the talking, and I let him talk. He first dealt with the general situation, and then went on to speak very highly of the French medium-heavy artillery, especially the 155 and 210 guns. He said that the French shells were far superior to the German, because they had a heavier charge, broke up into more fragments, and killed more men. He preferred the medium to the very heavy guns—305, 380, and the 420—which were chiefly for the diversion of the public and the Press. It was possible to have more of the medium calibres, and they were much more effective. He granted, however, that the Germans had the advantage of the longer range of some of their guns, many of which were quick-firers.

I then turned the conversation into the question how many British divisions had been promised to the French, and he assured me positively that he had nothing written on the subject, and had only been given general indications. He wanted as many troops as we could spare. But his particular request was that we should keep our troops now in France up to their full strength. I said that I supposed we were about 40,000 short in France, and he said, emphatically, ' More.' I afterwards learnt that we were 78,000 men short abroad, of which 55,000 in France. I told Joffre the situation of our divisions in England, as I had done to Pellé and Castelnau, and told him why they were not to come over yet. As an example of the disadvantage due to lack of men, Joffre told me that he had recently asked Sir Douglas Haig to carry out certain preliminary work for an eventual offensive, but that Haig had replied that he could not do it for want of men. We discussed the state of our Army at home, in Egypt, and at Salonika. As for the latter, Joffre declared that it was a political and diplomatic question. He did not attempt to suggest, and in fact contemptuously denied, that there were any military grounds for the operation, so I remarked that as this was his point of view, there was nothing more to be said. Our

Armies had only to carry the policy of Governments. However, he went on to argue that the Salonika detachments might bring Rumania in and keep Greece quiet. His main complaint was not the absence of troops from France owing to their retention in England, but the state of our effectives now in France. I told him that the question had never been presented to me in that way, and that I heartily sympathised with his views. I told him that as we had over 1,000,000 men at home, 200,000 in Egypt, and an Army in Salonika, I thought we ought to be able to make up the Armies in France, and that I would do my best to get them hurried out.

I then opened up the question of French losses, and said I wished to state them to the English public, as I thought nothing would move them more. He was very sympathetic and understood the point, but, after some reflection, said that as the losses had been concealed so long from the French public, it would be difficult to announce them now. He asked me what I thought of the general position, and I gave him my views, as concisely and clearly as I could, telling him that from what I had seen of his troops I felt confident and happy.

We went into the question of an African Army. He listened attentively to my views, and said that the French would have 100,000 black troops in France this year, but that he thought that they were no good in the winter, and that they could not stand being shelled ; they were only good for an attack. I asked him how he got on with Robertson, and he spoke very nicely of him, saying that he admired his frankness and his will power. We neither of us mentioned Lord K.'s name.

We parted on cordial terms, and Pernot, who was present at the talk, congratulated me on the way I had managed Joffre and brought him out.

Joffre impressed me favourably. He is a bigger and a stronger man than I thought. He struck me as being shrewd, prudent, broad in his views, and with a great many of the best qualities of the French peasantry. He warmed up gradually as we talked, and I should say that he is well worth talking to.

Motored on to Paris after a word or two with Henry Yarde-Buller, and arrived at 8 P.M. Sat up late writing about Verdun.

Sunday, April 2. Met Le Roy-Lewis in the morning. We went to the Embassy. I saw Lord Bertie, and told him what I knew. He evidently thinks very small things of Lord K. He came from Dubail, who had just been appointed Governor of Paris, and is said to belong to the Caillaux group, or what Bertie calls 'the Rue de Valois lot,' in politics, which is bad news, but Bertie says that even if the party got back to power, they would not make Caillaux premier. Bertie very amusing about his experiences with a British Assist-ant Provost-Marshal in Paris when the Ambassador was travelling to London. He told me that several French soldiers were against Joffre. I told him that a commander-in-chief always had enemies. Met Lady Granville, but missed Lord G.

Lunched at the Café Voisin on the way back. It seems to have fallen from its ancient glories, and there was hardly anybody there. Le Roy-Lewis gave me a tabular statement, expanding what I had told him about the system of the French G.Q.G., and showing the French W.O. system, includ-ing the command in the field. Lewis says that the French have 2,300,000 men at the front, and 1,900,000 behind, but allows that this includes sick and wounded, and odds and ends. It is, in fact, not the fighting strength, but the aggregate figure of men drawing rations. He places the French losses at 800,000 killed and 200,000 missing, and imagines that the total casualties may be 3,000,000.

Went to the French W.O., and saw General Bard, *chef du cabinet* of the new French War Minister, General Roques. Made an appointment to see the latter to-morrow morning.

Called at the *Times* office, 2 Chaussée d'Antin—nice rooms. Then on to see Mrs. Leeds, and had a pleasant talk with her. Tony Drexel there at first.

Hubert Walker dined with me at the Ritz. General Ferdy Stanley and his wife were there. He is back on short leave from his division, which is on the Somme. We talked with the Lewises after dinner. Lewis said that he had reported in June 1915 that the French had lost 1200 guns by using drilled shells instead of forged, and that the English had made the same mistake, and had lost 38 guns at Loos from the same cause. Lewis told me about the meeting between Lord K. and French at the Embassy in August 1914.

Monday, April 3. Saw General Roques at 10.15 A.M. I knew the *huissier* very well by sight. He has been there twenty-seven years, and has seen thirty-two Ministers of War in his time. He hopes to live to see his fortieth. Found Roques very pleasant. He is not tall. He was in plain clothes, because he had to attend Parliament that day. Roques said that he had long wished to meet me, and that he had read all my articles. He said that although I was often a severe critic, severity was often required.

He impressed upon me that he was an intimate friend of Joffre's, and had come to the War Ministry to protect his friend from *coups de langue*, while Joffre was giving the *coups de sabre* to the enemy. I said that I remembered all the work he had done for aviation in France. He replied that during the years 1909 to 1911 he had spent 12 million francs on this service, although he only had a vote of a few thousand francs. I asked him why he was not hanged by the Parliament, and he replied that all his friends had told him he would be, but thanks to his knowledge of administration, which no doubt meant cooking the estimates, he had managed to pull through. I congratulated him heartily on the fine work of the French War Office, examples of which I had seen in all the French Armies. We discussed a number of matters, and parted on very friendly terms. Lunched with the Lewises.

In the afternoon went to the French Foreign Office to see Monsieur Berthelot. He was apparently with Briand when my card went in, and Briand at once sent and asked

me to come and see him. I was struck by his resemblance
to Lloyd George. About the same height and build, with
the same cut—or want of cut—of hair, and the same
captivating smile and manner. He was extraordinarily
cordial, and said, as others had done, that he liked to meet
a man whose ideas he had so often read, as it made all the
difference in the world knowing the man who wrote them.
He asked my views on the situation, and the state of the
French Army. I gave them as briefly as possible. He then
launched out into a long and interesting account of the
diplomatic situation. Of course I knew that we would
soon arrive at Salonika, which has been his particular
pigeon, and sure enough he reeled off all the old arguments. We had saved the Serbian Army; we had prevented Germany from dominating the Orient; we had kept
Rumania and Greece from joining Germany.[1] I told him

[1] It is only just to M. Briand to give in his own words, from the *Loire
Républicaine* of August 1919, his view of the Salonika story :

C'est en janvier 1915, exactement le 1er janvier, à l'Elysée, que M. Briand,
qui était alors garde des sceaux et ministre de la justice dans le cabinet
Viviani, a fait au président de la République et aux members du gouvernement la proposition d'organiser, en collaboration avec les Anglais, une
expédition de 300,000 hommes qui, débarquant dans un port de l'Adriatique
serait allée joindre les Serbes, dont l'armée venait de remporter sur les
Autrichiens une grande victoire, consacrée par la prise de plus de 50,000
prisonniers.

L'idée fut adoptée en principe par les membres du gouvernement, mais
MM. Millerand, ministre de la guerre, et Delcassé, ministre des affaires
étrangères, ont fait des objections et ont demandé que le G. Q. G. fut
appelé à donner son avis. Il en fut ainsi décidé.

Quelques jours après, le G. Q. G. adressait au gouvernement un rapport
dans lequel il concluait à l'impossibilité absolue de cette expédition.

Plus tard, la Bulgarie ayant attaqué la Serbie et celle-ci se trouvant en
péril, on dut envoyer des troupes à son secours, mais il était trop tard ; elles
ne purent pas joindre l'armée serbe, qui fut menacée d'une destruction
totale. C'est alors que les Anglais voulurent renoncer totalement à toute
intervention dans les Balkans et ramener les troupes en France. Beaucoup
d'hommes politiques étaient de cet avis, et l'on se rappelle toutes les
attaques violentes qui furent dirigées contre M. Briand, alors devenu président du conseil, lorsqu'il persistait à maintenir les troupes françaises en-
voyées là-bas, à en augmenter le nombre et à obtenir des Anglais qu'ils
consentissent à suivre cet example.

On sait qu'il parvint à triompher des résistances du maréchal Kitchener,
et c'est là la véritable origine de la grande expédition de Salonique qui, dès

that I had objected to the expedition last October, because
it was too late then to save Serbia, and that the saving of
the Serbian Army, so far as it had been accomplished, was
not due to the Salonika expedition, but to the subsequent
relief sent to the Adriatic, and to the use of Corfu as a
repairing base for the Army. I told him that I was not
opposed to the presence of our troops at Salonika on principle, but only to the absence of a quarter of a million of
our best troops from France at a moment when they might
enable us to win a decisive battle. I told them that in
their absence, instead of having a *bonne bataille* this year,
we should only have an *bataille ordinaire*. He listened very
attentively to the argument and then admitted, in reply
to some further remarks of mine, that no military offensive
was to be expected from the Salonika base. In this case,
I said—following Castelnau's idea—that the time had
come to compel Greece to march, so that some useful result
might accrue from the costly expedition to Salonika. He
agreed, suggested that Venizelos was no longer of leading
importance, that financial pressure should be applied, and
that the Skaloudris should be replaced by a Zaimist Government. He also agreed that pressure on the King was
the main thing ; he added that this pressure had already
begun, and I said that I was glad to hear it. I suggested
that the great diplomatic fault of the war was the promise

l'année 1916, libéra le canal de Suez des entreprises de la Turquie, barra à
l'empereur Guillaume II. la route de Constantinople, sauva l'armée serbe
de la capitulation et permit de s'emparer de Florina et de Monastir.

Pendant ce temps, nos alliés russes, libérés des troupes turques rappelées
vers Salonique, s'emparaient en Arménie d'Erzeroum et de Trébizonde ; les
Anglais reprenaient Kout-el-Amara et prenaient Bagdad ; et le roi du Hedjaz, rompant avec les Turcs, se rangeant à nos côtés, s'emparait des Lieux-
Saints et de la Mecque, ce qui eut, dans le monde musulman de nos possessions algérienne, tunisienne et marocaine, une influence considérable.

Une autre conséquence—et non des moindres—de l'expédition fut que
la Roumanie déclara la guerre à l'Allemagne. Enfin, on sait qu'en 1918 ce
sont les victoires éclatantes de l'armée d'Orient qui ont fait capituler la
Turquie, la Bulgarie et l'Autriche-Hongrie.

Le mur qui protégeait, en Orient, l'Allemagne était tombé. Le maréchal
Hindenburg écrivit la fameuse lettre dans laquelle il disait : ' Il ne nous
est plus possible maintenant de résister. Il faut demander l'armistice.'

of Constantinople to Russia, to which he assented, and added that the second fault was the failure to send an Army to Salonika instead of to the Dardanelles in Feb. 1915. These two errors ruined our cause in the Balkans, but he was trying to re-establish it. He had advocated the Salonika *coup* early in 1915, just as Lloyd George had done. I told him that the military situation in France was now good in my opinion, and that we held the Germans definitely, but I thought it necessary to explain to him our recruiting difficulties. He was evidently possessed of a very poor opinion of Lord K., and declared that the latter had ruined everything in Greece by assuring the King of the Hellenes that we should withdraw our troops. Monsieur Briand added that a soldier should not be charged with diplomatic missions when completely ignorant of diplomacy.

Briand is a charmer, and I now understand his power. He has the appearance of strength, a great deal of fire, and much affability.

I talked with Berthelot, who gave me an extraordinary version of the Constantinople affair. He said that this affair had begun, as I knew, in England. The project was made known to the French, who were informed that the attack was to be purely naval, and so they desired to take part in it. Up to this point Russia had been told nothing of the attack, had not asked us to intervene, nor had there been any question of any promise to Russia, which seemed content with the idea that the Straits should remain in Turkish hands unfortified and free after the war. But one day Isvolsky, the Russian Ambassador, had happened to be with Delcassé,—at that time French Foreign Minister—and had mentioned incidentally a rumour that had reached him about a coming Allied attack on Constantinople. He said to Delcassé that he supposed there was nothing in it. Delcassé replied, ' Why, surely you know all about it, don't you ? ' Isvolsky expressed complete ignorance, and did not conceal his astonishment ; he then cabled off to Petrograd, thinking, no doubt, that we and the French intended to make our *coup* behind

Russia's back, and were playing a trick on her. The same point of view must have been taken at Petrograd, and very naturally. In any case, there came a wire back in almost harsh terms, exacting the concession of Constantinople to Russia after the war, and there was nothing for Delcassé to do but to agree. The whole fault lay in the neglect to inform Russia of what was being done. Isvolsky and Russia were not to blame in any way. It would be incredible to them that we should prepare an expedition against Constantinople—the aim of Russia's hopes for centuries—and yet not inform Russia when she was our Ally.

Berthelot also told me that Sazonoff, against all his promises, practically gave away the Franco-British project to the Duma people, and then, of course, the news soon got round, penetrated to the Balkans, and infuriated Turkey, Rumania, and Greece. This negligence was the main cause of our undoing in the Balkans. Berthelot declared that the Franco-British union should remain the basis of all our policy in the future. I went back to the Embassy and saw Lord Granville, to whom I communicated these conversations confidentially. He knew nothing of the proposed pressure on Greece, nor of the origin of the promise of Constantinople to Russia. He said that he thought Lord Bertie knew nothing also, but H. E. was in the habit of writing private letters without communicating the contents to the Embassy. He therefore could not be sure, but he was much interested.

Dined with Mrs. Leeds in her rooms; then joined John Baird, and we started with the 11.40 P.M. train from Paris for Calais.

Tuesday, April 4. After a frugal meal found the car which Prince Alexander of Teck had sent for us, and motored to La Panne at breakneck speed. We had just time to clean ourselves up a bit before being commanded to go to the Palace (*alias* Villa), for an interview with their Majesties. Baird was late as usual, so I did not wait for him.

I found the Queen and King alone in the same modest

little villa on the beach. He was in khaki with putties. I told him of my recent experiences in France. We were getting on to interesting subjects when Prince Alexander came in with Baird, and we had to break off. We then had tea. The Queen had to go and fetch it because the bell would not ring. The worst of it was that unless one can get the King or Queen alone, or unless one is alone with the two of them, the conversation is limited to *banalités*. Baird and I both felt it, but the audience had been arranged, and it was too late to alter it ; also Countess Ghislaine was not there to help to arrange matters.

The Queen as charming and as witty as usual. She thanked me for keeping my promise to come and see her next time I went to France. The King looked very well. We all had a lot of talk about nothing of special interest ; five people meant formality. Royalties in a company and Royalties alone are totally different people.

I had a talk with Major Gallet, the King's Military Secretary, and also with Commandant Prud'homme, on my way to Boulogne next day, as well as with Prince Alexander and Captain Bridge of the British Mission. It appears that the Belgians have six divisions of infantry and two of cavalry, but I do not think that the divisions are strong. They have 70 heavy, and 300 field guns. They have 18,000 men training at Havre as reserves, but could take in many more men if they were available. The inundations on their front still hold, but there is a gap of 300 yards at Dixmüde, and the front is also open at Steenstraete, where they join on with the French division which is still between us and the Belgians. The Army has now khaki and the French casque khaki-coloured. The cavalry take their turn in the trenches. Their horses look in capital condition. The French have the *Groupement de Nieuport* on the left—more than a division—and another division at Steenstraete, making in all the 36th Army Corps. Foch at Amiens commands the Armies in the North, but what he does I do not know, as all his troops have been sent away. I do not approve of this Anglo-

Belgian-French salad in the North, and must state the fact clearly. There is a British naval commander with four 9·2-inch and some 6-inch guns acting with the French Nieuport group.

Dined with the Mission. There were the Prince, Bridge, two English ladies from the Queen's Hospital, and two naval officers. While we dined the telephone rang, and we heard news of the Zepps. in England, and also that others were coming towards us from Nieuport. One came over us, if not two, but they kept their bombs for Dunkirk, doing some damage there, and killing some people. We had a merry dinner and a lot of chaff.

Wednesday, April 5. Started at 9 A.M. with Prud'homme to Boulogne. Got on board the boat all right, thanks to Major Comber, the British Intelligence officer, who was most obliging. Lady Angela Forbes turned up. Saw the masts of a torpedoed ship off the harbour mouth. We were very full of troops returning on leave. All wore life-belts. Prud'homme reminded me that the Belgian constitutional law of 1832 only allowed the Belgian Government to call out eight classes of the Militia for the active field Army, so they only have men from 18 to 25 in the ranks. Efforts had been made to change this, and the King was most keen about it, but the Ministers at Havre could not see their way. The King has never once been to Havre since the war began. It was thought possible to take all Belgians in England by an agreement between the British and Belgian Governments. I must talk to Madame Vandervelde on this subject. I learnt that the Belgians had all they wanted—money, equipments, uniforms, etc. All that they wanted was more men.

We had a good crossing. When I came over by Havre the German submarines were off Boulogne, and when I returned by Boulogne they were off Havre.

Friday, April 7. Saw Mrs. Townshend at three. She showed me a wireless from her husband, thanking me for my letters. She was, of course, delighted with the progress of Gorringe's relieving force. I went on to the *Times* and told

Northcliffe the story of my visit to France, and what I had learnt. He thought, and I agreed, that we could not take up either Joffre's complaint of the weakness of our effectives in France, or the story of the Russian claim to Constantinople, without documents to support us, and, of course, there are none. However, I must find some means of seeing that the effectives are put right. Talked with Steed. Washburn just back from America on his way to Russia, and with Edward Marshall just returning to America. Marshall was on the *Sussex* when she was torpedoed.

CHAPTER VIII

RECRUITING AND SUBMARINE TROUBLES

Lord French's Commanders and troops—General Robertson's diffi-
culties about men—Verdun silences French demands for Salonika—
Sir Mark Sykes's visits to Tiflis—Mr. Balfour on the naval situation—
The submarine depredations—Mr. Bonar Law unconvinced about
the need for a Military Service Act—A crisis in recruiting—Mr.
Churchill on events—Turkish distribution—Stories of the late Lord
Salisbury—A visit to Beaconsfield—General Robertson on recruiting
and oversea campaigns—A visit to Hartsbourne Manor—Sir F. E.
Smith's views—Italian defeat in the Trentino—Sir W. Robertson
on the situation—Necessity for us to attack in France—Commodore
Sueter on past naval policy—The R.N. Air Service—The Jutland
Battle—Lord Kitchener drowned.

Saturday, April 8.   My article on 'The Heart of France';
many congratulations about it by telephone.   Will Rothenstein came in this morning to suggest the despatch of artists
to the front to make sketches for regimental histories and
the H.Q. of county regiments—a good idea, and should be
worked.   I will try Lady Cunard.

Lunched with Mrs. Astor; Mrs. Lavery, the wife of the
artist and a pretty woman, another American woman,
whose name I did not catch, Lord Basil Blackwood, and
another man.   We had an amusing talk.   Mrs. Lavery
asked me to come to her husband's studio about five any
day.   Went on to see Lord French at the Horse Guards,
at his request.   He has got on a bit with Home Defence.
He will be happier a month hence.   It is true that Lord K.
was blocking his proposals.   French had to go to the P.M.
in order to get Arthur Paget and Bruce Hamilton for his
two Armies, and Simon Lovat for his cavalry.   His defensive system, as far as I can see, mainly concerns itself

with the coast south of the Wash. Hamilton commands
the Northern Army, Paget the Southern. There are ten
battalions entrenched on the coast, and the two cavalry
divisions, each with 7000 cyclists, as a reserve. The two
Armies have four and six divisions respectively as their
main force, while French has two in reserve under his own
hand. Lawson organises the defence from Berwick to the
Wash, while French considers that Scotland is sufficiently
protected by the Navy. French considers that he has
absolute control of the whole of the troops in the United
Kingdom, the only exception being certain schools, and he
has the trains standing ready to move the troops in any
direction.

All the aircraft are manœuvred from a ' dug-out ' at a
certain place. He thinks he stopped two Zeppelin raids
last week from getting to London. The defect of his position is the low number and the poor quality of his troops.
The divisions have only from 5000 to 7000 men each ; moreover, 8000 men have just been taken away and replaced
by untrained Derby group men. He has his guns and horses,
including howitzers and heavies, but ammunition is short.
He counts a good deal on machine guns, of which he has
500 now at the schools, where the new machine gun companies are forming, and he thinks that he can count upon
their machine guns for three months longer. He admits
that his troops are not much good in an attack, but supposes
that they will do well in trenches. He has never believed
in invasion, and does not believe in it now ; but the Navy
will give no guarantee, as they cannot be off the coast for
forty-eight hours, and probably not for seventy-two ; but
he says that we must take risks somewhere, and he is prepared to take them at home. With this point of view I
absolutely disagree, and I must put my views on record in
a letter to him ; however, he thinks that he can take on
100,000 enemies. He thinks that London is all right for
aircraft guns, but that the arrangements for the rest of the
country are pretty sketchy ; however, he has been thanked
by Hull for having defeated the raiders.

Sunday, April 9. Sir William Robertson came up to my house, and we had a good talk. I told him first of my journey to France, and of my talks with the French. He had not heard that Haig had told Joffre that he was unable to carry out the wishes of the latter for want of men. He had no news from Antwerp, nor of events from Holland. No news also from Kut, but we have over 50,000 men in Mesopotamia, including 30,000 infantry, and plenty of guns, so he hopes for the best. Gorringe is in command, not Lake. In war good news travels fast, not bad. (Joffre had made the same remark to me.)

He had come up to see me about recruiting at home. Did I know the position ? I said Yes ; I believed we were 78,000 men short abroad and 50,000 short in the thirteen Territorial 2nd-line divisions at home. We had taken 250,000 recruits since Jan. 1, but we should have taken 540,000 to meet the W.O. plan agreed to by the Cabinet Committee of February last. It is three months, he says, since he laid the whole situation before the Cabinet, and he says that in effect nothing has been done, and we are as badly off as we were three months ago. Out of 195,000 men called up under the Derby scheme, 54,000 had failed to appear. We could carry on till August, but then the machinery would crack up, and we were threatened with increasing deficits from now on.

He said, It is impossible to go on unless something is done. Did I know what had already passed ? I said I had heard that he had written a strong short paper, dated March 21, and that it was very direct, and ended by urging that publicity should be given to the state of recruiting. Yes, said R. ; and he had further assembled the Army Council, and told them that they ought to express an opinion if they considered themselves a Council at all.

Robertson was determined to put the matter through, and thought that no good could be done with the present Ministers. It was useless to have a S. of S. for War who was not determined to get the numbers. There was only one remedy, namely, a General Service Law, but even this would not affect the situation for five months. He had seen Lansdowne, who was too old and indefinite. Balfour and Chamberlain no good; Curzon, he heard, was weakening. The only thing that he could see was Lloyd George. He was to lunch with the latter to-morrow, and meant to tell him to put the red cap on, and get going with revolutionary tactics. He thought that Lloyd George was all right, and L. G. and Carson had been together, so he supposed that the Carson party knew all the essential facts. Robertson's paper of March 21 had been struck out of the agenda of the Committee every time since March 21. I asked him why he did not refuse to attend until it was considered. He said that you never knew what was on the agenda paper until you arrived. Maurice Hankey arranged it to suit the Prime Minister. The question was how to get a move on and what machinery to employ? He hoped that things would come to a crisis in Parliament this week, but the question was how to proceed to get the men? What did I advise? I said a General Service Law, a sharp revision of the list of exemptions, which the Board of Trade Committee pretended to have curtailed, but appeared to me to have been made longer than ever, certainly in the amount of paper it covered; prolongation of military service for all serving men, Regulars and Territorials alike; and some other reforms.

He approved of these ideas. He was absolutely determined to see the thing through, and would not budge an inch from his position as stated to the Cabinet Committee in February. He was much hampered by the difficulty of getting men moved from one regiment to another. There had been a revolt on Salisbury Plain the other day on this account, and the men had ' boo'd ' their colonel. He was a poor man, but he was determined to resign if he could not get the men in the numbers accepted by the Cabinet Committee of February, numbers agreed to by the Board of Trade, and due to be found by the Government. It was too critical for him to accept any compromise.

I chaffed him about the Society ladies who pursued him. He told me that he had been the recipient of innumerable invitations to lunch from one lady, who in her importunity pursued him to the War Office, but that he had succeeded in resisting her blandishments. His 'pursuer' had tried to work on his wife, but had failed : but he understood the game, and was determined to stand clear of politicians, their wives, and the other great ladies who sought to lionise him for their own purposes. I heartily congratulated him.

Monday, April 10. Lunched with Lady Pembroke, Lady Anglesey, Lord Wimborne, and Sir John Cowans. We had some amusing and interesting talk. Wimborne very Guestish, and tried to find excuses for the Government for doing nothing about recruiting. The Army Council have drafted a hot memorandum to the Government, and it will be in this afternoon, so Robertson has triumphed thus far. Bee delightful on the subject of my *Heart of France*, and raved about it.

Wimborne seems to take his Irish duties very seriously, and to be full of good intentions. He complained that he was not told when the Irish regiments were short. There seems to be no connection between the recruiting branch and Dublin Castle.

Dined with Colonel Brinsley FitzGerald and Mrs. Tony Drexel at 63 Duke Street. We had a good talk about their position. It is a pretty good mix up, and I think that they would be wise to settle amicably. We sat up rather late talking about the case.

Tuesday, April 11. Dined with the Scarbroughs. Sir Mark Sykes and his wife and Lady Lytton were there. Very pleasant dinner. Mark Sykes very full of his visit to Tiflis. He had been twenty-seven days continuously in the train. He told me that the Grand Duke had only 120,000 men in the field, and that if we did not do something he would very likely be turned out of Erzeroum when the Turkish reinforcements came up from Constantinople. He said that the Turks had men at

Alexandretta. We were both in favour of a blow at this point. I passed this on to Archibald Murray in Egypt, from whom I have had a most interesting letter full of his ideas of the coming campaign.

Friday, April 14. Dined last night at Madame Vandervelde's, 10 Norfolk Square : she is the wife of the ex-Socialist Deputy, now Minister. She is English, I should think about thirty-five, good-looking, Rossetti type, very clever and intelligent. She has been speaking in America, where she made £60,000 for the Belgian refugees.

Mrs. Rothenstein was there, and I had a great talk about Belgium and the war. Madame V. is a great admirer of the Queen of the Belgians and still more of King Albert. She thinks that the Belgians are making things uncommonly unpleasant for the Germans, whom they appear to insult in every way. She does not think that the Germans have any intention of keeping Belgium. She says that Gallieni's resignation is not in the least due to health, as Bertier made out yesterday, and she declares that she has known about it for the last ten days. Her husband comes over about once a month from Havre. We compared notes about La Panne, and the strange, simple life of the King and Queen in their little villa. She agrees with me that Major Gallet is the best of the Belgian officers about the King. I thought she showed a tinge of jealousy about de Brocqueville, so perhaps her husband aspires to the leading rôle. She says that the Belgian Government have got all they want, including money, and that the French and English Governments support them. She was lost in wonderment at England supporting her Allies financially.

Lunched to-day with Arthur Balfour, Lord Robert Cecil, and Mrs. Sedgwick, and told them all they wanted to know about my visit to France. They were much interested, and asked me shoals of questions. As they left for the Cabinet, I told Balfour that he was going off to decide whether we should win the war or only draw it.

I found him still very unhappy about the naval situation, owing to the depredations of the German submarines, which have been unusually bad since I saw him last. He said that it was a matter that he could not discuss publicly, but it evidently harassed him very much. He said that some of our Allies were doing no good in their zone of operations. They limited themselves to hunting for the shore bases of submarines, whereas the sea was the only place to hunt them, and all our successes have been gained there. He says that the German nets and other preparations in the Sound had made it difficult for us to put more submarines into the Baltic. We had five or six there which had done splendid work, in fact all the work. The Russians, fifteen in number, had scarcely done anything. The Russians sent effete people to our boats, who learnt nothing, and they would not allow us to send our young officers on their boats to teach them how to handle them. This pride of the Russian Navy was a very serious disadvantage. On the other hand, it had been rather useful at Archangel. One set of Russian authorities had asked us to take over Archangel, the port, and all arrangements about everything. Balfour accepted, much against the grain, because he thought that the Russians would refuse him labour, and bungle all other arrangements, and then lay the blame for want of ammunition on England. Fortunately a second set of Russian officers had objected to the plan, and so Balfour was relieved of an unpleasant responsibility. We talked a lot about recruiting.

I asked him if he had any news about Antwerp. He had none. I advised him to try and get it, as I was sure the Germans were up to no good there. I reminded him that it was the best equipped continental port in Europe, and as we had made Zeebrugge and Ostend such unhealthy spots, he could be sure that the Germans, who had been eighteen months at Antwerp, were preparing an armament there. He thought that I referred to invasion. I said that this was important too, as a lot of ships were in the port when the Germans conquered it, but that I was referring to submarine warfare, and I said that when the Germans were ready they would violate the Lower Scheldt and come out. I did not think the Dutch could stop them, and I thought they could only make an ineffectual protest.

I am every day more profoundly impressed by the exemplary conduct of our Merchant Navy under the submarine menace. There has been no shirking at all, and if we pull through it will be mainly thanks to these fine fellows. Balfour does not believe in a military success in France ; he evidently thinks that by raising a large Army we are pouring men into a sieve. We had an argument on this point, but it is too long a story for me to set out in full. Balfour is always charming, and always interesting. He has more moral courage than any other of our statesmen, and therefore he is a great asset to us.

Saturday, April 15. Sir William Robertson and I lunched together at the Naval and Military Club. He was still very much exercised about the recruiting. Things could scarcely be worse. Down to the end of February we were 250,000 men short, including the recruits expected during the first two months of the year, and we were 75,000 men short on our establishment of troops abroad. The Derby scheme is simply not working out. Of 195,000 men who should have appeared between certain dates, only 38,000 have been accounted for. Of the remainder 27,000 had become attested, 33,000, I think, were rejected for unfitness, 19,000 were missing, and I think 27,000 unaccounted for. Generally speaking the unfit average 25 per cent.

Robertson has not got the Derby scheme written out yet, but we drew the broad general conclusion that recruiting was a farce.

Macready, the new A.G., I knew, had suggested the following measures : abolition of the ' starred ' lists, and every man of military age to justify himself before Tribunals ; power to the police to stop and arrest, if necessary, every man of military age without a certificate of exemption ; a Bill to restrict all men from taking a discharge until the war is over ; also a fresh Registration Bill on account of the long period of time which has elapsed since August last. Those are the main proposals. There are probably some other which I have forgotten.

I told Robertson that I agreed with Macready, though I thought 'bounties' to the time-expired Regulars would be fairer. Not many Territorials would care for a 'bounty.' What they want is two months' furlough to come and look after their affairs.

I told him the story[1] of John French, and Lord K.'s figures. Robertson capped it by another. He said that K. had told him that they had taken 175,000 men one month—I think it was January or February of this year. Robertson had queried the figure, and they had called in the A.G., and had it out. The real figures were only 62,000. K. had counted in all the people who *ought* to have come in under the Derby scheme ; this was quite another pair of shoes. He said that K. was very much upset at the discovery, and gave the late A.G. a bad time. Robertson left them, and went out for a ride, leaving K. to do the clerking. What a Government and what a War Office !

Macready would pull things round in time, and, at all events, the Government would know the facts in future. But Robertson was very anxious about the whole situation. His view and Macready's was that recruiting should be entirely in the hands of a civilian, and the War Office merely responsible for stating what they wanted. As things stood, the War Office got the odium for all the mistakes.

He had found Joffre all right this last visit, but he, R., was still unable to get any troops out of Salonika. Robertson was inclined to look into the Alexandretta raid question. Murray was doing well ; he would still have 200,000 men under him when the five divisions had come back to France from Egypt. The second of these—the 29th Division—was now landing, and the other three were following. R. had refused to send Joffre any more

[1] See Diary for March 10.

from England at present. His view is that once they are in France they are out of his hand, and he has no strategic reserve left to throw in anywhere. There are at present only two of the New Army divisions left in England, and the thirteen 2nd-line Territorial divisions. He hopes to squeeze Joffre into taking away the troops from Salonika after a bit. Verdun had silenced the cry for more troops for Salonika. He thought the Germans were all out at Verdun, so the French were all right. In the first three weeks the French had 60,000 casualties, and the Germans, he imagines, at least double.

He said he must keep a good force for Home Defence : he could not afford to be anxious when any German ship put to sea. As to Kut, he had taken Aylmer away and given Gorringe the command, and had also sent Lake up to the front. He thought Townshend could hold out till the middle of next month. Aylmer's last fight was fought with only part of the force in Mesopotamia ; most of the last division sent out from India had not come up. The situation was delicate because the river was rising, and it was uncertain whether any offensive could be carried on very soon. He was disposed to put Townshend in command of the advance afterwards. He thought there might be 60,000 Turks in Syria. He had asked the Grand Duke to squeeze the Turks on the Tigris.

Saw Mr. Bonar Law one day at the Colonial Office, and had a talk with him. Told him all my news from France. He is evidently not at all convinced that we want a law for Compulsory Service, and evidently agrees with the Cabinet Committee, which made out that they can get 1,000,000 men by a series of half measures. I did not argue the point with him, as he did not give me the estimates. He told me that in case his party would not follow him, he would come out of the Government.

All this week there has been a raging crisis over recruiting. Robertson has been very firm, and has dragged K. and the Army Council with him. They try to enmesh him in politics, but he stands out and says that it is his business to tell the Government how many men they want, and their business to get them.

I have seen a good many people almost every day. X. and I had tea with E. and Doris Keane one day. Doris had decided that X. was the only man left in England who interested her, and she had asked to meet him. She was perfectly charming and very amusing. She told him that she had expected to see an old man, with a face like a Wall Street broker, whom she would have to fawn upon, and she found a boy against whom she would have to defend herself. She gave me two photos, with a nice inscription.

Tuesday, April 18. Met Commandant Bertier and Lieut. Pernot at my club; General Egerton and McGrigor there also. The Frenchmen were at a loose end, so I telephoned to Lady Cunard, who allowed me to bring them on to lunch at Cavendish Square, where I was due. There were Lady Randolph, young Asquith, Yeats the poet, the Duchess of Rutland, and three or four more. An amusing lunch. Lady C. in very good form as usual. She is tenant of the charming house of the Asquiths. Lady Robertson came in after lunch and told me that Willie was keeping a stiff upper lip about recruiting. The P.M.'s statement on the subject this afternoon is to be postponed in order that an agreement could be sought, but it will be precious difficult. Mrs. Asquith told a friend that the P.M. will be out of office to-morrow, but I doubt it.

Wednesday, April 19. Lunched with Lady Randolph; Lady Juliet, Lady Cunard, Miss Joan Campbell, and another lady; W. H. Davies the tramp poet, and Eddy Marsh. Amusing as always. All pleased at the fall of Trebizond. Marsh, who is now secretary to the P.M., left Downing Street to-day before the Cabinet had risen, so he could not tell us what the decision was. Juliet very charming. Miss Joan very pretty and amusing. Lady Cunard full of fun, and of the scheme of painters' and poets' visit to the front. She has quite a long list of artists who want to go. The tramp poet appears to be a Welshman. He is short and very lame, and came in rough country clothes. Such a contrast to the immaculate and inscrutable Eddy !

Lady Cunard extolled the poet's works. None of the rest of us had read them, which was awkward for the poet. He spoke broadly—perhaps in Welsh. At periods he began extolling the virtues of ' Cat,' saying how mysterious and wonderful it was. We were all in Mesopotamia, and his pronunciation was so peculiar that we imagined he referred to Kut. Finally we tumbled that he was extolling the animal cat, but Lady Randolph did not see this, and at last we had to tell her, after getting hot and cold in turn. We discussed the vices and virtues of man and woman. Lady R. said that no woman ever loved a good man, and Juliet agreed, saying that it was the last thing that gave any satisfaction. Lady R. said that man had terrible advantages over woman, as he came into the cradle fully armed. I said that the woman did too, but I was howled down. Lady Cunard thought that a woman ought to have romance and a man sense of humour, and then we tried to define what sense of humour was, and on going round the table we found that every one thought they had it. A good lot of feminine political talk. Lady R. very pleased that every one had patted Winston on the back in the House yesterday. Lady X. had made a very audible remark in the gallery of the House yesterday. Mrs. Y. had hissed her down, where-upon Lady X. had said that she would not be hissed down by any woman. Miaou !

Thursday, April 20. Went to see Sir Ian Hamilton, who gave me an account of his journey to France to be ' Grand Crossed ' by Joffre. A division was paraded for him and looked very fine. Joffre made a great and very loud speech. He then hung the Grand Cross round Ian's neck. Ian then suddenly found the arms of this large person thrown round him, and himself kissed on both cheeks. The famous *accolade*! He had forgotten, and was taken aback by it. I said that I thought that they ought to appoint a pretty woman to do these things to avoid shocking our feelings.

We discussed the Eastern Mediterranean. Joffre had told Ian that the Turks had 52 divisions in all, each of 10,000 men. There were 11 against the Grand Duke, of which 6 had been more or less destroyed, and 9 more had been sent up from Constantinople, there were 2 at the Dardanelles, and 5 against us in Mesopotamia. There was no formed division now in Syria, as the two in the north had gone to Anatolia, and the two at Beersheba had gone north. I suppose the balance were at Constantinople, in Thrace, Smyrna, etc., but Sir Ian had not got the story quite pat. The Grand Duke had only 3 Army Corps, which corresponded with Mark Sykes's estimate of 120,000 men, and we agreed that things might be warm for the Russians presently. We also agreed that it was quite absurd that the Allies should have four Armies opposing the Turks, and that there should be no real co-operation between them. Ian is a little dubious about Murray, and doubts whether the latter will be able to do anything big. He thinks that he must have at least 200,000 men still, but admits that they are a very miscellaneous lot.

Dined with Lady Randolph. Winston and Lady Juliet were there, and Mrs. Winston came in just for dinner. We had a good yap at dinner, and up to midnight. Winston and I did most of the talking ; two very sympathetic listeners. Winston in good form, but getting rather bald. His battalion is going to be disbanded and broken up owing to shortage of men ; this will enable him to say that he has not left his battalion, because his battalion has left him.

All the boys from France have got extension of leave until next Thursday, so they will be present at the debate postponed by the Government till Tuesday next. Nothing is yet settled. Winston seems to want to form a strong opposition, and spoke in high terms of Carson.

Winston's mess of the last Navy debate has made his women folk very anxious for him to be prudent, but I was against this, saying that the recruiting demanded hard hitting and no compromise. Winston opposed hotly the Runciman policy of a half-war followed by a bitter peace ; he wants, as I do, war to the knife till we get what we want, and then a good peace and the pacification of Europe. He likes no more than I do Asquith cooing in answer to Bethmann Hollweg.

We talked of the Eastern Mediterranean, and I told him my Constantinople story from Paris. He did not deny it, but at the same time told me that before the naval attack on the Dardanelles began, he had communicated with the Grand Duke, then, of course, in chief command, who had made ready two Army Corps to help. But, of course, it does not necessarily follow that the two *Foreign Offices* had communicated with each other. We gave each other points for a big debate next Tuesday, and Winston gave me bits of the sort of remarks he would make on the points—very good and penetrating and clever, with some fine language. I was told that he had sat up until 4 A.M. with Garvin before his Navy speech. This accounts for the mess he made of it. I think he will speak next Tuesday ; he half protested that he will not, but, of course, much depends on the statement to be made by the Prime Minister. Winston declares that since he left the Admiralty, the submarines have been allowed to languish, and nothing has been done. He spoke bitterly of Balfour, but I told him he must keep off that lay, and that it was much better to leave Balfour alone. The big thing was to go for recruiting. I told him nobody could afford himself the luxury of personal jealousies in this war ; that the cause was much more important than the individual ; and that he must go for the big cause, and forget all rivals and animosities.

He said that he thought I had taken the right line all through the war. He had had a good send-off from the trenches. The soldiers all mad keen for him to go, hoping that he could do something for them in Parliament.

He does not think that we are strong enough to attack yet. Robertson, he thought, was doing very well; in fact had been perfectly splendid. We discussed old times in the Sudan and South Africa. We thought that Lord K. was no worse than old Buller. Winston very angry about Monro's despatch, and said that he had decided to evacuate after looking at the position for a couple of hours, but I did not argue this point. He spoke without enthusiasm of Douglas Haig. I wonder where we are to find any one better. We both agreed that French, in the sacred fire of leadership, was unsurpassed as a commander, and that Haig ought to have been made French's chief staff officer. Juliet described how French went to her hospital in Grosvenor Square, and the very charming way he talked to all the soldiers, and knew what their regiments had done, and where they had been. The soldiers acclaimed him, and raised cheers for 'Lord French of Wipers.' We heard some more odd names given by the Tommies. Their French for Etaples was 'Eatables.' Winston thinks we ought to make up our minds that, owing to the delay which has taken place, we should not be able to do a big thing until next year. He thought I would disagree, but found that I did not. He contemplates coming back to politics, and professed not to care what people say about it. I am very dubious on this point and let him see it. However, he says that he has been five months at the front in command of a battalion, and he thinks it gives him the right to speak. He still thinks Fisher worth all the rest of our admirals, but I advised him not to harness himself to a corpse. I said, You must find good young men among the sailors. He said that Oliver was splendid; he arranged all the movements, and always had ammunition and coal ready. Sturdee, after his action off the Falkland Islands, had only twenty-five rounds per gun left, and so wired to the Admiralty. Winston was horrified, as the *Von der Tann* was supposed to be loose, but he learnt that Oliver had an ammunition ship waiting at the Azores to join Sturdee. Sturdee had fired off nearly all his ammunition because he had engaged at such extreme range.

Good Friday, April 21. Went down to Wilton Park, Beaconsfield, to stay with Mrs. Astor. Found in the train Baroness D'Erlanger, young Rumbold, Professor Ross, now in the Intelligence Department,—one of the finest linguists in Europe—and Vansittart of the Foreign Office, and one other. Ross, Van, and I got into the fly, leaving the Baroness and two other men to go in the car. The flyman looked rather dubiously at us, and asked whether he should go to the front or the back entrance ! I could not stop laughing all the way to the house. They were both quite cross. I found Seymour Fortescue already there, and there joined us, at various times during the week-end, Lady Randolph Churchill, Lady Cunard, and Mrs. Phipps, a delicious little sister of Waldorf Astor. She is small and very pretty and all on wires, dances divinely, and sings charmingly to a guitar. Mrs. Cecil Higgins drove down from London with the American, Mr. Griscom, who is shortly returning to the States. Prince Wolodiecki, a Pole in the Russian Diplomatic Service, also came down with Wolkoff from the Russian Embassy.

A very nice big house in a charming park ; everything very comfortable. The fair Ava a perfect hostess. We had tennis, fishing, walking, Bridge, charades, music, and games, and fooling of every description. The Baroness a very pleasant woman, and still very good-looking. Mrs. Phipps dances extremely well. Both the Russians told me that Sazonoff had insisted upon 200,000 Russians being sent to Asia Minor to help the Grand Duke. More political strategy. We had a most cheery party, and were all very friendly and young. A capable cook and a good cellar did no harm. With Ross, Rumbold, and the two dancing ladies to act for us, and with Wolkoff at the piano, the evenings passed very pleasantly. Ross is a great loss to low comedy; he is most amusing; and Rumbold is a very clever fellow and a delightful mimic. Hinds, the pro, came down from Prince's, and there was some first-class tennis. Van is also a tip-top player, while the hostess and Mrs. Higgins were quite able to live in this good company, and both played admirably. Altogether a most successful Easter party. All my letters went to the wrong Wilton, or perhaps we ought to say to the right Wilton.

Tuesday, April 25. Picked up Lady Cunard, and went to lunch with the Duchess of Rutland in Arlington Street. The Duke was there and Lady Diana, also the fair Ruby Peto, and a wonderful Rumanian singer who looked like a young beau of the early-Victorian period, and two or three more. Lady Diana's last appearance in her hospital clothes, which suited her so well; she is very sad about it. Mrs. Peto in very good form, and always brilliant. After lunch I went into the Duke's sanctum to telephone, and he came too. We began talking about Lord Salisbury as a chief; we had both served under him, and knew his value. The Duke said that Salisbury was a very fine tennis player in his earlier years, that he was the kindest-hearted man he ever knew. He said that he often forged his signature by order. An immense number of the sprawling S.'s which I used to see over the despatches in the old days were written by him, the Duke. Salisbury used to like to lie at full length on his blue velvet sofa in Arlington Street, and have the despatches read to him. He would then dictate the answer, and get his friend Henry, the Duke, to sign them. The Duke said that Lord Salisbury used to be out shooting to the last, even rabbit-shooting in the park, in a tall hat and frock coat. I told him what a splendid chief he was to me when I was running the Secret Service. He said he loved very short despatches, and those that were to the point. He could not stand the long Treasury minutes, they made him quite ill. We also talked of Arthur Balfour, and vowed that he was one of the finest figures we had ever known. The Duke taxed Arthur one day with going about armed when he was Chief Secretary for Ireland. A. J. B. said that he was made to carry a pistol by the police; he pulled it out of his coat-tail pocket and threw it on to the dinner table, when the Duke, to his horror, saw that it was not only loaded *but cocked*! We went upstairs to Lady Diana's bedroom, which is in the back drawing-room, and the Rumanian gave us some music. A beautiful, rich, mellow voice.

The Secret Session duly took place this afternoon, ostensibly on the recruiting question.

Saturday, May 6. Went down to Coombe in time for dinner. Large party for the week-end. The Grand Duke Michael, Countess Torby and her two girls, Lady de Trafford and her girl, Mrs. Keppel, the Duchess of Westminster, Mrs. Bingham, and various others. Eighteen to lunch on Sunday.

Had a long talk with Sir Arthur about his defence arrangements. He tells me that they have at last stopped taking drafts away from the division which he has available on the coast. But still only half his troops are properly armed.

He had nine hours' notice of the Lowestoft raid. He is going to practise defence manœuvres on Tuesday.

The Grand Duke very snubby because I had not been to pay him a visit in response to his request. He apparently regarded it as a command, and he told me that he was greatly surprised that I had taken no notice of it. I made some lame apologies.

The Countess very charming. Her little daughter Nada, who is to marry young Battenberg, very pretty and pleasant, but shy. Weather bad; some of us spent our time playing Bridge, while the boys and girls played and danced and sang. The Grand Duke joined them, taking his coat off. The Countess plays a good rubber. Went for a walk,

Sunday afternoon, with Mrs. Keppel. Returned Monday morning to town.

Tuesday, May 9. Went to see the Grand Duke Michael at 3 Whitehall Court in the morning. General Yermoloff was there, and I had a talk with him. He agreed that the strategy of the Allies in the Eastern Mediterranean is not the way to make war, but he wanted me to go and discuss it with General Gilinsky, who is at Claridge's, and is leaving for Paris to-morrow. I did not follow this advice, because Gilinsky's opinion is of no value, as I learnt at The Hague long ago, and the Chantilly people merely sneer when his name is mentioned.

Went to see Sir William Robertson at his rooms. We began by talking about the Service Bill. R. told me of all the trouble he had had during the crisis, of the constant meetings of the Army Council, and of the splendid manner in which Lloyd George had held out for General Compulsion in the Cabinet. Now we have got what we wanted, and he asked if I was satisfied. I said, ' Quite satisfied, provided the proper separation allowances are made to the families of married men who join, and provided also that certified occupations are not allowed to block the way.' This is the line I took in the *Times* in an article yesterday. He said that he had told Macready, the new A.G., that he would now have to pan out for himself, and study the situation months ahead, with the view of producing a mass of men for the autumn, when the Germans tired, and not to come to R. unless he was in a difficulty. R. complained that all his time had been taken up lately with this recruiting crisis, and that he had not been able to concentrate on the strategy of the war.

He had been over to France, and had visited the depots at Etaples, Rouen, and other places, and had ordered up to the front a great number of men, leaving us only 29,000 men short at the front. He said that Haig had taken twenty divisions out of the line for training purposes, and that he was a shrewd Scot who would not do anything rash. He did not know what Joffre meant to do. At one time

Joffre was for an attack on May 1, and wanted us to co-operate, but no Germans had moved from our front, and it was at length agreed that the time had not arrived for the attack as we were faced by a practically equal force of Germans well entrenched. But R. said that we would have to do something if the French made a move. He told me that after my visit to France the French had suggested a move on Alexandretta, and he had replied that only a week before they had refused to let any men go from Salonika, and that he could not understand what they were driving at. I thought this rather a pity, and told him that the only way to get the troops away from Salonika was to give Sarrail the command of the Alexandretta operation, which would meet the case of keeping this hero out of France, which was Joffre's great object. I told him that I thought it very bad that we should have those four Armies fighting the Turks, and there be no co-operation except between two of them. I said, ' Leave 50,000 French with the Serbians at Salonika, take the rest to Alexandretta by sea, and let Archie invade Palestine.' I was still dead against all these sideshows, as he knew, but as we were not allowed by the French to take the troops away, it was better to frighten the Turks than do nothing. I told him that, if he did not watch it, the Grand Duke would be overwhelmed. I told him what the Russians had told me about the 200,000 more Russians, but Robertson did not think they were coming, and did not put the Grand Duke's force at over 150,000 men. We then discussed the horrible organisation of the Meso-potamia expedition, and R. said that he was considering taking over the control of India. I think he means to do it, but he said, ' Of course, we can only send directions and not orders to India.' He complained that in every depart-ment, in the India Office and elsewhere, people thought it necessary to write long papers on the strategical position, but that he had stirred them up in the War Committee, and made them cable direct to India. Barrow, in the India Office, had wished to send ' orders ' instead of R.'s suggested ' directions,' so R. had told them that they would then be entirely responsible and not Duff, so eventually R.'s paper was cabled out.   R. did not see why India should not be under him, as the Dominions were, for strategical purposes.   I told him my project to visit Italy and Portugal ; he thought of going to Italy too, and promised to take up my idea of raising six divisions of Portuguese troops. He was satisfied with his position.   People did what he suggested, and he had K. at the War Office completely under control, but munitions were not doing as well as was hoped, and many contracts were six or seven months in arrears, especially rifles, while the French were behind in their promises of shells for Russia.   He grumbled a great deal about the Russians, and said that he never knew where he was with them, or what they could do.   He was still strongly in favour of concentration in France, and thought the dispersion of our forces was our great weakness.   All these Turks and Bulgars would have remained quiet had we let them alone.   R. seemed very fit and well.   His visit to France had done him a lot of good.   He only spent one night with the G.H.Q. ; the rest of the time he was on the L. of C. and with the commanders of the 1st and 2nd Armies.   Not a German had been moved from our front since Verdun began.[1]   There was still no sign of fresh formations from the interior of Germany, but he had had to raise his estimate of German reserves, owing to the employment in Germany of prisoners and Poles.   Consequently Germany can still go on for quite a long time.

Wednesday, May 10.   Lunch with Winston Churchill, his mother, Jack Churchill, and his wife.   Winston in good form.   His battalion has been disbanded, so he becomes Mr. Churchill again, and is in a politician's kit.   He thought with me, that L. G. had missed a great chance in not coming out of the Government when the latter brought in the still-born Service Bill.

---

[1] Though we did not help the French at Verdun directly, we responded promptly to Joffre's appeal when Verdun was attacked, and, by taking over the front held by the 10th French Army, increased Joffre's reserves by ten divisions.

We went into the question of the P.M.'s 5,000,000 men, and I gave Winston the correct figures of what we had. He said that he was with Carson when my letter arrived before the Secret Session, advising him not to take part in it, and Carson was much disturbed. However, they had gone in, but fortunately the whole thing was a perfect farce, and most of what happened had already been told.

Winston will speak on the third reading, and I promised to help him with his notes. I told him that we ought to organise the whole of the resources of the Empire, especially India and Africa, as the Romans would have done in our case, and he says that he will adopt this line when he speaks. He was very excited over this idea, and stumped up and down after lunch, when we made point after point which he is to make in the speech.

Thursday, May 11. Lunch with Lady Strafford; the Spanish Ambassador, Mr. Lutyens the architect, Mrs. Higgins, Mrs. Keppel, Daisy de Brienen, and a pretty Mrs. Clyde married to some rich American.

Had a good talk with Miss Daisy about Holland. She said that some inferior German prince had written to Queen Wilhelmina, and not the Kaiser. This letter said that Germany was much incensed at the action of Holland, and threatened trouble about it. There was a hasty Cabinet meeting. Kühlmann used the opportunity to spread the idea through the Dutch Press, and even to telephone to the hall porters of the hotels, that, as a result of the Conference in Paris, England was going to deliver an ultimatum to Holland. There was a general racket, and it took some time for matters to cool down. Meantime Kühlmann is trying by every means to irritate Holland against us, and uses the most insidious provocations. She complains of some man of the *Daily Mail* doing a lot of harm by spreading silly stories.

Pretty little Mrs. Coke turned up after lunch. Drove back with the Spanish Ambassador. We discussed German atrocities, and he asked whether they had been any surprise to me. Considering that the principle of frightfulness had been preached before the war, I said that the only thing that had surprised me was that the Germans should be such idiots as to challenge the whole public sentiment of the world by their villainous acts, and that Germany had gained nothing by it, and lost more than she had any idea of. The Germans did not yet know how loathed they were, and how their name will stink in everybody's nostrils for generations.

The Spanish Ambassador said at lunch that there were only 50,000 Germans left in Spain, and he criticised the system which allowed the Germans to have a double nationality. They could be naturalised in England, and yet by their own laws they remained German subjects if they returned to Germany once in ten years. This would have to be stopped after the war. I quite agreed.

Went to the Russian Embassy to see Sevastopoulo, the Councillor of the Russian Embassy in Paris, who is over for a few days' leave. We were both a good deal happier than when we last met in Paris, for we had now got our Compulsion, and Verdun still held. We thought that the French were very tired of the fighting, and agreed that we and the Russians would have to relieve them. He was inclined to agree with me that we might have to wait till 1917 to carry things through with a strong hand. He surprised me by telling me that the Russians were prepared to lose Poland, which will become autonomous in one form or another, but that they would seek compensations in Asia Minor, and at Constantinople, which they were bent on gaining.

We discussed Asia Minor, and I told him my views : namely, as the French would not let us bring our troops west, to leave the Serbians and 50,000 Allies at Salonika, and to put 150,000 Allies from Salonika at Alexandretta ; for Murray to sweep up Syria, and for us to assemble a quarter of a million men south of the Taurus. I said, if we did not do something the Grand Duke might be overwhelmed. I told him that I was entirely in favour of concentration in France, but that as we could not get permission from our Allies to take the troops away, it was better that we should use them fighting somebody. He agreed very much with this plan, and said that he would try to promote it. He had been in favour of making peace with the Turks, but this was now at an end, as the Russians were bent on gaining the Straits. He agreed that if Sarrail went in command to Alexandretta much of the French opposition would vanish, and especially that of the French G.Q.G. He said that the Russians were very badly organised, and that there were even complaints from landed proprietors of lack of men ; the depots, on the other hand, were crammed full.

The French wanted more Russians sent over to France, but apparently this would not be practicable, though the French offered to arm them when they arrived. He confirmed Berthelot's story about Constantinople to the extent of admitting that he, Sevastopoulo, knew nothing about the attack before it began, nor did his Ambassador.

I promised to lunch with him and Berthelot in Paris if I went to Italy.

Monday, May 15. Dined with Mr. and Mrs. Ernest Cunard, 27 Portman Square ; Lady Paget, Mrs. George Keppel, Lady Sarah Wilson, Seymour Fortescue, and Lord Lurgan. A charming house, done up in excellent taste, the dining-room newly built out, and of a very perfect shape, with some attractive pictures. The dinner table decorated exclusively with old Waterford glass of a very fine quality. Most amusing talk ; all the ladies in very good form, and told some capital stories.

Wednesday, May 17. Lunched with Olive and Sir Vincent Caillard. He told me that three attacks had been made upon the East Coast, and that German transports had been sunk, but I don't believe it. We had a good deal of talk about the war. Went on to see Lady Byng at 14 Clarges Street, and heard all her news. Maxine Elliott called for me about 7 o'clock, and drove me down to her home, Hartsbourne Manor, Bushey Heath, about twelve miles from London. A very charming house, unpretentious outside, but standing in a fine position, with an uninterrupted view of hills, valleys, and woods. Beautiful gardens, with two of the new red sand tennis courts, and several grass courts. Very nicely furnished inside, and everything extremely well done. We had time to walk round the place before dressing for dinner. The Duke of Rutland, Sir F. E. Smith, the Attorney-General, Sir Forbes Robertson the actor, Mrs. (Margaret) Montagu, a pretty woman with very fair hair, and another lady were the party. F. E. was in great form. He rather astonished me by saying that after the war all the belligerent Powers would repudiate all their war debts, and that this measure would be universally approved. Not very good news for the holders of war stock. He had succeeded to-day in getting Sir Roger Casement sent for trial. He said that he had heard that I knew Casement, and did I think him normal? I said that I had only met him once at Brussels before he went off to the Congo, and that he was then apparently normal and very intelligent. He thought that Casement would certainly be convicted, but that whether the sentence would take its course would depend upon the Executive. He told me that a recent article of mine urging prudence before a general attack was undertaken by the Allies had created a deep impression on the Cabinet, and he urged me to repeat it, as he said there was an intention to begin an offensive soon, and he thought we should lose 300,000 men and do no good. I did not give any undertaking. F. E. said that for the last six months the soldiers had been running the war. He said that everybody had been wrong about everything during the war, that he, F. E., had been wrong as well as the financiers, politicians, soldiers, and sailors, and that Robertson had been wrong too. I attacked him upon the decision of the Government to feed the Poles, telling him that I had just learnt that 2000 railway wagons full of potatoes from Russian Poland had reached Austria and silenced the complaints of the people who wanted food, and that the *Reichspost* said that this operation was to be continued. I said that we were being made fools of, and that we should be

feeding the enemy and not the Poles. He replied that it
was not the Government's fault, it was a Russian decision.
The Cabinet had objected very strongly, and had telegraphed
again to Petrograd, pointing out the dangers, but that the
Russians had insisted. This is strange, as one of their
best economists has opposed this step most strongly in
the *Novoe Vremya*. We all agreed that the conduct of
the war by the Government has been lamentable, and some
one wondered how England had ever attained her present
position in the world. I suggested that we were the special
confidants of Providence, but the Duke said that Providence
had got tired of us and had found us out. F. E. said that
the capture of Casement was the only bit of luck we had
had in the war. We went to bed rather late. Maxine
a charming hostess. There were some beautiful pictures
of her in various parts during her career on the stage.

Thursday, May 18. Returned early to London.
Dined with General and Mrs. Bingham, 40 Hertford
Street ; Lady Wolverton, Lord and Lady Essex, Lady
de Trafford, Sir Fritz and Lady Ponsonby, O'Beirne,
Lady Granard, and Lord Ribblesdale. Very pleasant
party. We had some interesting talk, and some good
Bridge. I cut out and had a long talk with Cis
Bingham about his experience at home and abroad.
We went through the battle of Loos again, and discussed
the cause of the trouble that we got into at the end of the
fight. Cis is devoted to Lord French. Looked in to have
a talk with Mrs. Leeds about the Drexel divorce case. I
should judge a settlement probable now. Saw Mrs. Astor
in the afternoon. Ribblesdale came in later.

Friday, May 19. Gave up my visit to the Scarbroughs in Yorkshire, owing to pressure of Tribunal work,
and went off to see Winston Churchill in the morning at
41 Cromwell Road. We had a long talk over his proposed
speech for next Tuesday, and it should be a good speech if
he leaves it as we shaped it before I left. I begged him
to leave out all personalities, all reflections on the past,
and all egotistical remarks, and to take the big line. I

said, ' You have brilliancy to the point of genius, but we distrust your judgment, and you 'll have to correct that impression.' I told him that he ought to have a ' foolometer,' like Palmerston had ; that is to say, a man who would give him the opinion of the man in the street before he made a speech or wrote a despatch. He is going to discuss the whole conduct of the war, its future, and to bring in all my points about India, Africa, and the Eastern Mediterranean. He has a good library, and some nice books very well bound and cared for. Lunched with E. and Mrs. Grahame White at Claridge's. The latter full of fun as usual, so we had quite a merry luncheon. They drove me down to the Horse Guards afterwards, where I saw F.M. Lord French. He could not tell me much about the offensive in France, as he hears little from that theatre now. Murray also has not written to him from Egypt. He did not think that we were strong enough to attack, and said that not even an archangel from heaven could attack under present conditions. It was so frightfully expensive of men. He never went to Lord K. now, as the latter was quite hopeless and most obstructive, but Robertson told him everything that was going on. The troops in England were coming on well ; there were more rifles now, and also more guns and maxims, but he was still far from satisfied, and said he had only eight divisions on which he could count, now that one had been sent to Ireland. He admitted that he had been so wrong about the German reserves that he could not even suggest how many there were now. He asked me to come round and see the Home Defence system with him, so that I could write about it later on, and, of course, I agreed to do so whenever he liked to invite me. He had been testing his troops in the eastern counties, using trawlers to represent hostile destroyers, and was rather surprised to find how close they could lie in to the beach. They got in within 1300 yards of some of his trenches, which he had to deepen in consequence to avoid the effect of 6-in. gun fire. He told me that George Moore would not be back for some months. The case against the *World* would not be given up until the paper had disclosed the origin of its malicious article. The printers of the paper had come to heel, and agreed to pay a heavy fine, but he was determined to discover the names of those who inspired them.

Tuesday, May 23. Saw Winston at his house at eleven, and went through his speech, which he read to me. We discussed the points. It is all on the conduct of the war, and there is less of Winston in the speech than in any that I have ever known of his. He is going to speak after Asquith to-day, and I think it will have a very good effect. He is taking up most of my points, especially about Africa and India, and has fortunately eliminated from the beginning of the speech his dictation of the strategy.

E. picked me up and took me to the Flower Show, where there was the usual crowd, but fewer new plants than most years. Commander Thurston lunched with us; he is in the Naval Flying Corps, and goes round to look after the aeroplanes and seaplanes. He is just back from Dunkirk, where we have 200 machines. He considers the limit of the aeroplane carrying bombs to be about 150 miles, and admits that the aeroplane cannot compete with the Zeppelin for long-range scouting. He says that he is scrapping 100 machines a week, many of which unfortunately have never been used. We spoke of Commodore Sueter, and in the evening he telephoned, asking me to call on Sueter at the Admiralty. Thurston deplored the disunion between the Army and the Navy Flying Corps, and said it was all due to the jealousy of senior officers. Wrote an article on the Italian campaign. The Italians have had a nasty knock in the Trentino, and have lost 20,000 prisoners and over 100 guns. I met one of the Italian Embassy lunching with Mrs. Grahame White, Lady Ashburton, and Mr. Chilcot. They were all very jolly, and I sent word to Imperiali about my Italian visit.

Saw Sir William Robertson, 6.30, at 4 South Street, a pleasant furnished house which he has taken, as he says, until he sees whether he is kicked out or not. I told him that one of the Ministers, whom I did not name, had asked me to write against an offensive this year, and had said that we should lose 300,000 men and do no good. I told R. that I could write nothing of the sort until I knew his views. I also told him that the ministerial pose just now was to say that the whole war was being run by the soldiers. Robertson said that Joffre had first wanted the offensive in March, but that we had held out as we were not ready. Joffre then wanted it May 1, but this time he postponed it. R. was fully aware that we were not yet ready, but we had now nearly fifty divisions, 2300 field guns, 18-pounders, and 1200 heavy guns, including 4·5-inch howitzers, so we were double as strong in guns as we were at Loos. We should steadily grow stronger, especially in heavy guns, and it was impracticable to say to our Allies that we should wait till next year to attack the enemy. The French had lost a great lot of men, especially at the beginning of the war, and at Verdun they had had perhaps 150,000 casualties already. They were not rich in reserves for drafts, and it was certainly true that the German attack had done something to exhaust the number of French divisions in reserve,[1] for there were thirty-nine when Verdun began three months ago, and there were now only twenty-five. There was also a very natural feeling in France that it was time we did something. The Italians were also now shouting for their Allies to set to work, while the Russians told him that though they knew they were not ready, they thought it better to attack as the Germans might concentrate quicker than they could on some point of the 700-mile front, and make things unpleasant. Therefore, when everything was put down, and all consideration given, he did not think that the offensive could be ruled out, and he left me with the impression that it would come fairly soon. He was to see Joffre on Friday, and perhaps he would then be told where it was to be, but this part of the affair he left to Joffre and Haig. He thought, as I did, that the southern part of the line we held offered the best chances, and we both pre-

[1] Seventy-two French divisions were used at Verdun from first to last.

ferred that the two Armies should fight shoulder to shoulder than that there should be two widely separated attacks. We both deplored the continued absence of the Allied Army at Salonika, where it had done no good, and R. did not wish to attack the Bulgarians, who are well entrenched and will probably do nothing if we leave them alone. But at present the French were as obdurate as ever, and I reminded him that I had told Briand that history would be very severe upon him in case of failure in the West for keeping a quarter of a million men doing nothing in Greece.

R. said he was getting back all the troops he could from Egypt, but we still had 200,000 men there. They were rather a nondescript lot ; he did not think that Murray could march into Palestine. He hopes that the Grand Duke will be able to maintain himself. The Turks on the Tigris had detached a force against General Baratoff, and the Grand Duke wanted Lake to march about 120 miles over a horrible country without food and water to help Baratoff who had gone to ground. A nice prospect ! R. is still entirely for concentration in the West. With regard to Ireland and the late rebellion, R. said that if the civil power required troops to suppress rebellion, it was their duty to ask for them. All he dealt with was external aggression. He was bringing up to-morrow the question of the General Staff taking control in India. He did not understand the position of the two forces on the Tigris, ours and the Turks, and had cabled an inquiry to-day. We have from four to six divisions there. He said, ' This is the general position as it occurs to me, and if any better ideas occur to you, put them on paper and send them to me.'

R. looks uncommonly well, and is quite at his best. He says it is no good worrying, one can only do one's best, and he referred to Wellington's visit to Blücher before Ligny. The old Duke said that Blücher would be damnably beaten, and then rode off, and went to dinner without troubling himself further upon the matter. R. gave me his opinion of the Italians, and chuckled about the Prime Minister having come back full of enthusiasm about them just before they had been licked. He thought the position serious, as the Austrians had sixteen divisions in the Trentino on a twenty-mile front, and were within thirty miles of the Italian railways.

Wednesday, May 24. Wrote an article yesterday on the Austrian attack upon Italy from the Trentino, and to-day wrote another on Verdun, gently hinting that the question of an Allied attack depended upon a set of considerations which were very complex. Nothing in it to guide the Germans at all. Met de la Panouse at my club. He was very anxious to know what resources for recruiting would be immediately available under the new Act. Would all the time-expired men be brought in ? I said I thought they would. How many would this mean ? Would there not then be a large number of men who had been trained for three or four months at the depots, and would not the 2nd-line Territorials in England be available for drafts ? I told him all I knew on these subjects, and said that the Act would now give us plenty of men, but that there were two faults, namely, the list of certified occupations which still permitted the *embusqués* to escape service, and, secondly, the Barrister Commissioners which might be a cause of great delay. We had a little talk on the strategy of the War, and I found him very keen that our Armies should do something. We also discussed politics, and agreed that our respective Labour men were much more useful than the Radical-Socialists in France, and the Radicals here. We agreed that things looked unpleasant in Italy.

Went to the Admiralty to see Commodore Sueter. An agreeable sturdy-looking sailor with a bright eye and a good head. He had evidently been much gratified at my remembering all about his book on submarines and his various prophecies which had been so well justified during this war. He had great difficulty, he said, in publishing that book, and had been made to cut out a great deal of it. He deplored the departure of Winston, who, he said, kept them all on the move at the Admiralty, and compelled them to be constantly at work and on the alert. He and Winston had practically run the Air Service between them. Now there was chaos. The young men could not get their way. No one, in his opinion, controlled the Naval Air Service, and that was the way we were making war. He had been a strong supporter of the dirigible ; and at a time when I was preaching it in *Blackwood* and being criticised by a pack of fools, he was preaching it at the Admiralty and had been turned down in succession by Sir Arthur Wilson, Prince Louis of Battenberg, Admiral Bridgeman, and Admiral Pakenham. It was impossible to get the new ideas through the old men. As a result our Navy was now blind, and the Germans had an enormous advantage over us. The Zeppelins watched the North Sea all the time. They could see up to seventy-five miles on a clear day, and whenever any of our ships put out, their number, type, and course were immediately reported to Germany. They held us under constant observation, and so, knowing where our ships were, could slip over when they pleased, and carry out such attacks as that at Lowestoft. Count Zeppelin had been ten years experimenting, and had lost many dirigibles before he got the right type. Now there were a great many, and we could not catch up during the war.

He showed me two specimens of the Zeppelin petrol tanks that had been dropped in Essex from about 2000 feet up when they were empty. They were sixty-gallon tins, beautifully made of aluminium, and so light that one could lift them with one finger. One of them was only a little dented after its fall, and the other only slightly broken. The sea and aeroplanes could not compete with the dirigible for long-range scouting, and, apart from engine endurance, the physical strain of piloting a plane was very great, whereas in a Zeppelin the pilot could sit in an arm-chair. He did not think it could quite be said that the Zeppelins had no military effect, for they caused work to stop, held up the railways for thirty hours sometimes, and made all the workmen run home to look after their families. He thought that a visit of forty Zeppelins would do a rare lot of harm.

But, of course, the scouting at sea was the main thing. We had eleven rigid dirigibles under construction, including one of the Italian type, the drawings of which had been sent to him by Delmé Radcliffe. There were some twenty non-rigid and a lot of little ones. The first rigid would be ready in June. We should have four or five by next spring. He agreed that the Germans, though bested at sea, would try always to be superior in the air. He thought that our future Navy would be above the water and below it. We should have submarines coming along one day with 12-inch guns on board. He said that the other day a sea-plane, one of ours, had attacked a German submarine near Harwich and driven it under water. It lost its bearings, ran aground, and was left high and dry when the sea went down. It was then captured intact apparently. I said that it should be shown to American correspondents and he agreed. Most of the German submarines which we had destroyed had been caught in nets, or bombed under water, and will never be seen again. At present the R.N.A.S. at Dunkirk was under the Admiral at Dover. Sueter wants an Air Ministry which would control the whole service, handing over to Navy and Army the resources which each required, and organising raids, reconnaissances, etc. I spoke to him of our failure to know what was going on at Antwerp, and of the danger of the Germans coming out by the Scheldt. Why did the First Lord not know what was going on there? Sueter said, because no one had asked us to go there. We can do it. Mahan, I reminded Sueter, had criticised our Navy for never producing any written work of any sort. We agreed that we would meet at the end of the war and see if we could not get on a bit.

Went to the Leicester Galleries, and saw Will Rothenstein's collection of drawings. They included one of me, not very good, and others of H. G. Wells, Madame Vandervelde, Johnny Hamilton, Mrs. Rothenstein, W. B. Yeats, Tagore, Gosse, and many others. A good lot of people there. We all had tea in a stuffy little Lyons' restaurant adjacent.

Week-end, June 3 to 5. Sat on the Advisory Committee all the morning. Went to see Miss Muriel Wilson in the afternoon in order to advise her about her brother, Jack, who was captured by the Austrian submarine in the Mediterranean with despatches.

He is anxious to be exchanged, but she is doubtful whether it is not all best left alone. We finally agreed that I should sound the Foreign Office and see how they regard what he has done, and that she would sound Lord K.'s FitzGerald and find out the War Office view. Her little house in 25 Charles Street very perfect and in excellent taste. I thought Laszlo's last picture of her perfectly charming, and very finely painted.

Went to Lady Sarah's, and she drove me down to Maxine Elliott's. Very jolly week-end, only spoilt by vile weather. Winston Churchill and his wife, Sir Forbes Robertson and his lady, Lord Drogheda, Sir F. Sinclair, Captain Foster and his wife, Millicent, Duchess of Sutherland, and Mrs. Montagu ; Miss Muriel Wilson came down on Sunday.

A little tennis the first evening. Sunday morning Winston and I spent going through the Dardanelles story, which appears to me to implicate the whole Cabinet as well as Balfour in the scheme of the attack, and also involves Lord K. in full responsibility for all the decisions. Lord K.'s letter of instructions for Sir Ian Hamilton is one of the most infantile papers that I have ever read, and will be the laughing-stock of the whole of the Staffs of Europe if it is ever published. We had a good talk over the whole question practically all the morning.

Had a long talk later with the Duchess over all her experiences in France and Belgium during the war. Her story of Namur was most interesting. What a wonderful woman ! She could easily be taken for twenty-five, and takes most of them down for good looks even now. She told me that she was not in the least missing the gilded halls and all the pomp of Stafford House, and found such a deep interest in life and in events that she was perfectly contented. She thought that she was still an adventuress seeking new experiences. Her hospital is now outside Calais by the Gravelines Gate. She disturbed me to some extent by declaring that the spirit of our men, judging from the cases which came under her hands, was not as good as it formerly was; but she excepted the Australians, who have only just arrived. I told her all about affairs here.

Winston was full of the naval fight off Jutland. He had been asked to issue the semi-official *communiqué* which appeared in Sunday's papers, June 4, and was not quite sure whether he had done right or not. Balfour's private secretary had made the demand, whereupon Winston had consulted L. G. and Rufus Isaacs, who said that he could not refuse, so he returned to the Admiralty, and said he would draft something if Balfour personally asked for it. This Balfour did.

Winston thinks that the success of the German Battle Cruiser Squadron against our superior squadron of similar type is a very serious matter and requires investigation. I agreed, but we are evidently very badly informed of all these events as yet, and cannot draw conclusions.

Maxine's party very delightful. There were six of the prettiest women in London there, and she says that she always has the prettiest women at her parties. Winston said that the dinner party on Sunday night was like an orchid house, so lovely were the feminine flowers and so varied. We played some amusing games after dinner.

I thought Forbes Robertson very charming and with a beautiful mind, and I liked talking to him. Mrs. Winston is a very sweet lady.

Friday, June 9. The torpedoing or mining of the *Hampshire*, and the drowning of nearly every one on board, including Lord Kitchener, O'Beirne, and FitzGerald, is a great tragedy. They were on their way to Russia, and were blown up off the Orkneys. The news came while many of our friends were selling at a bazaar in the Caledonian Market, and the women of the East End shed tears at the news. We hoped against hope, but no doubt now remains. A great figure gone. The services which he rendered in the early days of the war cannot be forgotten. They transcend those of all the lesser men who were his colleagues, some few of whom envied his popularity. His old manner of working alone did not consort with the needs of this huge syndicalism, modern war. The thing was too big. He made many mistakes. He was not a good Cabinet man. His methods did not suit a democracy. But there he was, towering above the others in character as in inches, by far the most popular man in the country to the end, and a firm rock which stood out amidst the raging tempest. In FitzGerald we lose K.'s best staff officer, and in O'Beirne, a man who must have gone far in diplomacy. A very sad day's work.

CHAPTER IX

A TOUR IN ITALY, JUNE 1916

The Salonika offensive temporarily abandoned—Preparations for our attack in France—Havre—Colonel Driant and General Joffre—Lord Esher's Mission—M. Berthelot on the last London Conference—Verdun losses—Views at Chantilly—Journey to Italy—Venice in war time—Italian strengths and dispositions—Udine—Italian and Austrian forces—Russian plans—General Diaz—A visit to the Isonzo and Carso fronts—General Porro—The Carnia front—A mountain fight—Audience with the King of Italy—The General Staff Bureaus—Bulgarian and Turkish dispositions—Aquileia—Visit to the Trentino front—General Pecori Giraldi—A talk with General Cadorna—The administrative services at Treviso—Colonel Enkel's views—The Cadore front—Italian Alpini—General di Robilant's views—The Asiago battlefield—News of our Somme attack—Return to Paris.

June, 1916. Early in May I represented to Geoffrey Robinson, the editor of the *Times*, that it would be a good moment for me to go to Italy. The worst crisis at Verdun seemed to me to have passed, and we were not likely to do anything very big in France till late in June at the earliest. I told them that it would take three weeks after they had come to a decision on the subject for me to make all the arrangements. They could not make up their minds at the *Times*, but, about a fortnight later, there came a letter from Delmé Radcliffe, head of our Military Mission in Italy, begging me to come, and saying that he would arrange it all. This helped matters a good deal, and ultimately all the arrangements were made.

Monday, June 12. Before starting I called upon Robertson at his house, 4 South Street, Mayfair, in order to see if there was anything fresh. I found him very anxious that the Italians should press on as fast as possible, and drive the Austrians out of Italy. He told me that the Conference in London with the French had resulted in the decision to abandon the offensive at Salonika. But he said that a paper was going forward, suggesting the possibility of an attack later, when possibly the two more British divisions required by General Sarrail would be available. Robertson had not changed his views, and still wishes to withdraw our troops. The 4th Australian Division from Egypt was now arriving in France, and the 5th was following it. We should then have fifty-one divisions in France, with some others to come later.

In reply to a question of mine, he said that he hoped that all our troops in France would attack and not only one Army. The French would go in on our right, but there would not be so many as he had hoped, and he supposed that the French could not spare more men from Verdun. The Russians were to make their main offensive to-day or to-morrow in the North. He thought that they had done very well, for Brussiloff had not many guns, and this success was quite unexpected. He thanked me for having sent him a private account from France of the fight at Vimy on May 21, and said that he would always be glad to see similar reports.

He declared that we were ready to fight long before the French, who had been putting off the attack ever since May 1. With regard to the successor of Lord K., Robertson would prefer Lord Milner, but did not expect to get him. It was impossible to carry on with Asquith at the War Office. He had been away since last Thursday, June 8, and had only come back for a moment, and was now away again in North Britain on a political tour. Meanwhile shoals of telegrams kept coming in, and many things had to hang about for the Secretary of State's decision, and R. thought that war could not be carried on in this sort of way, and I don't wonder.

Tuesday, June 13. Started at 9.30 P.M. from Waterloo to Southampton, and went on board the boat. Arrived at Havre at 10.30 A.M. next morning.

I met General Asser on board. He has been transferred from Boulogne to Havre, and promoted major-general to make up for his disappointment in not going to Egypt. He is a first-rate man at his work.

There was no train to Paris till 5 P.M., so I went round and called on some of the Belgians, whose political H.Q. are now at Havre.

Most of the Ministers are away, but I saw General Jüngbluth the King's A.D.C., and Vandervelde's *chef du cabinet*, besides some others, and had some interesting talk. They are short of news from Antwerp, and it is odd that they cannot find out from any one what is happening there, nor does any one in England take any interest in the fact that the Germans have been in possession of the finest port in Western Continental Europe for the better part of two years, and have certainly been up to no good there. Jüngbluth thought that things were looking well, and that the Kaiser must know that the game was up. He was satisfied with the political and military outlook.

Slow journey to Paris, arriving twenty-four hours after leaving London. It is quite evident that the desire is to discourage travelling and to throw every obstacle in the way of travellers. Put up at the Ritz and saw various friends. It appears that Briand is in trouble, and is likely to have a warm time with the Chambers. It seems that the late Colonel Driant, Boulanger's son-in-law, who was killed before Verdun and was a member of the Chambers, had come to Paris on Dec. 18 of last year, and had given full information to the Army Commission of the bad state of the Verdun defences. Joffre had replied on the 22nd contradicting Driant's statement, and making some harsh remarks about this fashion of going behind his back. However, Driant had been proved to be in the right, and the Opposition intended to attack Briand, whose fall would mean that of Joffre, and probably that of Castelnau, which would be a very serious matter.

Thursday, June 15. Went to see Lord Esher at Meurice's at 9.30 A.M. He is on a special mission, and I expressed my curiosity to know what it was. The real aim was, it appears, to give Lord K. information of what was happening, and no one is better able to do that in Paris than Esher, who knows all the soldiers and politicians, speaks French well, and is very shrewd, discreet, and industrious. Now that K. was dead, he was doing the same work for X. We had some talk about affairs, and agreed that the best person to be at the head of the British Peace Delegation would be Lord Lansdowne, whose knowledge of French and great experience would be priceless.

Lunched with Countess Greffuhle and Countess Ghislaine de Caraman Chimay. A beautiful house with some fine French furniture, decorations, and pictures of the eighteenth century. We talked of her convalescent establishments, and she told me that 2,000,000 Frenchmen had passed through the hands of her societies. Jules Roche the Deputy came in and talked in an interesting way. I am glad to say that he thought that Briand was safe this time, and Roche is a pretty shrewd parliamentarian, and likely to be right. Went off with the Countess G. to see her exhibition of eighteenth-century French art in the Champs Élysées. Some fine tapestries from the Ministries, and furniture, clocks, and pictures from various collections. I was so interested that I was late for an appointment with Esher, who was to have taken me to the *Matin*. Went on to the French Foreign Office and saw Berthelot. Everybody tells me he is so anti-English, but I have never seen a trace of it. He said that the last Conference in London had dealt with three subjects, namely, Salonika, Greece, and the Great Offensive. He said that the attack at Salonika had been postponed, mainly because we would not find the two more divisions demanded by Sarrail, but he has hopes that the difficulty will be overcome, and that an offensive will be undertaken late in July or early in August. There was a negative result on the discussions relating to Greece, but yesterday and to-day telegrams have been sent to London by the French, recapitulating and giving fresh instances of Greece's duplicity towards the Allies, and urging strong action, failing which the French propose to take it alone. On the subject of the offensive in France, Berthelot admitted that we had done everything that the French had asked of us.

I saw Lord Granville at the Embassy before and after my talk and had a good chat with him. Philippe Millet came to the Ritz before dinner. He is at the Maison de la Presse, and I must try and pay a visit there. At dinner were the Lewises, Eshers, Ian Malcolm, Lord Newton, Sir Walter Lawrence, and the Aga Khan. The latter was as well informed as usual, and appeared to know all about the arrangements for the offensive. Talking with various people in the evening made me fear that both our own and the French share in the offensive would not be powerful enough to lead to decisive results. Berthelot had told me that the French had lost 197,000 men before Verdun, and the Germans 450,000. The German figures were known accurately because the French had found out the German cipher.

Friday, June 16. Started at 8 A.M. for Chantilly. Had a talk first of all with Yarde-Buller. Then went to see General Pellé. We discussed Italy. He said that there were thirty-three Austrian divisions on the Italian front, of which some fourteen were in the Trentino. There were three south of the Danube, and then forty others on the Russian front, twenty-six of the latter having been already engaged and severely mauled, losing 150,000 prisoners up to this date in addition to other casualties. Pellé thinks that the Austrians are now securely held in the Trentino by superior forces. He imagines that Italy could attack simultaneously on both fronts if she wished. But an officer in special charge of this theatre came in and said that the Italians would not attack on the Isonzo when their hands were full on the other front. Pellé expressed his great satisfaction with the British preparation for the offensive, and spoke of the wonderful improvement that had been made in the training of our troops, and in the number of our heavy guns. But he still complained that too many of our divisions were left in England, and thought that, after the Jutland fight, any further talk of invasion was absurd. But then Pellé has not the responsibility for defending England. He said that there were now fifty-two British divisions in France, and that there were a few more to come. He felt fully assured that we should go in with all our weight. I told him of my qualms concerning the amount of the French support, but he assured me that Foch would have all the troops that could be spared, and a particularly formidable artillery. He admitted, however, that there were fewer troops with Foch than originally intended, but he said that others would come up in order to admit a continuous and persistent advance. The Russians, he said, were on the point of attacking in the North. Dupont, head of the French Intelligence and a capable man, showed me the map. Hindenburg has taken seven divisions out of his line and has posted them in a semi-circle east of Vilna, evidently anticipating an attack at this point. The 3rd Guard Division from the Austrian front is now in Champagne. The 7th German Corps from the British front is now before Verdun as well as the 1st Bavarians, but the 3rd Corps, formerly at Verdun, is now resting at Charleroi. According to the German official casualty lists, this Corps lost 15,000 infantry before Verdun.

Pellé gave me some important papers showing that the German 1917 class was now arriving at the front, and that many of them had been taken prisoners. The class of 1918, who are seventeen years of age, were now beginning to reach the German depots. It was also shown on these papers that the German regiments in France were being filled up from the depots of the German regiments in Russia. Another paper gave interesting extracts from letters of prisoners, judging from which there is real want, approximating to famine, in Germany, at all events among the lower classes. Dupont was unable to give me the figure of the German reserves still available, owing to the way in which the Germans had compelled the Poles and the prisoners of war to work in factories and in the fields, but he thought that the use of men of the age of seventeen and eighteen showed the state to which Germany was reduced, and that there were only the *récupérés* besides. The French appear to think that the Italians have fought well on the Isonzo, but that the partisan fighting in the mountains was a bad preparation for the tremendous bombardment with which the Austrians opened their offensive from the Trentino. It is thought at Chantilly that all the Austrian divisions in the Trentino, except one, have now been engaged, and that the Austrians are completely checked. I was told that the Italian Reserve Army in Venetia is now grouped round Bassano, and that a good Army Corps—the 20th—is now attacking in the Brenta Valley. I always enjoy my visits to Chantilly because I find the French G.Q.G. well informed and with clear-cut ideas.

Lunched with Sevastopoulo, 27 bis Quay d'Orsay. Colonel Ignatieff the Russian military attaché, M. Grosclaude a *Débats* man, M. Bidou who writes their military articles, and a Russian secretary. Wrote a short article to the *Times* in the afternoon, and gave it to Adam to send over. It contained a budget of letters found on German prisoners, almost all complaining bitterly of want of food in Germany. Adam dined with me, and Esher came and talked with us. Left Paris for Italy at 8.25 P.M. A good sleeping-car service, most comfortable, and an excellent train.

Saturday, June 17. Arrived at Modane at 10 A.M. Lieut. Lazzarini, station commandant, helped me through the Customs, and was very agreeable and useful. The French and Italian crops look uncommonly well. Much snow still on the hills quite low down, and it snowed last Monday. Mountain streams moderate, main rivers fairly full, notably the Adige. Roads in good order. Saw much Italian hay on the way to France. Went by Turin to Milan, where I dined at the Hotel Cavour, and so on to Bologna, where I put up at the Hotel Baglioni. Saw an immense number of young fellows not yet in the Army. A general air of well-being and content, and very little mourning to be seen about. I was harried late at night by several reporters whom I refused to see. One, a local editor, knocked at my door at 1 A.M., and asked to see the 'most illustrious Colonel Repington,' who refused to get up.

Sunday, June 18. One of the reporters caught me in the hall as I was leaving. I said a few words to him, and he spun it out into two columns of pure invention. These Italian reporters are terrors. Left at 9.30 P.M. for Mestre, near Venice. Warm but cloudy day, lunch in the train. The news in the papers continues to be good from all fronts. The Italian crops look so fine that I expect the Austrians are after them. Many people travelling, and a general air of gaiety prevails, so different from France. It is obvious that the Italians have felt the burden of the war very little hitherto, or else they are uncommonly light-hearted.

Arrived at Mestre at 3.15 P.M. Heard that Delmé Radcliffe was expected at Venice to-night from Rome, so I went on there. Took a gondola from the station to Danielo's Hotel. We traversed the Grand and other canals. The population of Venice seems to have fled, nearly all the big palaces are shut, and scarcely another gondola was working. It is delightful. if selfish, to have Venice to oneself. The place is looking very beautiful, and the weather is divine. I have a large window overlooking the lagoon, and a certain number of people turned up in the evening to walk about on the front. Delmé came in when I was dining, and after dinner we went out in a gondola on the lagoon for a couple of hours. It was very beautiful and still, a fine night, the moon rising a little before midnight.

Delmé told me that the Italians had mobilised 2½ million men, and that their total casualties had been between 600,000 and 700,000 men in one year of the war. They have forty-eight divisions in the field, besides special troops. There were probably nearer one million than three-quarters in the field. Strengths were well maintained, and the depots were full. The field depots contained up to 50 per cent. of the effectives at the front. The new Army Corps were numbered 18th to 26th Divisions, average only 32 field guns each, and all told there are probably no more than 500 heavy guns.

The Italians gave 400,000 rifles to Russia at the time of her greatest need. Delmé appears to have done much to help this matter on. The Italians are now producing one Deport field gun per day and ammunition to suit. General Cadorna did not believe in the Austrian offensive from the Trentino, as he did not think that the Austrians would risk it just as the Russians were getting up steam. There was a good deal of excitement when the Austrians attacked. The people pulled long faces over the first defeats, but Cadorna kept his head, and has now twenty-two divisions ready for the counter-attack, and other troops of the 4th Army are moving round wide on the right from Cadore. The blame is apparently laid on Brusati. A friend of Sonnino's has a daughter married to Di Robilant, commanding the 4th Army, and the latter is regarded the rival to Cadorna. The real reason of the Italian defeat, apart from their weakness at the moment, is that thirty-three Austrian 12-inch guns and seven of the German 17-inch guns opened on each of the Italian sectors in turn from a central situation, knocking the hills and the defences to bits, and surprising the troops who had only been accustomed to guerilla warfare in the mountains and could not stand such a bombardment. On the Isonzo there are six Italian Army Corps in the first line besides the reserves. Only two divisions from the Isonzo had been taken away to meet the attack on the Trentino. In Carnia there are seventy Italian battalions, but they form only one Army Corps. The 18th and 20th Army Corps are now attacking astride the Brenta. Delmé thinks that only the Italian 35th Division and two others gave way, and not six as the French Staff had told me at Chantilly. There has been some agitation against Cadorna, mainly got up by the Giolittians, but Delmé is helping to resist it. Delmé thinks that the value of an Italian Army is only about 50 per cent. of that of the Northern European nations. They fear to lose ships, and have not the habit and the traditions of

the sea as we have. Their ports are bad, and they were
short of almost everything at the beginning of the war,
because Giolitti had let things down. There is a great
shortage of coal, which is very dear, and the metal industries cannot be compared to ours. Delmé thinks that
the Italians might use more men, but cannot yet find arms,
cadres, and guns for them. Italy has not yet felt the strain
of the war like France and England, and food prices are
little changed. It appears that the main Russian Army
is delayed a good deal owing to the bad roads.

Monday, June 19. Went by gondola to the station with
Delmé at 8.10 A.M. He left me at Mestre and went to
Bologna by car on some committee work. Went to Udine.
My travelling companions were the Duca di Gallese of the
Household of the Queen Mother, and Princess Ruspoli,
the latter still very good-looking. The Duke vowed that it
was wrong to say that the Blacks of the best Roman families
were not fighting. He said that they were all at the front
in various capacities. He confirmed Delmé's story about
Sonnino, and his relation with Di Robilant. He said that
General Brusati, who made such a mess of things when
the Austrians attacked from the Trentino, was imposed
upon Cadorna by the Court. Brusati's brother is A.D.C.
to the King. He described General Brusati, who was in
command, as the *type accompli d'un imbécile.* The Princess
was very pleasant.

I was met by Colonel Count Barbarich of the Staff,
a most agreeable companion, chief of the Press Bureau,
who is to be my guide, and by young Rennell Rodd,
son of our Ambassador in Rome, who speaks Italian
fluently. Drove to the house where our Mission resides.
It is in peace-time a sort of home for people with weak
minds. It looks over a piazza, and possesses some large
marble baths, which were, of course, a joy to us all, and
prevented the Mission from moving elsewhere, in spite
of the bombs which seem pretty frequent. A large bomb
had killed five people outside my window, and made marks
all over the ceiling of my room after coming through the

window. Evidently a cheerful spot. About fifty people had been killed and two hundred wounded in this little town by bombs, but nobody seems to care very much. The town is full of people and soldiers. The Austrian aeroplanes come most mornings and evenings. The hooters sound and people get under cover until the aeroplanes have left. Very little damage has been done to the town. Found at the Mission an intelligent man called Routhe, who was civil, but looks a very ill man. Barbarich took me to his Press Bureau, where a lot of Italian correspondents were at work, and lined up to shake hands with me. There was a good deal of photography, and of sniping with cameras wherever I went.

The Press Bureau seems to be well organised. I obtained a book of their rules. The political and military summaries from the Foreign Press are admirable, but our English papers arrive very late, taking five or six days to come. Barbarich showed me everything, including some excellent maps and diagrams, giving the distribution of Austrian, Italian, and Russian troops, which I was allowed to take away and study. Delmé had told me that the Italians are rather sore because we did not show them the distribution of our troops, and I think that reciprocity ought to be the rule. However, Barbarich said nothing about it, so I said nothing. Italian information shows that there are sixteen Austrian divisions between the Lagarina and Sugana Valleys, besides five others from Stelvio to Monte Croce, and one from Monte Croce to Plezzo on the Isonzo. In more detail, and counting from left to right, there are two Austrian divisions west of Lake Garda, namely, the 89th and the Giudicaria detachment ; then Kövess's Army—consisting of the 48th, Landeschutzen, 57th, 59th, 8th, and 3rd Divisions in succession—stands between Lake Garda and the Astico Valley ; Dankl's Army covers the ground from the Astico Valley to the north of the Val Sugana, and consists of the 44th Division, 1st Mountain Brigade, 34th, 43rd, 28th, 6th, 22nd Divisions, 2nd Mountain Brigade, 88th, and 18th Divisions in succession. The 90th Division continues the line to the Pettorina Valley, followed by the Püsterthal Division, and the 91st Division continues the line to Monte Croce. The last three divisions form the 14th Corps of Tyrol.

The 10th Austrian Army, General von Rohr, extends from the source of the Piave to Tolmino on the Isonzo. It includes six Mountain Brigades on the Isonzo. The rest of the Isonzo front is held by the 5th Austrian Army under General Boroevic. This Army has the 16th Army Corps, consisting of the 62nd and 68th Divisions, from the river down to Gradisca ; then follows the 7th Army Corps, consisting of the 20th, 17th, 61st, and 106th Divisions, while the Nabresina Division is on the Austrian left between the Carso and Trieste.

Turning to another theatre of deep interest just now, I see from the Russian distribution diagram, dated the end of May, that the four Russian Armies under Brussiloff consist of 44½ infantry divisions and 12 of cavalry. They are opposed by the 5th Austrian Army with 35 divisions of infantry and 8 of cavalry. The above form the Russian Southern Armies. North of Czartorisk, General Evert's fiveArmies of the West or Centre have 50 divisions of infantry and 12½ of cavalry. They are opposed by five German Armies or groups between Dvinsk and the Pripet, with a strength of 35¼ divisions of infantry and 9 of cavalry.

Kuropatkin's four Armies of the North hold the rest of the line up to the Gulf of Riga, with 45 divisions of infantry and 9 of cavalry against 15 German infantry divisions and 4⅔ of cavalry. Thus the Russians along the whole front appear to have 140 divisions of infantry and 33½ of cavalry against the Austro-German 85 divisions of infantry and 21⅔ of cavalry. This is a very considerable superiority, and it becomes the greater when we remember that the Russians have killed or captured the equivalent of 15 Austrian divisions, and that the Russian division has 16 battalions to the Austrian 12. I wish that we had such a superiority in the West, but we have not, for as well as I remember we have about 154 Allied divisions against

120 stronger German, and we have no Austrians against us at all. The maps of the Geographical Institute in Florence are very good indeed.

Went to see Commandant Grüss of the French Mission, who seemed a capable man. He thought with me that the Austrians would now withdraw part of their forces from the Trentino to meet the Russian attack, and Grüss thought that they were probably doing so now, as they had made no great attack for the last fortnight. But it will take a long time to withdraw divisions, because of the poor railway facilities, and because Italian guns command the Püsterthal railway from Toblach to Sinnian, and practically everything has to go round by Innsbrück. I could not talk intimately with Grüss, because Barbarich's assistant, Colonel Claricetti, was with me. I dined at the mess of the Director of Operations and sat on the right of General Diaz, who is head of the branch. There were some twenty or thirty officers, and he introduced me in a kind speech, saying that my work was favourably known. The mess was in a palace with a courtyard, and in the garden at the back here was signed the Treaty of Campo Formio by Bonaparte. I had a lot of talk with General Diaz about the war, and found him a good, clear-headed, capable soldier. He thinks that the rigid mentality of the Austro-Germans was the cause of the blow from the Trentino, and that General Konrad had an obsession about this operation and pursued it regardless of what the enemy might do.

General Diaz thinks that the Austrians hoped to enter the plains and to cut the communications of the main Italian Army, but as the Austrian columns spread out fanwise they grew weaker and weaker, and an Italian *communiqué* says that the enemy has had 170,000 casualties. The Italian inferiority was due to lack of heavy and machine guns. General Diaz, like Joffre, prefers heavy guns of medium calibre to the very heavy types. He strongly approved of the Allied plan of simultaneous action.

Tuesday, June 20. Started at 7.30 A.M. with Barbarich

and motored via Cividale and by the new road N.E. of this place to the hills over Tolmino, whence there is a beautiful view of the Isonzo Valley and of the Austrian and Italian lines. There are many Italian batteries, including one of 295-mm. howitzers very well concealed in a pit where it is practically immune from fire. As we came up to a col near this battery, the Austrians opened fire and burst a heavy shell just at the col. We continued our journey and met the chief staff officer of the 7th Division, who pointed out the position to us from an observation point on one of the highest peaks. Tolmino Bridge is still standing over the Isonzo, and the Italian lines run down close to it, but lower down the Austrians hold a great slice of the right bank, and should be put out of it as they have no right to be there.[1] They opened on our hill with shrapnel. The 7th Division is now holding a front formerly occupied by an Army Corps. They hold strong positions, and there is much wire. Italian 295-mm. howitzers were brought up to a hill 1000 metres high in seven hours from the plain ; the platforms were laid and the guns mounted in five hours more. The guns weigh 11 tons, the carriages 8, and the platform, which was in sections, 22. The Italians had been ordered to destroy the Tolmino Bridge, which I thought unwise, as it would give away the fact that the Italians were on the defensive on this front. The local commander thought the same, and the bridge was left standing. We had a fine view all down the valley and over the hills to the East. A conical wooded hill faced us across the river, and is apparently crammed full of guns in galleries, with howitzers behind, but it could be flanked and rendered innocuous if the Italians took the Becenica and Santa Maria heights which the Austrians hold on the right bank here. All the Austrian trenches on the low ground near the river can be seen right into and ought to be smashed to bits. We had an exciting journey back, as the Austrian batteries opened on us and placed three shrapnel quite

---

[1] The Germans used this bridge-head in October 1917 for breaking into and through the Italian line.

close to us at a turn on the road. This artillery sniping of
motor cars must be great fun for the Austrian gunners.
They lay on an angle turn of the zig-zag roads and let
drive as the car gets to it. The chauffeur was more alarmed
by tne shrapnel than by the precipices below, and went at
break-neck speed. The result was, when the game began
again, that we came round a corner too fast and ran into a
transport wagon which was sheltering from the fire. We
bumped off it on to the precipice side, and must have fallen
1000 feet or so, if it had not been for a pile of boulders which
had been placed there to mend the road. In these we
fortunately jammed, and took some time getting out.
Our chauffeur is a very fine driver, but he goes down these
zig-zags at about 60 miles an hour, and seemed generally
to have at least one wheel over the precipice.

Returned to lunch at Udine, and started again at 2.30 P.M.
for the Carso. Arrived at Gradisca, where we had to leave
the car and walk. There is an interesting old citadel
here, and all the official residences have the Austrian arms,
and the notices are in German. It was pleasant to be
in the enemy's territory, and I liked the notice written
over the Millitärwacht Zimmer by some Italian wag—
Evitare di fumare esplosive. The town is practically
uninhabited, and there are no troops in it, so that the
Austrians may have no excuse for bombarding it. There
is a good view from the upper windows of the citadel
well up the river. I think that the name of the general
is Marchetti. He was very pleasant and a very keen
warrior. We crossed the river by a foot-bridge, which is
shielded by mats on both sides, and for some reason, known
to themselves, the Austrians have not destroyed it. I
visited a dressing-station, and also a magazine of bombs.
There are three types in use : one shaped like a quoit,
the second resembling a pine-apple, and the third a carrot.
Viewed from the river all the Carso here is in Italian hands
except at Mont St. Michele. The 21st and 22nd Divisions
took these positions, and have been here since Oct. 16
last. They work in three reliefs, and the regiments spend

fifteen days in support, fifteen days in the trenches, and fifteen resting in reserve. The Italian trenches are very near the Austrian, in some cases as little as eight or even two metres. The enemies talk to each other and send one another presents. The Austrians ask for bread, and apparently want this more than anything else. It is considered quite good form to throw over first a packet of cigarettes, then half a loaf of bread, and then a bomb. I asked the general why he did not mine the trenches that were so near and blow the Austrians up in the air ; he said that he did not because when he began the Austrians began mining back, which did not strike me as a very good reason. All the villages along the Isonzo were very little damaged ; at all events there is no comparison with the destruction of the villages in France and Flanders. We came back to tea with Marchetti and his Staff at Gradisca. Stray bullets have the facetious habit of coming through the windows during meals. We thought that we had left our car in safety under cover at the western end of the town, but when we got back to it we found that it had been bespattered by shrapnel. The chauffeur brought us a handful of the bullets that had fallen.

Returned to Udine. Delmé Radcliffe and I, with Barbarich, went to dine with General Porro, Chief of the Italian General Staff, and his Staff. We were photographed together before dinner. Porro showed us a large model of the Carso, the rough, bare, limestone plateau where we had been that afternoon. He pointed out to us the Vallone as the first objective of the Italians in this district. It is a depression in the hills eastward of where I was this afternoon, and is, no doubt, much used by the Austrians for artillery, reserves, and ammunition. Porro was rather didactic at dinner, but afterwards we walked together in the garden, when he improved and became more communicative.

We spoke about the Allied offensive, which has, of course, his hearty approval. He considers that the Austrian offensive from the Trentino is now definitely checked, and he tells me that in addition to the Italian Army Corps of the 1st and 4th Armies, he has five Army Corps in reserve on the plain in case the Austrians manage to debouch. There seemed to be every reason for his confidence. I asked him whether he would hear if the Austrian troops began to go back. He said that he had good information from Innsbrück, but that it took four days to reach him owing to difficulties made by Switzerland. From this source he had no information at present of any Austrians going back, but he says that General Konrad has left the Trentino for the Russian front and Porro imagines that troops may be following. He says that the 34th Division is already reported on the Russian front. The authorities seem to agree that it will take a fortnight to disengage one Austrian divisional unit from the Trentino and to carry it to Lemberg.

Porro thinks that the Austrian attack was miscalculated. The Italians expected the attack last autumn, but the Balkans took its place. A great deal of information points to the fact that the Austrians thought that the Russians could not possibly strike for another three months, and that therefore there was time for the Trentino stroke. Porro thinks that the Austrian attack may be pressed. The Italians were short of heavy guns everywhere, and especially of medium calibre heavy guns from 6 to 8 inch. He said that the Austrians employed thirty of the 12-inch guns in the opening of the attack. I told him how keen we were in England that no change should take place in the G.H.Q.'s in France and Italy, that we knew the men we were dealing with now and had confidence in them, and would, if necessary, support them. He quite understood and says that he will accept Bissolati, who has been appointed a sort of civil inspector of the Army by the Italian Parliament, and Porro will gladly see him take over the civil work performed by the Army in the occupied territories of Austria. This work includes agriculture, from sowing to harvesting, repair of the roads, religion, births, deaths, marriages, and every other sort of civil job. I told him that I expected an Austrian retreat. He spoke of the work that had to be done when the Austrians attacked. He had to move the Italian reserves, a quarter of a million strong, from the Isonzo to the Trentino front, and he also had to move 150,000 of the civil population from the territory temporarily lost by Italy, and to distribute them all over the peninsula. Porro declared that the whole country was united, and he seemed quite content with affairs. Delmé told me something in the evening of his difficulties in supplying the Italians with guns and munitions. He said that they are now turning out 2000 rifles a day from plant which he bought in England.

Wednesday, June 21. Started at 7.30 A.M. with Barbarich and visited the Carnia front, going via Tolmezzo, Arta, and Paluzzo, to Mount Timau, where we found the Italians engaged with the enemy on the Mauthen side, and also with the infantry, who were 800 yards off. On the way up I saw General Lequio at Tolmezzo. He commands the Italian Army in Carnia. He is a bluff Piedmontese engineer who impressed me favourably. He told me that he had 100,000 men in all and a front of 100 kilometres to defend. It was by his advice that we went to Timau and were well repaid. We had a glorious day amidst wonderful scenery. The forests on this part of the hills run up to 2000 feet, then come pastures, and above them are the arid peaks with some patches of snow on them. I found the Friuli and Carnia ladies most attractive ; they have good figures, fine eyes, and warm complexions. They wear black dresses and hoods of an original type, and I wish that Rembrandt or Velasquez were here to paint them. I found that the Tagliamento, as an obstacle, was almost as great a fraud as the Piave, and it will remain so until October. The But Valley, called the Canale de San Pietro in these parts, is very beautiful. At Timau there is a German patois-speaking colony. We found the Sicilian division in occupation, and I thought them very taking and hardy-looking fighting men. We found 290's on the road, and two more in position west of Timau in a wood. They were firing at Mauthen from a

position about 820 metres above the sea and over the
Timau Mountain which rises to a height of 2221 metres!
There are mountain guns on this crest, and field guns
behind, while there are some anti-aircraft guns further
back. The Austrians have two 305's at Mauthen. The
Gail Valley is commanded by the Italians both here
and lower down, while in Cadore to the westward other
guns strike with their projectiles the Püsterthal between
Innichen and Toblach.

The *filovia*, or telepheric air railway, has been established
in many places on this rugged frontier. The car and its load
weigh 400 kilogrammes, and cover in twenty minutes an
ascent which would take three or four hours to walk. They
have been in use ten years. The upper pair of chain lines
carry the car, and the lower pair do the haulage, and are
worked by machinery at the base of the hill. There are
other Austrian guns in caverns in the hills round Mauthen.
A staff officer, who turned out to be an aviation enthusiast,
said that we should long ago have bombed Essen and Vienna,
and that the air tactics of the Allies had been contemptible.
We found the Alpini holding the highest Alps. General Lequio
told us that to hold an Alpine crest of this character meant
three mules for every one man. There was good telegraph
communication, and the Italian hold upon the crest gave
good observation of the fire.

The best lorries are those of 1½ tons or about half the
capacity of ours. They are well-engined, and manage
the hills well. Small and handy steam tractors bring up
the guns. The way that the heavies are man-handled
round the zig-zag turns is very clever. Some 150 kilometres of new railways have been made in this sector
since the war began. The line held by the troops is
divided into divisional, brigade, and regimental sectors
of defence. On the whole, I found no reason to alter
my view that the Carnic Alps are practically impassable. They are most rugged and forbidding, and there is
no pass for wheel traffic except Monte Croce di Carnia. We
got back to Udine for lunch. General Diaz told me that

it was confirmed that General Konrad has left the Trentino, and that the Archduke Joseph Ferdinand has been relieved of his command owing to his defeats in Galicia. Delmé told me that no less than eighty Italian generals had been *dégommé* by Cadorna, whose enemies were consequently very numerous. I am inclined to think that the Italian Alpine warfare is very well conducted, especially considering the somewhat sparse means at disposal, but that this war of detail somewhat prevents the situation from being regarded from a large point of view. I was struck by the amount of work done on the roads, railways, and bridges. North-East Italy is certainly wonderfully attractive; it is so varied and so rich; one is struck by the comfort and the well-being of the people, and they certainly hate the Austrians pretty thoroughly, because they have been under their heel. We had news to-day that 24,000 Austrians had left the Isonzo front, leaving only 67,000 men on this side. There is no change yet in the Trentino, on which front to-day's Italian report gives the Austrians 227,000 men all told.

I had a private audience with the King of Italy at his villa near Udine at 6 P.M. It was a humble residence with a small garden, not differing much from the abode of the King of the Belgians at La Panne. There were three or four officers about, and a sentry at the entrance gate, but I saw no other guard. I was shown up at once to the King's bedroom, in which he appears to receive especially favoured guests. It was the humblest kind of room imaginable. There was just a low camp bed with a soldier's blanket over it; a small hard table, and two small hard chairs, made up the rest of the furniture of the room. The King met me at the door. He is even shorter than I imagined, but he was very cordial and spoke volubly and well in English. We each sat down on one of the hard chairs; he inquired what I had been doing, and what I had seen, and meant to see. I told him briefly where I had been and made some complimentary remarks about various things that I had noticed. He approved of my programme for the rest of the trip.

He then told me all sorts of details about the war. He did not believe that the Austrians had lost more than 100,000 men at the outside during the Trentino offensive. He asked me if I knew how many the Italians had lost since the campaign began, and I said that the estimates given to me varied between 200,000 and 400,000. He said that it was an intermediate figure, and when I suggested 300,000, he said, 'A little more, about 320,000.' But this was the total casualty list, and more than 50 per cent. of the wounded returned to duty. They had only 3000 cases of amputations up to January last.

I told him that I expected that the wounded would make good recoveries on account of the great sobriety of the people. The King agreed that this was the case, and told me that during the two years of his command of an infantry regiment, he had only one case of drunkenness brought before him, and the man got fifteen days for it. His men came from five different regions, of which two, namely, Piedmont and Friuli, did a bit of drinking. I asked him how he reckoned up the military value of the soldiers of the different regions, and he said that his best soldiers were the peasants and that it made no difference from which part they came. When I told him that I liked the look of the Sicilians, he reminded me that some of the best of the Roman legionaries came from Sicily. He said that the peasant who seldom ate meat was now getting from 300 to 350 grammes a day, and was having the time of his life. They also gave wine to the men, and the food was excellent.

We talked about the crops, and the King said that Germany's system of agriculture had not stood the test of war very well, because it depended on artificial manures drawn from abroad, notably the nitrates of Chili, and that these had failed owing to the blockade. Italy had followed her own practice of growing corn, wine, oil, and fruit, and had a very good harvest. The prices had risen a little in wheat, but not much in other kinds of food. He said that in a bad year Italy had to import wheat, because people were so well off now that they ate less maize. The harvest had been gathered in the south and was excellent. It was being gathered in central Italy and promised well. In the north the harvest would be gathered in about a fortnight's time.

He told me a story of a priest who had been a chaplain in the Austrian Army. He was not satisfied with the treatment, so one fine day he deserted in a boat, after taking away some of the parts of the guns of the battery. He landed all right, and went to the nearest Italian battery, in order to get it to fire at the house where the Austrian general lived, with whom the chaplain had quarrelled. The battery commander was quite willing, and hit the house with the first shot, to the immense delight of the chaplain, who jumped about and clapped his hands. The King told me that the Austrian prisoners told many stories of the severe discipline maintained in their Army. Three men had been shot for eating their iron ration without orders. The King said that it was inconceivable how little the Austrians knew about geography. The men had been told when they reached the Trentino that they were in Russia, and quite believed it.

The King asked what my medals were; he knew the decorations, but not the campaigning medals. He wore three or four only, including one only worn by officers and men who had been a whole year at the front. I opened up the question whether the Italians could raise a larger number of divisions, but he said that they could not raise a larger Army for want of cadres, and he even asked if it was not already too large, since it had been doubled since the beginning of the war. He deprecated any allusion to the fact that he was often with his men in the front trenches, but he admitted that he had often been under close fire, and showed me the base of an Austrian shrapnel which had burst over his head, and had been mounted as a souvenir by the Queen. He told me that his little house only took four people; there were four more in a second house, and three in another near by. This seemed to be all his field staff, and I saw no

servants about. He showed an extraordinary and varied
knowledge of his officers and men, and of all their likes
and dislikes and wants in the field. He seemed to me a
thorough regimental officer, and his thoughts seemed to
run much more on regimental lines than on those of high
politics and strategy. He certainly takes a real and warm
interest in all his men, and he struck me as being intelligent
and very well informed. He did most of the talking, and
was very pleasant and agreeable. He impressed upon me
that the country was entirely united in waging the war.
I dined at General Diaz's mess in the evening.

Thursday, June 22. A comparatively quiet day. Went
at 11 A.M. to the General Staff Bureau, and to Aquileia
in the afternoon. At the former I visited first the mapping
section and saw specimens of their maps, plans, and pano-
ramas. The whole frontier is well mapped on scales of
1 over 25,000, 50,000, 100,000, and 200,000. The Florence
establishment has done wonders. I liked best the 1 over
100,000, which is good and clear. It is issued to all officers,
and is that on which all orders are based. The photographs are very fine, and so are the plans compiled from
the airmen's photographs and reports. I inspected some
of the detailed plans of the Austrian position on the Isonzo ;
most of them were quite close to the river and only guns
were in the second line, but there were many lines of
trenches, notably on the Carso, which is the section most
strongly held. I saw also the maps of the Russian frontier
showing the dispositions of troops on both sides. There
is still no definite news of the withdrawal of Austrian
troops from the Trentino, but the Italian counter-attack
makes some progress. I also saw the distribution in the
Balkans. This showed that eight Bulgarian divisions were
on the Salonika-Monastir front, three on the Bulgar-
Rumanian frontier, and one, the 13th, in reserve. The
Turkish distribution map showed twenty-two divisions on
the Asia Minor front, six or seven in Mesopotamia, four in
the Yemen, two in Syria, and four near Smyrna, besides
about four marching towards the Turkish front in Armenia.

This leaves about nine divisions over in Constantinople and Thrace. Thus the Russian coup in the Caucasus has placed the Turkish Army out of the way during this critical stage of the campaign. The Information Branch considers that there are 500,000 Austrian effectives on the Italian frontier, or 1,000,000 in all, including all arms and branches, but they still declare that there are 400,000 men in the Trentino, though the main attack there is only by fifteen divisions.

Went on in the afternoon with Colonel Claricetti to Aquileia. On the road we came across some strong lines of trenches near Medea, built with reinforced concrete, and I got out to look them over. They were well flanked and well concealed in the woods and orchards, while there was plenty of barbed wire. This forms the fourth line of defence. The Museum at Aquileia has a really beautiful collection of Roman statuary and antiquities of all kinds, while the Church mosaics are marvels. I found that the Prince of Wales and Prince Arthur of Connaught had been here last month. We did not escape the inevitable photograph. We were snapped among the amphora, and it looked as though we had been drinking rich Falernian. The curator of the Museum amused me by telling us that he had received a warning to be ready to remove the contents to the interior of Austria in *March* 1914, so somebody evidently knew what was going to happen. However, nothing was done, and when the Italian attack came, a man arrived in haste from Vienna and took away what he could carry in four bags. All the rest is in perfect order, and has not been injured in any way. A very hot day.

Friday, June 23. The Austrians to-day have 67 battalions between the sea and Mount Sabotino, 39 from Sabotino to Plezzo, 23 on the Carnia front, 55 on the front of the 4th Army (Italian) in Cadore, 225 on the Trentino east of Lake Garda, and 38 west of the lake. These figures include 69 field battalions marked doubtful, and also 63 battalions of volunteers and rifle-club men.

Started 7.15 A.M. with Barbarich and motored by the main road to Vicenza and thence on to Verona, where we lunched with General Bompiani, commanding the so-called fortress. He accompanied us up the Val Pantena via Grezzana, and thence on to Castelbert (1758 metres), where his main position is. It is at present a second-line position, and his front extends from the Adige to the Val dei Romiche. The last 13 miles of road were made by the general in three months, and formed the best mountain road that I had yet seen, being an easy gradient and very broad with easy turnings. We had a good view of Monte Baldo and Monte Altissimo to the west, and of Passo Buole, Gugna Torta, and Coni Zugna to the east. We also saw Pasubio, and the valley down to the Adige. The Castelbert position is fairly strong, and has six batteries of medium calibre well concealed, including a battery of Armstrong guns. There are lateral roads and communication trenches, and this section should be pretty safe [1] if there is any fighting here. I saw that Buole was pitted with marks of Austrian shells. The defence of Verona has practically been removed to Castelbert. At Verona itself there is an old wall, the line of the old Austrian blockhouses is in front, and some miles in advance again stands the semicircle of Italian forts with armoured cupolas on commanding positions north and east of the town, resting on the Adige on the left. These works appear to have been disarmed and the guns taken farther north, but the old Italian position forms a good line in case of need. General Bompiani has his guns and few troops, with 2000 workmen. He thinks that he needs a division in case he is attacked to make him safe.

In passing Vicenza, I visited General Pecori Giraldi, commanding the 1st Army. A cheerful old warrior, but deaf. He told us that they were working night and day, especially to accumulate heavy guns, and he spoke hopefully of the impending advance. Colonel Albrecchi, his Chief of Staff and a smart fellow, showed me a capital

---

[1] It was never taken.

model of the Trentino, and explained why the Austrian attack had succeeded. The Austrians had brought up twenty-five 12-inch guns on to the Lavarone-Plezza front, and had used them like machine guns. He admitted that Col Santo should not have been lost, but said that it had been heavily shelled from Plezza. The Austrians were now very strong on the Asiago plateau. The Italians had massed a battery of 100 guns at the outlet of the Astico Valley upon the plains, and were developing their counter-offensive westward and northward. Cengio was in Austrian hands, also Asiago and Arsiero. It became clear on talking to Albrecchi what great difficulties the Italians would meet with in reconquering these positions if they were pushed right off the foot hills into the plain. This is a point not to be forgotten on our Indian frontier.

I saw General Cadorna at 7 P.M. on our return journey. He was at a quiet house at Vicenza, and I had a talk with him alone in his garden, a tranquil and shady spot. He is a man of medium height, broad shouldered and energetic. He impressed me favourably. I asked him what best we could do for him to help him, and he said that what he wanted most was heavy and machine guns. He told me that the Austrians had 400,000 men in the Trentino, with some 300 heavy guns. He had not expected the Austrians to commit such a folly, but had been prepared to meet this attack if it came. He admitted that the attack had been well organised and well launched, and said that General Konrad had been planning this coup for many years. The Austrians regarded it as a punitive expedition, and hatred had proved a bad councillor. He did not think that the Germans had approved, still less advised, this operation. He, Cadorna, had replied by strengthening his front and by massing five Army Corps in the plains in case the Austrians debouched. When they seemed checked, he had sent up these Army Corps to help his front-line troops.

Italy, said Cadorna, was short of many necessary things when she entered the war, and especially of heavy

guns. Except a few batteries they had practically
no siege-train, and so he had to withdraw guns from
fortresses and coast defences, and to make them as mobile
as he could, but Austria had still a great advantage. He
hoped in a few days to push on,[1] but he said that it was a
slow business. One short advance by one of his divisions
the day before had cost him 2000 casualties. He believed
that two Austrian divisions at Trent had left for Galicia,
and that the Austrian march battalions were also being
taken away. Of these there were two for each regiment,
and so the Austrians were able to make good their losses
up to date. But Cadorna said that it would take the
Austrians long to alter their dispositions, and he intended
to hold them on the Trentino, and also to begin something
serious on the Isonzo. He declared that if he had had
enough heavy guns he would have broken the Austrians
on the Isonzo before now. He sent messages to Lord
French and to Robertson. He told me that the Russian
main attack was planned for June 13, but had been postponed for various reasons. It would now begin, and the
numerical superiority of the Russians was of good augury.
Cadorna said that this mountain fighting was very hard,

---

[1] DISTRIBUTION OF ITALIAN ARMIES, JUNE 18

1st Army.	General Pecori Giraldi.	(Vicenza), 3rd, 5th, 10th, 14th, 18th, 20th, 24th, and ' Z ' Corps.
3rd ,,	H.R.H. the Duke of Aosta.	(Cervignano), 2nd, 4th, 6th, 7th, 11th, and 13th Corps.
4th ,,	General di Robilant.	(Belluno), 1st and 9th Army Corps.
5th .,	General Frugoni.	(Noventa Padovani), 8th, 22nd, and 26th Army Corps.
Carnia Force.	General Lequio.	(Tolmezzo), 12th Corps.
Special Force, Albania.	General Piacentini.	(Valona), 16th Corps.

Note.—The force on the plateau of the Sette Comuni consists of 24th,
14th, and 20th Army Corps under General Mambretti, with H.Q. at
Braganza.

and that it was only on the Isonzo front that superior numbers could be deployed, and only there with superior artillery. I told Cadorna that I should be asked when I returned why Italy had not declared war on Germany, and that I wished to have the answer from him. He replied that this was a political question, but that for practical purposes Italy was at war with Germany, and had fought with Germans. We got back to Udine late, having dined at Treviso on the way, and having covered nearly 600 kilometres in the day.

Corps.	Divisions.	H.Q.	Commander.
1st	1, 2, 19	Auronzo	Segato
2nd	3, 8	Ipplis	Barioni
3rd	5, 6, 37	Brescia	Camerana
4th	7, 18	Creda	Tassoni
5th	27, 35, 44	Valdagno	Bertotti
6th	11, 12, 45	Brazzano	Capello
7th	14, 16	St. Valentino	Tettoni
8th	13, 43	Limeria	Ruggeri Laderchi
9th	17, 18	Massari	Roffi
10th	9, 20	Thiene	Grandi
11th	21, 22	Medea	Cigliana
12th	26, 36	Tolmezzo	Lequio
13th	31	Campolongo	Ciancio
14th	28, 30	Gobbaro	Mossolin
15th	not yet formed.		
16th	38	Albania	Piacentini
17th	not yet formed.		
18th	10, 15	Arsie	Etna
19th	not yet formed.		
20th	4, 25	Bassano	Montuori
21st	not yet formed.		
22nd	24, 47	Montegalda	(?)
23rd	not yet formed.		
24th	32, 33	Sarcedo	Secco
25th	not yet formed.		
26th	23, 46	S. Piedro	(?)
' Z '	29, 34	Valstagno	Zoppi

=50 divisions, of which 3 uncertain, 39 to 42 allotted to cavalry, but not yet given to them, and 48 to 50 unformed ?   42 sure.

Note.—37th Division is by itself in Ala direction.   Also note that there are the equivalent of 6 divisions of Alpini and 2 of Bersaglieri outside A.C. formation.

Saturday, June 24. (Anniversary of Custozza.) Went in the afternoon to Treviso, which is the centre of the administrative service in the war area. Saw and had a talk with General Lombardi, the Intendant General; General Morrone, Vice Intendant; and the Director of Transport, Col.-Brig. Fiastri. They all seem to me to be good men. Major di Orestis of the Staff gave me a long explanation of the whole system. In Italy all the *services de l'arrière* are under the Intendant General except drafts and aviation, both of which come under the H.Q. Staff. The Intendant General has a representative in Armies and Army Corps. An Order of Movement comes to the Intendant General by telephone, and he arranges for transport, food, and ammunition. The transport includes the railways, which are mainly under the State; motor lorries, carts, mules, and porters, and big contractors' lorries worked on all the main roads. Then there are the middle-weight lorries taking a useful load of 2400 kilogrammes, and the light, which take half this amount. The engineers have special tractors for heavy guns. They do fine work and are very handy and powerful. The lorries form an Army Service, and each park has a group per Army Corps. Each group has two sections for each division, which equals two in a two-division Army Corps. There seems to be no material difference between the general arrangements of the rearward services in the Italian and other foreign Armies. The mules allowed are 200 per regiment of infantry, and fifty for an Alpine company. Di Orestis throws doubt on Lequio's tall story of three mules per man for mountain warfare. He gave me a paper showing me the war rations. The normal ration is 750 grammes of bread, 300 of meat, 150 of pasto or rice, 350 of potatoes, and also cheese, coffee, sugar, wine, salt, pepper, and vegetables. In winter the meat rises to 375 grammes, and pasto to 300. The total calories is about 3950. In case of severe work, wine, rum, and bread are added, increasing the calories to 4730. I had a long talk with Fiastri, who told me that between May 17 and June 22 the Italian railways had carried 18,000 officers,

522,000 men, 74,000 animals, 34,000 carriages and guns, including 71 field, 34 mountain, 81 heavy, and 38 very heavy batteries.

This makes : $71 \times 4 = 284$ guns

$34 \times 6 = 204$,,

$81 \times 4 = 324$,,

$38 \times 2 = \ \ 76$,,

Total   888 guns

Fiastri also told me that Italy had 5000 locomotives and 160,000 carriages when war began, and that, on mobilisation, 120 trains were cleared a day on the two Venetian lines. The train travelling was thirty-five kilometres an hour. He explained many other technical matters, but I had not time to go into aviation.

Claricetti on the way home surprised me very much by blurting out that the Treaties with Austria had prevented Italy from doubling her lines into Venetia. I had a talk with Delmé later, and he agreed that I should stick to Cadorna's view about the question of Italy declaring war against Germany. For all practical purposes Italy was at war with Germany, German prisoners had been taken, and German guns had been used against Italy.

Sunday, June 25. Wrote most of the day. Very hot. Colonel Enkel, Head of the Russian Military Mission with Cadorna, came to see me at 4 P.M. An exquisite and a man of the world, immaculately dressed, and about as clever as they make them. I found him extremely well informed. He thought that there were no more than twenty-nine Austrian divisions on the frontier, and many of them composed of such bad material that they were worthless. He went through the Italian lists of the Austrian divisions, and explained this point to me. He said that Italian officers were brave in a fight, and that the N.C.O.s lead their men well. He said that the Italians were best in an attack, but were not so good in the defence. They were always shot out of the trenches which they captured from the Austrians by the guns in two, four, or six hours. He agreed with me that the attack on the Isonzo was practicable, but he thought that it would not do with an Italian Army to work by phases ; it was advisable to take the whole position by a rush without stopping. He thought that the Austrian attack from the Trentino had been a success, because it had prevented a grand attack on the Isonzo front. There was nothing of much value in the Austrian Army in the Trentino, except fifteen Austrian first-line divisions, which delivered the main attack.

The Austrian Mountain Brigades were formed now anyhow. The Austrians would take battalions at random from other regiments, and the formations were difficult to follow. The Austrians appear to be accustomed to this happy-go-lucky system. Enkel said that Brussiloff's attack [1] had been meant as a demonstration to draw off the German and Austrian reserves ; it had succeeded. He did not know why the main Russian attack had been delayed. He regretted the departure of the Grand Duke Nicholas, and thought that the G.D. and Alexeieff would have been a perfect combination.

Dined in the evening with the Prefect of Friuli and Signora Luzzati, Signor Gioge of the *Corriere*, and a lot of others ; many came in afterwards ; it was evidently the meeting-place of the society of the town. The Prefect told me that out of 24,000 men absent abroad before the war, almost all came home before the notices had been sent to them to rejoin.

---

[1] RUSSIAN DISTRIBUTION AT THE END OF MAY.　RIGHT TO LEFT

NORTHERN GROUP OF ARMIES

	Kuropatkin,	45 divisions of infantry,	9 of cavalry.		
6th Army.	*Gobatovsky,*	4　,,	,,		
12th　,,	*Radko Dimi-*				
	trieff,	25　,,	.,	$3\frac{1}{2}$	,.
5th　,,	*Romeko*				
	Gourkho,	12　,,	,,	$3\frac{1}{2}$	,,

Monday, June 26. Started at 7 A.M. and motored by Gemona, Stazione per la Carnia, Tolmezzo, Passo della Morte, Passo di Mauria, and Pieve di Cadore, to Cortina d'Ampezzo. Thence back by Pieve to Belluno, and so home to Udine. An extraordinarily beautiful motor drive through gorgeous scenery, especially in the passes. We found the sources of the Tagliamento, and at the Mauria Pass we picked more specimens of wild-flowers to the square yard than I have ever seen anywhere before. The road was also quite good for motoring, and the air divine and very refreshing. Later on in the day it came on to rain, and ended in a drenching thunderstorm, so we had all varieties of weather. We found an Alpine group at Cortina, and made friends with them. After an indifferent lunch a quartette of soldiers gave us some music, and ended up with 'God save the King,' possibly played here for the first time in captured Austrian territory. We went up the hills west of Cortina, and saw the position of the Alpini. A few miles out of the town on the Dolomite road the Italians were holding the crest to the right of the road, except at one isolated peak called Castelletto, whence the Austrians fire upon the road on which we stood, and also hold a commanding rocky hill which looks right down the road. To overcome the Castelletto the Italians have driven

CENTRE GROUP OF ARMIES

	Evert,	50	divisions of infantry,	12½	of cavalry.
1st *Army,*	*Litvinov,*	8	,,	,,	3 ,,
2nd ,,	*Smirnov,*	10	,,	,,	3½ ,,
10th ,,	*Radkievic,*	10	,,	,,	2 ,,
4th ,,	*Ragosa,*	10	,,	,,	1 ,,
3rd ,,	*Lesch,*	12	,,	,,	3 ,,

Evert's right faces Eichborn's left, and Evert's left corresponds with Linsingen's right.

SOUTHERN GROUP OF ARMIES

	Brussiloff,	44½	divisions of infantry,	12	of cavalry.
8th *Army.*	*Kaledin,*	10	,,	,,	3 ,,
11th ,,	*Sacharov,*	4	,,	,,	1 ,,
7th ,,	*Scherbaceff,*	6½	,,	,,	2 ,,
9th ,,	*Leschitsky,*	24	,,	,,	6 ,,

long galleries through the rock and have already got under
the position, and have placed 32 tons of explosive ready
for firing. They intend to blow the whole mountain into
the air.[1] In these mountains the Austrians have galleries
built into the rock, and their practice is to shift their pieces
about to alternative outlets from the galleries. We were
advised not to stand up on the road to admire the scene
as we were within range of the enemy, and shortly afterwards there was some shooting, but nothing to hurt. There
was an Italian entrenchment across the valley with bomb-
proof shelters for the men to sleep in, but they are not
very strongly constructed. This particular Alpine group
consists of seven Alpine battalions from the 3rd and 7th
regiment of Alpini, and two line infantry battalions, making
nine in all, with a great many guns of all calibres ; in fact
an Alpine group is almost a division. The hill to the
right of the road is about 7000 feet above the sea. There
are about 4000 women in Cortina whose men-folk are away
fighting. The Italians surprised the place, and now they
have got the ladies on their hands.

We had tea at the billet of the commander of one of
the battalions ; nice quarters with the rooms all panelled in
pine, furniture and pictures all German. Here I was shown
at my request the kit of the Alpini, which I had not seen for
many years. They have strong hobnailed boots made at the
factories of the depots of the reserve regiments. In the winter
the heels of these boots are taken off, and an iron heel with
ice-nails is substituted. The *gavetta*, or mess-tin, is shaped
like ours, but is slightly deeper, and has a tin for spirit
at the base, and a lamp which enables them to boil their
coffee and to warm their wine. For climbing the highest
peaks the cat-shoes, or *scarpe da gatto*, are often used ; these
have string soles with felt tops and binders, and are stronger
than the Pyrenean straw sandals. The Dolomite formations are very slippery in parts, and one has to be careful
how one is shod. The Alpine soldiers use racquets and

---

[1] This was actually done a few weeks later, and all the Austrian
garrison perished.

skis. They carry either the Alpenstock or the ice-axe (*piccozza*), and also carry spare nails and dubbing. They have invented a wire-netting basket about 3 feet long, 1 foot 7 inch broad, and 2 feet deep, in which there is fixed a wooden loophole ; this is placed in front of the firer in any position taken, and filled with earth. It seems to me too weak to keep out a bullet, unless it is filled with rock, which splinters. The officers of the Alpini were young, captains of twenty-four to twenty-six. They were very smart-looking fellows, most of the officers spoke French, and the men looked very handy and businesslike. The battalions were of three companies, and each group has its men locally re-cruited, and gets its reinforcements from the French frontier. The officers told me that the Austrian artillery was not very wonderful, but that the enemy's riflemen were good. The war of manœuvre appeared to be at an end in the hills, as the two sides are cheek by jowl everywhere, just the same as in the plains, and often a few yards apart. There are good fur bags for sleeping in in the mountains, and in general all the Alpine equipment is very serviceable. I was amused to find some Bridge scoring cards. I wonder what Lord St. Davids would say about it ! We could not evade the inevitable photographer.

On our return I called on General di Robilant at Belluno. He commands the 4th Army. He is a bearded man of uncer-tain age, and seemed pretty shrewd. He explained to me his plans quite openly. He had two Army Corps with 110,000 men to protect his 100 miles of front, and he was opposed by 84,000 Austrians. Both sides hold groups of works facing each other at critical points, and here the fighting tends to concentrate. The general hopes to get on, but says that he needs more men in order to push through. He is not involved in the present operation in the Trentino, and requires a fortnight to perfect his operations before he moves. We discussed the strategy of the campaign in Italy, and I found that he thought that the Trentino should have been attacked first. He wants it to be attacked now, and this line of invasion to be followed. We had a good talk over it all. He asked me to stay to dinner, but I could not manage it, and we only got home at midnight after a long day.

Tuesday, June 27. Motored to Vicenza with Claricetti. Lunched at Treviso. All the people seemed to know who I was, and there was more photographing. I found that I was billeted at the Palazzo Querini. General Grimaldi, husband of the owner of the palace, kindly called to know if I was comfortable. We had some six or seven large and sumptuous rooms with marble staircase, but there was no bath. I could not get out to the front this day, so walked about the town and admired the architecture of Palladio, who was a native of this town. The Piazza is a dream. There was nothing in the shops. Dined at the Roma and met Mrs. Waterman, a rather good-looking American woman aged about thirty-five, who is the *Times* Milan correspondent. She and Sidney Low dined with me and Claricetti. Delmé was there with Larking, our naval attaché in Rome, and the Serbian and Belgian military attachés.

Wednesday, June 28. Started at 7 A.M. for the Asiago battlefield with Claricetti. We motored via Marostica, and thence by zigzagging mountain roads, which were covered by artillery and supply wagons, to Lusiana; here we left our cars, and walked beyond our artillery to a point overlooking Asiago. Mrs. Waterman and Sidney Low we found held up on the road as we came along, and only our presence enabled them to get on. I was very much bored with taking a lady to the battlefield, which was certainly no place for her, and also she had velvet shoes on, but she insisted on coming. We got out to look at the Austrian trenches in the woods, where the Italian artillery was firing. The Austrian trenches were rather trumpery affairs without much cover, the parapets revetted with tree trunks, and the head cover also made of wooden supports. It was very much like the trench made in the American Civil War, and as it ran through a wood it cannot be located by the Italian artillery, and is best attacked by trench mortars. The

Count of Turin passed us as I was examining the trenches. He saw the lady and was very much surprised, and asked whose party it was. They told him that it was Colonel Repington's, and he then asked who the lady was, and when they said that they did not know, he said, ' *L'attaché du colonel sans doute!* '

We got out of the wood and proceeded across the open to some low hills covered with grass, where we crawled forward to see the fun. There was a good deal of shooting going on, and Claricetti was furious with us when we exposed ourselves. Mrs. Waterman was as brave as a lioness, and paid absolutely no attention to the shooting. Austrian shrapnel gives out a pink and white smoke, so one can always distinguish them. We heard a good many blind shells whizz by and plunge into the ground without bursting. Asiago is a large straggling village, which looked as if it had not suffered much, but on closer inspection we found that a good deal of it had been burnt. It lies in an undulating plain resembling the Campagna of Rome. The Italian infantry were over the Assa in one place and across the Posina, but were held up by the Austrian rearguards on the higher ground. These rearguards gave no sign of being stampeded though our guns on the woods behind were very superior and hard at work. I imagine that the Austrian heavies, if any of them had got so far, had been withdrawn. There was a pretty constant stream of wounded going past us all day, and at one dressing station we found about 300 wounded, who were very patient and quiet. We stayed on the ground a good while watching the battle through our glasses. In the wood through which we returned a shell had burst and had laid out thirty Italians, but Mrs. Waterman took no notice of it. We lunched with a regiment in a hut while the rain poured down. Visited one or two Staffs to learn all the dispositions.

On reaching Vicenza, Delmé told me that the bombardment preceding our great attack on the Somme had begun, and I decided to return at once to Paris. I said good-bye to

General Pecori Giraldi and his Chief of Staff. The former said that the idea of the Italian public that Italy had won a great victory was absurd. He said that he and I both knew perfectly well that the Austrians were not a routed Army. He thought that things would go slow; and that it was risky to embroil oneself in the extensive fortifications of the Trentino. He then asked me to say frankly what I thought of the Italian troops. I said that I was very pleased with them, but that they had the repute of being better in attack than defence. 'Ah,' he said, 'what can one do with an Army which cannot be trusted to hold a position!' I fancy this expressed his feelings regarding the success of the Austrian attack and the loss of prisoners and guns which resulted from it. I tried to make him give an opinion upon the question of going on with the Isonzo offensive, but he would not be drawn. The liaison officer who shepherded us to-day said that the Austrians were good troops, that they were united by a deep devotion to the Emperor Francis Joseph, and that they would go on fighting. He had seen many prisoners, and thought them good men, well fed and clothed; nearly all had medals commemorating the Emperor's Jubilee. When I asked him how he accounted for the *esprit de corps* in such an Army, he touched his pistol and smiled. He said that the races of Austria were much mixed up in the Army, and that the German element spied upon the rest, and acted as a kind of battle police.

Dined again at the Roma. Talked with Delmé before dinner.

Thursday, June 29. Went off to wire to the *Times*, with a summary of the situation here. Started at 10.30 A.M. for Turin, and arrived at 7.45 P.M. A hot journey, no restaurant car, but some good iced orangeade at some of the stations. Met a pleasant captain of the Alpini in the train. He told me that he had been wounded five times and that his regiment, the 4th, had been almost destroyed; but the numbers had been kept up, and peasants from the Abruzzi and Calabria had been incorporated in the Alpini with good results. As he had fought in so many different places, I suppose Piedmont Alpini are shifted about according to needs. He told me the grim story of the Austrian corpses on Monte Nero which had fallen in the snow, and had suddenly reappeared after the thaw in the spring, frozen and lifelike. He gave me an admirable panorama map of the Trentino. He said that the serious moment in the high Alps was when the snow defences melted, and the others were not completed. This was the moment chosen by the Austrians for their recent attack. He spoke highly of the Kaiser Jäger. He told me that on Monte Pasubio the snow fell up to the end of May, and will fall again at the end of August. Thus there are only three months of good campaigning weather. Went to the Hotel de l'Europe, and had my first real bath since leaving Udine.

Friday, June 30. Got my passports *viséd* by the French and British Consulates. Went to see an old curiosity shop, Orazza's, Via Maria Vittoria 17. I admired a lacquer room, a statue of Perseus, and a fine overmantel. Lunched with the British Consul - General, Major Chapman, his wife, and an attractive daughter, the latter a *blonde aux yeux noirs* who was capital company. A good lunch and a pleasant talk. The impression at the Consulate seemed to be that Piedmont is less enthusiastic about the war than other parts of Italy. It is a question whether this is due to the cold-bloodedness of the people, or to the fact that they have not been under the Austrian heel, or to the influence of Giolitti and his friends. Left Turin at 3.15 P.M., and arrived at Modane at 6.45 P.M. Here I had to put back my watch one hour. Cool at last. Lieutenant Lazzarini very kind and managed to get me a sleeping-car. Dined on the train.

CHAPTER X

THE SOMME BATTLE, JULY 1916

Lieut. Pernot on the situation—Discussion on Rumanian affairs at
the Rumanian Legation—M. Millerand—Chantilly again—General
de Castelnau's opinions—Our objects in the Somme battle—Journey
to Amiens—Brig.-General Charteris's views—General Sir Henry
Rawlinson—A visit to the battlefield—A conversation with General
Foch—His use of artillery—Visit to the captured German position
round Dompierre—Visit to Beauquesne, Sir Douglas Haig's Headquarters—Visits to Generals Hunter-Weston, Snow, and Hubert
Gough—General Allenby at St. Pol—Sir Charles Monro at Choques—
Sir Herbert Plumer at Cassel—Views of various officers.

Saturday, July 1. Arrived at Paris at 8.30 A.M. after
a good journey. Finished three of my articles on the
Italian front, and sent them off. Esher came with the
joyful news that we had taken the first-line German
trenches north of the Somme on a front of 20 miles.
Maurice Brett told me later on that the French had
been equally successful south of the river. Lunched with
the Le Roy-Lewises, Esher, and Dr. Dillon. Worked in
the afternoon. Saw the Aga Khan, Adam, and others.
Went to the Crillon in the evening and was presented to
General Belaieff, Chief of the Russian General Staff, by
Brigadier-General Waters. I did not find him particularly
interesting, so I did not detain him more than a few minutes.
He mentioned to me what flattering accounts of the British
Army he had received from Russian officers attached to it.
The news in the evening seemed to show that only half
of our attack had been successful, and the rest of it a very
expensive failure.

Sunday, July 2. Various newspapers tried to interview

me. I only saw the *Temps* man, who undertook to give me the text before he published it. Worked and wired to the *Times*. Went to see the Countess Greffuhle and found a large party of distinguished French people and foreigners. Dined with the Lewises. I was unable to get into touch by telephone with the French G.Q.G. at Chantilly to-day.

Monday, July 3. Our offensive is not doing quite so well; we are hung up by some fortified villages. Lunched with Sevastopoulo at his rooms ; Isvolsky the Russian Ambassador, Joseph Reinach, and a few more. A pleasant lunch. Reinach said that General Pétain wanted to know my views on the question of amalgamating English and French troops in the same Army Corps, and he had apparently told Reinach that if he had had a British division in the Bois d'Avocourt, he would never have lost it. I said that there was the Portuguese precedent in the Peninsula, and that I had no objection from a tactical point of view, but that if we suffered any reverse each nation would blame the other, while there would be the difficulty of our communications, which, in order to reach the Channel, would have to cross those of the French, so I thought it would be best to leave well alone. Isvolsky and Reinach went at me about Salonika, as I thought they would, and we discussed it on the usual lines, they approving the operation and I opposing it. The impression seems to be that Rumania will come in. The Ambassador said that our five divisions had orders not to go beyond Salonika. There is one Russian brigade in France, and another arriving to serve at Salonika. I was not particularly impressed with Isvolsky's conversation, and I should say that as a diplomatist he is overrated.

Lieutenant Pernot came at 3.15, and is to make inquiries when I am to go to Chantilly and to Foch's H.Q. He told me that the British had twenty-six divisions, and that Foch had the 6th Army in the present attack, but that other troops would prolong the French front eventually, including the 5th and 10th Armies. Pernot said that the

British artillery preparation had not been so successful as had been hoped. The defended villages had not been sufficiently overwhelmed. He put down the German divisions as twenty-six against the British, and thirteen against the French. He thought that a hard and long fight for months was in prospect, and that only the sum of the efforts would count. I learnt that Robertson was here to-day and returns to London to-morrow. Harry Rawlinson is in charge of the main attack. Picked up Countess Ghislaine, and we went to see Countess de Montebello. A distinguished and well-informed woman, whom I found dead against Salonika, and very critical of our Embassy. Boni de Castellane came in and made a good story of something that had passed between me and Berthelot. It was at our last talk. Boni declares that I had said, ' Monsieur Berthelot, you are jealous of us,' and when Berthelot had protested and had raised his hands, I had replied that the French *must* be jealous, because we thought that we had made the greatest mistake possible at the Dardanelles, and now the French were trying to make a greater one at Salonika. Boni, with his inimitable phrasing and powers as a *raconteur*, made a capital story of it. Dined with the Adams's, 87 Rue Taitbout. Went on afterwards to see the pretty Mrs. Bliss of the American Embassy, at 4 Rue Henri Moissan, Quai d'Orsay.

Tuesday, July 4. Esher came in the morning, and we had a talk. Sent a wire to the *Times*. Lunched with Monsieur and Madame Lahovary, Minister of Rumania, and their three daughters; Countess Greffuhle and some others were there. We had a lot of chaff about Rumania and Salonika. The Rumanian military attaché talked at me about the Army at Salonika, and said he could not conceive why 300,000 men were standing there doing nothing looking at the skies. They all laughed and looked at me, so I said that they were not doing nothing, they were waiting to see which way the wind was blowing in Rumania. All talk seemed to be that Rumania would come in. The military attaché took me aside afterwards, and showed me tables which made out that Rumania had about 1500 guns, including 600 good quick-firing field guns, but only 600,000 shells. They had 200,000 more shells from France at Vladivostok, and 200,000 more shipped at Bordeaux. He said that many difficulties had been raised by the Allies in the way of Rumania receiving her shells. He very naturally said, in answer to my suggestion that Russia did not trust Rumania, that if Rumania had wished to join the Germans, nothing would have been easier than for her to have obtained her shells from Germany, who had provided both her guns and her shells. Rumania has 572,000 good modern rifles and enough ammunition to last five months, but he considers that she must have 500,000 shells a month before she comes in, or she may be overwhelmed. Rumania has eleven Army Corps, each of two divisions, or 600,000 men fit to fight. She has 500 machine guns and others making in Denmark, which she may not be able to get if war is declared. I promised to do my best to represent the situation.

Countess Greffuhle and I went off to the Marquis de Breteuil's. Charming people and a very nice house. We discussed the unavoidable Salonika.

Monsieur Millerand came at his own suggestion to see me at the Ritz at 4 P.M. We discussed the French Army and the operations, and also changes at the War Office in London. I hope that I made as good an impression on him as he did on me. I found him a very pleasant and straightforward man. I told him how much we owed him for his good work at the French Ministry of War. We had a long and cordial talk covering Italy, munitions, and political and military personalities. He thought that French politics did not now matter a rap, as the main current of the war could not be changed. He said that the only change made at Chantilly had been the removal of General Buat, who was a good man to speed up General Joffre. I fancy that Buat was removed because he was a crony of Millerand's. Received a wire from General Charteris inviting me to go to the G.H.Q. in

France ; as I am to go to the French G.Q.G. to-morrow, I reply that I will go to our people on Thursday.

Wednesday, July 5. Did some commissions in the morning, and saw Granville and Phipps at the Embassy. Pernot called for me at 1.30. Motored to Chantilly, and talked first with General Pellé, who got in the officer charged with following the Italian operations. I explained the situation of the Italian Armies on the different fronts. They were much interested in my experiences, and asked a great number of questions. They think as highly of Enkel's ability as I do.

They think that eight Austrian divisions have now gone to the Russian front, and that the Italian Army of reserve is now on its way back to the Isonzo.

I then saw General de Castelnau, who explained to me the object and the scope of the great offensive on the Somme. It was part of the general Allied offensive, and its object was first to pierce the enemy's line and then to enlarge the gap by continually bringing up fresh troops on the flanks. The movement aimed at Bapaume, Maubeuge, Liége, and Luxemburg. Castelnau said that we Allies in the West could not fight on a broader front because we had not the artillery means, but as the Germans brought up fresh divisions we should add their opposite numbers from our line, or else take advantage of their absence and make another push. We should not be hypnotised by the German lines, as it was not the trenches nor the barbed wire that stopped us, but the men. Pernot told me that sixty-four battalions were opposed to us at first, and thirty-nine to the French. Cavendish, a liaison officer at the French G.Q.G., told me that Rawlinson had fifteen divisions all told, but that ammunition was still a consideration, and we could not afford to be prodigal of it. He said that we were using up shells faster than we were getting them. Pernot said that our artillery preparation was too dispersed, and was not so crushing to the first line as the French was. Castelnau said that the co-operation was perfect, and in-stanced regiments on the flanks of the two Armies which went so far as to have liaison N.C.O.s and men. He reminded me of his last talk with me. Verdun had held out. He did not think that Germany would be able to stand long the strain of the three battles of the Somme, Verdun, and the Russian front. We had enough men and ammunition to continue the offensive until the winter quarters of the late autumn.

I asked his opinion of the amalgamation of the two Armies so much discussed just now in Paris. He wanted the British to have a French staff officer with their divisions, Army Corps, and Armies, and French staff officers attached to their artillery brigades. He did not like a large amalgamation scheme, and did not see the need of it. I asked Cavendish what he thought of this proposal, and he did not like it, saying that we had nothing to learn from the French except the manner in which they served their guns, and he reminded me that at the battle of Loos we gained several miles while the French on our right made no progress. Castelnau told me that our naval fight off Jutland had probably prevented a combined land and sea expedition against the Russians and Petrograd in the north, and that Russia was now free to act. Evert's Army was now coming further south to strike. This confirms what Cavendish tells me, but neither Cavendish nor I are best pleased owing to the time which Russia will take to shift her troops. Castelnau says that we shall prevent attacks upon our flanks on the Somme by echelons which will keep coming up. Broadly, we were starting out on the best highway to the Rhine and Berlin. He said that the French losses had not been high on the Somme owing to the excellence of their artillery preparation. There were periods of activity, and periods of quiet for preparation. He did not say much about our attack, but Cavendish told me that Haig had given up the frontal attack from Gommecourt to Thiepval, and proposed to advance north on the front from Montauban to Fricourt, thus attacking the line of defended villages in flank and rear. Castelnau said that there had been a steady drain of all the spare troops on the German front from Verdun to the Somme, and Brett told us in the evening that both German men and heavy guns were beginning to leave Verdun. Castelnau declared that there were no more fresh German troops to pour in at Verdun, but two new German divisions had been created from the surplus troops of others and by adding new artillery. This seems to be the line of future German progress. From a large-scale map in Pernot's room, I gathered that we had a good hard nut to crack, for there is a second line just behind that which our troops have now penetrated. The French have taken part of the second line south of the river, and are consequently ahead of us. It is apparently correct that the attack on the French front was unexpected. We have 55 divisions in France now, and Cavendish says 9 German divisions came from East to West before our attack began. Castelnau said that there were 125 German divisions in the West at one time, and that there are now 118. He also laid stress upon the point that the French had been holding up the Germans at Verdun all this year while the English Armies were forming and training, and while the Russians were re-forming themselves.

[An article in the *Matin* of July 6 gives a very good idea of Castelnau's argument, and must, I think, have been written by Pernot, who was present at the talk.]

Thursday, July 6. Lord Esher had arranged this trip to the Somme for me. The invitation having come, I set out and left for Amiens at 10.5 this morning. I was met at the station by Colonel Hutton Wilson, who was in charge of the Press, and I put up at the Hotel du Rhin. Brigadier-General Charteris, now in charge of the Intelligence in Macdonogh's place, came to lunch, and said that I was free to go where I pleased, the only stipulation was to show anything written, which I agreed to do while I was in France. Charteris said that our present action was to kill Germans. The strategic objective in this area was a secondary consideration. There were about 60 German battalions against us, and 30 against the French, when the action began on July 1. There are 120 battalions against us now, all the German troops eastward to Verdun having been milked. At present the Germans were afraid to milk their front to northward for fear lest we should make another attack there.

Rawlinson was in charge of the 4th Army, which was making the attack. He had been given fifteen [1] divisions, but Gough, after the attack, had been placed in charge of the 8th and 10th Army Corps, which, with Snow's 7th Army Corps, had made the unsuccessful attack between Gommecourt and Thiepval. Since the beginning some divisions had been taken out of our line and replaced owing to the failure and losses of our attacks at Gommecourt, Thiepval, and Orvillers. Charteris said we had lost 55,000 men, and put down the German losses at 75,000, which I did not believe. He is going to say officially that the Germans have lost 60,000, and says that I can safely say 50,000. When the northern attack failed, Douglas Haig arranged to take advantage of the success between Fricourt and Montauban, and to make a fresh attack in the South. This is to begin to-morrow, and will have the support of 270 heavy guns. Rawlinson will only have three Army Corps. The total available number of divisions for the operation is 23, but 3 more may be drawn upon.

I asked him if this was as many as could be spared out of the 55 which we had. He thought it was, because there were 65 miles of front to be held in addition to the front of attack. He said that they knew the German positions well, and the troops that held it, and declared that there were only 3 more much-harassed German divisions, which had already been used at Verdun, still in reserve. This seemed to me an extraordinary hallucination, as the Germans had 120 divisions in the West. However, I said nothing, and went off to Rawlinson's H.Q., and had a good talk with him. He said that he had attacked with 29 brigades simultaneously, and Foch with all his lot. Nearly all had got in, but at Thiepval, Beaumont, and Gommecourt, they

---

[1] Sir D. Haig's Despatch shows only thirteen at the moment of the attack on July 1.

were not able to succeed. He had found the number of divisions under him too many to handle. He said the ground was a chalky plateau, but that the streams that forced their way through this plateau had deposited much soil on the banks which were not chalky. He said that Montauban had been taken by the first rush, by the 30th Lancashires of the New Armies, which I had admired so much on Salisbury Plain, and had held out against counter-attacks on three sides. He meant to approach the German lines to-morrow, and to gain a few woods and slopes, so that he might be able to prepare an attack on a second German position which extends from Longueval to Bazentin-le-Petit Wood. I asked him about our guns, and whether he was satisfied with the artillery preparation, but he turned the question by saying that we could never have enough guns and shells. He said that the French thought that we ought to concentrate more fire on the first objectives of our infantry, but the French had not to face Germans in the second line as we had. He did not fear a German counter-attack on Montauban, because his guns could protect it.

Afterwards I met General Wanless O'Gowan, whose men had done gloriously, and had marched straight through the *tir de barrage*, but he had lost 5000 men, and had been taken out of the line. He gave me his views.

I then visited Sir William Pulteney, commanding the 3rd Army Corps. He had had the devil of a fight for La Boisselle, but now held it firmly, and was joining up to-day to the 12th Division, which was to attack Orvillers to-morrow, and would find it a very hard nut to crack. He was not sure of the 12th, and was putting out a strong defensive flank on their side in case they failed. He was to attack Contalmaison, and hoped to take it. The troops on his right were attacking Mametz, which was full of Germans. Pulteney told me a story of the N.C.O. in charge of the prisoners taken by his Army Corps. This man met a party of thirty Germans taken by a neigh-bouring Army Corps. He went up to the man in charge and made him an offer of 10 francs for the lot ! He also told me that when some other Germans were being marched off to the rear, a Tommy called out to them, 'Well, Fritz, how do you like being here ? ' whereupon one of the Huns replied in perfect English, ' You would not be here at all were it not for your b—y fleet.' Putty showed me the new German gas mask, and said that it was much more effective than ours. It is carried in a tin, and the mouth-piece screws on. All the prisoners declare that it is abso-lutely proof against our gas. Putty says that this is more than ours is, and that in a recent German gas attack we had 900 men knocked out, of whom 18 died. He also showed me the listening and overhearing machines of the Germans, which seemed very good. When one of the German positions was taken, he found some of his own messages, which had been overheard and written down in German.

Dined at the hotel, and met Perry Robinson of the *Times*, whom I congratulated on his reports. The German prisoners appear to be a mixed lot ; the Bavarians bad, the 14th Reserve Corps good, and also the 2nd Guard Reserve Division ; but the quality is irregular.

I met X., commanding the artillery of the —th Division : he said that he had enough shells, but that the supply of the heavies had to be nursed. He considered that the fault of our attacks was that our infantry were given too many objectives. The artillery had to shell them all, and its effect consequently was dis-persed, which is exactly what the French say about us. Some of the German bomb-proofs were too deep for any shell to reach, and the only chance was to bury the enemy in them, and this was not easy, as there were so many bolt holes. The German machine gunners hid in these pits, and rushed out when our artillery lifted and the infantry attack began. He said that there were 200 Germans with ten machine guns taken at Fricourt. I saw four 10-inch Minenwerfer at Rawly's H.Q. to-day. They were of wood wound round with wire, and rested on a large wooden block to fit the breech. They had elevating and traversing gear, and the gun moved on a fairly wide arc. These instruments did a lot of harm. Putty told me that since the German drachen balloons and the observation posts had been knocked out, the Germans had made very poor practice. The moral of the enemy was not as good as it was, but individually they were still fighting well, and their machine-gun detachments and miners were very good. Putty said what an astonishing thing it was that he and I should be examining all these extraordinary instruments, and how surprised we should have been twenty years ago, when both of us were backing 'stiff-'uns' for the Stewards' Cup, if we had been told what was in store for us.

Friday, July 7. The general scheme of attack to-day is that, while Snow in the north with the remains of his 7th Army Corps makes things lively about Gommecourt, Gough, with the 8th and 10th Corps under Hunter-Weston and Morland, acts more or less defensively, and Rawlinson, with the 3rd, 15th, and 13th Corps from left to right, makes the main attack from the south, reinforced by fresh divisions from the north, which replace those used up in the first attacks.

Went off at 7.30 A.M. to the heights of Carnoy, and witnessed the bombardment of Mametz Wood, Contalmaison, and other parts of the German line which we propose to occupy next. Captain Roberts, Captain Stewart, Perry Robinson, and I went as far as we could by car, and then walked forward over the brow between 500 and 1000 yards in front of our heavy artillery. This looked like being a lively spot, but I was very much surprised to find that our artillery had all the fun to itself. I have never seen such inequality of artillery since the old Natal days, and I cannot swear that a single German shell came over us, while the mass of our artillery was hard at work. Our bombardment was heavy, and after two hours of it, from 8 to 10, an infantry attack took place, and captured Contalmaison and part of Mametz Wood. The former place was on a mamelon, and was exposed to the artillery from both sides, and on this occasion our infantry had to withdraw. We made steady if slow progress all along the front, and the artillery kept on advancing. We watched the scene for a long time, having a capital view of the whole ground, which made up to us for not being so far forward as we should have liked. Caterpillar Wood was just visible over the horizon, but only parts were visible from here, and it looked as if it were crawling along the horizon, hence probably its name. I wonder whether history will retain all these names by which we have christened features of the battlefield. Montauban was scarcely visible from where we stood, but the long ridges towards Albert were marked features. The German artillery was mainly concerned in barraging the villages and woods which we were attacking.

I went off later to lunch by appointment with General Foch at Dury, south of Amiens. He commands the Armies of the North. We were three quarters of an hour late, but he and his Staff were most agreeable, and his Chief of Staff, Weygand, was most kind. We had a great deal of chaff and interesting talk at lunch. Afterwards I talked with Foch alone in his sanctum, where all the maps are spread out. He attributes his success to the use of his artillery. He has 500 heavy guns, which he used on a front of twelve kilometres, in co-operation with his field guns and trench mortars.[1]

[1] The intention had been to give Foch 42 divisions grouped in three Armies, with 1700 heavy guns and great supplies of ammunition. This force would have allowed an attack on a front of 27 miles from the Somme to Lassigny, prolonged to the north by the British offensive up to the Hébuterne district, a total front of attack of 44 miles. But Verdun had drawn 57 French divisions to the Meuse by June 1, as well as a large part of the heavy artillery at disposal, and therefore Foch was at first limited to the 6th Army alone on a front from Maricourt to the road Amiens–Péronne. He therefore engaged with only 5 divisions in the first line, and with 11 others at his disposal. The Russian offensive began to take effect in mid-June, and thereafter, from July 1 to Aug. 23, 14 fresh divisions were placed under Foch, making 30 in all, of which 15 had not attacked, 6 had been engaged but were to engage again, and 9 had been withdrawn from the battle. In July 1 Foch had 700 heavy guns on a front of attack of 8 miles; these included 580 guns of 95 to 220 mm., and 120 pieces of 240 mm. or larger calibre. His front extended to 16 miles by Aug. 20, when he had 1200 heavy guns.

The German first line in front of him extended north and south immediately west of the villages of Dompierre, Fay, and Estrées, which were included in the defensive line.   He said that these villages were smashed to bits.   His guns had orders to fire at nothing but the first line, and his infantry had orders to take this first line, to consolidate it, and to go no further.   He says that when he is asked to attack a position, he no longer inquires how many divisions he will be given, but only how many heavy guns.   He considers that each Army Corps of two divisions should have 100 heavy guns over and above its normal field guns and howitzers.   I find that he is opposed to any amalgamation of our two Armies, but he says that our artillery preparation was ineffective, because we dispersed it in depth instead of concentrating it, as he did, upon the enemy's first line.   He considers our losses excessive, and due to this fact.   Our failure was particularly noticeable in the north, where the infantry had too many distant objectives given to them ; for example, in a depth of three miles in front of our 8th Corps, where so many shells were uselessly expended.   He thought that we should attack on a wider front, the wider the better.   He wants 3000 rounds per heavy gun per month, namely, 200 per gun for ten fighting days, and fifty rounds per gun per day for non-fighting days.   He said that French was a great leader, and why had he been changed ?   I said, for political purposes, and with the idea that he would help the Government, which was rather weak.   Foch thought that the moral of the enemy was falling.   We had a long talk about many matters, and finally he gave me permission to go on and see the German trenches just captured by the French, and he again asked me to come and see him whenever I was over.

I motored on as far as I could towards Dompierre, and we then got out and walked.   The ground was clay, and not hard chalk, almost of the consistency of limestone, which was found in the ground we were attacking.   The trenches whence the French first attack started were within 30 yards of the Boche barbed-wire entanglements, which were very broad.   The German trenches in front of the village were like a rabbit warren, with very deep communication trenches, made rather broader than ours.   The dugouts were deep, but only a few had escaped from being blown in, and only here and there did I find steel shields which had escaped destruction.   In general, the ground looked like a tumbled sea, and the whole system of defence of the village was smashed to bits.   We could scarcely distinguish where the church had been.   It was a scene of most utter ruin and desolation, while the smell was awful, and the dead horses were still lying about.   The Germans were still shelling the place, and the French artillery were still busy behind us, but the main artillery action was now taking place towards Estrées.   The trenches were full of unexploded shells and live hand grenades, while the ground was very slippery in the trench, and it was very hard to keep one's footing.   Foch told me that he had used his trench mortars to wreck the German wire and all the front line, while his heavies pounded the others.   His 75's set up a barrage behind the village to keep back German reinforcements, and his long-range guns counter-battered the German artillery.   It was a good lesson in the manner of attacking modern entrenchments, and certainly the devastation was very complete.   Foch had as many heavy guns on his eight-mile front as Cadorna has got in his whole Army on a front of 400 miles.

Saturday, July 8.   I went by invitation to G.H.Q., which are at Beauquesne, north of Amiens.   Haig is living at a château in a wood on the right-hand side of the road, a mile along the Marieux road.   I found Haig with Kiggell: the latter was very pleasant, but spoke little.   Haig explained things on the map.   It is staff work rather than generalship which is necessary for this kind of fighting.   He laid great stress on his raids, and he showed me on a map where these had taken place.   He said that he welcomed criticisms, but when I mentioned the criticisms which I had heard of his misuse of artillery on July 1, he did not appear to relish it, and denied its truth. As he was not prepared to talk of things of real interest, I said very little, and left him to do the talking. I also had a strong feeling that the tactics of July 1 had been bad. I don't know which of us was the most glad to be rid of the other. Esher, who was staying at H.Q., asked me afterwards what I thought of things, but I said that I would tell him when I had been all along the front and had obtained more information. I should add that Haig referred to an old telegram of mine from France, of which he had thought he had cause to complain. This gave me an opportunity for explaining what had happened, and I thought it came as a new light to Kiggell that my telegram has been passed by the Censor. Went back to Beauquesne and saw Charteris, who was very civil and helpful. I am to get him to meet Northcliffe when he comes to London. I returned to Amiens to lunch, and then went on with Bobby Ward, the King's Messenger, to visit various H.Q.

We first saw General Hunter-Weston at Marieux ; he commands the 8th Army Corps, and is established in a pleasant château. Hore - Ruthven is his General Staff officer. The 8th Corps had attacked on July 1 from Beaumont Hamel to Serre, and had suffered a loss of 50 per cent. in the four divisions, namely, 29th, 31st, 4th, and, I think, 48th. The latter was the Corps reserve and was scarcely engaged. The 29th and 31st Divisions had tried to ' pinch ' Beaumont by attacking it from the south and the north, while the main agglomeration of the town was held under our heavy artillery fire. Despite an extremely heavy barrage fire of the Germans, which wrecked our two first-line trenches, all the troops got in. The German barbed wire was here well cut by the artillery. The small trench mortars, with a range of only 400 yards, did not carry far enough. Our medium trench mortars killed a lot of our own men, and there were too few of our large mortars, which carry 1000 yards. I asked Hunter-Weston about our artillery preparation. He said that on the first four days he fired exclusively at the distant objectives, and only gave up the last three days to the bombardment of the German first line. The Germans appeared to have sixty-one batteries in position opposing him, and their fire came from the east and north-east along covered valleys, and could not be mastered. Some of his men got to Serre, and the 29th Division got well into Beaumont, but the Germans, though still under his heavy fire, came out with their machine guns from their shelters, and cut the attack to pieces. There was a desperate struggle, and all the troops fought gloriously, but the opposition was too much for any troops to overcome, and they could not pull it off. He attributes his failure to the plucky fighting of the Germans; to the very heavy fire of the enemy's guns; and to the tremendous defences and bomb-proofs, some of which had twenty-seven steps down to them, and were 30 feet down in the hard chalk. He said that there were no shirkers at all, and that all arrangements, telephones, water, food, and the medical services, which he described to me in detail, were as perfect as anything could be. I examined his arrangements and his orders, and was struck with the immense care and thought which had been displayed in his preparations. He said that he had 100 heavy guns. He would personally have preferred to have concentrated his guns on the first line alone, but he defended Haig against the charge of having dispersed the fire of his guns over distant objectives by saying that if the enemy gave way it was necessary to get further on, and that on the Loos precedent we might have expected to get on. He said that his troops were in excellent heart in spite of their hammering, and would be ready to go on as soon as they were filled up again to full strength. He reminded me that the French had failed to take these positions.

Motored on to see Snow, commander of the 7th Army Corps. He had three[1] divisions and had tried to ' pinch ' Gommecourt in the same way as Hunter-Weston had tried at Beaumont. His flank attack got home except in one case. His attack was heavily struck by artillery

---

[1] Sir D. Haig's Despatch names only two, the 56th and 46th

and machine-gun fire. It was the maxims and guns and the fighting of the Germans which stopped him, but he said that he very nearly got through. He was entirely in favour of the creeping method, that is, to go on close behind the shells in the French manner, and wondered why this simple idea had not penetrated to the higher command. I did not see Morland, commanding the 10th Army Corps, which failed at Thiepval, because I had not time, but I saw Hubert Gough, to whom, since Saturday last, has been given the 5th Army, composed of the much-harassed 8th and 10th Army Corps, and to whom has been allotted a defensive rôle. He could not do much against the positions in front of him, but he said that he would hold on. The 10th Corps was still hanging on·gamely to the end of the spur running south-west from Thiepval, and was working up to Orvillers, and hoped to gain the village. Snow had forty heavy guns only, and now held 18,000 yards of front with 20,000 men. In general, my conclusion was that the attacks failed for the reasons given by Hunter-Weston and Snow. The fire was so hot that, in running back to our lines, one quarter of the German prisoners were killed by their own barrage fire, and one quarter wounded. It is to be noted that the distances which had to be covered by our men before they reached the German lines were much greater than for the French at Dompierre.

When the 8th Corps lost Serre, Snow was much harassed on his right. He told me that there was a very powerful German artillery engaged on all the northern front of attack, and it looks to me as if the Germans had expected an attack on this part of the field and not further south.

Sunday, July 9. Had a talk with Lord Crawford, who has been serving in the medical branch since the war began. I found him very intelligent and interesting, and we arranged to meet in London one day.

Started about 10 A.M., but, owing to blocks on the road again, could not manage to see Morland, whose H.Q. were at Senlis, near Albert, and went on by the main road to St. Pol to see General Allenby, commanding the 3rd Army.

A good deal of military traffic on the roads, all the police and traffic regulation being in British hands, and very well done, but the road was not very good owing to the wear and tear. I passed through Doullens and found Allenby in a small house at St. Pol, where General D'Urbal had been before. I found Generals Holland, Bols, Pratt, Lord Dalmeny, General Sillem, and others. We had a very pleasant lunch. Allenby looks uncommonly fit and well. He has nine divisions, and his three Army Corps stand on a 20-mile front from Hébuterne on the south to Zouave Gap on the Vimy Ridge, where he connects with Sir Charles Monro's 1st Army. Allenby says that he has not many heavy guns left, and he is not very anxious to be attacked, but he can go on worrying the enemy, and is doing so. He has with him some of the divisions drawn out from the fight in the south, which are very weak, but he has also the new 60th Division just out from home, and is training it. He is very busy mining, and has had good results from it. He takes all the responsibility for Snow's attack at Gommecourt. Other officers to whom I spoke entirely agree with Foch's artillery ideas, but add that the things that we had all learnt took much time to penetrate to the mind of the G.H.Q. I liked the look of Bols, whom I have never met before. I had a private talk with Dalmeny afterwards, and found that our ideas agreed on the subject of Allenby. I have no doubt in my own mind that Allenby is an absolutely first-class chief. I went on about 3.30 P.M. to the H.Q. of the 1st Army, which is at Choques, called 'Chokes' by the British, and is near Béthune.

Charles Monro came in from a ride about 5.30. We had tea and a talk at his H.Q., which has a little artificial pond in front of it. Monro's three Army Corps take up the line from Allenby to a point south of Armentières. He can hang on, but thinks that the Lens bit of his ground is very nasty. He does not see what troops the Germans have to attack with now, nor did Allenby. Monro says that many German heavy batteries which had been located on his front are now silent, and the guns may have been taken away, but all he can say is that they are not firing. They made a great burst of fire about a month ago near N.D. de la Lorette, and have been silent ever since. He thinks that if we could take the Vimy Ridge, we should have to take also the villages beyond it, or we should have trouble, and our observation points would not be secure. He thinks that the Boches are fighting well, but are decidedly tired, and, on the whole, are not fighting with their old fire. They appear to be exhausted, and make very poor counter-attacks, the Guard excepted. Most of the Guard prisoners, it is generally agreed, are fine fellows. He listened carefully to Foch's ideas of artillery, which I passed on to him, and he did not differ from them. Monro says that his mining companies are doing finely. They are recruited from all over the world, and he has done a good lot of damage to the enemy by mining and by raids. One of the latter had killed ninety and captured forty Boches. Monro's mind and brain are as good as ever. He has first and second lines, then groups of defensible posts, well wired up, and then a *last* line. He does not think that the Boches could do more than make a slight indentation. But all Army commanders agree that the Boches can wreck our front trenches whenever they please. Monro told me that ten Germans had been cornered in a mine, and were called on to surrender or they would all be blown up. They refused to surrender, and up they went. I find a difficulty in understanding what happened to the many thousands of men who must have been left in the Boche trenches after the failure of all our northern attack on July 1. So far as I know, only 840 prisoners were claimed officially by the enemy. There must have been many thousands on the ground. What happened to them? I note that Allenby mounted the attack of July 1, but that then he was shifted north, and Rawlinson was brought down to conduct it—not a sound course, I think. It seems to be agreed that the enemy knew where the French left rested, but did not expect to be attacked south of this point by them owing to the supposed French exhaustion after Verdun.

I see that I have missed out something that Foch had told me, namely, that we had destroyed twenty-four (?) German drachens in forty-eight hours, at the beginning of the fight. These were brought down by rockets fired by electricity, the invention of a young French naval officer. The aeroplane has to shoot from within 300 yards, and then to escape from the falling balloons as best it can. The loss of these observation balloons at the opening of the battle tore the eyes out of the head of the German command.

Monday, July 10. Motored on last night to Cassel, and put up at the Hotel Sauvage. There were a lot of our boys who had walked up to the top of the hill for dinner, and some of them played the piano. A beautiful moonlight night, and a fine view from the balcony at the back of the hotel across the plains. In the morning, at 9.30 A.M., I visited Sir Herbert Plumer, commanding the 2nd Army. His H.Q. are at the big official house at the top of the hill, approached by some rocky steps from the town side. Plumer has the 14th Canadians, the 5th, and the Anzac Army Corps from north to south, but the Anzacs appear to be trekking south very soon. He agreed with the other Army commanders that he can hold on, and that the Germans are not strong enough to attack, but he is being skinned of his best troops, and will want some more heavy guns as well as troops if anything serious happens here. He is satisfied that everything is secure. The Canadians and the Anzacs were both very cock-o'-hoop when they first came to this front, but all of them have now had their lesson. Even the Anzacs have learnt that they do not know everything, but they are excellent at raiding. Plumer said that in all the low-lying Flanders country the Germans could not construct deep dug-outs on account of the water, but he said that they could do so on the Wytschaete-Messines Ridges.

I had meant to go on to La Panne to call upon the King and

Queen of the Belgians, but could not spare the time, so motored on to Boulogne. Here I met Lynden Bell, Manifold, and others, returning on leave from the Staff in Egypt. I had a good talk with L. B. about his chief, Archie Murray. L. B. said that they had four divisions in Egypt, only averaging 7000 men each, and that one of them, I think the 42nd, was earmarked for India. There were also the mounted brigades, of which the Anzacs, as Murray himself writes to me, are perfectly admirable in the desert. L. B. says that we can put 70,000 men into the field in case of attack. He describes the state of Egypt as dangerous, but Archie had rounded up Shepheard's Hotel the other day and had seized fourteen intriguing notables, and had deported them to England. The Foreign Office had been much perturbed, and had asked Archie for his reason. He had replied in a crisp telegram that he acted under the powers conferred upon him by Martial Law.

On my way to London I met Colonel Rundle commanding a group of guns near Albert. He said that he fired 38,000 shells from twenty guns during the seven days' bombardment, or 250 shells per gun per day. He compared this with the preparation at Fromelles in May 1915, when the preparatory artillery fire was reduced to 1900 rounds on account of the shortage of shells. The result, of course, was very heavy infantry losses. Rundle's guns have been firing fifteen rounds each per night during the battle. He thought that the bombardment of German roads, billets, and supposed sheltered areas during the night had done them a lot of harm, and he said that the aeroplanes reported that the road about a quarter of a mile out of Pozières was black with destroyed German transport. The German communications have also been well shelled, and many German guns hit by our counter-battery work. But our artillery have used up many of their guns, and are short of springs. Rundle thinks that each battery should have another behind it to replace losses, as well as artificers to repair guns. He says that we still have a lot of prematures, the 60-pounders about 1 in every 500, the 4·5 howitzers about 1 in 200. He had lost eight men through prematures, and some French 75's, which were operating with us, were very cross at having lost five men from the same cause. He described the difficulty of getting guns forward, owing to the want of roads and to the barrage fire of the enemy.

A fair crossing, and I arrived at Victoria about 11 P.M.

CHAPTER XI

MR. LLOYD GEORGE AS WAR SECRETARY

Mr. Lloyd George War Secretary—Sir William Robertson's opinions
on the military situation—A Warren House party—Some Irish stories
—A luncheon with Mr. Lloyd George—His opinions and plans—No
victory till 1918—The disabled soldiers and the Statutory Commis-
sion—Sir Nevil Macready and the reinforcement of our Armies—
Vast numbers of exempted men of military age—A visit to Fulwell
Park—Lord French's dissatisfaction with the authorities—Scene at
Headquarters in London during a Zeppelin raid—Sir W. Robertson on
the Somme battle, the Channel Tunnel, and Portuguese assistance—
The Indian Police and Lord Curzon of Kedleston's reforms—Lord
Wimborne on recruiting in Ireland—A luncheon for King Manuel—
General Geddes on recruiting—General Alderson and the Canadians—
Mr. Beck on America.

Tuesday, Wednesday, Thursday, July 11-13. Spent the
time in getting straight, and finding out all that had happened in England since I had left. Scarcely any letters
or papers have reached me in Italy or France. I found,
generally speaking, that people were not aware what a
terrible battle had been fought on the Somme, nor of our
losses.

I went to see a friend on the 12th. He told me that the
losses were 83,000 by Sunday. He also said that L. G. was
a doubtful quantity as War Secretary at present. He has
been full of International Munitions work these last few
days, and has scarcely begun War Office work yet. But he
has shown a disposition to consult subordinates instead of
the heads of departments, and this will never do at the War
Office. Also, he is said to wish to put in Eric Geddes, the
railway man, as Quartermaster-General in France instead
of Maxwell. Geddes knows nothing about any part of

this work except the railways, and, if L. G. insists upon it, Geddes should be made Director of Railways in France. The general impression seems to be that L. G. is rather a wild man, and they are rather uncertain how he will frame out. However, Derby is Under-Secretary and knows the ways of soldiers, and military members invite him to their meetings. I saw Derby. He is just off to France for twenty-four hours. Poor Lord Haldane is still being abominably treated, and the Duke of Buccleuch went at him in the Lords just before Haldane began a speech on education. It is all very mean, and cruel, and stupid, for no one has done more for the Army than Lord Haldane. The public are like a lot of rooks; when one appears to be a bit ill, all the rest peck him to death.

Went to see Lord French the morning of the 13th. I found him very upset about the losses of the Army in the battle. He was also, I regret to note, not pleased with Robertson, who, he thinks, is trying to become Commander-in-Chief of the whole Army, and French talks of resigning. I implored him not to do so, but he declares he will unless he is allowed to have his own way in Home Defence. I am afraid there are troubles ahead, and it is a great pity.

We went on together to lunch with Lady Paget. Mrs. Whitelaw Reid, Lady de Trafford, Lady Ridley, Lady Herbert, Mrs. Astor, and some men. I sat next to Mrs. Whitelaw Reid, and found her very agreeable. She told me that she owned the *Tribune*, and interested me a great deal about it. I told her how much I admired Simonds and his editorial arbiters.

Lady Ridley looking rather worn out with all her hospital work. Lord French and I remained after the rest to discuss the war. Lady P. simply *shovelled* the others out of the house. We all three had the same point of view about the war. She had not the least idea of our losses, and thought that we had had only 500 casualties among the officers, whereas I suppose we have several thousand. French says that he is sending off trainloads of officers every day to fill up gaps. Robertson has asked him to spare a lot of men 'from his 200,000,' and French is very irate, because he only has 150,000, and one-third of them are not armed. I suppose the depots cannot yet provide enough trained men from the conscripts.

Met the Wimbornes at dinner at Olive's. He and I discussed Ireland and the war at some length.

My four articles on Italy have now appeared. Some people want them republished with maps and photographs, but I do not think that they are at all suitable for such a purpose.

I am writing two articles on the battle in France, but am delayed by having to send them to Haig to be censored ! What will they be worth afterwards ?

Saturday, July 15. Went in the morning to see Lord French, and had a talk with him and his Staff. They were all very happy with the news that our troops had broken the German second line yesterday.

Went on to see Sir William Robertson, and found him in his new office on the north side of the building, in what was formerly a committee room. I like it better than the old room. We had a good talk about events. He is pretty happy about the developments in France, though he thinks they are inclined to be in too great a hurry in reporting captures of positions, when our troops may only have taken certain elements of the line. However, we have apparently secured the German second line from Longueval to Bazentin-le-Petit, and there are rumours that our patrols are on the outskirts of Pozières. All this is good if the gains can be maintained.

The French have not done anything to-day. R. thinks that their main trouble is want of railways. They have only got a line made as far as Bray, and apparently are rather hung up. Lord French pointed out to me this morning that all the ground from the Somme to Péronne is very swampy, and that Mont St. Quentin, which is very strong, commands all this region. R. appears to have heard from Foch the same things about our artillery preparation that I have heard, and R. agrees with them.

He thinks Foch's attack was fine. He puts down our total losses up to the present at between 80,000 and 90,000 men. Those of the enemy at about 60,000. He agrees that we have only enough heavy guns for one Army and a half, but says that the rest are coming on, and we shall be all right by November. The drafts are also doing well. He has sent out 58,000 trained men to fill up. There are 15,000 more standing by. He has taken several thousands from the Home Defence Force.

L. G. is doing well, and he saw no reason to suppose that they would not get on together. He is still in exactly the same position with reference to him as he was to Lord K., and he had handed him a paper much in the same sense. L. G. had been quite amenable. Since he had come in, L. G. had been mainly occupied with International Munitions, Ireland, and Politics, so one could not tell how things were likely to go.

R. had seen Haig and usually went out every two or three weeks just to look round. He did not interfere with Haig. He did not ask him for plans in detail, as he did not wish to know them. He only discussed the broad subjects with him. He thought, after all, that the hole that we were making in the German line was not much more at present than a mere dent. But to-day it was calculated that we had 100,000 men against us, and the French the same number.

Macdonogh was rather disturbed because German battalions were turning up from all parts of the line, including Verdun. I said that this was sure to happen if we did not attack along the whole line, but so long as we had heavy guns for an Army and a half, and had five Armies in the field, we were bound to have some without use or employment. All the same, I said that I thought that the Northern Armies ought to be more busy. He was inclined to think the same, but said that the use of the Northern Armies had not been left out of calculation. We had plenty of men at the depots now. But after this first batch of drafts there will be a shortage for about three weeks. We should get all our heavy guns by November. He thought that the Germans were getting a bit strained. He disappointed me about the Russians, who, he hinted, were getting short of ammunition again. It is correct that the Russian Central Armies have sent down a strong reinforcement of twelve divisions or so to Brussiloff, but it looked as if the Russians were not going to get on much further at present. They have done very well.

Mesopotamia, he said, was an awful mess, and they could not get it right. The trouble was the transport. The river was very low, and they could not get the stuff up. They had neglected to make railways. Now they were making two, one of which, from Basra, would reach Nasariyeh in seven months, while the other would span the most difficult section of the Tigris line and be ready in four months. We had about 100,000 men in Mesopotamia. It was difficult to say who was responsible for the muddle. He asked me to suggest a name for some one to replace Duff, and I said that I would like to think it over. Charles Monro was in my mind. We discussed the question of Military Administration in India, and I implored him not to allow the old Military Department to be resurrected, as I warned him the *Times*, Curzon, and a lot of old Indian officials might do their best to bring about. I told him that he must keep the Commander-in-Chief in India his nominee, and that there was no reason why a Sub-Chief should not sit on the Viceroy's Council, just as Whigham sits on the Army Council at home. He had not had much luck in getting control of things in the East, as Austen Chamberlain would not look at it, but he was going at it again. He wanted general control of the strategy, but we could not control administration which India paid for. The War Office, he said, knew nothing of dhoolies, and coolies, and ghi. It was a difficult question, but he was determined to have the higher appointments in his hands.

He thought that the Germans still had a couple of million men to come on, and that we were not near the end of them yet. It was a long affair, and would go on well into next year, but we were all doing very well. I told R. that I thought that the attack of the 7th, 8th, and 10th Corps, on July 1, was a very glorious failure, and that all the generals concerned had done their best. I should deplore punishments of subordinates for what I did not consider their fault. He did not know of any dismissals except X. and Y., but Granville Egerton told me afterwards of several others, which grieved me very much. But I hope his information is wrong.

Saturday and Sunday, July 15 *and* 16. Went down to Coombe. A large party for the week-end. The American Ambassador, and the American Mr. Beck, who has been so active for the pro-Ally propaganda ; Percy Thelluson, from Salonika, where he was on Mahon's Staff —and ran the mess as admirably as the capable representative of Pommery's might be expected to—Sir William and Lady Robertson, Sir John Cowans, Sir Starr Jameson, Mr. and Mrs. Maguire, Lady Mar, Lady Leicester, Mrs. Duggan, and Mr. and Mrs. Lavery.

Sir Arthur came over for the Sunday morning. We had a talk about France and about his defence arrangements. He runs from Sheerness to Dover. He had five divisions, but two have now been taken away, and the others drained of several thousands, including most of the cyclists. He has represented it, and says that it is Lord French's job, and he can't do any more. We happened to walk through the dining-room, where there was luncheon laid for about twenty people, and he said, ' Good God ! ' and went off.

Had a long talk with Sir Starr in the morning, and then a walk with Dr. Page and Mr. Beck for a bit, but the rain drove us in. Lady Ripon still ill in bed, and could not see us.

A very cheery lunch ; sat between Mrs. Duggan and Lady Leicester, who were both charming. Mrs. Duggan's little girl had had a bad operation, but is getting over it. Lady Leicester I met in old days ever so long ago. She was the most beautiful English girl I remember at that time, and still has very good looks. She is very keen to get our wounded either employed or dealt with in some way properly by the Government, and wants me to look into it. There seem to be a great number of very hard cases, and some of these heroes are on the rates. She says it is entirely want of organisation, and I expect she is right.

Mrs. Duggan tells me that she is going out to Argentina in September, but will be back by Christmas. She is a very pretty woman, most charming and restful, but has got many enemies, probably because she is such a success.

Beastly wet afternoon; played Picquet with Lady Mar, and talked at the same time. She was very nice and pleasant, and wants me to stay at her place at Alloa, when I fix up to meet Jellicoe. This will suit me very well, as they are within forty miles of Rosyth, where Beatty and the Battle Cruisers are now. She says the sailors talk a great deal to her, and she has the feeling that the Battle Cruiser Squadron feels that it was not sufficiently well supported by the Battle Fleet in the Jutland fight.

An amusing girl came over to tea on Sunday—Miss Wiborg. She is known as 'Hoity,' and her sister as 'Toity.' A very self-possessed young woman, and rather attractive. She sang some first-rate songs without music, sitting at the tea-table, and made us all laugh enormously.

The contretemps of the week-end was the fact that Dr. Jim and Tommy Maguire were asked to meet each other. Dr. Jim had been appointed Chairman of the B.S.A. Company in preference to Tommy Maguire, who quite expected to get the place. They had sat on the Board together for two years, and Maguire had never said one word to Dr. Jim. They never spoke now, but Mrs. Maguire was most agreeable to Dr. Jim, so the thing went off all right. We talked until 2 A.M.

Monday, July 17. Jack Cowans drove me back to London early. We discussed the Indian question. He thinks, as I do, that the Mesopotamian muddle is not due to any defect in the system of administration of the Indian Army, but solely to the men who are running it just now, especially to Beauchamp Duff, the Commander-in-Chief, and General Bunbury, who has been Q.M.G. since the war began, and has now been replaced. Cowans said that they were all baboos in India at H.Q. Robertson, says Cowans, shows signs of being rather imprudent about India, of which he knows nothing. Jack says that except himself no one on the Army Council knows where India is.

Lunched with Sir John and Lady Leslie and Olive at 46 Great Cumberland Place. Very pleasant house. Lady Leonie as gay and amusing as ever. Many great Irish stories. One of an old woman who was found stealing potatoes out of her neighbour's garden. She was caught and asked the reason. She said, 'Shure, we have got martial law and can do as we plaze.'

There was another good story from the Galway coast. Some one tried to get a boat for fishing, and was told by Timothy O'Hara that he could not lend him a boat for fishing as he was getting £3 a day from the Germans for dropping mines. 'Oh,' says the man who wanted the boat, 'then I will try Michael Flaherty.' 'He's no good,' says Tim, 'he's getting £10 a week from the Government for fishing the mines up.'

Jack Leslie's battalion at Enniskillen is down to 600 : it was 1900. I don't know how these Irish regiments are to be kept up.

Hacket Pain is in command at Ulster. He was Chief of Staff to Richardson in the Ulster Volunteer Force, and is a good man.

Went to see Sir John French at the Horse Guards. He had just got word from the War Office that our losses up to Saturday evening were 103,000, of which between twenty and thirty thousand were missing. Sir John asked me whether I thought the game was worth the candle. The bit of ground we have gained is about the same as we had gained at Loos at half the cost, and we now had twice the Army. He said that the Kaiser and 200,000 men were now facing us. R. also told me that we had 100,000 against us, and the French the same number. He does not think that we can win at this rate. Nor do I, but where are the thirty new divisions which I said we should want in 1916 ?

He tells me that my French articles have been censored and will not be allowed to appear. I suppose that they don't want the truth to be known. He wants me to see L. G. and have a talk with him. He, L. G., and Haldane are dining together to-morrow night. I cannot get to hear yet whether there are any more generals who have been kicked out, besides X., Y., and Z. I hope there are no more ; it is not at all satisfactory.

Tuesday, July 18. Went to see Sammy Scott in the morning at 78 Mount Street. Heard some of his experiences in the East, and I told him some of mine. I am afraid that he will have to go out again on the 26th. He is too old for the Yeomanry, and too short-sighted, but he does not want to leave the East Kent Yeomanry and take a Staff appointment. It is the right spirit, and Sam is a white man.

Arrived rather late at Mrs. Arthur Wilson's for lunch. I sat between Muriel Wilson and Sevastopoulo. There were also there Mr. Laszlo and his wife, Lady Leslie, Lady Essex, Sir Louis Mallet, Major Baker Carr, whom I have not seen for twenty-three years, and Soveral.

Very pleasant luncheon, with a lot of chaff. Soveral in good form as usual, and very amusing. I told Miss Muriel how impossible it was to exchange her brother Jack, who was captured by an Austrian submarine from a big ship. Neither the Foreign nor War Office is at all pleased about it, and Vansittart at the Foreign Office warned me that it was best in Jack's interest to leave the matter alone, especially as he is near Vienna, and is well treated.

Heard that Delmé Radcliffe was in London, and came upon him at the Bath Club. Went to his rooms near by. He showed me a memorandum he was writing, advocating that Italy should declare war against Germany. But I did not approve of our taking any action in this matter, as I think, with the Russian Colonel Enkel, that it may upset the equilibrium of the Italians. He tells me that the Italians have now some twenty divisions back on the Isonzo, including the reserve Army and some nine divisions which have been engaged on the Trentino front. The Austrians have drawn a good many divisions from the Trentino, and everything seems to be going well. I arranged with Delmé Radcliffe about Lord Northcliffe's visit to Italy.

Wednesday, July 19. Find that my articles on the first phase of the battle of the Somme, have begun to come back from G.H.Q. The first article has no alterations. I got forward in completing the other two.

Lloyd George lunched with me at the Carlton at 1.30. Derby was also there lunching with Charles Montagu. The place was very full. We began talking about the Somme at once. He did not appear to believe that we should be very successful, as the casualties were already so numerous, and there was every chance for the Germans to bring guns and troops from the North and from Verdun. I told him I also doubted whether we should have great success until we were able to equip with heavy guns all our Armies. At present we had only enough for the 4th Army. I told him Foch's standard for the guns and shells, which made him look serious, and he told me that in seventeen days we had fired twice as much ammunition as Douglas Haig had reckoned to fire in a month. I told him about the defect in our artillery preparation, and he agreed on the subject. He was very anxious to get more 6-inch guns for counter-battery work. We had only thirty at present, and it was not nearly enough. I suggested that he should take them out of coast defences, as Cadorna was doing. He thought it a good plan, and also promised to get some from any old cruisers which were not wanted. He is going over to have a talk with the French gunners, and will then talk to Balfour on the subject. He says that the French were greatly outgunned at Verdun, and he heard that local French commanders were becoming a little pessimistic. If Fort Souville were taken, the

Germans will practically have taken Verdun, and they would then shift round 2000 guns on to our front and hammer in. It was a very serious moment, and he was evidently anxious. He doubted if this was the right way to win the war, and preferred to wait till next spring, when we should have all our guns and a lot more trained men. He said that Rumania wanted to come in, and he was for extending the front to weaken the enemy. I told him about Rumania's wishes about the shells, and that I had been commissioned to speak about it. He agreed that we could trust Rumania, for the reason which I gave him.

(French had telephoned me in the morning, and had told me that our casualties were now 110,000.)

I told L. G. how our divisions had been taken out of the line and sent up North and fresh ones supplied, and how this process made the Northern Armies weak, as they were already shorn of most of their heavy guns; but he reminded me that the 2500 heavy guns which he had ordered would be about right for fifty divisions on Foch's scale, and that we should get them by November. He said that, including trench-mortar projectiles, we were now turning out 200,000 shells a day, but he thought Germany was turning out more. He did not think it possible to beat Germany this year, and we both gave the war till 1918 to finish. They would not surrender because they could not give in, so the grinding process must go on, and could go on better the more guns we had and the larger the surface which we compelled Germany to defend. He evidently still favours the Salonika offensive for this reason, but he thinks that we can do nothing there this year unless Rumania comes in; then we shall have to move to keep the Bulgars employed.

We should end this war, he said, by being the second greatest military Power in Europe, and he thought that we had got a great deal out of the war in the way of defence equipment, national discipline, etc. He wanted our Dominions to do more, and he had also written a memorandum about African and Indian help. He had to defend

the Mesopotamian campaign ; he did not know how he was
going to do it, as he was thoroughly dissatisfied with it.

I asked him who there was at the War Office who had
his entire confidence, since he was such a busy man that
I did not like to trouble him often. He said Arthur Lee
was the best man for me to see, which will suit me very
well. He was getting on with Robertson capitally, and
with every hope to continue to do so. Robertson had
been capital over the Compulsion wrangle ; in fact, L. G.
and he had practically carried it between them. Robertson, like a cunning old fox, merely stated how many men
he wanted and when he wanted them, and refused to
express any opinion how they were to be found, since he
regarded this as a political question. This attitude completely defeated the politicians. L. G. had sent a memo.
to the Cabinet before the war in favour of a Swiss system
in the Army. Asquith, Grey, and Haldane had supported
it, and I think he said Crewe, but the Cabinet would not
have it.

He kept on returning to the war. He did not see how we
were going to win on the present lines. The Germans would
not give in, and by next year we should have a lot more
men and guns, and the Russians the same ; we should
begin breaking the Germans down. He did not think we
should do it until 1918. We discussed India and Mesopotamia, and I advised him to keep off the Indian Army
question as it was full of pitfalls, and when he asked whom
I should suggest for India if Duff went, I proposed Monro,
who had a good head and was very dependable. He asked
me whom I preferred if there was a change in France,
and I said Allenby, as he combined youth, physique, and
character. L. G. did not remember him. They met when
I was at the cavalry manœuvres some years ago, but only
one day when there were a lot of other officers about.

He did not like this Government, and said that he had
just come back from a meeting of ' the Duma,' meaning
the Cabinet.

He thought that he had some good men under him at the

War Office, and I advised him that if he would work through the soldiers, and consult them as Haldane did, they would all eat out of his hand before long, but they were kittle cattle and not to be treated like civil servants in other departments. He must carry them with him, or he would get beat.

He said that he was not going to move in a hurry, and I strongly recommended him to do nothing for three months, until he got to understand the machinery. He wanted very much to bring over Johnny Du Cane from the Ministry of Munitions, and asked where he could put him. I told him that he must make him M.G.O. We agreed that Von Donop would suit Munitions best. He was a very competent technical authority. L. G. said that he liked Du Cane very much. He had a quick mind which worked like his own, and he had big ideas and could grasp things. He was also ready to say when he changed his mind.

We had a very cordial talk and discussed many other matters. I gave him Cadorna's message about wanting heavy guns and machine guns, but he told me that Dall' Olio, the Italian representative for Munitions, had assured the Committee that Italy wanted for nothing, and made no demand for guns! I told him that I could not understand this, as Cadorna had been quite explicit to me, and that I should warn Delmé Radcliffe.

Dined with Mrs. Duggan at 32 Grosvenor Square. The party had grown from six to nearly twenty. The Prime Minister and Mrs. Asquith, Lord Curzon, Harry Cust, Frank Curzon, Dr. Ross, the Duke of Rutland, Wolkoff, Mrs. Ward, Lady Strafford, Lady Cunard, and a few others. Too many for the room, which was rather low, and we were too crowded, and it was frightfully hot, while the dinner was too long.

The Prime Minister very interesting after dinner. We discussed Eton and the Provosts, and tried to find a Provost for the P.M. to appoint, but we could not fix on one.

George Curzon looking much better; but his left arm

is still bad; he can scarcely raise it. He sat next to Mrs.
Duggan on a low chair. She was looking very pretty and
very happy. Her little girl is ever so much better.

Thursday, July 20. Finished and sent off my second and
third articles on the first phase of the battle on the Somme.
They have to go to the G.H.Q. in France, which I think
an absurdity.

Lunched with Winston Churchill at 41 Cromwell Road.
We were alone. He showed me his latest works of art,
and I must say that Lavery is right, for he has made an
extraordinary advance, and several of his pictures are
quite worth buying, notably an interior of Blenheim.

He knew all about the battle and the causes of our heavy
losses. He has always been against this offensive, and
thought it would come to no good. But we agreed that
something had to be done, and we could not sit still. He
was very pleased with his journalistic success. He had
got £1000 for writing four long articles in a Sunday paper,
and felt sure that he could make £5000 a year, and place
himself on the right side in matters of finance. He said
how sad it was that while he was slaving at Plug Street
in front of the battle, his reputation kept going down and
every one scoffed at him, whereas when he was talking on
the front Opposition bench, and getting a lot of money for
fiction, he was increasing his fame daily. We had another
long talk about the Dardanelles, and he told me what he
was going to say this afternoon. It struck me as very
good and true; in fact, unanswerable. I hope he may
get the inquiry which Carson is going to demand, both for
Mesopotamia and the Dardanelles.

Winston admits that he approved of the Mesopotamia
expedition, and the advance on Bagdad. He declares
it was because Nixon so strongly recommended it, and none
of the other military authorities opposed it. Had he had
the faintest conception that Townshend was against it,
he would not have touched it with the end of a barge-pole,
and it was very wrong of Nixon not to have let the Government know. I said, 'Well, that covers it as regards military

opinion, but I still can't conceive why any body calling itself a Government could send a single division of 11,000 men to attack a populous town at the heart of a military Empire, while we had insecure and bad communication over a line 600 miles from the sea.' I regarded it as lunacy, and told Archie Murray as much when he wrote to consult me on the subject at the time.

Winston is going to speak on the 'Conduct of the War,' and the debate on the next vote of credit, and will consult me beforehand. We discussed the question which L. G. raised yesterday about the gain of England during the war. It was an interesting subject, and I think that I must write about it when I feel in the mood. Winston thinks of going out to France and Italy to look round, and I told him that there was no difficulty. He told me that I ought to have had one of the highest commands, and that no one had my brain. I wonder whether he says this to everybody. I took the compliment for what it was worth. He is very lively and looks very well.

Friday, July 21. Dined with Lady Granard at Forbes House, Halkin Street. Found a large party. The King and young Queen of Portugal. He very agreeable, and she very charming and nice looking. Lord and Lady Chesterfield, the Duchess of Roxburghe, Belle Herbert, Lulu Harcourt and his wife, Soveral, Jack Cowans, Lord Lurgan, Lady Victoria and her husband. Sat next to Lady Chesterfield and found her very agreeable. We made up three Bridge parties afterwards.

Had some talk with the King, who asked me to invite myself down to Fulwell next week to lunch. Very pleasant party. Everybody animated and talkative. Lulu much chaffed and criticised about his petrol restrictions, which hit all motorists very hard.

Saturday, July 22. Had a lot of letters about an article which I had written about Belgium for her Independence Day, including one from the Belgian Minister, M. Paul Hymans, and another from M. Carton de Wiart. Both very enthusiastic and appreciative.

Went by train to Beaconsfield to pass a quiet week-end with Mrs. Astor. Olive, Vansittart, Lady Johnstone, young Davignon, son of the Belgian Foreign Minister, and Cecil Higgins also came.

We played lawn tennis and a good deal of Bridge.

Monday, July 24. Came back early. Mrs. Townshend lunched with me at the Berkeley. She was raging, as the Turkish and Bulgarian Governments had given her permission to go to Constantinople and join her husband, but the Foreign Office this morning had withdrawn permission. Lord Hardinge had even refused to see her. She found the excuse was that she had Austrian relatives. She wants me to get L. G. to work it. I think that considering Enver is making up to Townshend it would be quite worth while to let her go and bring back news of the situation in Constantinople. However, there are wheels within wheels, and one never knows what is at the bottom of it all.

Dined with Sir Ian and Lady Hamilton. Dr. and Mrs. Prothero, Lady Kitson—wife of my old friend, Gerald Kitson, who is home from India and at a loose end —Colonel and Mrs. Ronny Brooke, two hard-featured Australian officers, one of whom was a general, young Moncreiff whose submarine ran ashore on the Dutch coast causing him to be interned, and pretty Miss Pollen.

Discussed India with Lady Kitson, and other matters with Mrs. Ronny, whom I found quite charming. We had a good talk about the war.

Tuesday, July 25. We are not getting on very fast in France with the attack on Guillimont.

Lunched with de la Panouse and M. Floriau, the Chancellor of the French Embassy, at the Café Royal. We had a great talk about the war, and they wanted to hear about all my experiences in Italy and France. We discussed possible peace terms, and arrived at the usual conclusion, that there was nothing to be done with Germany until she had suffered military defeat.

Saw Sammy Scott at 72 Mount Street, and had a long

talk with him about Egypt and political matters at home. He returns to Egypt on Friday, and will not take any job at home as he wishes to stick to his Yeomanry as long as he can be of any service to them. He reminds me of Cardigan's ' Here goes £40,000 a year ' at Balaklava.

Afterwards went to 2 St. James's Square, Lady Falmouth's house, and met her, Lady Leicester, and Surgeon-General Jenkins to discuss the state of affairs with regard to the pensions of disabled soldiers. Those suffering from lung trouble are also in a very deplorable condition, and there seems to be a total lack of organisation on the part of the new Statutory Committee, and great bitterness has in consequence been caused among the men who fought for us. After a lot of talk it was decided that I should consult Keogh and Derby at the War Office, and then go and see Lyttelton or Charles Crutchley at Chelsea about the pensions. Then, that we should reconsider the whole matter. I was also to see Cyril Jackson, who is at the head of the Statutory Committee, and apparently confesses that he has no scheme, and that the whole matter is chaos. I think that we should run this affair through the County Associations, and have a central body formed by the old Council of County Associations. We need a big hospital for 2000 cases of tuberculosis patients, and to have county hospitals for disabled men, who should not be discharged until they can find work. We must also work through the Labour Party, as there is great difficulty in getting work for the disabled men who have pensions and can work at a lower rate than other men. The ladies want me to talk to Wardle, M.P., of the Labour Party. This affair kept me so long talking that I was late for dinner at the Locketts'.

Friday, July 28. Went to see the Adjutant-General, Sir Nevil Macready, and to speak about the complaints which I have received from the front respecting the indifference shown to regimental feeling in the allocation of the drafts. Macready said that it had taken him nearly three months to study the matter, and to change the chaos which existed in the A.G.'s Branch when he came to it.

He had found a bad Staff, and bad arrangements. So he had made great changes, and proposes to transform the whole matter of man-power.

The root of the trouble lay in the fact that when the expansion of the Army began, Kitchener had accepted battalions and other units from any district and from any authority that offered to raise them, without any regard to the question whether they could subsequently be maintained. Many evils resulted from this want of system, and from the fact that recruits and reserves were restricted to use in their own regiments. Some regiments could not be kept in the field and fell away to nothing, while others were full, and had large reserves which could not be utilised. From this source arose the disadvantage that we had an immense number of troops at home out of all proportion to the men in the field; in fact, the whole thing was very slipshod and inefficient. He had now decided that all recruits in regimental districts should be incorporated in training battalions, and should not be posted to any regiment until they had completed their training. He proposed to retain the Special Reserve battalions exactly as they were without any change, and also one Territorial battalion in each regiment, in order to preserve the continuity of the existence of regimental formations, but there would be, in addition, four or five or more training battalions located in each regimental district, distinctly *not* forming part of that regiment or of any other. The training units, in fact, would form a vast pool from which men could be drawn and sent wherever they were wanted, and the regimental *esprit de corps* would be inculcated in the regiment to which the men were sent.

I told him that, on the whole, I approved of these arrangements, but that they would probably meet with considerable opposition unless the subject were fully explained, and I undertook to enlighten the public if he would give me a copy of the order. He promised to send me an early draft of it so that I might explain to the public what was in the wind, and the very serious reasons which rendered this measure necessary. I told him that the main objection which occurred to me was that a great many men would not be serving in their county units, and that the Territorial system would be abrogated. He replied that the regimental system would be followed as far as possible, and that he fully understood the objection, but that his main business was to complete the effectives and furnish a constant supply of drafts, so that strengths might be maintained. He said that people must understand that the Army came before the regiment. He could see his way a year ahead, but much had to be changed in the attitude of the Government departments towards the whole question of man-power. Many thousands of men of military age were being sheltered in the Government departments, and the Admiralty was among the worst. There were about a million and a half men of military age exempted from service whom he thought it necessary to get at. Tribunals were also in some cases very slow in getting the men, and affairs were not all on a proper footing as yet. He said that L. G. had opened his eyes as wide as saucers on being told of things that had been going on in his late Department of Munitions, and this was only an example of what was going on elsewhere.

Saturday, July 29. Lunched with Mrs. Leeds, Lady Portarlington, Miss Joan Campbell, Bogey Harris, and a man from the American Embassy.

Went off to Coombe in the afternoon. Sir Arthur came down on the Sunday. We had a long talk, and he told me that his Home Defence troops had been so drained that he did not believe that we could resist an invasion of 40,000 men. He had been asked to find 10,000 men for France from his weak units, but had not that number of men trained. The number had then been reduced to 6500, which he had now to find as well as many officers, and they were trying even to take away his instructors, which he has resisted. I advised him to state the case fully to Lord French, and see that the latter represented it. I promised to go down to see his troops when he wished.

He told me that Douglas Haig wanted a demonstration on the Belgian coast to attract the attention of the Germans. Admiral Bacon was going to carry it out, but troops are also to be concentrated, and on Sunday next the cavalry division will cross the Thames by the patent bridge, and other troops will march down the coast, and there will be ships. He is telling his commanders to make their wills, but whether anything further will come of it, and whether the Germans will be alarmed, or even be informed of what is happening, is another question.

The party consisted of the Spanish Ambassador and Madame Merry del Val, the young Duchess of Sutherland, Lady Pembroke, Miss 'Hoity' Wiborg and her mother, Sir Seymour Fortescue, Lord Bertie Vane-Tempest, Jack Cowans, young Somers Cocks, Mrs. Leeds, the twins, and a few more. Some good tennis, much talk, and much Bridge. In the evening a great rag. We got to bed about 3 A.M., and the next night was almost as bad, if not worse.

Jack is very sick about Markham's accusations. There is going to be an inquiry, and a Bill is to be presented to allow evidence to be taken on oath. It is a great bore for him, and a wicked waste of time. He is now feeding and supplying 3,400,000 men, and the best part of his time will be taken up for three months over a trivial and idiotic case.

Monday, July 31. Went on from Coombe to Fulwell Park to lunch with King Manuel and his young Queen; Viscount Asseca and a lady-in-waiting were also present. Fulwell is rather a nice place, a fairly large and comfortable house with about forty acres of ground and nice gardens not overlooked in any way. The King's room very pleasant and full of some valuable pictures, china, and so forth, representing relics saved from the smash in Portugal. The Queen was very agreeable, and we had some amusing talk at lunch, after which the King and I retired into his room, and we had a long talk on Portuguese matters. He still holds that a National Government must be formed in

Portugal before affairs can right themselves. Late in the afternoon he motored me into London.

Tuesday, Aug. 1. The editor of the *London Magazine* came up to ask me whether I would write for him as Northcliffe wished me to do. He said that I could state my own price for an article of 3000 words. I said that I would let him know.

Lunched with Mrs. Leeds. She showed me the Boldini portrait for which she sat for a month in Paris and paid £2000. Boldini always makes his ladies six feet high and like successful cocottes. She likes the portrait very much. I was not struck by it, and there is no resemblance to her at all. Laszlo's portrait is out and away the best.

Went to see Winston at the House of Commons. He showed me a memorandum which he had written on the Somme battle. It was to be fathered by F. E. Smith. It showed our heavy losses and the probably slight comparative losses of the Germans, and was critical of our arrangements. I told him that I could take no exception to it, but that I did not see the use of taking this line at present. It was a good paper as Winston's papers usually are, but I did not see the utility of it at this stage. I thought that we were bound to attack and to suffer in the general cause.

Long sitting of the Tribunal, and we got through many cases.

Wednesday, Aug. 2. Worked most of the day. Dined with Lord French and Brinsley FitzGerald, at 94 Lancaster Gate, at 8.30 P.M. Spent most of my time in trying to soothe the Field-Marshal, who was in his best bantam-cock form. I told him that he must remember that Robertson was put in when Lord Kitchener was alive, in order to make good the latter's deficiencies, and that he was not put in in any way as a slight upon Lord French. I told him that R. had a difficult hand to play, and was quite right to support Haig so long as Haig was in command in France. I begged French for the sake of the country not to quarrel with him. 'Oh,' said the Field-Marshal, 'you used to say just the same kind of thing to me about Kitchener, when I did not get on with him.' I replied, ' Yes, I did, and I should say the same thing again.'

He has represented the weak state of Home Defences, and has the copies of all correspondence. He has told Robertson that he cannot resist a landing in strength ; that he knows that he will be hanged ; but that he has taken care that R. will be hanged with him. I saw no objection to this, but said that he ought to make sure that his views reached the War Council and the Cabinet. I also found out that French had no liaison of any sort with Jellicoe, and that neither knows what the other is doing. French thinks that Jellicoe is in the same position as Haig, and that therefore he, French, has nothing to do with him. I disputed this, and said that he and Jellicoe had a common task, should be hand and glove, and that then their combined representations would be listened to. I asked permission to bring these views before Jellicoe when I could meet him up in the Forth, and to suggest that each should have a high officer of the other's Staff in order to keep in touch. The F.M. agreed. Brinsley very useful in backing up my views, and in trying to soothe the F.M.'s outraged dignity.

About 10.30 P.M. came the news over the telephone of the imminence of a fresh Zeppelin raid. We all went off, and I had an opportunity of seeing the whole of the anti-Zeppelin arrangements working at full pressure in the stables, or cellars, at a certain place. General Shaw was there in control of a Staff of about twenty or thirty young officers, naval and military, clerks, telegraph and telephone and wireless operators, etc. The telephonic and telegraphic system very complete, and messages came in with few delays.

I went first to the Chart Room, where the position of most if not all the Zepps. in the North Sea before the raid began was shown. This is done in the following manner : Zeppelins cannot navigate at night with any certainty of knowing where they are. They, therefore, send by wireless to Germany the number of their ship—L 29, or whatever it is—and two German wireless stations, at a wide distance apart, get the message and send back at once the exact bearing of the airship, which they can do by one of the many inventions of this art. The airship officer plots the two bearings, the intersection of which then gives him his position. But *we* also pick up the airship's number, and, by cross bearings from our wireless stations, can plot in the Chart Room the exact position of each Zepp. We continue to do this every time a German Zeppelin calls to its friends, as it frequently does. A map in the Chart Room showed all the positions of all the airships which had called up their friends at different hours of the night. We knew, for example, to-night, that there were six or seven Zeppelins about to attack. We cannot attack them at sea, because we have no dirigibles, while the seaplanes are too slow in rising, and both seaplanes and aeroplanes have a very short radius of action, while it is considered dangerous for them to fly by night. Also, there is no moon. We are, in fact, on the defensive, and the only chance of defeating them is by insuring that wherever they go they find darkness, and if they run into our guns so much the worse for them. As each Zepp. crossed the coast, messages of all kinds poured in. There are sometimes a thousand in a night during these raids, and Shaw, or whoever is directing, telephones warnings to each district liable to be attacked. First they make preliminary preparations against the raid by sending to each menaced district the order to stand by, and then they give the order to bring into force the full anti-aircraft arrangements. A transparency in the office in front of Shaw shows all the districts into which England is divided. When the preliminary notice is given, the district warned becomes coloured pink in the transparency, and when the second warning comes it becomes green-coloured. By the end of the raid there were six or seven counties coloured green from Lincolnshire to Kent, and a fringe of counties to westward, including the London area, coloured pink. On large maps, hung on the wall, the course of each Zeppelin was shown by large square red blocks, and each message relating to it was forwarded to any Government department, or naval or military or civil authority, likely to be concerned.

The organisation is very perfect, with the result that these last two nights, during each of which six to eight raiders have come over us, they have been surrounded by darkness, and have done no harm, nor even killed anybody, although they have dropped bombs all over the place. The German report about last night makes the most fantastic claims, namely, that they had bombed London and done much military damage. This pleases them and does not hurt us. It was not even necessary to send the second notice to London, while at Harwich and Dover, which were visited by Zepps., and at a few other places, the anti-aircraft guns came into play, as well as the searchlights, and drove the enemy off before he could do any harm. One night we shall get a brace or so; meantime the system of opposing them seems as good as it can be in the absence of dirigibles. I think a few seaplanes and aeroplanes went up at one place. They asked permission to light up an aerodrome, which was granted, whereupon the Zepps. immediately bombed it. I got home at 3.30 A.M. A very fascinating evening. The weirdest experience of science and ingenuity applied to a new art of war. The scene during the night will always remain with me.

Thursday, Aug. 3. Had the very curious experience of finding myself the thirteenth at lunch with Lady Cunard, and the thirteenth at dinner with Mrs. Maguire, in both cases owing to my servants not having sent my messages accepting the invitations. I would not stay at Lady Cunard's, and fortunately the dinner misunderstanding was cleared up in time.

A long sitting on the Tribunal, and did not get in till 9 P.M. The Hampstead Tribunal have worked like niggers. The Mayor is an excellent chairman, and they sit on very steadily, showing excellent judgment and great patience. I wish that all the Tribunals were as good.

Friday, Aug. 4. Went to see Sir William Robertson

at 5 P.M. at the War Office. I told him that I had come just to ask him his views on three subjects : the course of the battle, the Channel Tunnel, and the affairs of Portugal. I told him the points, on all three subjects, on which I wanted his opinion.

He said that we had had about 150,000 casualties in France, which were certainly very heavy, but that 60,000 of these had happened on the first day, and that we had not lost lately more than 20,000 men a week. The Germans were very strong, and had now brought up against us and the French thirty-six divisions, or their equivalent. The result had been that we had no doubt killed a great lot, that there had been only one attack on Verdun since we had started, and that the enemy had suffered 750,000 casualties in the course of the past two months on all fronts. We went into these figures, which included the 382,000 mainly Austrian prisoners made by the Russians, and I found no reason to quarrel with them. He said, of course, that there were a great many people buzzing about who were trying to interfere with and to run the war, but that we were under a mutual obligation to go on, and that we could not tell Paris that we had had enough and meant to stop. We were now using less ammunition per day than we could supply daily, and the pressure would be continued. The best thing to do was to regard the question from these points of view, and not to give way to the busy-bodies. I said that I thought that this opinion was very sound, and that I would follow it. He said that he had heard that I had written about the fight, and supposed that my articles had come back unaltered. I said that the second article had not come back unaltered, and that Geoffrey Dawson and I considered the corrections dishonest and should not publish the articles in consequence, but that I was not going to bother my head about it just now, and that the war was too big for me to trouble about such trifles at present. He agreed that the great thing was to win the war, and that nothing else mattered.

He had not made up his mind about the Channel Tunnel,

but at present he saw no reason to allow it to be made.   I told him that I had always said that I would cease my opposition to it when we had a National Army in this country.   We had such an Army now, at all events abroad. But should we have it after the war ?   I did not know. Also, until the sailors could deal with the submarines, there was no getting over the fact that the tunnel, or tunnels, would be very useful to us, but that for the sailors to admit, by now backing a tunnel, that defence at sea had broken down, was to give away the case for the Navy.   He said, would not the submarines blow the tunnel in ?   I said that I thought that it was too far below the bottom of the Channel for them to do so, but that this point would have to be considered before any plans were passed.   I told him that all the people who were running the Channel were very busy.   He said that he would look into the matter, and let me know in a few days.

As for Portugal, he told me that since I had first spoken to him on the subject, they had been busy, and that one Portuguese division was nearly ready.   But when the second came up it was found that they had to use the officers and cadres of the first to push it along.   Further, the French had butted in and had suggested that as the Portuguese would fight in France, they, the French, should take charge of the arrangements.   Grey had even written about it to the War Office, saying that this would save a great deal of trouble, but he, R., was of the opinion that the Portuguese, being our ancient Allies, should be left with us.

I asked him to meet King Manuel, and arranged a lunch for next Wednesday.

Busy with all sorts of correspondence.   Had lunch with Lady Allendale, 32 Queen Anne's Gate. Sir Ian and Lady Hamilton, Sir George Murray, Sir Henry and Lady Cunningham, Mr. Fleming, M.P., of 27 Grosvenor Square, and one of the P.M.'s secretaries, whose name I forget.

We had some talk about the war and about finance,

Fleming thought that matters were getting serious, but George Murray thought that we could go on for ever so long, if we did not exceed £5,000,000 a day. The disputed point is whether we will ever get back the loans from our Allies. Murray gave me his views about the Statutory Committee and Cyril Jackson.

Met Mrs. Leeds and Joan Campbell, the former all the better from her month in Bath, and the latter looking very pretty indeed.

Saturday, Aug. 5. Sir Arthur Markham's death is a great loss to the country. He has been the most fearless and independent man in Parliament since the war broke out, and I regret his death very much. He has done incalculable good, and the Government were frightened to death of him. It is a great pity that he took up the case against Jack Cowans in the last days of his life, for he was on the wrong track. But I am sure that if he had known the facts, he would have been the first to apologise and recant. There is no one of any value to take his place. The odd thing is that he was liked though he was feared, but I expect that the Ministers in their hearts are glad that he is out of the way.

Went down to Hallingbury for the week-end. Some good golf, croquet, and Bridge. Weather heavenly. The Locketts are perfect hosts. Hughes-Buller, late Inspector-General of Police in Bengal, was there, and told us many interesting things about the condition of India. I heard from him that Valentine Chirol is in great trouble about the case brought against him by Tilak. Chirol's charges were based on confidential information from the Government of India, and he cannot bring them in evidence, consequently he is at his wits' end for proofs, and has been ranging India for a year in search of them. Hughes-Buller says that things were pretty bad at one time in India, but are now much better. The Germans have been doing their best to raise the country, but we had wind of all their doings, and knew of all their attempts to land arms, money, and agitators. We put our hands on most

of the rascals, if not on all, and he supposes that if our
police arrangements had been equally as good in '57, we
should have had no mutiny.　Curzon's Police Commission
Report reforms are having an extremely good effect, and
Buller now has a great many smart young fellows under
him, and the Government is accurately informed of all that
is going on.　He is an admirer of Curzon, and thinks that
the effects of his reforms have been excellent.

Tuesday, Aug. 8.　Lunched with Lady Cunard at 20
Cavendish Square—the Asquiths' house.　Lord and Lady
Wimborne, Mr. McKenna, Lady Douglas Dawson, Mrs.
Hunter, Lord and Lady Islington, Lord Carnock (late Sir
Arthur Nicholson of the Foreign Office), and some others.
We went up to see the new blue drawing-room, which is
in very exquisite taste and quite charming.　The state-
bedroom is alongside.　The hostess as full of life as ever.
Her daughter, Nancy, is engaged to a young man, Fairbairn
by name.　But I don't think that Lady C. much relishes
being a potential grandmamma, for she is so indescribably
young.

I had a serious talk with Wimborne about recruiting in
Ireland.　I told him that we ought to have Conscription
in Ireland, and that it was only the rank cowardice of the
Ministers which prevented us from having it.　He said it
was impossible, for the people have no intention to fight
England's battles.　But I said that they were not England's
battles, but those of civilisation, and, unless something were
done, many Irish battalions would have to be disbanded
for want of men to keep them up, and Ireland would be
the mock of mankind hereafter.

He promised to assemble his old Committees again, and
said that they were very representative of Ireland, and
that he would take them in hand again.　He thought that
he could get 500 to 600 men a week, but I don't believe
it, and even that would not be enough.　I promised to
try and get to Ireland and have a talk with him later on.

Had tea with Mrs. Leeds.　We had a great talk about
Tony Drexel's affairs.　Lady Strafford came in and took

part in it. The muddle is greater than ever, and neither side will give way, but when two American citizens decide for one of them to get his divorce in Paris, and the other to get hers in London, when both could and should get it in America, there is bound to be trouble.

Dined with Princess Clémentine and Prince Victor at the Hans Crescent Hotel. We had a great talk about the war, French politics, and the state of affairs in Belgium. A band was playing. Presently I noticed that all the people in the place were standing up. It was the Brabançonne, and I had not noticed it. I must be getting as bad as Franky Lloyd, who does not know 'God save the King' when he hears it.

Wednesday, Aug. 9. King Manuel, Soveral, and Sir William Robertson lunched with me in a private room at the Carlton. The King rather deaf on one side, after an operation to his left ear. Various intrigues to exclude us from all control of the affairs of our ancient Ally had been in the wind. The King said that a Spaniard of position had been to him, and had suggested that England's Alliances in the past had been with the House of Braganza, and not with Portugal, clearly seeking to make a rift through the King between Portugal and England. But the King had told him that though the Alliance had been made with the House of Braganza, he, as King, had presented it to Portugal. This and certain observations made by Soveral, who was in good form and was very communicative, made more clear the drift of a recent communication from France, suggesting that the French should organise the Portuguese military contingent, because it would fight in France. Soveral had had wind of this missive, much to Robertson's surprise and to mine, and he strongly opposed it. The King wants R. to send me to Portugal as his, R.'s, emissary, but I told R. afterwards that I was not keen about it, though I may go there later on and look round. We had a lot of talk about Portugal and Portuguese politics. The King very frank, and delighted in his luncheon party, which he wants repeated, and says he will come up from Eastbourne whenever I like.

Went to the War Office to see General Woodward, of the A.G.'s Branch, about the new Training Reserve. I told him and Colonel Lewis that the establishment did not seem to me big enough, but Lewis told me that only half the picture was given. The total establishment of the Regimental and the Training Reserve was over half a million. Woodward introduced me to Brig.-Gen. Auckland Geddes, who has been put into the recruiting branch under Macready. He seems a capable man. He said that he had been in despair about recruiting for the first two months after he had come in, but that in the last month he had begun to see light. He agreed with me that the Army ought to have been expanded from the Territorial Force, and said that the A.G.'s Branch at the opening of the war had recommended this, and had warned K. about the deep water in which he would find himself. Lord K. would not listen, and our present trouble was due to this fact. Geddes thinks that the changes will not be popular, but that they are the best that we can adopt in the circumstances.

We talked about Tribunals, and he said that the A.G. was dead against the Barristers' Commissions, which have practically done nothing since they were instituted, as I said would happen. I told him that in attacking these barristers I thought that I was opposing the A.G.'s Branch, but he said that, on the contrary, they agreed with me, and that the whole matter was due to Walter Long's obstinacy. It had become a personal question. He showed me a paper which disclosed that there were 3,800,000 men of military age who had not yet been touched, and we agreed that, this being so, we should outstay Germany in man-power. He thought that we had done a big thing in getting a small Committee on man-power with full authority to act. But the A.G.'s Branch had to fight all departments of State to get men, and some of the departments were very strong.

I finished an article for to-morrow's *Times* on the ' Training Reserves.' Lady Paget came up to Maryon about 9. We had dinner and talked till 11.30.

Thursday, August 10. Dined at the Wellington Club with Generals Grove and Alderson.

We had a good talk about the war. Alderson told me the reason why he had left the Command of the Canadians in France. He is now Inspector of the Canadian troops in England, of whom there are some 50,000 to 60,000 still here.

Friday, August 11. Dined with Mrs. Leeds, Lady Paget, and Mr. Beck, the American.

Beck held forth during dinner on the whole subject of his visit here, which had been very successful, and upon American feeling towards England and the Allies. I think that there is no doubt that 75 per cent. of American feeling is strongly pro-Ally, and certainly Beck is very much to be complimented upon the useful line which he has taken all through. We then branched into the question of the reunion of the English-speaking races, and we found that we were all four keen on the subject. But we had to go off to a play, and promised to meet again and continue the subject. A hot night and a small theatre—the Ambassadors. It was a Revue, and I did not look forward to it, but we were very late, and in spite of the heat we all found the show most amusing. Madame Delysia and some French actor; both quite excellent.

CHAPTER XII

RUMANIA TAKES THE FIELD, AUGUST 1916

A visit to Sandbeck Park—Imminence of Rumania's action—General
Maurice on the military position—A story about the Channel Tunnel—
An American opinion of President Wilson—The German Fleet out—
Mr. Balfour imitates Drake—Our Admirals and the Channel Tunnel
—Allied and enemy divisions on various fronts—A visit to Watlington
Park—The Dutch Minister's views—Lieut. Pernot on the situation—
Rumania enters the war—Sir Charles Monro, C.-in-C. in India—His
plans—Hindenburg succeeds Falkenhayn—Colonel Olivant on Meso-
potamia—General Maurice on Salonika and the Rumanian plans—
Mr. Lloyd George displeased with our strategy in France—General
Robertson's views—Chances that Hindenburg will attack Rumania—
Formality of Royal circles—Sir W. Robertson on the Somme battle,
Rumanian strategy, and Salonika—Indian Army affairs—Recruiting
difficulties.

Saturday to Monday, Aug. 12-14. Went off to Sandbeck Park, Rotherham, to stay with the Scarbroughs.
Train to Maltby and motored on. Met General Mends
in the train, after Doncaster. He has been far from
well. Sandbeck a large and handsome house dating from
about 1720, standing in a fine park with a pretty lake well
stocked with Loch Leven trout. The other visitors were
Mr. Fisher, Vice-Chancellor of the Sheffield University, a
fascinating savant and a good talker ; Lady Arran and her
daughter, Lady Winifred (Betty) Gore ; Lady Bradford,
Scarbrough's sister and Lady-in-Waiting to the Queen,
and little Lady Serena Lumley.

The Scarbroughs are both delightful people. He has a
great position in the West Riding, and is one of the hardest
workers and most unselfish patriots in England. I have
always known him to be working for the good of his country,
and always without advertising or self-seeking. He is

also a great gentleman, and of a type that is becoming
much more a *rara avis* than it used to be. She is a very
nice woman, and has, I believe, done an immense amount
to beautify Lumley, where I must go and stay one day.
Except some pictures of the Lely period and one Reynolds,
there are not many nice things in the house. It was
apparently cleared of treasures for the profit of a Savile
lady, who took them to Rufford and managed to keep
them. Sandbeck is very comfortable all the same, and
there are beautiful gardens, especially Lady S.'s secret
garden, with a nice summer-house at one end of it. It was
a perfect blaze of colour. There are also other gardens,
and a great expanse of glass. There has been the usual
trouble about gardeners, who are now all boys, and the
foreman is only seventeen. We had some long talks about
the war, and the future of education, on which Mr. Fisher
is very keen. He has had the breadth of mind to propose
Will Rothenstein for Art Lecturer at the University, but
I am not sure how it will work out. Certainly he could
not do better for Sheffield, for there is no brighter mind
than Will's on all artistic subjects, but I wonder whether
the name will not cause the proposal to be negatived. We
went over on Sunday afternoon to see Tickhill Castle, a
fastness of John o' Gaunt. Very imposing, with its walls
and keep and beautiful gateway. Scarbrough and his
brothers and sisters were all born there. We also saw a
model mining village for the workmen at the mine opened
seven years ago. Very excellently planned, all the roads
radiating from a common centre, and the houses well
built. They get down to the 5-feet seam at a depth of a
thousand yards, which is three times deeper than my 7-feet
seam in Warwickshire, and it cost the company a quarter
of a million to sink the shafts and get to work. It is good
steam coal they say, and the seam descends towards the
North Sea, and reappears somewhere on the other side of
it—perhaps in Westphalia. A German company had also
started in the neighbourhood, but their works are now
derelict. We went on to Roche Abbey, which stands in

grassy meadows at the confluence of two streams in a sequestered and quiet spot protected on all sides by hills— an ideal place for peace and contemplation. Only the west end of the Abbey remains, but enough to show the great beauty of the building, which dates from the twelfth century. Scarbrough has opened it up enough for one to see the form of the building and partly of the cloisters. It belonged to the Cistercian order, and must have been a superb place once, but it was destroyed in Henry VIII.'s day. It is a place that makes a great impression on one, especially when seen upon such a glorious afternoon as to-day.

I showed them in the evening the absurd trick with the three coins which I learnt at Maxine Elliott's. They all became intensely interested, and tried for two hours to do it, without any success, until at last Scarbrough lighted upon the secret. It is the most absurd and maddening little trick, and the Vice-Chancellor was completely baffled by it.

I liked the ladies very much, and found little Lady Betty very interesting, as well as attractive. I believe that Lady Arran is no longer with Princess Christian, but I am not sure. Lady Bradford had just come back from duty with the Queen. Short skirts do not appear to have won the Royal favour. Lady S. and Lady A. and the daughters travelled up with me to London. It is a long journey, too far for a week-end. We ate our first grouse of the season on the night of the 12th.

Wednesday, Aug. 16. Major-General Fred Maurice, the New Director of Operations, dined with me at the Savoy at 8. He says that the French declare that Rumania is coming in in a few days, and though he is not so sure as the French, he thinks that it is quite probable. He suggests that I should use this event as a peg on which to hang a comparison between the situation of May and August 1916. We went all through the different points, but as these will be in the article when it comes out, it is unnecessary to refer to them here. I wrote down a rough

sketch of the article on my return home. He thinks that
the situation at the War Office is now good, and spoke
very highly about L. G., whom he had accompanied on
his recent visit to France. L. G. and Thomas were very
thick, and an animated conversation went on between
the two through the interpreter, who, it appears, is a cousin
of M. Thomas. Maurice laughed a good deal about L. G.'s
description in the House of Commons of his visit to the
front, as though he had been everywhere and seen everything. Actually, said Maurice, L. G. only reached H.Q.
at 3 P.M., dined at Rawlinson's H.Q., and returned. But
L. G. will go there again soon for ten days. Maurice said
that the figures that I suggested to him of the number
of divisions in the West on the two sides were correct.
But he places the Germans in the East at fifty divisions
owing to the arrival of some newly formed divisions. He
thought that the Austrians were badly smashed up. He
told me that the Russians had practically abandoned the
central attack at Baranovitchi, and sent more reinforcements south of the Pripet, where they now had ninety-six
divisions. Hindenburg had made a parallel movement.
I was rather dubious about this move, which gives the
Germans the advantage of fighting on a shorter front.
Maurice is also a little uneasy about the situation in the
winter, when Hindenburg, with his superior railway system,
may try some move in the North, or again may transfer forces
to the Western front. However, we shall see how this
stands later.

We discussed the Channel Tunnel, and agreed that we
could neither of us support it until we were sure of getting
a National Army after the war. Some of the Channel
people have sent a memorandum to the Government in
favour of the scheme, and it has been forwarded to the
General Staff. Maurice has put in a reply in answer to it,
and it is now before Robertson. This is as far as the matter
has gone at present. I advised Maurice to get on terms
with the Admiralty on the subject, as united opinion was a
great strength.

He told me that crossing the Channel one day with Robertson, the latter was very sick, whereupon Maurice had said to him, 'After all, General, we were glad during the retreat from Mons, that we lived on an island,' and Robertson replied, 'By God, yes!' We agreed that had the tunnel existed when war broke out, the Germans would have seized the Calais end of it. We should have then destroyed our end of it, if possible, and supposing that the Germans had retired from Calais, they would have destroyed their end of it, so the utility of the tunnel would not have been great. Also, in the retreat it would have been a nice point whether we should have retired upon Calais or upon Paris. The main thing is not to let this scheme proceed until we are sure of our National Army. We were quite in accord on the whole subject.

Thursday, Aug. 17. Published two articles on the Russian campaign, bringing it down from June 4 to the present date.

Dined with the de la Panouses, 5 Princes Gate, at 8.30. He and his wife and two daughters, Sir Arthur Lee and his wife, and three or four secretaries from the Embassy. Quite a pleasant dinner, and a good deal of chaff afterwards with the girls and the secretaries. Had not much chance of a serious talk, but arranged to meet Sir Arthur at the War Office. He told me that he was sorry that we had not been able to prevent thirty more divisions going off against the Russians, but this must be an exaggeration, for I don't think any have gone from our front in France since we began fighting on the Somme. Panouse highly approved of my comment on the Russian campaign, which appeared to-day.

Friday, Aug. 18. I began writing a couple of articles on the 'Unity of Fronts' in accordance with Maurice's talk to me. Lunched in Belgrave Square; Lady Paget, Lord Carnock, Mrs. Leeds, Mr. Beck, Mrs. Whitelaw Reid, and Dr. Ross. Beck did most of the talking—all about Wilson and the Presidential campaign in America. He thinks that Mr. Hughes will get in, on account of the shame of the Americans of the figure Mr. Wilson has made America cut in the war. But he admits that any incident that may occur between now and November may be exploited by either party, and may make all the difference. He is opposed to Wilson, and, on the whole, gives a favourable sketch of Hughes, and thinks Teddy Roosevelt may become his War Minister, and Root Secretary of State. Beck speaks well, and is worth listening to about American politics. The trouble is that all our friends here seem to be Republicans, and we only hear their side. Mrs. Leeds thinks that he will not become Ambassador here. Mrs. Whitelaw Reid told us a great many interesting things about America. She appears to keep the *Tribune* going for the sake of her boy and for the political influence which it will give him. She has just bought a big villa on the Riviera. Went off with Mrs. Leeds after lunch to various places; to the Vine Street Police Station and the Westminster Town Hall, to complete innumerable papers which the wretched alien—even the 'friendly' type—in these days has to put in order. She says that the police are always sending for her, and that she tips them whenever she goes to the Police Station. She says that she is always getting telephone messages asking her to come. I said, 'Well, you should not tip them,' and I took care that she did not on this occasion. We will see how this works.

Larking, our naval attaché at Rome, sent me the first of two papers by the Italian Admiralty on the work of their Navy in the war. The Italians both wrote it and translated it into English, as if it were going to appear in the *Times* straight away, but it is heavy, cumbersome, and involved, and I shall only use it as a basis, and wait till the second article turns up, and see where it all leads. All the same, it is interesting as an indication of the general lines of thought along which the Italian sailors have proceeded during the war, and I may make something of it.

Saturday to Monday, Aug. 19-21. Went down to Coombe, and found Mrs. Astor, Miss Muriel Wilson, Evan Charteris,

Vansittart, M. Bardac of the French Embassy, and a few others. The General, the twins, and Somers Cocks came down on Saturday, but were recalled owing to activity in the North Sea. Mr. Balfour came down on Sunday, and also Mrs. O'Neill, a fine tennis player, who wins tournaments. A very pleasant party ; Balfour played very well. We had heard that there had been a scrap in the North Sea, and that one light cruiser had been sunk. He told us that this had taken place on Saturday. He had heard nothing from either Jellicoe or Beatty before he left London, and though he imagined that Beatty had communicated with Jellicoe, he could not understand why Jellicoe had not communicated with the Admiralty, and he was rather sore about it. He told us that no word had come of transports with the German Fleet, but that most of the German ships were apparently out. I admired the coolness with which the First Lord, emulating Drake, decided to go on with his game, although the Armada was at sea. He stayed until 7.45. He asked me a great many questions about the Rumanian Army, which I answered to the best of my knowledge.

I asked him about the Channel Tunnel, and what view the sailors took of the resuscitated project. He appeared to think that the Admirals were so upset by the German submarines, that they would be very glad of the tunnel. He expressed his utter astonishment that the Germans had not made any serious effort during the whole course of the war to interfere with our troops and materials going across the Channel. We had some good tennis, and I returned to London with Van on Monday morning. I then heard confidentially that Rumania was coming in on the 28th, which is very good news. It is said that Rumania had asked, first of all, that the general offensive of the Allies should be taking place on all fronts, and, second, that we should be busy at Salonika for a week before her intervention. This accounts for the initiation of an offensive movement from Salonika on our part on the 20th. I was also given the figures of the divisions on the different fronts, which are pretty much as I thought. Rumania is credited by our people with 1,000,000 trained men and 1440 guns,[1] which will be a pretty useful addition to our joint forces. There appear to be only sixty Austrian Landsturm battalions on the Rumanian frontier.

Tuesday, Aug. 22. Wrote an article on the Rumanian forces in preparation for the day when Rumania declares herself. Dined with Mrs. Leeds at Grosvenor Square; Lady Sarah and Dr. Ross also there. A very amusing talk at dinner, and afterwards we went to the Palace. Graves, and a good company, kept us in fits of laughter all the time. Mrs. Leeds goes away to the Grand-Duchess George to-morrow.

Wednesday, Aug. 23. Grimthorpe and a pretty friend came up to tea at Maryon, and stayed a long time. Both very pleasant and much interested in all the pictures and treasures.

Thursday, Aug. 24. Went down to Mrs. Astor in the morning to Wilton House, Beaconsfield. Only Lady Cunard there, but she went off in the afternoon to see her daughter, Nancy, who is at Lady Northland's. Had some capital sets of single tennis with Mrs. Astor; we got so hot that we nearly died of it. Lady C. came back for dinner, and we had a most amusing talk afterwards. Lady C. thinks that the P.M. is very disgusted with some of his colleagues, and complains that he is not being properly supported by several of them. She says that his hint, given in the House, that he might not be in office next year, was meant quite seriously, but I shall believe his going when he goes, and not before. She told us about the house that has been lent to the P.M. at Bognor. She says that it holds eight people, and that Mrs. Asquith thinks nothing of putting in eighteen, and they sleep where they can. The sea comes up to the garden; Lady Diana was staying there the other day, and insisted upon midnight bathing. We had a good talk about current gossip.

Friday, Aug. 25. My second article on the 'Unity of

---

[1] Compare p. 225.

Fronts ' has been massacred by the Press Bureau. The original article contained a comparison of the number of divisions on all the different fronts, which shows better than anything else the necessity for further efforts before we can obtain annihilating superiority. For instance, in the West we have 56 divisions, the French 105, the Belgians 6, total 167, while the Germans have 122. On the Eastern front the Germans have 55, the Austrians 45, total 100, against the Russian 141½. The Italians have 50 divisions, all included, against the Austrian 27½ at present. The Bulgarians have 12 against Sarrail, and south of the Danube. The Bulgarian divisions average 22 to 24 battalions each. The Russian divisions are 16 battalions, the British 13, the French 10 to 12, the Italian and Austrian 12, while the Germans are reduced to 10, and in many cases only 9, as Jäger battalions are being used as the nucleus of new divisions. My conclusion from this and from the relative proportion of heavy artillery on the two sides, where the Germans have the advantage, is that, though we have a good superiority, it is not enough to promise early victory, and this comparison would, I think, have heartened up the people, and brought out all their sporting instincts to get further in front in the race for victory. However, the censor—or rather the fellow who inspired him—thought differently, so the public are still kept in ignorance of what they are really up against.

Lady Sarah lunched with me at the Berkeley Grill, which, with the Ritz, appears to be the best place for lunching just now. The Lyttons were there, and the Lutyens with Robert and Barbara, also ' Scatters ' Wilson with a friend. He told me that the explosion in the munition factory, which occurred this week, was at Bradford, and that he had to go up to see about it, as many of his workmen were homeless. So far as he knew, it was the result of an accident. Last night's Zepp. raid did a little more harm than usual, as one Zepp. got into South-East London and killed a few people. Began a draft of an article on the Channel Tunnel.

Saturday, Aug. 26. Revised an article on Rumania and sent it in. We all hope that Rumania will come in up to time next Monday.

Lunched at the Ritz with Bertier, ' Scatters ' Wilson, Mrs. Montagu, and Lady Sarah. It was Mrs. Montagu's party. A great many people there. ' Scatters ' told me that he was returning to Egypt on Friday. He said that he was devoted to Archie Murray, and believed in him very much, but that he made himself unpopular by telling some senior officers that they were damned fools, which is Archie's way with incompetents.

Went off in the afternoon to Mrs. George Keppel's house, Watlington Park, Oxon, with the Dutch Minister, Van Swinderen. His servant took my luggage with him, and lost his master's, which did not turn up until Sunday night. I wonder if our secret service were looking it over ! Found a gay party consisting of George and Alice Keppel, their two daughters Violet and Sonia, the Hwfa Williamses, Lord Ilchester, Lady Lilian Wemyss, Baroness Daisy de Brienen, Mr. and Mrs. Nicholson, and Sitwell and another young fellow in the Guards. A nice house standing well at the top of the Chilterns, and a beautiful glimpse of the distance through a wood. A nice park, grounds, and gardens. The weather was bad, but I managed to get a few sets of tennis on Sunday afternoon. We had a great game of hide-and-seek in the house during the wet morning. The girls hid Van Swinderen over a calorifère, and he was nearly roasted alive. We also had some music and dancing, and played a lot of Bridge.

Had a great deal of talk with Mrs. Keppel about the war, and with the Dutch Minister about things in Holland. I told him that I thought things were working up to trouble between us and the neutral countries that were still holding out from the war. He evidently knew nothing about Rumania's intention to come in, and threw cold water on the idea. I told him that all neutrals would soon have to make up their minds what they were going to do, for we could not afford to let them feed our enemies, and I said I thought that opinion was hardening against Holland, and that sooner or later we should have to say that he who was not with us was against us. He was evidently a great deal exercised about this, and asked after dinner one night whether there was any animosity against Holland. I said, No; I was only talking of general tendencies, and things they had to look out for; that I, personally, did not wish Holland to come in at present, as I did not wish the Germans to get hold of the Dutch supplies east of the Water Line, but that I thought Holland would have to come in eventually and take her part. He was inclined to agree, and told me that if there was any idea of the Germans remaining in Antwerp, the Dutch would certainly fight. I said that I was very glad to hear it, for Antwerp and the Scheldt really formed part of the Dutch position and were inseparable from it. I reminded him how I had tried in old days to bring about a military understanding between Holland and Belgium, and how the Belgians had fallen in with the idea, while the Dutch had absolutely refused to accept it. He thought that the advantages would have been all on the side of the Belgians, which I entirely disputed, and said that if the two little States had been united, and had been able to put 500,000 men in the field at the outbreak of war,—as they easily might have done—Belgium would never have been invaded.

Miss Daisy told me that Amsterdam was very pro-English, Rotterdam equally pro-German, and all the rest of the country rather pro-French than pro-Ally. This was owing to the fact that England had to put into force all the disagreeable penalties of the blockade, which injured the Dutch trade, and that we consequently got the odium for what was really the decision of all the Allies. There is no doubt that the French everywhere are increasing their popularity, while we certainly are not. But we have set out to be feared and not to be loved, so it does not much matter. Had a lot of racing talk about the past with Hwfa, with many reminiscences about horses and jockeys, especially of the Derbys of Sir Bevys and Ormonde. He thinks that the Bard would have won the Derby in Ormonde's year if the jockey had ridden to his orders, and had been leading at Tattenham Corner. The Bard's trial had been very severe, and had made the Derby look a gift for him. It was certainly precious unlucky for him to run up against such a great horse as Ormonde, who was never beat.

Monday, Aug. 28. Returned to town early with the three young men, and instead of discussing soldiering we talked of nothing but pictures, Palladio, and palaces. They were all three extraordinarily well informed, and knew Italy well. The war has brought a strange medley of capacities and incapacities into the Army.

Lunched at the Ritz with Bertier and Pernot, who leave for France next Wednesday. Pernot says that they talk a great deal about me at Chantilly, and that they want me to come across and talk matters over with them, which I said I should be glad to do, especially before I went to Portugal, if ultimately I decided to go there. I asked how things were going, and they said well, on the whole. They were not best pleased with our tactics in France, but thought that we were doing much better now, using our guns better, and losing fewer men. They thought that it was absolutely necessary to continue the offensive, partly because we were under a moral obligation to do so, and partly because the supply of ammunition now admitted of it, whereas, in the old days, our attacks in Champagne and at Loos had to be stopped in order to allow the ammunition reserves to be accumulated. They said that we must not talk of a lull, or even think of it. If one did come, the Germans would like to take their troops over to Russia just now; and later on, when the Russians might allow themselves to be arrested by the winter, the Germans might like to jump upon us, so we must all keep on, and keep on keeping on. The Germans were certainly suffering very badly, and we had now a good superiority all round. The first public report of Rumania having declared war

came out while we were at lunch, so we drank Rumania's
health. We were none of us best pleased that Italy was
not more pressing after her Gorizia victory, and none of
us knew the reason. Things in Persia had been pretty
bad, but were apparently mending. Bertier rather surprised me by saying, in reply to my suggestion that we
might take over more of the French line next year, that it
was not at all a popular idea with the French that we
should do this. I hope it only means that they want us
to develop a strong offensive along the whole front, and
not simply to hold a long line so that the French may
undertake an offensive. We all agreed that Rumania
intended to attack Hungary through Transylvania, and
Bertier said that a strong force of second-line Russian troops
was on its way from Odessa to the Dobrudcha, where they
would help to keep Bulgaria quiet, and prepare for the
eventual Russian attack upon that rascal Ferdinand of
Bulgaria. I introduced them both to Muriel Wilson and
Soveral, who were lunching near us. Miss Muriel talks
excellent French. I wrote an article in the evening on
' The Boche Mind.'

Tuesday, Aug. 29. Finished article on ' The Boche
Mind.' Went down to see Sir Charles Monro at the Buckingham Palace Hotel at 5.30 P.M. He was, to my great
pleasure, appointed a week ago Commander-in-Chief in
India, vice Duff, who is coming home. Monro tells me
that he was not even asked whether he would take the
command ; he was simply ordered to take it, and says
that no one can refuse to do anything that he is told during
the war. He is going out entirely alone, and starts on
Sept. 8, via Marseilles. We had a talk about India and
the war. He tells me that there is no question at all of
making any serious change in the administration of the
Army in India. I said that I was very glad to hear it.
He personally agrees with the changes made by Lord K.
in India, as I do, and thinks that it would in any case be
fatal to make a change at this moment. He is going out
to look round, and has the idea of choosing his Staff

eventually, or part of it, from men who have been with him in France. He hopes to go to Mesopotamia and look round and see where the trouble is. He fancies, as we all do, that it is a question of transport. He has not been in India for twenty years, and was then only a company commander. He does not seem to have had many serious talks with Robertson or anybody about the larger questions of strategy and organisation, but he is immersed in all sorts of papers from the India Office, and has a tough job in front of him. He says that Duff will not return to India. He was very anxious to talk to me about the war. He does not seem to be as well posted as I should have expected an Army commander would have been in the things that are going on on the various fronts, and of the number, plans, and dispositions of the German and other Armies. I told him what I knew on the points concerning which he required information. He was very full of the big line taken by Lord K., when the latter first came into office. He says that a great lot of heavy guns have been reaching his late Army recently, and that this Army would now be in a condition to make some sort of push if necessary, but he did not know how the supply of ammunition stood until I told him. He wanted to know what I thought about German plans. I said that I did not think that they had any, as they were all fighting as best they could where they stood, and had no formed reserves. He said that they were extraordinary people, very docile, and would do anything they were told. There were no people like them in this respect. He thought that they would be up to some new game soon. On his front it had been chiefly raiding and mining. He had kept all the Germans in front of him expecting an attack during the first fortnight of our offensive on the Somme, but by that time they had smelt a rat and had begun to slip away. He did not think that the Bulgars could do us any harm where they were at Salonika. He was most anxious to know when the war would end, but I could not tell him, and thought that it depended upon the Germans and not upon us. He thought that it might go on for a year. I told him that L. G. and I gave it till 1918, if the Germans wanted to go on fighting so long. We agreed to write to each other while he was in India. This was the main object of my visit to him. I told him that I had corresponded with the Staff of Lord K. all through the latter's time in India.

We hear to-day that the Rumanians are attacking all along their frontier with Hungary. They have not wasted much time. We also hear to-night that Hindenburg has succeeded Falkenhayn as Chief of the General Staff. A very interesting piece of news. I expect, as I have already suggested, that there has been rivalry [1] between these two men. It may mean a change of plans, for which we must look out. It may also mean a shortening of front, or even an intention to make peace, in which latter case the prestige of Hindenburg will enable the Kaiser to do things which he could not do without it. I don't think that the conditions are at present favourable to any serious alteration of the war in Germany's favour.

Wednesday, Aug. 30. Wrote an article upon Hindenburg for to-morrow's paper, expanding the above ideas, and anticipating a Boche stroke against Rumania.

Thursday, Aug. 31. Looked in at the Horse Guards, and had a talk with Sir John French. Found him not more pleased than before about the conduct of the campaign in France. He thinks that we have lost over 200,000 men by now, and that the Army is being ruined without any commensurate results. He says that there is going to be a fresh effort to the northward in about a fortnight's time. He has had fresh drafts made on the Home Defence Forces, to supply the wastage of the Armies in France, and he says that he would be in despair about Home Defence if he believed in invasion, which he does not.

Wednesday, September 6. Called at the War Office in the afternoon, and found that Lloyd George and Arthur Lee had gone to France. Saw Lieut.-Colonel A. Olivant of the M.O. Branch, who was with Winston at the opening

---

[1] Fully confirmed by the Memoirs of Ludendorff and Falkenhayn.

of the war and is now one of the two officers in charge of an M.T. branch, under Sir William Robertson. A very clever and amusing fellow with a pretty wit. We fell to talking about Mesopotamia, and he said that when the question of the advance on Bagdad was mooted, the General Staff were not consulted, nor had they been about the expedition at the start. The whole affair was in the hands of India. When Nixon advocated the advance, a committee of thirteen members was assembled at the War Office to consider it, and among them were only two soldiers, of whom one was a young officer of the M.O. Branch. Olivant says they proceeded as though they were dealing with a problem of statics and not of dynamics. They took two months to ponder the matter, in spite of the protest of the young officer that while they were pondering the Turks would be moving. When they had finished pondering the Turks had got down to Bagdad from Constantinople, and it was too late. Nixon insisted and went on. Olivant has no doubt, in the light of the information in his office, that had the advance begun when Nixon recommended it, Townshend could have reached Bagdad, might have raided it, destroyed the boats and railway, and returned, but he could not have held it long. The information of the M.O. Branch about the march of the Turkish reinforcements was fairly accurate, but Nixon trusted to his local information, which was wrong, and perhaps he had his mind set upon the project and closed his ears to advice which countered it. Olivant also said that the staff teaching about river operations was faulty, and that the staff work, generally, was very bad in Mesopotamia owing to bad men at the top.

Olivant had been in the Mediterranean, and latterly on one of the islands. They were all right, he said, in the days of Sappho, but had not many attractions now. He thought that Austria was, like England, a bad beginner and a strong finisher, but certainly on the evidence she was nearly all out. We agreed to meet at lunch one day and talk more. He thought that the Bulgarian offensive had been very elementary.

Looked in to see Major-General F. Maurice, the new D.M.O. Things in France are going well. The extension of the French attack on the right southwards was good, and I understand that it will be followed soon by the extension of our attack to the northward. Maurice admitted that two German divisions had gone East since July 1, but one had been severely mauled. We hoped that the increase of pressure would prevent more from going, and we were watching intently. Cadorna should go on, but was waiting to store up big-gun ammunition. Dall' Olio's information given here had been all wrong, as I had told L. G. We branched to the Balkans, and I gave him my opinion that Sarrail should have tried to move ten days ago from what Olivant calls the Salonika eel-trap, *i.e.* one which an Army can enter easily, but not easily quit. I said that I feared that the Russians in the Dobrudcha might be beat unless Sarrail was more active to hold the Bulgars on his front. Maurice said that their information was that the Bulgars had still eight divisions in front of Sarrail. The latter had placed his troops wrong. There were only three roads out of Salonika, and the only thing that Sarrail could do was to advance on Monastir, but he had placed the Serbs here, and they were not very good yet, and had no reserves to fill them up. So Sarrail was bringing three French divisions to the left. This move would be completed to-day, when Sarrail would have ten divisions on the Monastir front against three Bulgarian, the latter equal to six of ours numerically. He hoped that this would attract more Bulgars in the Monastir direction.

The Rumanians had three Armies entering Hungary, one, the Army of the North, three divisions, 106,000 men, head now at Gyurgyo, was hung up at the Toplica Pass. The 2nd Army, four divisions, 132,000 men, was in the centre, and doing well. The 1st Army, five divisions, 142,000 men, on the Orsova front, and had got through; but all the columns of these Armies were not through the passes yet. The general objective was the Maros line. The left of Brussiloff's Armies aimed at Bistritz, and

the Russian line would extend northwards to Marmaros
Sziget *if* they could get through the hills. The Russians
were very short of heavy guns, but had plenty of field
guns, which suited this country best. The Rumanians
had a 3rd Army of six divisions, 146,000 men, mainly
reserve formations, along the Danube, and finally a reserve of 51,000 men at Bukharest. The Russians marching
into the Dobrudcha were $2\frac{1}{2}$ Army Corps and a cavalry
division. The latter was in contact with the Bulgars,
while the Army Corps had reached the level of Constanza.
They could hold the narrowest line across the Dobrudcha,
where the Turks had their lines in 1877, and be supported
by the sea and the Danube. Maurice thought that there
were not more than two to three Bulgar divisions attacking here, but he expected that three weak Turkish divisions,
30,000 men, might come up, and not more.

Maurice told me that $4\frac{1}{2}$ defeated Austrian Army Corps
had been sent to the Baranovitchi front, and regarded it
as a proof that the Germans had no offensive designs here.
He also said that the rains had begun in the North.

Thursday, Sept. 7. My article much cut about by some
ass as usual. Finished and sent off an article on ' The
Channel Tunnel,' opposing the scheme until we knew what
sort of an Army we should get after the war. Doris Keane
has found her £10,000 pearl necklace, which slipped out of
the pocket of her dresser at the theatre. A scene-shifter
had picked it up and had waited a week in hope of the
offer of a large reward. At the end of a week he produced
it, and the police insist upon his arrest and prosecution. Went to England's Lane, Hampstead, to see a
theatrical portrait of Doris as Cavellini in her rainbow
dress, from the first act in *Romance*. Striking and bold.
Very suitable for the theatre, and for posters, and very
like her. Buchel, the artist, had not made her pose, but
had made sketches of her at the theatre. Doris most
amusing about the letters and poems from her admirers.
She says that the gallery and the pit make or mar a play,
and have the finest instinct for a good piece ; this class

crowds to see *Romance* nightly. She says that Sheldon must have made £45,000 by his royalties on *Romance*.

Sir William Robertson had telephoned in the morning asking me to come and see him, so I looked in at the War Office at 4.30 and had tea with him. We covered much ground in our talk. He says that Lloyd George declares—not to him, but to Fred Maurice—that we have been all wrong in our offensive, and that we ought to send more troops to Salonika. I hope that Haig will help to disabuse him of this idea, but Lloyd George and Briand will be sure to goad each other on upon this thesis. Robertson asked what I thought, and I said that I saw no reason for changing our plan; that although Haig's tactics were bad and expensive at first, they had improved, and that now things were going better, and the French were doing remarkably well. There was nothing better than to continue the pressure on all fronts. We agreed that it was absurd to run about wherever the Germans attracted us. They could send divisions more rapidly to the Balkans than we could, and even if we sent more divisions to Salonika they would be badly placed in the eel-trap and could not easily debouch, while it would take us many weeks to put fresh divisions there; they could only come from France and the Somme, and it would take very long—months—to find mules, packs, and mountain guns for them. If Sarrail could do nothing with 400,000 men, why should we give him more? He ought to attack, and we thought that a Bonaparte might do so, and that, if Sarrail did not, the Bulgars would make use of their central situation and of the help of Germans and Turks, to punish the Rumanians.

What would Hindenburg do? asked Robertson. I said that his idea had probably been an offensive in the East, and that he would not be able to go back on it now. He might take troops from the Somme and Verdun front and attempt to crush Rumania as Serbia had been crushed, and our best way to stop it was to continue the general attacks on all fronts in order to prevent

him from shifting troops about. Robertson thought this
probable and agreed. He said that 4 divisions had been
taken from the German Western front since July 1, namely,
2 from the Somme, and 2 from Verdun. They had gone
to the northern German front in the East, where the
$4\frac{1}{2}$ convalescent Austrian divisions were also recovering.
We agreed that if Hindenburg decided on an offensive in
the East he might take away more divisions from Verdun
and the Somme—say 10. Then, as things had become
stationary on the northern front in the East, he might
take his 7 divisions from his reserve in the Vilna region,
and $8\frac{1}{2}$ from the eastern front, which would be replaced
by a similar number of the German and Austrian convalescent divisions. He would then have $25\frac{1}{2}$ divisions,
which might equalise matters on the south-eastern front.
Some Austrian divisions might also be drawn from the
Trentino now that the snow had begun to fall, and in all
we must consider the possibility of 30 more divisions
being at disposal. We did not name all these, but this
is my general idea of the situation. Robertson did not
want the general plan of ours changed, especially at the
enemy's bidding. I heartily agreed with him. Robertson
did not think that Hindenburg was a General Staff man
or very suited for the post. Neither of us knew much of
Ludendorff. I said that I thought that politics came into
the matter, and that H. would work with the Chancellor.
The suppression of Reventlow's paper was a symptom.
Robertson thought, as I did, that Hindenburg would go
for Rumania, and I said that he must, in this case, bring
250,000 men to attack this front, and that if we and the
Russians and Cadorna were pressing, it would be all the
harder. We discussed a German offensive on the Somme,
and I said that in two months the Germans must have
made many fresh trenches behind. Robertson said they
had, and that there were as many red lines—of German
trenches—in the German back lines on the newest plans
as there were in the original front German line when our
offensive began.

We then discussed India, and Monro's appointment. Robertson still harped on having more control over India, and was especially severe on X., who was endeavouring to bring up the old criticisms of the K. scheme again. Robertson thought that the Military Secretary at the India Office should not have his present powers of traversing everything and interfering as he did. Duff had complained much of him. Robertson also said that Nixon had asked for a railway a year ago, and that Sir W. Meyer, or the Government of India and the India Office between them, had rejected the proposal on financial grounds.

We discussed Ireland, and agreed that Compulsion was desirable. Robertson said that he had a real good Staff now.

Friday, Sept. 8. Wrote an article showing that if Hindenburg adopted a frankly defensive strategy in the West, he might accumulate a fresh Army of thirty divisions against Rumania, and that, with the Bulgars, he might make things unpleasant owing to Sarrail's inactivity at Salonika. Saw Flanagan, the excellent *Times* leader writer, at Robinson's request, showed him my MS., and advised him what to write. Met a smart Australian Light Horse Brigade commander at the Rag, and he told me all about the Katia fights. He said that the Turkish advance was very clever ; they marched by night, and lay up under the palm groves by day, thus deceiving our airmen. The Light Horse had borne the brunt, as the infantry could not march and fight in the great heat. He was very sarcastic about the Yeomanry in the first Katia fight. He was for taking El Arish. There was lots of water, he said, everywhere within 10 miles from the coast at the depth of a few feet, and further south there was none.

Dined with Lady Cunard at the Carlton. There were also Mrs. Brinton, the Duchess of Rutland, Princess Bibesco, Lady Randolph Churchill, Eddy Marsh, Lord Athlumney, and Sir Arthur du Cros. Had a talk before dinner with Sir Arthur and Mrs. Brinton about the now abandoned cinema of the Cabinet, which had promised to bring them in £100,000 for their plan of building houses for widows of poor officers. They had tried to publish an explanation of their aims in the *Times*, but the letter had not been published, and they thought it very unfair. Princess Bibesco I found attractive, with much charm and intelligence, and with a wide knowledge of things. She knows Briand well. She said that the Greek Royal Family gave Princess George —although a Bonaparte—a bad time because of her descent from M. Blanc of Monte Carlo, and that the Royal Family all held together and formed a caste apart. If a commoner married a Prince she would be treated like Princess George, and only be Princess to her *femme de chambre*. We had news to-night of the defeat of the Rumanians at the Turtukai bridge-head, where they seem to have left troops which could neither be withdrawn nor reinforced, and suffered in consequence, but the Princess was very calm about it. She told me much about the Rumanian generals, and speaks highly of Avaresco (1st Army), who is a Don-Quixote type physically. She is leaving for Petrograd and Bukharest to-morrow with the Red Cross plant. We all went on to a play at His Majesty's; it was the Ali Baba story, with wonderful dresses and good light effects, but absolutely inane otherwise. Lady C. drove me back to Maryon, and we stayed talking at the gate until 12.30 A.M.

Saturday, Sept. 9. My article did not appear, but the leader came out. No news why my article was not put in. Lunched at the Ritz with Mrs. Duggan, Lady Cunard, and Lord D'Abernon. We agreed that we ought to have a great opera house, and Lady C. said that her friend, Sir Thomas Beecham, would put down £300,000 if the Government would give the site. Lord D'A. also said that a new collection of Foreign Art was about to be started to complete the Tate collection. We all agreed upon the desirability of cheering up and lighting up London ; having restaurant cars on trains, holding exhibitions, and emulating the French coolness, instead of remaining gloomy in sackcloth and ashes as the *Times* has advocated. They want me to move in the matter.   Mrs. Duggan looking very pretty, and her mourning is growing less : she leaves for S. America on the 21st.   She told us that Mrs X. had written her an extraordinary letter advising her not to marry Curzon, whom she—Mrs. X.—described as finished and done for : it was a long letter all underlined, and ended by saying that if she married him she would lose all her ‘ nice new Radical friends ! ’   We agreed that this was beyond the limit of the sufferable.   Mrs. Duggan had showed the letter to Curzon, who must have been much amused.

Jack Cowans lunching with the Duchess of Marlborough, Mrs. Cecil Higgins, and Evelyn FitzGerald.   They came to talk to us after lunch, and Jack told me that he was doing well on the inquiry and was sure to get the best of it.   Went on to 16 Arlington Street to see the Duchess of Rutland's house organised as a hospital.   It opens on Monday.   All very nice and well arranged.   We found Mrs. Leeds and Lady Islington there.

Monday, Sept. 11.   Sent off a revised proof of an article on ‘ The Danube Front,’ and finished and sent off another on ‘ Russia's Recovery.’   Lunched with Lady Randolph at 72 Brook Street, which she is about to sell, to her great regret.   It is a delicious little house.   Winston Churchill and his wife at lunch.   We talked Dardanelles Inquiry, and I told him that the Committee looked like scamping the work.   He said that he would present papers and insist on making a full statement which might take three or four days, and he had sent in a list of the witnesses whom he wished to call.   He thought that Nick (Field-Marshal Lord Nicholson) would be helpful on the Committee.   Winston still objects to our offensive in France, which, he says, will ruin the Army and do no good.   He also talked of our casualties being 300,000, which is too high.   I told him that we had to attack, and that though we had probably suffered 50,000 casualties needlessly through bad tactics, the attack had to be pressed, and it was no good taking the line he did about it.   He said that he certainly would not discourage the men fighting by any public announcement of his views. Lady Randolph and I discussed other matters when they had gone, and agreed that if we could not have everything we wanted now, we had had a pretty good time, and had lived in a most interesting age. She said that she had had the pleasure of seeing both her husband and her son leading the House of Commons,—Winston once did so for a fortnight—and the pain of hearing them both make speeches when they resigned.

Called at the War Office to see Sir William Robertson. Lloyd George still away in France, and had been away about three weeks in all of late. Robertson approved the comment of the *Times* this morning on a *communiqué* relating to the doings of Lloyd George and Montagu in Paris. It had talked of the ' conclusions to be drawn from the operations on the Somme,' and we had pointed out—I had been down to the *Times* yesterday to see about it—that operations appertained to the General Staff, and that no representatives of the French or British General Staffs were at the Conference. Robertson said that we would begin again in France about the middle of the month, and that fourteen fresh divisions which had been six weeks in training behind the lines would take part. Another German division, making the fifth, had been moved east from our front, and the equivalent of eleven divisions in all, counting separate battalions. He agreed with me that a hundred German divisions were quite enough to hold up the Allies in the West, if a frankly defensive attitude were taken up by the Germans. I saw on a map in his office a red line showing a new German defensive line, running from Miraumont eastward nearly to Bapaume, and then turning south to Sailly, and so (probably) on to Mt. St. Quentin. He had no doubt that Hindenburg meant to go East, and he would attack one of the three Rumanian Armies which were covering an immense front. The Russians in the Dobrudcha were *only one* division, but there was a Serbian division with them, and two Rumanian (9th and 19th). There had been a Rumanian division at Turtukai and

Silistria, and the first had now been scuppered. The 8th Rumanian division was on its way from the Rumanian Northern Army to the Dobrudcha. Robertson thought that the King of Rumania was in command, and that the strategy was rotten. There were 200,000 Rumanians or more scattered all along the Danube, and 350,000 scattered along the Western front. It was not possible to advance into Hungary without disposing of the Bulgarian threat. Sarrail was not getting on much, though he, Robertson, and the French were sending him urgent telegrams, and had been doing so for a week past. Robertson said that the Salonika advance was neither fish, flesh, fowl, nor good red herring. He had been saying all the time that the Army there was too strong for defence, and not strong enough for attack. I agreed, and said that I found it hopeless to teach the politicians strategy, as they could not understand. He was of the same opinion, and had told Lloyd George that the latter must just take his, Robertson's, opinions without long explanations, because Lloyd George, to understand, would have to have had Robertson's experience, and no amount of explanation could make up for the want of it.

Robertson and I then discussed Indian Army affairs, and agreed that there should be no change of system, but that the Secretary for India should take the opinion of the Commander-in-Chief, and that if a second opinion were needed, it should be that of the Army Council, and not of the Military Secretary at the India Office. We claimed for the General Staff in London the same control over Indian Army strategy that it exercised over the Dominion troops. We thought that the Commander - in - Chief in India, when absent, should be represented on the Viceroy's Council by the Sub - Chief - of - Staff, and we examined the opinion that the Indian Army system should be altered as regards officers, to conform with the system of Egypt. The last is the only point that I am dubious about. But I should think that if the G.S. take this general line, they will answer completely all Barrow's arguments, which resurrected some of the old Military

Department views, and that they will send in a good, sound, firm paper.

We then talked of recruiting. Robertson was going to inform the War Committee to-morrow how the matter stood. Our 450,000 men under training would carry us on till the middle of March, when we should want 450,000 more, but we could not see them, and Ireland was only finding 1500 men a month, and we needed 7000 a month for the Irish regiments. What were we to do? I said that as the Prime Minister's Committee had agreed to 1,400,000 men being taken this year, it was necessary to see how many had actually been taken, and then to throw upon the Cabinet the onus of finding them, as this was Robertson's sound policy. He agreed, but did not know how many we had, but he thought not a million. He had been given Austen Chamberlain and Lord Midleton to preside over the Man-Power Committee, and hoped much from it. I said that it was a question of their reference and their powers. He had not wanted a Cabinet Minister to preside, but Austen had been forced upon him on the plea that only a Cabinet Minister would know all the facts of the case, and he did not know precisely how the reference and powers stood, but the matter would be settled to-morrow, and there might be some public announcement. He said that the Tribunals were working indifferently except in London. One Tribunal in Wales had exempted all but six of 2000 men. I said that when such things happened, the Government should nominate the members of the Tribunal, and R. agreed. He said that we had 1,600,000 badged men, and that with other exempted classes there were 3,400,000 men of military age who escaped service. I said that I was quite aware of it. I told him that if we devoted our energies after November to making guns for Russia, the latter Power might dominate the situation at the end of the war, whereas, if we raised fresh divisions *we* should do so. Robertson said that our number of guns per division had been raised, which was good news, and I hope that it is to the Foch standard. We had now 56 divisions in France, 11 at home, 4 in Egypt, 5 at Salonica, 3 in India, and 5 in Mesopotamia, but the latter only partly British. I said that I wanted 100 divisions in France next year. We seem to me, as I have often said publicly, to be preparing to prolong the war and not to win it.

Robertson told me that the railways to Amara and Nasariyeh would be finished by the middle of November. They were getting on one mile a day. He would chuck the whole campaign, and risk the loss of prestige, but for the Russians. We could not win the war in Mesopotamia if we lost it in Europe.

Tuesday, Sept. 12. Northcliffe gave us this morning a wonderful bird's-eye view of Spain. His articles from Verdun, Italy, and Spain have been really admirable, very penetrating, and yet very light and readable. Revised some articles and considered how best to take up the recruiting question.

Lunched with Mrs. Leeds, Lady Islington, and Lord D'Abernon. Lady Islington very good company. Said good-bye to Mrs. Leeds and promised to meet her in Paris if I can get away. Saw Lord Midleton at the War Office, and congratulated him on being appointed to the Man-Power Committee. But he says that he will be away for two or three weeks, which is wretched news when every hour counts. Saw Lord Derby for a moment, but he was full up with chaplains, so I fled.

CHAPTER XIII

FRANCE, SALONIKA, AND MAN-POWER
AUTUMN 1916

General Geddes on our Man-Power troubles—Mr. Asquith on German power—Lieut. Robinson's destruction of a German dirigible—Lord Wimborne on recruiting in Ireland—A visit to Wilton—The Kaiser's cedar broken—Proposed changes on the L. of C. in France—The transport of ammunition—A talk about the Tanks—Mr. Churchill as artist—Queen Amélie on Portugal—Losses of the Guards on Sept. 15—Mr. McKenna on the finance of the war and Mr. Lloyd George's character—General Robertson on the strategy of the war—Plans for reinforcements—General Callwell on the Russian Army of the Caucasus—Sir Herbert Miles on Gibraltar in war time—German submarines off the American coast—Our effectives at Salonika—French request for more troops at Salonika—Differences in the War Committee—Lord Northcliffe supports the soldiers' view—A temporary truce arranged — Details of our Man-Power situation — Brig.-General Bingham on shell expenditure on the Somme—General Geddes on the causes of our Man-Power difficulties.

Wednesday, Sept. 13.   My article on 'The Danube Front' appeared six days after it was written.   Modern journalism up to date !   I met de la Panouse at the War Office.   He was rather plaintive about the article because it had been sarcastic about Salonika, and he said that the Embassy hoped I would not criticise it any more, because Salonika was the apple of the eye of the French Government.   I asked him to tell M. Cambon to let M. Briand know that the article was not aimed at the French Government, but at certain British Ministers whom I did not name, who declared that our offensive in France was an error and that we ought to transfer more troops to Salonika.   De la Panouse agreed that this would be absolutely fatal, and was much relieved.   We agreed to lunch at 'The Rag' next Monday.

Wrote an article on 'Man-Power,' and went to see General Geddes about it in the afternoon. Found the A.G.'s Branch a little upset because the *Times* had published an article criticising rather severely the round-up of young men of military age to catch out the slackers. I explained that I had nothing to do with this particular leading article, but they were not so communicative as usual. Geddes told me that he did not see his way at present till next March, as Robertson had told me, and he also said that Robertson's figure of 450,000 men under training did not correspond with any figure that he, Geddes, knew, and he did not know where the C.I.G.S. got it from. Geddes was inclined to blame the Tribunals for the slow arrivals of recruits, and for the many exemptions. He confirmed the figure of 1,600,000 badged men, and said that there were vast numbers in the mines who were not working full time, and should either do so or come out and fight. The Tribunals in the agricultural districts were the worst. The figure given me for one Tribunal by Robertson, namely, all exempted but 6 out of 2000, is very near the truth, but it is an extreme case. Some of the departments were still very bad in sheltering men, the Admiralty especially, but also the Treasury and the Inland Revenue. Getting men was like drawing teeth out of a head. There was too much local and not enough national sentiment. I asked him how many of the 1,400,000 men guaranteed by the Asquith Committee in February last for this year had turned up, but he would not give me the figure, and would only say that there was a margin, but he thought that if all the men exempted by the Tribunals came to hand, we should get our men. A large order ! The Man-Power Committee was not finally decided upon yesterday at the War Committee, but after the next meeting some announcement might be made.

He said that the men were there, and there were enough for munition work and to expand it, for the Navy and to increase it, for the Army and to add fresh divisions to it, but the men must be got and were not now being got. I asked about the young men who became liable at the age of eighteen ;

he said that they were allowed to run off to munition work a month before they became liable. When I asked if we should get the half, he said he thought we would be lucky to do so. He was not for enlisting older men by legislation, but we must prevent the young men from becoming badged, and enforce National Service upon older men, who would then release the younger ones. I talked of a Landsturm for Home Defence, and he thought it a good idea because it would not be in a form of industrial compulsion, and I said it would also give people a force for Home Defence, which could not be constantly changed as it was at present, and so will become efficient, which is not the case now. Geddes thought that we might have my 100 divisions in the field if we altered the constitution of our divisions. He said that we were pouring in large numbers of men; the battalions sometimes went into the fight 1400 strong. I said that I had never found such battalions, but that if such numbers were the fighting strength, that was too much, and he said that the French were reducing the numbers of their infantry in a division. He thought that they were withdrawing a battalion from each regiment. But he said that the French fight mainly with the gun, and we fight mainly with the bomb and the bayonet. The vast numbers that we had to maintain at home were largely due to extravagant use of infantry in battle. He said that they could not tell me precisely their policy yet because it was not settled. There would have to be a compromise of all the interests involved, and then we could all shout together.

Lunched with the Islingtons in Chesterfield Gardens. A nice big house. I was late. The table very crowded. I sat between the Duchess of Rutland and Lady Cunard— almost on their laps. There was also Sir Charles and Lady Monro, Mr. Austen Chamberlain, Sir Louis Mallet, Lord Basil Blackwood, Lady Curzon, and Mrs. Churchill. A pleasant lunch. I told Mr. Chamberlain that I thought we had given him about the best man in the Army for the job, and he agreed, and thought he was very fortunate.

Monro also seemed very pleased with his chiefs. He went on to say good-bye to Robertson afterwards, and leaves for India to-morrow. Lady Curzon seems to have grown taller. A very fine figure and a marvellous complexion, which, with the golden hair, make an interesting combination, and most people rave about her. The Duchess full of stories of her wounded officers who have arrived in the hospital. She told me that Guy Brooke had been badly wounded, and I was very sorry to hear it. He reaches town to-morrow, and will go to Queen Alexandra's hospital.

I met the Marquis Imperiali, the Italian Ambassador, in Pall Mall, and told him that people were grumbling because Cadorna was not advancing, but that I knew it was only for want of shells. He had read my article this morning with interest. I told him that in British opinion if the three Rumanian Armies in Transylvania did not keep within supporting distance, Hindenburg would attack them in turn and defeat them. I asked him to let the Rumanians know what we thought about this. Imperiali said that General Avaresco had been transferred to the 2nd Army. Possibly the King is with this Army as it is in the centre.

Thursday, Sept. 14. Completed an article on 'Man-Power' and sent it in for proof. Lady Randolph and Austin Harrison lunched at Maryon, the former grateful to meet the latter, who is one of Winston's most bitter opponents, and she took him away with her afterwards. A very pleasant lunch, the house looking delicious, bathed in sunshine. Lady Randolph very cheery and amusing, and brought her book of reminiscences. We skated over the thin ice of political differences.

Dined at 8.30 at Lady Cunard's, 20 Cavendish Square—a large party which had grown from six to twenty. The Prime Minister and Mrs. Asquith, Lord Curzon of Kedleston and Mrs. Duggan, Mr. and Mrs. McKenna, Winston and Mrs. Churchill, Lady Randolph Churchill, Lady Diana Manners, Sir Mark Sykes, Sir Lionel Earle, Lady Granard, Lord and Lady Wimborne, Lady Paget, Lord Fairfax, and there came in afterwards Mrs. Astor, Lord Basil Blackwood, and one or two more. Winston came in late and told me that he had written a short answer to the *Times* leader about Service Members. I advised him not to answer, and he telephoned to withdraw his letter. The Prime Minister spoke to me before dinner about his visit to France. He had been nearly caught by the German guns, and had to take refuge in a bomb-proof. He had seen a great deal and seemed fairly satisfied. After dinner he spoke very impressively about the good quality of the German prisoners that he had seen, and the importance of not assuming that Germany was anywhere near the end of her resources in men, an opinion with which I very thoroughly concurred, and have always done so. He and Curzon gave us a most moving description of Lieutenant Robinson's attack on the so-called Zeppelin. It was really a Schutte-Lanz and not a Zeppelin at all, and had been built before the war. Robinson had been attacking another Zeppelin above the mists and had not been able to get it. He then dropped down and met the L 21. He had to attack it from below, owing to the way in which his gun was mounted. In the rarefied air he could hear nothing of the airship's motor, neither could it hear him. He emptied a whole drum of explosive bullets into the airship, and presently saw a glow of light. He had not the least idea that he had succeeded, but presently the glow of light became a mass of flame, and slowly the airship dropped past him towards the ground, a perfect furnace of fire. He only just escaped being caught in it. Then he became so excited that he discharged every projectile he had in every direction, and set alight all his flares, and began looping the loop and generally playing the devil in the air. The P.M. said it was the most romantic episode of the whole war.

Wimborne told me that it was impossible to apply compulsion to Ireland without general assent, which we should not get. He had discovered, with the assistance of the Registrar-General, that there were 200,000 men of military age in Ireland who might be roped in, but it would require 150,000 troops to get 150,000, and then the un-willing ones might desert, so he thought the game was not worth the candle, but he said the Irish might join a French Foreign Legion. What they hated was to fight a war for England. The old story, and my old answer covered it. The number of recruits which he anticipated he could get was, he admitted, not forthcoming. The rebellion had created a very bad spirit. Sir Arthur du Cros drove me back to Maryon in an open car ; a nipping wind from the north, and the first signs of winter.

Saturday, Sept. 16. Went down to Wilton for a quiet week-end. Only Lady Pembroke, Lady Chetwode, Mr. Baker of the War Office, and Bear Warre the architect, besides the children.   There were 2000 people in the grounds, which were arranged for a Red Cross fête which brought in £145. Walked Sunday morning with Baker and Warre, and we went round the pictures, which are a never-ending joy. Warre is responsible for the entrance porch and some other changes. Baker and I both criticised the porch. We had some capital tennis. As the sun was going down on Saturday evening, the effects of the lights on the Palladian bridge were indescribably beautiful. We wished that Sargent were there to paint it. Lady P. is going to shut up Wilton for the winter and come to London. She still has forty wounded officers in the house. They occupy all Bachelor's Row and her sitting-room, and the smoking and dining-rooms. The servants cook for ninety-six people every day. I hope that history will acknowledge the splendid work for our heroes which is being done by devoted women in most of the great houses in England. We had a look at the cedar which the Kaiser planted. It has broken in two—a bad omen for him. When he planted it, his suite insisted on a red carpet being laid from the house to the river bank where it stands above the bridge on the lawn side. If it had not been for the Wilton carpet factory, the red carpet could not have been procured.

Monday, Sept. 18. Baker and Warre returned to London early. I went up with Lady Pembroke and Lady Chetwode later. Just in time to meet de la Panouse at 'The Rag.' We discussed my idea of a fresh Conference of the Allies to decide how many divisions we should all keep in the field next year, and I am to find out whether it will be agreeable that the French should take the initiative in the matter. We also discussed recruiting, and I told him our position so far as I knew it. Saw some friends who gave me the latest news of the Eric Geddes affair. The thing is settled. Brigadier-General A. R. Montagu-Stuart-Wortley, who has been Director of Movements since the beginning of the war, will be sacrificed. He has done admirably, and has moved millions of men and tens of millions of tons of stores to all parts of the world without a hitch or complaint, and now he is treated like this. Sir John Steevens, Director of Equipment, and some others of the Ordnance Branch may also be evicted because of the Pimlico Army Clothing scandals. If L. G. puts Sir Ernest Moir in as Director of Railways in France, I expect that Maxwell, Clayton, and Twiss will all go, and our very efficient system will be dislocated.

Dined at the Savoy with Dudley North and Mr. Brinckman. Dudley leaves for France to-morrow, and was overjoyed. I saw the Somme cinema at the Scala afterwards. Most interesting.

Tuesday, Sept. 19. Northcliffe and X. came up to Maryon at 10 A.M., and we exchanged confidences and discussed the changes at the War Office. N. drove me down to London and was most amusing about Mrs. Waterman. She had accompanied him and Steed to Venice, and Countess Gleichen, now with the Red Cross in Italy, had invited 'Lord and Lady Northcliffe' to come and see her. So the photo of me and the lady on the battle-field, and the Count of Turin's pleasantry, are avenged! N. says that the Italians were greatly pleased by my visit. I saw Dudley North off to France from Waterloo. Holford, Penrhyn, and all the officers of the 1st Life Guards, except the Orderly Officer, had come to see him off, which was charming of them, and a great tribute to the lad, who was in tearing spirits. Spent the afternoon with Henry Nicholl and Leo Currie settling up our stewardship as executors. Then sat on the Tribunal from 5 to 8.30. Robinson 'phones me in the evening that there are fresh developments of the Geddes case to-day, and hints that the railway executive council are kicking. Heard about Raymond Asquith's death in France, and sent my sympathies to the P.M. A sad affair, and I am so sorry for Mrs. Raymond.

Wednesday, Sept. 20. Wrote a short article on ' Sour Grapes,' showing how the German critics were wilfully depreciating all our successes on the Somme. Lunched with Lockett, Sir A. Lee, and Mr. Carstairs, and had some talk about American opinion on the war with Carstairs, who returns to America to-morrow. Went down to the War Office and had a private talk with Lee. I told him of our serious doubts about the changes which L. G. contemplates on the lines of communication in France and England. He tried to throw the whole responsibility for any changes upon Douglas Haig, who had insisted, he said, upon these changes being made. He declared that the men in France could only handle 4000 tons a day of ammunition at the ports,—Calais, Boulogne, Havre, Rouen—whereas the amount would presently total up to 7000 tons a day, and when he was at the Munitions Ministry our L. of C. people in France had indicated that they could not deal with this quantity, and that therefore the supply of ammunition should not be so large. He admitted that he had not anything in writing to this effect. He also said that the want of light railways was a great disadvantage, and, further, that they had often a vast quantity of shells piled up awaiting transport to France. I said that the question of the responsibility of Maxwell, Clayton, and Twiss, depended upon whether they had been asked to arrange for 7000 tons a day and had failed to do so, and also whether they had been given orders for the light railways. I told him that I could not see any clear reason for the commotion that would be caused by the change. I investigated the matter, and found that it is incorrect that Maxwell and Clayton were only ready to take 4000 tons. They had arranged to take 5500 tons by the end of August, and this amount had never been approached on the average, although the Channel had been closed occasionally on account of submarines, and during such days accumulations of shells had been piled up, as they always must be in such cases. There would be no insuperable difficulty in arranging for more, and the endeavour to shift the responsibility for the changes on to Haig seems quite gratuitous. I don't know how the affair will be settled, but Northcliffe telephones to-night he is going to bring it up in the House of Lords.

Arthur Lee showed me a list of filled shells sent to France in the weeks ending Jan. 8 and July 15. The first figure was 248,000, and the second about 1,175,000—a notable advance, and it seems that we are working up to 2,000,000 a week. Very interesting in view of Falkenhayn's order, quoted in Haig's *communiqué* of to-day.

Thursday, Sept. 21. Lunched with Lady Cunard, Winston, Lord and Lady Frederick Blackwood, and Lieutenant Hermann of the French War Office. The latter said that he had read all my articles, and that I had been right all through about the war. We had a great discussion about the famous Tanks, which made their first appearance in the field in last Friday's battle. Winston said that though he had in his mind H. G. Wells's predictions about them, they really developed from the armoured motor car, which trench warfare had rendered useless. They were taken up by the Admiralty. He found that he had some money to spare, and he applied it to this purpose. To that extent the initiative and responsibility rested with him. Winston had wanted them to wait until there were something like a thousand Tanks, and then to win a great battle with them as a surprise, but, as Northcliffe said the other day, nothing keeps whether in journalism or in war. W. was rather excited at lunch, and began a most voluble speech at Hermann. I forget what point he was making, but he could not speak French well, and most of his genders and tenses were absurdly wrong, but he stumbled along to a conclusion, and got there in the end very valiantly, laughing and apologising for himself at the end. Hermann wanted to speak, but Winston never gave him a chance. We walked back from Cavendish Square to Whitehall together, when Winston complained how difficult Northcliffe was to deal with. At one time he was friendly, and the next was attacking him. If Northcliffe attacked Lloyd George, the latter would coalesce with Asquith for mutual protection; did Northcliffe wish that? Also the natural course was for Northcliffe to support the incipient opposition which Winston and Carson had begun, but he did not do this, and Winston did not know how to take him.

I was given some interesting statistics about the number of men and the amount of tonnage sent to France each week. It amounts now to 128,000 tons a week of all kinds of stores and ammunition, so Arthur Lee's suggestion that Geddes's appointment was partly due to the fact that the Q.M.G.'s Branch could not place in France 3000 more tons of ammunition a day, is absurd on the face of things.

Here are some of the figures for five representative weeks during the battle of the Somme, showing men, horses, food, ammunition, etc., sent weekly:

18/19 June to 25/26 June 1916

Officers.	Other Ranks.	Horses.	
1,293	40,088	6,824	To France

9/10 July to 16/17 July 1916

1,755	40,089	5,990	,,

13/14 Aug. to 20/21 Aug. 1916

929	24,636	2,254	,,

20/21 Aug. to 27/28 Aug. 1916

788	23,437	1,606	,,

3/4 Sept. to 10/11 Sept. 1916

1,154	23,929	655	,,

Supplies (in tons)

Food.	Forage.	Fuel.	Ammunition.	Explosives.	Oil (gals.).	Petrol (gals.).	Canteen Stores.
10,852	8,706	686	21,980	631	517,053	443,664	1,469
9,045	9,936	548	26,813	375	203,045	788,584	3,028
9,815	8,399	698	28,343	84	118,479	987,836	1,573
10,760	10,460	748	30,973	361	181,440	——	1,398
9,607	10,726	375	27,483	732	94,728	249,048	1,032

besides some 16,000 *to* 20,000 *tons a week* of stores, clothing, equipment, guns, saddlery, etc.

If they can do this, is it likely that Lee's 3000 tons more are likely to be the straw to break the camel's back ? It is only a $2\frac{1}{2}$ per cent. addition !

Friday, Sept. 22. The *World* published on Wednesday a complete apology by Fenton for his attack on Lord French and George Moore, and Lady Cunard tells me that the original draft submitted to Lord French contained other names, but that French asked that they should be cut out. It has been practically agreed that Sir E. Geddes is to confine his work to France, but he is to have an office in London. Stuart-Wortley has been induced to stay. It is thought that Clayton and Twiss will both resign. I asked more about the question of light railways, which is another cause of indirect complaint against the Army. They tell me that it is on record that the W.O. implored our people in France to start these railways more than a year ago, and that they steadily refused—French, Haig, and all the rest of them being wedded to the broad gauge. Geddes has insisted that he shall make his own contracts, so apparently does Rothermere, who is to be the new Director at Pimlico. There seems to be a scheme on foot for ousting from the Q.M.G. Branch all the soldiers as soon as they dare, and, as the Q.M.G. is spending about a million a day, it is an enormous responsibility to transfer to people who will be immune from the supervision of the contract branch. At present no soldier in the Q.M.G. Branch has anything to do with contracts directly or indirectly.

Saturday and Sunday, Sept. 23 and 24. ̍ ̣nt down to Warren House in the afternoon to spend the week-end. A large party coming and going, including Queen Amélie of Portugal, Lord and Lady Drogheda, Arthur Balfour, Winston and Mrs. Churchill, Lady Granard, Mr. and Mrs. Lavery, Dr. Ross, the twins, Somers Cocks, Lord Blandford, Lady Cynthia Graham's boy, Lady Meux, Mrs. Cecil Bingham, and a few more. Some capital tennis on Sunday ; Lady Drogheda and I took on the twins and nearly beat them. Watched Winston painting in the Japanese garden. He is developing real talent, and Lavery is enthusiastic. Sat next the Queen and had a long talk about Portugal. I told her that I thought of going there next month. She advised me to see the north and the Alemtejo, Cintra, Lisbon, and Oporto, and to get Soveral and Asseca to make an itinerary for me and to give me a list of the people worth talking to. I told her that I did not propose to take introductions to the men of the King's party as I should then be *brûlé* with the Republicans with whom I should have to deal, and she quite approved. She made me laugh by saying that the Republican Minister in London was quite respectable, as he was neither a thief nor a murderer ! All Portugal, she said, was honeycombed by secret societies, and the situation of the country was terrible. Dr. Ross had a talk with her about the Germans who had persuaded some of the Monarchists that they had more to hope from the Kaiser than from England. The Queen's answer was that she and King Manuel lived in England, which was proof of what they thought of it. Had a talk with Balfour about coast fortifications, and told him of Mahan's views, which coincided with A. J. B.'s. I am to send him the volume in which they are to be found. (I see it is *Naval Strategy*, chap. xv.)

We discussed why it was that British sailors had added nothing in our time to naval literature. We were all very pleased with the destruction of two Zeppelins during the night of Sept. 23-24. We heard the guns and watched the distant lights and flares. Balfour says that the

Admiralty cannot imagine why one of the Zepps. landed, as its engines were in perfect order, and they are inclined to assume an intention to surrender.

Found that Lady Paget had been very anxious about Sir Arthur's meeting with Winston, as the two had not met, she said, since Winston's famous message to Sir Arthur when the Ulster row began. She said that she had the original locked up in the bank, and I suppose it must have been something rather damning by the way she spoke of it. However, Sir A. and Winston were quite friendly, and both agree in anathematising the strategy in France, which Balfour also does not pretend to approve.

Monday, Sept. 25. Returned with Ross. No particular news except about the Zepp. defeat. Lunched in Cavendish Square : Lady Cunard, the French Ambassador M. Cambon, Arthur Balfour, Winston, Lady Randolph, and Lady Kitty Somerset. Cambon had been to see the fallen Zepp. and had brought back a bit of the outer envelope, which I made him show to A. J. B., who declares that the outer covering is made from the bladders of cattle, and that 300,000 cattle only find enough material for one Zepp. The outer envelope looks to me more like American cloth. Cambon enthusiastic about the wonderful construction of the Zepp. Balfour and Winston very interesting at lunch. We discussed Irvingites, taxation, tanks, the war generally, and other matters, Lady C. occasionally throwing in her usual impromptu and startling observations, such as that Balfour was an abstraction and not a man, and that the *upper* part of his face was like Christ —which made A. J. B. laugh consumedly. Balfour and Winston still harping on the uselessness of the Somme battle. I asked them to state an alternative, and they could not suggest one, but Balfour admitted that it had become absolutely necessary that we should do something to help the French out. He said that now we had shown ourselves capable of sacrifice and Verdun was safe, he thought that we need not go on, but the whole thing was in the hands of the soldiers. The Guards lost 190 officers and 6000 men in the last attack on Sept. 15, and there is much lamentation. It is the first time since the early days of the war that Society has been hit quite so hard. Balfour says that he has sent D'Eyncourt over to France to see how the Tanks have fared, and he admits Winston's large share in their beginnings. Sat on the Tribunal all the evening, and could not get away to dine with Lady Granard and Mrs. Cis. Heard with much regret of the death of my contemporary, Lord Essex, and wrote her a letter of condolence.

Wednesday, Sept. 27. I was to have lunched with Sir William Robertson to-day, but he put me off because there was an Army Council in the afternoon; and on these occasions L. G., Derby, and R. meet at lunch and practically settle all the points before the meeting. I suppose L. G. has taken this from the practice of the Inner Cabinet of Asquith, Grey, Haldane, L. G., and Winston, which used similarly to settle Cabinet affairs before the war. So I saw R. in South Street and had a talk before dinner.

R. had left Haig before the attack of the Guards, but he had found very long faces at Windsor over it, and no wonder. R. could not yet give the cause of the heavy losses, but said that war was a bloody business anyhow. The attack was doing well. There were still some fresh and various rested divisions which could be used, and lots of guns coming on and plenty of shells. Haig hoped to get a good deal further and to occupy still better ground before the weather stopped him. He calculated on having another month, when the rain and the soft ground and the short days would prevent large movements. R. thought that the Germans had lost a lot of men. We had had 260,000 casualties and the French under Foch 130,000, but we ought to have had 50,000 less if the mistakes made on July 1 had been avoided. R. still thought that Hindenburg would go for Rumania. R. and Joffre had made some tactful suggestions to Alexeieff, but they were not sure how they would be taken, as Alexeieff did not care much for advice. R.

agreed with me that the Russians should now stand fast on their main front and send a lot of divisions down to crush Bulgaria and open the way to Constantinople. He said that there were only 70,000 Bulgars and, perhaps, 50,000 Turks in the way. The presence of Turks in the Dobrudcha had not yet been confirmed beyond doubt. The Bulgars still had 8 divisions (equal to 16 of ours) on the Greek front, of which 4 were now on the Monastir side. They were all concreted up and bent on holding Macedonia. There was immense difficulty in feeding Sarrail's 10 divisions which were attacking Monastir, and only the adaptability of the French troops prevented a collapse, as roads and transport were wanting. Yet the Prime Minister of Serbia had asked R. to send another 100,000 men to help the Serbs. R. would not do it, nor would he consent to send troops, as some people wished, to help the Sherif of Mecca, who was howling for them : R. advised me that this affair might grow like the Dardanelles and our other side-shows. R. said that the Serbs were fighting well, but that Sarrail's reports were designed to encourage Rumania. We certainly held up some Bulgars, but Mackensen might take away three or four more Bulgar divisions from our Salonika front if he wanted them. The Rumanians were not fighting too well, but it took time for new troops to become accustomed to modern artillery. The Russians in the Dobrudcha complained that the Rumanians could not fight, and the Rumanians complained that the Russian general could not command. At the Vulcan Pass the Rumanian Central Army had retired before one German brigade, but had since thought better of it and had re-occupied the Pass. The Russians should act against Bulgaria, but there seemed to be no love lost between Russians and Rumanians.

R. was having some fun about Mesopotamia. He had not been able to trace any orders to our commanders in Mesopotamia informing them of the intentions of the Government. All our other commanders, since he, R., had come on the scene, had received definite instructions.

We then talked recruiting. The Man-Power Committee had had a first meeting, and Macready had been before them. Macready, said R., did not know the politicians as well as he did. They had not been too friendly, but Midleton meant business, and had given up his holiday. Balfour of Sheffield also seemed a good man. We had sent out a quarter of a million drafts since July 1. R. still talks of 400,000 men training here. I asked about fresh divisions for 1917. R. said that there would be a row in the Cabinet if this were proposed, so he and L. G. had agreed to bring on for service the 5 divisions still at home, to place in them all the general service men, and to make small divisions, each with 24 guns for Home Defence, out of the men posted to Home Defence by the Medical Boards. L. G. would stand the racket of doing this. Sam Hughes had promised another division from Canada, so in the spring R. hoped for 62 in France, apart from anything he might get from Egypt, Salonika, and Africa.

He was to see Desborough to-morrow about using the volunteers, but did not expect much from people only prepared to give partial service. The best way was to put all men needed under the common obligation to serve.

R. did not think that the Germans would go back of their own free will in the West, but only if they were kicked back. They could not afford to retire, though they probably wished that they could. I told R. that we had done well in the German colonies, and that the shade of Chatham would be pleased, as we had secured one million square miles of territory oversea, and had effected an equilibrium of force on land in Europe. This was the Chatham policy, but we had not yet humbled Germany's pride enough nor turned her out of Antwerp. A question for us was whether we should be able to keep all the German colonies at the Peace. R. said that he had advised the Government to settle up with Australasia and South Africa about the colonies, and then go to Briand and make a settlement with him. Briand was the leading figure in the war at present.

Thursday, Sept. 28.   Saw Joey Davies, military secretary, at the War Office.   He told me that at the beginning of the Somme offensive they had 5000 supernumerary officers in France, and that, after making good all losses up to date, they still had a surplus of 1500.

Friday, Sept. 29.   Finished an article on ' Autumn War,' and sent it off to Robinson, hoping that it might not be mangled in the manner my last article was.   Lunched with Mr. and Mrs. McKenna at 36 Smith Square, Westminster. Nobody else there.   A Lutyens house, built for them.   No basement, the kitchen and offices on the ground floor, drawing-room, dining-room, and library on the first floor. A very pleasant house with good proportions.   We had a great talk till nearly 4 P.M.   I told McKenna that I had not asked to see him before during the war because I did not like to bother a busy man, but that now I wanted to know his point of view with regard to the future, and especially with regard to finance and our powers of holding out.   He said that we were spending five millions a day and that our power of holding out rested largely upon America, from whom the Allies were now purchasing materials on credit and on securities to the tune of 80 million sterling a month, or nearly 1000 millions a year.   The figure had already doubled since last year, and would go on increasing.   I asked why this was so, since the Allies had now got all their munitions machinery in full swing.   He said that the expenditure was less upon munitions than upon raw materials of all sorts, including steel, cotton, copper, and every sort of other thing.   I asked why we could not increase our output of steel.   He said that it was shortage of labour which stopped us. This dependence upon America had been more fully realised by German critics than by ours, and he thought that the German financial criticism was much better and more acute than ours. The Germans had not thought that we should be able to go on so long, but McK. thought that we could always go a bit better than the Germans, and that they would be exhausted before we should be.   But he said that owing to the riches made by America, her consumption was going up very fast, and after a time she would not have the materials to send us. We could continue the war for a long time, in fact, for ever so long, but not this kind of war that we were waging now. If the war continued for a long time the extravagant, if effective, system of the present would have to cease, and we should have to finance the war on what we could produce. He had been educated in Germany, and thought that the Germans were better educated, better organised, more thorough, and more disciplined than we were. The State system was superior, and the Germans were an extraordinarily docile people and lent themselves to anything. I asked him what the Germans would do after the war. Would they repudiate their internal debts ? He thought not, and did not see why they should. But they would effect the same purpose in a more gentlemanly way, namely, by abandoning the gold standard. The mark would fall to sixpence or threepence, and then from 50 to 75 per cent. of their internal debt would be wiped off. He did not think that if we had allowed them to import goods, and thus forced them to send gold abroad, it would have shortened the war. I asked him about our loans to the Allies. He said that his real difficulty was that out of the five millions a day that he was spending, two millions had to go abroad either in gold or its equivalent. How did we manage it, I asked, when our gold reserve was so small ? He said that we borrowed it from Paris and Petrograd to a large extent, and in reply to a further question he professed to have no doubt that our Allies would repay both capital and interest. He could see his way over next year, and thought that economic pressure would never bring Germany to terms, but that the killing of her men would. He considered that our estimate of the German reserves at two millions in the beginning of this year was pessimistic, but even taking it at this figure they had since lost at least a million, and he did not think that they could go on for more than nine months ; that is to say, that after this lapse of time they would be unable to keep up all their existing units. He seemed to think that this estimate took into account the substitution of prisoners, Belgians, Poles, and Frenchmen, for the German munition workers, of whom a million, it was calculated, had been put into the field.

I told him my views about the Balkans, and about the need for twenty Russian divisions to march upon Sofia and then Constantinople. He heartily approved of this plan, and I told him what Joffre and Robertson had done in the way of communicating their views to Alexeieff. He agreed with me that England ought to be the strongest Power when we began talking about terms of peace, but he admitted that he had opposed the seventy-divisions scheme at the beginning of the year, as I knew. He had no fear of the result of supplying Russia plentifully with guns and munitions, because the Russians were so inefficient that they would kill three Russians for every one German. He doubted that the war would end by a great Russian offensive into Germany, because he was sure that Germany would consent to any terms rather than allow this to happen. I said that after their experience in East Prussia I did not wonder.

He told me many things of great interest about Lloyd George. McK. thought that L. G. was out for power. The greatest defeat that L. G. had ever suffered was when he had tried to make terms on taking over the War Office and had been beaten by Robertson, who had insisted upon and had obtained the same powers that he had enjoyed in the time of Lord K. McK. knew L. G. well, and thought that he would never forgive this defeat. What L. G. loved was to be always in the limelight. It was for this reason that he had quarrelled with Winston, when the latter enjoyed popularity, and if he had now made friends with him again, it was because he no longer feared him as a rival. For the same reason he never rested until he had completely undermined Lord K.'s position. L. G.'s object was to pose before history

as the organiser of victory. He found unexpectedly that
Robertson stood in his way, and McKenna thought that
he was attacking Cowans, because he regarded the latter
as an outwork of Robertson's position. L. G. had no
personal animosities, and was not likely to dislike Cowans,
for the latter was not a popular favourite with the country,
and not an eagle, though an excellent man at his work.
McK. thought Robertson a first-rate man. On the Asquith
Committee, at the beginning of the year, Robertson had
made all the best points possible for his case, and had put
his finger unerringly on all the weak points of McK.'s case.
Robertson had much more power than he knew. I said,
'Do you mean with the Government or the country?'
He said, 'With the Government, for the country did not
know much of him.'

I said that I could not conceive why L. G. should seek
to oust Robertson, since the latter was really indispensable
to L. G.'s success in his post, but McK. said that L. G.
really believed himself to be inspired and to have a divine
mission, and would not let any one else stand in his way.
McK. thought that I probably did not know how L. G. was
overshadowed and silenced by Robertson, who was the real
Minister of War. He instanced a case when some scheme
had been brought up for some subsidiary operation. Robertson, as usual, stated his views very fully and clearly, and
L. G., also as usual, sat perfectly silent. But Robertson
had an appointment at 1 o'clock, and the instant he had
left, L. G. advocated the course directly opposite to that
which Robertson had recommended. As Minister of
Munitions, L. G. had talked to his heart's content, had
recommended strategical plans, and had constantly turned
Lord K. inside out. Now he was an extinct volcano, and
the nature of the man could not stand it.

McK. thought that the French had conceived the idea of
Salonika from L. G.'s constant advocacy of it in private,
and were very much surprised to find such opposition to
it over here. I asked McK. if any Minister kept a diary.
He said he thought that only Lulu Harcourt did, and that

the Harcourt memoirs would be a feature of this period. We discussed the question of men at some length. McK. said that he was not now standing out against the men being taken for the Army, because by a natural process we should gain an equilibrium between trade and war. The prices would rise so much that we should be forced to curtail our call upon men. He thought that we could fit out the Russians with guns and so on by next May. I said I hoped this might be soon enough, because not much campaigning was to be done in Russia before May.

I have received two very interesting letters on this subject from General Callwell, who is now in charge of delivery of supplies to Russia. He says that Russia's $2\frac{1}{2}$-million field army is not more than $1\frac{1}{2}$ million in terms of French or British troops, for lack of adequate war material, especially heavy artillery, aeroplanes, and mechanical transport.

McKenna told me that he had stood out against war in 1911. It would have been fatal, as we should not have had the Belgian case to unite our people ; most of the Liberal Party would have been in opposition, and the South African War conditions would have been repeated. He could not imagine why Winston was so bent on the Dardanelles Inquiry, because he could only show that other people had made mistakes as well as he, and this would not help him. Winston, he thought, had great qualities but lacked judgment. We then discussed how the captured colonies could be retained by us at the peace, and not be used for bartering against Germany's conquests. McK. made the excellent suggestion that we should say that we refused to begin negotiations while any part of the territory of our Allies remained in German occupation. This would close the mouth of America, and would prevent all question of haggling over our colonial conquests.

Saturday, Sept. 30. Major-General Charles Callwell dined at Maryon, and we talked Russia all the evening. He has paid two visits to the country lately, and has been in the Caucasus, where, he says, Russia has a splendid Army, and Yudenitch is a great leader. He found the Grand

Duke very impressive, especially in appearance and at first sight, but he did not think him a very great man as the impression wore off. He says that the losses of the Russian Army have been frightful—probably not under 5,000,000 including prisoners lost, and it is mainly due to want of heavy guns. He talks of 500 6-inch howitzers being enough, — but this seems to me too small a figure—and he declares that aeroplanes and motor lorries to carry up shells are the two other chief needs. The Murman line should be ready by Jan. 15 next, and we can then have a regular flow, but not so full a stream as when Archangel reopens next May. Alexeieff can only speak Russian, which is a great disadvantage.

Monday, Oct. 2. I am refusing all invitations to dine out and stay away as I want a little quiet. Last night the Zepps. came again a little before midnight. I heard no guns, but only some loud talking in the streets, followed just before midnight by a hoarse and prolonged cheer, and a servant came down to tell me that a Zepp. had fallen in flames to the north and had lit up all the top rooms. We afterwards heard it was the L 31, which had fallen at Potter's Bar.

Tuesday, Oct. 3. I went to have a talk with Sir William Robertson, who told me that it was difficult for him to carry on when he ought to be giving his whole mind to defeating Hindenburg, and yet when such a lot of his time had to be given to the S. of S. He thought that we all ought to be pals and work together. He would go on quietly in his own way and would stick to his own job. He would not brook interference in his sphere, and had made the fact known to the P.M. He said that the War Committee story of McKenna's was perfectly correct. It was over the Mecca campaign, advocated by Austen Chamberlain, supported by Curzon. L. G., after R. had left, had supported the plan and had advocated reference to India, to Murray, to McMahon, and others. All these opposed it, but Chamberlain had stuck to this point at the next meeting. The P.M. had turned to R. and had asked him what he thought, whereupon R. said that ' he had nothing to add to his former statement,' which was dead against the proposed new campaign. There was then a minute of dead silence, and finally Curzon laughed and the question was ended. R. said that, though a poor man, he was determined to resign if his advice was not followed.

On the other hand, he said that L. G. had been splendid about the men, and had fought like a tiger, even for compulsion in Ireland. R. said that the victory of Falkenhayn at Hermannstadt was only over one Rumanian division. The other divisions were all scattered about. There were now three Russian divisions on the Danube, and the Rumanians had twelve preparing to cross, and they ought to beat Mackensen if they held together and did not commit follies. Mackensen had only 70,000 men, and had lost a good lot. There was only one Turkish division with him, and two in Galicia, and only four more can come up. Then it will be necessary to draw other Bulgarian divisions north from Greece. He told me that the French *communiqués* from Salonika were exaggerations. We were still all hung up there, and Milne had reported that the Bulgars were all concreted-in and strong.

Wednesday, Oct. 4. Saw Geoffrey Robinson, who goes to France to-morrow. Also saw Northcliffe and told him what I know about the L. G. and Geddes cases. He asked me to tell Robertson that he would support him. N. also said that Rothermere's new post would make no difference to him (N.). His chief fear was that L. G. will give Winston some appointment at the W.O. N. said that he was giving Winston £500 for each *London* article.

Lunched with General Sir Herbert Miles, Governor of Gibraltar, who is at home on short leave. He told me that he went out the day war was declared, and had to stand in the corridor all the way from Paris to Bordeaux, as the train was so full. He found, on arrival, that Spain had stopped our supplies of cattle and coke, being terrorised by the German Minister at Madrid. He, M., had made a row and complained to our Minister. The Spaniards first wanted to send cattle and coke by boats to meet a ship from Gib. at some clandestine rendezvous and to transfer the supplies. M. would not do this, and insisted on the normal system. Finally it was allowed, *sub rosa*, on condition that M. did not ask that the Spanish order should be openly rescinded. M. also found that there was a run on the Gib. banks, which were on the point of being broke. He cabled home for £100,000 in cash, and was told that he could not have it and must do the best he could. So he put up a printing press, collected some ordinary paper, and struck off enough paper money to carry on, making it legal tender by his edict as governor. He also stopped the eviction of aliens, which helped to stop the run. He was dictator, and could do as he pleased. He fixed the prices of all foods. He took all the sugar on the wharves for Government, paid $3\frac{1}{2}$d. a lb. for it, and sold it back to the merchants for $4\frac{1}{2}$d., and they sold it for $5\frac{1}{2}$d. So every one was pleased, and M. got £1000 as a poor-fund. The Gib. people were now all rolling in money, and had made a fine harvest. He had stopped sixty ships a day (? a week) in the Straits at first, and had procured trained stevedores from home to help search the ships. Gib. was full of contraband collected in this way. He had £1,000,000 of copper alone at one time, and he took even the rubber tires off motor wheels. The value of Gib. in war was apparent now. He was careful not to arouse Spanish ire by being hard on the coasting trade. He thought that not more than twelve German submarines had entered the Mediterranean by the Straits. The water was too deep and the current too strong for net defence, and the question of Spanish waters was difficult.

Friday, Oct. 6. Dined at Lady Herbert's; Olive, Sir Seymour Fortescue, Lady Ridley, and Wolkoff. Very cheery, and we had a lot of chaff. Lady R. cheering up, and violent against Radical politicians whom Seymour tried to defend. I could not get to Doris Keane's anniversary night of *Romance*, but others went there and enjoyed it greatly, saying that Doris played exquisitely. When called on for a speech she held out her arms to the audience and said, simply, ' Thank you all so much for loving me.' We were also too late to go on to Lady Cunard's party.

Saturday, Oct. 7. I lunched with M. and Mme. Vandervelde at 98 Knightsbridge—the same house where I had a mad supper party once with Lydia Kyasht and her Russian dancing friends. General Orth, the new Belgian military attaché, and some others. We had a nice friendly talk, but were too many for confidences. Refused two invitations for this week-end.

Sunday, Oct. 8. I was amused to hear that Eric Geddes had placed some contracts without the consent of the Treasury when told that he could not. Geddes said that he had L. G.'s permission to go ahead, and that he was not worrying about the Treasury. Perhaps he will later.

Saw a letter, dated August 31, from Joe Maude, the new G.O.C. in Mesopotamia. He hopes to get the railway from Basra to Khamsieh on the Euphrates by the middle of this month, and then it will be easy to send on supplies by river to Nasariyeh. The railway progresses one mile a day. The Kurna-Amara railway is getting on. He would like to run it on to Sheikh Sa'ad, which will practically double his communications and give a railway from Kurna up to Sinn, where his advanced lines are now. This is a 2 feet 6 inch gauge : the Nasariyeh railway is a metre gauge. He says that the heat was intense in June and July, 120° to 126° under cover, but that it is now cooler, and the British division (13th), which had most sick, now has the best record. McMunn in charge of L. of C. and doing well. Maude hopes to have a fine force ready when he has straightened out his transport difficulties, and intends to teach the Turks a lesson.

Monday, Oct. 9. News came of German submarines off the American coast at Nantucket and nine ships torpedoed. The Yankees won't like this much. The German submarines also seem to be busy worrying the Murman line.

Met Count Sala at lunch with Lockett. Our soldiers tell me that though we have sent out 250,000 drafts since July 1st, we are short of 75,000 men in France. They are cross about Rumanian strategy. The Austro-Germans have 21 divisions against Rumania, of which 7 are with Mackensen, and 13 in the main Army about Brasso. The Russo-Rumanians have 26, and should win, but the dispositions are bad. Our soldiers think with me that it is Alexeieff's job to run this part of the war, and that if he does not take it in hand, it may be serious. The Germans kill two birds with one stone if they march into Rumania and then turn the Russian left flank and advance on Galatz. We can do little from Salonika except hold the 8 Bulgarian divisions in our front, as the roads are so bad, ground so difficult, and transport so poor. Saw 'Bockus' Nicol just home on leave from Salonika, where he has been commanding a division of Briggs's Army Corps (27th, 28th and 10th divisions) on the Struma. He says that 'Fatty' Wilson, with the 22nd and 26th, is on the Doiran front. We can do little as we have had to send our mules back to Salonika for forage : the road is worn out and sickness severe. His late brigade only 2400 strong, the next strongest 2100, and others less. In fact, they are only about 50 per cent. of their proper strength owing to malaria and dysentery. His division has had to send back 1000 sick a week. O this tomfool expedition ! what lives it has cost uselessly ! 'Fatty' Wilson has three tremendous positions in front of him on the Doiran front. Even if Monastir falls it will do no good. Milne wants 25 divisions to advance on Nish, and does not think we can get on with our present force.

Bertier asked to see me, and after dining with Lockett, I went on to the Ritz and had a good talk with him. He produced a paper drawn up at Chantilly, to induce us and the Italians each to send two more divisions to Salonika. A similar paper had been given to Robertson, with whom Bertier confessed he had had no luck, and the War Committee had supported Robertson to-day in the matter. The French want us to send two divisions from the four in Egypt, and to abandon Murray's plans for Palestine.

I told Bertier that I entirely agreed with Robertson: that as we were 75,000 men short in France and 50 per cent. short at Salonika, we should concentrate upon France; that we could not spare the troops from Egypt just now; and that if Sarrail could do little with his 17 divisions (5 French, 5 British, 6 Serbian, and 1 Italian), there was nothing to show that he could do better with 21, as it was less the want of troops than communications and transport that stopped him. Bertier said that the Serbians had lost 25 per cent. of their strength, had no reserves, and could not go on much longer. The Bulgarians had 2 divisions on the Struma, $1\frac{1}{2}$ against the British left and the Italians, 3 German regiments next on the right, and 4 Bulgarian divisions on the Monastir side. I told him that in holding up 8 Bulgarian divisions,—equal to 16 of ours—we were helping the cause, but that even the fall of Monastir would not affect the Germans, or influence seriously the campaign of Rumania. I told him that Brussiloff had 71 divisions from Kovel southwards, and could easily spare 12 for Rumania. This campaign, I said, was Russia's pigeon, and I was against our wasting any more troops there. We had only gone there to please the French. Bertier told me that the French G.H.Q. had been told nothing about Eric Geddes, and that the French commandants at Havre and Boulogne had been annoyed because Geddes had inspected these ports and had never called upon them or consulted them in any way.

Tuesday, Oct. 10. This morning I heard that at the War Committee yesterday, the question of sending more divisions to Salonika had come up, and that Robertson had opposed it. The Committee were with him. But Lloyd George had drawn a lurid picture of Rumania's downfall, and had asked that eight Allied divisions might be sent. It seems to have been left to R. to ask Joffre's opinion about L. G.'s proposal, which he did. R. sent to ask to see me later, and told me that, on thinking it over, he saw that he could not go on, and had this morning drafted a letter to L. G. restating his objections, and saying that as L. G. constantly opposed his military opinions at the War Committee, he, R., saw no use in remaining where he was. He asked for my opinion on the letter. I read it carefully and pondered it a little. I then said that he should not have sent the telegram to Joffre, but, as he had, I advised him to await the answer and then have it out on the War Committee, telling the P.M. to-night that he meant to do so. He would then get the support of the Committee, whereas, if he sent his letter to L. G., the latter had him in his power, and could accept the resignation, and appoint a new man in the morning. It was too great a risk, and I said that a resignation was a confession of failure. R. did not much relish this advice. He wanted to have it out with L. G., and preferred to do it in his way. He said that he would get no good from Joffre's reply, as J. would only write 'namby-pamby stuff,' and the Committee would not take sides between R. and the Secretary for War. Finally R. said he would think it over.

I caught Northcliffe at the *Times* office, and told him what had happened. He was much exercised. He had just been appealed to by the P.M., through some man, to support the Secretary for War and the Government. He now telephoned to this man to tell the P.M. at once, to-day, that he would support L. G. if the latter did not interfere with the soldiers. This may help a bit. Northcliffe agreed with my advice to R., that he should see the P.M.

N. had been speaking without reporters at a lunch in Aldwych to a lot of city and business men. N. had told them that there were two great dangers, one that the politicians might interfere with soldiers, and the other that the Government might make a secret peace.

Much talk to-day of the submarine depredations off the coast of N. America. The Yankees are much stirred.

Thursday, Oct. 12. Jack Stirling lunched at Maryon, and then I went into town with him. Dined with Sir Arthur and Lady du Cros at the Carlton in a private room.

A party of eighteen, including Lady Gwendeline Churchill, Lady Paget, Arthur Balfour, Mr. and Mrs. McKenna, Baron and Baroness Aleotti (she was the lovely Countess Fabricotti), Winston and his wife, Harry Cust, Sir F. E. Smith and Lady S., and Lady Cunard. A good dinner and all very cheery. I sat between Lady Gwendeline and Mrs. McKenna, and was much amused by them. We talked people, politics, books, painting, and scandals. Talked with F. E. after dinner. He thought that all was now well between L. G. and Robertson, and before dinner McKenna had told me the same thing, as had Robertson over the telephone, but McKenna had said that there was nearly the devil of a row, and that L. G. would not change his manners as he honestly thought himself appointed by heaven to win the war. F. E. very contemptuous of the soldiers and very flattering to me, especially approving my article yesterday against the amalgamation of the French and British Armies. The best scheme would have been French, with Haig for Chief of Staff. F. E. thought that we were still expending life too prodigally. He asked to see a memorandum on the war which I had written, and said he would tell me where it was wrong in the facts if he found any error. He was getting on all right with Macready. The Cowans case was not going so well, as Nick was being contumacious, and F. E. feared that Cowans might suffer. I gathered that the suggested despatch of large reinforcements to Salonika was off. Robertson told me that L. G. was furious with Northcliffe now. He said that N. had spoken to L. G., and R. wondered how N. knew anything! The innocent! I suppose N. has warned L. G. to keep his hands off the strategy. We also had a shot across his bows in a leader to-day. Lady Cunard has spoken in the same sense to the P.M., and she has again urged him to be conciliated with N., and he answered, 'Nous verrons.' R. told me that he had not sent to L. G. the letter which he had shown me, but had sent another. He did not tell me what was in it. Everybody gloomy about Rumania.

Friday, Oct. 13. Northcliffe telephoned in the morning to ask for news, and I told him how things stood, and that all was well for the moment, but that R. had still to see the P.M., and that L. G. was angry with N. The latter said he did not care, and told me that he had not seen R., but had seen L. G., and had warned him in plain words not to interfere with the soldiers. He also told me that he had sent word to the P.M. through a mutual friend that he would support him on the same conditions. I wonder if this will end the trouble. Anyhow it is a good mark for N.

Monday, Oct. 16. Occupied in looking into the question of Man-Power. Out of the 7,200,000 men of military age existing in civil life before the war began, there remained on Jan. 1, 1916, 4,300,000 men, of whom about 900,000 have been obtained for the Army under the Military Service Acts, leaving a balance of 3,400,000 still nominally available.

Of these 3,400,000 men, 1,500,000 have been badged and exempted by Government Offices, mainly the Ministry of Munitions : 1,100,000 have been exempted by the Tribunals temporarily, mainly on account of the list of certified occupations ; 500,000 are due to undergo fresh medical examination ; about 170,000 are waiting to be called up ; and the balance, about 130,000, are absentees. In fact, the 170,000 men are the only resource left unless some change is made. The deficit in the *infantry* in France is about 100,000. This is in establishments of some 650,000. The losses on the Somme, July 1 to Oct. 15, are 300,000 roughly. There are 350,000 men under training at home. We need 350,000 more before Dec. 31, and 1,000,000 in all by Sept. 30, 1917, to keep up existing units. This wastage is based on the assumption that, proportionately with effectives, the losses in winter and summer will be of the same character as in the previous year. We are short by 350,000 men of the numbers guaranteed by the Cabinet in Feb. last before the end of the current year. Salonika has at present the priority for drafts, in spite of the deficit in France ; and, in addition to the 23,000 drafts just sent to Salonika, 10,000 more are going out now.

It is very discreditable, but 20 per cent. of the men working in the mines are absentees, and some deliberately limit their work to a wage which keeps them below the income-tax level. All men of military age under twenty-five should be given up to the Army, no matter where employed, and eventually we must come to Compulsory National Service for every man up to fifty-five, when power will be obtained to release the younger men for the Army and to put the older men in their places.

Went to the Munitions Ministry and saw Mr. Montagu. He admitted—but only after naming a smaller number and refreshing his memory at my request—that his Ministry had badged 1,400,000 men, but he could not tell me how many were of military age, nor how many were skilled workmen. Neither could he give me any definition of what was and what was not a 'skilled man.' His secretary, Mr. Barlow, declared that not one-fifth of the badged men were of military age, but this I subsequently ascertained to be a mistake. Montagu expressed his desire to release all unskilled workmen, if he were given time and if substitutes were found. He expects the Army to find them from men not in the 'general service' category.

We had a talk over the supply of munitions to Russia and the provision of the new programme of guns and shells for our own Army. We agreed that the War Committee must lay down a *modus vivendi* on this subject. He told me that 32,000 men had been unbadged by his Ministry since May, but did not tell me how many were still being badged. He rather led me to believe that the substitution plan had been initiated by the Ministry of Munitions, whereas, I am told elsewhere, it has been forced upon them. My impression is that Montagu is all right, but Barlow was obviously hostile and probably represents the inner views of the Ministry.

I went to see Brigadier-General Frank Bingham, who

has taken General Du Cane's place at the Ministry as Military Technical Adviser. He is a good man. He showed me the expenditure of shells at the Somme battle, which included over 14,000,000 18-pr. shells expended, and 5,000,000 4·5-inch howitzer shells, besides all the rest. He also showed me a graphic which indicated that we had trenched on our shell capital in France to a considerable extent, but the echelons behind the line and on the L. of C. are still all full up. Haig had asked him last week whether he could continue his present rate of expenditure of shells, and he had told Haig that he could not. But all the same the figures are wonderful and the position not too unsatisfactory. We discussed the new munitions programme, and the new scale for guns demanded by the Army. This gives some 40 heavy guns per division, which is nearly up to the scale which Foch said he wanted, but Bingham says that the guns cannot *all* be provided until Dec. 1917. If Russia is to be assisted before next summer, then our Army must moderate its demands. We had sent 400 4·5-inch howitzers to Russia and a lot of motor lorries and 500,000 shells, but the Murman line is only expected to take 3000 tons a day, and as we are, for example, now sending 5000 tons of ammunition a night to our Armies in France, we cannot do big things for Russia until Archangel reopens. Bingham described to me the awful time he had gone through during the first two years of the war, and the anguish which he had suffered from the shell shortage.

I saw Stephenson Kent in Whitehall Gardens. I found him anxious for National Service for men up to fifty-five. He talked a great deal, but did not add much to my information except by raising the question of semi-skilled men, which may prove a fresh obstacle. I found him somewhat hostile to the Admiralty and the Man-Power Board, and critical of Admiralty methods.

Saw Brigadier-General Auckland Geddes at the N.L. Club, the new office of his branch, the Directorship of Recruiting. He is one of the best men of the new lot. I told him my figures, and he confirmed them. He said that I could have no conception of the tremendous fight which he and Macready had had with the Government Offices, of which the Board of Trade and the Home Office were the worst. Lloyd George, occupied in other matters whilst at the M. of M., had ignored what was going on in badging. The Labour Exchange section of the Board of Trade had gripped the Munitions Ministry firmly, and had simply shovelled out badges to any firm that had asked for them. There had been trafficking in badges and exemptions all over the country. Similarly, at the Home Office, the so-called Advisory Committee of the Mines had taken charge and had starved the Army. Samuel was not so bad as Runciman, but he had allowed these men to rule. Several civil permanent servants had helped in obstruction. The A.G.'s Branch had found itself up against a gang of anti-militarist and pacificist fanatics. In fact, the whole machinery of Government was acting in a manner to starve the Army. All these people, when in a corner, played the card of 'labour troubles,' and this had always frightened Lord K. from taking drastic measures. Geddes had settled the question of who was a 'skilled worker' by the Army Order of this month, and said that he would prevent any tricks being played—as I suggested they might be—by issuing an Army Council Instruction to say that the 'skilfulness' of the workers should depend upon their description as such under the Registration Act, *i.e.* before Aug. 15, 1915. In a week or so Geddes will establish seven Boards to arrange the badging, though the Munitions Ministry did not yet know of this. He was delighted with the work of the Man-Power Board. This Board took all their decisions to be passed by the War Committee before being published. I told him that I thought some of the departments hated the Board and meant to catch it tripping, if they could, and to destroy its usefulness. He quite agreed, but said that as the edicts are practically Cabinet decisions, we ought to be safe on this side.

As to the number of men of military age badged by the

M. of M., the figure was over 700,000. He knew this from the consolidated returns which he showed me, compiled by his central registry where every man can be traced, and they had been through every badge and man on the lists, except a certain number which might add 100,000 to the above figure. I looked over this registry. It is very complete, and all new since Geddes came in. There was no efficient Recruiting Branch before. Geddes is also completing his plans for substitution, and making them widely known. From all these arrangements he hopes to get 500,000 men from the M. of M. The yearly contingent will only give 100,000 men this year, as so many young fellows have already enlisted, but next year we should get our full amount, *i.e.* some 350,000, I suppose. There will still be a flow from the Tribunals as exemptions expire, but he thought that the M.-P. Board would take steps to set free for the Army nearly all men under twenty-five, and that Compulsory National Service for all men up to fifty-five was bound to come. He expected a long war and agreed with my views about Germany. I consider that we are very fortunate in having Macready and Geddes in the A.G. Branch, and have recommended their strong support. They, and the Man-Power Board, are our best hope. The Tribunals must not be criticised for the faults of a few of them. It is the erring Tribunals that we must trounce. They are not all exempting on their own initiative, but because Runciman's list of certified occupations leaves them no opening in most cases. It is the remote provincial Tribunal that does the harm. In the Orkneys men are said to be asked whether they want to join the Army or not ! Our real danger comes from Runciman and the pacificist gangs at the B. of T. and the Home Office.

I found general agreement wherever I went that the needs of trade, and especially munitions, must be a matter of fair compromise between departments. But it ought not to be left, as it is now, to the strength or weakness of personalities in one department or another to gain this end or that. The War Committee, advised by the Man-Power

Board, must decide and hold the balance fairly and firmly, and it is especially necessary for this Committee to decide how far we can and must help Russia with munitions. The munitions people declare that they are still short of 30,000 skilled men. On the other hand, Macready told me that we had exempted from service seven men for every one Frenchman exempted, and we must note that the demand for 1,000,000 men during the next twelve months only aims at replacing wastage, and not at the creation of fresh divisions. There are some businesses, *e.g.* blast furnaces and the branches of munitions dealing with shells of 6 inches and over, which must have hefty men of military age left to them, but the vast bulk of munitions work can be done by women, and by men over and above the military age. For us to leave our infantry in France with a deficit of one-sixth of its strength at such a moment as this is criminal.

CHAPTER XIV

MR. LLOYD GEORGE AND THE MILITARY MOLOCH

Some *Observer* articles—Lord Northcliffe and Lord French—Germany's new divisions—Mr. Lloyd George on the situation—He wishes 'to knock out the Turks '—His opinions on some soldiers—Two books still worth reading—The Military Moloch—Tales of the authorship of my *Observer* articles—General Robertson on Rumania, the Somme, Home Defence, and the Balkans—General Geddes on Army wastage—M. Nabokoff on the Russian situation—An article on ' The Lost Legions '—Lord Tullibardine on Egypt—A coming Conference in Paris—The Rumanian campaign—Our losses—Our numbers in different theatres of war—The German reserves—Our inability to raise fresh divisions—Lieut. Pernot on events—The question of convoy.

Tuesday, Oct. 17. Busy writing out result of my investigations yesterday and sending it to Robinson. Lunched with Sir Edward and Lady Carson at 5 Eaton Place. Colonel Frewen there too. An amusing lunch, Carson full of stories, and I told a good many. Carson on the Cabinet at the Coalition very humorous. He said that he told them that they were twenty-three blind mice. Robertson, after his first Cabinet, walked off with Carson and asked whether he had been attending a Cabinet or a committee of lunatics. Carson said that he would not advise that Ulster should have Compulsory Service unless the rest of Ireland had it too, as it would not be fair, and this disposes of current rumour to the contrary effect. I asked Carson what the law was concerning Press comments about the Dardanelles and Mesopotamia Inquiries, when both questions were under investigation. He said that legally they were not *sub judice*, but that for the rest it was a matter of taste. I told him much about the Geddes case and the question of Man-Power, and am to send him my two memoranda on these subjects. He told me that a man who had been on board the *Fanny* was writing the story of the famous voyage and the gun-running exploit. Lady Carson and Colonel Frewen very agreeable. Frewen and I had a talk before lunch about the Home Divisions.

Wednesday, Oct. 18. Busy writing. Dined at 3 Tenterden Street with Lady Ridley, Lady Alistair Ker, and Evan Charteris. Most agreeable dinner. Lady R.'s mother's house, and a gem, with delicious panellings and very quiet. Both ladies delightful companions.

Thursday, Oct. 19. Garvin being ill, I have, at his urgent request, taken on the big article in the *Observer*, and find it a pleasure to have such scope after the shabby manner in which I have been treated by the *Times* of late. Garvin writes that I am the only man whom he can trust to replace him. I shall probably continue the *Observer* article for three weeks or a month. Garvin wants 5000 words, which is rather a lot, but there is a lot to say.

Lunched with Lady Randolph ; Lady Gwendeline Churchhill, Lady Ridley, Mrs. Sheridan, Winston, Lord Stanmore, Lord A. Thynne. Very cheery, and Winston in great form. A good deal of Dardanelles Inquiry talk, Winston standing up for his point of view, and I taking the line that it was folly to send 60,000 men to fight 240,000 Turks. Winston also exclaimed as usual against the old Regular Army officers still all having the higher commands, and pretended that with all the intelligence of the country now in the Army, some of it should be in the commands after two years of war. I argued that some privates had already risen to command their regiments, but that in no profession would apprentices be at the top after two years. What new member would be in the Cabinet in two years ? Lady Ridley down on the Radicals as usual. Walked to the House of Commons with Winston. We were hailed into 55 St. James's Street, where we found Lady Diana, Mrs. McKenna, and others selling things for the Red Cross, and we were made to buy.

Dined with E. and went to the Bull Dog Club, in

Edgware Road regions. Very full of soldiers, including Australians and Canadians, also a general gathering. I had to make a speech on the war. Sir Frederick Pollock, who had spoken before me, had not got hold of his audience. I made a homely speech about soldiers and sailors, and got a great reception. I never spoke from a stage before. I made them turn off the footlights. Perhaps if Balfour had done the same when I saw him speaking at the Palace Music Hall one day he would not have appeared so horribly shy and uncomfortable.

Dined with the McKennas and Lady Paget at 5 Smith Square. I was three quarters of an hour late. A good dinner. McKenna told us the story of the *Goeben*. He also said that America would have all the money and the knowledge how to make munitions after the war, and would be the greatest Power in the world. He had found J. P. Morgan and others had learnt a lot about finance, and were now less provincial. He had shown them that England had 4000 millions sterling of collateral securities outside the U.K., which ought to be good enough to borrow on, but the trouble was, as he had told me before, that America had all the money, and was increasing her consumption and could not find the things we wanted. He said that if the U.S. came in, all his difficulties would be removed : he would get a loan of 1000 million dollars from the President, who would get it from the State. He thought that the British banking system was far superior to all others in the world.

Saturday, Oct. 21. Revised the proof of my first *Observer* leader : nearly six columns, and about the best summary of the war that I have written. Garvin and Bell send me most flattering messages about it, the former wiring that it is ' just the thing, and displays breadth, grip, and judgment. Thanks indeed.' Why does not the *Times* occasionally praise ? Got through much reading and went down to Coombe in the afternoon. Found the Duke of Alba, Lady Cunard, Sir F. E. and Lady Smith, Winston and his wife, the twins and Somers Cocks, Mrs. Ward,

Mrs. O'Neill and her boy, Mrs. Grahame White, Baroness Aleotti, M. Bardac, and Count Charles de Noailles, assistant to Bertier and a charming young fellow. Some excellent tennis. F. E. and Mrs. Churchill quite good. Everybody seemed to know of a recent visit of mine to Lord French, so he must have been talking. But he had telephoned to me in the morning to-day to say that he was not going to mention the matter to the King, so all is well. Sir Arthur came on Sunday. He told me that he had now three divisions, and Bruce Hamilton, with the Northern Army, only two. Sir Arthur had 93,000 men all told, but few fit to fight or march, and that he could not stop 30,000 Germans if they came. He had had to give up the idea of opposing a landing seriously on the beach, and could only occupy the London positions, but he could throw 3000 men anywhere on the beach in a few hours, and had placed Lovat at Ipswich with 4000 mobile troops for this purpose. Three of Sir Arthur's provisional brigades had been taken from him to form the nucleus of three new divisions. He had given up warning the authorities as no one attended to him. I hear that Germany is making twenty-seven new divisions, representing an additional field strength of 300,000 men. It is said that Brussiloff's offensive has definitely failed. The situation in Rumania is anxious. A German Army Order has been found, telling commanders in the West that they were not to attack without explicit higher orders, because even the defence on the Somme is so costly of men. Alba asked me to stay with him in Madrid if I went to Portugal. He thought that Northcliffe had been unwise in attacking the clericals in Spain. F. E. and Winston most gay and amusing. Lady Cunard raised some awful subjects in a general conversation, and Mrs. Churchill was visibly put out. F. E. spoke to me about Winston when I motored back with him on Monday morning, and thought he was most stimulating to listen to. Winston read me his December article. It was full of interesting ideas. We walked over to see Lady Ripon, but she was too ill to see us. We saw Ripon for a few minutes. Everybody much interested in the *Observer* article. Much talk about the Censorship. Personally I think it is improving. At the beginning of the war it deleted all my remarks about Chatham, believing him to have been a naval port.

Tuesday, Oct. 24. Lunched with Sir George Murray at 50 Grosvenor Gardens. Theresa Lady Londonderry, and Lady Lilian Grenfell also there. I had not seen the former since the death of her husband, and she is now lamenting the death of Lord Feversham, who was killed in France the other day. She was full of interesting talk, and carried me away to tea at Lady F.'s house in Pont Street, where we talked of people and things for a good while. I liked her description of a man who had married a certain great lady: ' C'est un homme qu'on reçoit ou dans son lit, ou dans son anti-chambre, mais jamais dans son salon ! ' perhaps a quotation, but I do not recall it.

Wednesday, Oct. 25. Lloyd George lunched with me at the Carlton, 1.45. He was looking well, and was in good form. We plunged at once into the war. He told me that the War Committee had agreed to send another division from France to Salonika, and that he had also sent the best part of another division, mostly from Egypt. Robertson had not stood out against it : had he done so, the Committee would probably not have consented. L. G. thought that these fresh troops would do no good. It was all much too late. Two months ago it might have had some effect, and if we had gone to Salonika, as he asked and advised, in Feb. 1915, we might have had the whole Balkans with us. At all events this reinforcement will hearten up the Rumanians, and proves our willingness to bring help. He thought that Sarrail was no good, and that the offensive towards Monastir was childish. However, he said that our people at Salonika thought that we were holding up 250,000 Bulgars, and if this were so, it was something. He was very much down on the soldiers, generally, for not having made better plans when Rumania entered the war, a point on which I heartily agreed with him, saying that I supposed

Rumania and Russia must have come to an arrangement on the subject, but he said he knew absolutely nothing of what had been arranged. We agreed this was a most extraordinary manner of waging war. I said I hoped that the detachment from Egypt would not prevent Archie Murray from carrying out his plans. L. G. thought we ought to knock out the Turkish Empire. I agreed so long as we did it with Indian and African troops, and set free all our white divisions for the West. He said that Smuts was of opinion that there were no black troops to be provided, but I said that Smuts only knew one part of Africa, and that naturally the Boers did not want their blacks, who were in such an enormous numerical preponderance in South Africa, to be trained to arms, but that there were plenty of warlike races in other parts, and that the Allies held all Africa and were making no use of its resources.

L. G. said that he was getting on well with Robertson, but that he was very disappointed that R. would not go to Russia to visit Alexeieff. He could have done the whole thing in a month, and it would have made R. more Eastern and Alexeieff more Western. If they had sat together and talked things over quietly for a week or so, it might have had a great effect.

L. G. thought that both the General Staff of the War Office and the Adjutant-General's Branch were very well manned just now. We did not get on to the Q.M.G.'s Branch, I am sorry to say, but we discussed Geddes, and I told him broadly my objections to the replacing of soldiers by civilians. L. G. then rather launched out and said that he could not recognise any difference between soldiers and civilians, and was going to take the best man he found wherever he discovered him. He evidently thought that the soldiers had muddled the campaign, and was very uncomplimentary about several of them, both French and British. He had still not met Allenby, but he liked the look of Tom Bridges, and thought Gough a good man.

He was evidently by no means satisfied with the general

situation, and thought it was worse now than it had been for a long time. What did I think ? He said, 'Do you see your way to winning the war, and if so, how do you propose to do it ? ' I said that I would ask him to define what he meant by winning the war. He said that he meant if we thrust the Germans out of France and Belgium. He would consider that winning the war. I said that winning the war was difficult, but that it was a question of the strongest will-power, as Hindenburg had truly said, and that we had nothing to do but, in the language of the Prize Ring, to keep on punching. I said that my view was that we wanted a very much greater superiority of force than we possessed to win the war in the ordinary way. We were perhaps as six to five in the West, but we wanted to be stronger to annihilate the enemy. I told him that I thought that the leading statesmen of the four Great Powers of the Alliance should meet in London, review the whole situation, and lay down the policy to be pursued. But he said that there was no one in Russia to be trusted or who was trusted by the Tsar. Briand was very good and quick, but he was like a golfer who hits the ball very hard, but never gets it very far. There was no ' carry through ' in his stroke. However, I said the thing has to be done because this is really a little over the heads of the strategists, and he said, ' Yes, they will meet and discuss things without any knowledge of politics and economics, and we shall not get on.' He did not think that Asquith would be of much use at such a meeting as I suggested, ' because he was a lawyer.' As to the division to be sent from France to Salonika, it would be replaced from home, so Haig would be no worse off. We discussed G.H.Q. ideas on policy and strategy, and I promised L. G. to write on the subject. He asked me whether there was any single military book published before the war which I found worth reading. I said, ' The Book of Joshua and Clausewitz.' ' And Clausewitz is only principles,' added L. G. ' Yes,' I said, ' but they survive all the changes.'

As for the rest, we had to discard all the baggage of our previous learning and teach ourselves by our new experiences, and not allow ourselves to be hampered by anything. He agreed, and said that he found soldiers in command only concerned with their special fronts, and not able to take broad views.

L. G. said that we were in a serious position. The Australians, according to Murdoch, were dissatisfied with the discipline of the Army and the manner in which they had been handled. It might be that our people at home might begin to ask questions, and it might be difficult for us to get the men and to carry on, especially if we had to ask for older men. Not a very encouraging talk. He burst out once, and said that we were all asked to keep silent and bow the knee to this military Moloch, but that he was responsible, and as he would have to take the blame, he meant to have his own way. So the antagonism is even deeper than R. suspected, and I am not best pleased with the situation. I fancied that the bit of venom that L. G. put into his conversation was partly due to the attack on him to-day by the *Daily Mail* on the question of the pledge to men of forty-one. L. G. said that Northcliffe had abused him for not bowing to the soldiers in strategy. Now L. G. had supported the soldiers about the men aged forty-one, and Northcliffe had rounded on him. He said that N. was like a flea ; he hopped about and you never knew where to catch him.

Dined with Sir F. E. and Lady Smith in Grosvenor Gardens, 32 I think it is. Sir Max Aitken, Maxine Elliott, General Salmond, and another man. Max asked me a lot of questions after dinner about the war, and promised to show me the Canadian diaries when I called. I found him shrewd and capable. Sir F. E. told me that Carson was wrong about the Dardanelles Commission. It had all the powers of a Court of Law, and any attack upon it was a breach of privilege. They had nearly got Marlowe, editor of the *Daily Mail*, for blackguarding the Committee, but George Hamilton had made a mess of it.

Maxine very jolly, and looking very handsome. She is off to America till April, and is doing a course of banting. We played Bridge till 2.30 A.M. and had some wonderful games, forcing each game up and doing much doubling. I never remember more interesting Bridge or stranger hands.

Thursday, Oct. 26. Lunched with Mrs. Astor, who is back in town and not looking very well. Sir Alan Johnstone and Lady J., Lady Cunard, Seymour Fortescue, Vansittart, and Lady J.'s boy. A gay party, and Lady C. in her best form. Her description of Mrs. X.'s account of her to Sir Arthur du Cros was quite killing. I told them that seven Cabinet Ministers had warned futurity in their wills that all Mrs. X.'s diary stories about them would be quite untrue.

Friday, Oct. 27. Lunched with Lockett at the Ritz. He also had Laszlo, the artist, and Mr. McFadden, the American cotton man and collector. Two Cabinet Ministers at the next table; Sir Ian, Lady Annesley, and Ronny Brocke and his wife at another, while General Whigham had a party for some Russians. McFadden told me all about his great collection of the early English painters which he has taken thirty-four years to amass, and how the Velasquez did not consort with them. Laszlo has bet Lockett £300 that the war will be over before April, and if Lockett wins, Laszlo has to paint a portrait for him, but Laszlo claims the right to choose the sitter, and says that he will select me. Laszlo looked long at X. and did not like his roving eye. He said that he looked like a nan who had no foundation under him but only a morass. I promised to go to his studio next week. Got home to finish the article for the *Observer* on German politics and economics.

Saturday, Oct. 28. Amused to read in the *Nation* a note by Massingham ascribing the last *Observer* article to Winston. He says that the internal evidence is conclusive ! Churchill's light, he adds, is never long hid under a bushel, and ' in the *Observer* its gleams shone like the shaded lamps of our city ! ' He says that ' the form of the article is extremely good—the pessimistic conclusions wrought up with skill of presentation and argument, and the writer's feelings suggested with a freedom to which our timid, suppressed, impersonal journalism rarely attains.' He declares that ' the intellectual quality of the article is remarkable.' This has given me a real good laugh, not lessened by the *Evening News* blackguarding the article now that they believe it to be Winston's. Went down to Coombe for the night to meet Sir Arthur and some soldiers. Lady Granard also there, and we had some good Bridge.

Sunday, Oct. 29. Motored down to Doris Keane's country house ; a delicious house, standing high, and with a fine view.

Monday, Oct. 30. Lunched with Sir W. Robertson in South Street. He told me that Alexeieff was sending four or five Army Corps to Rumania, but that only two would arrive by Nov. 1. The Rumanians insisted upon retaining the command because they had stipulated for it in their convention with Russia. But there was then only question of a few divisions, and now circumstances were different. R. did not think much of the Russians, and said that the Rumanians at Orsova would be cut off unless they moved. He did not think operations any longer practicable on the rest of the Russian front. We laughed about the raid of the German destroyers into the Channel, and R. said that he would make the Admiralty talk about it at the War Committee to-morrow. He had been told nothing about it, and I told him that Paget was not warned when it happened. R. was sarcastic about the Navy doing nothing for so long and having no offensive plans. Haig was to have attacked on the 25th, the day after the Verdun stroke, but the weather had stopped him. Some of his horses had been so deeply embedded in the mud that they had had to be shot. It would take five days of good weather before he could go on, and they expected a big result and some 5000 prisoners. The Navy still refused to say on paper that they could defend the country from 70,000 men and under, and R. was not going to send his five good divisions out of England until the four new home service divisions were fit for something. They would then join French, who had, beside them, five other home service divisions, a lot of provisional brigades, seventeen yeomanry brigades, 15,000 cyclists, and 160,000 men in the fortresses. These include Ireland, where there is one of the five good divisions. There are 30,000 men at Newcastle. French had half a million men all told, and could fight with 200,000 to cover London. R. admitted that all would go if London went, and he would take no risks, although he thought an attack unlikely in the winter. He had thought it right to give way about the division to be sent to Salonika, and had made up most of another division by odd battalions from various places. Maurice had been cross because he had given way, but I thought him right to compromise at this stage. He had told the Cabinet that the divisions would be unfit to fight before January on account of the delay needed to find mules and equip the troops for mountain fighting. He still thought a great campaign in the Balkans a mistake from every point of view. His time was much taken up by having to explain every detail to the War Committee. L. G. was always holding him personally responsible, and he felt that he would not get his support in a difficulty. It was a difficult war to fight. We were not winning it at present, and he had told the War Committee so. He was finding five spare lots of divisional artillery to help Haig out and allow the gunners a rest. He feared that we might have to reduce our infantry in our divisions next year, so it was not worth while following the German plan just now. He thought that the Germans increased the number of their divisions to enable them to move more troops about. He wondered whether there were enough reserves to keep the new German divisions going, or whether it was just a splash in Rumania to make things look well before a peace. The French had had to reduce twelve of their divisions to nine battalions.

Wednesday, Nov. 1. Got on with my third *Observer* article, which will be on the conduct of the war. It is going to be a lively one. Immensely amused by the discussion in the Press and elsewhere about the authorship. Winston has now publicly denied that he wrote the first article. Lovat Fraser amused me by telling me that one of the compositors at the *Times,* who works for the *Observer* on Sunday, declared that he set up the article from Gerard Fiennes's MSS.! All sorts of other names suggested. I wish that I had not told any one. Lunched with Lady Randolph. Lady Gwendeline, Winston, Lady Leslie, and Benson the novelist. Cheery as always. Drove off with Winston and begged him to make L. G. have proper men round him. Saw Geoffrey Robinson at 'The Travellers,' and told him my grievances against the *Times.* He was quite nice. Saw Corbett, manager of the *Times,* at the office. They have done well, and have repaid by bonuses the £4000 previously deducted from salaries. This is the first that I have heard of it. Lovat Fraser told me the story of the last Boulogne Conference—true or not?—that Pellé had asked for a general examination of the position and had been suppressed by Joffre, that Thomas had done the talking in favour of more Salonika troops, that Haig had made an angry speech, that Robertson had supported him, and that the P.M. and Grey in bad speeches had done the same. Nothing decided: then Thomas came to England and got Montagu to run round and move people, with the result that Robertson gave way as above. L. G. appears to have laid low.

Thursday, Nov. 2. Went to see Auckland Geddes at the National Liberal Club. He showed me that our wastage for a year would be 944,000 men, and that if we did not take another recruit we had 1,044,000 men of 'A' category and returned wounded, who would be available. Better than I expected. He thinks that it is want of organisation as much as anything else that is wrong. We can talk of the deficit of 150,000 men abroad, and then there is the need for more divisions. He can manage five more, but he says that the number of men of military age is constantly found to be larger than known, and that they are in many funk-holes all over the country. I had met Daisy de Brienen on the way, and she had talked of the English abroad not having been called on. I thought this a useful point and mentioned it to Geddes, who agreed and said that he had written to the F.O. to-day asking them to agree to a short act to cover the ground. We cannot take these men as they are not 'normally resident in Great Britain,' as the Service Act stipulates. Geddes wants more men mainly for infantry wastage, which works out to 75 per cent. per year, and to 50 per cent. for the whole Army. He told me that he could not find out anywhere from any branch of the War Office, what the establishments were in France, and what the wastage. The A.G. Branch was chaos before he came into it. We had over 1,500,000 men at home. We ought, with the five good divisions now at home, with five more which might be raised, and with two Dominion fresh divisions, to be able to give the Germans a good surprise in the spring.

Friday, Nov. 3. Lunched with Lady Cunard. Lady Sackville, M. Nabokoff of the Russian Embassy, Winston and Mrs. Churchill, Mrs. Bonham-Carter, Herbert Asquith (wounded and getting better), Lady Gwendeline, the Duchess of Marlborough, Nancy Cunard and her fiancé, and a few more. Arranged with the Duchess a plan for explaining what Americans have done for us during this war. Lady Sackville has given up the plan of buying the fine Hampstead site. She is living quietly at Knole, and only putting up four guests at a time as things are so bad. Nabokoff told me that the internal situation of Russia was amazing. A revolution against reactionary bureaucracy was certain, but the Tsar would stand apart, and no Russian peasant would look at any one who spoke against him. He said that the *Almanach de Gotha* was right in describing the Government of Russia as an autocracy with a constitutional Government. The organisation of the food supply was most defective. The people were all heart and soul for beating the Germans, whom they loathed, and for taking Constantinople, and nothing else mattered to them. The revolution might wait, but if the bureaucrats became too impossible they would be put out.

Took Mrs. Churchill to see the picture in silk of Lord French. It was made in the interior of China, and is a great curiosity. Mr. McFadden, the American millionaire, has bought it. He came up to Maryon to-day, and I showed him the pictures, which he liked very much, and I then took him up to Judge's Walk to show him the scene which Constable painted of Hampstead Heath, which picture McF. now has. He brought up a photograph. The gravel pit in the foreground can still be identified, and the lie of the land and the distant view, but much wood has grown up since Constable lived.

Called at the War Office, and saw General Macdonogh, to ask about the situation in Rumania. He tells me that there are ten German and nine Austrian divisions now in Transylvania, and he thinks that the Predil Pass will be their main line of advance. If they can be checked for ten days, all the Russians will be up. The Dobrudcha, he thinks, will be all right now, and here the Russians have the best of the communications, but on the mountain side it is different. He doubts that the season will stop the fighting after our experiences of the Masurian Lake and Erzeroum campaigns. Nabokoff said the same thing. Macdonogh does not like the Rumanian efforts at the Vulcan Pass any more than I do those at Orsova. If the Germans get through, these forces may be cut off. He said that the bulk of the oil district was between Ploesti and Predil, — five-sixths of it — and this road was the shortest to Bukharest. Hindenburg was obviously attacking in Galicia to hold the Russians there.

Sunday, Nov. 5. Two terrible days of rain and howling storms, which make it impossible ever to forget the men in the trenches. A lot of letters and messages about my article in the *Times* of last Monday on ' The Lost Legions '— a tribute to the old Army, including a sweet one from

Lady Grosvenor, who recalls happy days at Clouds. I publish my third *Observer* article.

Wickham Steed, foreign editor of the *Times*, and his brother came to lunch at Maryon, the brother to discuss Tribunal work and volunteers. The latter said truly that the Government were asking the Tribunals to be in advance of national policy, and were throwing upon them the onus of unpopular measures.

Dined at Belle Herbert's in the evening. Reggie and Bee Pembroke, Lord and Lady Crewe, Lord and Lady D'Abernon, Foster and another man in the Blues, Sir Seymour Fortescue, Dick Molyneux, Lady Colebrooke's pretty daughter, Lady Juliet Duff, the Duchess of Roxburghe, and Lady Granard. A pleasant talk at dinner with Bee Pembroke, and we mutually raved about Lady Bessborough's letters in the new Granville memoirs. She tells me things are bad in Ireland. Reggie confirms this. They have just come back from a short visit there. Neither Mr. Duke nor Wimborne satisfies the middle parties in Ireland, but all speak well of Lady W., who is very popular. Mahon's substitution for 'Conky' Maxwell is announced. The latter takes Bob Lawson's place on the Yorkshire coast and gets a G.C.B. Lady D'Abernon in great good looks, and very decorative. Seymour, the Duchess, Lady Granard, and I made up one of two Bridge tables after dinner. These ladies are the two best lady Bridge players in London. The cards were mad, and we had some extraordinary games. Seymour and I cut together and beat the two experts in a hard-fought last game, and we talked and chaffed all the time. I was very sorry to say good-bye again to Reggie, who returns to France to-morrow. He is looking older, and one sees the effect of the strain. Bee is a very gallant lady and keeps up her wicket in these hard times. Went with Seymour to his rooms, and we talked stories of King Edward till late.

Monday, Nov. 6. Lunched with Lockett to meet Sir Arthur Lee. We talked for two hours, controversially about Sir Eric Geddes, and quietly about volunteers and man-power. Lee evidently inoculated with L. G.'s views of the 'military Moloch!' I did not wish to discuss the Geddes case as Haig has come to heel to L. G. about it, so I regard it as a *fait accompli* and not worth discussing any more, but I let Lee see plainly what I thought about the matter. Lee knew nothing about volunteers or man-power, so he was not useful.

Went afterwards to see Lord Tullibardine in Eaton Place. He is just back from Egypt. He was not keen about Archie's plan about going to El Arish, and says that Lawrence does not like it either. We shall have the inundations behind us, a long line to defend, and long communications, while, when the spring comes, the Turks can attack over the desert to southward, and will not be restricted to the El Arish route. The French hate us touching Syria, and will try to steal Murray's troops for Salonika, as they have done already, and I do not feel sure that we are doing the right thing unless we can send Murray a lot of native troops from Africa and India. Bardy spoke of the proposed plan of sending a Yeomanry brigade to help the Sherif of Mecca as a piece of folly. We should have come up against two Turkish divisions had we done so. He says that the Sultan of Egypt had told him that he was going to abdicate, and that he, Bardy, had stopped him from doing so. All the Egyptians were anti-English. He thought that Murray was doing well. The Scottish Yeomanry have been badly treated. They have all been broken up and made into Black Watch, Camerons, used to make up the depleted Irish battalions, and others of them make a 'liquid pool' at Salonika. Bardy says that his work and Lovat's of sixteen years has been lost. He has told the King, and showed me the paper which he has sent to Stamfordham on the subject. The W.O. should have formed a Scottish Yeomanry brigade on foot, and the rest have been kept for filling it up. The Household Cavalry have been much better treated. He says that Murray is furious about it. I advised him to take a turn at the House of Commons in order to stir people up.

More amusing reports about the *Observer* articles. One man swears he knows that Cromer wrote them, and others say Milner, Rosebery, and Carson. I am in good company. Arthur Murray has asked Olive to find out from me who wrote the articles as the Government wish to know!

Saturday, Nov. 11. Made some additions to my article on Poland and returned it, and went on with the Man-Power series. Lunched with Lady Paget and her two sisters-in-law. She is full of new schemes for making money for the Red Cross. Mish-Mish (the Grand Duke Michael) has got forty-two Royalties to dine with him on the night of his daughter's marriage. We wondered where he has swept them all up, but Lady Minnie says that if you go down to Battenbergs it is quite easy. Had a talk with Generals Kitson and Peter Granet at the Club, who more or less confirm my views about the war.

Went on to see a well-informed man. We began about recruiting. He thinks, with me, that we cannot talk openly about the number of divisions that we are going to put into the field, but thinks that Lloyd George might mention that we shall want a million men by next June, as that will not teach the enemy anything. He says that we ought to take power to bring in men up to forty-five, but that we need not do so if the Trade Unions play up and actively assist in the process of substitution. I told him, following Geddes, that I thought organisation was at fault, and he was inclined to agree, but said the doubt they were in with regard to the number they were going to get hampered the work of recruiting very considerably. He told me that the chief soldiers were going to have their annual conference at Paris this next week. L. G. was also going to have a conference of Allied Statesmen. Joffre had been asked to postpone the soldier conference till later, which I thought quite reasonable, but Joffre had refused. L. G. was still a very dangerous factor. When L. G. had been abroad before, all had been well, but last time some unpleasant things had happened. It is thought that Haig will have one more smack at the

Germans, and will then close down about the end of November in order to get his divisions out of the line for training as he had done before. The Navy still refuse to give any assurance about stopping an invasion between the Wash and the Medway. If the Germans came there, the Navy said they would have twenty-eight hours in which to do anything they liked, and consequently the Army problem was how many troops the Germans could put ashore in those twenty-eight hours. This compelled Robertson to keep the 5 good divisions at home, besides the other 4, and this also gave him a reserve for emergencies, which is a sound thing to possess. I said that we ought to have 100 divisions in France next year, and my friend said he would be content if he got 70, but not because he did not want more.

We then touched on Rumania. The Russians are extending their line southwards as far as the Buzeu Valley. This sets free the Rumanian Northern Army to reinforce the central sector, and the Rumanians should now have 21 divisions of their own from Buzeu to Orsova, while the Russians have sent 4 Army Corps and have 2 more behind. With these they intend to begin on Monday an attack over the mountains to take the Germans in flank ! Falkenhayn has 10 German divisions and 11½ Austrian in Transylvania, but it is thought that they may spare some 6 more from France and may bring 9 in from other parts of the Eastern front. This will make 35 divisions in all, which is about the figure I anticipated a month or two ago. The Rumanians are fighting well, but have only field artillery. In the Dobrudcha, Sakharoff has now 9 divisions and a good lot of cavalry. Mackensen has 8 against them. Only two of Sakharoff's divisions are Rumanian and one is Serb. Our General Staff suggested to the Russians that they should make their main effort through the Dobrudcha against Mackensen, but this has not been done. We still hold up 9 Bulgarian divisions round Salonika, but can really do nothing during the winter. There will be three Venizelist Greek divisions ready by January, when they will try and retake all the Kavalla district occupied by the Bulgars. I spoke about an Eastern move of the Salonika Army, but Milne reports that not more than 9 divisions can be fed if we take this route owing to poor harbours, and the Admiralty agree. When the frost comes campaigning can go on all the winter along the Western-Rumanian frontier. Our people are fairly happy about Murray. When I spoke about sending him black troops from Africa I was told that we had now 17 black battalions which we might send when East Africa is settled up, but that the Union Government object to our raising black troops in South Africa, and the local people elsewhere report that we cannot do much more without compulsion. I doubt this very much.

Sunday, Nov. 12. Spent two hours investigating man-power questions again. We have now 2,054,000 troops in the field in the various theatres of war, and 1,502,000 at home. These include Colonials. Our losses on the Somme have been 370,000 since July 1, that is to say, on the Somme front only. The numbers in Egypt are 164,000, and we have about the same number at Salonika. Our forces at home include 944,000 Regulars and 179,000 Colonials. The Royal Defence Corps is 39,000. We have 368,000 of administrative services at home, a figure difficult to defend. Lord French's 500,000 men include the garrisons, the R.D. Corps, Ireland, etc. His field troops do not amount to 200,000 men even in the aggregate. Some want to reduce the Home Defence Force, but I tell them that it is not safe until the Navy can give firm and written guarantees and make different dispositions. The Germans have now 201 divisions in the field, and the Austrians still 1,000,000 men, making 5,500,000 in all, including L. of C., but not including depots. The figure of 2,000,000 for the German reserves is thought to be an outside number, and will not keep up the German strengths for a year ahead when there would be nothing left but the young contingent and the returned wounded. The new German divisions have meant a drain of 380,000 men on the German reserves.

Some of our people dubious about Sir Eric Geddes's appointment and others think that three men on Haig's Staff are all second-rate chaps, and that another in a higher post is not very strong. Clayton has been sent home, and is a great loss.

The Man-Power Board have just sent in their new report and proposals. The W.O. refuse to consider them before the P.M. and L. G. come back from France, so the War Committee will not legislate upon it until next Friday, Nov. 17. The main proposal is to take all unskilled men under twenty-five, and soldiers are satisfied generally with the other proposals. The report admits the unpopularity of the Tribunals, and says that they are helpless under their instructions. The taking of British subjects domiciled abroad is recommended, but the F.O. have been very obstructive on this subject.

Monday, Nov. 13. Went on with the Man-Power articles. Lunched with Will Meredith and his partner Mr. Kyllmann at the Bath Club, and talked books, war, and politics. Meredith says that the Publishers' Association want the Government to put down quite a modest sum [1] to enable the publishers to oust German books from their present predominant position. All the plans are made, but the Treasury will not act. Meredith says that trade follows the book, and that we are letting slip a golden opportunity. He also said that the Ministry of Munitions had done wonders about optics, and that we now, thanks to Professor Herbert Jackson, led the Germans. They want me to prepare a book on the war, but I see little chance of doing so.

Saw Sir William Robertson at 4 South Street at 6.30 P.M. He leaves to-morrow for the Paris Conference, and may be back Friday. He asked if I had noticed how the War Committee had met of late without any naval or military representatives. What were they up to? Perhaps a stocktaking all round in preparation for Paris. R. is still sore about India taking so little part in the war, and thinks, with me, that they ought to take on all the Eastern cam-

[1] This appeal had no result.

paign and set free the white divisions. R. said that they were still at him to go to Russia, but that much might happen in a month, and he did not like to be away so long. When Lord K. started for Russia he took something in his hand, namely, guns, but the supply of guns for Russia had now been settled for six months ahead, so R. had nothing to offer Alexeieff. R. had heard no more than was in the papers to-day about Haig's attack this morning. Gough was making a push with seven divisions and all the Tanks. R. talked of figures. We agreed about the figures at home and that they were indefensible, especially for the Administrative Services. I told R. that the old A.G. point of view and the cult of 'states' had dropped out from the Army since the General Staff was formed, and that it ought to be restored. The G.S. had neglected this side. He agreed. He wanted to form as many new divisions as he could, but with a deficit of 150,000 abroad he could not form fresh divisions. He had 450,000 men on the lists at home under training, but when he examined the figure he found only 200,000 infantry, and much of the rest were redundant artillery or cavalry. He was asking all departments of the W.O. to study the question of numbers with the A.G., a course which I heartily approved. But I told him that he must not complain of his deficit abroad while he had 1,500,000 men at home, as a politician might say that if the W.O. could not make good the deficit with such numbers, he would find another War Office that could.

A thick fog, but I found my way down to the Hyde Park Hotel, and dined with Bertier and Pernot. The latter discussed the *Observer* articles at length, and thought the writer a friend of Robertson's. He had summarised them for the G.Q.G. I told him what, in my view, the object of the writer was. He liked immensely my definition of the rôle of policy and strategy, as Robertson had done. The latter had congratulated me upon the articles, and thought them first rate. Pernot said that he had most flattering reports about Alexeieff from the Head of the

French Mission in Russia, and he also said that the Russian Munitions were coming on well. Pernot had been in Italy, and thought Italian opinion discouraged and not very firm. A certain well-known Italian deputy, X., had got one of Cadorna's Staff officers to write a memo. criticising Cadorna. A deputy had taken three copies to Rome. One had been sent by one of the Italian Cabinet to Cadorna, asking as a *quid pro quo* that his nephew might be excused service. It was given out that this copy had been found in a train. Cadorna had tried the Staff officer, and he had got a year's seclusion, whilst the deputy who took the report to Rome had been sentenced to two months' imprisonment, and X. had been asked not to go to the Army again. Cadorna had been ordered to Rome and had replied that he was too busy. A characteristic story! Pernot told me that Castelnau shared my views about an Eastern move from Salonika, but had been overruled, whence the Monastir move. Crawled to the tube in a pea-soup fog. On reaching Hampstead, found a clear night and a lovely moon.

Tuesday, Nov. 14, *to Sunday, Nov.* 19. On Tuesday the P.M., L. G., and Sir W. R., with Fred Maurice, went off to Paris for the Conference without beat of drum. I spent the week in writing three articles on Man-Power and a leader, and also wrote a short sketch of the position in Rumania, and a review of Sidney Low's little book on Italy. This kept me fairly busy. On Tuesday I lunched with two friends, and we all told each other stories of the iniquities and intrigues of various politicians. The W.O. have made out the cost in shipping of a scheme for carrying ten divisions to Salonika. This showed that it would take 279 ships five months to do the job, and was an effective stopper on Eastern adventure. The report had been laid before the War Committee before L. G. had seen it, and the latter was angry about it.

Dined on Wednesday at Lady Leslie's; Lady Horner, Lady Juliet Duff, Professor Morgan, and Sidney Leslie. The ladies very gay and amusing, but we forgot that Sir John Simon was a friend of Lady Horner's, and castigated him badly.   Morgan, a captain in khaki : he seemed at first rather hard, but talked well after dinner when the ladies had gone, and seemed to hold some strong and sound views on political matters.   A warning had come of a Zepp. raid, and no taxis were to be found, so I walked with the ladies to their houses.

Lunched on Thursday with Mrs. Astor ; Seymour Fortescue, Wolkoff, Mrs. Bellville, Major Mortimer, Mrs. Phipps, and Marjorie Higgins.   Met Sir L. and Lady Jenkins at E.'s in the evening.   He was formerly Chief Justice in Bengal. He thinks that from the frontier, from the native States, and from other warlike resources of India, a much greater military reinforcement can be drawn.

On Friday lunched with Mr. Massingham, editor of the *Nation*, at Claridge's.   E. and Dr. Ettie Sayer also there. Massingham seems now to have heard that I wrote the *Observer* articles, and we had some fine fencing on the subject.   We went off to see M. Fauthier, 131 Cheyne Walk, Chelsea.   A black-haired artist, very young.   His painting of Zogheb too awful, but some of his sketches and many of his drawings show talent.   Lieut. Pernot and the MacColls dined at Maryon.   The MacColls charming and cultivated people. Pernot full of good talk, and a most interesting companion. He is still trying very hard to bring me round to Salonika, but he admits that the advance towards Monastir is all wrong.   We stayed up late talking over the war.

Monday, Nov. 20.   Wrote an article on the Ancre battle, and replied to the German General Staff criticism, in the German papers of Nov. 3 and 4, on our Western strategy.

Lunched with Garvin at the Carlton Grill, and we had a two-hours' talk.   Took tea with Mrs. Long at 55 Seymour Street, which she has done up with great taste.   We discussed the pro-German tendencies of the Russian bureaucracy at Petrograd, and Lady Muriel Paget's reports thereon.   Saw a Mr. Logio at Maryon.   He is anxious for General Radko Dimitrieff to go to Salonika and form the Bulgar prisoners into a fighting force, and get touch with the anti-Ferdinand elements in Bulgaria.

Dined with Lady Pembroke, who has taken Mark Fenwick's house, 22 Bruton Street, till January ; Belle Herbert, Admiral Sir Hedworth and Lady Meux, Sir Francis Hopwood, and Lord Tweedmouth, the latter leaving for France again to-morrow. Mrs. Rupert Beckett came in after dinner, looking worn and tired after her hospital work. Her brother has been terribly wounded and is at her house. A good deal of Navy talk at dinner, and a lot of good stories. Hopwood seemed critical of Balfour. We were told that the difficulty of arming merchant ships was that the Americans refused to allow armed merchants to enter port and remain long enough to clear and load up. The same difficulty seems to have arisen in South America. We all thought that we should have to come to convoys as in old days. The trouble seems to be that such a mass of ships is kept with the Grand Fleet, that there are few to spare for other purposes. The idea seems to prevail that the Germans may attack our Grand Fleet at its bases, but this seems improbable, if our scouting is worth a rap. Bee Pembroke most amusing about her experiences in waiting at a canteen. Some of the soldiers call her ' my girl,' and others ' waitress ' ! She was asked by one of them for ' two Zepps. and a cloud-burst,' which left her transfixed with surprise until she found that this meant sausages and mashed potatoes. Another asked her for a veal and ham pie. She brought it, but a minute or two later the soldier shouted to her to come back. He said that the pie was bad. ' What 's the matter with it ? ' said Bee. ' Look here,' said the soldier, ' I ain't got time to argufy with you *why* it 's good or bad ; just you 'op off and get me two 'alfpenny buns ! '

Tweedmouth discussed the Tanks. Opinions vary about them. He said that the regiments would be very glad to have their deeds made known.

CHAPTER XV

MR. LLOYD GEORGE PRIME MINISTER
DECEMBER 1916

The November Conferences in France—The old strategy to be continued—General Robertson on the Cabinet and the Press—Mr. Balfour on naval affairs—Admiral Jellicoe First Sea Lord—Admiral Beatty gets the Grand Fleet—No change in naval strategy—Mr. Balfour's answers to criticisms of the Admiralty—The Q.M.G.'s difficulties—Captain Paget on the orders of the cavalry for July 1—Count Benckendorff on Russian politics—The Rumanian defeats—Depression in London—Brig.-General Yarde-Buller on the French strengths and 1916 casualties—The political crisis of Dec. 1—Mr. Lloyd George Prime Minister—Course of events in Rumania described by General Robertson—The first War Council of the new Government —General Joffre in difficulties—The Kaiser offers to negotiate for peace—General Nivelle replaces General Joffre—The Italian Day at the Ritz—Mr. Harry Cust on the war—A German raider loose in the Ocean—The Duke of Connaught on the new French attack drill— Sir Ernest Cassel thinks that we shall outstay the Germans—The Kaiser's offer refused—The strain of Salonika—The raider and submarines hold up our drafts for the East—The Dutch Minister on Holland's attitude.

Tuesday, Nov. 21. Began to study the new German Kriegsamt. Is it the biggest thing of the war, or bluff ? How will it go down ? If it is business, how will our people reply ? Lunched with Lord Grimthorpe, Miss Fairfax, and Mrs. Ralph Beckett at the Carlton. G. had heard that we had differences at the Conference in Paris, and that they were serious.

Wednesday, Nov. 22. Got through a lot of reading. The soldiers held their conference at Chantilly last week, and the politicos in Paris. It was the best conference that has yet been held, and there was agreement on the military side at all events. The Serb and Rumanian tried to press for more in the East, but Joffre was very firm—firmer than Robertson himself, and in the absence of the French Cabinet closed down all discussion on further despatch of reinforcements. It has been agreed that the old strategy should be continued, and the new Russian representative has been very amenable. All has been well, and R. has only been compelled to make two or three short speeches. So we shall press on in the West after a delay for training and repairs, and shall do what we can in the East as well. Murray's movement is likely to be interesting, and the Monastir business has been well done. The Germans have sent their $1\frac{1}{2}$ divisions to restore matters, but they have arrived too late. But all admit that we cannot affect any strategical purpose at Monastir. There is no change in Rumania, so far as numbers are concerned. There are still 12 German divisions and 10 Austrian, besides the 3 Bulgarian and the 3 or 4 Turkish with Mackensen. Our G.S. think that, strategically, Falkenhayn had failed owing to the good Rumanian defence in the Predil Pass. All the Rumanian divisions at Orsova, with possibly the exception of half a division, have already broken clear and are out of danger of being cut off, but the accounts of the Rumanians are not very encouraging, though the men are fighting well. They have been marched off their legs in all directions and very ill-handled. The Russians are still not further south than Buzeu. It is still hoped that a good resistance may be put up, and that the Russians will get more and more control. Our people have never thought that the Turks and Bulgars would do more than they could help.

Saw Robertson, who grumbled most about the Cabinet, which, he thought, might succumb to any opportunity of an early peace. I said to R. that he must not let them have an armistice. R. had thought of that, and he and Joffre were dead against it. I asked R. what he thought of Admiral Jackson, the First Sea Lord. R. said that he was a good mathematician he believed. The Navy was allowed to do as it liked, and the War

Committee never hauled it over the coals or asked any question about it. R. thought that the Press had been good. He always had thought the contrary before the war, but he had changed his views now. The Press had led well, and had kept the Government up to the mark. He did not speak at all confidently about Jack Cowans, and made me uneasy about the report on the case just investigated. We shall never get a Q.M.G. like Cowans again.

Had tea with E., Count de Zogheb, Missaievitch the pianist, and his pretty Australian wife. Zogheb told me that the Syrian Christians were dying of hunger. The names of the leaders of the Syrian revolutionaries had been left, he says, among the French archives by the French Consul at Beyrout, and most of them had consequently been hanged. The Syrians considered that the French had deserted them, and Syria would welcome the English now. It was Italian claims, he said, that kept France from Alexandretta, and the Russians had also opposed.

Haig is going to the South of France for three weeks. Rawlinson is back on leave here. Robertson thinks that January to March must be given up to resting and refreshing the Army. He hopes to fill it up next month and to have a lot more men behind it. We had more guns with Gough's attack on the Ancre than on the whole Somme front on July 1. Gough had accounted for 20,000 to 30,000 Germans.

R. also told me to-day that 60 per cent. of the Austro-German supplies for Bulgaria and Turkey took the Danube route, and that the loss of Orsova by the Rumanians might open this route again.

Thursday, Nov. 23. Wrote an article on the Rumanian campaign. Saw General Pilcher at the Club and walked down to Carlton Terrace with him. He told me briefly his experiences in France, and was critical of cavalry and artillery generals, who knew nothing of what infantry could do.

Lunched with Arthur Balfour, his sister, and Gerald Balfour. A. J. B. told me that Jellicoe was leaving the Grand

Fleet to be First Sea Lord instead of Jackson, and that David Beatty would have the Grand Fleet. I said I was sorry that Jellicoe was leaving the Grand Fleet, but Balfour said that he was a tired man ; that the Grand Fleet was now unimaginably large, and that the strain even of looking after it administratively was very heavy. Jellicoe was a good office man and would do well at Whitehall, while Beatty was quite unsuited for the position. Beatty had the confidence of the Navy, which was the thing that mattered most. Balfour hoped to make the announcement next Monday, but Jellicoe was at sea and had asked that the announcement might be postponed till his return. It was a little hard on Jackson, but he had taken it very well. He was not an easy man to deal with, and it was necessary to have some one with whom relations were more easy. The change implied no change of naval strategy. He was curious to see how Beatty would now deal with the Battle Cruiser Fleet. It was a fleet and not a squadron, hence a certain rivalry between the two, but the Commander of the Grand Fleet could issue orders to it without reference to the Admiralty.

All this was said before we went in to lunch. I then told Balfour that he had a bad Press, that the Admiralty was accused of lack of vigour, that many desired an offensive policy, that our lack of merchant ships hampered us, that people could not understand why the Germans had broken through the Straits, that the depredations of the submarines had caused a very uneasy feeling, that we seemed to lack destroyers where they were needed, that questions of convoy or arming merchant ships were exercising men's minds, and that his attitude towards the Air Board was not understood. I told him that I was in favour of the present strategy, and only desired to have answers to all the complaints.

Balfour said that all the sailors were in favour of the general strategy now pursued, and that all hinged on the efficiency of the Grand Fleet. This was an immense task. We had repaired some 20,000 ships since the war began.

We had now 360 destroyers, because we had to escort all ships by destroyers, and the Fleets absorbed so many that there were not enough left, although we had been building six or seven a month since the war began. We were now catching up with the Fleet needs, and could then do more with other wants. Even the cruisers needed destroyers. The submarine influenced everything. We were and are short of everything—men, ships, guns, mines, nets, etc., and no one had really foreseen the war conditions, not even Germany. It was right to have begun with a big building policy for the Navy, and now it was the turn of the mercantile marine. We had decided to go in for the smaller classes of ships, but if the war lasted long, and Germany was gambling in big ships, we should find ourselves in difficulties.

Balfour thought that it was still five to four against the Germans coming out. Even apart from which side would win, it was sure that Germany would lose so many ships that she would be beaten by Russia in the Baltic. Also, by keeping her fleet safe, Germany compelled us to keep a large Army at home, and this would be set loose if a naval action were fought. It was impossible for us to get our submarines into the Baltic by sea now, so they had to be taken round and sent by canal to the Baltic, in sections he thought. Lord Beresford and others had advocated sending a Fleet to the Baltic, but the hydrography made it impossible, and all other sailors of experience were opposed to this scheme.

The public, said Balfour, were under the impression that the Straits of Dover were mined and netted and so forth, but the storms and currents swept all away, and the marvel was that the Germans had done so little all this time. Zeebrugge was now being bombed, and could be attacked by a conjoint expedition.

Macnamara had stated that our loss of ships was $2\frac{1}{2}$ per cent., but this was after taking on the credit side the ships we had captured and the additions made to our merchant fleet. It was much more if this was left out. I must look up the text of the speech. I told Balfour of the ideas of some of the younger sailors about sailing in company and convoy.[1] He was much interested and thought progress likely on these lines. He said that a huge branch watched the course of all our ships and recommended courses to be followed. This had saved much. We could not do the same even by friendly neutrals, as any skipper could give us away, and then there would be German submarines on our appointed trade routes. The neutral shipping was worse protected than ours, and the Norwegians had lost 18 per cent. of their shipping.

The idea of a naval offensive against the German coast was not shared by the best sailors. We could no more make the Germans come out and fight than the sailors could in the old wars, and the character of coastal defences, including mines and submarines, was now very formidable. We had done a great deal to meet the submarine menace round our coasts, but the ocean-going submarine and the submarine mine-layer were difficult problems. Last week the Germans had mined the approaches to Havre. The French had not kept their water sphere clear. We could do it better, but the French desired to take their part, and we could say nothing when they failed.

Balfour said that he seemed to be in a minority of one on the air question. The Air Board and David Henderson were united against him, though separated on other matters. Balfour's position was that the Navy had been given certain duties to carry out in the air. So long as this was so, the air must form part of the Admiralty sphere of action, and it must train its men and make its aircraft. There was no evidence of overlapping. If there were an Air Ministry the Admiralty might be able to hand Air Defence over to it, but the Air Board was not a Ministry and had no responsibility. It only delayed matters by calling for interminable reports. Balfour thought that

---

[1] The first convoy reached England on 20th May 1917. On the following day the Admiralty adopted the system for all merchant shipping.

Curzon's position was illogical, and said that Curzon had had no experience of administration at home. Balfour did not hold a very high opinion of his own air branch. Churchill had kept it all in his own hands as a toy, and it had not grown naturally. Is Balfour going too ? I did not ask him, but when I reminded him of how he kept his head in the Black Week in South Africa and of the debt we owed him for it, he said, rather pathetically, 'Ah, but that was sixteen years ago !'

Saturday, Nov. 25, to Monday, Nov. 27. Wrote a paper on the new German effort,—the Kriegsamt and the Auxiliary Service Bill—explaining their importance. Sent it off by post, but it did not fetch up on Saturday. Lunched at the Ian Hamiltons'. Ian and I had a good talk. We both came to the conclusion that Egypt was the right base for all our Eastern operations, and that we should drop the rest when we could and start afresh.

Went down to Coombe in the evening. A large party, including Sir Arthur and Lady Paget, Bertie Paget (home on a week's leave from France), the twins (both now passed for service again), Sir John Cowans, Lord Alec Thynne, Lady Pembroke, the Duchess of Marlborough, Lord Annaly, Lord Blandford, Lord and Lady D'Abernon, Mrs. Ward, Miss Wilmot, while about a dozen more who had proposed themselves for lunch on Sunday were put off. Jack tells me that it is just all he can do to feed the twenty-three divisions now at Salonika, as on the British Struma front the rail communication is wretched and the road worn out. He also says that he has had to give up ten good transport ships from the Channel to fetch wheat from abroad, and that whereas a division could formerly be sent across the Channel in four to five days it will now take a fortnight. There is, however, shipping for a division always kept in reserve at Southampton in case it is needed anywhere. He says that the Navy keep continuously employed about a million tons of merchant shipping, which he thinks preposterous. Jack has been exonerated by his Inquiry, but they have taken exception to some of his private letters, and Sir F. E. Smith has been to him to suggest his resignation, which I strongly advise him not to hand in. An illustrious person has written declaring that the use made of these private letters, which Jack handed in quite voluntarily so that nothing might be concealed, is an outrage, and so it is.

Bertie says that the orders for the infantry on July 1 were to reach the high ground at Courcelette that day. They actually reached this objective on Sept. 25. The cavalry were ordered to reach the front, Péronne–Bapaume–Irles, the same night, July 1! During the fighting on the Somme the cavalry were three times brought up to break through, and on one occasion five cavalry divisions were massed in depth for this operation. Bertie thinks that when Lesboeufs was taken the Germans were much demoralised, and threw away their rifles, a thing never before known. He says that the reserves of the Armies are kept too far back to intervene effectually, and that fear of bringing them within the shell zone, and the distance from the front of the Army commanders, are the main causes. He thinks that the Corps and Army commanders must be closer up, or that at all events decisions should be taken by some one in the front. As things are, the favourable moments are lost by the delays in reporting and obtaining decisions. He says that Hubert Gough is the exception : he is always well in front. Bertie says that the 4th and 5th Armies are now 13 divisions each, and the 1st, 2nd, and 3rd Armies each 10 divisions. They will have about half their troops in the line during the winter, and the rest training and repairing, Dec. 1916 to March 1917 inclusive. The cavalry divisions the same. They will each have a brigade training all the winter, and battalions made up to help in the line on pioneer work.

Sir Arthur told me that again he had no reports from the Navy of the German destroyer raid on the Downs. He was at Deal on Friday and no one mentioned it to him, although it occurred the previous night. There are only seventeen of our destroyers, out of the 360 we possess, allotted to the Channel, so no wonder the Germans can do as they please.

We played tennis. The new red court holds well in the winter. D'Abernon still plays a very good game. Walked with Bertie in the morning, and we called on the St. Georges who live near. Jack and Bee went to see the Ripons, but Gladys is still in bed. In the afternoon I took a good walk with Lady Helen. She has a talent for making one confess all one's views. The Duchess of Marlborough very pleasant and an interesting personality. We all sat up too late as usual. A good story of Mrs. Asquith, who is reported to have said that if she had been Christopher Columbus and had discovered America, she would have taken very good care not to tell any one. Thynne told me a lot about Carson and Devlin which I found to be incorrect later, or at least G. Robinson said it was.

Met Count Benckendorff, the Russian Ambassador, at Olive's, Monday afternoon. He is very pleased with Trepoff's succession to Stürmer. He says that Trepoff is conservative, and will not admit that he is reactionary or Black Hundred. B. has always disliked Stürmer. The change means that all thought of conciliation with Germany is at an end. B. says that we must not expect a rapid march towards Parliamentary Government, and reminded us how long it had taken in England to settle the question of the prerogative of the Crown in a democratic sense. B. knows nothing, he says, of the plans made for the defence of Rumania, but hinted that Alexeieff at first had only agreed to send a small force, and declared that Rumania had retained a quantity of rolling stock lent by Russia. He does not seem to be much disturbed by the idea that the Germans intend to throw all their weight on Russia, and declares that they lost their chance by not continuing the attack at the close of 1915. Went on to see Mrs. Long. Toby is made a Brigadier-General. We had a good talk over politics and war matters.

Tuesday, Nov. 28. This morning two raiding Zepps. were brought down on the N.E. coast. An aeroplane bombed London before noon and did little harm. I began to rough out an article on the conduct of the war. Lunched with Lockett and Eddy Wortley : saw a lovely Romney sepia drawing of Lady Hamilton at Lockett's and also two new Romneys, and one of Eddy's, very fine. The Rumanians meant to defend the Aluta and counter attack in the north, but the rapid advance of the enemy and Mackensen's passage of the Danube put them off. There are now 20 Rumanian divisions of 3 Armies facing West, against 15 Austro-German in Rumania and the equivalent of 4 to 5 Bulgar divisions of similar strength. The Russians are due to begin their attack across the mountains to-day—good if the Rumanians hold, but not otherwise. Mackensen only threw two regiments across the Danube. Heard a great deal more of the share which Major-General S. S. Long, C.B., late Director of Supplies and Transport, has taken in the Cowans case. All this affair makes me anxious. There is a regular set against Jack, and what they are out to do is difficult to define. I should say that the aim is to get rid of all soldiers in the Q.M.G. branch and on the Army Council, and to substitute civilians, but with what ulterior motive can only be guessed. I begin to think that it may become impracticable to conduct the war successfully if this sort of thing is permitted to continue.

The news from Rumania continues to be bad, and the Germans claim to have repelled a great attack by Sarrail north of Monastir.

Went down to the *Times* in the evening to talk to Geoffrey Robinson about War Office affairs. G. R. not keen about my going to Egypt for Archie's January campaign.

Wednesday, Nov. 29. I dined with the Beresfords ; Lord and Lady Charlie, the French Ambassador, Lord Hardinge of Penshurst, Sir Hedworth and Lady Meux, Lord Islington (she is laid up), Lady Leslie, Lady Herbert, Lady Maud Warrender, and one or two more. Islington and I discussed India. He thinks with me that India can do much more, but says that the force of inertia in the public offices sterilises all energy.   He saw nothing against my proposals regarding Egypt, and thought that the Territorial divisions in India, after two years' residence, could supply from their intelligent elements many good officers for new Indian units. He seems to have made many suggestions which Austen has not adopted.   A good talk with M. Cambon, who was very agreeable.   He declared that we should all be bankrupt States after the war.   He thought that Russia had twenty-eight divisions in Rumania, which I think may be an exaggeration, but like Benckendorff he professes to know nothing of what was arranged with Rumania.   Belle and I talked family matters after dinner.

Thursday, Nov. 30.   Lunched with Lady (Archibald) Murray at her little flat, 61 Iverna Court, Kensington. We compared notes about Egypt and Archie's prospects. He is now at Cairo.   I gave her my views of the future prospects, and told her what people were saying.   She is unable to go out to him as he cannot have all the ladies out.

The course of the war this week has brought the Austro-German invaders of Rumania close to Bukharest, and has seen the Russians open a counter-offensive on the Carpathian front from Bukovina to the Buzeu Pass. Our attack from Salonika reached Monastir but gets no further.   On all other fronts the war has died down, but at sea the submarines of the enemy cause many losses, and there is much depression in London, and much talk of changes in the Government.   Few, if any, people see the end of the war except by stalemate, and there is no public guidance by statesmen, who for weeks past have left many vital problems unsolved, such as man-power, food, the submarine menace, etc.

Friday, Dec. 1.   Lunched with Smiler Kennedy, late Black Watch, at the Naval and Military Club.   There were several other men, including Colonel Gordon, V.C., long a prisoner in Germany ; Turner, the Editor of the *Globe* ; a judge from St. Lucia, and various others.   Gordon a man of great charm and nobility of character.   He told

me the story of the surrender of the Gordons, all except
the last stage, and of the Dum-dum accusation of which the
German Press made so much. Dined the same evening
with the Pagets. The General in good form. Lady Ridley
came, and she and I, with Bertie and Lady Paget, went to
the Alhambra to see the *Bing Boys*. It was very funny,
and we laughed heartily all the time. I took Lady Ridley
home. She is now looking very well again. Bertie returns
to France in the morning.

I have begun three articles on ' The Land War,' restating
my views about the Western front and explaining what
I want done in Egypt, which is the only other campaign that
really concerns us.

Saturday, Dec. 2. Lunched with the Baroness Daisy
de Brienen at a charming flat, 5 Old Burlington Street, and
heard some interesting Austrian news. The Yarde-Bullers
were at lunch, and I walked to his hotel and had a talk with
him. He says that the French have 105 divisions all told,
and 2,900,000 men drawing rations. Of the 1917 class 50,000
are incorporated after ten months' training, and 150,000 more
are in reserve with the *récupérés*. That is all, and each
year only 180,000 of a new class. He says that most careful
estimates make the German casualties 670,000 at Verdun
and 600,000 on the Somme. He thinks that Russia will
be able to do no more than hold the German-Austrians
now in front of her, and that Italy will not be able to do
much more. He says that we English must finish the war
and produce 2,000,000 more men : we agree to the figure
of 60 fresh divisions in the West, of which we can get 12
from England soon, 4 from Egypt, 15 from Salonika, and
3 or 4 from India and Mesopotamia, so there will be 25
to 30 to be freshly formed here to give us any good chance
of winning. He says that the Germans have 126 divisions
in the West. We are agreed about Salonika. Y. B. regards
Pellé and Dupont as the two best men at the French G.Q.G.
He quite thinks that Briand may fall if Rumania is knocked
out. Bad news from Greece to-day. An armed conflict
has begun at Athens.

Sunday, Dec. 3. Last Friday began a great internal crisis when L. G. wrote to the P.M. that he could not go on unless our methods of waging war were speeded up. He proposed a War Council of three, including himself, Bonar Law, and Carson. The two latter are with him, which means the Unionists too. The P.M. sees the King, and eventually at midnight to-day a statement is given out that the Cabinet is to be reconstructed. The main complaints are the inability of the Government to settle the question of Man Power, Food Directorship, Submarine Menace, and other matters. The smashing of Rumania has caused deep depression, and everybody feels it very much. It is L. G.'s opportunity to become P.M. and he is seizing it.

Lunched with Sir Edward and Lady Coates at Queen Anne's Lodge, to see his unique collection of English coloured prints. A charming house, owned by the Hankey who built Hankey's folly (Queen Anne's Mansions). Various ladies, and Lord Edmund Talbot and a doctor last from Russia. Talbot thought that H. of C. would support the P.M., and that if L. G. came in by dispossessing Asquith he would not last long. Coates agreed. We had a good talk over the crisis and the war.

Monday, Dec. 4. Went to see Mrs. Leeds in the afternoon. Her news from Paris and Switzerland is not particularly good.

Tuesday, Dec. 5. Lunched at Lady Hamilton's. Sir Ian and the Winston Churchills there. Winston full of talk, and declares that he will not take office in the new Government unless he can take effective part in the war. A long talk about the Dardanelles and Salonika. Winston tells me of his case before the Dardanelles inquiry. He seems to have proved that the naval attack was undertaken on expert naval advice.

Wednesday, Dec. 6. Bonar Law fails to form a Government. The Cabinet go to Buckingham Palace but fail to agree. Lloyd George agrees to try and form a Government, and Bonar Law is to support him. Most of the Radicals are to follow Asquith into Opposition. Had a talk with Derby. He expects to become War Minister, and we might do worse.

Lunched with Olive; Bridget, Harry Cust, Lady Cunard, Lady Leslie, Sir Vincent Caillard, and Mrs. Marshall. Harry and Lady C. in great form. We were very cheery in spite of all the depressing circumstances. Cust and Caillard both wish Asquith to remain. In the afternoon we hear that L. G. has squared the Labour Party.

Went to see Sir W. Robertson at York House, where he is now established. He has the big room at the east end of the house for his library. We began with Salonika and Rumania. R. thinks that there are no more Austro-German divisions coming along, and that there are in Rumania 10 German, 8 Austrian, 5 Bulgar, and 2 Turkish divisions. There are 25 to 28 Russian divisions near the Sereth and on the Moldavian frontier. He expects our Allies to hold the Sereth. The course of events, according to R., was something as follows. We had tried to make the Rumanians come in in June at the time of Brussiloff's victories, but they would not. When they agreed to come in, the only stipulations were that Sarrail should begin to push ten days before, and that we and the Russians should be engaged in our respective offensives. Rumania attacked Transylvania because this had been the plan to accord with Russia's projected advance over the Carpathians, and no change was made when it should have been made. Rumania was tricked by Ferdinand of Bulgaria, who pretended peace and then attacked. R. had asked the Rumanians to defend their western hills and to attack Bulgaria, but they trusted Ferdinand, and then spread out their armies on a 350-mile front in the West 'with a man and a boy in each pass.' R. had wired to Rumania, Sept. 9, saying that Hindenburg would defeat them in detail, and they had replied that they were concentrating forward. But they could not do so before they were attacked and beaten. We thought that now they must go right back to the Sereth, and R. thought that the enemy could not force this line. But we agreed that our position at Salonika was now bad.

Joffre is in trouble again, and possibly Briand may now fall owing to the collapse of his Balkan policy. R. had strongly warned Joffre that a decision was needed at Salonika, but Clive had only brought a verbal answer and nothing satisfactory. I said that Briand did not dare quit Monastir which he had boasted about so much, and that consequently Joffre could not act. There might be 70,000 Greeks fit to attack us, but he hoped he had interned 12,000 in the Morea and had asked our sailors to destroy the Thessaly railway, but all was at sixes and sevens at Athens. The Allied Ministers feared for their lives, and were afraid to irritate the Greeks. The French Admiral did nothing. We had no reserves handy, but most of our new divisions had arrived at Salonika and this would help. It was all a horrible entanglement, and had been entered into contrary to his advice and mine.

He then asked for my views on the general position, and I told him that we needed 60 more divisions in the West : that we should mass a great Indian-African force in Egypt : introduce the German *levée en masse* for all men seventeen to sixty, and get hold of the men of military age needed for our new formations. I developed this on the lines of the articles which I am now writing. He quite agreed, and said that he was promised 30 more battalions from India but that Africa was coming on slowly, and I told him my ideas of how things should be speeded-up. I found him entirely of my opinion on all these questions, but the difficulty was the new formations of artillery. I said, reduce the programme for guns to supply the new divisions, and then fill up with guns later. I said that the time was past for makeshifts and that we must now do things on a grand scale. If Colonial Governors would not act they should be recalled, and I advised R. to take over all the troops under the Colonial Office, and to get on quickly. We must do big things in the West and in Egypt, and no other theatre counted. R. entirely agreed with all this. He told me that the Government had fallen mainly over a *levée en masse* Act, which was news to me. He said that the Navy wanted 4000 guns for the merchant ships, and that the Munitions could not supply them without stopping work on the 18 prs. Even had we the guns— and he has fished out a lot of various sorts—the mountings would take weeks and months. He was disturbed about the submarines, and thought the war was going on for a long time.

We discussed the crisis. R. would like Derby at the W.O.

Saturday to Monday, Dec. 9 to 11. Motored down to Coombe with Lady Sarah Wilson. Sir Arthur in bed with a bad cold.   Lady Paget's maid left her to-day after twenty-four years, and Lady P. much upset. She had charge of everything. Before she left she brought out six lockets of Lady P.'s old admirers before she married with their photos in them, and Lady P. found that she had forgotten all their names. There came the twins, Lady Cynthia Graham's boy, Mr. Roberts, Mr. Davis of the American Embassy, Mrs. George Keppel, Mrs. Rupert Beckett, the Spanish Ambassador and his wife, Joynson Hicks, M.P., Maurice Rothschild, Lord Bertie Vane-Tempest, Mrs. Leeds, and a few more. The red court was covered with frozen water and we could not play. Walked with Mrs. Keppel. We called on the Ripons and saw him, but Gladys is still in bed and, I fear, very ill. Mrs. Keppel in great grief for the Asquiths, with whom she has been so intimate. The Asquiths are going to the Granards for three weeks and then to their own house, now occupied by Lady Cunard. We discussed the war and politics. One of the ladies is just back from France and is all for peace, saying that the French cannot hold out beyond the autumn of 1917, but I said that they must and that we must go on. I asked Joynson Hicks to see Bonar Law in the morning about Salonika. All our party agreed that our Salonika policy was disastrous.

Jack Cowans writes to me that he is to be Q.M.G. in France, and that a ' great civilian ' is to take his place.

The alleged reason is that L. G. cannot defend him in Parliament from having written 'indiscreet private letters'! We have all done that, including L. G. and all his friends.

Motored back, Monday morning, with Lady Sarah. Found that I had to write the War Review of the year at short notice. Went to see a friend before dinner to ascertain how the first War Council of the new Government had got on. The first meeting was last Saturday, and I feared that L. G. might have stampeded the Council into some wild action at Salonika. But I heard that L. G.'s views had become calmer since his position was altered. He had not pressed for anything more to be sent. I heard that R. had spoken to the War Council as I had spoken to him last Thursday. He had fully explained to them the danger of the situation, and had told them that their first duty was to their own troops. He had thoroughly frightened them, and there was no question of sending another man, so that for the moment all was well and there was no chance of a change of policy. If there were, it is supposed that R. will come out. It is thought that the shipping question in itself prevented the dispatch of large reinforcements to Salonika. It had taken two months to send the last division from France by Marseilles, partly owing to want of ships and partly owing to the enemy's submarines. One of the transports had been sunk, but fortunately it was empty. The only officer on board had been *dégommé* and sent home from Salonika and was taken prisoner by the submarine. He was evidently dead out of luck. My friend thought the position at Salonika serious, but said that he was not sure that the enemy could do much against us in the winter. We might have to fall back, but there need be no evacuation, though he would like it, and thought it might come later. Much depended on how many troops the Germans could send down, and how far they had prepared their communications and supplies for this movement. The Greek situation made the Council anxious. The trouble was that the Allies could not agree what to do with King Tino, and that the various Powers were alternately for and against stern measures with him, and never in accord. Some thought that the German submarines would try to cut us off at Salonika by sea when the attack came by land.

The Council had asked Robertson to tell Joffre what he had told them, but he had already done so, and he was now going over to talk about it all with Joffre. The future position of the latter was not yet clear. Apparently the Chantilly G.Q.G. was to be broken up, and Joffre would be at Paris, but whether as a C.I.G.S. or in some other capacity was not yet certain. Meanwhile replies to our wires came regularly from Joffre, and nothing was yet changed. On the whole, R. was satisfied with the way that the Council was shaping. It was not very different from the old War Committee, and there was still a great deal of talk. The soldiers want badly to get on with the Man Power and other great questions, and will no doubt get their way. It is doubted whether Derby will replace Cowans by a civilian, as D. means to be master in his own house and would not allow interference with the personnel of his department. All this is fairly satisfactory, but progress is precious slow.

Tuesday, Dec. 12. Lunched with Mrs. Long: Toby now a General, Sir Lionel Earle, and an A.D.C. of Lord French's. Earle says that the German prisoners love work. Earle has to find the wood for the Allies, as much as 30,000 standards a month, each standard representing 40 tons. He has 3000 Canadian lumbermen at work in the Jura. Toby not at all optimistic about the Western front. He complains that they lose a lot of men and never get their bayonets into the enemy, who either runs or surrenders. His battalion lost 75 per cent. in one fight and 65 per cent. in another : he is under Tom Bridges. Tried to see Bertier at the Ritz but missed him. Saw Yarde-Buller at the N. and M. Club. He is going to Norway as M.A. He left Chantilly yesterday morning, and says that Nivelle has refused the succession to Joffre. He thinks that Joffre will remain and defeat the politicians who clamour for his blood. In the afternoon came the surprising news that the Germans had to-day offered to negotiate for peace with the Allies. Dined with the Harry Higginses: Lady Ancaster, Lady Ridley, Fritz Ponsonby, Lord Richard Cavendish and Lady Moyra, and an Intelligence man. All the talk of the peace offer, which Ponsonby had seen at the Palace before dinner but did not know thoroughly. The Intelligence man said that there were 100 peace meetings a week throughout the country, chiefly in Wales, and that they were not reported. We agreed that the German terms would have to be very carefully handled, and Ponsonby said that they were favourable in the West but unfavourable for Russia, and so meant to divide us. He was not sure about Antwerp. However, we shall know all about it in the morning. The ladies were looking like roses in a June garden.

Wednesday, Dec. 13. Germany's Peace Proposal fills all the papers, but nobody thinks much of it, for no one trusts her or supposes that any peace worth having can be made yet. Lunched at the Carlton and then went on to see Fred Maurice about the change in the French Command announced to-day. Joffre is to go to Paris, and Nivelle is to command the Armies of the East and North-East. Maurice no better pleased than I am, and thinks it political. He regrets the break-up of G.Q.G. Chantilly is to be abolished. Castelnau gets an Army Group again. Pellé stays with Joffre. Little doubt that Joffre is expected to be more closely under the French Government. I don't like it. There are now 64 German and 44 Austrian divisions on the whole East front, or 75 German including cavalry: of these, 12 German and 11 Austrian on the Transylvania-Rumania side besides 3 Turkish and 80 Bulgarian battalions, say 6 divisions, equals 32 divisions in all, which is about what I calculated long ago. One more Turkish division has turned up on the Struma front. Difficulties of transport may make a great Bulgarian attack hard to carry out. We are well entrenched and wired in on the Doiran and Struma fronts, but Monastir is a weakness and Sarrail may hold it too long. He should rest on Lake Orsova. Maurice is for getting out, as I am.

Thursday, Dec. 14. Met Sir Ernest Cassel at lunch, with Lady Fingall my favourite dancing partner of Viceregal Lodge days, years ago. She is still attractive in spite of all these years, and complained that people would ask her admirers of the year before to meet her, instead of this year's admirers. Cassel thought that the difference between us and the Germans was still too great for peace.

Sat on the Tribunal all the afternoon. Horrible process of sending fathers of families into the Army. Then to the Ritz, half an hour late, to dine with Lady Strafford's party for the Italian Day. We were a large party, and had a huge round table in the centre of the room. Lady Herbert, the Laverys, Joan Campbell, the American and Spanish Ambassadors and their ladies, Lord Ludlow, the Danish Minister, Sir Sidney Greville, the Duke of Argyll, and one or two more. The contrast between the afternoon and the evening made me sad. Found myself between the two prettiest women of the party. Other people having parties included the Italian Ambassador, Prince Victor Napoleon, Lady Bagot, Lady Massereene and various others. Afterwards a Vaudeville, and Lady Constance Stewart Richardson posed and contorted and danced, in few clothes and with bare feet. She looked like a white dervish. Lady Strafford declared that she was playing John the Baptist, and that the contortions represented her attempts to find locusts and wild honey. Had a short talk with Prince Victor and Princess Clémentine. Many fled when Lady C. danced, including Sir William Robertson, who, when asked whether he did not think that she had a very fine leg, replied that 'it was just like any other damned leg.' Imperiali, the Italian Ambassador, told me that when I had warned him on Sept. 13 that, in our opinion, the Rumanian armies were too scattered and that unless they kept within supporting distance Hindenburg would fall on them and defeat them separately, he had telegraphed to Rome the same day, and Rome had passed on the message to the Rumanians.

But all to no purpose, and events fell out as we had warned him. Saw Macleay just back from China and now at the F.O. His wife had reached Marseilles, her ship chased by submarines, and all the passengers had remained fully dressed for six days and nights. Mrs. Leeds, Lady Sarah, Joan and I adjourned to Grosvenor Square. Much talk of the Curzon marriage. Mrs. Leeds kindly lends me her house for the Mayfair Hospital Supply fund an afternoon in February.

Friday, Dec. 15. Lunched with Lady Cunard: Princess Hatzfeldt, Lady Paget, Lady Randolph, the McKennas, Winston, Harry Cust, and Lord Wimborne. A gay party. Afterwards the men discussed the war: a serious talk, and we all held different opinions. Walked back with Cust, who was all for fighting on, and would rather not live if we do not win.

Saturday, Dec. 16. Worked, and then lunched with Mrs. Harry Higgins: also there Lady de Trafford, the Countess Torby, Lord Lurgan, Lady Florence Willoughby, and a French count who had been Ambassador at Constanti-nople, and was very flattering about my work and its influence all over Europe. A thick fog. The Countess took two hours to get home, and the Grand Duke kept ringing up all the police stations to find out what had happened to her.

Sunday, Dec. 17. Lunched with Olive and met Lady Fingall again, and Captain Norton who was blown up in the *Hogue* of the 'live-bait squadron.' He starts to-morrow in command of the *Laurentic*, a fast 14,000-ton White Star liner, armed with eight 6-inch guns, in chase of the latest German raider loose on the Atlantic and said to be of 5000 tons and armed with 6-inch guns. He thinks she may have coal endurance for four weeks or so, but may be an 'oiler' and may also have a rendezvous with colliers. Norton says that we can now go through a minefield, owing to some new invention, without risk. The Duke of Devonshire on his way to Canada had the great luck to pass untouched through a minefield laid the night before by German submarines. Norton thinks that we must arm all merchant steamers fore and aft. He declares that owners and skippers will not obey Admiralty orders and so have caused many losses, *e.g.* the *Lusitania*. He says that when the U 53 reached the American coast there were six or seven of our ships due to arrive, and belonging to rich lines, which had no wireless, and that all his time was taken up in finding and warning them. Had tea with Mrs. Keppel, Miss Violet, Lady Randolph, and Lord Ilchester. Much talk of the engagement of Lord Wilton to Clare Sheridan. We discussed the war and politics. Walked home with Lady R. Her last night in the Brook Street house.

Monday, Dec. 18. Began my annual review of the war, which takes much spade work. Lunched with Lady Pembroke to meet General Tom Bridges and his lady. He was looking well, and was fairly confident about next year if the men and guns came along. His division lost 7000 in the July offensive ; he was not filled up till a fortnight before he went in again at the Ancre, when he lost 5000, and would not have lost more than 2000 had the men been sent to him earlier to train. He wants 6-inch howitzers beyond everything. Met the Duke of Connaught at Olive's in the afternoon. He told me that he had seen the new attack drill of the French infantry while over in France. It was wonderful. With one quarter of the men formerly used they developed twice the fire, and all specialists were well used—bombers, riflemen, m.g. men, and bayonet men. We discussed Max Aitken's peerage. Max had said that he was sure something was coming, for he had cut himself shaving in the morning and his blood had been blue.

Tuesday, Dec. 19. Worked, and then lunched with Sir Ernest Cassel at Brook House. We had a long talk on the finance and resources of the belligerents. He cannot see his way financially far into 1917. England had really gone off the gold standard as well as Germany. Egypt had possessed only two millions in her banks when war broke out. The Treasury could not help, and there was no money to buy the cotton and wheat, but paper was used and was accepted by the Egyptians, and there were now 25 millions in the banks. It was a question of confidence. He thought that we should outstay the Germans.

L. G. made his great speech to-day, on the policy of the new Government. The House crammed. Germany is told that we will not negotiate as there are no terms, and she must offer reparation and guarantees before we meet her.

Wednesday, Dec. 20. President's Wilson Peace Note, presented to-day, caused astonishment and much criticism. Worked, and then there lunched with me at the Carlton : Sir Ian Hamilton, Sir William Robertson, Mrs. Astor, Lady Ridley, and Miss Campbell. A very pleasant lunch and much interesting talk · all these pretty women very agreeable and full of ide₄s. The first war lunch : only two courses, but we did very well on it, and it is a mercy to be spared long meals. Neville Chamberlain, Mayor of Birmingham, placed in charge of National Service. Joan Campbell says she will do anything but plough. Ian after lunch had a talk with Robertson and advocated the campaign from Egypt.

Thursday, Dec. 21. Worked, and then lunched with Mrs. Keppel. The hostess, Lady Randolph, Sir Ernest Cassel and I at a small table. Sonia and a young party at a large table. They went off to a matinée and we talked. Mrs. K. says that Winston is to be Air Minister. Lady R. hopes so but has nothing definite. I hear from other sources that the Tories will not allow Winston to join the Government, a decision I should deplore if it were the Air Ministry that he had charge of, as his energy in that office would be of great public utility.

Saturday, Dec. 23. Worked, and then lunched with Mrs. Leeds : Lady Paget, Mrs. Cis Bingham, Lord Charles Montagu, and a Highlander. Lady Nunburnholme will not allow Mrs. Leeds to lend her house for the Guild if she is away.

Sunday, Dec. 24. Finished the Review of the War in 1916. I am going to write something of the work of the Q.M.G. Intrigue is still rampant round this branch which political hangers-on are still endeavouring to fix their claws into. General Clayton, late I.G.L. of C., has been disgracefully treated and has come home. His appeal to the King reached G.H.Q. in November, but has not yet reached the W.O. or the King. Why? Sir Eric Geddes is building a regular village near Montreuil for his new branch : he is taking over 1000 clerks, and has 77 motors for his staff. The soldier in France calls the town Geddesburg. Stuart-Wortley will probably be pushed out, and Jack too, as Derby is very weak and as clay in the hands of L. G. The Q.M.G. work has been admirably done, without a hitch or complaint, and all the delicate machinery is liable to be thrown out of gear if a pack of civilians without knowledge of military affairs are dumped down to run it. It is difficult to get to the bottom of this intrigue which seems very widespread.

The strain upon us of Salonika is concealed from the public. We can only just feed our troops on that front as there is only one single and bad line, and one bad road, and if any more men are sent they must remain at the port or be starved. At present we have 69 ships of 420,000 tons (=three tons a man), permanently engaged in supplying our troops at Salonika, besides 8 ships of 33,000 tons lent to the French, and we are now asked to equip and supply 30,000 Venizelists. It takes 20 ships to carry one division to Salonika, average 4000 tons a ship, =4 tons a man. If we send ten more divisions they will require 740,000 tons of shipping to keep them going, and we shall then have 1,193,000 tons of shipping on this beat, and, further, we are losing one ship every other day in the Mediterranean from submarines and mines.

The mass of horses in France is another drain. We have 700,000 horses there and have to provide 2000 tons of oats and 2000 tons of hay *a day*, and we have only six days' reserve in France. Jellicoe says that the Navy is no further advanced in countering the submarine, and that the latest German submarine has a range of 5000 miles and can stay out 52 days. We lost three ships torpedoed in the mouth of the Channel last week. We cannot use some of our Western ports on account of the submarines and the commerce raider now loose. We have 50,000 drafts for the East waiting to be sent out and we cannot send them by sea, while France can only send to Marseilles 500 of our men a day. It will take a month to take away our divisions from Salonika, and at least three months to take away the whole Allied Force. There is the off chance that the Germans will come down on us, and some folk believe that the submarines are going to beat us. All this comes of the late Government weakly permitting this Salonika folly, which I opposed before a man was sent there and have consistently opposed ever since. But it must be admitted that the Navy have been remiss in their anti-submarine preparations.

Thursday, Dec. 28. The Dutch Minister, M. van Swinderen, brought up Captain Dunlop, his new naval attaché, to be introduced to me. Van Swinderen did not think that the German offer of peace arose from weakness, but on account of the Kaiser's nature. He impressed upon me again that Holland would fight with any one who violated her territory, which, I replied, was all that we asked. Dunlop declared that the Dutch were strong in Zeeland on the left bank of the Scheldt, that mines were laid in the river covered by batteries, and that any infraction of Dutch neutrality would mean war. I said that this was very satisfactory. Saw Maurice at the W.O. in the afternoon. He tells me that Joffre is finally *dégommé*; that Lyautey will be the French soldier of most importance now and will have the handling and arranging of the war, but Nivelle has claimed complete liberty for his plans on the Western front, and he will concert with Haig. The Russians have a position ready on the right bank of the Sereth, which seems rash. The Rumanians have only four divisions in good order, but promise to take the field with 400,000 men in April.

M. hopes that the Russian 28 divisions with the 4 Rumanian will hold up the enemy. The latter will try and capture the Sereth line, perhaps the Pruth, and anyhow the lower Danube, when they will be able to pass their submarines down the river into the Black Sea. The position at Salonika was unaltered, and he still wishes that we could get out.

CHAPTER XVI

THE QUESTION OF JAPANESE CO-OPERATION
JANUARY 1917

General Robertson, Salonika, and the War Cabinet—A victory while you wait—The new military decrees in France—Transport losses in the Mediterranean—Generals Haldane and Hull on our troops in France—The Kaiser tells his Army that he will impose peace with the sword—Our position respecting drafts—The *Daily Mail* helps about Salonika—Lord Northcliffe opens fire—A talk with Lord Derby—He promises to support Robertson—M. Briand fails to stampede us into more Salonika follies—Joy among the anti-Salonikans— A dinner at the Dutch Legation—The question of Japanese co-operation—A talk with General Inagaki—Sir James Willcocks's early history —Count Benckendorff's death—Stories of Mensdorff and Lichnowsky —The German raider busy—I make a speech to the Unionist Agents— Mr. Balfour and Lord Robert Cecil on the freedom of the seas—The Russians to be consulted respecting Japanese co-operation—Mr. McKenna describes the German Peace Terms—M. Nabokoff on Japanese aid—General Dessino's views—General de la Panouse on changes in France—Captain Norton's account of the loss of the *Laurentic*.

Saturday, Dec. 30.   Robertson wrote this morning to say that he had been through a hell of a week and sometimes had despaired.   Would I come and see him ?   I went down to see him at York House at 5.   It was of course the old story—Salonika.   MM. Thomas and Ribot had been over here and had almost succeeded in stampeding the new War Cabinet against their better judgment. They had drawn lurid pictures of Greece invaded, and the Russians were also howling through Gourhko, whom R. described as a good field general, but a man out of his depth in the position of C. in C., where he now was. The Serbs also threatened to break up if we did not send more troops. The French wish to save Monastir, which is Briand's ewe lamb, and Robertson does not care a hang for Monastir, the retention of which is outside the limits of the defensive position which Sarrail ought to hold. The French, under their new régime, are sending two more divisions, though R. says that the two which they promised to send in October last are not all there yet, and they have wired to Sarrail to ask if he wishes two new divisions to be sent first or the 30,000 drafts which he needs! R. feels sure that we ought not to go on with this folly at the risk of our campaign in France next year. He says that we are on the defensive at Salonika, and that twenty-three divisions already there are ample for defence, even on the exterior line of works which exist, in fact twenty would do. But the Cabinet are impressed by the French: they criticise Haig: do not believe in the spirit of our troops in France: declare we have lost too many men: and have no clear ideas about anything.

L. G., says R., is always L. G., and I know his views. Milner has been so long away from affairs that he is little help. Henderson cannot be expected to know military affairs and is a cypher, while Curzon is the best of the lot and always tries at all events to understand the soldier's point of view. R. says that the Cabinet are taking a special house where they will be all together. They sit twice a day and occupy their whole time with military plans which are R.'s job. They take up his time but do not take his advice. Jellicoe has already had to tell them that he cannot conduct the war at sea and attend their meetings all day, and in short, in England as in France, a little body of politicians, quite ignorant of war and all its needs, are trying to run the war themselves. R. thinks that he will have to resign if two more divisions are sent. There is also the Hedjaz operation which Curzon favours. It cannot be done without emasculating Murray's force. R. has stated the force needed, and has said that if the Cabinet lay down the policy the necessary force will be sent. But the Cabinet wish to send only half the force needed, and are trying unsuccessfully to get some authority or other in Egypt to agree to the smaller force. R. says that this is a small affair but a great principle is involved in it. Amery back from Salonika acting as Milner's secretary, and said to be full of Salonika schemes. His ship was sunk on the way back and he got to shore in a small boat.

R. says that all our drafts for the East are still held up. The German raider has disappeared, and the knowledge that she is loose on the Ocean stops everything. Jellicoe says that he has to use so many torpedo craft for escorts that he has none for the offensive. R.'s only hope about Salonika, apart from the pressure which he can bring to bear, is that the ships cannot be found for more troops, and if found cannot be sent. The Navy are dead against Salonika, and would rather have the Germans there than be charged with the protection of our troops and supply ships.

There is also the question of men. The Asquith War Committee decided on National Service for all men from sixteen to sixty before going out, and Asquith intended to bring it into Parliament before Christmas. But first Runciman objected, then Asquith began to wobble, and finally L. G. upset him.

Nothing has been done since L. G. came in and cannot now be done until February, when even if we get the new law in a month, allow another month before it is applied, and the time necessary for training the men, it will not begin to produce men at the front before June or July at the earliest. Meanwhile we got 30,000 men this month in place of 100,000 needed, and we want 100,000 in January. Derby is very good and helpful, and all the office is very satisfactory now, but Derby seldom attends the War Cabinet to which he does not belong. R. said that the King had asked him if he had read my articles on ' The War on Land ' and had declared that they were very good. The King thought that R. must have inspired them, but R. said that they were merely a paraphrase of what I had written a year ago in my article on ' The Western Front,' which still stood as the expression of my view of our correct strategy. But it was true that I agreed with R. The point is that all our best soldiers agree, and yet the politicians will not accept their opinion. R. thinks that it is high time for Briand's Cabinet to fall, and I agree, because they are subordinating strategy to politics, and are imperilling our success by the *engouement* for Salonika, where 500,000 of our Allied men are held in play by a few Balkan cut-throats.

R. also says that L. G. wants a victory quickly, a victory while you wait. He does not care where. Somewhere where opinion will be impressed, like Damascus. R. has told him that Damascus may come in time, when rail and pipe lines are laid, and meantime what about Beersheba ? L. G. didn't fancy that Beersheba would catch on, but Jerusalem might ! This is War Cabinet strategy at the close of 1916, and if we can win on it we can win on anything. I gave R. my views on all these matters.

Sunday, Dec. 31. Laid up with a chill. The fates are against my helping Robertson. I telephoned to Lovat Fraser, one of the *Times* leader writers, to come and see me on his way to the office, and he promised to come at 5 P.M. He only turned up at 9.30, too late, and it was useless. Meantime I had telephoned to Geoffrey Robinson to tell him the position and he promised to help, but he had dined with Milner, Friday night, and M. had made him understand that the Cabinet would not go against the General Staff, as it was too great a responsibility for them to incur. So Robinson is not so fidgety as I am about the situation.

Monday, Jan. 1. Nothing in the *Times* to help. Fraser had told me overnight that M. Thomas had been telling people here that Sarrail had only 130,000 bayonets at Salonika. I replied that M. Thomas was misinformed. We had 500,000 men there including 230,000 infantry. A happy New Year's day. Went to tea with Maude Cassels and her girl, 17 Langham Street, and discussed Canadian affairs. She told me how Max Aitken was regarded in Canada and why.

On reading my French papers this evening I see that the Decree of Dec. 13 appointing Joffre 'Conseiller technique en ce qui concerne la direction de la guerre' has been cancelled, as well as that of Dec. 2, 1915, which made him C. in C. of all the French forces. The duties hitherto performed by the French G.Q.G. are to become part of those of the General Staff of the Army at the War Ministry. Thus it seems to me that the French Cabinet intend to run the strategy of the war, as L. G. obviously intends to do here. This is very serious. At the same time I get a 'projet de résolution' from Steed, drawn up by the French Deputy, M. Hennessy, in favour of an Allied General Staff, which seems to be part of the plan for concentrating the real direction of the war under the French. I rang up Steed to-night and found that he and I absolutely disagreed on all this affair, he holding that there was no distinction between policy and strategy (!) : that Robertson and Joffre had been obstructive : that there had been a military dictatorship under the Asquith Cabinet, and so on—the usual fustian. All this because Robertson has kept strictly within his legitimate duties and has tried to keep the Cabinet from committing follies. Steed also complained—and all his ideas obviously come from Thomas and other French politicians—that Joffre and Robertson had made their plans together before the Conferences. So they did, because they would not trust them to 60 or 100 people, and they were quite right. But evidently all this is even more serious than I thought, and I am much perturbed to know what I can do or ought to do to help to save the country from the danger which has so often nearly ruined it before, namely, of having its strategy directed by a pack of ignorant politicians. Steed also told me that Haig and Kiggell have refused to prolong their lines beyond the Somme until more divisions have reached them, and had suggested to the Cabinet that they should bring back to France the divisions from Salonika, advice which I heartily agree with, but Steed was furious about it. Robinson has had to go away to Yorkshire.

Northcliffe is in France, out of touch. I doubt whether any leading member of the late Government will take up the case for soldiers. Balfour is a Minister, but not in the War Cabinet. Shall I try Balfour, or shall it be Marlowe and the *Daily Mail* and a public row ?

Tuesday, Jan. 2. Lunched with Marlowe and H. W. Wilson at the Automobile Club and posted them up in all the Salonika question. Marlowe promised a leader on it to-morrow.

Wednesday, Jan. 3. The *Daily Mail* leader duly comes out—not strong enough, but still on the right lines and quite useful.

Thursday, Jan. 4. I finished last night an account of the work of the Q.M.G.'s Department during the war. Things continue lively in the Mediterranean. I hear privately that the *Ivernia*, of 14,000 tons, has been torpedoed east of Malta. We had 1800 troops on board, and the ship was escorted by destroyers. All but 130 were saved. A bad business, but might have been worse. Our people have not yet grasped the fact that the German submarines have made these oversea expeditions highly dangerous, but I can only hope that after the *Gallia*, the *Gaulois*, and the *Ivernia* even the blindest will see the folly of the Salonika expedition. If the Germans had threatened to attack Salonika, had thereby drawn more of our troops there, and then had massed their submarines off the port we should have been in a nice mess. However, it is quite bad enough as it is.

Friday, Jan. 5. The article on Cowans's great work duly appears. It is not a literary *chef d'œuvre*, but is full of detail. Either the *Times* or the Censor cuts off the head and tail of it. I am thereby not permitted to warn the public of the danger threatening the efficiency of the Q.M.G.'s Department. Lunched with Lady Murray at the Berkeley Grill, and we exchanged news about Sir Archie and the campaign in Egypt. He has told her that he hopes to get to Jerusalem.

Afterwards I saw Generals Haldane and Hull, commanding

respectively an Army corps and a division in France, and also Nicoll who had a brigade in Salonika, and Joe Fyers back from the same quarter. Haldane and Hull declare emphatically that the spirit of the troops is splendid and that the men want to go on and smash the enemy. Hull wants at least one battery of 6-in. hows. with each division. He also suggests that the T.F. C.O.s should be made Brevet Colonels. His great difficulty is to get good platoon leaders : he says that they have too many courses at home and not enough practical handling of troops. He says that with the 2-in. trench mortar, he keeps the German wire down and can get into the front German trenches when he likes. A long talk with Haldane. He thinks that our attacks have lacked depth. Haldane does not worry much about the new German trenches, as the deeper the dug-outs the more the prisoners. It was Haldane who seems to have carried out Rawlinson's remarkable night attack on the German second line on July 14 which I admire so much. The French had told him that it could not be done with our raw troops. Haldane is all for more divisions, and agrees that we might copy the German system of reducing the infantry in each division and increasing the number of divisions. He says that the A.G. has now sent out 250,000 drafts and that the strengths are made up again. But it is all a question of fire. We can smash our way in anywhere with guns and shells, and wreck all defences. He is for automatic rifles like the French, who now attack with a brigade on a front of 600 yards, and he is now using the Lewis gun fired from the hip while advancing. Nicoll and Fyers agree that there is nothing to be done from Salonika. Nicoll says that only with the greatest difficulty can our 40,000 men on the Struma get their rations, and we have not been able to get *one* day's reserve up to them. He thinks we require 250,000 men to hold Salonika defensively.

Saturday, Jan. 6. The Dutch Minister came up to consult me about the personages to be asked to a dinner which he is giving to the officers of the Dutch Military Mission now in England. He showed me the list and I suggested an alteration. He thinks peace may come, and says that he has found hardly any one except Steed to discard emphatically and *a priori* the idea of peace. A good mark to Steed. I told him that I doubted whether Germany had suffered enough to sicken her of war, and in this case peace might only mean a truce. He says that Alan Johnstone is furious at being dismissed from his post at The Hague. Van Swinderen says that Johnstone has done very well, but that Lady J.'s long absences from Holland have done him harm. He said that I was right in thinking that Sir Walter Townley would get the post, for he has now been appointed. Swinderen thinks him more than *le mari de sa femme*, and says that he is not at all a weak man.

Lunched with Mrs. Leeds: Fox McDonnell, Lady Sarah, and some other people whom I do not recall. The conversation turned on the Court.

This evening there came out the Kaiser's answer to the Allies' refusal to negotiate. He tells the Army that he will impose an understanding with the sword, and before God and Humanity throws the whole responsibility upon the Allies of continuing the war. The offer came at a bad moment. Trepoff was on his trial with the Duma, and Briand in difficulties with his Parliament. Both made violent anti-peace pronouncements before we spoke, and so did the Tsar, who claimed a free Poland and the possession of Constantinople. The ground was therefore cut from under us before L. G. spoke, though Sonnino made a good moderate speech in Italy. The Allied reply to the Kaiser was verbose, declamatory, and a patchwork.

Monday, Jan. 8. Saw the A.G., Sir Nevil Macready, at the War Office, 10.15 A.M. I told him that I wanted to know whether the position had changed since we last met, and that it was no good launching out into fresh commitments until we knew what we had in the bank. He said that we had sent 500,000 drafts to France since July 1, including 380,000 infantry, and were now full up there. He was also sending 5000 men a day, and the losses were now only 200-300 a day, so a certain reserve was piling up locally. But he had reduced the reserve cavalry regiments at home to eight, and so had obtained 5000 cavalry to help the infantry, especially with N.C.O.s, and he had done the same with the Engineers, from whom he had drawn another 5000. Our losses on the Somme had been 460,000. He had now 200,000 infantry drafts left at home, while for the East there were 53,000 drafts of all kinds waiting to go. He said that the Mediterranean was now closed, but drafts for Egypt, Mesopotamia, and India were going out round the Cape—10,000 men in a convoy. The trouble was that we were doing nothing at home. He needed 100,000 men a month to keep existing units going, and had taken 28,000 general service men in December. In the first five days of January we had taken 10,000. It was not possible to think of forming fresh divisions until the new Director of National Service (Neville Chamberlain) got to work, and at present he was a great disappointment, although a good, straight, honest man. He had tried to start a lot of useless machinery, had prevented a fresh revision of the list of certified trades, and had not used the 94,000 substitutes which the A.G.'s branch had ready for him. The best course, thinks the A.G., would be to put in Geddes (A. C.), as he has the whole thing at his fingers' ends, a complete register, and a knowledge of what should be done. Macready had revised the establishments of all the training branches at home, basing himself on the experience of the war only, and had cut off 100,000 men. There were hardly any general service men or artificers to be found now among the home service men. His department had investigated further the number of civilians of a military age still in civil life, and had worked out results by four different methods, all of which brought the figure to 4,000,000 or thereabouts. But I noted that 990,000 are men excepted by virtue of the provisions of the Act—parsons, theological students, etc. etc.—and Macready doubts whether L. G. will dare to tackle this class. It is, in any case, absolutely necessary for the new Cabinet to move at once, and Macready intends to alarm Derby and get a move on somehow. He thinks the expansion of the Army may best be carried out by taking field battalions and doubling them in the field with drafts. This will save most trouble respecting cadres, and new artillery will present few difficulties. Macready does not intend to use the Tribunals if he gets his compulsory National Service Bill, because the country Tribunals are not severe enough, and he will have special panels. He thinks that if Geddes were in Neville Chamberlain's place he would within a week begin to get a good flow of recruits even voluntarily.

The papers to-day say that the Conference in Rome [1] is ended, and — of course — that there is general agreement amongst the Allies, which looks like some compromise over Salonika. I saw Maurice to ask why Robertson's name had been omitted from all the telegrams : he did not know, but thought that R. might have wished it. No more news from Salonika, except that all the other Bulgarian division has now reached the Monastir front. Thaw has set in on the Struma, and Thomson reports the Sereth country impracticable. Maurice thinks it open to Hindenburg to stop on the Sereth line and send troops to Salonika.

Lunched with Hacket Pain at the Senior. He commands in Ulster and has 25,000 men under him, including the Special Reserve. Recruits are few. The feeling strong against the Sinn Feiners. I find that his ideas and mine on the war agree. He wants compulsion for Ireland, and says that there will be a squeal and then all will agree. It will be the saving of Ireland. The great mistake of the English, he thinks, is that they take the Irish seriously. It is comical that the late Chief of Staff of the Ulster Volunteer Force should now command all the King's troops in that province. H. P. says that all the rifles of the U.V.F. are well looked after, and that the Ulster men will never give them up. They feel that they cannot be trifled with so long as they remain armed.

----

[1] The story of L. G.'s 'Laibach campaign' is omitted here, but should be told some day, as it is a gem.

Tuesday, Jan. 9. A strong article on Salonika in the *Daily Mail* of yesterday made me realise that Northcliffe was back. I went to see him this morning at 22 St. James's Place, 11.30 A.M., and found Sir Philip Sassoon there. We all exchanged impressions on things that had happened in France and England recently, and we all agreed that Briand's Salonika policy was disastrous. But Northcliffe and I agreed in thinking that great prudence was now necessary, because the Allies at Rome appeared to have agreed on a certain course of action and it would never do for us to suggest a different course. Also I pointed out that all the alternatives at Salonika were necessarily bad, and we should not therefore tie ourselves to any one of them. It was for the people who had got us into this mess to get us out of it. Lord N. thought that L. G. would make great play with the smaller nations, and therefore we could not take a strong contrary line in the Press.   I said plainly that I thought, unless Briand was beat or changed his views, that we had to decide between losing Briand and losing the war, and that the prosecution of the Salonika enterprise, concurrently with the failure to expand our military establishments at home, threatened to ruin the campaign in France. Sassoon agreed. I said that we needed 60 new divisions, and Sassoon declared that we could win the war if we had them in France. Northcliffe appears to have given L. G. a good piece of his mind in Paris. He also snubbed Thomas when the latter, who was sent to him by Briand, began to declaim to him about the merits of statesmen and the demerits of soldiers. Lord N. asked to whom M. Thomas referred. The latter looked surprised and said—Briand and L. G. Lord N. replied that these were not statesmen but only politicians, and that the soldiers had always been right about the war and the politicians always wrong. Altogether Lord N. has been very helpful. He is also withdrawing all the reporters from L. G. and other Ministers, and does not propose to see the War Cabinet men until he knows whether he may have to oppose them or not.

Lunched with Lady Beresford and a small party. The Admiral has been laid up, but crawled down, and was as full of fun as ever. Arthur Stanley stuck up for Jack Cowans most nobly, and Mrs. Maguire thought that the whole inquiry in the Barrett case was an outrage.

Wednesday, Jan. 10. Lord Northcliffe and his Radical brother and M.P. came up to Maryon, 9.45 A.M. Lord N. has seen Derby and has told him that he will not permit any injustice to be done to Jack. He wants me to find out what happened at Rome, and also to ascertain what truth there is in the Bavarian complaints of being given all the hardest work in the West.

Lunched with Lady Paget ; Mrs. Beckett, Lord Dudley, and Arthur there. We discussed Derby. I said that I liked him at the War Office. Mrs. Beckett told us a lot about the private hospitals. Hers cost £90 a week in food, medicines, and nurses, for twenty beds. She only got down to this figure by going to Lipton's for her groceries. She says she gets them wholesale prices, which are about a quarter of shop prices. There is a wonderful shop, Garrould's, in the Edgware Road, where all hospital requisites, bandages, etc., can be had very cheap. We went to look at Lady Minnie's latest purchase, a picture of Lady Diana Manners in a Velasquez dress by Sir Philip Burne-Jones. He had written to say that it was going to be sold at Christie's and had asked Lady M. to bid for it.

Went on to the War Office and saw Derby, 3.15 P.M. He was very cordial and outspoken. He distinctly told me that Cowans would not be moved from his post. I told him that I did not like what was going on in the Q.M.G. Branch, and that people ascribed to L. G. the initiative in all the recent changes. Derby said that this was of course true of Sir E. Geddes, but that he, Derby, was responsible for other changes, including that of Stuart-Wortley. He said that instead of 140,000 tons a week we had to expect to send across the Channel 240,000, and unless things could be changed we should get into difficulties. I told Derby that the responsibility was his and that I did not mean to criticise, but he had to beat the best, and that he could not do better than had been done and might not do so well. I told him that soldiers looked askance at the dispossession of soldiers of some of their important functions and were surprised that he should be responsible for it. He kept on reverting to this, and was obviously anxious about it. All that he said about Robertson and strategy was most encouraging. He said that he would not interfere, but would support Robertson, and that if the War Cabinet did not take Robertson's advice on strategy, and Robertson had to go, he, Derby, would go too. I said that he would make a great name for himself if he stuck to this. I asked about the War Cabinet. He said that it worked all right now. He saw all the papers and decisions. He could attend when anything which concerned his Administration, *e.g.* recruiting, came up. I told him my ideas about the 60 new divisions needed in France and how to get them, and he made notes of my suggestions. He thinks he can get a great lot of men by administrative machinery, *i.e.* by arranging to take all men of certain ages from all trades, beginning with nineteen and working up. He also suggested that many B men might line the trenches defensively. There is something in both these proposals. He told me in a roundabout way that the Salonika danger was ended and that no more troops would be sent there.

I saw Sir W. Robertson for a few minutes. He was wreathed in smiles. He said that Cadorna had been splendid and had refused to send a man to Salonika. He, R., had been very firm. L. G. had resented his attitude, and Northcliffe's visit to him, but he had given way, and R. told me that he, R., was *perfectly satisfied*. No wonder that the papers give out that there is to be no statement regarding decisions ! R. said that Briand tried very hard at Rome to stampede people but failed. Sarrail had been there, also Milne, the latter very good and helpful. Sarrail a *beau sabreur*, in immaculate English-cut uniform with a wide skirt and wonderful breeches and boots, his hair all brushed up, and the very devil of a fellow to look at. He quite awed L. G., who was much impressed by him. Robertson's private secretary tells me that R. dominated the military conference and took the lead all through.

I went back to Northcliffe to tell him the joyful news. We were as happy as sandboys and immensely relieved, but we have still to dig out the garrison of Salonika. N. drove down to the *Times* and left me intending to publish an article headed 'Good News from Salonika,' praising the decision and not saying what it was! But Marlowe wisely did not put it in the *Daily Mail* as it would have told the Germans too much. I took his car on to Hampstead. Sat on the Tribunal till 7.45. Arrived at the Dutch Minister's dinner half an hour late. The Dutch Mission under General Burger, whom I remembered at Dutch manœuvres in old days: some other Dutch officers, including Colonel Roell; Admiral Jellicoe, whom I liked very much, Lord Robert Cecil, and two or three ladies. Had a good talk to Burger, who seems quite alive to all the Germans may do. The Dutch are prepared, and can place 500,000 men in the field, and have all the water out in twenty-four hours. The German garrisons are weak and they are entrenching on the eastern frontier of Holland. Burger has been taken round our war factories, etc., and is much impressed by the calm confidence in victory, and by the total absence of all signs of war. Jellicoe said that he had had an awful time the first few weeks of the war. He had no safe harbour to lie in, and had to slink in at night, coal, and be off again before morning. He thought the German a very good Navy. Captain Dunlop told me that the Dutch officers reported that ship for ship the Germans were better than we, but we had more experience and a larger navy. I asked the Italian Military Attaché, who was there, to tell his Ambassador that Cadorna had been splendid in Rome, and to present my *félicitations*.

Thursday, Jan. 11. Dined with Mrs. Lionel Guest: Lady Paget, Sir Francis Hopwood, Colonel Swinton, and Johnny.

Friday, Jan. 12. All my allusions to Salonika are banned by the Censor. Lunched with Mrs. Keppel: Sir Walter and Lady Susan Townley, Mr. McKenna, and a few more. I liked Lady Susan. A cheery lunch. Discussed finance and politics alone with McKenna after lunch. He would not believe that Salonika was off, and asked if I had it from any one except L. George. McK. said that he had opposed Salonika throughout, and that it was the main reason for the fall of the late Government. Salonika was a terrible drain upon us, and everything overseas had to be paid for in gold. He told me that his plan for the loan just out was to have been 4 per cent. at eighty-three. Bonar Law's plan was more favourable for the investor. He said again that we could go on almost indefinitely in our war expenditure except in America, where our real difficulty lay.

Saturday, Jan. 13. Lunched with E. Colonel Winter and General Haldane there. We talked of the war. Both scoffed at the Tanks, or rather at the way they were used, and Winter said that forty were derelict before his guns. They both attributed our want of a great success to lack of depth in attacks, and disliked the utter destruction of the German trenches by our guns, as this left us no cover. The French only knocked out the main points and left the intermediate German trenches intact, then using them to shelter their men. Winter is using Airedales as messengers from the O.P.'s, and says that they do well.

Went to the War Office to see Sir W. Robertson, to try and get him for Lockett's dinner next Thursday and to make a speech in my place, but doubt that he will come. He says that he can give them no constructive policy, as nothing has yet been done about the men, and the discussion has been put off twice in the War Cabinet. General Nivelle is coming over on Monday. I advised R. to give way on all small points to L. G. and only oppose him when it was a vital matter. It would not do for him to gain the reputation of being an obstructionist.

Sunday, Jan. 14. Wrote an article on the 'Will to Conquer' showing the need for sound strategy, more divisions, and more men, pointing out that we had not followed the Kitchener plan as explained by me on Aug. 15, 1914. Sir James Willcocks and General Inagaki, Jap. Military Attaché, came to lunch at Maryon. I consulted the latter on the subject of Japanese co-operation. He told me that Japanese soldiers wished to come and fight, but most of the politicians did not wish it, because their chief interests were in the East and they might have to act in China at any time. He thought that Japan could spare ten divisions, and that they could arrive on the Galician front in two months. The want of ships would render the sea route inadvisable. He doubted whether Japan had enough ammunition for such fighting as that on the Somme. Japan had sent many guns and the men for them to Russia. The rolling-stock, etc., on the Trans-Siberian was not very good. Inagaki was for the evacuation of Salonika, and said that he agreed with all the views of my articles in the *Times*.

Willcocks told us that he had been born during the Mutiny in India and had been hidden by a native near Delhi. His mother had died at the time. Later in his life, when Brigade Major at Delhi, the native, then old and blind, had come with all his family and had blessed him by all the Christian and Hindu gods and had prophesied his success in life. He had obtained a high position for the old native and for his children. Later, when he was commanding the Northern Army and was a great swell, the family had come again with all their relatives and he had given them a great reception. He also told us that he had been two years at sea as a common sailor before he joined the Army. He was very unhappy at not being employed now. He would like to go and raise new Armies in India or Africa, but as he did not appear to be wanted he thought of retiring. I advised him not to do so, for no one could tell what might happen before the war ended. He is a first-rate fighting general.

Monday, Jan. 15   Went to the *Times* to talk with

Messrs. Corbett and Parker about the *Documentary History of the War*, which seems to be a great enterprise. But it will be of tremendous bulk. Dined with Mrs. Leeds, Lady Sarah, a young American, a lady-in-waiting of the Grand Duchess George, and the young Count de Noailles. A pleasant dinner. We went on to the Palace to see a Revue. The Grand Duchess and her attendants were in the house. De Noailles very sick about the treatment of Joffre and the change of command. He is now under Nivelle. One of my best articles in the *Times* to-day on 'The Will to Conquer.' Many letters about it.

Tuesday, Jan. 16. Not much war news. Lunched with Olive at the Berkeley. She was in great sorrow for Count Benckendorff's death, which had been very sudden. His girl told her that Benk's last hours had been spent partly in making plans for going to Torosay—Olive's château in Mull—and partly in composing imaginary replies to imaginary American notes to Russia—the Ambassador using most opprobrious language to America all the time. Maude Cassels writes to tell me of Emmie's engagement. She is to be married on Thursday.

Wednesday, Jan. 17. Worked, and then lunched with Lady Strafford at Chandos House: the Dutch Minister and his wife, the Marchesa Imperiali, General Cavendish, and a couple whose names I forget. Van Swinderen and the Marchesa told stories of Count Mensdorff and Prince Lichnowsky, recently Austrian and German Ambassadors in London, and of Kühlmann. Van Swinderen said that at 4 P.M. on Aug. 3, 1914, he had visited Mensdorff, who had told him that he was not going to leave and that there was no chance of war. He was furious when he got his passports. The Lichnowskys also absolutely refused to believe that we should go to war, and left everything in the house all standing as Mensdorff had done. The Princess took away nothing but seven canaries, a cat, and a dog. Took a present to Emmie Cassels. Met a friend who drove me down to the War Office, where I saw Whigham and Macdonogh to ask about Switzerland and other matters.

Macdonogh thought little of the Swiss mobilisation, which he considered only a wise precaution, but I said that though this was my view we could not overlook the strong pro-German sympathies of many chiefs of the Swiss Army which had come to light during the war. Macdonogh said that no particular changes had occurred recently, and that I could take the pre-war organisation as still in force. M. did not like the changes in the French Higher Command at all, but he said that Nivelle had created a good impression over here. He arrived Monday last, and left for France yesterday. M. said that the Russians had been very slow in reaching the Sereth, but had twenty-six divisions there now, with more behind to come up. He could not say what the Germans would do next, but thought with me that they were kept fairly busy on the Sereth, and said that there were still no signs of a concentration against Sarrail. Saw de la Panouse, who tells me that he really believes that the news of German exhaustion and internal trouble which reaches him is at last true.

We hear to-night that the German raider has sunk ten ships of some 60,000 tons in South American waters. I hope Norton will catch her. Robinson asks me to see McLeod, Chairman of the Reserved Occupations Committee, and also Perry Robinson, as the latter is off to Switzerland.

Thursday, Jan. 18. I heard from Egypt last Tuesday, complaining that none of the authorities at home had taken any notice of the labours and successes of the Army in Egypt, and that Murray had been passed over for promotion. I passed this on to Derby, saying that I heard that the Army in Egypt were sore. Derby replied to-day most cordially, and the matter will be put to rights, either now or at the next success. Derby was very grateful for the hint.

Went to the wedding of Emmie à Court Allan Cassels with Captain Wallis at St. James's, Piccadilly. The bride looked lovely in a Lucille dress—such a graceful figure. So sorry for dear Maude, who now loses a daughter who has never left her since she was born. Walked away with Lady Byng, who is at 22 Princes Gardens. Then to lunch with Lady Paget, to meet the Grand Duchess George of Russia : Mrs. Leeds, Wolkoff, Max-Muller, Dr. Ross, Lady (Ralph) Paget and a lady-in-waiting. Madame seemed a human being and was quite agreeable. Leila Paget a great heroine, and she impressed me very much. No one has done finer work during the war. She now acts as messenger between Copenhagen and London because, she says, it is unsafe for men to come! Sir Ralph is now Minister to Denmark.

Lockett entertained some 250 Unionist Agents at the Criterion, 7 P.M. Main object to say good-bye and to make a presentation of plate to Steel-Maitland, late Chief Whip, and to welcome Sir George Younger, his successor. After they had spoken I addressed them on the war, no reporters allowed. I commended to them Balfour's fine despatch published to-day, then went into the naval position and discussed the submarine question and our naval losses, and showed the various causes of our losses of trade at sea, and the remedies. I quoted 1803-14 experiences to show that we had equal losses in the old wars. I then discussed the various military operations, condemned the whole proceedings at Salonika, demanded a stronger support of Murray in Egypt, and asked for sixty more divisions for the West, showing that until we got them we could not expect a decision, and that the war would probably be prolonged till 1918. Then I told them how the numbers stood at home and that we had 4,000,000 men of military age still in civil life, and that we wanted about half of them this year to keep up strengths and create the new formations, the manner of which I explained to them. Finally I showed that we had, at all events, followed the Chatham plan of securing the balance of power on the Continent while mopping up all the enemy's colonies, and that we had nearly completed our military equipment, etc., so that we would not be attacked again in our time. I was well received. A horrible room with wretched acoustics and music outside, which made speaking a strain.

Friday, Jan. 19. *Le Temps* of Jan. 17 refers to my demand for sixty fresh divisions in the West and says that they will be welcome, but that the Allies have already strength enough to have serious chances of success. No doubt, but it is assurance I want, not chances. I have had some more correspondence with Derby about the Army in Egypt, for which I have taken up the cudgels. Jack Stirling came to luncheon at Maryon and we discussed the Western front. He returns there to-morrow. Dined with Lady Scarbrough at 21 Park Lane to talk with S. about Territorials. Only Sir John Hewett there. He is under Neville Chamberlain, and was very reserved about his new master and not sanguine about progress. S. and I agreed to support Derby over his Territorial plans.

Saturday, Jan. 20. I was very pleased this morning to read congratulations to the Army in Egypt from the King, Derby, and War Cabinet. Murray gets a G.C.M.G. If I had not taken action nothing would have been done. My correspondent must be smiling over the prompt result of his letter to me.

Sunday, Jan. 21. Wrote an article on Army Expansion. After dining in London, no tube, bus, or taxi to be found, and had to walk as far as Regent's Park, wet and slippery, till I managed to get a lift beside the chauffeur in a taxi in which were an officer and a girl. They had bad luck. I suppose that it was a thousand to one against their taxi being stopped and the door opened at 1 A.M. !

Monday, Jan. 22. Much amused to see that General Malleterre, the critic of the *Temps*, rats at last about Salonika, and throws for the Western front and the Rhine ! He says that I have more authority in England than any military critic has in France, and he quotes from my article on 'The Will to Conquer.' I hope that this may mean the beginning of a change of opinion in France. A pleasant dinner at Mrs. Maguire's, 3 Cleveland Square, St. James's : a sister of Lady Crewe, some Sassoons, Mrs. Keppel, Mrs.

Astor looking a dream, Lord Lurgan, Mr. Balfour, Mr. and Mrs. Walter Burns, and some others. Balfour talked a good deal after dinner of Foreign Affairs and Admiralty business, and was very interesting. Had a long talk with Mrs. Keppel, who says that second youth resulting from a man of fifty-eight marrying a pretty woman is only transient—a St. Martin's summer ! She says that Violet's engagement is not yet decided. Violet wants to wait for three months. We played Bridge, all except A. J. B., who now has an hour's work at night with his despatches when he gets home.

Tuesday, Jan. 23. Lunched with Arthur Balfour, Lord Robert Cecil, and Ian Malcolm at 4 Carlton House Gardens. President Wilson's speech to the Senate published this morning. Balfour not much impressed by it. He did not know what America meant by the freedom of the seas nor why Wilson should resent a victory at the end of a war. Bob Cecil said that the Americans did not know themselves what they meant by the freedom of the seas. All of us anxious about the submarines. Balfour said that his despatch had been kept back in America, and that Wilson had not replied to his point that we could not, in the light of experience, trust the Germans to carry out any treaty obligations. I was given permission to write something nice about Alan Johnstone, who has committed no fault and has been savagely assailed. The reason for the change is simply that a first-rate man is wanted at The Hague and that Alan is not an eagle. Balfour had never seen Alan, and evidently knew nothing about the change. Cecil puts it on the War Cabinet. I spoke about the Japanese and Inagaki's views. When the others had left, Balfour and I discussed this matter, and it was finally decided that I should consult Nabokoff of the Russian Embassy to see whether the Russians would accept Japanese support and what they would give for it. I suggested the northern part of Saghalien. I am not sure if A. J. B. knew where it was, and neither of us was sure whether we still occupied Wei-hai-Wei. I am then to see whether

Inagaki will get his people to move, and I am to report progress to Balfour. These are matters more easy to initiate unofficially than officially. Saw Lord French after walking to the F.O. with Balfour. The F.M. does not think that we are making the proper arrangements for winning this year, but he says that Haig and others including Nivelle believe that the Germans are demoralised and that we can walk through them. So we are going on strongly, although we have infantry drafts for only two months' normal casualties.

Dined with Mrs. Leeds: the Grand Duchess George, the McKennas and Winston Churchills, Lady Paget, Mrs. Keppel, Lord Charles Montagu, Bogey Harris, Lady Sarah Wilson, Mrs. Bingham, and others. Talked politics with Winston and McKenna after dinner. Home rather late. McKenna told me that he knew the German Peace Terms. They include the evacuation of Belgium with indemnification, and of N. France: also a territorial satisfaction to Italy in the Trentino, the neutralisation of the Dardanelles and of Trieste and another Adriatic port. McK. assumed that the Germans would recover German East Africa, but not the other lost colonies. McK. assumed that we should not accept these terms. He also said that the French had tried to obtain full command in the West for Nivelle and had failed. Winston in favour, while McK. did not think it would work.

Wednesday, Jan. 24. I saw M. Nabokoff at the St. James's Club, 2.45 P.M. I told him that I had come to talk with him on a confidential matter that had no connection with the *Times*. I said that I was led to believe that the Japanese might be willing to co-operate in the war if they were properly approached, preferably on the Russian front owing to the tonnage shortage and the submarine risks. Would it be too much for Russian pride to accept such help, and would it be agreeable and practicable? If so, then what *quid pro quo* could be given? It was no use for me to proceed further with my Japanese friends until I knew the Russian view, and I mentioned the figure of ten divisions, which General Inagaki had suggested to me on Sunday last. Nabokoff listened carefully as I developed this theme and said that the war with Japan had left no bitterness in Russia, where the Japanese were highly respected. The manner, for example, in which Baron Rosen had been seen off by the whole Japanese Cabinet in 1904, and had been presented with a bouquet on leaving, was contrasted in Russia with the odious treatment of the Russian Ambassador in Berlin by the Germans, and with the indignities heaped upon the Countess Woronzow and other ladies. The co-operation of Japan would be agreeable, but he thought that Russia did not lack for men and that her real need was for guns and rifles. The passage of so many troops would encumber the Trans-Siberian, already so much used for goods from America and Japan, while the special rations of the Japanese might be a difficulty. Would it not be best that the Japanese assistance should take the form of war material ?

I said that I was glad to hear that Russia did not lack for men and was sure that Nabokoff knew much more than I did, but that I should like him to be positive that Russia could afford to do without the help of 250,000 fresh fighters of the Japanese stamp, who could be maintained by regular drafts and by their own war material. I said that the transport of the troops would only take two months. I thought that the Japanese soldiers would like to demonstrate their military virtues on European battlefields, but that obviously we must appeal not only to the Samurai spirit but to the commercial classes in Japan, and whether we asked for war material or for men we must find some form of material satisfaction for our Allies. Nabokoff admitted that the Russians had lost 500,000 men in the two attacks on Kovel ordered by the Tsar in August last. He agreed to take military advice concerning his opinion, and said that he would consult General Dessino, the Russian liaison officer. I suggested that if he cared to cable to Petrograd to be sure of his ground it might do no harm. As to compensation, Nabokoff thought that if he suggested it to the third-rate men at Petrograd they might become suspicious of England, because the only country which could give Japan advantages of a territorial character, or concessions, would be Russia. I did not mention Wei-hai-Wei. Nabokoff mentioned Saghalien (Sakhalin). He admitted that the Moscow merchants had made nothing of it as it was too far away, and that Japan was developing its resources which included coal, but declared that the southern part ceded to (America for) Japan at the Peace of Portsmouth was chiefly remarkable for containing billions of bugs. I replied that as we were all enthusiasts for the principle of nationalities just now, it might be wise to reunite the Northern with the Southern Saghalien bugs and provide Japanese insect powder. We agreed that if it came to war material it would be a question of cash. Russia had heavy commitments in Japan already and all had to be paid in cash, and Nabokoff doubted whether the British Treasury would prove very keen to help. I said that any reasonable price for 500,000 to 1,000,000 rifles, which would bring into the field an equivalent number of Russian troops, would be worth paying for. It might enable us to win the war this year, and in my view it was at present a question whether our armies could win the war before our navies lost it. But I mentioned that the Japanese were mainly exercised about China. Would there be any danger for Japan from China if our Ally depleted her arsenals? Nabokoff thought not, and said that no Chinese Army now existed, but that the Germans in China would at once try to make trouble when the news got out. Nabokoff is to telephone to me when he is in a position to know how the question is regarded by his friends.

Saw Wolkoff at the Club. He was thrilled when I told of McKenna's account of the German terms. He told me that the Embassy were still without official notification of Sazonoff's appointment. Met a naval officer of the I.D. in the afternoon. He is in charge of some anti-submarine work, and after entering into various details he told me frankly that he knew no way of combating the submarine menace.

Thursday, Jan. 25.   We have had an Allied Naval Conference these last two days—England, France and Italy—and the usual *communiqué* is published to say that everything is satisfactory.   It needs to be, as we lost 300,000 tons of mercantile transport in November, and over 400,000 in December.   Lunched with Lady Murray at her flat, and we exchanged views and letters on the subject of Egypt. Evidently, what she feels most is Archie being passed over for promotion to General.   Robertson gets his G.C.B. to-day, Whigham a K.C.B., and Macdonogh a K.C.M.G. A late sitting of the Tribunal.   I dined with Lockett to play Bridge.

Friday, Jan. 26.   A good article in the *Chronicle* to-day on Mercantile Marine losses and the remedies.   Sent to Balfour, as requested, a copy of my article of 1904 on Bushido.   Nabokoff telephones to ask me to meet him again to-morrow.   Lunched with Winston, his wife, and the Duchess's younger son, Ivor Churchill.   We spoke of the coming session and of political and military affairs. Winston was copying a Sargent landscape.   We discussed points for a speech on the address.   Mrs. Churchill drove me to my club and told me that W. was very sick about his position.

Sat on the Advisory Committee in the afternoon.   Dined with the Scarbroughs and Lady Ridley at 21 Park Lane. A most pleasant little dinner.   Scarbrough had been at Derby's Territorial meeting, and was pleased by the bluff manner in which he trounced Sir R. Temple of the Worcestershire Association, who may have been put up to criticise the War Office by one of the Staff.   Scarbrough and I agree that Derby is doing well at the War Office.   Lady Ridley very charming.

Saturday, Jan. 27.   The Kaiser's birthday.   He has a gathering of all his satellites at the German G.H.Q.   I wonder whether it will be bombed.   Lunched with Nabokoff at the Ritz.   He brought General Dessino with him.   We at once resumed the conversation of Wednesday last. Nabokoff said that Dessino—who speaks English only moderately—did not agree with him that Russia was not in want of *trained* men, but that railway, political, and financial considerations made the co-operation of a Japanese Army on the Russian front a difficult matter. Dessino admitted that the Russians were short of trained men. He had seen the British drafts at home and in France, and they were incomparably superior to the Russian. Yet when he had seen a fine draft and had asked why they were not at the front he was told they were not ripe. If he could have had such a draft in his Army Corps he would never have forgotten it. I said that in these circumstances it seemed to me that Russia might be well advised to take a quarter of a million trained Japanese if she could get them, and that it was of enormous importance to us, on naval and financial grounds, to finish the war as soon as we could. Nabokoff and Dessino agreed to consult their employers by cable in cipher. Dessino is to cable to Alexeieff, who is at Yalta, and is returning to the Tsar to command under him as soon as he is well enough. Nabokoff is to consult Petrograd.

I suggested three questions. Would the co-operation of the Japanese be agreeable? Should this co-operation take the form of divisions? Should it take the form of guns, rifles, and ammunition? I did not think it prudent to suggest a reference about compensation until we had got on further, but we discussed it, and I found that Dessino was quite agreeable to the Saghalien deal and had nothing to say against it. The two Russians said that Japan had been acting as a paid servant of the Entente and not as an Ally, and I said that the failure to use the magnificent Army of a warlike Ally with 77 million people was an incredible error, and that if M. Motono was correct in his speech reported in to-day's *Times*, the advantages to be gained by Japan by an Allied victory were surely worth an effort on Japan's part. I suggested that this speech would form a useful peg on which to hang an official conversation if we ever got so far. I pointed out that we were not asking the Japanese to save us. We had saved ourselves, but time was an object and Japan should help. I promised to appeal to the chivalry of the Japanese in an article, but still thought that we should make it worth Japan's while to lend a hand. The appearance of a fresh Army in the field this spring would cause immense depression in Germany when she was already so hard hit. It was bad enough for the Allies to have been without the imagination necessary for exploiting the martial races of Africa and India : we really could not afford to forget Japan any longer, and Motono had given no real reason for Japan's abstention.

Nabokoff was all for Japanese co-operation on the Russian front, if it came at all. He was against the appearance of the Japanese in Egypt and Asia Minor. He thought that they should be kept out of the Turkish theatre, and I agreed. I gather that Dessino and the Embassy work together. This is more than can be said of the Grand Duke Michael and General Yermoloff, about whom the Embassy people are always so sarcastic. Dessino reports direct to Alexeieff for the Tsar, but he and the Embassy work as a team and show each other everything. Dessino has been much impressed by his visits to our munition factories. He had a great reception in Scotland wherever he went. Even the maid at his hotel tried to make herself agreeable, and thought that she was talking Russian when he said good-bye and she replied ‘Danke schön !’ He said that more officers spoke Russian in our Army than in any other. Very few French officers could speak it. I feel sure that all Dessino's reports will be very favourable to us, but his view is that our attacks in France have been too timid (!), and he is misinformed about our losses on the Somme.

The French railways are congested, and some rather panicky telegrams are pouring in from Haig, Eric Geddes, and the Director of Ports, asking for all the despatch of troops and stores to France to be stopped. Is this the result of six months of the Eric Geddes régime, and of his 100,000 more workmen ? It has never happened before. Waghorn, the manager of the N.W. railway in India, has resigned his appointment as Director of Railways in France. He says that he is sensible of a political atmosphere all round him, and of blank cheques flying about. He does not know what is going on, and prefers to get out with clean hands and while there is a plank to walk over. He is evidently thoroughly alarmed at the proceedings, and he is one of the best railway men we have. Derby is curtailing his holiday and returning to-morrow, Sunday, morning. He told a friend of mine last Thursday that he does not see eye to eye with L. G. and does not know how long he will be at the W.O.

Olive telephoned to me to-day that the *Laurentic* was torpedoed by a submarine on Thursday, but that Captain Norton is saved. No word of it in the papers yet. This is a 14,000-ton White Star liner, and was equipped as an auxiliary cruiser with 6-inch guns.

I heard to-day a characteristic story of contemporary politics, but do not know if it is true. The Irish Party had asked L. G. to take over their railways as they could not afford to pay the 10s. a week bonus to employés paid by the Government in Great Britain. L. G. was advised that this meant the payment of £500,000 a year by the British taxpayer to Ireland, and that the railways were not needed, so he stuck out against an Irish deputation which tackled him on the matter. But during the political crisis Redmond went to see L. G. alone, and the next day appeared an announcement in the Press that the Irish railways would be taken over, and the Railway Executive Committee were duly informed. Is this part of the price of Irish support for L. G. ?

I must add that Dessino told me that the Russians did not like their troops to serve in the West as they became spoilt. Their men only received 6d. a month pay, so I do not wonder.

Sunday, Jan. 28. Maude Cassels, Generals Kemball

and George Cockburn lunched at Maryon. A pleasant party. Kemball told me and George all about the operation of October 8 in Mesopotamia for which he had been blamed, and explained it on a map. I thought that he made out his case.

Monday, Jan. 29. Lunched with Colonel de la Panouse at the Club. We discussed the changes in the French Command. He thought that the secretiveness of Joffre and his failure to tell his government what was going on had had a share in his downfall. Panouse shares my views about the illogical character of the present system, but says that everything political is illogical, and he regrets with me the disappearance of G.Q.G. He allows that Salonika has become a bankrupt policy, but will not admit evacuation on account of the moral effect which would be produced. I told him plainly that I was for evacuation and feared the consequences of remaining. However, he admits that all the plan is now for concentration in the West, and that I ought to be satisfied ; he deplores the articles in the *Daily Mail*, which he considered aimed at the French Government. The cap certainly fitted them. He praised Lyautey, whose particular gift was to surround himself with proper men and to leave them much independence. He told me that de Castelnau has accompanied M. Doumergue to Russia with Milner's mission, and I am pleased with the choice. He says that Nivelle has the merit of being able to explain and defend any plan he makes, and in this is superior to Joffre and to Haig. He thinks that we are bound to throw for a great victory this year, and feels that the enemy is weakening and that peace is in the air. I told him that our delay in preparation aimed at victory in 1918 rather than in 1917. We mutually lamented the submarine warfare and its consequences, as well as the railway breakdown in France. He paid a handsome tribute to Jack and the Q.M.G.'s branch in the past, saying that whenever he had gone to them they had settled the most difficult matters in five minutes and always in accord with his wishes. He deplored the departure of officers like Stuart-Wortley, the Director of Movements, who had done so well. He thought Benckendorff a great loss, as he had a great position and was so intimate with and trusted by M. Cambon. Panouse thinks that the Russians will never be ready. He cannot suggest what the Germans will be up to next. He discredits the reports of a German concentration in Alsace, and disbelieves in a German advance through Switzerland, which would place all the neutrals in antagonism without doing Germany any good as the Jura are so defensible by France. I suggested that Germany might place all her inefficients in the trenches and mass her armies for a break through, but that we might do the same.

News came to-day of Toby Long's death in France. I am much grieved. His wife telephones to me in a calm clear voice to tell me about it. She is a brave woman, and I am very sorry for her and for Walter Long, and sent a short appreciation of Toby to the *Times*.

Tuesday, Jan. 30. Wrote an article on officers' grievances, based on reports furnished to me by Major Seymour, whom Derby has appointed to investigate the cases. Met at Olive's at lunch Lady Powerscourt, who was full of stories of the Irish rebellion, and Captain Norton whose ship the *Laurentic* was sunk off Lough Swilly last Thursday evening. He thinks it was due to two mines which struck his ship at an interval of thirty seconds. He was steaming out of harbour at full speed without lights to escape submarines, but one of these pests must have laid mines outside, probably moored some 20 feet below the surface, and as he went out at low tide he ran the worst risk. He described the whole scene. There was a strong easterly wind and it was bitterly cold. He was the last to leave the ship, after releasing the prisoners who had been forgotten by the sentry. Fifteen boats got clear, but only seven were saved : the others were swamped or blown out to sea, and the men died from exhaustion. His wireless was destroyed by the explosion, but he got one rocket off, and the trawlers came out and saved him but could not find the other boats in the dark. He was seven hours in the boat, baling hard, and the water was up to his knees in the boat when he was picked up, but he looked little the worse for his experience. I think that 330 of the crew were drowned. This is the second time that he has had his ship sunk during the war.

Wednesday, Jan. 31. The cold continues: the hardest winter I remember since 1880-81. Lunched with Lady Pembroke at Lord Grey's house, 22 South Street: the Duchess of Marlborough, Lady Juliet, Mrs. Cecil Higgins, Jack Cowans, and Harry Cust. The Duchess gets on with her list of American heroines. Juliet said that everything went back to love, even in her conversations with Cabinet Ministers. I do not wonder with such a lovely lady. Harry and Jack full of fun. Lady Pembroke expecting Reggie back next week. Sat on the Tribunal all the evening.

CHAPTER XVII

MR. LLOYD GEORGE AND MAN-POWER, 1917

The German submarine threat—America breaks off relations with
Germany—General Robertson on the French railways—The first
Dardanelles Report—Lord Wimborne and Irish politics—The
Household Cavalry battalion — A proposed Irish settlement—
The men demanded by the Army Council not forthcoming—
Mr. Lloyd George's views—His criticisms of the Admiralty—His atti-
tude regarding men for the Army—A difference of opinion—His views
on Ireland and the Wimborne scheme—A quaint story of Lord
Northcliffe—F.M. Sir D. Haig's assurances to French journalists—
An indictment of the Allies from Greece—The proposed plan for
unity of command on the Western front—Lord Derby on Man-Power
—Lord French's Home Defence cripples—General Inagaki on Japanese
co-operation—My speech to the Unionist War Committee at the
House of Commons—My letter to the Prime Minister about Man-
Power—Mr. Balfour thinks the price for Japanese co-operation is
too stiff.

Thursday, Feb. 1. The rascally Huns tell lying tales of
our hospital ships carrying troops, as a pretext for sinking
them as they now to-day threaten to do. An Admiralty
communiqué threatens reprisals.

Friday, Feb. 2. The Huns announce to-day that they
will sink at sight all neutral vessels approaching the Allied
coasts. Much interest to know what the United States will
do. Lunched with Lady Beresford and discussed the submarine question with the Admiral and Charles Whibley,
also the breakdown of the railways in France. Charlie is
preparing broadsides for the Government, but he approves
of Carson. A late Tribunal.

Saturday, Feb. 3. I was asked by the *Times* for a paper
on the American Army. Drew blank at the Embassy.
Colonel Lassiter and the Ambassador both away. Went
on to the War Office and received some useful notes from

Sir G. Macdonogh and some of his officers. His idea is that if America comes in we could more rapidly absorb American volunteers in our Army than the U.S. can in hers. Had tea and a long talk with Mrs. Leeds, whom I found very disgusted with the cool way in which Mrs. Moore's death in Paris was taken by ladies who had constantly been her guests, and vexed that a Bridge party at her house to-day was going on. She feels her loss a great deal. To-night came the great news that America had broken off relations with Germany and had sent Bernstorff his passports.

I went down to York House at 7 P.M. for a talk with Sir W. Robertson before the news arrived. He was very fit, and was just back from the soldier hospital at Brighton. We discussed man-power. He told me that the War Office had fully done its duty last November and had clearly shown the late Cabinet what was wanted. The delay had been most serious, and he fully agreed with my remark about the Army winning the war before the Navy lost it. That was, in his view, the exact position. We could not now meet heavy casualties for longer than a month or two, and I told him that though the idea was not realisable I thought that there was a good deal to be said for postponing a serious offensive until 1918. R. told me that the French had made a serious endeavour to get our Army placed under Nivelle, but the proposal had never reached R. and possibly the War Cabinet had turned it down. Nivelle was anxious to attack at once. R. said that, except man-power questions, all was going fairly well. But L. G. had no enthusiasm for Haig and Kiggell. The latter had travelled in the train with L. G. on his return through France from Rome and had been examined by L. G. Kiggell had told him all the truth, and all the things which L. G. hated most, about the West and Salonika. R. said that one had to manage these politicians, to give way on small points, to postpone larger questions which were awkward, and to temporise if the politicians were promoting them. In this manner time was gained, and it was also 7 to 4 that the politician went off at a tangent on some other lay, or entirely forgot about the first affair. Haig and Kiggell did not know how to deal with the politicians, and so were out of favour. R. did not think that the congestion in France was the work of Geddes. It was the fault of the French. They had not repaired their lines nor their locomotives, and had suddenly thrown the whole business on us, saying that they had only promised to supply six divisions! This after 2½ years of war and the steady growth of our armies! It is inconceivable! We had been obliged to send 400 locomotives and some 20,000 railway wagons to make good, and a big railway man would have been necessary for us in France in any case.

Sunday, Feb. 4. Lady Juliet telephoned that her mother was so ill that she could not meet me at the Hospital. Went in the afternoon and played Bridge in Belgrave Square with Lord Dudley and the Ladies Headfort, Ridley, and Paget. Lady Headfort is good-looking and clever, and no actress-peer marriage has been so entirely successful. Lady Ridley looking more like a Hoppner portrait than ever. More heavy snow. Sent off an article to the *Times* on the U.S. Army.

Monday, Feb. 5. No fresh news from America, and the German papers are stopped on the frontier to-day. Lunched with Sir Ian and Lady Hamilton. He told me that some four nights ago he met Asquith and McKenna at dinner. They were discussing the interim Dardanelles Report which Lord Cromer signed before his death, and they described it as 'grossly unfair.' I said that in this case I imagined the Report must have discovered the *fons et origo mali*, namely, the failure of the late P.M., the War Committee, and Lord K. to produce a plan of operations, and that I expected that the Report had been most scathing on this subject, as it certainly would have been had I had anything to do with it. We wondered what L. G. would do with the Report. Would he publish or hold it over Asquith as a rod in pickle to keep the new Opposition in order? I did not care to take a strong line until I knew what was in the Report, but my preference was for publicity. Sir Ian had sent the Commission the drafts of all his private letters to Lord K.

Dined with the Wimbornes at Wimborne House, Arlington Street. Only the Winston Churchills and an engaged couple there. Had a good talk with Lady W. at dinner, and she was most charming and agreeable. After dinner we discussed the war. Winston has become more Western. He did not enlighten us much about the submarines and did not seem to have clear ideas about the maximum attainable under-water speed of these craft, nor to have heard of the new hydrophone. When the Churchills had gone the Wimbornes and I discussed Irish affairs. W. said that the Nationalists were ready to give Ulster a half share in the government of Ireland, and that they would be all the more amenable on account of the result of the North Roscommon Election, announced to-night, in which Count Plunkett, the Sinn Fein Candidate, had been returned by a large majority. W. also thought that the Ulstermen, and especially Belfast, were mitigating their old animosities, and were now more swayed by their commercial interest which would profit by a Concordat with the South. But W.'s trouble was that L. G. was so inaccessible that W. could not get at him. It was an absurd position. Here was a Viceroy of Ireland, ten days in town, and unable to see the P.M. ! We agreed that this was an unique opportunity for a settlement, now that America was almost fighting with us, and I said that I would try to help. The trouble is that L. G. seldom answers letters and is as inaccessible as Asquith was the reverse. As for Ulster, I said that W. was much better informed than I was, but that I was convinced that religion still counted more than anything else with Ulster, and that Ulster's resolutions on this subject were insuperable. L. G. had told W. that Ulster did not want to join in an Irish Government, and that to offer her compulsory service, which Ulster also did not want, if she joined with the South, was to offer Carson two things which he and his friends disliked, and the offer could not therefore be attractive.

Wednesday, Feb. 7. Not having heard more from my

Russians, I sent off this morning to Mr. Balfour a copy of my diary, of Jan. 24 and 27, containing the conversations on the question of Japanese military assistance. Balfour has written to thank me for sending him my Bushido article. Lunched with Mrs. X. and discussed current affairs. We went together afterwards to see Jack Cowans doing his rest-cure in 7 Mandeville Place. He said that the rest of the 58th Division had got over to France, Feb. 4 to 6, but that Haig had wired that none but divisional troops could be received yet. We had just lost another big transport in the Mediterranean conveying the refrigerating plant and aeroplanes to Mesopotamia. Jack and I doubted the wisdom of reducing so much the only good troops at home. Derby had also expressed doubts on the subject to Jack. We agreed that this was the sort of moment the Germans would choose for a rush attack upon us at home. On Tribunal all the afternoon.

Thursday, Feb. 8. Busy looking into the Japanese question. Lunched with the Pembrokes; Reggie home till Monday from France. Mrs. Beckett and Mrs. Lindsay also there, and Rupert Beckett and Bear Warre. A cheery party. Reggie says that the attack will be on the Arras front towards the end of March, and that the cavalry will be used dismounted this time. The Household Cavalry infantry battalion can now only put 270 men into the trenches, though it went out 1100 a few weeks ago. It has suffered from the want of experience of its officers, and has had heavy losses from frostbite. Reggie is so furious that he can hardly speak on the subject. Dined with Lord and Lady D'Abernon at Foley House, Portland Place. A party of eighteen, including Sir Ronald and Lady Graham, Lord Richard and Lady Moyra Cavendish, Mrs. Percy Wyndham, Lady Rocksavage, Lady Colebrooke's girl, Sir James Barrie, the Maguires, Lord Hugh Cecil, and various others. Found my neighbours, Lady Graham and Mrs. Wyndham, very good company. The latter quite recovered from her loss to all appearances. She says her father, Lord Ribblesdale, is living in a garage. The Cavendish

Hotel seems to be shutting down, and the famous Mrs Lewis giving up. Barrie told a story that in a club in America there was posted up a notice : ' To English actors. England wants you — we don't ! ' Played Bridge with Lady Rocksavage, Lady Moyra, and Graham. A good talk after dinner with D'Abernon, whose views and mine about the war usually agree.

Friday, Feb. 9. Went down to see the Wimbornes in the morning. We discussed a possible Irish Settlement and reduced it to the following :

1. Supremacy of the Crown. (Army. Navy.)
    (Veto of Viceroy.)
2. Colonial Self-government of United Ireland.
3. Equality in the Irish National Parliament for the two parties.
4. Representation in Westminster in inverse proportion to degree of self-government.
5. Civil Service Commission.
6. Provincial Autonomy in local government and education (with concordat).
7. National Service if operative in Great Britain. Crown to be empowered by Order in Council to set up Irish Government on these lines.
8. Details, but not principles, to be subject to Parliamentary review at conclusion of war.

I said that I should have to consult Carson about it and learn his views. W. thinks of a nominated Senate, and suggests that certain honours might be given to ease matters, on the Castlereagh precedent I suppose. Lady W. was helpful about the plan.

I hear that the men asked for by the Army Council have not been obtained. The Army Council tell the War Cabinet that the need is now 420,000 men by the end of April, and 800,000 more through the year, and they place the full consequences of any failure to provide the necessary numbers upon the Government. They further say that Germany raised 37 fresh divisions last year, have 6 more now ready, and probably 11 forming in the interior, total 54, which means an increase since the beginning of 1916 of 700,000 field troops. To this we have scarcely made any reply, though ample men are available. Thus my demand eighteen months ago that we should raise 30 fresh divisions, and my demand a month or two ago that we should raise 60 new divisions, have been followed up by Germany but not by us. We are asking for a defeat.

Went down under the impression caused by this news to No. 10 Downing Street to lunch with the Prime Minister. Only Sir Arthur Lee and Mrs. Lloyd George besides. We lunched in the little room where Gladstone used to prefer to take his meals. L. G. said that Asquith always dined in the big room, even when he was alone. The table was laid for five, and as we were only four, Mrs. L. G. removed the other *couvert* herself. Only a maid to wait. The simplest food— cutlets and vegetables, milk pudding and French plums—and water. Just what I like. Mrs. L. G. told us that there had been a division in the family about the move from No. 11. The P.M. and one of his daughters had wished to stay at No. 11, and the others had wished to move. L. G. said that No. 11 was much more comfortable, and that No. 10 would have suited Bonar Law better, as he had more money than L. G.

We began on the Navy. L. G. said that the Admiralty had been awful, and the present submarine menace was the result. We had scarcely any mines even now, and those we had were bad. Thus we could not use at sea the stonewalling system of the Germans in France. He thought that the apathy and incompetence of the naval authorities were terrible. I asked him why he did not hang somebody. He said that, at the time of the French Revolution, the heads of the incompetents would certainly have fallen. I reminded him that he and his friends had always given everything that the Navy had asked for, whereas the Army had always been starved, yet now the Army was winning the war while the Navy was losing it.

We then went into the Man-Power question, and I

was thoroughly alarmed by the P.M.'s attitude. He
seemed to me to be influenced by sentiment and pre-
judice, rather than by a reasoned view of the military
necessities of the case, and although he had been the
head and front of the demand for men under the
Asquith leadership, he now seemed to me to be adopting an attitude which threatened danger for the success
of our arms. He said that he was ' not prepared to accept
the position of a butcher's boy driving cattle to the slaughter,
and that he would not do it.' In making this sort of
statement he assumes a kind of rage, looks savage, and
glares at one fiercely. I suppose that his colleagues and
toadies quail under this assumption of ferocity. I said
that he must place himself in the position of the soldiers
who had a definite military problem before them, and must
know, not only how many men they could have now, but
also how many during the rest of the year. All organisation, strategy, and even tactics, I told him, hinged upon
this decision. I said that I thought we might be faced
in the West with almost an equality of forces, and that,
apart from the possibility of German economic exhaustion
and the cracking of German moral, I saw no reasons on
military grounds why he should expect a decisive victory
in the West this year. We seemed to me, I said, to be preparing, at the best, for 1918.

The P.M. said that the country could not spare the men
that the Army wanted, and that we could not denude the
shipyards, the farms, and other essential national industries.[1]
He had been told that the present decision to give the Army
all men aged eighteen to twenty-two would compel certain
munition works to close, but he was prepared to face this as
the supply of steel was so short that we could not at present
keep going all the works to their full capacity. Certain
decisions, he said, had been conveyed to the Army Council,
and it was their business to ascertain what the results in
men would be. I agreed that the A.G.'s branch could
do this, but it would be only a partial guide to the Army

---

[1] See Clemenceau's answer to this argument, Vol. II. p. 208.

Council, and very little use to the General Staff. I thought he should give the soldiers a more comprehensive understanding and make the situation clear to them. If the War Cabinet said that the Army Council should have 100,000 or 1,000,000 or 2,000,000 men this year, or that they should have none at all, then this would be a political and governmental decision before which the Army Council would necessarily have to incline, and they could then cut their coat according to their cloth, and perhaps make more use of the 1,500,000 men at home. But at present it seemed to me that they had no such decision, and that their position was therefore almost untenable. He did not admit that the soldiers did not know exactly where they stood, and asked me to make inquiries and to let him know, which I promised to do. He made no claim that he expected a decision this year, but thought that if the Germans found by the autumn that they would get worse terms, *i.e.* be in a worse position, by going on, they would come to heel. He admitted a shortage of men on our side, but affirmed that this was due to the excessive waste of men on the Somme, and that the difference between the 460,000 casualties of Haig and the 220,000[1] of the French represented our present deficit. I did not think this point worth discussing now.

L. G. only counts upon the Russians to hold up 1,000,000 Germans in the East—front line and reserves—and was not disposed at first to agree to my ten divisions of Japanese, saying that the Russians would not have them, and that if the Japs came and victory followed it would be considered cause and effect. I told him that this did not matter, that the Russians would accept Jap help, and that I did not think that anything should be allowed to keep outside the war an Ally with 77,000,000 warlike people : in the end L. G. was inclined to agree on this point. We discussed the African and Indian question summarily. He said that R. threw doubts upon getting men from Africa, but L. G. wished for black

---

[1] The P.M. omitted the French losses at Verdun.

labour and thought they might be used in the artillery columns and trains, to which I replied that the artillery relied on these for reinforcements. The P.M. stated that he thought of sending Jack Poynder (Lord Islington) to India with full powers and with men under him to act, but was hampered by red tape and the relationship of such a mission with the existing authorities—and I do not wonder. He agreed that it was necessary to support Murray.

We then branched to Ireland and I put forward the Wimborne scheme. L. G. told me that Duke had been for a similar scheme, but after going to Ulster and consulting all classes of people in the North he had come to the conclusion that it was not acceptable to Ulster, which did not want an Irish Parliament even if Ulster had supremacy in representation. The P.M. said that he himself shared some of Ulster's prejudices. I said, Yes, the Ulster folk are mostly dissenting Radicals like the Welshmen, despite their present Unionism-cum-Toryism. The P.M. agreed, and said that they were not Irish any more than he was, and that he would never consent to an Ulster dragged into a settlement against its will, and had so informed the late Cabinet. We discussed the North Roscommon Election, and I found the P.M. of the belief that there was no need to worry about a Revolution in Ireland as the people were all so well off. The P.M. proposes to speak on T. P. O'Connor's motion which is due to come on soon, and he will take a strong line and fight the Irish on it if they wish to fight. I must go and hear him. We ended by discussing the re-union of the English-speaking people as the result of the probable entrance of America into the war, and I found that the P.M. was very keen about it. Towards the end a servant announced that two well-known men were waiting to see the P.M. He sent down a contemptuous message to say that they had no appointment with him.

I saw Sir W. Robertson afterwards to begin the inquiry which L. G. had asked me to make. R. said that he did not intend to lose the war by giving in to the politicians, and that the Army Council had taken up a strong position on which they would stand. His view was that if it were true that we could not guarantee Haig his drafts after April—which was the present position in the event of serious fighting—then we should so inform Haig, who could then lay the matter before Nivelle, and the two would then be able to revise their plans. I strongly agreed with this line, and it may bring the War Cabinet to their senses. R. told me that Neville Chamberlain was doing well, and that Austen, as Head of the late M.P. Board, had also weighed in with a useful paper. N. C. was working closely with Macready and Geddes. N. Chamberlain had shown that the men could be found for the Army, and wants a short Bill to call out men by blocks of classes, all exemptions for these classes being withdrawn, but R. says that the Cabinet have not accepted this view yet, and he thinks that L. G. will not face the music. R. said that we could not win battles without men : that was the kernel of the situation, and he advised me to see Derby about the question which L. G. had asked me to investigate. R. agreed that we should be near an equality if the new German divisions, and the spare reserves from Rumania, all turned up in the West, and did not think that I had overstated the case to the P.M. He said that I was right in believing that we did not deserve to win this year, and that he continually told the War Cabinet that they were not winning the war. We considered what we should do. R. asked if I intended to make a row. I replied that the matter was extremely serious and that I would like to reflect upon it. I thought that we had already lost the campaign of 1917 by our delays, and that therefore it might be unprofitable to harry the Cabinet, especially considering that English opinion liked to give time to a new Government to find their bearings. I thought that it might be best for me to wait a little to see how he got on.

Sunday, Feb. 11. I have sent off two articles to the *Times* on ' Officers' Grievances ' and on 'The Maximum Effort,' the latter saying as much as can be said of the new German formations and the need for a reply here, but I hear that the

Censor has turned it down.   Thus concerning the two most critical questions of the hour, Salonika and Man-Power, I am muzzled, and the question arises what is best to be done?

Lunched with Olive to meet the Alan Johnstones just back from The Hague, the Dutch Minister and his wife, and Lulu Harcourt.   Alan very dignified about his treatment, and said that if his dismissal was in the public interest. he could only agree with it.   Lulu told me a quaint story of Northcliffe in his younger days.   He had to write an article on Eton for some cheap weekly paper, and sent down to Eton to ask if he could come.   The boys said yes, and prepared a lot of strange, new, and ridiculous games for which they dressed up, and these games, under various absurd names, were performed for Northcliffe's benefit. He was quite taken in and wrote three articles, describing these games and Eton as he had found it.   These articles were bound up and given by Lulu to the Eton library, with the title 'Eton as she is not'![1]   Lulu says that N.'s name is on the fly-leaf as the author.   Had a good talk with Lulu after lunch and told him of my anxieties about Man-Power. He gave us an amusing description of taking his seat in the Lords.   Outside a harlequinade there seems to be nothing more comic.

Monday, Feb. 12.   Mrs. Leeds and the McKennas, Sir W. Robertson, and Sir Gerald Kitson lunched with me at the Ritz.   A war lunch.   Had a pleasant talk.   McKenna is going to criticise the Government on the Vote of Credit to-day, and believes that L. G. intends to have a General Election.   I was to have dined with Mrs. Bischoffsheim to-night, but she was ill and put me off.   Busy the next three days with Tribunal work, as all my colleagues are ill. Northcliffe wrote me a long letter about the failure to use the brains of the nation by the Army Chiefs, and threatens to join in a row about it.   I must see him.   It is all gammon.

[1] I saw a copy of this amusing little book later in the Eton College Library, but not Harcourt's copy.   It was dated 1883, when Alfred Harmsworth was 18.   The paper which profited was, I believe, called *Youth*.   It sold so well that I wonder whether the young Editor took in the boys, or vice versa.

Thursday, Feb. 15.   I went to York House to lunch with the Robertsons : Sir Ivor and Lady Maxse and Lady Loch also there.   Could not talk much of important matters, but R. told me after lunch that the G.S. had passed my article and that it went back to Swettenham, one of the Head Censors, yesterday morning. R. told me that the War Cabinet had held two long sittings on the question of the men, and that L. G., though haggard and anxious, had said at last that Labour had been so splendid that he could not impose this strain upon them, or words to that effect, and, in short, that we were not going to get the men we needed.   R. hopes that my article will bring things to a point.

I went on to Northcliffe's house, but he was only up for the day, and left word that he had thirty people to see, so I did not go on to the *Times*.   R. told me to-day an amusing story of L. G. R. reminded me of my remark that ' it was a question whether our Army could win the war before the Navy lost it.' I had said it to him, to Derby, and to L. G.   Well, R. said, the P.M. had given out that a distinguished military critic had warned him that if we devoted all our resources to the Army we should find our Navy beaten, thus completely travestying my phrase.   R. looked at Derby who smiled back, but neither spoke, though both recognised the origin of the observation and the manner in which L. G. had inverted its sense.   The worst of it is that Haig is reported to have given some bombastic assurances to the French journalists that we shall break the German lines this year and defeat the enemy.   R. was very vexed about it, and I have not heard one good word for it.   My own impression that Haig will disown a good deal of the supposed interview which appears in different forms in different French papers.   I hope so. He who putteth on his armour should not boast as he who taketh it off.

Friday, Feb. 16.   The article on ' The Maximum Effort ' appeared, this morning, with a strong leader, to which all my allusions about the Neville Chamberlain scheme had been transferred to save space, so Fraser telephoned to me.

I had written to tell Robertson that the article had been turned down. But it came back untouched, Wednesday night, and now I have done all I can to warn the country of the danger. Fraser wrote the leader. Lunched alone with Mrs. Astor, who was looking better and was good company. We discussed America, politics, and private matters. She gave me the idea to assail*the Government about Man-Power from as many different quarters as possible, and I think that this is sound. Went on to see Winston who was just off to his new country cottage. He told me that the Dardanelles Report had been in his hands and may appear Wednesday. He is pleased with it as it covers him in the main, but it is very critical of the War Committee, of Lord K., of Asquith, and of the failure to use the General Staff. We then discussed Man-Power, but I soon saw that Winston had been forgathering with L. G., as he began to talk about driving cattle to market and so forth, just as L. G. had talked to me. I told Winston that this sort of talk was all very well for the baser sort of politician, but was unworthy of responsible statesmen at such a crisis as this. I told him that if L. G. mistrusted Haig he ought to change his Commander, but that he should see that we could not win the campaign without men. Winston much down on Haig about the interview, and said that the House of Commons were very much annoyed about it. Bonar Law has promised to make inquiries.

Dined with the Wimbornes. Owing to a series of accidents the party had shrunk from twelve to six : Lady Cunard, Mrs. (Venetia) Montagu, and Sir George Prescott. I admired the fine newly decorated rooms, and we had a good and gay dinner. A long talk about Ireland and the war. I said that I did not see how the war was to be won if leading statesmen refused to give us the men, and we talked on this theme for long. Much Irish and political talk too. Mrs. Montagu made many acute and interesting observations on events, and I began to understand the interest that the late P.M. took in her.

Everybody down on the Haig interview. Mrs. M. said that L. G. had never asked Montagu to remain at the Munitions Ministry.

Saturday, Feb. 17. Received H. G. Wells's new book on *War and the Future* from the author. He has written on the fly-leaf, ' To our one and only British Military Expert from H. G. Wells.' Austin Harrison rang me up to ask what I thought about the Haig interview, and I told him that I deplored it. A. H. was just back from France, and said that the French were furious, and incensed at Haig's patronising tone towards the French. Saw Jack Stirling in a nursing home in the afternoon. He says that 25 per cent. of the German heavy guns have shifted from the Somme front. I saw to-day a long letter from Athens giving the Greek Royal Family view of recent events in Athens. It is one long and severe indictment of the Allies, and particularly of the Allied Ministers at Athens and of the French Admiral, since recalled, and French troops. It purports to give the history of the affair of 1st December last at Athens. It declares that the Allied Ministers received numberless warnings from all sides that the Greek troops would not allow themselves to be disarmed, but that they paid no heed to them and sent an absurdly inadequate force. The writer says that the French attacked first. He says they found on a captured French officer a plan of the attack, and the places marked in red which were to be destroyed. These included the Palace. The Queen and children had taken refuge in the cellars. Out of sixty-one shells fired from the sea, eleven fell in the Palace grounds. The Allied Ministers, and particularly Demidoff, were terribly alarmed. The writer alleges that a long succession of what he calls acts of tyranny and injustice have caused the sentiments of the Greeks to change, and that now they naturally look to the Germans, who have left them alone in peace, which was all that the Greeks asked. I made no comment, but suggested that a typed copy should be sent to Balfour. Had a talk with some people about Briand, and some one said of him ' qu'il a connu les femmes du monde trop tard.' I thought that Lady Ethel Baird, who was among the party, had a shrewd wit.

Sunday, Feb. 18. Lunched with the Ian Hamiltons: Jack Cowans, Colonel Freyberg, and Lady Scott, widow of the Arctic explorer. Her boy Peter coldly clad, and down is forming thickly on his neck, arms, and legs as nature's provision. I suppose that we should all be furry if we survived going about naked. Our ships in the Mediterranean are not suffering much now, but Jack says that the raider has reached the Indian Ocean, and submarines are at the Cape. After our wheat ships from Australia I imagine, and it was Runciman who said we were counting on them. Jack lost 18,000 tons of oats last week by having his ships torpedoed at the mouth of the Channel: nine days' supply, and he has had to draw 10,000 tons from England, his main difficulty being to get the sacks. He says that we have heaps of meat and plenty of wheat in the country, and that he cannot imagine why the Government are making such a fuss about food.

Monday, Feb. 19. Spent most of the day reviewing conditional exemptions at the Town Hall, and called up a large number of men for further investigation of their cases. Dined with Lady Beresford and a small party including Mrs. Astor, Lady Johnstone, and Edmund Gosse. Bertier came in later. Sir Alan told me that on August 3 last the Emperor Karl of Austria had gone to see the Kaiser at Brussels, and had told him that unless the Germans threw in more troops the Austrians would have to stop fighting. Alan says the Kaiser goes to Brussels because there lives there a Belgian singer. Alan is sure of the facts, which he has from one of the Princes de Ligne. I said that I thought Caesar was above suspicion on this count. Alan replied that men of highly nervous temperament could never long keep away from the fair sex. Bertier told me of Pernot's impending arrival here and of his wish to see me again.

Tuesday, Feb. 20. Commander J. Wedgwood, D.S.O., M.P., came to lunch with me at the N. and M. Club. I told him that I had asked him to come because he was one of the few capable independent men left in the House of Commons, and that the position was serious. I took him all through the Man-Power question and posted him up. He was much concerned about it and will think over what is best to be done. He thinks that Curzon counts for more than Lloyd George. Wedgwood has been to America and wishes America to guarantee the future peace and to help in the garrisoning of Constantinople.

Dined with General Fred Maurice at the Savoy. He thought Bonar Law's explanation of the Haig interview to-day very lame. I said that it was a case of hoping for the best in France and preparing for the worst here, and that I never blamed the C.-in-C. in France for being or appearing sanguine, but that I did not approve of Haig's declaration. M. said that the War Cabinet were all down on Haig and somewhat on Robertson, and that there was a scheme afoot to place X. and Y. in their places. Z. had let Haig down by passing the interviews over here and not telling Haig about them. Man-Power plans have been virtually blocked, and we have only 250,000 infantry drafts now at home. M. said that the German effort would be even larger than I had suggested in the *Times* last week. On July 1, 1916, the Germans had 1334 battalions in the West and 675 in the East. Now there were 1344 in the West and 886 in the East, but there were certainly 150 more in Germany and probably 93 others, total 243. Thus Hindenburg could hold his additional length of front in the East and still have available for a strategic reserve as large a force as that which he sent to Rumania last September. As to guns, we have a good preponderance in field artillery, but not in heavies. Our own guns of all sorts were now 6000. The Germans had 256 divisions altogether, namely, 137 in the West, 89 in the East, and 30 strategic reserve. We should have 60 and the French 105, but of the latter only 60 were *troupes de combat* and the rest were *troupes de défense*. The combat troops were nursed and withdrawn after fights, pampered, and their officers ablaze with decorations. They were very fine troops. M. thought that the Germans were undoubtedly aiming at the West : all the indications pointed that way. He thought that they wanted us to attack, and that when we got forward on to bad ground the Germans would launch great counter attacks. M. also said that Haig had been ordered [1] to conform with Nivelle's wishes, and the latter has been anxious to attack at once before the German

[1] I did not receive the text of one of the proposals which followed the Calais Conference till a later date and from a French private source. I insert it here as it explains matters :

PROJET D'ORGANISATION DE L'UNITÉ DE COMMANDEMENT
SUR LE FRONT OCCIDENTAL

' 1. Par délégation du Comité de Guerre britannique avec l'assentiment du Comité de Guerre français, et dans le but d'assurer l'unité de commandement sur le front occidental, le Général-en-Chef français aura, à partir du 1er mars, 1917, autorité sur les forces britanniques opérant sur le front, pour tout ce qui concerne la conduite des opérations, et notamment :

' Le plan et l'exécution des actions offensives et défensives.

' Le groupement des forces en armées et groupes d'armées.

' Les limites entre ces grandes unités.

' La répartition des moyens matériels et ressources de toute nature entre les armées.

' 2. Le Général-en-Chef français disposera d'un Chef d'Etat-Major Général britannique qui résidera au G.H.Q. français. Ce Chef d'Etat-Major Général aura sous ses ordres :

' (a) Un Etat-Major Général chargé de l'étude des questions d'opérations et des rapports avec le Comité de Guerre britannique.

' (b) Le Quartermaster-General.

' Il sera chargé de tenir le Comité de Guerre britannique au courant de la situation et de lui transmettre les demandes émanant du Commandant-en-Chef français au sujet des besoins de ces armées.

' Il transmettra au Commandant-en-Chef britannique aussi au Commandant d'armées ou de Groupe d'armées opérant isolément, les directives et instructions du Commandant-en-Chef français.

' Sous l'autorité du Chef d'Etat-Major Général le Quartermaster-General sera chargé de répartir les ressources de toute nature entre les armées britanniques, et de donner au Directeur Général des Transports les instructions nécessaires à son service.

' 3. Les questions de personnel et de discipline générale dans les armées britanniques seront réglées par le Commandant-en-Chef britannique, les Commandants d'armées, ou de Groupe d'armées opérant isolément, et le Chef d'Etat-Major Général britannique, suivant les attributions qui lui seront fixées par le War Office.

' 4. La composition et le fonctionnement de l'Etat-Major Général strategic reserve got up.   Robertson had said that, as this had been done, the responsibility which formerly pertained to Haig had been assumed by those who gave him these orders, and this had made the Cabinet anxious and they were now trying to get out of it.   The G.S. would now tell Haig, who was not for an early battle, that he could not count on drafts for more than two months' fighting.   Haig would have to tell Nivelle, who would tell the French Government, which would wish to consult us again, and there would be another Conference, probably at Paris.   M. and I are convinced that nothing will teach our politicians what war means.   I told him, as I had told Wedgwood, that I began to think that L. G. had too soft a heart for this war.   I also said that it seemed to me that we should play the German game by attacking now, and that I thought we ought to wait till near June for the Russians and Italians to bear a hand.   M. was inclined to agree that we should wait till May in any case, for if the Germans checked us in the West, after only employing a fraction of their reserves, they would then fall on Lombardy with the rest.   M. supposed that the Russians would come along with more guns and much more ammunition this year.   He imagines that the War Cabinet is inventing pretexts to keep Milner in Russia, and that if Milner were here he would help us about the men.   We in the West were now 3000 yards south of the high road to Péronne south of the Somme.   Nivelle is to attack from our right to about Berry-au-Bac.   M. and Wedgwood agree with me that there is nothing for it but to call up blocks of groups of men, *e.g.* men of eighteen to twenty-two and so on, without any exemptions, and to tell employees the dates, and ditto for further levies, say twenty-two to twenty-five and so on.   Then everybody would know what was coming, there should be no exemp-

britannique détaché auprès du Commandant-en-Chef français seront fixés par accord entre le Maréchal Sir Douglas Haig et le Général Nivelle.

'5. Au cas où le Commandant-en-Chef français disparaîtrait, ses attributions passeraient au nouveau Commandant-en-Chef français à moins de décision nouvelle des deux Comités de Guerre.'

tions, while a compulsory national service levy should find the substitutes. I was told by X. that my article on 'The Maximum Effort' had alarmed the War Cabinet and that I must repeat the dose.

Wednesday, Feb. 21. An experienced naval officer now at the Admiralty lunched with me to discuss submarine warfare. He told me that my prophecy in 1910, in *Blackwood*, of the submarine situation was astonishingly accurate. I had been right about the mine-laying by submarines, though my critics in 1910, including Carlyon Bellairs, had told me that the story should be told to the Marines. Also my allusion to the 'otter' was more apposite than I knew. We had adopted the 'otter' principle [1]—a poaching device which I had recommended— to our ships. Wires led out from the keel of ships each side to an 'otter,' and they swept mines aside and cut their moorings. The destroyers also fished for submarines with 'otters' containing an explosive charge, and some of our recent successes had been won with them. Our Allies were all adopting the device. Why was not the *Laurentic* fitted with it? He told me about the successful attacks of sub- marines which worked with trawlers. The submarine fol- lowed the trawler under the water and was connected with it by telephone. When the German submarine attacked the trawler, the submarine below counter-attacked, and they had got two this way. But one day a torpedo missed fire and the enemy got away, and was no doubt warned of what was happening by this experience. He is not at all sanguine about overcoming the menace, and thought that we should tunnel the Channel and improve our air transport service. What a prospect for our Navy! He thought that it had become a disadvantage to be an island.

Thursday, Feb. 22. Wrote all day till 5. Then to the Tribunal. A very late sitting, and we had many cases; several conscientious objectors, including Wyndham Albery, to whom we gave no exemption. Was fearfully late for

---

[1] I have since been told that the term 'paravane' was applied early in 1916 to the various types used by warships, while 'otter' was introduced at a later date to denote the type supplied to the merchant service.

dinner at the Ritz. We went on to see a Revue and had a very pleasant evening.

Saturday, Feb. 24. Went to see the Bardac-Carnarvon collection of French drawings. A truly wonderful lot, with the finest specimens of the best masters of this period. Lunched at 2 Upper Brook Street with Lady Cunard: the French Ambassador, M. Nabokoff, Masterton Smith of the Admiralty, Lady Lytton, and Mrs. Cavendish-Bentinck. Nabokoff told me that General Dessino had not yet heard about the Japanese affair and had cabled a reminder. N. did not think that the Japanese co-operation could be arranged, not on account of the railway transport difficulties, but owing to the general political situation, and because the price to be paid would be too high. Cambon also spoke about the subject, and appeared far from keen.

Went to see Lord Derby at the War Office at 3 P.M. I thanked him for Seymour's services about my collection of Army complaints, concerning which we talked for some time, when we branched to the T.F. and Scarbrough's work. Then we spoke of Northcliffe's desire that the intelligence in the New Armies should be better recognised. Maurice had told me that 40 per cent. of the G.S. officers at the W.O. were not Regulars, and that a high proportion of the Brigade Majors and 2nd class G.S. officers abroad were the same. Derby now told me that there were more of the new lot on the Staff at home than there were Regulars, and that ten of the Brigadiers at the front also were not Regulars. He thought that Lord N. drew conclusions from isolated cases. He was going to give figures presently.

We then discussed Man-Power and I told him my views, namely, that we should have compulsory National Service and substitution, and a calling out of groups of classes. I said that we could not fight through the year on last year's figures of casualties, and that strategy and tactics must be affected by our situation. He said that he agreed with me from A to Z, but neither of us could see what we could do to force the War Cabinet to act. I asked what I was to reply to L. G. about the soldiers. Was it true that they knew where they stood during the year ?   Derby said that they did not, that they could only bank upon the available drafts in hand and upon the youths of eighteen to nineteen ; all else was guesswork.   I told Derby how the numbers stood, and asked if it was correct that we needed 1,250,000 this year and had only 250,000 infantry for drafting.   He did not deny it.

I saw Lord French at 4 P.M.   He has still but few rifles for the Volunteers, and puts it down to shortage of steel. He has been to the War Cabinet and has told them that his troops have been so drawn upon for France that he refuses to be responsible for Home Defence.   But he added that if a risk had to be taken and he were in the War Cabinet, he would take the risk rather than allow the Armies in France to be short.   He asked me whether I did not think he was right, and I kept silence.   I asked his C.S.O., General Lowther, how many Germans he could oppose, and he replied ' about 450 ' !   Lord French says he has a bit over 100,000 men, of a sort.   He is placing them all on the beach to resist a landing, and if the Germans get into the country he does not think he can do much.

Sunday, Feb. 25.   General Inagaki came up at 5.   We renewed the conversation about Japanese co-operation. He had studied co-operation by sea, and estimated that it would require 200,000 tons to carry one Japanese division by sea to Europe, 150,000 tons constantly for supply, and 150,000 tons more to replace casualties at the high rate of 200 per cent. per year.   The Japanese had only 450,000 tons which they could devote to this purpose, and the scheme of an important Japanese despatch of troops by sea to the West consequently seemed impracticable.   I agreed, assuming his calculations to be correct.   The co-operation on the Russian front was, he said, a different matter.   If rolling stock were available Japan could spare ten divisions out of her twenty-one, and each would need fifty trains to carry it.   Afterwards one train every other day per division would be enough, *i.e.* five trains a day, to bring up 500 tons forage and supplies per division per day for ten divisions, and the manufacture of ammunition for Russia would have to stop. It might be difficult to keep up the ammunition supply from Japan for ten divisions.

The rice would have to come from Japan. Inagaki could not say what rolling stock was now available for a movement of this kind, but it was a question of the rolling stock and not of the railway lines which would carry the requirements easily, as he said I knew from the experience of 1904-05. He told me that thousands of railway wagons built for Russia in America were awaiting shipment, for the Russians were so stupid that they had not arranged for their transport by sea. I suggested that the 450,000 Japanese tons might be first devoted to this transport and then we might get on. Inagaki said that the main thought of the Japanese was always China, China, China. He admitted that public opinion in Japan, such as it was, was not in favour of more active participation in the war, but there was no real public opinion in Japan, and no union except in war. There were only parties. China had no Army or Navy to speak of, but Japan was anxious about Russia, who had a strong position in Eastern Asia. Japan wanted certain things, but felt that the war time was the time for sacrifice and effort and not for profiteering. If Russia offered certain concessions it would be a different matter. I asked what the Japanese wanted. Was it land ? Inagaki said no : he could only give his personal opinion, but his view was that the Japanese control of the railway to Kharbin and the dismantlement of Vladivostok and the Russian naval base at this port would give Japan all she needed. Japan had sold 700 heavy guns, mostly of old pattern, and 600,000 rifles to Russia. Japan's arsenals were depleted in consequence. No country but France had made any serious proposal to Japan for military support since the war began, and the French request dated two years back. I asked Inagaki to consider how Japan would be viewed by the Allies after the war if, when all the others, including perhaps America, had fought hard, Japan had done but little fighting. Inagaki said that this question was always in his mind, and he fully understood it. There was a weak Government in Japan.   M. Motono might be in favour of my views.   I was left with the impression that Japan would act if the concessions named were granted. North Saghalien did not appear to be much attraction to Japan.

Sir Ian Hamilton, Lady Alexander, and Marjorie dined with me at the Carlton.   We enjoyed ourselves very much, and went on to the New Gallery to see a cinema, which was very amusing.   We saw the ladies home afterwards.

Monday, Feb. 26.   Ronny McNeill telephoned from the House of Commons to ask whether I would address the Unionist War Committee at the House to-morrow at 5 P.M. on Man-Power.   I agreed.   It seems the best way to preach the gospel.

Tuesday, Feb. 27.   Lunched with **Mrs. Cavendish-Bentinck** at 4 Richmond Terrace :   Sir Lionel Earle, Lady Bonham-Carter who was Miss Asquith, Johnny Ford, Vansittart, and some others.   A pleasant party.   Lady B. C. very intelligent.   Earle told me that 1500 German prisoner woodcutters did as much work as 3000 Canadian lumbermen, and that the latter did as much as 7000 soldiers.   He also said that our prisoners interned in Switzerland lacked supervision.   Looked round the house and pictures and saw some of the Ford Velasquezes.   Saw Derby for a moment while I was talking to Macdonogh at the War Office, and told him about the Committee and my intention to address it.   Macdonogh has no doubt about the German reinforcements alluded to in my diary for Feb. 9.   They are still mostly in Germany, but many regiments have been identified by spies.   He said that Lord French had often chaffed him about ' celestial ' German divisions, but that they had always materialised. Went to the House.   A good attendance at the Committee Room.   Sir Frederick Banbury presided.   I was on his right at a raised dais.   A good room for talking.   They got through their business, and then Colonel Page Croft spoke on some motion of his about taking men from Home Defence for France.   I was asked to speak next.   I told them how glad I was to have the opportunity of telling what I believed to be the truth about Man-Power, and that my figures must be regarded as unofficial but confidential. I told them that they were not winning the war, and that I was sure that the G.S. had said the same to the War Cabinet. I said that I would explain why we were not winning the war, what our needs were, and how they could be satisfied. I explained the numbers of our troops at home and abroad, and was particular to show them how the 1,442,000 troops at home were composed, and that there were only 400,000 fit for drafting, of which 250,000 were infantry, equal to some two months' wastage only at the Somme rate of loss. I showed that except these drafts and the youths of eighteen to nineteen the War Office had nothing but guesswork to go on, and that it was impracticable for Robertson to regulate strategy on such a rickety foundation. I also spoke warmly against Salonika, and said I saw no chance of getting the fresh divisions needed for France. I told them the numbers of German and Allied divisions. I explained the weakness of the Home Defence Force, and said that I felt sure that Lord French must have refused to be responsible for Home Defence under our present arrangements. I said: 'This then is your position. You cannot keep up your armies in France for more than two or three months of serious fighting. You cannot form the fresh divisions which are needed. You may not bring home your seven good divisions from Salonika, and you are dangerously weak at home.' I told them that it took six months for any legislative reform at home to bear fruit in France, and that we had been behind our market all through the war. I then said that there were 4,000,000 men of military age still in civil life, and that Mr. Henderson had admitted that there were 3,500,000 men in non-essential trades. I said that I felt convinced that Neville Chamberlain must have reported that there were ample men to supply essential national industries as well as the Army. I told them that they were better able to say than I was why the War Cabinet did not act, or only by such eyewash as the Bill of last week.

Then I told them how to proceed, namely, to make the

N.S. Bill compulsory and then to call up blocks of classes, and was strongly for calling up the younger men first, but said that I wanted the men of forty-one to forty-five for a Home Defence Landsturm. Finally I asked how the necessary reforms were to be carried out. I suggested that a case had been made out for a secret session, but this was disapproved, members saying that there would be no secrecy, and others shouting 'Outhwaite!' I did not stop to argue the point, but passed on to suggest that the Committee should ask Robertson, and either Macready or Auckland Geddes, to attend one of their meetings. This they decided to do on Tuesday next, and then to invite the P.M. to attend.[1] The Committee were most attentive and civil to me, and applauded me very warmly. They asked me a number of questions which I answered. I remained for the rest of the Debate, and dined at Olive's and played Bridge with her, Mrs. Astor, and Sir Alan Johnstone.

Wednesday, Feb. 28. Lunched with Lady Paget: Lady Curzon of Kedleston, Dr. Page and his wife, Sir William Tyrrell, Mrs. Leeds, Belle Herbert, Mrs. Keppel, Lord Farquhar, and Arthur Stanley. Lady Curzon was very angry about reports that she had given a dance in London. It was not true. There was only a young party dance at Trent two months ago for the coming of age of Lady Irene. I told her about our Man-Power worries, and how I could not understand why G. C. let things slide. Did he know?

Mrs. Leeds drove me off and I went to see Jack Stirling at his nursing home. He is getting on slowly. Rather a levée, including Lady Leith of Fyvie, pretty Mrs. Butter, and some others. Then went to have tea with Theresa, Lady Londonderry, who was full of news, and then we were interrupted by the advent of Lady Beresford and Lady Antrim, whereupon there began a good old Irish gossip about everybody's misdeeds, male and female. Went off to see Lady Ridley a few doors on in Carlton House Terrace. Found a charming picture of her by McEvoy in her room, a little too dark but very characteristic and striking. I

---

[1] I believe that their request was refused.

told her all the news about Ireland and Man-Power, and we had a good chat.

Thursday and Friday, March 1 and 2. I stayed at home most of these days, and wrote a long account of England's share in the war for a supplement of the Russian *Bourse Gazette.* A sitting of the Tribunal Friday evening. Hugh Chisholm asks if I will be the guest of the 1900 Club and address them. I accept. Sir W. R., back from Calais, writes to say that he needs all the help he can get about men, so I suppose the War Cabinet still jib. Colonel X. from France called this morning.

Saturday, March 3. I sent off the following letter to the P.M. about Man-Power:

MARYON HALL,
FROGNAL LANE, N.W. 3,
March 3, 1917.

MY DEAR PRIME MINISTER,—When I last had the pleasure of lunching with you we discussed the question of Man-Power, and you will remember that I expressed my anxiety on the subject and suggested that the military authorities should have clear ideas of the numbers of men on which they could count during the current year. You told me you thought that certain decisions of the War Cabinet would have made this point clear, but you asked me to make inquiries on the subject and to let you know the result.

I have made inquiries and my anxiety is not lessened. I find that the recruits taken during the last three months are not the half of our requirements for maintaining our existing forces, and that there can consequently be no question of fresh divisions to meet the 56 or so new German divisions which have been created in the course of the past few months and are held over us as a rod in pickle. It appears to me that the military authorities cannot be sure of the future, and that beyond the men actually available for drafts and the young fellows reaching the age of eighteen in the course of the year, all the rest is pure guesswork. I calculate that on the Somme rate of losses you have only enough men in sight to continue a serious operation for two or three months. I do not know what the plans are and I do not ask, but if the Allies attack in the West, for example this month, and the attack peters out for want of men, I think the Germans will turn upon Italy and not improbably overwhelm her. My inclination, in the circumstances, is to postpone an attack until the Russians can join in towards the end of May, and so to regulate the attack that the operation may be continuous until October, by which month it should be too late to operate against Italy except on the Carso front. It appears to me that you are confronted by the possibility of an approach to equality of forces in infantry and heavy guns in the West this year, and I cannot but regard the position as being very serious. The Unionist War Committee invited me to come before them last Tuesday, when I gave them my views on the subject of Man-Power in a strictly confidential manner, and observing that the figures which I mentioned were not official and that the Committee must get such figures from the authorities. I am asked whether I will address the 1900 Club on the same subject, and also confidentially, without reporters.

I do not know and have not inquired what the point of view of the War Cabinet may be in all this matter. My impression is that this is your position :

> You cannot keep up your Armies in France for more than three months of serious fighting.
> You cannot form the fresh divisions which are needed.
> You are not allowed to bring to France your seven good divisions from Salonika.
> You are dangerously weak on land at home, and a blow may be dealt at you in this direction.
> It takes six months before any legislative action would produce results in France.

This is my reading of the situation, and I think it right to state it to you quite frankly without beating about the bush.

What in these circumstances is the course which you would recommend me to take ? I am always at your disposal if you want to see me.——Yours sincerely,

(Sd.) C. à C. REPINGTON.

Wrote to Northcliffe to ask why he did not help about Man-Power, and gave him details of the use made of Non-Regulars in our present organisation. Lunched with Mr. and Mrs. Montagu at 24 Queen Anne's Gate. I have not sized up Montagu yet, but we had a good talk.

He regrets his departure from the M. of Munitions as much as I do. He has kept the whole story of the political crisis of December from hour to hour. The change of Government upset everything, and M. could not understand, any more than I could, why L. G. had not gone on with the plan for compulsory National Training. M. said that the M. of M. were turning out 37,000 rifles a week when he left it : this was at home only. I told him that I had written a strong letter to-day to the P.M., describing our position as I understood it. I do not think that M. understands any better than I do what is passing in L. G.'s mind, but M. is rather a deep person and I do not really know him yet. Had a dish of tea with Mrs. Leeds in the afternoon. She was very cross about the criticisms of a dance she gave in January. A young Reuter there, Gordon Bennett's nephew I think. Some one talked about our submarines being able to submerge for ten hours. 'That's nothing,' said Reuter, 'one of our American submarines has been submerged for four months and has not come up yet ' !

Sunday, March 4. Lunched at the Ian Hamiltons'. Lord Haldane and Mrs. Lindsay there—and antagonistic. It appears that Cromer brought his draft Report down to the Dardanelles Commission, expecting them to accept it as it stood. They did nothing of the sort. Cromer fought for five days, and it practically killed him. Four of the original members are now out of the Inquiry, but it still goes on. I told Haldane the story of the numbers and of our anxieties, but got little help from him. He remains in the old ruts, and Ian declares that he is hopeless on this subject. Went to see Jack Stirling at his nursing home. Then to Lady Leith's to tea. Lord Leith of Fyvie a pleasant old gentleman but rather deaf. A nice house, 23 St. James's Place, looking over the Green Park. Went on to Lady Wimborne's. Saw the new McEvoy portrait of her, just home. I liked it. It is very lightly painted, but McEvoy thinks it his best work. It grows on one. We had a good talk about Ireland. Wimborne never saw L. G. after all. Dined with Lady Horner. Lord Haldane again, also Mrs. Alfred Lyttelton and Mrs. Aubrey Herbert who was Mary Vesey, and is absurdly like Emma Vesey whose picture hangs in my room with those of Sidney Herbert's other sisters. The type is a strong one and enduring. We had quite an interesting talk on politics and war.

I had a letter from Balfour about my communication to him. He thinks that the price suggested for Japanese co-operation by General Inagaki is too stiff, and he wants Russia and Japan to make terms by themselves. He does not mention the Athens letter which he returns.

Monday, March 5. Saw Lockett and Olive, who told me that they had both heard the nicest things about my speech to the Unionist War Committee, and that I had been very effective. My prompt answers to all questions had given much satisfaction. Went to see General Marafini, head of the Italian mission, who subjected me to a long harangue and gave me a paper about aviation, mainly with the idea of enlisting me to support big aeroplanes for long-distance raiding into Germany, a cause to which I am already won. He says that the Italians have 600 h.p. engines and are going on to 1000 or 2000 h.p. They propose to bombard Vienna and Buda-Pesth in May or June. Saw Geoffrey Robinson at the *Times*. His staff much reduced. He seems better, and is to see Milner to-night.

Dined with Mrs. Harry Higgins : Baron Michiels, the Max-Mullers, Olive, and a few more. Michiels has been eight months in Russia and has only recently returned across Germany, where he finds a great change for the worse in general conditions — especially in the railway service, which is slow and bad. He says that one cannot get from The Hague to Berlin in a day now, and that one has to stay the night at Hanover.

CHAPTER XVIII

MR. LLOYD GEORGE REVIEWS THE SITUATION
MARCH 1917

A speech by Sir Edward Carson on the submarines—The first Dardanelles Report out—It creates amazement—The port of Southampton—Our wheat and flour supplies—General Maurice on the situation—General Yermoloff's views—General Geddes on Man-Power—A talk with M. Albert Thomas—General Lyautey resigns—General Lawson's combing-out work in France—General Robertson on the Calais Agreement—His opinion of General Nivelle—Lord French on the German voluntary retirement—Princess Clémentine on journalists—A letter from Sir Archibald Murray from Egypt—The Scottish Office on the Army—The Russian Revolution—Lord Jellicoe and the War Staff—Lord Milner and the Russian Revolution—Mr. Balfour's views—Rumours of raids and invasions—My telephone keeps on ringing—A visit to the Russian Embassy—M. Wolkoff's amusing repartee—German and British figures of submarine sinkings—The Haig-Nivelle trouble—A luncheon for the Prime Minister and the Russians—Mr. Lloyd George's severity—Our food supplies—The Prime Minister's doubts about German reserves and invasion—His views on the general situation—Our ration strengths—General Robertson on Italy and Russia.

Wednesday, March 7. Lady Paget, the Ernest Cunards, and Sir Matthew (Scatters) Wilson lunched with me at the Ritz. Cunard tells me that his tramps now keep the submarines under water by their guns, and the pests dare not come to the surface within two miles of them. So their speed is reduced to that submerged, which is not much more than that of the tramp steamers. Also we now use smoke-producing devices, as the Huns did at the Jutland battle, and often escape in consequence. Scatters very much against remaining at Salonika, whence he has recently returned. He says that Milne and Sarrail are quarrelling, but Lady Granard and others tell me that Scatters has been at Lake Doiran and knows little of things going on at Salonika.

Thursday, March 8. Northcliffe and his brother, Sir Leicester Harmsworth, came up early, and we talked Man-Power, etc. My letter of March 3 to the P.M. was read to them. They started the surprising idea of having an Army Council of civilians. I poured scorn upon it. I went to the luncheon to Sir E. Carson, given by the Aldwych Club, at the Connaught Rooms, Great Queen Street. Northcliffe presided. Carson made a fine speech which was duly reported. A great gathering. I sat opposite to Carson and watched his style of oratory closely. He had five sheets of notepaper and referred to them often, in order, I fancy, to get the precise effect of words that he intended. He began slow and calm, without gestures, and gradually worked up, raising his voice, and then using first one arm and then both to enforce his point. He seemed to speak no louder than he would at a dinner table, but I found afterwards that he was well heard by all the several hundred guests. He appeared to me to be pessimistic about the submarines. On Tribunal all the evening.

Friday, March 9. Lunched with Mrs. Keppel: Lady Sarah, Sir Sidney Greville, and a few more. Dined with Olive to meet the Duke of Connaught: only Lady Leslie, Bridget, and Captain Arthur Murray, M.P., besides. The Duke was very charming, and was most flattering about my work. The Duchess is very ill with a complication of diseases. The Duke has refused the office of I.G. of the Overseas Forces, on account of restrictions imposed upon him, it is said by Lord French, and the King recommended the refusal.

Saturday, March 10. The Dardanelles Report is out and has created great interest and amazement. The public know at last how the direction of the war was mismanaged during 1914 and 1915.

Lunched with X. as Sir W. Robertson was ill in bed with a bad chill. X. did not know what had been settled at Calais, but says that the whole Army Council mean to stand and fall together. Man-Power was no better, and nothing had been done. There are at present 63 divisions in France, including 10 Dominion and 1 Portuguese, 6 at Salonika, 3 in Egypt, 3 in India, but there are the makings of another division at Salonika and a dismounted division of Yeomanry is in Egypt. We have nearly 2,000,000 men now in France in the aggregate, and there are 8 divisions at home, including those forming. We have not been allowed to send troops and supplies across the Channel at night while there is a moon. We had twenty-two days' reserve supplies in France last August, but it has fallen one day a month since. The railways in France are still in a bad state. Southampton has cleared 2,500,000 men going abroad, 600,000 horses, 600,000 vehicles, and 6000 guns from Aug. 4, 1914, to Dec. 24, 1916, on which day the 10,000th troop train steamed into the Docks. Going out and coming in the port has handled 3,350,000 men. McMunn wired from a point thirty-four miles from Bagdad three days ago that the supply was safe and that he had lots with him. I saw a return showing that the daily supply going up the river, which was formerly 200 tons, was now 2888 tons. We have 5 Indian and 1 white division—the 13th—in Mesopotamia, and 2 brigades of cavalry. Murray has 1 Anzac and 1 Yeomanry mounted division. Maude reports that he has only 5000 men in front of him. He intends to occupy the advanced posts Hit and Samarra on the two rivers, and can then maintain himself in Bagdad.

I saw a friend who gave me the figures of our wheat and flour supplies for the week ending Jan. 20 last, in quarters (? 320 lbs. each):

(1) Wheat, and flour as wheat, imported .	430,000	quarters
(2) Weekly consumption of foreign wheat	455,000	,,
,, ,, ,, home grown .	165,000	,,
(3) Total wheat and flour imported since July 29, 1916	10,535,000	,,
(4) Foreign wheat and flour in U.K. ports	1,625,000	,,
(5) British wheat undelivered , .	4,100,000	,,
Afloat and orders . . .	2,195,000	,,

(6) In farmers' hands, U.K. ports and
 afloat, and America and Canadian
 visible supply   .   .   .   . 28,271,000 quarters.

(This last figure was 21,000,000 two years ago.)

From this I gather that if the weekly consumption is 620,000 quarters, the yearly consumption is $620,000 \times 52 = 32,240,000$ quarters, and that this supply for a year ahead is practically assured, excluding all question of Argentine, Indian, and Australian wheat. I also recall the old Food Supply Report, which said that 10 per cent. of the trade normally plying on our maritime routes could bring us all the food we needed. There is plenty of meat in the country. Potatoes are short because the last crop was poor, and the price now is £9, 5s. a ton, and is to be raised to £10, 5s. on April 1, so farmers are naturally holding up for the higher price. I am told that there has been practically no variation in these figures during the war, and no visible sign even of the beginning of shortage. All this is comforting, except for the Huns.

Saw Fred Maurice, who wants me to write about the question of the employment of officers of the Old and New Armies. I must do so. He says that the idea that this war is different from any other has been said of all wars, and that it was the trained officers who shone in the American Civil War and not the untrained. He says that we have good trench officers, but that they are of little use outside it from the New Armies, and that the Mesopotamia railways are G.S. work and mean strategy. He still believes that the Germans are coming west. There is every indication of it, and none of anything else. The Russians have 3,500,000 men on their front, including 1,900,000 rifles, and ought to be quite safe against attack, but they are a feckless lot and their air service is putrid. They know nothing of signalling from the air to batteries. We are trying to teach them. They go up and drop bombs casually by night and return. They are better off for guns and shells than ever before. The German retreat in France is natural, but has thrown us out and compelled us to alter our dispositions more than the French understand, as the retreat at present affects us more than the French. We may now have to wait till the middle of May before attacking. The 'Hindenburg line' runs from Lens by Cambrai and St. Quentin to Laon, and has fifty yards depth of barbed wire in front of it throughout. It is not certain how long the Huns will stand on their position, but their aim is evidently to cut off their large salient and reduce the length of their line. M. thinks that they will mass a great reserve in the West, east of the Arras front, to counter-attack us, and if we fail they may send divisions to attack Italy. If we wait till late in May the Huns may attack near the coast and try to take Dunkirk. M. thinks that the Huns have not yet made up their minds where to attack, and he says that the intense cold in Germany, which has frozen up the waterways and the substitutes for grease in the axle boxes, has delayed German preparations more than ours. Briand, Cambon, Thomas, Ribot, Lyautey, and Nivelle are coming over on Monday for a fresh talk. M. thinks that Archie Murray is all right, though six Turkish divisions are concentrating against him. I hope he is right. Archie has the Welsh, East Anglian, and Lowland T.F. divisions only, and no Regulars or New Army people. Went down to Coombe. Only Mr. McKenna and Sir Fritz Ponsonby the first night, and we had a pleasant four at Bridge with Lady Paget.

Sunday, March 11. On Sunday there came down Lady Granard, Mrs. Keppel, the Edwin Montagus, Jack Cowans and Sir Arthur. Had a talk and a walk with the latter in the morning. He has only one good New Army division complete with 18 prs., three brigades on the coast each with 8 guns, 15 prs., and three divisions in formation but with no guns yet. There are also his Yeomanry and cyclists, while the training brigades are to join him in case of need, and he has just been given 200 Hotchkiss guns. Bruce Hamilton has two divisions forming, and two coast brigades. French has one New Army division in reserve at Bedford. I suppose that they make up the eight divisions at home by adding that in Ireland. A precious miscellaneous lot, and Sir Arthur thinks that the Huns can come any day. They have reconnoitred the coast four times and have opened fire, and each time have got away without interference. A wet afternoon. We discussed the question of Nivelle being given the command over our Armies in France. I opposed it warmly: so did McKenna. Montagu favoured it: so did Sir Arthur. I hear that the instruction is actually issued. Derby and Robertson were not at the War Cabinet when the matter was settled, but Robertson and Haig have initialed the instruction, agreement, or whatever it is. A bad business, and sure to breed endless mischief.

McKenna said that when Hardinge's private letter to Buchanan, captured by the Boches and published, was read out the other day in the House by Dillon, Hardinge, who had been satirical about McKenna, wrote to the latter to apologise. McKenna wrote back regretting Hardinge's ignorance of his (McKenna's) financial arrangements with the Russians. He had already fixed it up with Bark to give four millions a month to help the rouble and the Russian exchange. We heard that Maude had occupied Bagdad this Sunday morning, March 11. Drove back to town with Jack late Sunday night.

Monday, March 12. I looked in at Whitehall Court to have a talk with General Yermoloff, the Russian Military Attaché, whom I had not seen for a long time, and I found him more communicative than usual. He was very pleased about Bagdad and the situation generally. He thought that the German submarine campaign was a sign of weakness and an attempt to win the war by trickery. He did not think that it would succeed, and did not believe that the Germans, in spite of their new troops, had the momentum for a grand offensive. He thought that the German reserves would act as Reserves and be used for counter-offensives. We were neither of us prepared to say which way the German reserves would go, and agreed to let each other know the first news about them. Yermoloff did not fear a German advance on the Riga front, and had news pointing to the possibility of a German retreat on this side. I told him that the new German forces on the Dutch frontier had moved into Belgium, and supposed that the closing of the Dutch frontier was to prevent desertion. He could not understand the delay of the Germans to move, but I passed it on to him that it was probably due to the hard and long winter, and to the disorganisation of their railway and inland waterways owing to the frost. He thought that the German people were almost starving, and that the German leaders must know that the submarine campaign promised to be a failure. He supposed that the plan was for Yudenitch, Murray, and Maude to combine their operations, but did not know if this were so. We agreed to differ about Salonika, but he thought that the Turk was in a bad way and might make a separate peace. Y. said that the Germans wanted Verdun as a pivot, especially if they went back to the Meuse, and he quite thought that they might recommence their attack here. We discussed the ' Hindenburg line,' of which he had not heard.

I went on to have a talk with General A. C. Geddes about recruiting. He no longer works with Neville Chamberlain, with whom he has fallen out. He says that N. C. has got a jellyfish at St. Ermin's Hotel and will never turn it into a mammal. It is hopeless chaos. If Geddes thought that we were to postpone a serious offensive till 1918, he would be in favour still of compulsory National Service, but he does not think that the French can stand the delay, so he is in favour of (1) raising the age limit for service to forty-five, with power to increase to fifty by Order in Council; (2) making an end of all extension of exemptions by two months, as in the Service Acts; (3) medical re-examination within one year for men discharged from the Army, and within six months on other medical certificates. This would replace the whole business under the A.G. They had hoped to get a strong man to do the work which N. C. is not doing, and to make him the lightning conductor for public resentment at the sacrifices required. It was difficult for L. G. to quarrel with the Chamberlain interest. Geddes says that Compulsory National Service is the cleanest job, but it will take six months to organise before a man begins to come in for training, and that the delays which have happened no longer justify this course. He can get his men the other way, beginning a fortnight after the amendments in the Service Act are passed. There are 1,250,000 men aged forty-one to fifty, and Geddes would make a solid Home Defence Force with them, and use the rest as substitutes so as to get younger men out of munitions, etc. There are over 800,000 men of military age in munition works, and we have only got 10,000 out of them. There seem to be more A men in the home forces than I knew. There are 150,000, but mainly in Yeomanry, cyclists, Garrison R.A., and R.E., etc. We have actually nearly 1,600,000 men at home, including 200,000 in the hospitals. Geddes agrees that we should not attack till May 15, and says that it is written on the figures. Geddes has told N. C. his mistakes with almost brutal frankness, and has refused L. G.'s request to become N. C.'s deputy, urging L. G. to keep at least one part of his recruiting machinery clear of lumber. Geddes had seen much of the War Cabinet. He considers that L. G. is crushed with detail. Every booby who has some small personal or other grievance thinks himself justified in worrying the P.M. Milner, who has been away in Russia all this time, has his feet firmly on the ground and understands. It is necessary to convince L. G., Bonar Law, and Milner in order to get on. Geddes thinks that he can get all he wants by short amendments of the M.S. Act.

Wednesday, March 14. M. Albert Thomas, who has come with the French mission, telephoned to ask me to see him at the Ritz, and I went there at 3.30 after lunching at the Ian Hamiltons'. Found M. Thomas full of energy and activity. After mutual compliments we began to talk. We discussed operations first and gave each other our ideas about German intentions, I refusing to commit myself until the German reserves had moved out from the interior, but I suggested a postponement of our attack until May 15. I asked him if he was pleased about the decisions of the recent Calais Conference and of the Conference in London which finished yesterday. He thinks that the question of the Command has now been settled satisfactorily, and that Haig and Nivelle are in agreement. He admitted that it was impracticable to place 2,000,000 British troops under a French Commander, but spoke of 'directives,' from which I gather that Nivelle is to issue such directives and Haig to conform. But the two G.H.Q.'s are to be near together and the Generals are to confer instead of writing, and I also understand that there is some 'security' clause, which probably means that we are not to be asked to engage elsewhere the troops needed for holding our lines. I said that I hoped that some of the Salonika troops were coming away, and, when he asked how many, I suggested ten divisions as a beginning. He did not seem to believe we should much reduce the garrison, and spoke hopefully of the things about to be accomplished by Sarrail. Thomas said that he hoped he would not be regarded as a *sale politicien* when he visited the British H.Q. I said I hoped not, but that he was regarded as *un homme terrible* who was inclined to interfere in military affairs. He said that Millerand had allowed the French G.Q.G. to assume too great responsibilities, and had forbidden any one to interfere with them—T. suiting his actions to his words and fending off some imaginary persons with his hands. The result was that the G.Q.G. had almost monopolised diplomacy, and that policy and strategy had not been kept in their proper spheres. Nivelle's G.Q.G. was now quite different, and had been shorn of many of the old powers. We had a good deal of talk on these subjects and about the prospects of the war. I asked him about the French moral, and he told me that during the winter he had been much concerned about the attitude of the French troops, as they had become listless and there was much grumbling, but that now things were better, and it only needed one good victory to make things all right. He feared to postpone an attack and give the initiative to the enemy. He found that the

French and British politicos got on well after a good talk. He asked me Robertson's opinions on certain points, and I said that I could not take it upon myself to give them. He made me promise to come and see him in Paris and to visit some of his munition factories. I said I would come before the fighting if possible. He grumbled about coal, but on the whole seemed fairly well satisfied. Not a very attractive personality on the whole, but full of energy, and people speak well of him.

Thursday, March 15. News comes that General Lyautey has resigned, after refusing information to the French Chambers about confidential matters connected with aviation. The very sad news of the Duchess of Connaught's death also came this morning, and will cause great grief to the good Duke's many friends.

Dined with Mrs. Astor: Evelyn FitzGerald, Sir Matthew and Lady Wilson, Evan Charteris, Lady Essex, Charles Whibley, Lady Juliet Duff, and Mr. and Mrs. Laughlin of the American Embassy. Talked with Evelyn and Scatters after dinner. Stayed to talk with the hostess after the others had left. Juliet told me that her mother sees no one now but her and Mrs. Sneyd. On my way I thought what a wretched system it was to make the French War Minister practically Chief of Staff, for he had no permanence and was liable to be upset by any political side wind. It may please French politicians to have the War Minister under their thumb, but it is not the way to promote continuity of strategic plans. However, Robertson and I foresaw this situation when poor Joffre was given his congé.

Friday, March 16. General Lawson came up to Maryon. We discussed the war, and he then told me that he had been round in France on a combing-out expedition and had reported that from 100,000 to 200,000 men, young and physically fit, now serving in France as clerks, storemen, motor and lorry drivers, servants, grooms, bathmen, and laundrymen, could well be replaced by older men. For remount, veterinary, transport, and labour work coloured labour could be employed. The whites must be B and C men, and he thinks they can be set free at home. But the technical corps are under various powerful heads which think of their own services first. Lawson thinks that reserve and training brigades might set free the provisional brigades on the coast south of the Wash where they exist, and that the B and C men from them might go to France. He also expects to draw men from administrative services at home by substituting women. All good work if any one will take it up.

Saturday, March 17. Went to the War Office in the afternoon to see Sir W. Robertson. The 'Hindenburg line' of defence of the enemy appears to run from Arras south-east to La Fère : whether it thence runs to Laon or Soissons is uncertain. A direct line of trenches from about Lille cuts in east of Arras and joins the other. We must regard the recent German withdrawal to this line as voluntary. Found Sir William looking a bit worn from his fortnight's hard work. He said that the Frenchmen told him with tears that *our* people had raised the question of giving Nivelle the supreme command. It had come up at the Calais Conference, and R. supposes that our War Conference settled it beforehand without consulting him. He was very displeased with the result of that Conference. There had almost immediately been trouble between Nivelle and Haig, and the London Conference had been hastily summoned to make things better. Haig was not now under Nivelle, but I understand is to some extent subject to his general directions. However, R. thinks that there will not be much great change now. I asked him what he thought of Nivelle. R. preferred Joffre, who was a much bigger man and a great fixed point in the Entente system. He has gone, and now Lyautey has gone too. R. says he is the fourth who has got the G. or K.C.M.G. and has promptly vanished. R. will advise Fritz Ponsonby to be less lavish with these decorations, or there will not be enough to last out the war. R. has now again no opposite number, and will still have none if Painlevé is made War Minister. If the French appointed Castelnau as C.G.S. it would be better. Our system was much the best. It was bad to have a whole administration constantly disorganised by the fall of its Chief as the French W.O. had been. R. is of opinion that the Germans will keep their great reserves centrally situated and will use them for counter-attack, but Haig's staff think that Ypres may be attacked. He thought that possibly we were overrating the enemy, and he could not think where any more German drafts could come from. In this case a German division badly mauled could be ruled out. Nivelle had desired to attack, March 1. It was probable that this had become known to the enemy, who had begun to go back three days earlier to throw us all out. But actually we should not attack for several weeks. The disadvantage of having a War Minister in France as a channel for communications was that his references to Allied Armies had to go through the Foreign Offices, and heaps of copies were struck off and secrecy could not be expected. He and Lyautey had agreed, in spite of things, to communicate confidentially between each other directly, as it was the only way to preserve secrecy, but now Lyautey had been dismissed. R. said that the published accounts of the Russian revolution gave too rosy a view. Actually, it was not clear who was master or what would happen. It might be that a much more socialistic republic would emerge. No one could tell, but meanwhile all the services of the Army might be disorganised. Possibly many German divisions more might now come West. All that R. was sure of was that we were not doing our best. He and the Army Council continued to warn the Government, but without avail, and nothing had been done since L. G. took office to solve the Man-Power problem. There was no change. He could not tell me the excuse or even the point of view of the War Cabinet, but thought it would be a good scheme for me to see Milner.

We turned to the East. R. meant to stop at Bagdad. He allowed Mosul to be talked of, but did not mean to go there. When we had shepherded down the Russians from the Persian side and got them going, we had done all that was needed. We should just clear up the surrounding country, and that was all. He meant to bring away the 13th division and one or two Indian divisions, and to throw a lot of troops in with Murray this summer. Murray was all right, and in a month or so would get going again. I had met Lady Murray in the hall and she had told me that Archie had said, in reply to a question by her, that his birthday would be important. It is April 20. As soon as R. could get the troops from E. Africa they would also go to Murray, who was getting another nine battalions of Sudanese and Indian troops. R. saw no hope of withdrawing divisions from Salonika at present. Sarrail had some potty plan, but there was nothing to be done there R. thought.

I called on Lord French afterwards to hear about the Zepp. raid last night. The Zepps. had hung about in the Thames estuary and had probably lost their way. One dropped some bombs harmlessly in fields. Another drifted south, with engine trouble apparently, and had been brought down by the French at Compiègne, all the crew being burnt alive as usual. The Field-Marshal gave me his appreciation of the position in France. He said that the Germans had retired to confuse us, and to take up better ground and shorten their line. It was true that ours was shortened too, but the shortening was of more value to the defensive, and he reckons the enemy to be in that attitude. He thought that the enemy was awaiting the result of the U-boat war. If it failed, he considered that they would either resume peace negotiations or try a great blow at England as a mighty gamble, and sacrifice their fleet to try and get into England. I quite agreed. He said that they must try something great, as the vitality of the whole population was becoming dangerously lowered. Dined with Lady Juliet at 16 Upper Brook Street. Lady Pembroke and Cecil Lowther also there. A delightful evening: much amusing talk. These little parties *à quatre* are much the pleasantest in these times, especially when the ladies are as handsome and charming as these two.

Sunday, March 18.   Called to see Sammy Scott in Mount Street in the morning.   He was looking very fit after his two years' hard service in Gallipoli and Egypt.   Lunched with Lord Haldane.   We discussed the whole situation of Germany, and arrived at the conclusion that in her desperate situation a blow at England was a logical necessity.   The only question is whether the Boches think that the U-boats will do the trick.   Dined with Lady Granard : Mrs. Stanley, Mrs. Bingham, McKenna, Montagu, Lord Lascelles, Murray Graham, and one or two more. Pleasant dinner.   I had just begun a fascinating talk with McKenna and Montagu, the latter sharing Haldane's point of view about an attack on us, when in rushed the hostess to say that the drawing-room chimney was on fire, and what was she to do ?   We said ' Ring for the Fire Brigade,' and most brutally went on with the port and our talk.   When we went in we found one fireman squirting something down the chimney from the roof, and another squirting it up from the drawing-room.   The upper fireman put out the lower one, and then we cleared up and played Bridge.

Monday, March 19.   Lunched with E. and met General Dessino, who was still without news of his Japanese cable.   He was furious because he had made three attempts to see the P.M. and had not succeeded, nor even had any reply.   So like L. G.'s way of going on !   So Dessino had written to Petrograd that there was no use in keeping him here, and that a lieutenant would be more suitable than a Lieutenant-General as *chef de mission.*   We discussed the war together.   He says that a reactionary Russian General has arrived here with a bâton for the King and a trunk full of decorations, but as the Revolution has broken out, no one knows what to do with the man, or his luggage.   We decided to have another talk later.   Dined at the Carton de Wiarts' and met the de Lalaings, General Comte de Jonghe the new Belgian *chef de mission,* and Belle Herbert.

De Jonghe and I disputed somewhat after dinner, but I like a man who stands up for his opinions.

Tuesday, March 20.   Lunched at the Carlton with Sir Matthew and Lady Wilson.   He wanted to consult me about a speech which he was going to make during the Dardanelles debate to-day, and I gave him an unimportant suggestion or two.   It was quite a good speech, but he attaches more weight to the Whip's opinion of what he ought to say than I should have done.   He also gave me the paper on Salonika which he has given to various high personages, and I did not like it at all, for reasons which I gave him.   Tribunal all the evening, and was late dining with Olive.

Wednesday, March 21.   Revised two articles, and wrote a fairly long one on the military situation.   Saw Maude Cassels in the afternoon with her girl and the son-in-law, who seems a very nice fellow.   Went on to see Lady Ridley in the evening for a few moments.

Thursday, March 22.   Lunched with Princess Clémentine and Prince Victor Napoleon at the Berkeley Grill.   We had a great talk on the war.   Victor regrets Lyautey's fall very much, and they both fear that the Russian Revolution will spread in Europe, and are anxious about it.   He tells me that his brother, Prince Louis, is with Cadorna, and writes that the Huns will have to bring 100 divisions to overcome Italy.   We all agree that the advance down the Meuse is still the correct strategy for the French, but see no prospect of it being carried out.[1]   We had a gay talk.   The Princess, discussing the Haig interview, declared that 'rien n'est pire qu'un journaliste,' to which I replied that I was convinced that madame was right as I was one myself.   Of course she replied that I was a critic and not a journalist, and I congratulated her on the *adresse* with which she had *tiréd* herself from the *embarras*.   They are at Farnborough with the Empress,—who is now ninety-one—from Fridays to Tuesdays, and the Tuesdays to Fridays at the Hans Crescent Hotel.   There are few visitors at

─────────

[1] It was carried out in September 1918.

Farnborough now, they say, but the Empress is still in the full possession of all her faculties.

Dined with the Scarbroughs and Lady Lowther in Park Lane. S. is at Astral House in his new appointment, and is working up the Volunteers as he formerly did the Territorials. He says that they have 140 rifles per battalion, and will get 50 more a week each up to 400 per battalion.

Friday, March 23. Murray writes the following letter to me from Egypt :

GENERAL HEADQUARTERS,
EGYPTIAN EXPEDITIONARY FORCE,
11th March 1917.

MY DEAR REPINGTON,—Just a line to tell you shortly the situation. The Turks had taken up an enormously strong position in the neighbourhood of Shellal and occupied it with about 12,000 or 14,000 men. I had hoped that they would remain and let me attack them as soon as my railway reached Rafa, but when the line had reached Sheikh Zowaiid, within about 10 or 12 miles of Rafa, they retreated, and are now on the line Gaza–Tel el Sharia–Beersheba with about 33,000 men, either on that line or to the south of Jerusalem. On this line they are for the present outside my striking radius, so I have to wait until the railway is fully established at Rafa before I can strike. I do not believe they will stand on the line Gaza–Beersheba. They have a holy fear of our cavalry and, as they cannot place both flanks on an obstacle, fear the result of a general engagement.

I shall be glad to establish myself at Rafa, because here the desert is almost at an end, and the ground sound enough for wheeled traffic as long as it is not too heavy. Up to now I have not been able to use anything ahead of the railway but the old camel, who has done me right well, but is very slow.

For the moment the interest centres in the Hedjaz. I think the Turks wish to withdraw their troops from there in consequence of my advance. If they stayed they could no doubt hold Medina for some months against the Arabs until starved out. If they try to retire north I think the Arabs will give them a very bad time, using harassing tactics and interrupting the railway as much as possible. I shouldn't be at all surprised if that Turkish force never saw Palestine again. The G.O.C. the

Turkish 4th Army wants these troops to reinforce his army against me. In view of Joe Maude's successes the Turks are not in a very happy condition, and if the war should be carried on into next winter we ought, with the help of the Russians, to lop off Asia Minor.

Next month will see the opening of the Spring campaign in all western theatres except perhaps the Russian. We wonder where the blows are to fall, and whether Haig will be able to make good his public utterances.—Yours very sincerely,

A. J. MURRAY.

A. C. Geddes sends me an amusing letter about Neville Chamberlain, who, he says, has been slow to understand that he was called on to effect substitution, and the concentration of labour in essential industries. Instead, he has created staffs and departments without functions that G. has been able to discover, and has not yet got down to his real job. His functions should be ancillary to the fighting departments and their subsidiaries, munitions and shipbuilding. He also gives me a delightful instance of the way we are governed. He says that the Scottish Office has expressed an opinion that the Army's demands for men are in excess of requirements. The fact that this office is completely ignorant of the Army's requirements does not prevent it from laying down the law on the subject. A nice country!

The Russian Revolution which began on March 13 resulted in the formation of a Provisional Government under Prince Lvoff, the abdication of the Tsar, the imprisonment of the reactionary Ministers, the adhesion of the Provinces, and the consent of the chief Generals in command of Armies. Whether we are told everything is at present uncertain, and many fear the recurrence of trouble, but on the whole the change meets with general approval here, and also in America. It is a mighty big transformation scene, caused by the crass stupidity of the Tsar, Tsaritsa, and their cronies. Wilton at Petrograd has kept the *Times* remarkably well informed about it all.

Saturday, March 24. Spent the morning in reading.

Went down to see Lady Ridley after lunch, and had a good talk with her on political affairs. There then joined us Mrs. Ferdy Stanley and Lady Florence Willoughby, and we played Bridge till 6.30 P.M. Lady Gwendeline Churchill came in to tea. Dined with Lady Cunard: Lady Randolph, Arthur Balfour, Admiral and Lady Jellicoe, Lady Johnstone, Lady Essex, M. Nabokoff, Mrs. Keppel, Bogey Harris, and Lord Lascelles. Lady Jellicoe told me that during the first three months of the war, when there was no safe port, Jellicoe had coaled and victualled at sea and had only entered harbour twice. She was very critical of the way Balfour had announced the Jutland fight: she had to explain and excuse her Admiral's action. She thought the official Admiralty approval of Jellicoe's proceedings very cold. She said that the Admiral now skated in the morning at Prince's, but took little other exercise. The War Staff constantly rang him up at night, and as he was gun-deaf it devolved on her as a rule to wake him up. I said that she ought to stop the Staff waking him up except in case of real necessity, but she said that she could not oppose his wishes. The worst was that when he had given an order he turned over and went to sleep, while she lay awake thinking of the lives that would be lost. A woman of character.

Jellicoe did not encourage us much about the submarines, and Balfour said that yesterday had been an awful day, one of the worst. Jellicoe said that the Army must win the war. What else but an Army ever did win a war? We had some talk of Russia. Balfour said that Milner had been quite wrong about the Revolution on his return from Russia, and had said that it would not take place as there was no important figure round whom it could crystallise, but Balfour said that the French Revolution began without such a figure. Balfour says that he has given Buchanan a free hand, as he is on the spot and knows all. I said 'You are treating him as you should a General in the field.' He said, 'Yes, it is a parallel case.' There was still a good deal of doubt about what would happen, but to-day's news was better. Nabokoff said that he had warned Miliukoff, the Foreign Minister of the Provisional Government, not to give us so much news about the Tsar and his doings, but more of the political situation, the attitude of the Provinces and great towns, the feeling of the Army, etc. Balfour approved this very much. It is thought that the Tsar and all his family will come here, and Balfour hopes that they will be well protected until they start. Mrs. Keppel says that all the Imperial appanages have been sequestrated. What will the Grand Dukes do now? Especially the G. D. Michael, who has £30,000 from the appanages and £5000 a year from money invested in Germany. Neither source looks like yielding any more income. Many stories of the blank refusal of the Tsar to listen to endless warnings. Nabokoff thinks he had never thrown off the evil influence of Pobiedonotseff's training, but the Tsaritsa is undoubtedly responsible for much. Balfour says that no plenipotentiary ever gave a more serious warning to a great monarch than Milner gave to the Tsar. Many rumours to-night of raid and invasion and movements of troops. Drove down to the Horse Guards with Mrs. Keppel and Lady Essex after dinner to see if they had any news, but found all quiet.

Sunday, March 25. Walter Scott, the excellent assistant Foreign Editor, telephoned to me from the *Times* office this morning that Wilton had cabled from Petrograd on the 23rd that Alexeieff had told him that the Germans were concentrating on the Riga front, that the Provisional Government were issuing an appeal for unity on this plea, that the position was serious, and that Wilton was off to this front which would be the centre of interest. What did I think? I said that the weather was unpropitious for a German attack, that the political trouble in the Russian Northern Army had calmed down, that I knew nothing of a German concentration in the north, and that I supposed that the Provisional Government were using the rumours in order to promote unity. I then referred to Maurice who almost repeated my words, and added that so far as was known no German reserves from the interior had gone north. This I passed on to Scott, and told Northcliffe all about it when he rang me up this morning to ask about last night's rumours. N. says that all the wires were blocked last night and that there was a panic at Broadstairs, Margate, etc., caused by a schoolmaster and a squire, and that all the population and schools had taken wing. Marjorie rang me up from the Cliffords' place in Devonshire, anxiously inquiring about the rumours, which appear to have penetrated to the West of England. Later there came other inquiries from all sorts of quarters. What will it be like if one Boche lands ?

Monday, March 26. Spent most of the day arranging a Russo-British lunch for Thursday at Lloyd George's request. He and General Dessino had fallen out, while Northcliffe and Nabokoff had been put against each other by the stupidity of somebody. I managed to smooth them all down, and arranged the luncheon. Dessino tells me that Baratoff, who is advancing on the Tigris from Persia, has only a cavalry division and a scrap of infantry. He and Maude are not in communication, and Maude wired to our W.O. to know what Baratoff was doing. Dessino wired to Petrograd, and Petrograd to Baratoff, who replied, and the reply came back to Maude in forty-eight hours after the devil of a roundabout trip. Why on earth could they not have wireless ?

I had a long talk with Nabokoff at the Embassy. He evidently hopes to be left in charge, as the Government will have no authority to send an Ambassador with credentials, and he rather hinted that we might make known that he was doing well here, both in the Press and through the F.O. I am inclined to agree, as he is young, capable, and friendly. He made out all things in Russia to be satisfactory, but admitted that he had spent a miserable ten days, not knowing whether the whole of Russia would be plunged into complete anarchy. He wants to get rid of Yermoloff, who does not work in with the Embassy, but is in a difficult

position respecting him. We talked of the use to be made
of the Russians in England for war purposes. I told him
that I was still very uneasy about affairs in Russia. He
seems to stand well with the new Government, and hopes
that they will soon consult him and not only send him orders.
Passing out through Wolkoff's room I noticed the prints of
various Tsars on the wall. I said, ' Hullo ! you will have to
change these, my dear Wolkoff.' ' Oh, no ! ' said Wolkoff.
' This *was* a picture gallery. It *is* a museum.'

Tuesday, March 27. I was shown to-day the last figures
of our cereals (see diary, March 10). There is no material
change. The import is 455,000 quarters. The American
and Canadian visible supply is 17,550,000 quarters. It is
thought that Ministers are trying to scare us, and that our
main food supplies are assured. But I see that the German
Press on March 18 claim officially that they expected
to sink 600,000 Allied tons, and actually sank 780,000
tons in February, or much more than they expected,
and that our imports were reduced 30 per cent. They
regard our Admiralty figures as an imposture. Even so,
we have atoned for the falling off by forbidding non-essential
imports, and our main food supply is not yet seriously
imperilled. I went to the War Office. Whigham and I
discussed the West. He does not know what the Germans
propose to do, but assumes that they may propose to stand
on the line Lille–Douai–Cambrai–St. Quentin–La Fère–Vailly.
He says that the Man-Power problem remains unsolved,
and that we still have only drafts enough for three months'
serious fighting. Our casualties last month were only
20,000 in place of 100,000 expected, as we had no serious
fighting. So the deficit of last December is made good, which
is something. He says that Macready places the blame on
Arthur Henderson for the failure of the War Cabinet to
act. Robertson returns to-night from a visit to Italy
and France. He has been away a week.

Wednesday, March 28. I lunched with Sir Ian and
Lady Hamilton, Mrs. Lindsay, and the Comte de Noailles.
We had some talk about the Dardanelles. Ian is up

before the Commission for what he calls his 'finals.'
He quoted to them yesterday a paragraph in a recent
article of mine which stated that a division without drafts
and that had been hammered might be written off the
account. This is what happened to some of his troops at
Gallipoli. De Noailles and I walked back across the
Park together. He told me that the trouble which arose
between Haig and Nivelle after the Calais Conference which
had placed Haig under Nivelle was due to a crisp order
sent to Haig by Nivelle through d'Alençon, who is Nivelle's
Staff man. De Noailles says that French orders are
crisper, shorter, and firmer than ours, but I pointed out the
difference between *Befehle* and *Directiven*, and said that
people in Nivelle's place issued directions not orders. De
Noailles said that Huguet used to hocus Joffre's orders
and place them before Lord French in more acceptable
terms, and that it was d'Alençon's want of tact, and the
inability of the French liaison officer with Haig to speak
English, that caused the trouble. These matters were put
right by the late London Conference, which undid the harm
of the Calais decision, and though it was not quite certain
how the new arrangement would work, things tended to
return to the old practice. There was, however, a great
need of a C.I.G.S. in France, and there was no sign of one
being appointed. Pernot was now under Thomas, but why
the Controller of the Press should be under the Munitions
Ministry no one could explain. De Noailles also mentioned
a curious French scheme of dividing the British Armies into
two groups, with no Commander-in-Chief of the whole—
another attempt to divide up and diminish the importance
of the British Armies in France. I said that when the
secret history of these times came to be written, people
would be surprised to learn that far more time and energy
were expended by British and French soldiers in fighting
their own politicians than in fighting the enemy. If the
politicians would only go on leave and allow the soldiers
to carry on, victory was assured, but that I thought that
the politicians were doing their best to lose the war.

Thursday, March 29. There lunched with me at the Ritz, the Prime Minister, Northcliffe, General Dessino, Nabokoff, and Wolkoff. A private room and a most interesting talk. The P.M. a quarter of an hour late. We all began on Russia, and the P.M. discussed the events in that country with the Russians present. He had received bad news yesterday from Russia, and was very severe upon the indiscipline of the Army, plainly telling the Russian diplomatists that nothing was to be hoped from an Army without discipline. Nabokoff made the best of the situation, and Dessino declared that late last night he had received a long telegram from Alexeieff with much more favourable news, and he eventually promised to send the P.M. a copy. I asked Nabokoff why he did not call together the Russian journalists in London, and make them represent to their papers the state of feeling in England about the Revolution, but he said that their opinions were not valued in Russia, and that they seldom came to the Embassy. But Northcliffe said that they came to him, so he may be able to inspire them. We discussed some lighter subjects, including the Kaiser's pet ladies, of whom he seems to possess types in Norway, Venice, etc., as well as in Brussels. The P.M. much enjoyed this gossip, and his eyes twinkled as he listened to it. We then branched to food, and I found that Lloyd George shared my views about food in England. There were lots of meat, and a lot of wheat in sight, but he also said that there were oats, and that we could eat the horses that eat the oats, and then the oats too. The Welsh, he said, lived on oats, so why should not the rest of us ? But on the same principles he thought Germany would be able to squeeze through till the next harvest. He saw no reason why the Germans should lack guns and shells, as they had steel, coal, aluminium, etc., and he thought that we should see a great increase in the power of the German artillery this year. He threw doubt upon the German reserves, and said that some man had returned from Germany with a story that the Auxiliary Act in Germany had not had the effects anticipated, and, instead of releasing 1,500,000 men, had only added 150,000 men to the Army. I said that I preferred the deductions of Macdonogh and Dupont, who had always been so right throughout, but, of course, this last report suits the P.M.'s well-known views, and I must get Macdonogh to look into it. The P.M. asked me what I thought Germany would do. I replied that, assuming the German position to be on the verge of desperation, I saw nothing but an attack on England or on Italy. With the latter alternative the P.M. agreed, and we discussed Robertson's views, of which R. had sent me a summary last night. I said that we could throw troops from France into Italy as fast as we liked, and that the Italians had now a great many men in the field, but were short of guns, and had too old generals. The P.M. would not believe in invasion, and offered to eat a sausage for every German landed over 50,000. I told him that his Home Defence was very weak ashore.

The P.M. then gave us his view of the situation, and I was much struck by it. He thought that the Germans wanted peace, and that Hindenburg's view was that the Germans had already obtained more than they wanted. They could therefore afford to relinquish the territories which they did not desire to keep, including Northern France, parts of Belgium, and even a part of Alsace, besides Courland in the north. What they would cling to at all hazards was the route to the East, and the power of exploiting Asia Minor, which had enormous possibilities. They would then give up Courland, make Poland autonomous, offer to Russia a right-of-way through, but not possession of, the Straits, and would get as much foothold in Antwerp as they could haggle for. They would leave to us their colonies, except East Africa, which, he said, Smuts did not hanker after, although he had conquered it. In this case France might ask herself, and so might Russia, whether there was anything left worth fighting for; and if our Allies were satisfied, and did not much concern themselves about Antwerp, peace might come. He thought, however, that the French, from their high sense of honour, might not stop fighting unless Belgium were completely evacuated. This voluntary evacuation of Northern France and Belgium would save the face of the Belgian Army, and I suggested that in this hypothesis the line of the Meuse might be defended, and thence from north of Verdun by Metz to the Rhine. This evacuation, proceeding gradually, may work out to the Meuse by the end of the summer, and then we might all be so tired of fighting that we should more or less automatically accept the *fait accompli*, as it then would be. We should have Mesopotamia, and the French probably Syria, while the Russians would have Armenia, and Turkey would become a German fief. I wondered whether such evacuation as L. G. suggested, and the ravaging of Northern France, might not dispose the French to go on, but, on the whole, the project which the P.M. attributes to the Germans, or at least to Hindenburg, of whom he has a high opinion, is exceedingly interesting, and shows clearly the bent of the P.M.'s mind. The P.M. spoke very highly of Maude, and told us that Murray had just won a good victory in Syria. He was attacked by 20,000 Turks south of Gaza, had killed and wounded 6000 of the enemy, and had taken 900 prisoners and guns. I was delighted, and sent to Lady Murray the first news of it by telephone. I had a few words about Man-Power to the P.M. after lunch, but except the change in the Service Act about re-examination of the unfit, I found him indisposed to move.

I was given our ration strengths in the afternoon. They are :

1,710,000 in the U.K., including 326,000 in hospital.
2,000,000 (approximately) in France, including 55,000 in hospital.
  234,000 at Salonika.
  231,000 in Egypt, including 96,000 Indian troops.
   53,000 in East Africa—British, Indians, and Africans.
  172,000 troops and
  118,000 camp followers } in Mesopotamia.

4,518,000 Total.

Friday, March 30. Lunched with Lady Johnstone at 19 Seymour Street. Mrs. Cecil Higgins also there, and a Belgian military attaché marooned here. He thought that the German reserves in the Interior were at least twenty-five divisions, and he said that the Dutch would fight if their territory were violated in any way : they were very firm on this point. Lady J. told us many tales of the great want in Germany and of the numerous German desertions.

Dined with Lord Wimborne : Mr. Birrell, Olive, T. P. O'Connor, M.P., Sir F. E. and Lady Smith, and two pretty women, namely, Mrs. Esmé Arkwright and Miss Phyllis Boyd. Tact seems hardly T. P.'s forte, and he told the story of 'Birrell having become a Duke,' which Birrell did not relish at all. Also at dinner T. P. told us an interminably long yarn about nothing in particular, and F. E. was very caustic about it. The ladies charming. We discussed the Revolution after dinner.

Saturday, March 31. Jack Stirling lunched with me, and returns to France Monday. Went to the W.O. and told Maurice about L. G.'s spy story. Robertson came up, and they said that every politician was prepared to credit the talk of any one in khaki, if he were not over the rank of a captain. I went down to York House to see Robertson later. His small boy is ill with pneumonia. He told me that the P.M. had asked him to address 2000 Trade Unionists in the Central Hall, at Westminster, next Wednesday, and he wanted my advice as to what he would say. I gave him my views at some length, and he said that when I had gone he would jot it all down. We then discussed his Italian visit. Cadorna had wanted divisions from France ear-marked for Italy, but R. could not do this as divisions were always changing from the trenches to reserve, and *vice versa*. He had told Cadorna that before asking what the Allies could do to help Italy at a pinch, it was necessary to ask what Italy could do to help herself. He had told C. that he, R., would never pass a quiet night if he had to tremble at every report of a hostile division coming out of the Trentino upon his communications, and he advised C. to use his troops on that side to invade the Trentino and straighten out his line. He doubted whether C. would do it, however. All the plans had been made for Allied assistance, and we were going to send French and English officers to study the zone of concentration of the divisions to be sent. The Italians had stacks of men, he said, and though they had only fifty-three divisions they had 900 battalions, or the infantry for ninety divisions, and battalions were very strong. But the senior generals were too old and guns were too few. The Italians were in a great fright, for no particular reason, for there was no hostile concentration against them yet, but they thought that the German retreat in France might set free troops to come against Italy. I told R. of L. G.'s views of the general situation, and how I had worked them out in military terms. He was much interested, and said that when the last article of my 'chameleon' series came out, he would get his General Staff together, and discuss the plan credited to the Germans. I told him that I would fight the Germans with guns this year, and not play the game they wanted, namely, of constantly losing heaps of men against their prepared positions. He told me that the munitions were such a great store now that we could never use them, and he meant to limit the production. Maude and Murray were doing well, but he had not heard from the latter for four days, and had cabled for news. R. was very critical of the Russians. He said that Alexeieff was shooting men right and left, and could do nothing else, but the Provisional Government were trying to stop him. R. thought, still, that if the Russians could only hold the enemy now in their front, we ought to be thankful. More he did not expect, and he was anxious to know what might happen in the Caucasus, as our operations and Yudenitch's hung together. If things had not changed too much, we ought to lay out the Turk this year.

CHAPTER XIX

OPENING OF THE 1917 CAMPAIGN IN FRANCE

Explanation of forces at home—Our need of drafts—Every Department against the Army—Commander Grenfell harangues the Baltic Fleet—I address the 1900 Club on Man-Power and the War—General Geddes supports me—M. Sevastopoulo on Russian affairs—General Count de Jonghe on the coming attack—The American Women's Hospital—A letter from Sir Archibald Murray on his operations round Gaza—Success of the British attack of April 9 round Arras—General Robertson on the Russians—A talk with General Smuts—My objections to the Flanders operation—Smuts on German E. and S.-W. Africa—His ideas about the Teutonic race—A visit to Brentwood—Dispositions of our Southern Army in England—Miss Wilmot's gardens—Lord Derby's requests to me—General Nivelle takes the German first-line trenches in Champagne.

Sunday, April 1. Heavy fall of snow this morning. This winter seems endless. Here is the present distribution of the troops at home. Roughly they are :

> 320,000 in hospital, including Dominion troops.
> 400,000 administrative troops.
> 130,000 Dominion troops, mainly drafts.
> 400,000 Home Defence troops.
> 400,000 troops for drafting.
> 50,000 with other Government departments.

> 1,700,000 Total.

Of the Home Defence troops there are the local garrisons, 160,000; the Royal Defence Corps, some 40,000; and amongst Lord French's troops are included some drafting units. There are the Home Defence divisions, coast brigades, and all sorts of other troops. French's mobile troops are not much over 100,000 out of the 400,000. Of the 400,000 of all arms available for drafting, there are 230,000 infantry, but 180,000 of these on March 1 were either not trained or were young men of eighteen to nineteen. It is thought that by June some of the latter will have to be sent out. There were only 50,000 trained infantry drafts at home on March 1, and now, on April 1, we are 111,000 short of our right figures at home to keep up existing units. In France we are 15,000 over-strength on the whole. In March we had taken 35,000 A men, 26,000 A boys of eighteen, and 40,000 B and C. We want 500,000 men before the end of June, and do not see our way to them. Every department is against the Army, and every new director or controller attempts to get men from the Army. A new Director of Timber Supplies is the latest bureaucrat created, and he went at once to ask for 25,000 men, though he admitted having six months' reserve of timber in England. He has been referred to Neville Chamberlain. On the basis of last year's casualties we need from 100,000 to 120,000 drafts a month. Only 40,000 A men a month can be foreseen with any assurance. The Board of Agriculture last September admitted that 100,000 A men in excess of needs of agriculture could be taken, but when the W.O. tried to get some of them, there was a howl, yet these were the Board's own calculations. Agriculture has 500,000 men of military age, Munitions 800,000, the Admiralty a great many in supposed shipyards, but many really doing other work; and then there are all the certified trades. Railways have behaved well, but every man with a cabbage-patch is now claiming exemption on agricultural grounds. The Bill of last week was merely a clause of a larger Bill sent up to the War Cabinet by the Army Council. It has been so ill received that it seems useless to go on so far as agriculture is concerned. The War Cabinet will not face the music of the larger Bill,—increase of age, liability to forty-one, etc.—and everybody is mortally afraid of the Trade Unions. The Trade Card scheme is happily to be abolished. Its effect had been to enable the large Trade Unions to swallow the small ones. I asked recently if the National Service scheme had produced one man for the Army, and was assured that it had not. After four months' work ! The substitution part of the scheme has been handed over to the Labour Exchanges, which nobody trusts. It is all supposed to be working so as to go on with Compulsion, but I do not know what the scheme is, and have not met anybody else who knows. The Labour troubles at Barrow and in Wales are due to a few agitators who are well known, but on whom the Cabinet has not the pluck to lay hands. Every department is against the Army, and always says that if the department's needs of labour are not met, the country will be starved ! If they are fought, then they threaten labour troubles and strikes. As a result we are not winning the war. The A.G.'s Branch is capable—or at least Auckland Geddes is—of taking over the whole business of getting men for the Army, but it is not invited to do so, and our position may become almost desperate. The country knows absolutely nothing of all these facts, and I cannot tell them.

There came to lunch at Maryon, to-day, Lady Cunard, Lady Murray, the Comte de Noailles, and Lieutenant Pernot. A gay party, and much amusing talk. I had a little time with Pernot. We agreed that things were better between Haig and Nivelle, and that it was necessary that there should be an officer corresponding with Robertson at Paris, in fact a French C.I.G.S. I agreed to write about it, as Pernot said it might be helpful. Pernot and the Press were now under M. Thomas. The T.O.E. were established in Paris, but had now no chief except a civilian War Minister. If Haig and Nivelle fell out, there was no one in France, at least no soldier, to communicate with Robertson and put things to rights. Dupont was still with Nivelle, but obviously his place was with a French Chief of Staff.

Monday, April 2. Dined with Lord and Lady Beresford. Gwynne of the *Morning Post* was there, and Charles Whibley ; also Lord and Lady Lytton, Lady Leslie, Belle Herbert, and a few more. Gwynne told me of his visit to France, and I found that we were agreed upon recent transactions. Talked with Lytton after dinner. He frankly confessed that naval officers were only regimental, and that few had Staff training and big ideas about war. We had been very remiss, but he hoped that things were coming on, and that we should soon improve. Talked with Lady L. upstairs, and congratulated her upon Lord L.'s recent speeches in the House of Lords. We went through the other young or youngish men fit to lead and did not find our list overcrowded.

Wednesday, April 4. Lunched with Lady Cunard. There trooped in Wolkoff, the Fairbairns, Elizabeth Asquith, the Duchess of Rutland, Lady Diana Manners, Lady Anglesey, Princess Hatzfeldt, and a few more. The ladies kept up a hot fire of smart sayings, and one had no need to talk. I liked Miss Asquith's story of her mother writing to Miss A.'s maid one morning: 'Dear So-and-So, Elizabeth looks terribly old and plain and dresses anyhow. Please see what you can do. I am sure that she sleeps under the bed and not on it.' Lady C. gave an entertaining account of Nabokoff's singing, much to Wolkoff's amusement. Wolkoff swears it is not true that when he was playing *L'Après-Midi d'un Faune* the other day, Lady Farquhar begged him to stop and play a fox-trot dance; but nobody believed him. Mr. Asquith came in for his girl after lunch. Walked away with Wolkoff, who told me that the news from Petrograd was better to-day. Our naval attaché, Commander Grenfell, had been haranguing the Baltic Fleet ships, and had brought nine-tenths of them round. He had assured the crews that they were not right to murder their officers and petty officers, and that such things were not done in a good democracy; in fact, that it was very bad form.

Dined with E. and Doris Keane. Went on to open a discussion at the 1900 Club, 5 Pickering Place, St. James's Street, on Man-Power and the War. A good attendance, all M.P.'s or candidates. General Hickman presided and then Lord Portsmouth. I told them the whole story and concealed nothing.   General Geddes had come and spoke after me.   He backed me up splendidly, and we were both well received, and thoroughly aroused our audience.   Hannon, of the Navy League, proposes to call a meeting of members of both Houses and to start a campaign in the country, and other members vow they will have a secret session and either get the truth out of the Government or tell it to them themselves.   Sir W. Robertson made a good speech to the Trade Unionists to-day, but he could not speak as openly as Geddes and I did, as we had barred reporters.

Thursday, April 5.   M. Sevastopoulo, Councillor of the Russian Embassy in Paris, met me at 3.30 at the Naval and Military Club, and we had a talk.   He is despondent about affairs in Russia, and terribly down on all the Russian ex-Royalties, except the ex-Tsar and his brother, who were well brought up, he says, in English ways.   He puts the largest share of blame on the Tsaritsa, but says she had *la manie de la dynastie.*

All stories of pro-Germanism at the Russian Court are incorrect.   Even the French mission to Russia had admitted this.   S. laid much blame on the Grand Duke Nicholas, who had introduced spiritualism to the Tsar twenty years ago, had also been trusted by the Tsar in all military affairs, and was largely responsible for the unpreparedness of Russia.   S. says that Isvolsky has been confirmed as Ambassador in Paris by the Provisional Government, and he supposes that Sazonoff will come to London.   I told S. of our man-power troubles.   We discussed French Command questions, and I begged him to try and get a good soldier made Chief of Staff in France.

Friday, April 6.[1]   Played Bridge with Countess Torby, and she drove me back to Hampstead.   She was perfectly furious about the Revolution, and declared that all the Russian officers who came over here assured her that there would be a counter-revolution very soon, and that the Revolution would be put down.   She had to leave Kenwood, to her great regret, and would have to live more in the town,

---

[1] This day the United States declared war.

as she would have no motor soon. Curzon had been to see Kenwood.

Saturday, April 7. Lunched with Lady Byng. Met afterwards General Count de Jonghe, just back from France and King Albert's Headquarters. He was very critical of the Russian Revolution, and did not think that we were as safe with the present Government as we were with the last. He was most anxious for us to attack in France, and knows, as so many people have known for weeks past, that it is to be near Arras. The French are going in on the Champagne front again, and this looks like a repetition of the September 1915 plan. He says that the French will employ 60 divisions, but that it will be about their last great effort unless it goes well, and he declares that there are only five really good Army Corps left in the French Army. The Belgians are, however, always hypercritical of the French. We both thought that the right blow to deliver was one northward along the Meuse, in which direction alone a great strategic success might be gained. A blow at Mézières from Champagne was the next best thing to deliver.

Easter Week-End. Horribly cold, much snow. I had fortunately refused all invitations to leave town, and spent the time in writing some articles for the *Times*, notably one on 'American Aid,' which my American friends are pleased to approve of. On Monday night, April 9, came the news of Haig's success north of Arras, making us all happy.

Tuesday, April 10. Sir W. Robertson writes that he has heard nothing from the politicians about his speech, so I hope that they are not too vexed about it. He wants to enlist Americans in our Army, and I write back to try and dissuade him from suggesting anything so dangerous. Lunched with Lady Johnstone, Lady Leslie, Lady Randolph, Nabokoff, and the Comte de Grünne. The ladies entertaining. Lady Leslie's story of the nervous and dissipated diplomatist at the Court of Francis Joseph amused me. The Emperor asked where he lived, and he replied, 'À la

campagne avec deux sœurs, Sire ! '   ' Mais quelle charmante
vie de famille, Monsieur ! '—' Mais, pardon Sire, elles ne sont
pas *mes* sœurs ! '   Nabokoff told me before he left that he
had been offered a Legation in Europe.   He prefers London
or New York.   He is to consult Hardinge about it to-day,
and will write the result to me.   Lady Randolph drove me
down to the new American Women's Hospital in Lancaster
Gate.   Very well arranged.   Forty-two beds, thirty-eight
full.   Everything in excellent order.   Lady Harcourt taking
a leading part, and Mrs. Walter Burns.   A very good-looking
lot of V.A.D. ladies.   One of the patients told me that our
failures in the air in France were due to inferior aeroplanes
and guns.   The Huns had knocked him out because his
machine was slow and his Lewis gun jammed.

Wednesday, April 11.   General Count de Jonghe lunched
with me at the Club.   We had a good talk about the war,
agreeing about Russia and the French offensive up the Meuse.
The French attack still hangs fire and has not started, though
a heavy artillery fire has begun on the Champagne front.
De J. very pleased with the result of Haig's attack on the
9th.   Saw Lady Paget and General Geddes in the afternoon.
Murray sends me the following account of his operations
round Gaza :—

GENERAL HEADQUARTERS,
EGYPTIAN EXPEDITIONARY FORCE,
3rd April 1917.

MY DEAR REPINGTON,—I think you may like to hear of our
operations of the 26th, 27th, and 28th March around GAZA, of the
progress made, and of our estimate as to the enemy's forces.

My intentions were threefold : To seize the line of the WADI
GHUZZE in order to protect the advance of the railway from
RAFA to GAZA ; to prevent the enemy from retiring without a
fight, which we knew was his intention as regards his troops in
GAZA, TEL EL SHARIA, and BEERSHEBA, so soon as we approached
a little nearer than RAFA ; and, if possible, to capture GAZA by a
coup de main.

Dobell, who was in command of the whole force, retained two
Divisions as a Main Body to secure the Wadi, and support Chetwode, who, as Commander of Mounted Troops and one Division,

was to protect the march, and, if possible, capture GAZA.   My advanced Headquarters were at EL ARISH.

The probability of the Turks making off as soon as they got wind of our intentions necessitated the selection of starting points at some distance from the objective.   The Mounted Troops, therefore, started from RAFA, and the Infantry from oases a little to the east of it, where water was to be obtained.

On the morning of the 26th there was a dense fog until 11 o'clock, and this, though of value in screening our movements from the enemy aircraft, greatly hampered and delayed our advance.   By dusk, however, GAZA was enveloped and the first-line trenches taken.   The Commander of the Turks in GAZA blew up his wireless station, and prepared to surrender.   Von Kress, about 1 P.M., had started his relief columns from HUJ, SHERIA, and BEERSHEBA, whilst his 53rd Division was arriving at EL MEDJEL from LUDD.   Our Mounted Troops, assisted by armoured cars, all most brilliantly led, fought a delaying action all day, and inflicted very heavy losses on the separate columns without much loss to themselves, capturing, amongst others, the Commander and Staff of the Turkish 53rd Division.   (He was in his carriage.)

I estimate the enemy's losses on this day at over 5000.

It is probable that GAZA would have fallen before dusk but for delay caused by the morning fog.   As it was, however, Chetwode decided to run no risk of envelopment by converging Turkish columns, and drew off towards the main body, thus enabling GAZA to be reinforced during the night or early morning.

On the 27th the Turks delivered a fierce attack on Dobell's main position and Camel Corps, but were beaten back with very heavy loss, the Camel Corps nearly annihilating the Turkish 3rd Cavalry Division.   The Cavalry and Camelry then had to move back to EL BELAH to water, the horses not having had any for 24 hours, and the camels for 4 days.   The Infantry managed on their water-bottles, which is good discipline, considering that a hot wind was blowing and the thermometer registered over 90° in the shade.

On the evening of this day it was obvious that if we could advance, GAZA would fall, and the Turks retire, but want of water, distance of railhead, and the fatigue of the horses prevented it.   I estimate this day's enemy losses at 3000, making a total of 8000.

On the 28th the Turks would not advance to attack again, and mostly occupied the GAZA Defences. Our Cavalry remained in contact, and our Infantry withdrew, without a fight, behind the main prepared position.

Thus terminated a most successful operation, just falling short of complete disaster to the enemy. Our troops are exceedingly proud of themselves, especially a Division which had not been in action since SUVLA, and I am delighted with their skill, enterprise, endurance, and leading. At no time were any of our troops hard pressed or harassed, and the result of this fight proves conclusively to my mind that the enemy has no chance of success in the open, where the mounted troops simply do what they like with them. The Turk is, however, as of old, very tenacious in prepared positions. We have about 400 killed.

We now have opposed to us the 3rd Cavalry Division, the 3rd, 16th, 27th, 53rd, and 54th Divisions, so I think the Russians should be pleased, and Joe Maude's task made easier.

I would give a good deal to have even one more Cavalry Division, but whilst France can employ them I must resign myself to do the best I can with what I have got, and ever press on. Offence is the best defence.—Yours ever,

A. J. MURRAY.

Friday, April 13. An amusing lunch at Lady Cunard's: Winston, Masterton Smith, the Nicholsons, Isidore de Lara, and the Princess of Monaco. I received last night from Sir Philip Sassoon a pressing invitation from Sir Douglas Haig to go to France, so arranged finance and permit to-day, and propose to cross Tuesday next. Called on Sammy Scott, who is installed as private secretary to Derby at the War Office. Thence to York House, and, after tea with Lady Robertson, had a talk with the General, who is laid up with a bad eye. I found him consoling General Barrow, who has been *dégommé* by Gough. He was very pleased with the results of our attack in France. Haig's gains are already 13,000 prisoners and 150 guns. R. tells me that we have 60 German divisions opposing us on the whole British front, and that they are so thick that it is difficult to show the units on a map. R. shares my views that the Russian position is rotten, and that we cannot trust them to do anything this year. He doubts whether the Russians will do anything for a hundred years, for the nation behind the Army is no good for anything 'except music and dancing and tommy-rot love stories.' I said that if I were a Boche I would let the Russians alone this year, trusting them to dissolve and perhaps make a separate peace, while I took some 50 Boche divisions to the West. R. agreed, and said that yesterday they had the first indications that a movement West was beginning.

I said that as the Yankees could not come for a year, and we had not used our man-power, I thought that we should make a splash now, and then when the Germans began to arrive from the Russian front we should take up a good fighting position instead of our present line, which was bad, except on the Vimy Ridge and on the Ancre-Somme sector, dig ourselves in deeply, and wire ourselves up like canaries. Then we could hang on whatever came against us. R. was inclined to agree, and he said that my ideas on what the enemy was likely to do next were in his opinion near the mark. We were all right in France for the moment, and he thought Haig a good man and very determined. But nothing had yet been done about man-power. Maude was doing well but nothing could be got out of Alexeieff regarding his Caucasus plans, and the Turks might mass against Maude. R. had had to fight a battle for Murray before the War Cabinet last Wednesday, as they were displeased about the Gaza fight, and R. thought them very hypercritical. In a fortnight or so Murray would get going again. I again asked if he had enough troops, and R. assured me that he had. I still do not think it. There were 12 more Indian battalions to join him. R. is very uneasy about French politics, and declares that when Nivelle fights he will fight with a halter round his neck, as Pétain disapproves of the offensive, and he and Painlevé, with others, are said to be distrustful of Nivelle. R. likes Nivelle, and thinks him straight and frank, but does not know whether he has the qualities for his present position. If Painlevé succeeds Ribot, Pétain may get the Command-in-Chief, but R. says that it is absurd to change the Commander with every change of Government. He thinks our Government the only one on the Allied side with any stability. He says that people are always producing new bomb-shells. The French the other day desired to share in the Palestine expedition, but L. G. refused. Now the French want to quarrel with Greece, and R. does not see why we should. It was difficult to deal with such shifting plans, and R. wants us to take more control of the war. Another French demand is that we should send now to Italy the divisions destined to reinforce the Italians in case of need. General Foch has been sent to Italy to encourage the Italians.

R. continues to regret Joffre and the old G.Q.G. as I do. There is no one now in charge of the exterior operations in France. R. grumbles a good deal about the number of men under Lord French, and I should judge that trouble may be brewing over it. R. passed on to me some interesting advices from an important person. The latter does not think that we are taking the position due to us from our financial, naval, and military pre-eminence in the war, and complains that French policy is untrustworthy, and their plans always changing. He is disposed to think that after the present, or rather coming, French offensive ends, we should make the French take over more of our line and mass a force in the North to sweep up the coast and march towards Holland. He also says that France has drained us of all our troops, and that we have no great strategic reserve left such as the Germans now possess, and that, therefore, we cannot easily repair a mistake or strike a new blow. Much of which is very true, but I think a great attack in the North poor strategy.

I walked to the Savoy afterwards, and saw General Smuts. We had a good talk, and I drew him to talk of Holland, when he outlined some interesting schemes on this side. Then I told him that I was against a direct attack through Belgium towards Holland, as it would lead to the further devastation of Belgium, and because the Low Country positions amongst the rivers and canals, and with the rain and mud, **would** be difficult and costly to force. I was, and always had been, for the advance northward along the Meuse, and on both banks. Smuts thought that the French offensive, as planned, would lead to Mézières, but we both agreed that we should use the right bank of the Meuse in order to turn its defences as we progressed. Smuts feared a German raid on Holland for its food, and I told him about my promise [1] of 500 aeroplanes, which made him laugh a good deal. We discussed Man-Power, and I found he had a better opinion of the War Cabinet's plans than other soldiers have.

He then talked of Africa, and I asked him whether it was true that he, Smuts, did not hold out for the retention of East Africa. Smuts replied that this was not correct. He, of course, desired to keep German S.W. Africa, which was part of South Africa, but E. Africa was a British Empire question. The submarine, in his opinion, had played hell with sea power, and we could not afford to leave Germany local bases about the world to enable her to prey upon our trade in war. Germany's plan had been to create a Central African Empire, whence she could menace Egypt, the French in W. and N. Africa, and South Africa. The plan had collapsed, but we must not allow it to be revived. He thought that German E. Africa could maintain 25,000 good fighting men of the warrior class. These were the warrior tribes, and there was also a great mass of slave races, 8,000,000 or 12,000,000, who were of no use in mind or body. He had 15,000 blacks already in E. Africa, including 1000 men made prisoners from the German black troops. They did not mind for whom they fought so long as they were fed and paid. When the rains ended, he hoped that the German residue would be rounded up, but if they got into Portuguese E. Africa, they could live on the country, and the affair might be long spun out.

---

[1] The Dutch had told me that they were frightened about air-raids in their small country, and I had advised them to make aerodromes so that we could send them 500 aeroplanes in six hours.

General Smuts is an attractive character. He is not tall, but dapper, well knit, and athletic looking. He talks sound sense, reasons well, and shows excellent judgment on difficult questions. It will be strange if we do not find some even higher place for him in our Armies. He reminded me somewhat of General Pétain. I should add that Smuts declared that the Teutonic stock was still the dominant race, and that it threatened to flood and subdue Europe, as formerly it had subdued Rome. But, fortunately, in this war the Teutonic stock was divided. England, the Dutch, North America, and the Dominions were in opposition, and but for this division Germany would have knocked out the Slav and Latin races, who cannot stand up against her without us. An interesting point of view.

Saturday, April 14. Arranged for the journey to France. Lunched alone with Winston at his old house, which Grey has had for five years, 33 Eccleston Square. We talked the war up and down, and are agreed on the main lines. Winston wants me to make his peace with Haig, and to get the latter to invite him out to France. We plan a combined journey to the French front. We go through all the Man-Power points.

Sunday, April 15. Sir Arthur Paget called for me and motored me down to his house near Brentwood. Nice house, with good gardens and a mass of shrubs, fruit, and flowers of all kinds. This house is a sort of annexe of Miss Wilmot's house, Warley Place, where are her beautiful gardens, with so many wonderful specimens of plants of all sorts. We went first to Paget's H.Q. at an ophthalmic hospital, and he showed me the maps with dispositions of troops. He has some three divisions north of the Thames, and one south of it at Canterbury, also coast brigades and garrisons. An attack is considered by Paget to be most probable in Kent, or on the Norfolk coast. He has 90,000 men in the Southern Army all told, but his divisions are only nine battalions with twenty-four 18-prs. and eight 5·5 in. howitzers each. The Isle of Thanet seems much exposed.

We walked over to Miss Wilmot's after tea, and she showed us some of her treasures. She is certainly a very wonderful lady. She and some of Sir A.'s Staff and their ladies dined in the evening.

Monday, April 16. Returned to town early. Business in the morning. All the usual little things which one takes campaigning seem to have run out, and are not to be obtained, especially metal articles. Saw Lord Derby at the War Office in the afternoon. Our casualties are 43,000, to date, over the Arras fight. The Navy is not evacuating our wounded at the rate promised. They said 10,000 a day, and are doing only 3000. So there is a crowd of wounded in France, and even the convalescent depots will be full soon. We agreed that Man-Power and Russia were the black spots. Derby wants me to find out, and to write and tell him, whether our new aeroplanes are superior to the German ; whether our guns are better than the German ; how the 30th Division fared in the late fight ; also how the 8th Cavalry Brigade with the Blues and the 10th got into such a warm corner. Derby may be coming over this week, but finds it unsafe to leave his office very often. Saw Jack, who was angry with the Navy because a tramp steamer had fought for two hours with two German submarines off the Scilly Isles, and no help had gone to her. Maurice says that a telephone message from G.H.Q. says that the French attacked the enemy in Champagne this morning, and have captured their first-line trenches on a front of thirty miles. Only one German division has come West as yet, and it started before the Revolution began.

To-day the thermometer outside the window in my library registered 35 degrees in the morning and 85 in the afternoon.

CHAPTER XX

ARRAS AND CHAMPAGNE, APRIL 1917

Journey to the British front in France—Montreuil—Order of Battle of our Armies in France—Distribution of the German Armies—With Rawlinson's 4th Army—The devastated area—The question of guns and fuses—Visits to Generals Du Cane and Pulteney—German booby traps—Visit to Generals Gough and Birdwood—The 5th Army Trench Mortar School—Visit to General Allenby at Bryas—State of his 3rd Army—We visit the battlefield—Feat of arms of the 3rd Army on April 9—Bad condition of our horses—Plan of attack for April 23— General Allenby comes with me round his gas laboratory, survey company, and signal service—Description of these services—Visit to General Horne's H.Q. 1st Army—A visit to Vimy Ridge—Fine view from Hill 145—A call on General Byng—His capture of German guns and their use—Opening of the attack of April 23—The mechanism of the command at General Allenby's Headquarters—Visit to G.H.Q. at Bavincourt—Talks with Generals Kiggell and Sir Douglas Haig— German divisions, the new series—General Trenchard and the R.F.C. Headquarters at St. André—Trenchard's opinions—Major Cornwall's views of the German forces—Arrival in Paris—A talk with M. Painlevé, the new French War Minister—Motor to Châlons—Meet Generals Pétain and Nivelle—I give General Pétain my views at his request— He describes what happened before Nivelle's attack—A discussion of the present position—General Pétain at work—Studies of his Staff— A reconnaissance of Moronvillers—General Pétain's plans—M. Citröen's Munition Works—Renault's factory—A visit to General Nivelle at Compiègne—His explanatory note on his battle of April 16 —General Foch unemployed—I visit him at Senlis—His views— French G.Q.G.'s estimate of present and future German strengths— A lunch with M. Loucheur—Another talk with Sir D. Haig and General Pétain—A successful Conference—Admirals Jellicoe and Sims on the submarine war.

Tuesday, April 17.   Left Charing Cross 2.55 P.M.   Arrived Folkestone 4.30 P.M., and found that we were to wait for other ships, and were to sail in convoy.   Walked on the Lees with Bobby Ward, the King's Messenger, and we dined at an hotel. Left towards sunset with two hospital ships, one transport, and our mail boat. Some destroyers on each side of us. We all emitted much dense smoke, shrieked with our sirens, and did all we could to warn the submarines that we were coming. The four ships convoyed kept no order, though they started in line ahead. As it got dark, we saw ships coming over from France covered with lights of all colours. They looked, as a man said, like the White City at Exhibition time, and so they did. As two Hun submarines were yesterday in the Channel sinking our ships at their sweet will, I did not admire the arrangements. Reached Boulogne, and was met by Lieut. Burgess, Charteris's secretary, and motored to Montreuil, where I had a billet at the abominable Hotel de France. Talked with Charteris and his officers at and after dinner about the war.

Wednesday, April 18. Visited the G.H.Q. offices. Charteris gave me several interesting papers. I met General Trenchard in charge of the Flying Corps in France. We had some talk, and made an assignation for later. A good talk over affairs with Charteris. Our troops are at present organised as per table below.[1] The second table gives the

---

[1] THE BRITISH ARMIES IN FRANCE

HEADQUARTERS OF FORMATIONS AS LOCATED ON 14TH APRIL 1917

Formation.	Headquarters.
FIRST ARMY	Lillers (Adv. Ranchicourt).
Portuguese E.F.	Roquetoire.
I. Corps	Labuissiere.
6th Division	Cité de Braquemont (Nœux-les-Mines).
24th Division	Sains-en-Gohelle.
II. Corps	Aire.
18th Division	Steenbecque.
46th Division	Busnes.
XI. Corps	Hinges.
49th Division	La Gorgue.
66th Division	Béthune.
XIII. Corps	Ecoivres.
2nd Division	Marœuil Cemetery.
31st Division	Bruay.
63rd Division	Villers Chatel.
Canadian Corps	Camblain l'Abbé.
1st Canadian Division	A. 14 a. 9.2 (51 B).
2nd Canadian Division	Aux Riotz Caves.
3rd Canadian Division	F. 6 c. 5.5 (36 C).

Formation.	Headquarters.
4th Canadian Division	Château d'Acq.
5th Division	Château de la Haie.
SECOND ARMY	Cassel.
VIII. Corps.	Château Lovie.
38th Division	St. Sixte.
55th Division	Nine Elms, A. 25 d. 2.3 (N. of Poperinghe).
IX. Corps	Mont Noir.
16th Division	Locre.
19th Division	Westoutre.
36th Division	St. Jans Cappel.
X. Corps	Abeele.
23rd Division	Esquelbecq.
39th Division	Busseboom (28).
41st Division	Reninghelst.
47th Division	Hoograaf.
II. Anzac Corps	Bailleul.
25th Division	Bailleul.
57th Division	Sailly.
New Zealand Division	Steenwerck.
3rd Australian Division	Croix du Bac.
THIRD ARMY	St. Pol.
VI. Corps	Noyelle Vion.
15th Division	Duisans.
3rd Division	Russell Caves, Arras.
17th Division	Arras, Place St. Croix.
29th Division	Arras, Place St. Croix.
VII. Corps	Fosseux.
21st Division	F. 18 a. 2.6 (51 C).
56th Division	M. 3 c. 5.1 (51 B).
33rd Division	Blaireville Quarries.
50th Division	Ronville.
XVII. Corps	Aubigny.
4th Division	H. 14 a. 0.9 (51 B).
9th Division	G. 16 c. 3.4 (51 B).
34th Division	F. 29 c. 5.8 (31 C).
51st Division	Hermaville.
XVIII. Corps	Hauteville.
12th Division	Wagnonlieu.
37th Division	Lignereuil.
30th Division	Pommier.
14th Division	Warlus.
XIX. Corps.	Flers.
Cavalry Corps	Duisans.
1st Cavalry Division	Haute Avesnes.
2nd Cavalry Division	Henu.
3rd Cavalry Division	Gouy-en-Artois.
FOURTH ARMY	Querrieu (Adv. O. 31 Central S.E. of Villers Carbonnel, noon, 15/4/17).
III. Corps	Foucaucourt.
42nd Division	Péronne.
48th Division	Tincourt.
59th Division	Santin Farm (P. 23 a. 8.7).
IV. Corps	Nesle.
32nd Division	Aurior.
35th Division	Beauvois.
61st Division	Voyennes.

Formation.				Headquarters.
XIV. Corps .	.	.	.	E. 23 b. (62 D).
Guards Division	.	.	.	Maurepas.
1st Division	.	.	.	Chuignolles.
XV. Corps .	.	.	.	Suzanne Château (Adv. A. 29 d. 9.7).
8th Division	.	.	.	Gurlu Wood, D. 22 a. 1.7 (62 C).
20th Division	.	.	.	Rocquigny.
40th Division	.	.	.	Manancourt.
5th Cavalry Division	.	.	.	Guizancourt.
FIFTH ARMY .	.	.	.	Albert.
V. Corps .	.	.	.	Acheux (Adv. Bihucourt).
7th Division	.	.	.	Courcelles-le-Comte.
11th Division	.	.	.	Englesart.
62nd Division	.	.	.	Achiet-le-Grand.
58th Division	.	.	.	Bus-les-Artois.
I. Anzac Corps	.	.	.	Henencourt (Adv. Grevillers).
1st Australian Division	.		.	H. 35 c. 5.7 (W. of Bancourt).
2nd Australian Division	.		.	H. 15 c. 4.3 (W. of Favreuil).
4th Australian Division	.		.	Fricourt, X. 27 d. 3.7.
5th Australian Division	.		.	N. 11 Central (N. of Beaulencourt).
4th Cavalry Division	.		.	Marieux.
ROYAL FLYING CORPS	.		.	St. André.
TANKS .	.	.	.	Bermicourt Château.
G.H.Q. TROOPS	.	.	.	Hesdin.

G.H.Q., 14*th April* 1917.

SUPPOSED DISTRIBUTION OF THE GERMAN FORCES ON THE WESTERN FRONT, 14TH APRIL 1917

	DIVISIONS.			
	In Line.	Reserve.	Exhausted.	Total.
Beverloo area and unlocated . .	—	3	—	3
FOURTH ARMY (Flanders) . .	9	$5\frac{1}{2}$	—	$14\frac{1}{2}$
SIXTH ARMY (Artois) . . .	$17\frac{1}{2}$	2	6	$25\frac{1}{2}$
FIRST ARMY } (Somme) . . .	8	1	1	10
SECOND ARMY }	11	7	1	19
SEVENTH ARMY (Aisne) . . .	12	3	—	15
THIRD ARMY (Champagne) . .	13	5	—	18
FIFTH ARMY (Verdun) . . .	15	2	—	17
von STRANTZ (Woevre) ' C ' . .	$7\frac{1}{2}$	1	—	$8\frac{1}{2}$
von MUDRA (Lorraine) ' A ' . .	7	3	—	10
von GÜNDELL (Alsace) ' B ' . .	9	4	—	13
Total	109	$36\frac{1}{2}$	8	$153\frac{1}{2}$ [1]

Amounting to about 1471 battalions.

The following new divisions from Germany and from the Eastern front have been identified : 187th Div. and 15th Bav. Div.

              (Signed)   J. CHARTERIS,

G.H.Q., I., 14*th April* 1917.   *Brigadier-General, General Staff.*

---

[1] Ludendorff's *Memoirs* make the figures 154, which shows how accurate our information was.

German dispositions.   Motored on to the H.Q. of Sir Henry Rawlinson, commanding the 4th Army at Villers Carbonnel, south of Péronne.   The devastated district from which the Germans have retreated is like nothing else on earth. Every village, bridge, and tree destroyed, and large craters at the cross-roads caused by explosions.   The trees by the side of the roads in many places cut in rows to fall outwards into the fields, and not to obstruct the roads, showing a mere insane desire to destroy.   Even the library at Péronne has had the covers of its books torn off, and the pages kicked about.   The wells are filled in and defiled—in fact, a desert so complete that it has ceased to howl, and nature herself seemed to have given up trying to mend matters. There was scarcely a blade of grass anywhere.   Found Rawly and his Staff lodged in Nyssen huts, which are excellent, but the nights are precious cold.   Had good talks with R. about the war, and with Budworth about guns.   The bombardment of the enemy by our 1st and 3rd Armies in the North did not cease for one single instant during the night.   Rawly and his Staff busy digging and planting gardens and crops round their huts.   R. and I walked out to inspect the German positions, trenches, dug-outs, etc., in the neighbourhood.

Thursday, April 19.   Had another good talk in the morning with Budworth about the guns.   His only need is for the 106 fuse, which enables our shells, by bursting on impact before penetrating the ground, to destroy the German wire so well.   But he also wants a 9·2-inch gun on the naval mounting to plaster the Boche billets, railways, dumps, etc., for 28,000 yards in rear of their lines.   He considers that even if we do nothing we shall be superior to the Germans, admitting that the German field gun now ranges 2000 yards further than before, and that the Hun 5·9-inch howitzer is, on the whole, the best gun of the war.   Budworth likes our 12-inch howitzer, but not our 15-inch.   He says that we must keep on improving projectiles for our various guns, and not have too many projectiles of different kinds for each gun.   I motored and walked round Rawly's battlefield of July 14 of last year, and am confirmed in my impression that this was one of the finest feats of the war. The country is a scene of appalling desolation, all the trees cut to ribbons by the shells, and the remains of dead Boches, skulls, and equipments littering the place, especially the grim and gloomy Delville Wood, where I picked up a good Boche steel helmet. There were so many unexploded British shells that one could scarcely take a step without treading on one, and the whole place is a maze of shell craters.

Motored on to General Du Cane's Headquarters in Nyssen huts, north of Péronne, and lunched with him. He says that his battalions can only put 500 men into the field for a fight. He thinks that with the 1st and 3rd Armies the figure may be 600. Rawly has been told to expect no drafts, and as his Army has lost 6000 men this month the prospect is cheerless. Du Cane told me that the contract for the 106 fuse had been placed in Switzerland! After some months we were told that the people could not carry out their contract. Probably a Boche took the contract and called himself a Swiss. Du Cane says that he must have the 106 fuse before he attacks the Hindenburg line. He says that while at the Ministry of Munitions he also ordered a 9·2-inch on an all-round railway mounting. It had an 18,000 yards range. Rawly's Army has had most of its guns taken away for the profit of the operations further north. There is what is called a 'Travelling Circus' of 450 heavy guns, which is now with the 1st and 3rd Armies, and Rawly has only three 6-inch howitzer batteries and the 60-prs. with his Army Corps, leaving him too weak for attack. This is also the reason why only two Armies out of five are attacking.

Friday, April 20. I find that the troops are so delighted to be out of their muddy trenches that they make light of the bad billets. Rawly has Archie Montgomery for B.G.G.S., Pitt Taylor and Vivian are also on his G.S., and all good men. Sir Richard Sutton and Lord Methuen's boy are his A.D.C.s. In their spare time they dig and plant vegetables, assisted by some Boche prisoners, guarded by one *vieille moustache*, aged about sixty, who looks like one of the Old Guard, and keeps a stern and vigilant eye upon them.

Visited General Pulteney, as cheery and as fit as ever. He has still the same old 3rd Army Corps. He thinks it a mercy that the Boches destroyed the villages, as otherwise we should have had no materials for road-mending. He has two moderate divisions, and one good under Fanshawe, whose praises he sings. He is short of horses, and could not bring on all his guns except by motor haulage. He says that the Huns must have used 300,000 lbs. of explosives on their demolitions here. I saw an immense crater at one cross-roads. It was some twenty feet deep, and was being filled in with tree trunks and earth. The Huns have left many mines with some clockwork arrangement, or acid cutting through suspensory wires after a certain length of time, to cause explosions after a month or so has elapsed. Some have been found on the railways and removed; others have exploded, even in houses, and some of our officers and men have been killed by them. Putty is in Nyssen huts. His Staff in a house near. There is a German mine gallery with a spade temptingly placed, and possibly connected with a mine which will explode if the spade is removed, so nobody touches it.

Motored on to Albert, H.Q. of Gough's 5th Army. Lunched with him. Old Sir Pratab Singh in the Jodhpore breeches as usual, and his son, a smart boy. Pratab said that we were fighting four enemies—snow, rain, mud, and Huns. Gough has some thirty heavy guns, so that he may be able to help the 3rd Army. He attacked Bullecourt, hoping that the 3rd Army would come on, but I could not learn that he had received any promise that it would. His tanks had taken the lead, but were much exposed on the snow, and he had taken a knock, and only two tanks out of twelve did well. The Australians fought well, but lost 3000 men and were driven back. Then came the German attack on

April 15 against the Australian front. It was well beaten, except at Lagnicourt, where it got home and captured 48 of Gough's guns. The Huns had 20 charges ready for blowing up the guns, but only 5 were destroyed before 4 companies from the west of Lagnicourt and 2 from the east counter-attacked and brilliantly recaptured the guns. Gough's other guns were meanwhile barraging the exits through the German wire, and when the enemy fell back he got into trouble and lost 3000 killed. Gough hopes to take Havrincourt with help from Du Cane, but perhaps not for a month.

Went in the afternoon to visit Birdwood and his Australians. All very cheery. He can put 800 men per battalion into the field, and has 63,000 men in England, including men intended for the 6th Australian Division now forming. He is anxious about his future drafts. The Australians, after Bullecourt, say ' Na-poo Tanks.' Dined with Gough and his Staff at Albert.

Saturday, April 21. Neill Malcolm, B.G.G.S., and I visited the 5th Army Trench Mortar School at Valheureux. It takes 150 pupils for a fourteen days' course at a time, then three days' rest, and then another course. A nice farmhouse and grounds, with excellent arrangements. Our chief trench mortars now are the 9·45 - inch throwing a 150 lb. bomb 1100 yards, a 2-inch throwing a 50 lb. bomb 500 yards, and lastly the infantry Stokes mortar throwing a smaller bomb 500 yards, to be increased to 700. Types of all the German trench mortars are at the school : the heaviest is outranged by ours. Our Mills' hand grenade seems to be the best type of the war now. It is curious to recall the first trench mortar made by Willcocks's Indians in 1914, of barrel staves tied up with wire, and throwing a bully-beef tin !

Motored on to lunch at General Allenby's château of Bryas, near St. Pol, at which latter town the 3rd Army Staff is installed. Bryas a fine château, and the King stayed here when he was last in France. Allenby, Bols his M.G.G.S., Sillem, Kenyon, Dalmeny, Agnew, and others.

The state of the 3rd Army to-day is given in the foot-note below.[1] Went with Allenby beyond Tilloy, where we had a wonderful view of the battlefield. We were bombarding the Huns in preparation for next Monday's battle, and a few Hun shells came our way. The ground is very open, resembling Salisbury Plain without the trees, but lacking in grass and vegetation. All our batteries were in a long line in Battery Valley, and we could watch them well : the heavies were behind us or on the flank. We had much the best of the game of long bowls. We walked over the scene of Allenby's attack on the 9th. I was struck by finding so few unexploded shells, so different from the Somme battlefield, and pointing to the great improvement of our fuses. Monchy, where the 8th Cavalry Brigade had their fight, is perched in a very conspicuous position,

[1] THIRD ARMY, APRIL 1917

STRENGTH, CASUALTY, AND REINFORCEMENT STATE

Formation.	Strength, 21st April 1917.		Casualties, 10th to 20th April 1917.		Reinforcements from Base, 10th to 20th April 1917.	
	Off.	O. R.	Off.	O. R.	Off.	O. R.
3rd Division . . .	434	11,854	145	2,731	37	1,405
4th Division . . .	493	11,549	122	2,580	17	1,101
9th Division . . .	441	10,561	193	3,399	10	1,294
12th Division . . .	493	12,861	95	2,011	16	1,446
14th Division . . .	440	12,405	90	1,708	22	1,576
15th Division . . .	490	12,511	132	2,900	11	2,011
17th Division . . .	499	12,702	37	623	22	356
21st Division . . .	471	12,309	66	1,362	32	312
29th Division . . .	539	11,901	76	1,860	28	916
30th Division . . .	479	12,455	66	1,195	35	1,282
33rd Division . . .	536	12,873	29	380	13	851
34th Division . . .	396	11,401	140	2,138	51	1,437
37th Division . . .	435	12,395	121	2,552	34	2,790
50th Division . . .	538	11,893	45	707	32	379
51st Division . . .	534	12,608	107	2,707	10	1,470
56th Division . . .	484	12,875	96	1,850	9	1,218
1st Cavalry Division .	326	6,416	5	45	—	—
2nd Cavalry Division .	325	6,173	11	175	—	—
3rd Cavalry Division .	273	5,974	42	590	—	—
Totals . . .	8,626	213,716	1,618	31,513	379	19,844

and is a cockshy from all sides. We walked north to a point overlooking the Valley of the Scarpe. Here the Huns are hanging on gamely, with heaps of machine guns in all sorts of sequestered spots, reminding me of Cronje and Modder River. Allenby's guns had broken the wire of the first two German lines, but I found the wire of the third line only cut in places. The Huns were so petrified by the loss of their other lines that parts of the garrison of the third came out and surrendered, which was lucky, as the wire stopped us from getting at them.

I realised for the first time the immensity of the Arras battlefield, and the fact that the 3rd Army had accomplished a great feat of arms on April 9. It had attacked with three Army Corps abreast, and had captured over 8000 prisoners and 150 guns. Allenby had ten divisions in line that day, each Army Corps having two brigades in front line and one in support, with one division in reserve. His front ran from Croisilles to the Commandant's hut on the Vimy Ridge. He had 16 divisions altogether and 1600 guns, or 2159 including trench mortars. He bombarded for five days, and then on April 9, at 5.30 A.M., there was a furious ten minutes' counter-battery of all heavy guns, each Hun gun being attacked by an English gun of greater power. The result was that during the first quarter of an hour of our infantry attack no German gun replied. Our infantry took the first line easily, then the second, where the resistance was stronger, and then most of the third line. The losses of the 3rd Army were 29,000. Had a good talk with Dalmeny in the evening, and learnt some of Allenby's difficulties. Allenby and I discussed the condition of the horses, which had surprised and vexed me. He declared that our losses in horses were more due to ourselves than to the Boches. He traced it back to clipping, which had been imposed by the Vets., who had found it easier to detect disease when the coats were off. The want of shelter was also bad, and he thought that horses should have movable shelters, so that they could stand with their tails to them, and then if they had their coats on and proper

food they would be all right.   We were very short of horses.
They were overworked, and the oats had been reduced.
These were the causes of the bad condition of the horses.
Allenby's attack next Monday is to be in the following
order from left to right :—

2 divs. in support.	27th Division. 51st ,,	} XVII. Corps.
1 div. in support.	17th ,, 29th ,, 15th ,,	} VI. Corps→Enemy.
1 div. in support.	50th ,, 33rd ,, 30th ,,	} VII. Corps.

In Army Reserve, VIII. Corps, 4 divisions.

Sunday, April 22.   In spite of his coming battle, Allenby
found time to accompany me this morning round his gas
laboratory, and to the Survey Company H.Q. and the Signal
Service.   I admired the coolness and detachment of mind
which enabled an Army Commander to interest himself in
such matters at such a moment, but he said that all his
plans and arrangements for the following day were made,
and that he could only await the result.   At the gas
place, Mr. Hartley, an ex-college don, is in charge.
This scientist, no doubt, believed that all his life would
be spent in the cool shade of his university.   Now he
has become a dealer of death, and positively revels in
defeating and destroying the Huns.   He is always inventing something new and deadly, and he always tries it on
himself first.   The other day he made a new gas, put on
a Hun mask, and let the gas loose on himself.   He was
dragged out two hours later more dead than alive, and was
in hospital for some time, but perfectly delighted that
he had found something to defeat the Hun respirator.
The German phosgene ($COCl_2$), which we now use, kills
within a circle of 25 yards radius, and causes casualties
in a circle with diameter of 200 yards, unless men are
masked.   It is, however, not of much use in winds of over

seven miles an hour, as the gas disperses too quickly. Our box respirator gives complete protection, and so does the P.H. mask against all but lachrymatory. We use the gas in clouds from cylinders, in trench mortar bombs, and in shells, and there are many reports of the damage done by it. All sorts of cross-roads and communication trenches are to be gas-bombed to-night, and this will compel the Hun to keep his mask on, and it must be very hard to sleep in it. I expect that the Huns are cursing their chemists who invented poison gas.

At the Survey Company we found Colonel Winterbotham, a clever expert of the Ordnance Survey, who has many smart men of his trade under him. The rapid way in which all reports, from all sources, of the positions of the enemy's batteries are collected, co-ordinated, mapped accurately, and promptly issued to troops, is a real triumph of science applied to war. The R.F.C. photographs come here to help in the final stage of mapping, and are, of course, invaluable. I was surprised to learn that we had found the French maps, even the $\frac{1}{80000}$, quite untrustworthy. I told W. that I had regarded them like the Bible. So, he said, had he, but experience had shown that only the trigonometrical points were accurate, and that the details were often as much as 200 yards out. This had practically entailed a fresh survey of the whole ground, and he had amassed all the French mining and railway surveys that he could lay his hands on. The Germans had merely enlarged the French maps and had trusted them, and, in consequence, often hurled tons of metal on the wrong spot, day after day. While we had accurately located as many as 93 per cent. of the German battery positions, the German maps of our batteries showed that they had not located one-third of our batteries accurately. The sound-ranging and flash-spotting work of the survey companies is also very wonderful, and Winterbotham explained to us the most intricate mathematical calculations which were at the base of it. I am not sure whether Allenby or I understood it least. One of W.'s workmen told me that all the lithographic stones came from Bavaria, and were now most scarce. Our Government had commandeered the whole supply available at home. I found the Signals under an officer who declared that I had saved his life in South Africa by giving him breakfast one day. Visited the telegraph and telephone rooms. He gave us a lot of interesting figures. He has 90 tons of copper wire out on his Army lines. A very complete system, and I suppose that an Army can be better controlled from Paris or London with a perfect telegraph and telephone system than from a height overlooking the battlefield without one.

Took leave of Allenby, whose character I admire more the more I see of him, and motored on to General Horne's H.Q., 1st Army, further north. Here I found Horne, lame from a fall, but as cheerful and pleasant as ever, Anderson B.G.G.S., Heath C.R.E., General Mercer C.R.A., and others. We had lunch, and afterwards the A.D.C., Knatchbull-Hugessen, an active and capable young officer, took me on to the famous Vimy Ridge. We had to wear tin hats, which I found very comfortable. We made the best time we could through the ruins of Souchez, which the Huns persistently shell, and thence on to Stephens's Brigade H.Q. at the Cabaret Rouge, passing a number of our batteries in action. We here left our car under cover, and walked to the topmost point of the ridge, the Hill 145. The whole ridge is pockmarked with shell craters full of water, so close together that one has to crawl along the edges of the craters; and as the ground was still very muddy, it took us a long time. It must have been very hard for troops to cross this ground during their attack on April 9. We saw the remains of the Hun lines, which had for so long held up the French Artois offensives, and had become a nightmare to the French people. The Hun second line, which had held up the Canadians until the evening of April 9, was hard to find, but it appeared to be within about 200 yards of the crest on our side, well-sited, and with tunnels running back from it. All the trenches were knocked to bits, and almost all the wire was cut. I saw no preparations of ours for defending the ridge in case the Huns tried to retake it. It is most difficult, in fact almost impracticable, to bring our guns over this maze of craters, and so we are using the roads east and west of it, through Souchez and Thelus, for this purpose.

From the top of the ridge there is a wonderful view, and the visibility this day was perfect. We saw right away to Douai across the plain. At our feet, below the ridge, there was a broad fringe of field, and then all along the horizon from Givenchy, Lieven, and Lens on the left of us, and all along so far as we could see, an unending line of red-brick and red-tiled mining villages, which I thought good places to steer clear of if it could be done. It was clear why the enemy held the ridge so stiffly for so long. It is a remarkable observation point, and one sees everything from it, all spread out at one's feet. One could see into every part of Lens, where hard scrapping was in progress, and the guns on both sides were busy. The Huns keep on dusting the Vimy Ridge, which is still 'unhealthy'; but to-day they were civil on the whole, and we had a prolonged and quiet inspection of their positions. Stephens and a gunner colonel, P. de B. Radcliffe, out on observation duty, joined up with us. Stephens and P. de B. R. had been out scouting for the attack of Stephens's division to-morrow. We are getting round Lens, but it is a bit of a proposition, and will still want a lot of taking. Hun aeroplanes appeared over our heads not more than 1000 feet up as we returned, and fought a battle with one of our squadrons that turned up. The Huns were chased away, and some of our Archies aided. The way the Huns used the clouds was very pretty. I think that they were after our observation balloon, near Souchez, or else were reconnoitring our batteries which begin to turn up round the Cabaret Rouge. No harm seemed to be done by anybody to anybody else, and the Huns got away.

Going back I called on Byng. He thought that it was the winter training of the Canadians that had done the trick at Vimy, which, he said, was not a bowler's wicket, as

I must have seen. He told me that the Huns had only destroyed one of the guns which his men had captured, and that he had formed his 64 captive guns into a 1st, 2nd, and 3rd 'Pan-Germanic Group,' and had used up all their ammunition in shooting Germans. They were the only guns he had, as he could not get his own forward. Dined with Horne and his Staff, who are a very happy and united family, and had a good talk with him. His 1st Army have 360 heavy and 720 field guns. He was sorry that only one or two of his divisions could help Allenby to-morrow. It is uncertain whether the wire is well cut, and only a relatively small number of the new German battery positions have been spotted. There are six Hun divisions against the 1st Army, and two more are coming up with their guns. General Mercer only knows the position of a few batteries, while the 3rd Army this morning knew for certain the positions of 52 batteries, and in all of about 83, out of perhaps 110 German batteries left uncaptured on April 9. Reports also show that other Hun divisions are quitting the Northern front to come here. Horne and I talked of Lord K. Horne was with him on his trip to the Mediterranean, and told me of K.'s reply to the cable from the Cabinet inviting him to proceed to Egypt. It ran, 'Cable received. Am sending Horne to Egypt, and return via Italy to-morrow.' Horne said that K. quite appreciated the designs of the Cabinet and was very sarcastic about them.

It seems that we are bound to attack again, because Nivelle has got in a mess, has lost heavily, and has failed to get through. Otherwise we seem to have gained on this Arras front all we want at present.

Monday, April 23. At 4.45 A.M. this morning we seemed to be hit on the head by the thunderclap of the opening of our bombardment by 3000 guns. I took leave of Horne and went off to Allenby's H.Q. at St. Pol to watch the mechanism of the Army Control during a big fight, as Allenby had said I might if I liked. I found Allenby as cool as ever. Bols, Charles Grant, and the Operations

Staff were busy and full of work, receiving reports, and recording all information upon maps of various scales. Allenby and Bols in one room, Grant and another man in a side room, and the rest in another large room. The procedure was very thorough and businesslike. The whole Staff worked as a team, perfectly united, and with great coolness and rapidity. All reports, in and out, were transmitted to G.H.Q., the other Armies, and to Allenby's four Army Corps, nine copies of everything required. All the movements of our troops were shown as they became known, and also any movements of the enemy. The Signal Service kept us accurately informed. Congreve had taken Gavrelle with the 63rd Naval Division of the 1st Army, and held it throughout the day with great gallantry. Allenby's divisions made progress, but met with violent opposition, and Hun counter-attacks took place all along our front. This suited us well, as we had a tremendous line of batteries which searched all the open ground, and the Hun losses must have been immense. The progress expected had not been made by 1 P.M., so Allenby issued orders that the attack should be resumed at an hour to be fixed by the 6th Corps (Haldane); the hour selected was 6 P.M., and the line was at last attained, but not until many more counter-attacks had been repulsed. I thought that the Huns wished to retake Monchy. The 29th Division lost 2000 men in the village by shell fire alone, and on the slopes north and south of it some of the heaviest Hun attacks occurred. I doubt whether the enemy has ever suffered such loss in battle with us since the first battle of Ypres.

I motored in the late afternoon to F.M. Sir Douglas Haig's G.H.Q. at Bavincourt and found Sir L. Kiggell at home, so we had a walk together, and I found that we were in accord about questions of Man-Power and other matters relating to the war. I chaffed Kig. about his talk in the train with L. G., and Kig. told me that he had advised L. G. to make peace if he could not keep up the strength of our Armies. No wonder L. G. dislikes him! Haig is writing a fresh memo. about it, and is just putting the finishing touches to it. The Bavincourt château is small, and with little accommodation. Only Haig, Kiggell, Davidson, Fletcher, and Sassoon are there.

Haig came in at 7.45 P.M. He had been with Congreve and Snow on the two flanks of the attack. A few words with him and then a pleasant dinner, when we talked on a variety of topics, and I told him the political situation respecting men. We then had a talk alone after dinner. He wants me to show the connection between the Somme and Arras, and how necessary it was to wear out the German Armies in the field before doing anything else. He gave me the German *communiqué* saying that the retreat had begun on March 16, and pointed out that Gough had attacked and secured the observation over Miraumont on Feb. 24, this causing the retreat. I asked Haig when he thought that the Germans had decided on a retreat, and he said December 1916. He told me that his horses were 14,000 short, and that clipping should not be allowed after November. He had reduced the oats ration because his reserve had fallen to four days'. He thought that horses were plentiful in England, but could not be sent over. He told me that our Armies in France were now 42,000 short. On the basis of the number of men whom the W.O. had undertaken to supply, and allowing for casualties of 100,000 a month all told, his infantry would show a deficit of 198,000 men by Aug. 1. These figures do not include the Dominion troops. Very rightly, as I thought, he did not enter into any political discussion of how we were to get them, and merely said that now that I knew all the facts, I could work my own passage.

Tuesday, April 24. This morning we heard that Snow's 7th Corps had been driven back to its original line last night, and that the 63rd Naval Division had sent up the S.O.S. this morning and was being heavily attacked. Allenby came in during the morning and said that the Germans had had very heavy losses all day yesterday, as they were under the fire of our superior artillery in all their counter-attacks. I went to Charteris's local intelligence office. There are now 157 German divisions in France, of which 69½ are between the sea and the Oise. All the first 13 of the first new series of German divisions are now identified and located, while 3 of the second series have also come up. Vivian of the 4th Army Staff and others sent me shoulder straps, as I had requested, cut from the German jackets, showing the numbers of the new regiments so that L. G. might not rest any longer under any misconception. He would be reminded, I hoped, of David's proofs of his night visit to Saul's tent. We have exhausted 10 to 15 of the German divisions which were in the line against us on April 8, and have drawn in 12 out of the 18 divisions in reserve on our front. The G.H.Q. calculation is that a German division withdrawn from the line has lost 50 per cent. of its strength and is out of action for two months. This was the Somme experience.

After lunch with the F.M., motored on to Montreuil. Stopped on the way to see Reggie Pembroke to take him Bee's message and to hear his news of the Monchy fight. Found him at a little inn in a small village, very fit and well, and as full of spirits as ever. I asked a Blue trooper where to find Reggie, and he replied, 'At the third *hestaminet* on the left, sir.' He had been temporarily in command of the Blues on April 9th, and had ridden with them through the barrage, losing 30 or 40 men and 100 horses. As the Blues were in reserve, he had taken up his machine guns to Monchy to help the 10th and Essex, and had had a breezy time there. He was twice knocked down by shells, and once thrown down a staircase, but his steel hat saved him. The loss of horses occurred in the village. He said that the Brigade made a tremendous mark, and were shot at from all sides. We regretted poor Bulkeley-Johnson's death very much. I was glad to see Reggie again, and hope to goodness that he will pull through the campaign.

I motored on to St. André, the H.Q. of the Flying Corps, near Montreuil. Trenchard, its chief in France, is one of the few indispensable men in the Army. He has done wonders and deserves immense credit. The R.F.C. in

France now number 2500, including 2000 pilots. They were masters in 1916, but in the autumn General von Hoeppner was put in charge of the Hun Air Service, which came out in 1917 in the proportion of 6 to 4 against us. The Huns had two one-seater fighting aeroplanes to every one artillery scout, and with us the proportion was reversed. Trenchard pointed out that a great nation like Germany will not easily be cowed, and that we must not expect the conditions of 1916 to recur. He expects that we shall have ups and downs in the air as elsewhere. His policy is to seek out the German airmen and either drive or draw them away so that our artillery scouts may carry out their mission. This has led to heavy fighting and many casualties, but he has persevered. We have been all over them to-day, and have bombed Ath and Hirson. These bombing raids worry the Germans and draw them away from the front, but T. made it clear that bombing will not win the war.

T. says that it is no more possible to say which is the best aeroplane than to say which is the best type of ship. It all depends upon what each has to do. He thinks that great harm is done by finding fault with old and slow types, and thus discouraging the pilots, who are young and impressionable. T. is against the pilots selecting types of aeroplanes, as he would be against taking Tod Sloan as adviser in choosing a horse. Our great need is for plenty of fast one-seater fighting aeroplanes with two guns, or with three if we can have them. T. thinks that our latest S.E.5 is better than the latest Hun Albatross. A squadron of twelve of these new machines of ours had been out yesterday and had brought down three of the enemy without loss. A new French machine lent to us was even better, but it had only one gun. T. declares that a new type invented now will not begin to reach the Army in any numbers until May 1918, and that it is necessary to shorten the period which elapses between the decision respecting types and their utilisation in the field. T. says that an aeroplane lasts about two months on an average. A pilot takes two months of fighting to become an adept, but his nerve usually only lasts for three, six, or nine months afterwards, and a man who has had a rest is seldom good for much again. T. wants a squadron of eighteen aeroplanes with each Army, besides the H.Q. wing, which goes wherever the need is greatest. He is determined to act offensively in order to enable the artillery scouts and photographic machines to do their work. This they certainly do, for I am told that in four months the aeroplane observers reported 1589 direct artillery hits on German guns, and some 200 important explosions.

The best machine we have now gives 105 miles an hour 10,000 feet up, and, in choosing a new type for 1918, T. will be contented with an increase of 20 miles an hour. He talked of the immensity of the air, and of the difficulty of seeing planes in the air, and of distinguishing friend from foe. The 'Archies' were most useful in this way, as they saw the plane from below, while in the air the enemy might only be seen end on, and the shells bursting distinguished friend from foe. All the aeroplanes sent to bombard Ath to-day were slow, and might have been put down by any Hun Albatross or Halberstadt, but they never saw one. The space was immense and planes travelled fast. T. had 900 aeroplanes in the air on April 9. The Essen enterprise is a different kind of job which must come on later. In general, T. wants his one-seater fast fighters to go full speed for 3 to $3\frac{1}{2}$ hours only. Everything, he says, is a compromise in an aeroplane as in a ship. He instances the new German three-seater driven down by us near Montreuil to-day as a useless type, though it has two 260 h.p. Mercédès engines. T. thinks that a good aeroplane gun has not yet been invented. He says that from a large point of view he has not obtained what he asked for last year. We talked alone first, and he showed me some aeroplane reports. Then we went into the mess-room, where were some of his chief officers. Maurice Baring was there. It was rather felt than expressed that the home organisation was behind the times, but I did not go into the matter, as these officers were not the proper people with whom to discuss it.

Haig told me at breakfast to-day that he could take many more heavy guns, indeed as many as we could give him. Kiggell said the same, and resented very much the handing over of so many guns to nearly all our Allies when we needed them so much. People seem to give promises to Allies much too freely, and meantime the G.H.Q. demands have not been met, and we are short of 120 field guns and of a good proportion of guns of other calibres for our existing batteries, while the reserve of guns inspires anxiety.

Wednesday, April 25. At the Hotel de France again, and as abominable as ever. Walked round the ramparts this morning—a very attractive view, and a resort of nightingales. Montreuil stands finely, and the walls are very high. Visited the Intelligence Branch and had a talk with Major Cornwall, who has a rare talent for this work. He thinks that there are from 4,500,000 to 5,000,000 Germans on the two fronts and on the L. of C., besides 1,000,000 at the depots, and, in addition, the class of each year—the 1919 class is only now coming to the depots—and the *récupérés*. But he declares that combing is finished, and this makes an immense difference. He places 155 German divisions in the West, and says that all the Landwehr and Landsturm have gone East. There are still 10 divisions in reserve from the sea to the Oise, but 25 German divisions have had to be withdrawn from the front during the fighting since April 9, of which 15 from the British front. He says that the new Boche 08/15 machine gun, which is an answer to our Lewis gun, can be carried and manipulated by one man, and that, all told, the Huns have now 16 machine guns *per company*. C. thinks that the Germans are short of guns. Hindenburg asked for a doubling of the output, but has probably been disappointed. On the other hand, shells still seem plentiful.

Motored to Amiens in $1\frac{3}{4}$ hours—good going. Met the Duke of Sutherland at the station ; he is off to visit Birdwood. The train journey to Paris took four hours, and was very boring. Put up at the Ritz, where Dalmeny had fortunately taken the last rooms for me. Billy Lambton came and talked with me at dinner. His 4th Division had lost 3000 men, and he had only received 1000 drafts, and he is now 9000 instead of 13,000 infantry. Le Roy-Lewis came to talk over matters in my room later. He says that the French have lost 120,000 men, and that Nivelle is to go and Pétain will succeed him. Pétain had opposed the plans for the offensive on broad statesmanlike grounds, and the event had proved him right.

Thursday, April 26. Esher came in to talk in the morning. He told me a little more about the famous Calais Conference, and how the proposal to place the British under the French had originated with L. G. and Briand only, and that no one else knew of it. L. G. had tried to induce Lyautey to break the news to Haig and Robertson, but L. had refused, and had gone off to spend two hours with the 'Duchesse de Süderland.' We agree that if Pétain is appointed he should be C.G.S. in Paris. Completed my first article on my tour, all about the Boches.

I saw M. Painlevé, the French War Minister, in the evening. After some preliminary conversation he asked for my views on the general situation. I told him that the practical equality of the combatants in the West did not justify adventures or soaring strategy on our part, and that I was for a prudent offensive on the model of April 9, to place us in better positions all along the line, and that I did not believe in the aspiring offensive of the Champagne model until we had greater superiority. I thought that we should have to wait until the appearance of the British and American reserves of manhood came forward, and meanwhile not exhaust the strength and moral of our good Armies by trying to do too much. Painlevé told me that my ideas accorded with Pétain's, and he asked me to visit the latter, which I agreed to do.

Painlevé appears to have read all my articles, and even reminded me of my *Blackwood* articles on the future and certain domination of the submarine in the North Sea, written four years before the war. Haig came to Paris to-day at Painlevé's request. He would not mix himself up in the personal question of Pétain versus Nivelle, but deprecated any change in the plans arranged, and wished to continue his offensive. It was arranged that the old plans should hold good, at least for the time. Painlevé is having a hard time to induce his Cabinet to accept Pétain, and is furious because Sir H. Wilson came to see him uninvited, supporting Nivelle and criticising Pétain severely. Ribot is pro-Nivelle, and Briand angry at Nivelle being upset; but Nivelle has failed, and the Government have to meet the Chambers on May 22. There are already ten interpellations announced concerning the French offensive.

Friday, April 27. Finished an article and sent it off for Charteris to censor by Maurice Brett. Lunched with Le Roy and the Councillors of the Russian and Spanish Embassies. Poor Sevasto very low at being named Russian Minister at Copenhagen. Nabokoff goes to Berne. Sevasto gave us no comfort about Russia. He was rather good on the British and French parliamentary systems. He said that in England everyone knew that the Front Opposition bench would have all the sweets of office on a change of Government, and so there was no intrigue among the rank and file of a party, whereas in France any one in Parliament might become Minister, or even President of the Council, and hence the endless intrigues and changes of Government. Mrs. Leeds turned up at lunch from Switzerland, and I was glad to see her again.

Motored to Châlons in the afternoon via Meaux and im-perishable Montmirail—$3\frac{1}{4}$ hours. Road fairly good. Many troops at all towns and villages *en route*. Reached Pétain's H.Q., where several officers were assembled. I was shown into the garden, where Pétain and another general were walking about. Pétain greeted me kindly and then intro-duced his comrade as General Nivelle. I was at a loss to know whether Pétain or Nivelle knew of Pétain's new appointment, but, in fact, as it turned out afterwards, Pétain and I knew, but Nivelle did not. There was, there-fore, a certain comedy about the deference which Pétain and I showed to the supposed but already fallen Commander-in-Chief. Nivelle was looking very troubled and careworn, Pétain as calm and inscrutable as ever. Nivelle discussed the war. We then dined with some eight or ten other officers, I being on Pétain's right, and Nivelle opposite. We three monopolised the conversation, the rest of the party keeping silence, as usual at Pétain's table. Very unlike a British mess table! I believe that it was not etiquette in Joffre's day for any one to speak to the *généralissime* unless he spoke first, but, being a stranger, I omitted this boring formality.

Nivelle said that up to the present 34 German divisions out of 43 had been withdrawn from the line for repairs, and that previous experience had shown that this was done when a loss of 4000 men per division had been incurred. He thought that the Germans had already suffered 200,000 casualties in his battle. I asked how long the divisions withdrawn could be counted out, and Pétain answered, ' Three weeks at a minimum.' Nivelle was very pleasant and agreeable, but he lacks Pétain's character, and was plainly under the latter's influence. It was like pupil and master, and there was no doubt which was the dominant spirit. We told stories. Pétain discussed women and marriage. He said he was a bachelor but loved children, and after the war he would have to choose between matrimony and suicide. I said that it was often the same thing. Pétain thought that he would have to adopt some small children of about five or six.

About 9.30 P.M. Nivelle left, and Pétain and I adjourned to his working-room, where we were alone. I began at once by saying that the general situation was very delicate, and that I had come at M. Painlevé's suggestion to talk it over with him. Pétain asked me to give him my views first. I said that we could not count this year upon Russia, and that the best we could hope was that she should hold in her front the German troops now in the East, but that we must also face the possibility that Russia might make peace, or be ' down and out ' for the rest of the war. I said that Italy lived in terror of being attacked, and offered little assistance, though she had a mass of troops, and that the burden of the war fell upon France and England until America could help. How were we situated ? We had 169 divisions against 155 German. 'Yes,' interrupted Pétain, 'but as the French battalion has only three companies to the four German, and as the artillery comparison was also in German favour, three German divisions were the equal of four French.' I agreed, but said that the British divisions were stronger at present than the German, and that the point was that there was practically equality[1] on the two sides, a conclusion with which Pétain agreed. I then said that France had few reserves left but the *récupérés* and the yearly classes, and Pétain replied that this was correct. Our numbers, I went on, are not being maintained, and unless we did better at home we should have a deficit of 200,000 infantry in France by the end of July, and the loss of moral would correspond with the reduction of effectives.

In all these circumstances, I continued, I had watched with concern the plans for the summer, which did not appear to me justified by the relative forces in presence, and I thought that the promises held out by Nivelle and Mangin to break the German lines were sanguine, to say the least. It seemed to me that too little attention was paid to the mechanics of the war, and that our plans of a long-range offensive would only be justified if we had a much greater superiority of force than that which we actually possessed. I was, in the circumstances, for a short-range and prudent offensive, such as that of Haig's on April 9, and I reminded Pétain that this was France's last Army, and that Nivelle's failure had destroyed the half, at least, of the French class of the year in a few days. How could this go on ? We also had lost many men, and at the present rate might lose more a month than the 100,000 on which the War Office and Haig were tabulating. It seemed to me, therefore,

---

[1] According to M. Painlevé the superiority of the Allies on the Western front on July 1 only amounted to 100,000 rifles.

that the whole situation required to be reviewed, and action
to be taken to correspond with the realities of the position.

Pétain said that he absolutely agreed with me. He himself had often conducted short-range attacks such as those
of which I spoke, especially at Verdun. He had strictly
limited Nivelle at Verdun, but Nivelle was not apparently
aware of it. When Nivelle had succeeded *en sous-ordre,*
the Government had acclaimed him as a genius, though
he was only acting as a subordinate. In fact, the instrument had been acclaimed the master. This last Rheims
offensive, said Pétain, was prepared by Joffre last December.
It was originally meant to engage the four southerly British
Armies, the Army Group of Franchet d'Esperey, and Pétain's
own 5th Army. With such a long line the Germans would
have been highly tried, and could not have easily massed their
reserves as they did on April 16 against the French. But
the German retreat had thrown the plan out of gear, since
two British and one French Army had no enemy in their
front. Painlevé had visited Pétain a fortnight before the
attack began, and had consulted him about it. Pétain had
explained the position, had severely criticised the prosecution of the plan under the changed conditions, and had
foretold its failure. He was perfectly justified in giving
his opinion when the War Minister asked for it. Painlevé
invited him to Paris, where he met at dinner Ribot, Thomas,
Painlevé, and Admiral Lacaze. All were members of the
War Council. The conversations here led to the appearance
of Pétain before a full meeting of the War Council, at which
were present President Poincaré, all the usual Ministers,
Nivelle, and all the Army Group Commanders. Here Pétain
expounded his views ; most of the Army Group Commanders
agreed with him, and Nivelle, who was absolutely *acculé,*
offered to resign after being completely defeated in argument. But the War Council would not accept the resignation, and finally Nivelle took the 5th Army away from
Pétain and made absolutely no change in the dispositions.
In short, said Pétain, the Council had been a *parlote* ; and
I said that we knew the *genus* perfectly well.

After Nivelle's costly failure, there had been a question of what was to be done.   Pétain had been called to Council. He had refused to become the 'Major-General' (Chief of Staff) in Paris, because he could not issue orders, and besides, he knew that he was not popular with the Chambers, who were alarmed by his *boutades* at their expense.   The actual solution is to be announced on Monday, and the only thing sure is that Pétain is to be master.   But whether Pétain will go to Paris with full powers, or replace Nivelle at Compiègne, is still uncertain.   I must ascertain, as Nivelle has invited me to Compiègne, and it will be awkward to arrive there during the *déménagement*.   Pétain was severe upon Nivelle.   I remarked how much I had regretted Joffre, for though he was no eagle, had made mistakes, and had acted against his military conscience in the affair of Salonika, he was a solid asset to the Entente, enjoyed great prestige, and represented the only fixed point in French politics.   Pétain agreed, and said that he had always supported Joffre, but that the latter was very jealous, and as each new star rose in the firmament Joffre tried to snuff it out.   But the real cause of Joffre's failure was his inability to surround himself by the right men.   He had allowed operations to fall completely into the hands of Colonel Renouard, who had established liaison officers in all the Armies—a system of which the Armies disapproved; and I learnt, without surprise, that poor Renouard is to go.

Pétain then asked me many questions about our military authorities, generals, and Ministers, and I sketched out their characteristics at some length, assuring him, in particular, that he could place entire reliance upon Robertson and Haig, who would never fail him, even if for the moment stupid stories were current.   The argument used to Painlevé against Pétain that he was a pacificist and a cunctator, though absurd, must be met, as such phrases did harm and created a false atmosphere and impression.

Pétain was very wrathful on this subject, recounted to me his *états de service* during the war point by point, from regimental to Army commander, and asked, indignantly, whether he had merited the accusation levelled at him. I said that the phrase having been launched, I should be asked in London what he meant to do and in what manner his system would be an improvement on the past. It would be well for him to enlighten me on these points, even if I could easily guess the explanation. Pétain said that the practice of promising the moon and of the *surenchère* had entered the Army from French politics and had done an infinity of harm. Joffre had begun it by promising victory at the end of three months, by the end of which period everybody had forgotten about it, and then Joffre promised it again, while Briand traded on it. The foolish promise before the Rheims offensive was of this character, and he, Pétain, would never lower himself to such deceptions. He would tell the truth, and if politicians did not like it they could find some one else to lie to them. He was opposed to the practice of attempting to do much with little, and preferred to do little at a time with much. He agreed that Haig's day of April 9 was a good model, but thought that so were his attacks at Verdun. The situation required great prudence and great patience. He said that 'you cannot have strategy until you have exhausted the enemy's reserves.' He was for the short-range prudent offensive or for the aggressive defensive, for a further increase in the artillery, and for its use in the manner which he had explained to me at Verdun last year. It was necessary, in France's position, to economise men, while hitting the enemy as hard as possible.

He considered it of the first importance that England should keep her ranks well filled. He wished to incorporate American recruits in the French Armies until they were trained, and then to form companies and battalions of them until they were fit to go into the larger units. He had made a plan which he would show me in the morning, and had given a copy of it to the Americans. The merit of it was that we should have the support of our new Ally in the field without delay. Pétain agreed with me about German numbers and moral, as also that German combing

is at an end, and he does not for a moment count the Germans
to be beaten men. He expressed a great admiration for
British troops, and hoped and believed that the British
people appreciated him and would soon learn to know
him better. He also told me of the great effect which
had been produced in raising the moral of the French
Army by my report on the German manœuvres of 1911.
He confessed that it was a revelation to him that such a
report should have been written by an English officer,
as they were supposed in France to be ignorant of the
grande guerre.

He also told me that the French Government had consulted him about Nivelle's offensive, and he had advised
that it should be stopped in its original form as it would
only lead to the useless loss of another 40,000 men. I
asked what Pétain would do, as Haig wanted to go on, and
I also asked how Pétain would extricate his own troops
from the present position. He saw no reason why Haig
should not go on, and said that the French would continue
to fight and would not allow us to be overwhelmed. A
very satisfactory talk late into the night. We understood
each other, and Pétain asked me to keep in touch with him
by letter, and to come and see him often.

Saturday, April 28. Put up at the Hotel de la Mère Dieu
last night. Went round this morning to the H.Q. of the
Armies of the Centre and saw Pétain. I sat in his room while
he received all the morning reports, which were read out to
him by his Chief of Staff, Colonel Serrigny. I was struck by
the quick and businesslike methods of both, and by the acute,
pungent, and penetrating remarks of the General. He gave
me the evidence taken from prisoners. It shows a German
intention to attack as soon as our infantry come near,
and I remarked that this was what was happening on our
front. He also gave me the *mémoire* on American help
to France. His two principles are *agir vite* and *voir grand*.
It is dated April, and gives the whole plan for American
help, not only in men, but in artillery, aviation, etc. He
proposes 120 guns for each American division, including

40 field guns and field howitzers, and 80 heavies of 105, 120, 155, and 210 mm. He wants a great output of shells, and reserve guns to be made in proportion to shells turned out, so that wear and tear may be met. He calculates that he can get this new artillery ready in eight months, and he suggested the Creusot guns for America. It is a long and interesting paper, and my only criticism to him was that it did not touch upon the language difficulty.

General Pétain has maps hung round his room, with some graphics, showing at a glance by coloured labels the number of German and Allied divisions fighting, in reserve, and withdrawn for repairs. The Verdun front looked the most unsafe, and Pétain said that he had frequently warned the G.Q.G. on this subject. Pétain keeps his Staff busy. He makes them study all theatres of war, and thereby he will find himself well posted when he reaches Paris, and will have trained aids. I found him concerned about Italy and Switzerland. He thinks that if Italy is struck down, Germany will invade France through the Swiss plain, along which run four good railways and eleven good roads from east to west, all marked in colours on one of his maps. He also showed me interesting maps of the German railway lines, which show the main lines east and west, the normal gauge, old and new lines, on each frontier, and the metre gauge and 60 cm. Decauvilles which branch from them. It is all very illuminating, and explains the excellence of the roads in the ground which we have taken from the Germans, who must have little need of horses and lorries. We talked of Paris, and I advised him to trust Le Roy-Lewis, whose name he took down. He mentioned, incidentally, that Ribot had told him that by April 7 there would not be one sou left in the French Treasury, but that, providentially, America had come in on the 6th. P. said that he meant to make Serrigny head of the 3rd Bureau at G.Q.G., which would remain at Compiègne as it was a convenient spot. It had a fine building for offices, and he saw no reason for changing it.

After breakfast we motored off together to see the preparations for the attack on Moronvillers to-morrow. At the top of a high fir wood a little rustic look-out had been prepared like a nest in the topmost branches. We ascended by a ladder and had a fine view of the bombardment. General Vanderberg, who is literally *criblé de blessures*, told us that the haze beat the *avions* to-day, and that we should have to postpone the attack for twenty-four hours. Pétain means to throw for the heights with six divisions and a lot of heavy guns. We had another good talk motoring in and out. He said that Nivelle knew nothing of the coming change of command when he was at dinner last night, but that the announcement would be made on Monday. Pétain has already made all his plans, and I gather that there will be many changes in the higher commands. If the War Council changed their minds at the last moment, he said that he would write and let me know and tell me the reasons.

I asked why the Chambers feared him. Was it on religious grounds ? 'No,' said P., 'I am certainly a Catholic and respect my faith, but I am not *pratiquant*, and have not been to Mass for thirty years.' 'It is true,' he went on to say, 'that when Joffre went, I said that his successor should claim the control of all the French reserves, and should ask that Parliament should be prorogued until the war was over, but the latter remark was a joke. It, however, established a blue funk of me in Parliament.' Pétain's refusal to succeed Nivelle will now result in his being *nommé d'office*, and he thinks that this will strengthen his position. He intends to give the War Council the deuce of a time when he first goes before them, and proposes to make them all miserable. He is drawing up a *bilan*— a profit and loss account—and proposes to tell them the whole truth, which they have never heard yet. He says that he knows that with equal forces little can be done, and that he will be roundly abused by everybody, but he proposes to do what he knows to be right, and will not allow himself to be influenced by anybody.

We then discussed what I should do, and whether I

should go along the Armies and see all the commanders.
I said that in view of the stupid charges against Pétain,
I thought that I had better go back to Paris and try to
circumvent them. I could return to the Armies on another
occasion, and, also, I felt that as Pétain meant to change
the commanders, it was waste of time for me to see
any one but Nivelle, whose invitation I had accepted.
Pétain agreed, and away I went. Directly afterwards, a
Hun bombing squadron visited Châlons and gave it beans.

There are many good stories of Pétain's sarcasms and
boutades. He told me one himself which was very amusing.
Some one asked him if he agreed with the desiderata for
a French general. He asked what they were. He was
told that—un général français doit :—

(1) Avoir du cran ;
(2) Avoir du courage à prendre des risques illimitées ;
(3) Avoir une confiance aveugle dans le G.Q.G.

' Oui,' answered Pétain, ' je suis d'accord. Mais je
mettrai la dernière clause entre les deux autres *par peur
qu'elle n'échappe.*' All that I saw of the General confirmed
me in my belief that he is the best leader in France, and
combines the qualities of science, judgment, and character
to a higher degree than any other of the generals whom I
have met. I admire Painlevé—this deputy of the extreme
Left—for his courage in selecting him. We parted on very
good terms. Arrived in Paris. Esher and Le Roy dined
with me, and I posted them in all that had happened. Ribot
had been floundering about telling different people different
things, poor old man, but Painlevé thinks that he has pinned
him down to a formal undertaking to accept Pétain.

Sunday, April 29. I cabled to London a warm eulogy
of Pétain which duly appeared in the *Times*, and I wrote
to Lloyd George, Sir W. R., and Geoffrey Robinson to
counteract the anti-Pétain cabal. Motored out to Ver-
sailles in the afternoon with Le Roy, and walked about
the grounds. A glorious spring day, the first after many
months of the worst winter that I remember. Saw Mrs.
Leeds later. Went to see Painlevé in the evening, and heard

that Pétain had to-day been definitely appointed C.G.S. of the Army and would come to Paris. He had been offered this or C.G.S. to Nivelle, and had naturally chosen the first, and I feel sure that it will be with such extended powers that he will have full control. Painlevé asked me to describe the appointment as eternal, but said that it was, in fact, only temporary, and that Nivelle will be sent on a mission to Russia in a fortnight, when Pétain will succeed him. As Le Roy had no one to help him, I assisted him in figuring out the cipher on the appointment.

Monday, April 30. Reflected over all these matters in the morning. Joseph Reinach ('Polybe' of the *Figaro*) lunched with me. Either he or Lieut. Pernot told me a story of de Galliffet which amused me. When Galliffet received the command of the *division de fer*, all the Nancy authorities came out to greet him, the bishop at their head. The bishop recounted all G.'s exploits and expressed the great joy of the frontier town at receiving such a hero. He then went on to belaud the Comtesse, whose eccentricities were notorious, whereupon Galliffet stopped him, saying, 'Mais pardon, M. l'Évêque, je ne vous ai pas fait du mal!'

Went to the Ministère de l'Armement, 74 Avenue des Champs Élysées, and arranged for some visits to one or two French munition works near Paris. Dined with Le Roy. Met Baron Wedel the Norwegian Minister, M. Paul Cambon, and others. We admired Mme. de San Martino, sister to Mme. Letellier. Le Roy now declares that the Calais Conference was engineered by Bertier. Lyautey left it as his dying injunction to Le Roy to get rid of Bertier. Robertson agreed, and so he went. Le Roy says that Painlevé is rabid with General Wilson for opposing Pétain and interfering in French political affairs.

Tuesday, May 1. In the morning I went to see M. Citröen's *usine*, accompanied by Colonel M. Collin of the French artillery. There are 10,000 French workers, of whom 6000 are women, and also 2000 foreigners. Of the women 2000 are married, and half of them are war-widows, while nearly all the others have lost a brother or a brother-in-law. They work like beavers. This factory is a mushroom growth of the war and did not exist before. Now it turns out 40,000 shell cases a day, and could turn out 60,000 were not steel and lead so short, and M. Citröen says that there is no limit to his expansion, and that he could find 100,000 more women in Paris easily. A fine piece of extemporised organisation. In the afternoon went to Renault's factory, which turns out a great variety of war material, including shells, tanks large and small, 155's, and *camions*. I did not care for the large French tanks.

Saw M. Loucheur, U.S. of S. for Munitions, in the afternoon. M. Thomas is away in Russia. We had a long talk. The department employs 1,500,000 persons. Of these, 550,000 are mobilised men, of whom 300,000 are *réformés*. Thus while our Munitions Ministry shelters 800,000 men of military age under 41, the French only use 250,000 under 47. There are 450,000 young and old people, and 550,000 women. M. Loucheur has been to see the fighting, and agrees with me that the German reply to our guns is weak. He has no complaint against England for any failure to help France. In coal it is the bad distribution rather than any real shortage which is the difficulty. He only needs 300,000 tons of coal a month from us. M. Loucheur showed me a graphic, from which it appears that the output of guns continues to increase, and he told me that they had outstripped our figures by February last. Much, however, is being made for Russia. Spent the late afternoon with Mrs. Leeds. Dined with Baron Wedel and his wife,—who was Madame von André— Emilie Yznaga, and some others. Wedel told us that when the French Government fled to Bordeaux,[1] he and the American Ambassador were asked to go out to the Germans and to try to arrange terms for the peaceful surrender of Paris. Fortunately the victory of the Marne rendered the mission unnecessary.

Haig telephones that he is coming on Thursday to see Pétain, while Lloyd George, Robertson, and Jellicoe, with

---

[1] The Government were described in Paris as *tournedos à la Bordelaise.*

a *duma* of 28 persons, arrive from London the same day. I am a little sorry for Pétain to have to deal with all these people before he is firmly in the saddle and has had a chance of placing his *bilan* before his own War Council. However, I expect he will rise to the occasion.

Wednesday, May 2. Motored to Compiègne and lunched with General Nivelle and his Staff, including Colonel d'Alençon, who was the immediate cause of the Haig-Nivelle row. I walked with the General from his office to his house and talked, and after lunch we were alone together and had a long talk. I told him that I had come to ask what I was to tell our public about the battle of April 16 and following days. He said that his losses were 86,000, including 75,000 French, of whom 16,000 were killed, 4000 missing, and 55,000 wounded, of whom two-thirds only slightly.[1] He had 60 divisions, of which 28 remained unused. I told him that I had been given much higher figures of his losses, but he declared that Paris had estimated his losses from the medical returns, and that they had accounted for the same men several times over by reckoning men in the field dressing station, ambulances, hospitals, etc., as all different people, whereas wounded men passed down these various echelons.

He said that the Allies had agreed last November to attack early so as to forestall a German offensive which might have thrown out our plans. The attack was intended to take place on a front of 200 kilometres. Hindenburg retired to evade the blow, but the Germans were then subjected to attacks on the wings at Arras and to the east of Soissons. He had therefore, he claimed, imposed our will upon the enemy, had taken the initiative, and could claim a strategic victory. He had also obtained a tactical victory by occupying the enemy's first lines on the fronts attacked, contrary to the enemy's will, as shown by captured orders requiring a defence to the last in the first line. Nivelle

---

[1] M. Painlevé's figures are 116,000, April 16 to 25, including 28,000 killed, 84,000 wounded, and 4000 prisoners. See *La Renaissance*, November 1919.

claimed that he took the Huns' first line and parts of his second line.　The enemy had reinforced his first line in a most unusual manner, and the density of the troops of the defence was greater than that of the attack.　The enemy, therefore, suffered terribly from the French artillery fire, and instead of the 52 divisions in reserve, he had but 8 by April 23. There resulted an impossibility for him to carry out any offensive action for a long time to come.　The extent of the front of attack, in proportion to the rest of the front which remains passive, will not allow the enemy to relieve his relatively fresh divisions by those under repair, except for a period relatively short, four to five weeks at most. Nivelle said that signs of wear and tear and of confusion in the enemy's ranks multiplied themselves.　Hence the need to continue the pressure which had produced such good results.

Before I left, General Nivelle wrote all these points down on paper in my presence, and this curious document runs as follows :—

EXPLANATORY NOTE ON THE BATTLE OF APRIL 16, 1917
BY GENERAL NIVELLE

Pertes : 75,000, dont 16,000 tués,
4,000 disparus,
55,000 évacués,
dont les $\frac{2}{3}$ blessés légers.

Avantage stratégique.—Plan Hindenburg : Échapper à l'étreinte des armées franco-britanniques—d'où repli—l'attaque franco-britannique montée sur un très large front déjoue le plan ennemi —les armées allemandes subissent notre étreinte aux 2 ailes (Nord d'Arras—à l'est de Soissons).　Nous imposons notre volonté à l'ennemi et prenons l'initiative des opérations.　C'est la victoire stratégique.

2° *Avantage tactique.*—L'ennemi étreint aux 2 ailes, contrairement à sa volonté, donne l'ordre (ordres trouvés sur les prisonniers) de résister à outrance en 1ère ligne, jusqu'à la mort.　Partout nous brisons cette résistance.　Nous enlevons partout les 1ères lignes, les 2èmes en bien des points.　C'est la victoire tactique.

Résultats.—Pour pouvoir résister à outrance en 1ère ligne, l'ennemi avait renforcé cette ligne d'une façon inusitée.   La densité des troupes de défense était supérieure à celle de l'attaque.

D'où pertes considérables par le feu de notre artillerie— (évaluées à plus de 200 mille hommes).

Usure des forces ennemies qui n'avaient plus, le 23 avril, que 8 divisions fraîches, au lieu de 52.

D'où impossibilité pour lui d'entreprendre avant longtemps aucune action offensive.

Moyen de continuer la bataille.—L'étendue du front d'attaque par rapport aux fronts restés passifs, ne permettra à l'ennemi de relever les divisions relativement fraîches du front par les divisions usées que pendant un temps très court, évalué à 4 ou 5 semaines au plus.

Indices d'usure, de désarroi, se multiplient.   D'où nécessité de continuer cette usure, dont les résultats se feront de plus en plus sévèrement sentir.

Nivelle wrote this paper on his own initiative, and I did not ask for it.   It seemed best not to enter into a discussion with the C.-in-C. on the many contentious points of his *exposé*.   I had called to learn his views, and these he had given to me, so I thought it best to leave it at that.[1]   He also told me distinctly that the decision of the Calais Conference to place the British under him was taken on Lloyd George's initiative.   He approved of Pétain's appointment, saying that the Government would now have some one with them who understood matters.   This they certainly will.   I judge that Nivelle and Haig will press for the continuation of the attack.   Nivelle is very pleasant and a gentleman, but he looked dreadfully worried, and I often recalled Robertson's dictum, that he was either very elementary or thought that we were.

I stopped at Senlis on my way back to consult General Foch, who has been unemployed since December 11 last, and has his headquarters there.   He was just going out for a motor drive with his old C.G.S., General Weygand, but most kindly got out and came in to have a talk. We agreed that the situation was serious.   Foch said that he could not determine what ought to be done

---

[1] I did not publish this statement at the time.

without knowing exactly all about the state of our joint effectives, of our munitions, and of the prospects of the submarine war. But he was disposed to advocate the continuation of what we called the Somme tactics, as opposed to what he called, a little unfairly, the Verdun school. I see no difference if Pétain is considered the master of the Verdun school, but Foch seems to regard Nivelle and Mangin as its chief exponents. He said that the latter people criticised the Somme tactics as slow, and proposed to swallow the Germans at a gulp. The thing could not be done, he said. We must eat the wing, then the leg, and so on ; but if one tried to swallow the whole chicken at a gulp, one would be choked. He liked Nivelle, and said that he was well-intentioned, but did not think that he had the capacity to direct such a great operation as this. The British had done finely. Last time he had seen Lloyd George he had told the latter that if he gave the British Army time it would do England credit, and so it had fallen out. Foch thought that France was headless politically, and urged me to tell L. G. to take the lead and adopt a strong line after consulting Robertson and Haig. He is for the prudent, short-ranging offensive like Pétain. He thinks that the French and British troops are now superb. He regrets Joffre, and for the same reasons that I do. I asked Foch if it was true that he had been accused of being on bad terms with the English. He said that he had. I told him that I had made inquiries, and that there was no foundation whatsoever for the charge on the English side. He was very pleased, but said that when people wanted to do a thing they invented reasons for doing it. He evidently retains his old and cordial sympathy for us. We discussed operations in the West and elsewhere. I was struck by his opinion that in these days one needed a chief skilled in Staff work who could sit at his desk and work out problems with all the science of war at his disposal. I found that Foch had ideas about the low country near the coast, and I advised him to keep away from them. He got out the maps and we had a discussion on the subject.

General Dupont was not at the 2nd Bureau at G.Q.G. when I was there, but I saw a smart *locum tenens*. No one seems to know what the Huns have done with their 8-inch and other heavy material, little of which has appeared in the recent fighting. He thought that the first 13 of the new series of Hun divisions were good material, but that the other 10 were poor. He gives me 230 as the total number of Hun divisions, of which 155 on the Western and 75 for all other uses. He puts the Huns in the depots at 600,000, excluding the 1919 class, but there are the Arras-Rheims losses to be made good. He thinks that the possibilities of Hun criss-cross transport are much reduced. It takes 3000 railway wagons ten days to bring a German division from East to West, and only four or five can be carried over in a month, so no great or rapid transfer is practicable. The great distances which the Huns have to travel have much disorganised their traffic and rolling stock. He agrees that Hun combing is practically ended, but that Hun moral is still good. Hindenburg and the submarine are the Hun gods. Dined with Le Roy on returning to Paris. Esher and Lovat came to talk with us. Haig has arrived here to-night and is at the Crillon. L. G.'s caravan comes to-morrow.

Thursday, May 3. Finished my third, and last, article on 'The Western Front,' and sent it off to Charteris, via Maurice Brett. Lunched with M. Loucheur and a large party of Frenchmen at La Rue's Restaurant, Place de la Madeleine. Two Creusot directors, Bérenger the Senator, Charles Humbert the deputy (famous in munition matters and director of the *Journal*), and various deputies and other folk. Humbert convinced that bread will decide the war. Others expect a *coup de théâtre* on the political side from Germany. When they had all given their views I *optéd* for Armies and victories.

Went to see Haig at 3 P.M. He was immensely pleased with his first talk alone with Pétain to-day, and this gave me great satisfaction. They had got on very well, and had been entirely agreed, as I expected. Haig has lost

86,000 men in the Arras fighting, or, with the other and normal waste, 100,000, as anticipated. The Armies have recommenced to-day, and have taken Fresnoy, and are half in Bullecourt. Haig's deficit of infantry is now 60,000, and he says that Pétain tells him that the French depots have no more that 35,000 men. A nice situation in the first month of the spring offensive! However, our Government prepared for nothing else. Dined with Simon Lovat at the Café de Paris. M. Citröen and his pretty wife—in what looked like widow's weeds—at the table next us. Talked with Le Roy and David Davies, the Welsh M.P., in Le Roy's room later, and passed on to L. G., through the latter, Foch's advice about taking the lead here. We also discussed the Paris Embassy.

Friday, May 4. Saw Colonel Lucas, Robertson's P.S., at the Embassy in the morning, and inferred from his general tone that R. did not much like the changes of command, and had received varying reports of Pétain's views. Lucas asked if Pétain would attack. I said Yes, within his means, but we were neither of us in a position to attack and lose a lot of men, as we should be living on our capital. I learnt this morning that we were at last determined to get our troops away from Salonika, and that this was the reason for Jellicoe's visit. I was delighted, but said that the time for action was while the Bulgars were held fast in the mountains by the snow, and that now the operation would be hazardous. But it was a question whether we should remain and be starved, or depart and be sunk. We agree that the French have only come over to our views from shortage of men here, and not by conviction that we were right.

Adam dined with me. He doubts whether Ribot will be able to stand against the ten interpellations on May 22, and thinks Painlevé vain and imperious, and that he has many enemies. I was much relieved to hear later that the first conference of the soldiers had gone off famously. Pétain had told Le Roy that Robertson had evidently been put against him and was grumpy at first, but the air had soon cleared, and all had been as happy as marriage bells.   M. Hennessy had been to Painlevé to get the latter to name General Wilson as *chef de mission* for the liaison with Pétain, but Painlevé had absolutely refused, and with indignation.   I wrote to Pétain to congratulate him on his first day's work. The Mission dined at the Élysée to-night.

Saturday, May 5.   Meetings all day of the various committees of the Conference.   Lunched with Mrs. Leeds. Reggie Paget came.   He is on three days' leave from the front, and is busy moving Elinor Glyn's furniture!   Mrs. Leeds in great form and very amusing.   She crosses as soon as she can get her boy away to Switzerland.   M. Millerand, late War Minister, came to see me.   He is sure that France will go on, and that the spirit is superb, but she prefers to act with knowledge, and no one tells her with authority what she has to do.   He has been away lecturing in the South, and finds opinion as resolute there as elsewhere to go through with the war.   He wants the Yankees to come to France as soon as possible, and in any manner agreeable to them.

Saw General Pétain at 6.30 P.M. at the War Council Buildings, 4 bis Avenue des Invalides.   He thanked me most cordially for having helped him through the intrigues against him, and said that I had rendered him a great service.   He had, in effect, found that the British had a *prévention* against him, and Robertson showed it in his manner of *entaméing*—as R. would say—the conversation. So Pétain had taken the bull by the horns, had said that he knew of the stories current about him, and then proceeded to recount his *états de service* as he had done to me. He asked, finally, whether any one else had undertaken more resolute attacks, and whether he deserved the sneers of being called a pacificist.   He did not wait for the answer, and, having fired his shot, said, ' Now, gentlemen, we can begin business ! '   Robertson had been gradually won over, and had drafted the agreement on the Western front exactly as Pétain would have drafted it.   The offensive was to be continued, but it was not to be *à longue portée.*   Our troops were to be withdrawn from Salonika, but Pétain warned me that this operation was easier for R. than for him. It was a great disappointment for the French, and indeed a *situation angoissante*, because they had posed as protectors of Serbia and Greece. Pétain said that it would take him three weeks to bring over his people. He said that Robertson had just paid him a visit of courtesy, and had taken his hand and promised to tell him the truth and help him in every way. Pétain was much pleased and touched by the visit. 'Yes, I can do the right thing sometimes, can't I?' said Robertson with a smile when I told him how pleased Pétain was.

Dined with the Mission at the Crillon. Robertson said that he was better pleased with the Conference than with any other that had preceded it. We had taken the lead, and laid down the terms, and all the soldiers were in agreement. Admiral Jellicoe, who sat next to me, told me that the Huns were turning out 3 submarines a week and that we were catching 3 or 4 a month, and, on the whole, had destroyed 2 submarines a month since the war began. We build 6 to 7 destroyers a month, and lose 2 a month from accidents mainly. He wants 500 to cope with the submarines. There are 6 American destroyers now at Queenstown, and there will be 36 at the end of the month. He told me that he needed a good star-shell badly, and could not get one made until he had found an unexploded Hun star-shell at Ramsgate, when he had asked for it to be copied without delays for improvements. Eric Geddes goes to the Admiralty as Controller, and from General becomes Admiral! Jellicoe becomes Chief of the Admiralty Staff, and asks—what's in a name? All are very pleased with Pétain. L. G. stays behind to see his son, and the others leave, 10.45 P.M., for Boulogne, where we arrived 10 A.M., *Sunday morning, May* 6. A slow express, but comfortable, not to say luxurious. We each had a sleeping compartment to ourselves, good food, and regal saloon carriages. We intended to cross in the *Swift*, but a strong N.E. wind made Calais impossible, so we crossed in a boat that had just brought drafts over. Jellicoe not optimistic about evacuating Salonika as he has not enough destroyers to spare for escort duty. One is no use ; he should have two for each ship, and he prefers four. Bacon sends a strong escort for us. Talked with Robertson and Maurice on the way. R. thinks that the Russians are of no use to us. Nothing is doing on the Caucasus front, and the Turks may mass against Maude, who cannot now spare troops for Murray, who is mixed up in a trench warfare mess. I showed Maurice Nivelle's *mémoire*, and he was very critical of it.

I had a talk with the American Admiral, Sims, whom I thought a good and modern flag officer and sure to do well. He told me that he had been shown a chart giving the places where submarines had been seen and had sunk ships. The mass were in S. Irish waters, and off the Scillies, and a few near Brest. He is to work this area, and expects to drive the submarines 100 to 200 miles out to sea, as they are not dependent on local bases. He will soon have fifty destroyers, and will have supply and repair ships so that he can move on to wherever there is an aggregation of submarines. He will have general administrative charge, and all the boats will be under British naval command. He will get a lot more patrol boats and light craft, and the building of fifty more destroyers has begun. America is making 1,500,000 tons of steel shipping besides the wooden ships of green wood. He thinks that thirteen knots gives the tramp a fair chance, if she has a gun, against the submarine submerged. It is a dangerous problem,[1] but had we 500 destroyers we might have met it. Our Grand Fleet occupies 100 destroyers, and many more are needed for escorts. We caught two submarines last week, of which one was recharging on the surface by night. This makes a noise which can be heard five miles away, and one of our submarines heard it, stole up under water, and

---

[1] Admiral Sims's account of the U-boat war in the American *World's Work* for September 1919 gives a chart showing over 100 ships sunk by the U-boats during April 1917 in the Mediterranean alone.

sank the Hun, a few men only escaping. Sims thinks that nets and mines off the German coast would require watching and guarding, which means that both Navies would be gradually drawn in, and it is waste to expend ten millions and find a gap of 600 yards driven through the minefield. The plan was tried in the north, and too many watching craft were torpedoed, so it was given up. Sims considers the American battleships to be a reserve to be used in case of need, or if the area of operations extends, *e.g.* in the Baltic. He described life on a submarine as hell, from the smells and the rolling.

We reached London in the afternoon, and I was home by 4 P.M. and found all well.[1]

---

[1] The early part of the campaign of 1917 has been the subject of such serious dispute that I append the dates of the chief events for convenience of future reference :—

Nov. 16, 1916. The Chantilly Conference. General Joffre's plan accepted.

Dec. 16, 1916. General Nivelle succeeds General Joffre.

Dec. 21, 1916. General Nivelle's plan sent to Sir D. Haig.

Jan. 15, 1917. The London Conference. F.M. Sir D. Haig and General Nivelle agreed.

Jan. 25, 1917. General Nivelle's new plan. Vast scope and aims.

Feb. 26 and 27, 1917. The Calais Conference. F.M. Sir D. Haig placed under General Nivelle.

Feb. 27, 1917. General Nivelle's instructions to F.M. Sir D. Haig.

Mar. 1, 1917. The German retirement begins.

Mar. 2, 1917. F.M. Sir D. Haig consults the War Committee.

Mar. 6, 1917. M. Briand complains of Sir D. Haig to Mr. Lloyd George.

Mar. 12 and 13, 1917. A new Conference in London. The Generals in accord.

Mar. 15, 1917. The German retirement completed. Fall of M. Briand's Government.

Mar. 16, 1917. General Nivelle's fresh plan sent to Sir D. Haig.

Mar. 17, 1917. M. Ribot's Government succeeds.

April 6, 1917. The Compiègne Conference in President Poincaré's saloon carriage.

April 9, 1917. F.M. Sir D. Haig wins the Arras-Vimy victory.

April 16, 1917. General Nivelle attacks in Champagne and only takes the German first-line trenches with heavy loss.

April 29, 1917. General Pétain appointed Chief of the General Staff at Paris.

May 4, 1917. A Paris Conference. The offensive to be continued with limited objectives.

May 16, 1917. General Pétain succeeds General Nivelle in command.

CHAPTER XXI

THE AMERICAN PROGRAMME

General Murray's situation—Our horses—A recruiting talk with General Geddes—Where the 3½ million men of military age in civil life now are—Austrian and Italian strengths on Italian front—The Italian Isonzo offensive of May 12—Mr. Lloyd George suggests a defensive in the West—Low Country warfare—Lord Burnham and the Calais Conference—I address the Manchester Chamber of Commerce— A northern business audience—Some plain speaking—Foch says that *la grande guerre est finie*—Lord Hardinge on Russia—Plumer's victory at the Messines Ridge, June 7—Admiral Hall at the Admiralty—Sir John Cowans's advice for the Americans—Allenby replaces Murray in Egypt—Sir Edward Carson on naval affairs—The present military position in France—Lord Crewe's opinion of Lord Kitchener— General Tom Bridges on his mission to the United States—Probable course of American arrivals—Lieut. Pernot on French opinions and events—On Marshal Joffre in America—The Grand Duke Michael and the revolutionaries—A talk with F.M. Sir Douglas Haig at Eastcott—His view of the Flanders position—We agree about the War Cabinet's illusions—General Robertson's opinions—an amusing cartoon—The position at home.

A LETTER from Murray tells me how he is getting on—

> GENERAL HEADQUARTERS,
> EGYPTIAN EXPEDITIONARY FORCE,
> *22nd April* 1917.

MY DEAR REPINGTON,—I am in my train on my way back from Advanced General Headquarters at Khan Yunus to Cairo, to see the Mark Sykes' Political Mission, which has just arrived and is sure to prove a source of nuisance to me.

We are now close up against the Turks' main position, which runs from the right, which rests on the sea about Sheikh Hasan, and, roughly, on the arc of a circle with a radius of about 3000 yards, west and south-west of Gaza as far as the Ali Muntar Ridge. This section, which consists of a double line of trenches and redoubts, is strongly held by infantry and machine guns, well placed and concealed in the impenetrable cactus hedges, built in the high mud banks enclosing gardens and orchards which stretch back to the outskirts of the town.

Due south of Gaza is the main Ali Muntar position, which forms the key of the whole system of defences immediately covering the town. This position is our 'Vimy Ridge,' is very well wired, and has the natural obstacle provided by the cactus hedges. It is a nest of German-manned machine guns. The line then turns back north-eastwards along the eastern slopes of Ali Muntar for about 2000 yards, whence it bends south-eastwards to Hareira. This section of the line is a semi-continuous series of redoubts and trenches, well placed and well sited. Alternative positions have been prepared and fortified behind the whole of this line.

The bulk of the enemy's forces are in the neighbourhood of Hareira and Sheria. Both his flanks are absolutely secure : one rests on the sea and the other on a broken, waterless country impassable to wheels, the dongas of which have to be ramped for cavalry to be moved over. The enemy has at least five divisions and a cavalry division on this line, and, as far as I can gather, many more divisions are on their way to join him.

I am now engaged fortifying myself opposite Gaza so as to get all the troops I possibly can free for offensive action. Some way or other I must gain freedom of movement and not get stuck down to trench warfare. The problem is difficult because I am weak in troops, as you know. The reinforcements I am receiving from India will require a long training before they are fit to put in the field. Those from East Africa are absolutely riddled with malaria, and will have to be nursed. The whole problem is an interesting one, and not easy of solution. Philip Chetwode is my right-hand man—a very trusted, capable old friend.

I do not think it is understood by the few students of this out-of-the-way campaign how great are our difficulties ; the vast deserts with absolutely no water, a few scattered oases with a very little. For instance, my cavalry on the right flank is now watered once a day, and either has to go back ten miles to get it, or go forward and fight for it between the two lines. I long for Joe Maude's Tigris, and shall probably end this campaign with water on the brain.

We have really done well the last week or two, though it does not sound much. We have given the Turks some shrewd knocks, inflicting heavy casualties, and we are breaking in our territorial divisions to war under many aspects. I am very well, and perfectly happy, and the various problems interest me immensely. We are certainly pulling our weight, and ought to make the Russian advance easier and Joe Maude's position secure.

What splendid work has been done in France by both Haig and Nivelle. By the end of the summer, if we keep up our reinforcements, the war ought to have a very different complexion.—Yours ever,   A. J. MURRAY.

Monday to Friday, May 7 to 11. Occupied in writing and in Tribunal work. A curious example of the way the poor live. A woman in a small way as greengrocer and with five children was in receipt of 37s. 6d. a week separation allowance, and admitted that she took in 6 loaves a day, or 84 lbs. a week! Her proper allowance, according to the rationing rules, was 24 lbs., or less if she used flour. But one of our members said that people in her class ate bread at all meals, as it was the easiest form of food to eat and needed no preparation.

Lady Murray called, and is much exercised about Archie, whose recall is persistently advertised in conversation. I fear that the War Cabinet do not appreciate his difficulties, as explained in his last letter to me, dated April 22, which I have sent to Robinson and to Northcliffe to digest. Lunched one day with Lady Paget, who wants me to write for the American *Times*, *World*, *Tribune*, or *Herald*. Spoke to Northcliffe on the subject, who approves. Lady Johnstone still ill with her broken arm. Jack Cowans and I had a talk about the state of our horses in France, which had given me great concern. He said that owing to sinkings we were down to three days' oats reserve in France one day in January. Haig on Jan. 16 reduced the oats ration by one-quarter, *i.e.* from 12 to 8 lbs. for artillery draught horses, and for others in proportion, without informing the Q.M.G. Cowans agrees that clipping, want of shelter, overwork, underfeeding, and shortage of horses account for the trouble. We also discussed the soldiers' rations, which cause some complaints owing to the unpopularity of the biscuits, of which 20 per cent. are now provided, partly owing to transport difficulties; and we also went into the question of variety of rations and the better practices of the French. Certainly I have never seen our horses in such a state, and Birkbeck showed us that we had lost in France from Jan. 1 to April 14 as many horses nearly as during the whole of 1916. It used to be 1·7 per cent. loss a month, and has been 5 to 7 per cent. in the above period.

Saturday to Monday, May 12 to 14. Went down to Coombe for the week-end. Glorious weather. The Edwin Montagus, Lady Granard, Jack Cowans, Evan Charteris, and Lord Lurgan in the house party, and there came down Lady Johnstone, the Spanish Ambassador, M. Bardac of the French Embassy, Mrs. O'Neill the tennis player, Baroness de Forest, Wolkoff, Lady Alistair Ker, and a lot more ladies. Played some desperate single games of tennis with Montagu all the Sunday morning, and we tied, though he is twenty years younger than I am. Jack and I went over to Mrs. St. George's to see Lady Headfort, and found ' Scatters ' Wilson and some others there. We met Lady Massereene and Lady Curzon motoring on the way and had a talk. Jack tells me that the Americans have offered us 100,000 men, which I deplore, and he says that some lunatics suggest that they should be quartered in Ireland for training ! He says that he only learnt of the Salonika decision by chance, and was busy cramming in supplies there ! He goes to France, Wednesday, to investigate my criticisms about the horses. Montagu says that the whole attitude of the H. of C. towards L. G.'s optimistic review during the secret session was one of scepticism, but when Asquith got up and supported him the House was induced to accept the soporific. M. said that L. G.'s whole attitude before he took office was one of pessimistic criticism. He had done nothing since he came in, and yet his attitude was now one of the utmost optimism. M. thought that we had still not made up our minds what to do. We were neither throwing all our power into France nor accepting the fact that we had to wait till we were stronger.

Motored back to town with Jack in the morning of Monday. Met Lord Crawford, who said that our good imports of wheat had been obtained at the cost of the reduction of other imports, and that even munitions were now suffering. He read the position to be that if Germany could not beat us on the submarines before the autumn, we would make peace before Christmas.

Tuesday, May 15. Lunched with Lady Randolph at her new house, 8 Westbourne Street, W. She has done it up in an extremely clever and attractive manner. Winston there and four pretty women, including Mrs. Lavery. W. thought that L. G.'s speech was directed solely to create an atmosphere favourable to him in the Commons, and W. thought that events would soon do justice to the optimism. L. G. has talked of 800,000 recruits to come this year; but W. said that none of his, W.'s, facts and figures had been disputed and denied, and that men of all parties had congratulated him on his speech, which was about the best that he had ever made. Dined with Theresa Lady Londonderry, the young Lord and Lady L., Belle Herbert, Edmund Gosse, Hugh Cecil, and the Duchess of Marlborough. We discussed the cavalry at Monchy. Lord L. and his mother argued about Ireland at the end, and I find him very keen to throw himself into Irish politics with a view to a settlement.

Wednesday, May 16. This morning came the news that Pétain is to succeed Nivelle, and that Foch is to be C.G.S. at Paris in Pétain's place. This completes the plan, and I write an article on it. Spent the rest of the day in the country, which was looking very bonny. The show of blossom on all the fruit trees is unimaginably fine in all the orchards.

Thursday, May 17. My article on Pétain and Foch appears. I find that my article in the *Times* of May 11 is very widely quoted. I lunched with Madame Vandervelde, Edmund Gosse, and Roger Fry, at 48 Bedford Court Mansions. We discussed books, pictures, people, and the war. Then the Tribunal, and was so late that I had to go in uniform to Mrs. Astor's, where was a large party of some twenty people, including Sir J. and Lady Graham, Joan Poynder, the Winston Churchills, Lady Moyra Cavendish, Charlie Beresford, Lady Paget, Lady Cynthia Asquith, Sir F. Hopwood, Sir L. Earle, and others. Lady Graham interesting about her work in an attic. Talked with Earle and Hopwood after dinner, and we all agreed that the War Cabinet was incompetent, also that the Monarchy held all the Empire together as no President could. Played a rubber with Lady Graham, Lady Moyra, and Evan. Hopwood seems to have been in Scandinavia, and in some sort of touch, through an intermediary, with the Kaiser, whose civil advisers want us to destroy the military prestige of the Junkers or they never can make peace ! Our soldiers are doing their best to oblige !

Friday, May 18. Wrote most of the day. Interesting letters from Murray from Egypt, from Maude from Mesopotamia, and from Birdwood from France. Dined with Mrs. Long, Lord Derwent, and Baroness de Brienen, and played some good Bridge ; a most pleasant and quiet evening.

Saturday, May 19. Went to see General Geddes in the afternoon to talk recruiting. From Jan. 1 to May 18 they have collected 295,407 general service men and 172,343 others, a total of 467,750,[1] which is not bad in

[1] NUMBER OF RECRUITS OBTAINED BY DIRECT ENLISTMENT AND FROM GROUPS AND CLASSES

	General Service.	Others.	Total.	
1917.				
January . .	51,131	34,538	85,669	
February . .	75,930	42,911	118,841	
March . .	75,445	44,094	119,539	
April . . .	55,857	31,175	87,032	
1st to 12th May	25,267	13,423	38,690	Includes 573 for Ireland.
13th ,,				,, — ,,
14th ,,	2,272	1,274	3,546	,, 68 ,,
15th ,,	2,558	1,309	3,867	,, 57 ,,
16th ,,	2,693	1,446	4,139	,, 65 ,,
17th ,,	2,305	1,225	3,530	,, 54 ,,
18th ,,	1,949	948	2,897	,, 45 ,,
Total for current month . .	37,044	19,625	56,669	
Grand total from 1st January.	295,407	172,343	467,750	

itself, but between April 4—when Robertson asked for 500,000 men before the end of July—and May 18, they have only got in 93,000 men for general service, and this is less than 60,000 a month, at which rate R. will only have half his requirements at the end of July. Geddes seems to count on 100,000 more, however, from the new law for re-examination of the rejected, and on more men again by combing general service men from Home Defence, and from the rear in France, while he has designs on the boys of $18\frac{1}{2}$, saying that the German boys of $17\frac{1}{2}$ will be fighting this summer. By these shifts Geddes hopes to go a long way to get the men needed, but not all R. asked for and by the date he specified, and this is only to keep up strengths, and allows nothing for new divisions which Geddes and I concur in thinking necessary.

We then went into the question where the men of military age, 18 to 41, now are in civil life. There are $3\frac{1}{2}$ millions of them. There are 728,705 temporarily exempted, including 226,705 in certified occupations, 196,000 for domestic reasons, and 126,000 appeals outstanding. There are 628,000 under the Ministry of Munitions ; 527,000 exempted by the Colliery Courts ; 236,000 on the railways, including 50,000 under 25 ; 115,000 of low medical categories, C3, etc. ; 211,000 unexpired notices, etc. ; 85,000 men badged by the Admiralty, and 37,000 by the War Office ; 61,000 men holding trade cards, 88,000 men of the transport trades, 47,000 of the public utility services, and 40,000 absolute rejections. There are many other headings. Geddes thinks he ought to get 300,000 out of the M. of M., 100,000 from the railways, 200,000 from the mines, and so on. He reckons the class of the year to be 364,000, but only counts on 240,000 to serve, as some 60,000 will not pass fit, he thinks, and 60,000 will be in exempted occupations. Geddes still wants the men of 41 to 50. He put out the voluntary or Derby group system for these men as a counterblast to the P.M.'s optimistic speech in the Commons' secret session. He does not expect much from it. Agriculture is not shown specially in his lists, which is a pity, but I think it is about 500,000.

Sunday, May 20. General Dessino came to lunch at Maryon. He complains that we do not understand Russia, and that he feels everywhere, and even his daughter feels, a great decrease of confidence in Russia, almost amounting to neglect and rudeness. He is sure that Russia will attack next month. He says that desertion has been common in Russia all through the war, and mentioned that there were 50,000 French deserters in Spain. He also thinks that German divisions moved West from the East have been replaced by others, either tired or of less value.

Monday, May 21. Maurice tells me that the Austrians have 1400 guns and 300 battalions (16 divisions) against 2400 Italian guns and 450 battalions on the front of the new Isonzo battle. There are $36\frac{1}{2}$ Austrian divisions on the whole Italian front.

Saw Northcliffe and Lovat Fraser at the *Times* office. Went on to have a talk with Lady Ridley at her house. We discussed the war, Ireland, Smuts's theories about the Teutonic race, the future of France, American aid, and other matters. She has a remarkable capacity for rapidly analysing a situation and arriving at the truth, and I do not know any woman in London better worth consulting. She gave me many ideas worth thinking over.

Found Robertson at York House later, and we had a good talk. We were both pleased with the Italian offensive which began on the Isonzo on May 12. But R. was very scornful about Russia, and declared that we should get no good from her this year. He could not imagine why Germany had not drawn more on her Eastern troops, but apparently they had not done so yet, though it was true that she had mainly tired or second grade troops there. R. says that his 500,000 men demand referred solely to general service men, and he admitted that we were only getting 60,000 of them a month. However, we might get a few more from the re-examination of the medically rejected and discharged, and perhaps 300,000 to 400,000 altogether by the end of July. R. saw no difficulty in raising new divisions if we got the men, but the War Cabinet were not helping him to get them. They were busy with other subjects and left him alone. For instance, this morning, they had spent nearly all the time discussing the Socialist Conference at Stockholm, and it was not till 1 P.M. that Maurice was able to get a small matter settled. They were not really placing the war first, and when they did discuss it they understood little about it. L. G. had asked why we could not adopt a defensive in the West. I told him Montagu's opinion, that we were doing neither one thing nor the other. R. thought that this did not express the whole truth, and that we could not sit still and let Germany play tricks elsewhere. We agreed that there was practical equality in the West, and he could not see his way to winning the war either this year or next. He was much exercised how to get our troops away from Salonika. If he could get them away, then we might do something to clear up Palestine, but at present half our submarine losses occurred in the Mediterranean, which was a narrow sea favourable for submarine action, and the French and Italians were no good for sea affairs. Our losses on the Arras front had been, he agreed, 100,000 in the month following April 9, and about 20,000 more later, but in the last week only 1000 or so a day. He had no estimate of the German losses. I gave him a warning to keep out of Low Country fighting, and said that I had warned Foch when he disclosed ideas to me in this sense. I said that you can fight in mountains and deserts, but no one can fight in mud and when the water is let out against you, and, at the best, you are restricted to the narrow fronts on the higher ground, which are very unfavourable with modern weapons. I reminded him of our past failures in the low-lying lands, and urged him to keep away from them. He listened so attentively that I think that some operation in this sense may be in the wind. He gave me no hope of any offensive by the Russian Army of the Caucasus, and generally said that the Russians were no good and had let us down. He had received several letters or telegrams from Russian soldier committees, etc., full of tosh, and he had chucked them all into the waste-paper basket. He expected nothing of any serious value from Russia this year.

Tuesday, May 22. I publish a short article on the new Italian offensive in the Carso. Lunched with Lady Sarah Wilson at a nice little house, 2 John Street, where she is temporarily till her house is ready. Lady Curzon and Mrs. Belville also there, and Captain Keith Trevor. A cheery party. Lady Curzon declares that she is ill and cannot travel by train, but she looks the picture of health. Dined with Lady Granard and a large party. Mrs. Whitelaw Reid, Fritz Ponsonby, Lord and Lady Burnham, the Winston Churchills, Lord Lurgan, Mrs. George Keppel, Lord Richard and Lady Moyra Cavendish, Mr. and Mrs. Walter Burns, and half a dozen more. I found Mrs. Reid very well informed about American affairs, and we agreed to meet again. After dinner Burnham admitted that he had taken part in the Calais Conference to this extent, namely, that he had submitted the French views about unity of command to Lloyd George, but from London and not from Paris. Burnham offers to tell me the whole story when we can have a private talk.

Wednesday, May 23. Having accepted an invitation from the Manchester Chamber of Commerce to address them on the subject of Man-Power, I left St. Pancras, 9.50 A.M., with Mr. Hannon of the Navy League, and arrived Manchester, 2.47 P.M. Spoke for 35 minutes without reporters to a select audience of Lancashire business men, nearly all those who had been invited turning up. I took them through all the facts and figures and told them the real situation. Many got up to speak and asked me a number of questions, to which I duly replied. I liked the Northern business audience. They took nothing for granted, were very keen, asked the frankest questions, and explained the position in the Manchester district very clearly. They do not rightly know what the Government expects of them. They showed me that Manchester had been very strict about exemptions, and that their great need was shipping and labour. They cannot get their goods away for want of ships, and so cannot lodge the bills of lading in the banks to cover advances. They also have to pack cotton in bales instead of cases, and are short of men who can do it. Many told me that there were heaps of young men in certain circles there, notably munitions, who should go, and that the country districts also contained many young fellows who could be spared. They rose to the point about sporadic expeditions, and did their best to extract a promise from me that no more should be undertaken. I refused to go bail for the War Cabinet! They wanted the alien Jews brought to heel, were inquisitive about Ireland, wanted to know why colonial labour was not being more used, and asked the Army to dig out more young men in khaki from hospitals, etc. Several asked me when the Government meant to govern. On the whole, a very alert and well-informed audience, intensely patriotic, and several said that they would do anything to win the war if the Government told them what to do. Returned home by 11 P.M.

Thursday, May 24. Had a talk with Mrs. Whitelaw Reid about the *Tribune* and the war. Dined with the Ernest Cunards at 27 Portman Square. Billy Lurgan, Jack Cowans, Mrs. Ronny Greville, Mrs. Robert Grosvenor (Mrs. Cunard's daughter), Lady Cunard, the Duke and Duchess of Teck, Lady Sarah Wilson, and Sir J. Lister Kaye. Mrs. Greville most amusing and interesting, and we talked most of the dinner. The Duke agreeable. We discussed who was likely to succeed Haig if he were recalled, and I thought Allenby the nearest approach to the Wellington type in our Armies. A pleasant evening. Jack, back from France, says that the 270,000 artillery horses have suffered most. I put it down to the distance of the wagon lines from the guns, the absence of the captain of the battery, and the ignorance of the new officers of horsemastership.

Whitsuntide. I spent the days of May 26 to 29 with the

Lockett Agnews at Hallingbury, and had some delightful rides in the forest and good golf croquet. Wonderful weather. The country looks splendid. I never saw such a show of buttercups. The gardens looking beautiful. Is there a war ?

Friday, June 1. Lunched with Mrs. Robert Grosvenor at 88 Gloucester Place, Portman Square. Sir Sidney Greville, Dr. Dillon, Mr. Raemakers the Dutch cartoonist, Mrs. Astor, Mrs. Keppel, and the Duchess of Westminster. Mrs. Astor took me away in her little electric brougham, which she drives herself in a most workmanlike manner. She looks in it for all the world like a beautiful piece of Dresden china in a glass case. I saw F.M. Lord French later. He had received a visit from General Foch during the visit of Ribot, Thierry, Jules Cambon, and Foch to London, May 28-29. Foch had declared that *la grande guerre est finie*, and he ascribed it to the socialistic movements in Europe and the state of affairs in Russia.

Monday, June 4. Lunched with Marjorie at the Ritz. We went down to Agnews afterwards and saw two fine new Romneys of Lady M'Leod, and a wonderful Reynolds of Venus and the Piping Boy, in the best manner and dated about 1785. We went on to the Academy. The worst that I ever remember, and except the Orpens and two or three others, there was a terrible exposure of fifth-rate work. Everything quiet on the Western and Eastern fronts, but we are obviously working up for a big attack on the Wytschaete-Messines front, and perhaps on the Belgian coastline. The news from Russia continues to be bad. The Germans have apparently brought many guns from the East to the West.

Tuesday, June 5. Went to see Lord Lonsdale in Carlton House Terrace, to discuss the state of our horses in France, and found that we agreed as to the causes. He is going to tell me about the baths in which horses are now plunged to get rid of the mange and lice, and he approves of my suggesting to Derby that Lord L., Sam Hames, and a gunner officer should go to France to report. Dined with Olive ;

Professor Morgan, ' Dodo ' Benson, Mrs. Astor, and Lady Johnstone. Lady Leslie came in afterwards.

Wednesday, June 6. Lunched with Lockett Agnew at the Ritz. M. de Laszlo the artist, Marjorie, and another lady. Sir Ian Hamilton and two ladies dined with me at the Carlton, and we went to see a clever Revue which amused us all.

Thursday, June 7. Lunched with Lady Randolph; Jack Churchill and his wife, Belle Herbert, Mrs. Astor, Lady Johnstone, and some others. In the evening a large dinner party at Mrs. Keppel's; Mrs. Ronny Greville, Lord and Lady Granard, Lord Lurgan, Mr. and Mrs. Walter Burns, Mrs. Astor looking a picture, Lord Hardinge of Penshurst, Mr. Montagu, Violet Keppel, and some half a dozen more. An excellent dinner and some pleasant Bridge. Hardinge and I discussed Russia after dinner. He was very despondent, and expected any Russian offensive to fail. The sailors had been shot at when they went to the trenches to ask the soldiers to go on fighting. He thought that the publication of the Mesopotamia and Dardanelles reports could do nothing but harm, but Sir Ian asks me not to oppose publication, so perhaps I will not move in the matter. Lord Bertie is in town, and may have to give up the Paris Embassy. Hardinge considered likely to be his successor, but the Mesopotamia report has yet to see the light.

This morning there came the news that Plumer's 2nd Army had captured the Messines Ridge, and we are all happy in consequence.

Friday, June 8. The Prime Minister telephoned that he would lunch with me to-day, so I invited Lady Ridley and Mrs. Astor to join, but at the last moment the P.M. could not turn up. We had a very pleasant lunch all the same, and a great political talk. Both fair ladies very intelligent and penetrating in their criticism of Ministers. L. G. missed something. Went to the opera to Lady Cunard's box to hear *The Fair Maid of Perth*, by Bizet, never before given in English. Good in parts. Mrs. McKenna and her sister Marjorie, Wolkoff, Bardac, one of the Italian Embassy, and Sir Claud Phillips. No cars or taxis, and we all had to walk to the Tube. I liked Sir T. Beecham's conducting.

Saturday, June 9. Went to welcome Mrs. Leeds home from Paris, and had a good talk. She is going to take Kenwood, which is a great pleasure, as we shall be neighbours.

Sunday, June 10. M. Nabokoff, who has been appointed Minister Plenipotentiary, and Lady Townshend lunched at Maryon, and General Dessino and his daughter came in later. Nabokoff assured me that the Russian offensive would begin in three weeks' time, and that the 7th and 12th Russian Armies, which had been almost disintegrated, were now normal again. He says that he telegraphed most of my last article on Russia to his Government, and that the *Novoe Vremya* sent it almost verbatim. This article has been generally approved, but the *Times* cut out one of the best paragraphs in it, relating to the need for strict discipline. Dined with Lord Haldane; Sir John and Lady Horner, Dr. and Mrs. Prothero, and Miss Haldane. A pleasant evening.

Monday, June 11. Went to see Admiral Hall of the Intelligence at the Admiralty in the afternoon. A pleasant keen-eyed sailor. He advised me that the Yankee 110-ft. motor launches of which I desired to know the naval value were no use for sea-keeping, and that our sloop class were better, though of course of far greater displacement and much more costly. The type was not settled in America, but it should be about 1000 tons, 16 knots speed, with an armament of good 5-inch to 6-inch guns. The merchant ship to be built should have 12 knots speed, and be built with bulkheads, and have one gun able to range 10,000 yards at a minimum, and be able to compete with German guns, which may be 5·9-inch, and two of them in each submarine. We were getting on well with the Yankee destroyers, of which 24 were now here working with us. The submarine feared our destroyers because of their speed and armament, and plunged at once when they saw them. There should be a trained crew of 6 men to each gun. Admiral Hall showed me the photos of the damage done at Ostend by our monitors at 26,000 yards range. It did not appear to be very important, though some 15 shells hit the mark. The German submarines lie up under concreted shelter in the harbour. Our shells fell at an angle of 60°. It was like shooting at a pin's point at such a range. He showed me a paper to prove that it is the Prussian system, and not the Hohenzollerns, that we should get rid of, but what this has to do with naval intelligence I do not know. He has a *cache* of German naval prisoners here, and constantly examines them. One German officer, recently picked up, and with a very long name, was contemptuous of America because she had no *militarismus*.

Saw Jack Cowans, who was wroth because the Huns had sunk the *Hunstrick* off Gibraltar full of ordnance stores, including 1000 tons of barbed wire, and heaps of other things. We have taken a division away from Salonika at last, but only one, and Nabokoff told me yesterday that his people had made a row about it, and that he had defended us. Jack advises that the Yankees should send over engines, trucks, and carriages to France to carry their men up from St. Nazaire, and that they should begin now to amass stores, ammunition, and supplies for forty days for all the force to come, within reasonable distance of the front which they are to occupy. They must also prepare frozen meat stores, veterinary hospitals, bakeries, remount depots, and other depots of all kinds, and this must be done before the troops arrive ; guns and machine guns must also be sent in advance. This is sound advice and I shall pass it all on. Our last return showed 850,000 quarters of wheat received, and we have been asked to find storage for 1,000,000 tons of it ! And still they talk of wheat shortage ! Saw Sir E. Allenby, who told me that he has received the command in Egypt. I am pleased for his sake, and he is a splendid soldier, but am very sorry for Archie, and telephoned in the evening to condole with Lady M., who had been dining with Lady Robertson, who had broken the bad news to her. I think that Archie has been abominably treated throughout the war.

Tuesday, June 12. Lunched with Marjorie at the Ritz. She leaves for Hampshire to-morrow. Dined with Olive, whose girl, Bridget, has had a bad accident riding in Rotten Row, having been run away with. Lady Paget, the Murrays, Belle Herbert, and others.

Wednesday, June 13. Sir Seymour Fortescue gave us a nice lunch at Claridge's, which is becoming the best restaurant in London again under Charles's management. Lady Paget, Mrs. Astor, Olive, and Vansittart. A lot of well-known people there. Dined with the Wimbornes at Wimborne House. Jack Churchill and Lady Gwendeline, Mrs. Arkwright, Miss Boyd, Sir Eric Murray, Claude Lowther, and a few more. Talked about Ireland and the chairmanship of the Irish Convention. To-day 15 Hun aeroplanes, flying high, bombed the East End of London, causing a large number of casualties. People crowded the streets and tops of houses to look on. Nobody seems much concerned, and no panic.

Thursday, June 14. Lunched with the Londonderrys at Londonderry House. Lady Islington, Fox McDonnell, and a sculptor also there. Saw Mrs. Leeds afterwards. Countess Torby is preparing a surprise house-warming for her on July 1. Tribunal later, and then dined with some neighbours and met a pleasant Russian lady who was a warm revolutionary.

Friday, June 15. Lunched with Sir Edward and Lady Carson at 5 Eaton Place. He is looking very well, and is, on the whole, happier about our naval arrangements, and is getting new life into the Admiralty and stirring things up now that he has had time to look round. We have had a bad time again lately with the submarines, but he thinks that the figures given away by a Socialist in the Reichstag are not far out, and they gave the Germans 70 effective large submarines, 70 smaller, and 70 minelayers. He thinks that we shall get the American troops over. Now that the U.S. are with us it is easier to institute convoy.

This is being done after all the experts had first opposed him, and to-day[1] the first convoy came in with 20 ships, all of which arrived safely with food and munitions. Carson is making various changes at the Admiralty. He is stopping minute-writing, and is asking heads of departments to see each other more and settle things by word of mouth. He has started a thinking branch to make plans, and there will be a similar branch in the Grand Fleet. It is surely a sound thing to begin to think after fighting for three years. He wants to promote Tyrwhitt to be Admiral, and finds a rooted objection to promote any man out of his turn. He evidently thinks the Navy a fine old crusted service. He has found no one yet better than Jellicoe for First Sea Lord. The latter is very pessimistic, and Carson tries to make him and other admirals take a good rest. Carson thinks that the motor-driven craft are becoming more popular. He does not think that the German Navy will come out. In the bombardment of Zeebrugge the monitors fired from positions marked by buoys, and seaplanes directed them, while a line of motor boats kept up a smoke-screen to annoy the German coast batteries. They got in 115 rounds before the enemy could do anything. The range was 12 miles. Carson is dubious whether we are playing a good game with the Russian revolutionaries, and thinks that the Socialists in all countries will try to make all Governments impossible. He admits that there is no real food shortage, and adds that we are trying to amass six months' reserve supplies, which explains much. He is evidently very hostile to his colleague, X., of whom he has a poor opinion. We mutually admired Smuts, who, Carson says, will not express any political opinion, but never speaks without saying something worth listening to on military subjects. Carson is not sure whether the Germans are not already using the Scheldt for their submarines, and does not think, any more than I do, that the Germans will respect Dutch neutrality if it becomes a German interest to violate it. Carson is defending officers

[1] See footnote p. 396.

who destroy German ships in neutral waters. He has a great belief in the large new seaplanes, and thinks that they will help much in the submarine warfare. He also told me that there had been much more bloodshed during the Revolution than had been reported, and that there had been shameful scenes. He was delighted that the seamen had prevented Ramsay Macdonald from leaving England, and believed that the bluejackets might very well be inclined to do the same thing if asked to carry him.

Saw Winston before lunch. L. G. had first offered him Munitions and then the Air, but not firm offers, and when W.'s enemies had made a row, the thing had fizzled out. We talked of W.'s visit to France, which he greatly enjoyed, but he was not allowed to go to Messines.

I made some fresh inquiries about our position in France. There are now 158 German divisions in the West and 74 in the East. We Allies in the West have 9500 field guns, and 6500 heavies to the German 7500, but the latter figure has not changed since January and it includes all guns in reserve, so that comparison is not quite fair. Actually about 6600 German heavy guns have been located. We are now 46,000 men short on establishment in France, but 86,000 are ready to go abroad, and as our losses have been light lately we are fairly right on the aggregate until August 31. We British alone have over 6000 guns now, and shall have 7500 next autumn. We have about 3500 field and 2500 heavies. Gough's 5th Army is being reconstituted, and the attack in the North is not due for some time yet. Murray's organisation has been excellent, and there are no military grounds for his recall, the terms of which will have to be settled by L. G. Only five American divisions are expected this year, and only twelve by April 1918. I have seen photographs which prove the total destruction of the German positions on the Messines Ridge. Our mines only seem to have blown up the German first-line trenches, which were weakly held, but the explosions caused great alarm, and our infantry rushed the second line almost by surprise. Plumer had one field gun for every $9\frac{1}{2}$ yards of his front of attack: There was evidently something wrong with the German guns, which fired seldom, but whether it is want of guns or shells I do not know.

Dined with the Walter Burnses at 50 Grosvenor Street. Lady de Trafford, Violet Keppel, the Duke of Roxburghe, Lady Paget, Lord Crewe, Bear Warre, and one or two more. Talked to Crewe after dinner. He had no comfort to offer on the Russian situation, which we thought bad. Crewe said that Lord K., with all his faults, was a great personality, and that he would loom large in history. We wondered who would write his life, and I said that of the few men who knew him well, two were dead,—Hubert Hamilton and 'Conky' Marker—and that his life ought to be written by a syndicate of the others left, but that if George Arthur wrote it, it might not be so good, as he only knew the last phase well. We agreed that only when all the memoirs and diaries of this time came to light would the future historian be able to sum up. The Duke, Lady de Trafford, Walter Burns, and I played Bridge, and the rest played Poker.

Saturday, June 16. Spent the day gardening with E., and brought back masses of roses in the evening. Very hot. The garden lovely. A heavy thunderstorm in London.

Sunday, June 17. General Tom Bridges, our military representative, recently with Balfour's Mission to America, leaves for France to-day, and I went to see him in the morning at 27 Chesham Street. He had given his views to the War Cabinet, and Curzon had described it as the most depressing statement that the Cabinet had received for a long time. Tom thinks that the first American division will reach France in June or July, and that, thereafter, one division a month will probably come. We could only count on 6 divisions this year, say 150,000 men, and 12 more in 1918, total 18, with 360,000 men in the divisions and 140,000 in the services. This assumes that the present programme is followed. The Cabinet were expecting a million, and were proportionately depressed. I said that this report would incline the Cabinet to peace, but Tom said that this could not be helped as he had to report what he believed to be the truth. Tom says that 40,000 fine young fellows have joined the Officers' Training Corps in America, and he has great hopes of these camps ; the universities have been almost cleared to find the young men. Balfour, he said, had been splendid. He had never put a foot wrong, and his hosts had been delighted with his statesmanship and his intellect. Tom thought that the Americans wanted the French and English Missions to boom the war more than for anything else, and this they had done. He had strongly advocated Compulsion, and when Joffre arrived he had done the same thing, and this had greatly helped in getting the Selective Draft Bill accepted. He thought that the country was keen about the war, but there were elements which did not wish to fight. He liked General Pershing very much. The only other leading general, Leonard Wood, was put aside because President Wilson was politically opposed to him. Tom thought that they had New York solidly with them owing to the support of the three most influential men there, Mitchel, the Mayor ; Malone, the head of the port ; and Woods, head of the police—all men under forty and very energetic. He had made good friends in America, including Sunday, the preacher. Wilson had been admirable, but had never said a word to Tom about military affairs. Also, he says that Washington is like Cawnpore in the hot weather. There is nothing doing in the middle of the day, and people don't come out till the sun is down. There is no hustling, but rather the calm of a university town and little conception of the need for haste.

The divisions are to be made like ours—twelve to thirteen battalions. Tom and Pershing prefer to have our 18-prs. for the field artillery instead of the American 15-prs., and our guns can be made in the U.S. at the factories which we established there. The heavy guns are a difficulty, and Tom agrees that the French might make them. I told him of Pétain's views, which interested him much. He thought it possible that Joffre had made different suggestions, but the French defeat had taken place while the Missions were away. There is little hope of a big air success soon, as Tom says that there is little in the U.S. except practice aeroplanes, and he is not sure whether the first American battle-plane will appear before 1919! More disillusionment! Tom says that they can turn out standardised goods very fast in the U.S., whether it is sausages or motor-car engines, but that they are short of craftsmen, tool makers, and setters, and he would let us make the aeroplanes for them, and let the Americans make the engines for cars, etc. He has advised Pershing to have a good look round in France before he decides upon anything. Haig was asked to express an opinion about the field guns, but refused to do so, or at least did not. In these matters he is always most prudent and reserved. He sticks to his last. Tom, under instructions from Robertson, who did not take warning from my advice in this matter, began by asking for 500,000 American recruits for the British Armies, but had at once found that he was on the wrong path, and had had to drop the proposal like a hot potato! The Yankees would not look at the idea, so Tom and Joffre had agreed that all the support should be asked for France. Tom says that if we pass a law to reach our citizens in the U.S. we may get 100,000 men, but he only expects 5000 by voluntary enlistment. The American Regulars are now 180,000, and the National Guard 300,000. With the 500,000 selective drafts to come on Sept. 1, there will be a million, and the divisions at the front can be maintained. Pershing tells him that the National Guard, many of whom have been embodied on the Mexican border, are as good as the Regulars, if not better. They have not such long service, but have better men. It is not yet decided where the American troops are to take post in France, but the American soldiers would like to be near us. Tom thinks that after they have with-drawn the cadres for training, the U.S. troops which will come out first will have 60 per cent. of new material in the ranks. They will be strong in heavy guns so far as the first three divisions are concerned, and though Tom is not sure where the neck of the bottle will be, *i.e.* in transport, guns, or equipment, he is inclined to think it will be equipment and especially clothing. No cavalry will come out.

The Mission had strongly urged that no one else should be sent out till they had returned, but, all the same, Northcliffe passed them on his way out while they were at sea, and Tom was not at all sure whether it was wise to send him. He admits that America is a trifle disappointing, but sees no reason why they should do better with their New Armies than we did, and besides they have further to come. St. Nazaire will probably be their base, but Tom has advised Pershing not to get jammed up against the Swiss frontier, where he may be cut off if things go badly elsewhere. He thinks that Pershing can do just as he pleases in France. We discussed the war, the Low Countries, and changes among our higher commanders. Tom had been down to Walton Heath to see L. G., who had asked him shoals of questions about America, and seemed mad keen about capturing Jerusalem.

In the afternoon Lord and Lady Scarbrough and Olive came up to Maryon, and we had tea and talked. I took S. up to the top of the house to see the view over London, and then we motored up to Judge's Walk to see the Constable scene, and on along 'The Spaniards' to see the view towards Hendon through the trees of the pine clumps. S. thinks that many of our Volunteers are now superior to the pre-war Territorials.

Tuesday, June 19. I began a review of the British spring offensive of 1917. Met Philip Sassoon yesterday, who told me of troubles[1] in the French Army bordering on mutiny, from sheer war-weariness I suspect. Lunched with Lord

[1] The secret of these troubles was extraordinarily well kept and the truth was not known to the enemy till much later. These troubles explain the comparative inactivity of the French during the summer of 1917.

and Lady Islington. We talked India and politics. The Indian astrologers who prophesied this war give it six more years to run. The optimists! Islington says that India is quiet, but that we must give commissions to natives, and make a long step forward in Indian self-government. Afghanistan is being good, and the Amir has behaved very well. The Indian Government is weak and the Council feeble. Monro is doing well and rules the roast, as he knows his own mind, even if he does not know India. The Mahsuds may give trouble again at any moment. I. says that Maude cannot trust the new Russian commander in the Caucasus with secret matter. It is a great pity that Yudenitch has gone. We discussed politics; Lady I. very amusing about them, and about the characters of certain Ministers.

Met Lieut. Pernot at my club afterwards. He brought a charming message for me from General Foch. He said that Foch was not Pétain's nominee, but the latter was glad to have him in Paris, and the two got on well at present, and constantly visited each other. Pétain was looking after the politicians while pretending to despise them, and they were still a little afraid of him. I said that I saw in the German Press that Pétain was busy at Verdun, and Pernot did not deny it. There has been serious trouble in two French regiments, and the mutiny had been firmly repressed. Things were all right now. It was the Press making out that the French had been so badly beaten that caused the trouble. Many deputies sent scores of copies of the *Journal Officiel* to the front, and Pernot could not censor it. In this paper all the critical speeches of the deputies appear in full and do much harm. The French had been much cheered by Pershing's arrival, and had given him a great reception. I said that there was not enough of the *impresario* in the war, and that when the first Yankee troops came, they should be marched through Paris several times like a stage army. Joffre's report is more favourable than Tom Bridges's, as he gives the Yankees 150,000 this year, and 500,000 next spring; also he believes in the great air pro-

gramme in the U.S.   I told him to advise Foch to talk to
Bridges.   Joffre is at the École Militaire with a small staff of
five officers, and receives *rapports* on the situation.   He will
act as the go-between with the Yankees in their negotiations with the French.   Pernot is still under Thomas.
The latter sends very optimistic messages about the coming
Russian offensive, but Pernot discounts some of it.   He
says, however, that Foch is disturbed about the British
view that the Russians can be written off for this year,
and thinks it exaggerated.   Pernot approves of Brussiloff,
for C.-in-C., and describes Alexeieff as a trimmer.   I told
Pernot all about our affairs here.   Pernot says that the
French can keep up their 108 divisions this year if there
is no large general offensive.   Nothing was yet settled
about the position in the line of the Americans.   Pernot
says that Ribot returned from London full of Stockholm
and a Socialist gathering there, but was met by deputations of the pillars of French policy in the Senate and
Chamber, who called upon him to take a firm stand or
they would put him out.   They told him that he had
always deserted his friends, but that they would not let
him desert France.   Hence the ' strong ' line which he
adopted, to the confusion of his nice new friends in London,
who were left in the soup.   Pernot said that the state of
the public mind in France was generally sound, and the
censorship of letters to and from the Armies showed that
the arrival of the Americans and the English victories had
done much to cheer the people up.

I arrived late at the House of Commons to talk to Winston
about his speech next Thursday.   I agreed with a good
deal of what he means to say, but he was most sarcastic
about the attitude of soldiers, and declared that they
made up information to suit their book, a suggestion against
which I protested.   He was much depressed at the views
of Bridges about the Yankees, and wondered if it was worth
going on if they could do no more.   I earnestly urged him
to be strong, and not to take any weak line.   Sir F. E.
Smith joined us, and they went off together.   Saw Charlie

Burn, just home from France. The Lords' and Commons' War Committees have joined forces.

Wednesday, June 20. Busy writing a review of Haig's spring campaign. Dined with the Scarbroughs in Park Lane; Lady Ridley, Lady Titchfield, Dr. Dillon, and some others. Much talk of politics and the European unrest—gloomy on the whole; but I stood out for going on strongly. Dillon wants Austria to be divided up and I do not. Palmerston often described her as the pivot of the balance of power. Lady Ridley said much of interest about labour in the North, and wants a week's holiday for all controlled firms at State expense.

Thursday and Friday, June 21 *and* 22. Busy writing three longish articles. Tribunal in the afternoon. In the evening Madame Vandervelde and Lieut. Pernot dined at Maryon. Madame asked what effect Viviani's oratory had had in America. Pernot said that it had had none, but that at one dinner an American had said that Joffre, who could not speak a word of English, had made himself understood by the whole of America. This has vexed Viviani, who made magnificent speeches, but no one understood them, except a small minority of his audiences. On another occasion Viviani had belauded Joffre, who had risen and had begun to embrace Viviani across the body of the Chairman, who had thought that they were quarrelling, and had risen to say that order must be maintained while he presided. Madame says that her husband's letters are very pessimistic, and that chaos reigns in Russia.

Saturday and Sunday, June 23 *and* 24. Corrected various proofs. Lunched with Lady Cunard and found Mr. Birrell, Wolkoff, Dr. Dillon, Lady Paget, Lady Randolph, and Mrs. Cavendish Bentinck. Wolkoff very silent. In the afternoon went to Coombe, where there were the Grand Duke Michael and Countess Torby, the Countess Zia and her fiancé Captain Wernher, Lady Wernher, Mrs. Astor, Lord Charles Montagu, Baron Maurice Rothschild, Mrs. Leeds, Reggie Paget, Mr. Straker, etc. Bertie Paget still very ill indeed. We talked much of Russia. The revolutionaries and anarchists returning to Russia call on the Grand Duke for financial assistance on their journey ! Chaos still reigns, and the G.D. party have no hope of a successful offensive. Most of the trouble is at Petrograd, however, and the best families appear to have left for Moscow and the provinces. The Russian soldiers who come here from France on their way home, come to see the G.D. and Yermoloff with pipes in their mouths and their hands in their pockets. The G.D. is stunned by the collapse of all discipline.

Went at 11.30 A.M., Sunday, to see Sir Douglas Haig at Eastcott, Coombe Hill, Kingston, only 300 yards from the Warren House. Derby was with him when I arrived, so I had a talk with Lady Haig till Derby went, and she showed me over the house, which is very nice, with large high rooms, and there is a nice garden. She has a long lease of it. We got on to Haig's enemies. Derby and Haig then came in and we had a little talk together, during which Derby said that the taking of all men up to 25 was the only solution of the recruiting problem. He was much exercised about the standing of a soldier candidate against his son, Lord Stanley, at Liverpool.

When he had gone, Haig and I had a talk alone. I congratulated him heartily over his Messines victory. He got out the plans of the Messines-Wytschaete position, showing all the trenches and the British three objectives, marked as usual by differently coloured lines. It was the deuce of a strong place. The Germans thought it impregnable, and a German officer, taken at Messines during the battle, said that they expected the attack from the S.W., but that the Wytschaete positions could not be taken. At that moment there trooped in the first prisoners from Wytschaete, whereupon the German officer admitted that all was lost. Haig says that he has now a safe defence to his right flank at Ypres, and has all the ground cleared up to the Lys, while his Arras success enables him to approach Lille from the S.W. as well as from the N.W. We then discussed the coming coastal operation, and I gave him my views about the ground and the inundations. He brought out another map whereon are shown all the likely inundations which would make a broad band south of the German fortifications on the Belgian coastline. Haig thought that the Germans could not let out the water without isolating the coast defences. I doubted it, and said that the plan seemed to me to credit the Germans with too little water-science, and that they were more likely to inundate lines and sections of ground as the Dutch did, and that I hated the idea of thrusting an Army into such a dædalus of mud and water. Haig thought that the Belgians knew all the water-system well, and said that even if he only got forward a bit, it was all to the good, and that the best success open to us was to turn the German right on the coast. He said that he thought, and had stated the fact on paper, that had his Armies been kept up he would have pushed the enemy back to the Meuse this year. But he was very short of men, and two days ago Robertson had promised him 80,000 drafts, when the Armies would be only 30,000 short.

Did I know what had happened in London? Yes, I said, I knew. He asked me how I explained L. G.'s attitude about men and strategy? I gave him my views, and we agreed that German moral, numbers, supplies, guns, and ammunition had become reduced by the hammering which they were getting; that any change of plan would have a bad effect upon opinion in the Army; and I said that I was totally opposed to the War Cabinet's illusions. Haig likes Pétain very much, and says that he is a splendid fellow; but when I asked how Foch did and whether Pétain and Foch got on well, Haig was very reserved and said that the Frenchmen were funny fellows. We found the attitude of the War Cabinet inexplicable, and I said that I would see what could be done.

Maurice Rothschild, after a great gossip with Lady P., drove me home late on Sunday.

Monday, June 25. Got through a rare lot of letters. Lunched with Mrs. Leeds, Mrs. George Keppel, and Lady Sarah Wilson. A rare lot of gossip. In the late after-noon called on Sir W. Robertson at the War Office. A good new raised map comes in showing up well all the terrain in the North, and all the German lines. R. says that Clive is now liaison officer with Pétain. An excellent selection. R. admitted how they stood in regard to men, namely, as Haig had said. He did not think that L. G.'s attack on him would come to anything, but he was quite ready to go if he were not wanted. He thought that the War Cabinet idea about Italy was preposterous, and that it would fizzle out. The Italians had about 2,000,000 men more than they could usefully employ, and it would take six months for us to move in strength from one theatre to another. But it showed that the manners of the War Cabinet had not altered, and that they were always out for firework strategy. He saw nothing for it but to go on hitting the enemy with all the men and guns that could be had. I agreed. He thought that Pétain would soon help, and he was fighting hard now, though at the Boche instance. He thought that Pétain must be much exercised about the mutiny. He agreed that only two regiments were concerned badly, but some others had engaged in conversations.[1] All his news from Russia was bad, and he said that Foch had the same news from his man. In the Caucasus the 2nd Division had had a committee meeting and had decided to go back 50 miles and pass the summer in a place where there was a better water supply ! R. approved highly of my two articles and of the *Times* leader to-day on the spring offensive. He was immensely amused by a cartoon in *London Opinion* of L. G. and Carson, in which they were laughing, depicted as the monks in the famous picture of ' Une bonne histoire,' over Northcliffe's absence in America. Carson was made

---

[1] M. Painlevé has told us that 150 French soldiers were condemned to death by Courts-martial for these mutinies, but that the sentences were only carried out in twenty-five cases.

to say, 'If Asquith had conceived such a splendid idea, he would have been Prime Minister still!' Robertson thought that the Boches were short of men, and the artillery was certainly inferior to ours, though Macdonogh allowed them to possess so many heavy batteries. Perhaps ammunition was short, and some captured documents pointed to the fact. Perhaps they had difficulties in repairing their guns. Our divisions now aggregated 25,000 to 27,000 men, and in reply to a question of mine, he said that I could take three British to equal four German divisions now. We had a M.G. company with every brigade, and a divisional company, besides the regimental M.G.'s. We also had an increasing amount of heavy artillery, and it was all good and new. He had twenty spare artillery brigades outside the divisional organisation. R. also talked of the Admiralty. Carson had been over to talk with him about it. They would have to find a table man with good knowledge of his business to run the naval strategy. He thought of Colville, who seemed to him a good man.

I heard some good stories yesterday of the late Mrs. Moore of Paris, celebrated for saying the wrong things in French. To her *cocher* she once said, on starting for the opera: 'Cocher, prenez-moi du côté des *abandonnées*!' To her butler whom she was engaging, she once said, 'Eh bien, c'est convenu. Vous aurez 400 francs par mois, *et la blanchisseuse*!'

Generally speaking, people are deadly tired of the war and greatly upset at the Russian situation, which has probably saved Germany from a military disaster. The Government are too frightened of labour troubles to do the right thing in the way of man-power, and seek for some new strategy to spare them the necessity of acting vigorously in France. L. G. is not so popular as he was, and there is a talk of some additions to his administration. The people do not like the Review of Exemptions Act. Society is pessimistic on the whole. No Ministers talk in the provinces or give the country a firm lead. The losses continue to be high. American aid is seen to be a long way off. But, on the whole, the country is sound and steady; there has been little real suffering, and while we continue to win victories in France, there is not likely to be any violent change of attitude. On the whole, the worst danger is the dour, vengeful, and almost revolutionary attitude of labour, in the North particularly. The Government have broken some of the pledges about the Dilution Bill, the workers are physically exhausted and angry, they no longer trust their parliamentary labour leaders, and though they do not like Ramsay Macdonald, they like Henderson and Barnes even less, and stand half-way between these two extremes of thought, and are determined to participate more fully in the results of their toil and to dispossess all profiteers. There are many secret meetings which are not reported, and a strong feeling that we should make some move towards peace. All this accounts for the sour looks which Lady Ridley notices among the northern workers and miners, and as the revolutionary movement spreads abroad in various quarters, notably just now in Spain, the Reds and the anarchists feel that their moment may be coming. Not a pleasant situation, but Lloyd George goes north this week, and I hope that he may help to clear the air. This day the first division of American troops, some 30,000 men in all, landed safely in Western France. A great event.

CHAPTER XXII

MESOPOTAMIA AND EGYPT, 1917

General Maude's letter describing events of the past six months in Mesopotamia—Angry comments on the Mesopotamia Report—A visit to Glynde Place—Indian politics—General Harington on Messines—The Russian Southern Armies attack—A great relief—Lord French and Sir D. Haig reconciled—Reasons for the early failure in Mesopotamia—A German daylight aeroplane raid on London—Captain Charles Fox on his escape from Germany—Sir Archibald Murray's return—His account of the situation and of his organisation of the advance and conquest of the desert—We lose the Dunes sector at Nieuport—More details from General Murray about his campaign—A talk with General Smuts—His view of the War Cabinet system—His strategy for Palestine—Why it was negatived—His opinion about Man-Power—He thinks that the defeat of Turkey will end the war—New political appointments—Russian news bad again—The Southern Armies retreat without cause.

Tuesday, June 26. Wrote two long letters to Generals Monro and Maude. Lunched with Lady Leslie, and met there the Dowager Lady Londonderry, Mrs. Leeds, Jack Leslie, and Prince and Princess Radziwill, just back from Russia and uncommonly glad to be here. The Princess told me all about the Russian retreat, which stopped at Baranovitchi, close to where they lived. She thought that the situation was very bad, and that there was no chance of a successful Russian offensive. At the end, before she left Russia, the soldiers who had occupied their house made them understand that the Radziwills were only there on sufferance, and that the soldiers were the masters. The Princess expects a counter-revolution, in which all the officers will join, and says that it will take two years for things to come round.

The following letter from General Maude gives a fascinating account of his brilliant campaign in Mesopotamia :—

GENERAL HEADQUARTERS,
MESOPOTAMIAN EXPEDITIONARY FORCE,
7th April 1917.

MY DEAR REPINGTON,—Your letter dated January 22nd has only just reached me, so you will see what a long time our mails take, although I hope that this will not continue, for as regards delay in this country it has been mainly due to the events of the past few weeks. But still having to go round by Bombay, letters always take some time to reach us here.

You ask me for some news from these parts, and so I will try and give you a condensed narrative of the events of the past six months. I am afraid that it must be very much condensed, for, as you will understand, my hands are very full. Since I took over command I have had hardly a moment to myself, and since we reached Bagdad work seems if possible to have increased, for there is not only what there was before to do, but in addition there is the civil and military administration of the city to re-organise, and that takes a bit of doing.

When I succeeded Sir Percy Lake at the end of August, it seemed to me that the first step was to reorganise thoroughly and develop our resources fully ; much spadework had been done, but still there was an immensity more to do; and much as I wished to remain at the front, it was evident that it was my business to go down to the Base and get the foundations of our house placed on a sound and secure basis. Until that was done, it seemed unwise even to think of making a move forward. So from the end of August till the beginning of November, I was at Basra going into everything, and investigating how things could be improved here and there, how things could be developed, and where thorough reorganisation was necessary. There were many points that had to be dealt with—railways, ordnance, medical supplies, transport, communications, etc., all had to be taken in hand in turn. But every one was out to work with a will, and with the incidence of the cooler weather work was easier. So we all set to work zealously, and by the time that I left for the front after Sir Charles Monro's visit I felt that the foundations were secure, and it was only a question then of building up our reserves of supplies before it would be safe to move.

I was very glad that Sir Charles Monro came, for it enabled him to see a good deal, and it has been most helpful in our relations with India ever since. I only wish that he could have stayed longer and seen more, but I think he saw the maximum possible in the time at his disposal.

As soon as he left I dashed off for a hurried visit to the oilfields, and then to Nasariyeh on the Euphrates, for I was most anxious to see both the Karun and Euphrates fronts before I left for the Tigris front, so that I might have a certain grip of what was going on everywhere. Both were most interesting trips, and I felt that I learnt a lot by going there, even though my visits were necessarily hurried ones.

That done, it seemed to me that my place was once more at the front, for to command from Basra was an impossibility. To be that distance away, under the most favourable circumstances, appeared to me to be out of the question, and certainly with our precarious communications it was impossible. So I went right up to Arab Village—a proceeding which made some people shake their heads—but I feel confident that my decision has been amply justified by the results. Amara, where it was suggested that I should stay, would have been very nearly as bad as Basra, but at Arab Village I was in close touch with the troops. I could see them and feel their pulse, and could watch all that was going on from day to day, besides which I got the earliest and first-hand information of what the enemy was doing. Further, it seemed to me that Arab Village was only suitable whilst we were still accumulating supplies and stores at the front during November, and that when operations began it was my business to get still further forward. So when we started off in the middle of December, I pushed my headquarters—moving as light as possible—up to Sinn, which was about the centre of my battle line.

It was quite clear from the start what I should aim for. The Turks had in the previous spring relinquished very nearly their entire hold on the right bank of the Tigris, and only held a few systems of trenches on each side of, and opposite, Kut, as well as the mouth of the Hai. They had chosen their position cleverly, for they were well protected by rivers and marshes, and with the advent of the wet weather it was likely that their position would become stronger and stronger, as marshes would practically surround them. Still, though defensively strong, they had little power of offence. It was difficult, if not impossible, for them to strike my communications, as the detours necessary were so great, whereas if I could seize the line of the Hai it would be possible for me, even if I could not strike their communications directly owing to natural difficulties, to hammer away at their extreme right, in prolongation of which ran their lines of communication—a situation which appeared to me to be a most dangerous one.

So away we went in the middle of December, and we secured the line of the Hai with little difficulty. As soon as we had occupied that we wheeled to the right, and cleared both banks of the Hai up to Kut. We then sat down systematically and began the reduction of the two trench systems which the Turks still held on the right bank, and these we succeeded in capturing one after the other during January and the beginning of February. It was tough work, but the troops fought splendidly, and were full of dash and go, and nothing could have been finer than their performances. The Turkish losses were heavy, and as we kept on pressing at their tail, they had to string out more and more until they became weak everywhere. It then seemed to me that the moment was propitious for a culminating effort, and consequently we attacked the extreme left of their line at Sannaiyat, more as a diversion than anything, but still with the intention of taking as many trenches as we could, whilst feints were made all along the river line as far as Kut. Then having drawn the attention of the enemy in every other direction, we launched our main attack across the river at Shumran. The crossing was a real gallant performance on the part of the troops, and will stand high in the records of grit and determination of British soldiers. Having once established a bridge-head on the left bank the rest was comparatively easy. We threw our bridge and rushed troops across as fast as we could, till I had got the 3rd Corps practically severing the Turkish communications. I then pushed the Cavalry Division across, and from that moment the Turks were all in rout. The 1st Corps pushing along took trench after trench from Sannaiyat onwards, and the Cavalry and 3rd Corps pressed in pursuit of the flying enemy.

The scene on the line of retreat beggars description. For over 80 miles the countryside was littered with everything imaginable—guns, rifles, ammunition, stores of all kinds, equipment, food—everything was being thrown away. It was everything to press our pursuit as rapidly as possible, and I am afraid I got impatient. Naturally the change of our communications from rail and river to river only was bound to take a little time, and it is wonderful how quickly it was effected, but it made me chafe, as my eyes were always on the retreating Turks. Still it only made four or five days' delay at Aziziyeh, and off we went again in pursuit.

Directly I crossed at Shumran I wired for instructions from the Government. I said that meantime I was pushing on, and of course I would readjust my line according to any subsequent instructions I received, but I could not lose a moment under the conditions. In time I received a reply to the effect that I might press on into Bagdad provided that I was satisfied that my supply considerations and the security of my force would not be imperilled. I answered to both of these queries that I was satisfied, and so, as you know, we entered Bagdad on March 11.

I cannot tell you how magnificent has been the work of the whole force. It is a real pleasure to command such an Army. Everybody has worked with a will to make our operations a success, and the results achieved have been entirely due to their whole-hearted efforts.

The troops have fought like tigers, and with a dash and determination worthy of our highest traditions, but although all this has been superb we should have been doomed to failure if it had not been for the splendid work done behind the Army. The communications were magnificent throughout, river and rail transport running without a hitch, and my every need was met with the utmost promptitude. This was especially creditable when we consider the enormous amount of ammunition, for instance, that was involved, and this took a tremendous lot of moving up. The troops were practically on full operations scale of rations throughout, and it was only for a day or two when the advanced troops had to go in any way short, and then even on the worst occasion they had their emergency ration to fall back upon. This, however, was not the fault of the communications, but rather my own, as I was so anxious to go on and not to lose a moment.

Broadly speaking, since we started we have taken 9000 prisoners and 39 guns. The rest of our captures I cannot give you any estimate of. They are all being tabulated, but it will take an enormous time to sort out and realise, but it is sufficient to say that they are very considerable, though not so big as they might have been under some circumstances, for the whole countryside being littered as it was, the Arabs helped themselves freely, and we were too busy in other directions to gather everything up systematically as we went along. Still, we have taken thousands and thousands of rifles, immense quantities of ammunition, and stores of all kinds. The Turks were quite a broken force, and I do not think that the remnants of those who retired in front of us will give us very much trouble. In fact, although within comparatively close distance of us now, they bolt whenever we approach them.

The 13th Turkish Army Corps, which was retiring before the Russians, is, however, a different proposition, as they are quite unbroken, and have some good regiments. The Russians are coming along in a very leisurely manner, and effected a junction with us a few days ago near Khanikin, but apparently they mean to do little or nothing more in this direction at present. I hope, however, that further orders may be sent to them, as I have suggested that their rôle is to hunt the Turks in front of them whilst we continue to hunt those in front of us. The idea of their commander, Raddatz, is apparently that his mission is completed now that he has cleared the Turks out of Persia. I am, however, very anxious to give them another blow before the hot weather comes, and to establish the Russians on the TIGRIS. Whether this will be possible or not we shall see. It depends on whether the Russians are dilatory or not.

Our river transport is excellent now, and gets stronger day by day with the arrival of new ships and barges. So we feel quite happy on that score. By the middle of this month we shall have converted the Kurna-Amara railway to metre gauge, and so both that and the Basra-Nasariyeh line will be metre gauge. We are rolling up the Sheikh Sa'ad-Sinn [1] line as it is no longer required, and I shall bring it up here where it will be most useful. It was suggested that it would be best to utilise this plant for laying a line from Kut to Bagdad, as our water transport will find a difficulty in getting here when the low water season comes later on. It seemed to me, however, that it was essential to have a metre gauge line, and I have decided on this, and hope

---

[1] It is quite marvellous what this little line did for us during December, January, and February, and the tonnage carried by it must almost constitute a record.

to begin laying it before very long. So all our lines will be metre gauge, except the light railway which we shall lay for local use here.

Our medical arrangements, too, are most satisfactory now, and in all stores we are indeed well found. So everything rests on directing things on sound lines and keeping things up to the mark during the hot weather, which is always a difficult matter.

I am afraid that this is a very hurriedly dictated line and you must take it for what it is worth, but the mail is soon going and my time is so very fully occupied.

If you could give me any news from other fronts I shall always be grateful, as we do not hear much in these parts.

As regards the future, it seems to me that by capturing Bagdad we become so to speak the left flank of the Caucasus Army, and as they press forward, as I trust they will do vigorously, and establish themselves on the headwaters of the Tigris, our functions will lie more on the Euphrates, on which I have already established some strong posts west of Bagdad. The occupation of these posts means that we seal the middle Euphrates here and at Nasariyeh, and we hope to draw many and plentiful supplies from that region.

Here we have got into a land of plenty compared to the barren deserts to which we have been accustomed, and we hope to draw large supplies locally in the way of fresh meat, vegetables, fuel, grain, and fodder, which are all such important and bulky articles, so this ought to ease our supply situation considerably.

I have just established a new Local Resources directorate here, which will cover all Mesopotamia, and tap every area to the utmost, so that we may be able to live to a certain extent on the country. I have been working at it for some time, but it has only been finally launched during the last few days. A capital fellow is running it, and I look forward to great results from it. Hope you are very fit and well.—Yours sincerely,

F. S. MAUDE.

Wednesday, June 27. The Mesopotamia Report published. A terrible show-up of almost every one chiefly concerned in the initiation and conduct of the campaign in 1914, 1915, and 1916. Angry comments in the Press and a call for the heads of the delinquents. Lunched with Mrs. Ronny Greville, and found Max-Muller, the Duchess of

Beaufort and her two daughters, also her boy just back from Salonika, besides Sir Francis Hopwood, Lady Kilmorey, and the Count de Grünne. Hopwood not sanguine about the submarines. We mutually damned the War Cabinet, and agreed that Carson and Derby should be on it. The Duchess's boy told us much of interest of Salonika and about Sarrail's affairs. He says that the French troops are all colonial and bad. Only one of our divisions has gone. I judge that the relations between Sarrail and Milne are rather strained. Found de Grünne anxious about the German inundations in the Belgian front, and I do not wonder. It was he who opened up the question to me. Had an Ulster talk with Lady Kilmorey. Things in Ireland worse than ever.

Thursday, June 28. Wrote an account of the present situation in India and Mesopotamia, based on Maude's and Monro's last letters. It will be an antidote to the Mesopotamia Report, and will cheer up those who have friends and relatives in Mesopotamia. Lunched with the Lyttons at 10 Buckingham Street, S.W. I did not know where the street was, but found it at last. The Lyttons bought two or three lodging-houses and converted them, as some other people have done, into a single house. Mr. Lutyens, Lord L.'s brother-in-law, did the transformation, and his staircase and other changes will make people believe some years hence that the house dates from 1760. But the rooms are mostly small, and neighbours are building at the back of the house where much of the light will be shut out. Found Lady Islington and McEvoy, the artist, there. We had a lot of talk. Lady Lytton thinks that we all look exactly what we are, a very convenient theory for such attractive women as the Ladies L. and I. But I said that I did not believe it altogether, as the powers of deception of some women, trained as the sex had been to deceive to conquer for ages past, made it impossible to judge from their looks what they were. A talk of placing *The Leper* on the stage. Lady L. had never read it. Lady I. thought that the leper lady had no face or hands or feet, and that the play could not be given as it was too gruesome. I thought it could if it were not exaggerated. McEvoy interesting, and I congratulated him on his portrait of the Ladies Wimborne and Ridley. He is, though a trifle cadaverous, artistic looking, and very pale with dark hair, interesting but not good-looking. We heard more of the story of the two Canadian Adonises who met these two lovely ladies when they were marooned on the coast from their motor breaking down. The Canadians were in luck. They said that they would be late for their parade somewhere, but did not care, and the General would have to wait. Walked to the Admiralty with Lytton. We agreed that Derby and Carson should be in the War Cabinet, and that it was preposterous that they were not.

Dined with the Duke and Duchess of Sutherland at 39 Portman Square: Lord and Lady Londonderry, Lady Titchfield, the Solicitor-General for Scotland, and the Duchess of Marlborough. A pleasant evening. The house looks charming now. The great Romney of the Gower children is in the drawing-room and looks superb. The dining-room is enamelled dark green, with light gold panelling, very beautiful in itself, but a trifle hard upon the Romneys, Reynolds, and Hoppners which adorn the walls and are well lighted up. The Duke showed us some interesting sketches of the fleet of motor boats which he commanded in Egypt. They do twenty-one knots and must be useful in calm waters. He had also brought back from Rome a lot of paintings by a new artist, remarkable for their artistic properties and colour effects, and I was much struck by them. At Florence he bought a pearl necklace for the Duchess, and Garrard's value it at twice the price which he paid for it. She and Lady Londonderry compared their necklaces, which are nearly identical in length and shape. The Duke is now on the East Coast. He arrived at his H.Q. one morning to find that it had just been wrecked by a Zeppelin bomb ! We all praise the past above the present, but it occurs to me that the six ladies whom I have met at lunch and dinner to-day would hold their own, and probably win the palm, in any aristocracy of any age and country, for looks, grace, and charm.

Week-end, June 30-*July* 1. Lunched with the Ian Hamiltons, and we discussed Dardanelles and Mesopotamia. In the afternoon went down with Fox McDonnell to stay with the Islingtons at Glynde Place, Sussex, three miles from Lewes. We were met by Joan Poynder who motored us to the house in a taxi. Found also Lord Londonderry, Lady Rocksavage, Lord Hugh Cecil, and Lord Wemyss. A delightful house, partly fourteenth century, sheltered by the downs and woods, and with a lovely view over the Park towards Eastbourne, Newhaven, and the sea. The house is built round a quadrangle which is turfed like a college lawn. Julia James, the actress, came down on Sunday. She is acting for Lady I. somewhere. Walked over the Downs with L. in the morning, and discussed the Paris Embassy and the need for collecting all the best of the young men of the Tories to prepare a programme for the coming times. Later had a long talk with Islington about India and the Mesopotamia Report, which still holds the field of interest. It appears that Chelmsford's Council has sent back an ill-digested plan for extending Indian self-government. It increases the voting power on a territorial basis, but does not increase the responsibilities of Indians, and so would merely create more difficulties and solve none. The plan was submitted to a committee of Islington, Duke, Sir T. Holderness, and another, and was thrown out. The War Cabinet—Lloyd George being away in Scotland—decided to send a small Commission to India under Austen Chamberlain to arrange for a more satisfactory plan, and perhaps find this the best way to unload A. C., who says he will go out if they wish, but does not think that he can remain Secretary for India, which is probably what the War Committee thought he would think. It will be difficult for them to commence any action on the ' Messpot ' Report without alluding to A. C., who comes in for blame, and this seems the best way out. The Tories on the War

Cabinet do not seem to consider that any changes in India need be considered until after the war, but Islington does not agree. He thinks that Edwin Montagu may get the India Office, and asked me my opinion of what he, Islington, should do in this case. I felt sure that he would discard all personal feeling and do what best served the interest of the State. It seemed to me that his experience would be valuable to any S. of S., and that therefore he should remain on and help without regard to his personal feeling. We had some tennis, and then Islington and I walked on the downs with J. J., who told us about her stage experiences, the attentions of her admirers, and their letters. She is a nicely-behaved girl, with good eyes, a pretty mouth, and chestnut hair. An odd week-end companion for Lord Hugh! Miss Joan Poynder a charming fresh girl full of the *joie de vivre* and with much independence of character. Glynde belongs to a Brand sailor, and is full of Brand, Hampden, and Trevor portraits, besides old Dutch and other pictures. I liked a Jannsen, a Greuze portrait of the family, a Hoppner, and the Zoffanys. We talked war the first night, and on the second ecclesiastical lore and Speakers of the H. of C. All considered that Peel was the best Speaker of our day. We all came up by an early train Monday morning. It was crammed and there were few porters. Travelling in England is a trial in these days.

Monday, July 2. Met Plumer's Chief of Staff, Tim Harington, in the morning. He told me about Messines. All went to perfection. The leading troops all had orders to dig in on the ridge, and Plumer had no idea of going on in advance of the guns. G.H.Q. never pressed them to do so. It was a real advantage having had a good training especially in musketry, and having thoroughly rehearsed the scheme. The Second Army had been together for long, and were a family, and this told in the fight. The second line of troops went on through the first. The German counter-attack was very feeble. We had 54 guns knocked out by the German counter-batteries, but we believed we had knocked out 460 of theirs, and we destroyed 20 miles of barbed wire utterly. Now the Second Army had lost five of its divisions, which had gone to Gough for the coming attack in the north. We had 460 aeroplanes at Messines and cleared the air.

Lloyd George made a fine speech at Glasgow on Saturday, and another at Dundee, appealing for unity and resolution.

Yesterday the Russian Southern Armies attacked and took some 17,000 prisoners. A great relief to us all that they are able to do something after their long inaction and dreadful internal convulsions.

Wednesday, July 4. A rare lot of correspondence and documents. Met at Theresa Lady Londonderry's the Ronald McNeills, James Craig, and Lady Annesley. I liked Craig's story of an Irish M.P. who complained to him of the cooking in the House of Commons. He said he had never known such bad food—except at Kilmainham. 'What!' says Craig, 'have you been in gaol?' 'How the hell would I be in Parliament for an Irish constituency, Captain, if I had not been in gaol!' Craig very kind about my work, and said that I was one of the few concerned with the war who had maintained and even increased their reputation. Met Spencer Ewart, G.O.C. in Scotland, and had a talk about his affairs. He thinks Scotland well covered by the fleet. Too many units were raised in Scotland before the Service Acts, and it is hard to keep them up. He agrees that we should call on all young men under twenty-five. He says that the older miners in Scotland would be glad as the men are only working two days a week, and there would be more work for the older men if the young ones went. Went to the Opera at Drury Lane in the evening to Maurice Rothschild's box to hear *The Magic Flute*. A delicious treat, and very refreshing. With our party and Lady Cunard's there were the Italian Ambassador, the Chilian Minister and his wife, Lady Hamilton, Lady Kitty Somerset, Mrs. Lindsay, Wolkoff, Bardac, Prince and Princess Radziwill, Miss Kerr-Clark, and some more. Beecham's conducting I thought quite excellent, and Bardac said that it had improved immensely.

Thursday, July 5. Got through a lot of reading, including the speeches in Hansard by Dr. Addison and Montagu on Munitions. Quite a fairy story to read of what has been done in two years, but Addison might have given the contractors and workmen a little more credit. Lunched with Lady L. again, and met Lady Haig, F.M. Lord Grenfell, Sir Reginald and Lady Talbot, and Scovell of Geddes's Staff. Lady H. told me that Haig had called on French at his office and that all was peace between them, news which gave me great satisfaction. The F.M. said that Wingate was known in Egypt as Abu Hibr, the Father of Ink, and he wondered how the Sudan could be ruled from Egypt. Lady Talbot is going to think of a candidate for the Paris Embassy. Went to see Lord French : he may pay a visit to France, which will be an excellent thing. The F.M. is rather in favour of the coming coastal operation which I am dubious about. He says that he and de Jonghe and Winston worked it out once, and he thinks that the dunes can be cleared with the help of the Navy. He supposes that it is coming on soon now, as his flights of birds in Kent are going over to-morrow. He showed me his ' states,' which show an enormous difference between fighting and ration strengths, and he tells the War Cabinet that they may be right to accept the risk, but that he will not be responsible for saying that England is secured by the present arrangements. We talked over many other military matters. He says that the War Cabinet send to consult him unofficially.

Saw Sir W. Robertson afterwards about the Mesopotamia Report and the Indian Army system. We are in agreement about both. The men who made all the mistakes would, we think, have failed under any system. There was no reason why Duff should not have had an assistant, as R. has, to attend to the Council work, leaving Duff free to go about, but the latter chose to occupy himself with administration, which was not his job. Murray could not be blamed for not opposing the advance on Bagdad. He was only just installed in London ; the W.O. had not been in charge of the operation, and only had knowledge at second hand ; they also had no knowledge where the troops of India were. Even now R. did not know what troops India had on the frontier, and it was not his business to ask. We agreed that India had been severely taxed by the war, but that this did not clear Duff and Bunbury from responsibility for mistakes. Persia was now an example of divided responsibility, for the India and Foreign Offices as well as the War Office might send instructions there and they might not agree. The need was that, for Imperial purposes, the control of all the Armies of the Empire should be one, not for internal management, but for all oversea operations, and this power should rest in the hands of the C.I.G.S., subject of course to the policy of the Government of the day.

We had a little talk on other matters. Some French divisions are in the north to help Gough. I said that I did not think that the choice of Gough for this particular operation was good, much though I admired his gifts. R. was inclined to agree, and wished that Plumer, who knew every stone in the north, had been placed in charge.

Saturday, July 7. Between 10 and 11 this morning there was another air raid on London by Hun aeroplanes. It was a fine morning, with a rising easterly wind, but the sun still obscured by mist and drifting clouds. The gardener ran off to look after his wife, and the postman, much alarmed, flew in for shelter. I got my field glasses and went to the top of the house to see the sight. Our guns on 'The Spaniards' were at work, but at first I could not see where the shells were bursting. Then there came into view from the north, a little to the east of the house, and apparently from the Hendon direction, a great flight of Hun planes, looking like silver swallows, about 12,000 feet up, and appearing to fly slowly. They were in fan-shape formation and were heading south. I saw them very well and counted twenty-six, but a few may have been ours in chase. The shells were bursting all round them, and after reaching Piccadilly they turned south-east, and the formation became more broken. No bombs were dropped near us so far as I could make out. As they faced the wind the pace became slower, but only one nearly fell and then recovered itself. They made for the City, and by 10.40 the guns near us stopped firing and the planes were soon out of sight. The inevitable errand boy walked by whistling and quite unconcerned at the height of the racket. In the evening it was said that 37 people had been killed and 140 wounded, also that no serious damage had been done. Lots of sightseers on the tops of houses and in the streets, and everybody unconcernedly going about to do their Saturday shopping as soon as the guns stopped. London will soon be as accustomed to being bombed as Ladysmith was to being shelled. Major Blair of the Indian Army, lately in Persia, came up to Maryon to talk Mesopotamia, but the chief point of his argument, and a good one, was that the Egyptian system of attaching officers for periods was not suitable for India owing to the class-company system and the need for learning several languages, and the habits and customs of different races, acquirements which could not be expected under the Egyptian system, and further that the Indian Army would oppose any change which curtailed their Indian pensions.

Monday, July 9. One of the colonels of the Special Reserve came up to suggest that some of his colleagues should be given brigades or other acknowledgment of their hard work during the war. He had sent out 450 officers and 15,000 men from his own battalion. He also wants temporary commissions to be given to a few N.C.O.s in each battalion, and that they may remain with the battalions for training purposes. Very good suggestions.

I went to have a talk with General Sir O'Moore Creagh, formerly C.-in-C. in India, about Mesopotamia affairs and the Indian Army system. He is a convinced supporter of Lord K.'s system, and declares that he was often away for two months at a time, and that finance is the great stumbling block to progress in India. He is finishing a book on India which promises to be entertaining, and he says that the Government will never dare to publish his evidence before the Mesopotamia Commission. He says that the Council in India are usually all in want of a Lieut.-Governorship, or a seat on the India Council or something, and so never oppose the Viceroy or take any initiative. They should never be appointed unless they have already been Lieut.-Governors. He thought that he had ruined his own chances of a seat on the India Council by his plain speaking.

Saw Maurice in the afternoon and had a talk over the position of the General Staff concerning the Mesopotamia expedition. He told me that two new German divisions had appeared on the Eastern front, and that one from the West had also turned up there, making 155 German divisions in the West and 80 in the East. We discussed the coming attack in Flanders. He thinks that Allenby will be all right at Gaza. No more troops from Salonika have been taken away yet. From several sources I find that the War Cabinet have still refused to move about men until all A men for general service have left England. Korniloff's new offensive in Galicia seems to have struck a soft place where all the enemy were Austrians, and the Russians did well. Our guns, fortunately, continue to come on well.

In the evening Jack Stirling and Captain Charles Fox, both Scots Guards, dined at Maryon. Jack says that the Guards are in front line east of Ypres and will lead the new attack. Two French corps are on their left, the 1st and 6th. Gough will have 16 divisions or more, of which 12 in front line. The French attack next, and then Rawlinson on the coast, aided by the Navy. He says that the place swarms with our pontoons. I said that I disliked all this country very much and thought it bad ground for an offensive. The Boche guns are busy and are doing better than usual with their counter-battery work, while their planes have been all over us. Fox has just escaped from Germany at his third try, and was intensely interesting. He was taken on Oct. 26, 1914, and has been nearly three years a prisoner. His experiences on his 160 mile journey from near Hanover to Holland recall Jules Verne. He travelled at night by compass bearing, and lay up by day in young plantations where children and dogs were not likely to come. He had many close shaves of recapture, and at one place had to bury himself as Boches with dogs were after him. Fortunately a flock of sheep ran over his grave and put the dogs off the scent. He lay hid there a whole day and at night swam the Ems, where he lost his boots. He was not sure of the frontier, and the first man he saw was in field-grey, and he took him for a Boche, and went up close to him determined to throw him into the river if he were a Boche, but he turned out to be a Dutchman and all was well. He says that the Germans are very hungry but can still go on. He found the crops very poor in Germany. All were sick to death of the war and the Socialist spirit was increasing fast. The English prisoners were badly treated. When they were knocked about they always hit back, and then got two years' imprisonment. They practically lived on their parcels from home. The Boches still think that no ship can leave England. The Russians are regarded as coolies, and clean up for the officers' English orderlies. Some English are on the farms, many with only a girl in the house, or a few women. The Russians are not guarded and are very tame. He says that there are hardly any men to be seen in Germany where he happened to be, and he met hardly any on his long and adventurous cross-country journey. He walked about twenty miles each night from 11 P.M. to 5 A.M., and found many bridges unguarded. He located some new Zepp. sheds on the way. Fox says that my articles appear very fully in the German papers. The Boches consider the Russian troops to be herds of sheep and take little count of them. They are furious with the Austrians, who are always letting them in, and consider one Italian to be as good as several Austrians. They respect us, but are greatly misled about the facts of the war. The complete ignorance of F. on all that has happened at home and in our Armies abroad is remarkable.

Tuesday, July 10. Completed an article on the Indian Army system, defending it against assailants of Lord K. Lunched with Olive, Countess Pappenheim, the Dowager Lady Londonderry, Sir Vincent Caillard, and Professor Morgan. Later saw Easy Villiers, with whom I discussed East Africa. Villiers would not follow the German remnant into Portuguese East Africa, as it is not worth it and they can do no harm there. But we are raising 20 new native battalions to go after them, and 80,000 native porters. V. says that he can only put in the field 200 men of his Suffolk Yeomanry and that home defence is a farce.

Archie Murray returned last Sunday, and I had a talk with him to-day. He is furious at his supersession,[1] and I do not wonder. He told me all about the conquest of the desert, and showed me the position of his troops south of Gaza. His coming despatch begins by showing all the changes of policy of the War Cabinet, but we feel sure that they will not publish it during the war as it shows up their instability too well. He had sent away to France 9 of his 12 divisions, or 250,000 men, and then when he only had 3 left was ordered to advance on Jerusalem. He hopes that Allenby will ask for 7 before he moves on. With the 60th Division from Salonika and the 74th ex-Yeomanry Division Allenby will have 5 divisions on his east front, and should have two more. Murray had only four heavy howitzers when he attacked Gaza, and many more heavy guns are needed, while his planes are of old types. Only 6 of the 12 battalions promised from India have turned up, and all troops sent him from E. Africa and Aden are useless, the former being fever-stricken. He has his black troops along the canal, and 13 garrison battalions hold Egypt, the Western front,

---

[1] In Allenby's concluding Despatch the great services of Murray were handsomely and gratefully acknowledged.

and Khartoum. He has broadened the front for Allenby
by extending his pipe lines, and says that people will not
understand that there is neither water nor a scrap of food
to be had in the desert. He has prepared three days' reserve
stores of water every few miles along the railway and pipe
line, and his pipes bring him 600,000 gallons of water
from the Nile daily. They are 12 in. diameter most of the
way, and then twin 6 in. and 4 in. He says that the advance
on Jerusalem cannot go faster than the railway, which can
only be laid at the rate of twenty miles a month. Once in
Palestine, the water trouble will be at an end he thinks.
The Turks have 5 or 6 divisions on his front, with nearly
100 guns and many machine guns. Their line extends
from Beersheba on their left to Gaza. There is constant
surf on the coast, but he gets much up by sea. He hopes
to be able to have $13\frac{1}{2}$ trains a day soon on his normal
gauge railway, which will be able to supply 7 divisions
and the cavalry. All his sick and wounded, 20,000 in all,
are still in Egypt, where he has 18,000 prisoners to look after.
The men are very fit at the front and live in the open. The
losses from submarines have been heavy. The Yeomanry
just arrived from Salonika lost a ship with 800 horses on
board, and 700 mules were lost in another ship. He asked
every morning what losses there had been, and declares
that the passage of the Mediterranean is now a regular
operation of war. Egypt asked the Cabinet last year
whether it should grow corn or cotton, and was asked to
grow cotton. It will therefore require to be fed with corn
from the East.

Wednesday, July 11. Freddy Manners-Sutton (Lord
Canterbury) came up to Maryon to get an Oxford tutor
some work. Freddy was lugged off to gaol for not answering
a calling-up notice, placed in khaki, refused to take a commission, and did four months as a private, partly in France,
where he once went ' over the top ' and took part in a
scrap. He was then invalided, and I wonder he stood it
so long. It appears to be uncertain whether a peer or an
M.P. is liable to serve, but anyhow this one is not serving

now. Lunched with the Ian Hamiltons : Commander Wedgwood, Colonel Mola, head of the Italian mission, Mrs. Ronny Brooke, Lady Annesley, Lady Kitson, the Count de Grünne, Mrs. Tom Bridges, and Blow the architect. A very pleasant party. Wedgwood full of Mesopotamia, which comes up in both Houses for debate to-morrow. He is also full of reforming India. He has never been there. De Grünne anxious about the new offensive in Flanders, and says his King is too, and that it is a gamble. He does not like the presence of the French troops between us. Mola interesting. He admits that the last Italian offensive stopped for want of shells, and quotes Hamilton who commands our guns in Italy as saying that the Italians will not be able to begin a great attack again till the end of August for this reason. He spoke to me about an Allied offensive towards Laybach. I asked him how late we could fight in the Laybach area, and he said till the end of October. I said that I was entirely against the Allied participation in this attack until after the end of October, when little could be done on our Western front, but that during the winter I was all for Allied help to Italy on the Carso, where we could fight all the winter. To-night comes news that we have lost the dunes sector on the coast near Nieuport, and that a battalion each of the 60th and the Northants have been taken. I had an article to-day on the Indian Army system and Mesopotamia supporting Lord K.'s reforms in India.

Thursday, July 12. Wrote to General Pétain on our affairs here. Lunched with Olive and Lockett at Prince's Grill. On the Tribunal most of the afternoon. We are getting down to bedrock in men because the Cabinet will not call out the young men, and we are now mainly getting oldish men in low medical categories. The Tribunal work continues to fascinate me. Dined with Mrs. Astor, and found a party of twenty or so including the Italian Ambassador and the Marchesa, Lord and Lady Harcourt, Tommy Maguire and his wife, Lady Ridley, Prince and Princess Radziwill, Lord D'Abernon, Sir Seymour Fortescue, Sir John Cowans,

Fox McDonnell, and a few more. A pleasant talk with Lady Ridley at dinner. She is going north again soon for the holidays. Imperiali is pleased that Mola and I have met.

There has been the deuce of a row in Cabinet circles. The Cabinet wanted the War Office to take on the Mesopotamia Special Inquiry which is to investigate the affairs of soldiers and civilians, but the W.O. refused unless Lloyd George put it on paper. This he did, but the War Cabinet refused to let him send the paper out. Parliament is cross about the form of the inquiry. Austen Chamberlain has resigned. There have been several meetings of the Army Council to-day. I mentioned to Seymour the rumour about Carson leaving the Admiralty, and Seymour said it did not matter a hang who was First Lord so long as he did nothing ! I doubt whether a court-martial would convict the soldiers on the charges brought by the Commissioners, and it is hard to frame charges under the Army Act to meet the cases. Londonderry, whom I saw at Londonderry House this morning, has been reading the Roebuck Report after the Crimea, and says that the Report tallied with what we are saying now about our present governors. *Plus ça change!* I saw the Lawrences at the top of the house and advised L. to have them cleaned. There are four quite good about 1820. L. says that Reggie Pembroke had command in the line at one period lately and did right well. The Wilton sale has been somewhat of a fiasco and the armour is unsold, as wicked stories were spread about the two great suits which I have known for half a century.

Friday, July 13. A nasty little knock at Nieuport on the coast of Flanders. I write a note for the *Times* to explain that only two battalions were involved. This would have checked current rumours in London of the loss of thousands of men, but the foolish censorship, or rather its masters, cut out the allusion to the two battalions. Lunched with Lady Beresford, the Admiral, Austin Harrison, the Ladies Essex and Herbert, the Duchess of Marlborough,

Edmund Gosse, and some others. C. B. is to speak in the Lords to-day on this wearisome and futile Mesopotamia question. Dined at Mrs. Bischoffsheim's house. The hostess too ill to come down, so Lady Meux presided, and there were also Lady Mar and Kellie, Theresa Lady Londonderry, Mrs. Astor, Jack Cowans, the Maguires, Mrs. Lowther, the Countess Torby, Sir Victor Mackenzie, and others. Allenby has told the War Office that he must have 7 divisions and 50 heavy howitzers to attack the Turks in Palestine, and the W.O. does not know where to get them from. I am glad that Allenby has spoken out. Incidentally he has shown up the odious treatment of Archie Murray, who had 12 divisions for the defence of Egypt, was made to send 9 away, and then invited to attack Palestine with 3! It is lucky for the War Cabinet that there is a censorship and that we are muzzled! Played Bridge with Lady Mar, who was looking very handsome, and with Countess Torby and Mackenzie.

Saturday, July 14. Wrote all the morning. Lunched with Lady Paget and Mrs. Leeds in Grosvenor Square. We had a great discussion about the question whether American ladies should transfer their services, and incidentally their subscriptions, from British to American good works. I thought that American women with English husbands should keep on at our good works, but that others without English husbands should look after their own American people. Lady X. and Mrs. Lavery came in after lunch. Lady X. told us a good story of —— visiting a hospital. She was talking to a soldier who constantly brought in ' Wipers ' into his tale. Each time —— said ' Ypres ' rather sharply to correct the Tommy's pronunciation, and when —— had gone the Tommy was asked how he got on. He said that she was a nice homely woman and very kind, but it was very sad that she was troubled with such bad hiccups! Lady X. told the story well, making ' Ypres ' into a sort of hiccup each time. A *ben trovato* story I expect! I dined with Sir Archibald and Lady Murray at their new flat, 20 Lincoln Mansions,

Basil Street. He was delighted to hear of Allenby's appreciation. Archie has been a week in town and has never been invited to come and explain the Palestine situation to them. Yet he has all the maps, plans, and figures, and they cannot rightly understand the situation without consulting him. I should say that their shabby treatment of him makes them shy of him. He thinks that it will take three months to get the 3 divisions up to the Gaza front even if the 2 extra divisions can be found. We discussed the wanderings of the children of Israel in the desert and ours—and also Joshua's campaign and ours. He said that at one place in the desert, forty miles east of Ismailia, he had found 1,000,000 gallons of water stored of which we knew nothing, and this supply would have greatly helped the Turks had they marched this way. I thought of Moses striking the rock. Moses, after all, was *dégommé* like Murray. He thinks that the best way is to attack the centre of the long-extended Turkish line, about midway between Beersheba and Gaza. We also discussed October 1915 and the share of the General Staff in the first failure to advance on Bagdad. Birdwood writes to me from his Anzac corps in France to say that he agrees with my article on Mesopotamia in the *Times*. Mark Sykes in the Commons brings out well the two main points.

Sunday, July 15. Spent the day at the cottage with E. and Doris Keane. The latter has been offered a huge sum to do *Romance* on the cinema. She has great plans for the future.

Monday, July 16. Got through many letters. Lunched with Lady Strafford at Chandos House : Lady Yarborough, Lady Morton, the Victor Stanleys—he starting to-morrow for Petrograd—and Max-Muller of the F.O. Max-Muller has examined Charles Fox, and agrees that the Germans are suffering but not famishing. Stanley has an anxious time before him. He is just back from the Grand Fleet, and thinks the Boches would be fools to come out and fight as they are holding up our fleet by sitting tight. It appears that every Russian has still to be bribed before anything can be done, and Stanley's mission in the Baltic is an arduous one. Met the Mayor and Council at the Hampstead Town Hall to discuss air-raid warnings, and had an interesting discussion. We decide on maroons or foghorns at four places where there are fire stations, and make various other suggestions to the Home Office for uniform action, for Scotland Yard to telephone first as well as second warnings, and so on. Lady Strafford has taken Knebworth for the summer, and wants me to go there. Dined with the Dowager Lady Londonderry. Arthur Balfour had to dine with the P.M. and could not come. We had Lord and Lady Mar and Kellie, Lord and Lady Ilchester, Edmund Gosse, Lady Salisbury, and Jack Cowans. A pleasant dinner. We discussed Lord Haldane after dinner. Jack, Gosse, and I stuck up for him, and Ilchester was also kind about him. But all except Gosse doubted whether he would ever loom large again in our politics. Lady S. says that Salisbury is ill and at Hatfield. He has left his division, the command of which was a joy to him. I wish that he figured more in politics, as I trust him. Jack and I walked away together and mutually cursed all politicians. The only two investigations into the war have damned the War Cabinets to heaps, and if Egypt and Salonika were investigated the War Cabinets would be quadruply damned. We suppose that they have done their best but it has not been good enough. People are pessimistic to-day about tonnage again. The Greeks have asked us to fit out 180,000 Greek soldiers and I believe we are refusing.

Tuesday, July 17. Lunched with Lady Paget, and found the American Ambassador and Mrs. Page; Bee Pembroke's sister, Lady Ingestre, a very sweet lady, and her young fiancé, Mr. Pennoyer of the American Embassy; Mrs. Leeds, Arthur Stanley, and one or two more. Mrs. Leeds tells me that the Americans in France had no idea how bad things were with the French, and how much they would have to do: they now think themselves in for a three years' job. Dr. Page very cheery. We discussed affairs in America. Arthur Stanley quite hurt because our Red Cross has had only seven millions to work with, and the Yankees have given twenty millions right off. Most of the party left early for the Stanley-Cadogan wedding.

In the afternoon I had a talk with General Smuts, who has just been given a seat on the War Cabinet. He told me that he was only going to advise on military affairs, and would steer clear of politics. I told him that as he was the only man in the War Cabinet with military experience, we looked to him to keep the politicians straight, and also to safeguard the interests of generals, some of whom, like Murray, have been scurvily treated. I said that the War Cabinet had been twice condemned by the only Commissions which had investigated their proceedings, and that if other inquiries were made into Salonika, Palestine, and Home Defence, similar condemnations would result. I mentioned specifically the question of men, and asked him if he felt as happy about it as when he last talked with me. Smuts said that Lloyd George's original proposition was the right one, namely, that Asquith should be Prime Minister, with a Cabinet to deal with political and administrative matters, and that a small body under L. G. himself should manage the war. But this had broken down, and now, Smuts admitted, the War Cabinet were overwhelmed, and L. G. was trying to do the work of six men. He admitted that the machinery did not work too well. He had not known that Murray was in London, and would try to get him called in over the Palestine campaign. Smuts was not very keen about our present strategy in Palestine. He had suggested the landing of three divisions at Haifa and the interception of the railway, if troops were not available on a larger scale for the Alexandretta coup. But when he had failed to win the approval of people for this plan, he had refused the command which had been offered to him. I asked if he had been at cross purposes with the General Staff. No, he said, he liked

Robertson and had a high opinion of his rugged honesty
and good sense, while he thought the G.S. excellent and a
fine instrument. It was not that. I said that I was
glad, for Smuts's strategy was in line with my ideas and
was that which Pétain had agreed was the right course at
Verdun eighteen months ago. What was the cause then
of the refusal of his plan ? He said that after three years
of war people were worn out ; many disappointments had
made them cautious, and they had not the nerve to take
risks. I said I understood. As to the men for the Army,
Smuts admitted that he took a less rosy view than before,
but he thought that we had enough men to keep up our
Armies during the summer campaigns. In the autumn
we should see how things were, and the Government might
have to take a virile resolution and call up 500,000 young
men under thirty. I said that if they had been called up
before we should have them ready now, and might end
the war, whereas forces were now too evenly balanced for
decisive victory, and I cavilled at the continued retention
of our Army at Salonika. Smuts said that I knew that
Salonika was a French plan to which we weakly consented.
It was easy to get into a mess but not easy to get out
of it. Brussiloff wished us to remain because he was going
to invade Bulgaria as his main blow, when the offensive
in Galicia had gone further, and wanted our troops to hold
up the Bulgars. The Serbians also wished us to remain
and said that they trusted us alone, while Venizelos promised twelve Greek divisions if we would supply equipment
and heavy guns. Smuts did not consider the Turkish part
of the war a side-show. He thought that Turkey would
make peace if she were tackled, and that this would end
the war. I replied that certainly we had 800,000 men in
the East, and it was enough to crush the Turks if our forces
were properly directed by the War Cabinet, but they never
had been. I did not believe that the defeat of Turkey
would end the war. I said that I wanted the War
Cabinet to end the war with a great reputation, but
Smuts replied that every one connected with the war

seemed destined to lose his reputation. We agreed to meet again and discuss these points.

Wednesday, July 18. Some new political appointments. Winston gets Munitions ; Montagu goes to the India Office ; Addison the Ministry of Reconstruction ; Carson leaves the Admiralty and goes to the War Cabinet, while Eric Geddes takes his place. Am very sorry for Islington, who will, I hear, retire in spite of my advice to him. Lunched with Lady Juliet, Lady Cunard, and the Comte de Noailles. De Noailles and I discussed the war, and he told me that the Yankees promise thirty-three divisions by the spring, which will be a great deal more than any one here believes. The Russian news is not good again, and it is said that the Russians who did so well in Galicia have gone back without orders and without military compulsion because they thought that they had done enough. Dined with Lady Herbert ; Lady Manners, Lady Juliet, and Fox McDonnell. A pleasant evening. We discussed art first, and then fishing. Many tall stories. One of Fox's was voted the tallest since Jonah's tale. It was of a shark which swallowed a bucket which stuck in his throat, and all the food went into the bucket instead of into the shark. So the shark died. Jonah's whale was more masterful.

Thursday, July 19. Lunched with the Vicomte de la Panouse at the Café Royal, and we discussed the war. We both doubt the persistence of the Russian offensive, and his instinct is that we may reach the stage of negotiation in the autumn, but that much will depend upon the attitude of the new German Chancellor, Dr. Michaelis, who has succeeded Bethmann Hollweg, and upon the result of our coming offensive in France. I said that the Allied misfortune was the want of a great figure to dominate the war. Panouse agreed. We talked of France, Italy, and Greece, and were pretty well of one opinion, but the French obviously do not much like Italy's somewhat independent actions in the East. I gather that Pétain's next attack will be in the Verdun direction. Afterwards I visited Colonel Armando Mola, *chef de mission* and Military

Attaché to the Italian Embassy at Empire House, **Kingsway**. Captain Count Vicino Pallavicino, a very nice fellow whom I have known since his youth, also there. Mola is an intelligent and agreeable man. We agreed that there ought to be better co-operation on the Franco-Italian front which, rightly regarded, was all one. I repeated that I was dead against any detachment from our Armies in France to Italy during the summer, but that after October I thought that we might take part in an Italian offensive on the Carso and in the Adriatic. I said that if the Italians sent a few divisions to France now, or even one to the Vosges, it would be useful as a proof of co-operation, and suggested that as the Italians had heaps of troops our winter contingent should be mainly artillery. Mola agreed, and says that his War Minister controls $1\frac{1}{2}$ million men who are not under Cadorna. He thinks that the defeat of Austria, which he desires, would prevent Germany from going on, but I ventured to doubt it, and insisted that the defeat of Germany would end the war and that nothing else mattered by comparison. Alexander of the Indian Army, who is with our mission in Italy, came in. He complained bitterly of Steed's Jugo-Slav policy in the *Times*, and in general complained that our Press was not taking enough notice of Italian doings.

Friday, July 20. To-day there was published in the early afternoon papers the text of the Reichstag speech of the new German Chancellor, Dr. Michaelis. He seems to be the captive of the Junker bow and spear, but one can read his speech as one pleases according to one's temperament, and much of it consists of platitudes, combined with the old lies about the origin of the war, many hypocrisies, and a false estimate of our position. I do not think that the speech has brought an accommodation any nearer. Lunched with Olive, Lockett, and Laszlo at the Ritz. Laszlo told me that the Hungarian who had escaped from Donnington Hall came to him for assistance. It was a horrible situation for Laszlo, who is a British subject, and had the man been followed and been arrested in Laszlo's studio it might have ruined him. He refused help and informed the police. He is very keen about the pictures in which a friend is to figure. Laszlo also told me of his first study. It was to illustrate a Spanish poem translated into Hungarian. A young man lying on a bank of a lake sees the misty vapours materialise into a beautiful woman, and a conversation between them begins. She has a veil round her and a belt. She offers the youth all above the belt or all below it. He chooses the upper half, and she gives him all as a reward. How would we portray this episode ? We all guessed wrong. Laszlo's engraving showed the belt and the vanishing veil alone and left the rest to the imagination.

Printed by T. and A. Constable, Printers to His Majesty
at the Edinburgh University Press

www.ingramcontent.com/pod-product-compliance
Lightning Source LLC
Chambersburg PA
CBHW021656070726
47591CB00017B/1